Educating Adolescents
with Behavior Disorders

Educating Adolescents
with Behavior Disorders

Edited by

Gwen Brown   **Richard L. McDowell**   **Judy Smith**

Charles E. Merrill Publishing Company
A Bell & Howell Company
Columbus Toronto London Sydney

Published by
Charles E. Merrill Publishing Co.
A Bell & Howell Company
Columbus, Ohio 43216

This book was set in Times Roman and Windsor.
Production Coordination: Judith Rose Sacks
Cover Design Coordination: Will Chenoweth
Cover Photo: Greg Miller

Excerpts on pp. 242, 247, 253, 272, and 275 are from *Crisis in the Classroom: The Remaking of American Education*, by Charles E. Silberman. Copyright © 1970 by Charles E. Silberman. Reprinted by permission of Random House, Inc.

Photo Credits

pp. 16, 31, 64, 108, 147, 166, 180, 195, 215, 242, 281, 306, 340—Suzette Boulais
pp. 82, 367, 390—Paul Conklin
p. 127—Rohn Engh
p. 359—Alan Bagg

Library of Congress Catalog Card Number: 80-82608
International Standard Book Number: 0-675-08056-8
Printed in the United States of America
1 2 3 4 5 6 7 8 9 10—86 85 84 83 82 81

Contents

Preface

Throughout history, individuals with physical or behavioral differences have been abused, neglected, and excluded from important segments of society. The first real efforts in the United States to educate exceptional or handicapped persons started in the latter half of the nineteenth century, with the establishment of residential schools. Most of these schools, however, did not address the needs of behavior disordered students. As late as 1976, the National Advisory Committee for the Handicapped estimated that 81% of the nation's emotionally disturbed children were not served by the public schools. Of those served, most fell in the mild to moderate range, and almost all were of elementary school age.

Today, special education finally is coming of age. Educators now agree that public schools are responsible for educating all young people, including adolescents with deviant and disruptive behavior patterns. The question remains: How to deliver the appropriate education demanded by Public Law 94-142, the Education for all Handicapped Children Act? Programming for these adolescents has been a concern of educators for only a short time; much remains to be learned.

By presenting the ideas of leading educators who work with adolescents with behavior disorders, this text may help to begin filling the gap in special education. The book is intended for all educators interested in sharpening their thinking about educational programming for these students. The text begins with a discussion of normal and deviant behavior, its causes and a discussion of disturbed adolescents from a sociological perspective. From this background information, the text moves directly into practical chapters focusing on educational strategies—screening and diagnosis, classroom structure, work with parents, teaching and remediation approaches, and finally teaching in specific content areas.

The authors contributing to this text are professionals involved in personnel preparation, classroom teaching, clinical work, or administration of programs for teachers or young people. As a result of the varying backgrounds of the contributors, the chapters differ in depth and style and provide readers with a broad range of thinking within the field.

The editors express their gratitude to the authors who contributed to this book. Their cooperation, enthusiasm, and suggestions made editing the text a rewarding experience. Special thanks go to Sylvia Johnson and Donna Kraus for manuscript preparation and review, and to Esther and Wesley Blacklock, Gwen's parents, whose care of her child allowed her time to work on the manuscript.

Prologue

Richard J. Whelan

Another word for *prologue* is *beginning*. Other words which are synonyms are *debut* and *outbreak*. When it comes to emotionally disturbed adolescents, special education is making a debut, a beginning. It is indeed a new era for special educators, but it is an old story for many adolescents. They are out there with all their wants, problems, and antipathy toward adults. And why not, what have adults ever done for them except to criticize, force them into adult-prescribed niches, and then castigate them for not being properly appreciative? Realistic or not, many emotionally disturbed adolescents perceive adults in just such a negative manner. Our newly aroused recognition of their needs and a messianic desire to serve them won't change that perception; yet, we must make the attempt because to do otherwise will not ease the chronic and acute pain experienced by adolescents labeled as emotionally disturbed, behavior disordered, drop-outs, antisocial, chronically disruptive, and so on *ad infinitum*. However, our helping efforts must be carefully planned, implemented, and evaluated lest more harm than good be done. This is not to assert that programs should be error free before they are attempted: that is probably not possible or even desirable. Errors will be made during the search for excellence. In fact, errors often indicate that many are trying to do good; an absence of error usually reveals an absence of effort.

    This book is a beginning. It reflects the commitment of its contributors to share with others what they have learned and will learn in the future about the education of emotionally disturbed adolescents. It is hoped that the book will stimulate others

1

to take a first, second, or even tenth look at the problems and to act creatively in the search for solutions.

At best, a prologue can only set the scene. The scene is the schools—public, private, day, residential. The players are the young people and adults (educators) who must somehow discover cooperative, concerted ways for helping one another and thereby themselves. The scene includes brief glimpses at perspectives, human/environmental interactions, and some alternatives for program foci. The play will unfold in the following chapters.

PERSPECTIVES

At best it is ironic; at worst, tragic. When asked for recommendations to reduce or eliminate violence and disruptive behavior within secondary public schools, students, teachers, and principals tend to stress security devices, floating security patrols, and better discipline. Discipline is described as (a) enforcement of rules and suspensions, (b) watching and reporting troublemakers, and (c) strict enforcement of laws by police and courts. Equally enlightening are the considerations not stressed. These include (a) improved teaching, (b) course changes, (c) individual counseling, (d) student rights and responsibilities, (e) understanding behavior variance, (f) mutual respect, and (g) participation in discussions by those affected (National Institute of Education, 1978). Perhaps it is true that adolescents are neither fish nor beast. Therefore, they must be fowl. This attitude might be understood, though not condoned, when expressed by adults; but when the students react in the same manner, that is indeed surprising. Whatever happened to the "we vs. them," "stand together against those over twenty years of age" syndrome characteristic of many adolescents?

One interpretation is that most students, like teachers and principals, are so frightened of violence and extreme variance that they are supportive of responding in kind, e.g., using aggressive procedures to counter aggressive behavior. Responses of this type are known as "negative environmental practices" (Long, 1974).

Another interpretation is that the observation of violence in others is frightening because it provides visible evidence of the destructiveness that may only be thinly covered within oneself. Rhodes (1977) identifies this reaction as the "illusion of normality." That is, behaviors not within the illusion's boundaries must be purged in order to maintain it. Yet, those who are different serve those who are not by functioning as agents for vicarious gratification from display of forbidden behaviors. So, it is the classic double bind: behaviors which result in both gratification and punishment. Variant behaviors are at the same time frightening yet necessary for the maintenance of the illusion and the awareness that at another time that which is now considered normal may be labeled as crazy. As Rhodes has pointed out, this process is used to sustain existence of the self through time and under all conditions. The alternative is to acknowledge nonexistence, a condition too painful, except for fleeting moments, to contemplate.

Yet another interpretation is that the students, teachers, and principals do not recognize the power of the alternatives not stressed or do not understand how they might be implemented. There is evidence that individualized curriculum changes, for example, can reduce destructive behaviors by as much as two-thirds when compared with a standard curriculum applied to all students (Edwards, 1977). This is not surprising when it is recognized that a standard curriculum, taught within a specific time frame, will result in a substantial range from high to low scores on achievement tests. The same phenomenon occurs with measures of intellectual ability, hence the substantial relationship between intelligence and achievement test scores. However, this relationship decreases if time to learn and the curriculum are allowed to vary. More students then achieve desirable objectives, thus reducing the variation in achievement scores as well as the relationship between them and measures of intellectual abilities.

A simple, clinical example can be used to illustrate the effects of varying time. The Speed of Learning Evaluation (SOLE) is a ten item task that can be used to evaluate the speed at which students acquire accurate auditory-visual associations (Whelan, 1979). Each item consists of three to six letter-like symbols to which the student gives a word from his own language or vocabulary. Once a word is identified for each card, the cards are mixed and presented until all ten are correctly identified for two consecutive trials. The SOLE was designed for children and adolescents but can be used with teachers to demonstrate the association between opportunities to respond (time) and performance. A demonstration requires dividing the group into three member teams. Team members rotate roles of examinee, examiner, and recorder of correct and incorrect responses. Even with teachers, the competition to learn the auditory-visual associations in fewer trials than others is intense. Also, when difficulty is encountered in acquiring auditory-visual associations, avoidance and escape behaviors such as wiggling, giggling, and anger are noted. The competition and escape behaviors are mirror versions of the behavior children enact when confronted with a task they validly or invalidly perceive to be too complex. Nevertheless, it remains significant that all participants do reach criterion, though some may need only three trials while others require ten or more. To further illustrate, an arbitrary trial cut-off point can be used. For instance, the fourth trial can be selected in order to determine how many meet criterion at that point and how many do not. That is, time is held constant and the effect is a pass-fail distribution observed when standard curricula and time restrictions are in place.

Which interpretations are relevant is probably not the central issue for educating the behaviorally disordered adolescent, however. Nor is the issue one of whether to respond to deviant, disruptive behavior. The issue is really one of how, and when, to respond. Perhaps disruptive behavior is due more to the absence of certain alternatives rather than of punitive measures. These alternatives reflect a more humanistic approach to education than suspension, security guards, and the courts and, in fact, are those over which educators have some influence or power to implement. The sterner measures are really outside of an educator's domain of influence.

HUMAN/ENVIRONMENTAL INTERACTIONS

Adolescents who are identified as emotionally disturbed, behavior disordered, or chronically disruptive usually exhibit a wide range of social and academic behavior variance. The behavior, be it withdrawn or hostile, is, in many instances, a means to escape or avoid an aversive environment. For example, if an adolescent is faced with a complex algebra problem that is perceived as unsolvable, the reaction to the situation may be defiance, clowning in class, or going to sleep. These reactions reflect an attempt to escape from an intolerable situation while keeping intact a measure of self-integrity or control over one's destiny.

Emotionally disturbed adolescents have usually experienced many instances of academic and social failure and thus have acquired a variety of strategies for coping with aversive situations. The strategies vary from the primitive to the quite creative. A temper tantrum or causing a fight is a primitive example, even though it might be effective in avoiding the task at hand. However, it usually brings a harsh response from others, such as time in the principal's office or other punishment. Of course, if it leads to exclusion from school, the adolescent may then become part of an environment that is supportive of behavior that is not congruent with societal expectations. A more creative response is to feign an attempt at problem-solving, thus creating more empathy from others. The result is the same, though: avoidance and escape from failure-inducing situations while at the same time inducing pain in self and others.

How prevalent is emotional disturbance among adolescents? Simple answers to this question do not exist, but there are interesting patterns that have emerged over the years. Ullmann (1952) found that 8% of ninth grade students could be considered seriously emotionally disturbed. Some 25 years later, it was found that 26% of ninth graders were considered to be emotionally disturbed (Kelly, Bullock, & Dykes, 1977). However, it should be noted that this estimate, based on teacher judgment, was discrepant with the trend for secondary-age students, 8.8% for twelfth graders. If the 26% figure for ninth graders was an artifact of the study, then the prevalence estimate for adolescents has remained somewhat stable over the years. On the other hand, if the geographical area in which the study was conducted uses the ninth grade as the first year of high school, the transition from elementary or middle school to high school could function to exacerbate adjustment problems. Again, the prevalence of emotional problems reflects the extent to which the environment is able to either support positive coping behaviors or elicit negative variant behaviors.

Support for the position that environmental variables influence the frequency with which school-age children and youth are identified as emotionally disturbed has been provided by Ruben and Balow (1978) who found that 60% of the children in kindergarten through grade six had been considered by at least one teacher during a six-year period to be behavior-disordered or emotionally disturbed. However, over the same six-year period, only 3% of the children were consistently identified as exhibiting problems that interfered with academic and social behavior progress. It should be noted that the cumulative total of 60% exceeded the percentage noted for any one year by approximately 30% to 37% and that the 3% consistently classified as behavior disordered was considerably less by 27% to 20%. (That is, teachers identified behavior problems for any one-year range from a high of 31% in the first grade to a low of about 24% in the fifth and sixth grades.) This longitudinal study is a milestone in the literature on the prevalence of emotional disorders among school-age children and youth. Although the study did not include adolescents, there is no reason to assume that the data could not be extrapolated to that age group. The actual percentages may decrease with age because of drop-out opportunities and expulsion rates, but the relationship between inconsistent and consistent identification would probably not vary a great deal. This study provides information that may be supportive of one or all of the following interpretations:

1. Emotional disturbance is a function of the perceiver. That is, what is

disturbance to one teacher may not be to another. This could account for the pattern of inconsistent identification.

2. Similarly, teachers may have been responding to transient problems among the school population. Children do experience periods of stress during developmental stages and/or situational upheavals in their personal lives. So, the teachers could be quite accurate in their observations. This would be consistent with previous reports on teacher effectiveness in identifying emotionally disturbed children (Bower, 1960).

3. Chronic, serious behavior problems, as reflected by the 3% consistent identification, are easily recognized as children move through the various grades, even by people with little or no professional preparation. On the other hand, mild behavioral problems are more difficult to categorize. For one teacher mild behavioral problems may represent mere troublesome encounters whereas for another they may indicate deeply rooted problems.

While the interpretations may be valid, they do not entirely address the issue of environmental variables and their effects on the behaviors of emotionally disturbed children and youth. Another critical finding of the Ruben and Balow study was that the consistently identified group of behaviorally disturbed children scored substantially lower than the group with no problems in the areas of intelligence, achievement, and economic status. This finding tends to confirm the notion that when curriculum and time are held constant, a considerable number of children will not be successful. Thus, it would appear that the educational system actually creates avoidance and escape behaviors by ignoring an old philosophical credo— individualized instruction. The irony and tragedy is that the failure to provide for children's academic and social growth elicits conditions that threaten the system's stability, and the system then responds by developing a parallel system to cope with problems of its own creation. That parallel system is generally known as *special education*. This is not an indictment of special education nor a proposal for its abolishment. Indeed, for many children there is no alternative unless all education is reorganized to provide for small class size, highly specialized teachers, and a plethora of instructional resources. From an economic standpoint alone that change will not occur in the foreseeable future. However, when it is consistently found that in any one year 10% to 30% of school-age children and youth are identified as emotionally disturbed (Bower, 1960; Kelly et al., 1977; Ruben & Balow, 1978), it is obvious that general education must institute changes that will prevent problems. From an economic rationale, it is less costly to prevent than to treat; the educational system can improve in arranging means to reach desirable ends, optimal development, and growth for children to whom it is ultimately responsible.

Adolescents who exhibit avoidance and escape behaviors have not been served as frequently as those who display the same behaviors at a younger age. There are several reasons for this situation. First, as educators timidly accepted responsibility for the mental health of children in partnership with other helping professions (psychiatry, social work, psychology) the accepted strategy was to "catch them when they are young." This is not a bad strategy, only short-sighted in that it does not recognize that some children need support for many years and that others may encounter serious problems only during adolescence. Second, younger children are more easily managed, both psychologically and physically. They are supposedly less set in their personality structure, therefore providing more potential for change when external intervention is used. Should that intervention falter and a temper tantrum ensue, physical control until the tantrum subsides is relatively easy to provide. For adolescents, on the other hand, psychological and physical management is more difficult. Adolescents have had more years to develop hardened sets of behaviors, beliefs, and attitudes, thus requiring large amounts of time and personnel to elicit changes. Also, an adolescent on the rampage cannot be controlled physically by one or even two people without risk of injury to someone. Wrestling a 7 year old into a position where no harm can be done to self or others is far different from trying the same tactic on a 15 year old. Third, arrangement of instructional environments for children is less complex than for adolescents. Self-contained classrooms are the rule rather than the exception for elementary schools. However, most junior and senior high schools are departmentalized. How can one teacher be competent in algebra, biology, literature, history, etc.? Planning appropriate educational programs for adolescents is most complex, and unfortunately it has been put off except for some instances of self-contained basic skill classes, resource rooms, and alternative educational programs (a new label for day schools). Educators, like the adolescents who need support, also engage in escape and avoidance behaviors. Unfortunately, such behaviors lead to solutions by default. When nothing else is available, exclusion from school becomes a forced and only approach (Nelson & Kauffman, 1976).

ALTERNATIVE GLIMPSES

How can one even speculate about alternative patterns for caring educational programs when the need to begin at the beginning has only recently reached professional, collective awareness? There is a need to scrutinize alternatives rather than rely upon single massive efforts, such as self-contained classes, and to renew and sustain contacts with colleagues in the mental health professions, those who have striven over many years to serve emotionally disturbed adolescents. The 6-hour school day is only a part of the distressed adolescent's daily coping; the other 18 hours require attention, too. At present this much is known about educational provisions for emotionally disturbed adolescents:

1. School personnel are confronted with students whose behavior is so variant that it elicits counteraggression from representatives of the educational system. This aggression takes the form of suspension, extrusion, exclusion, and legal action.

2. There are sufficient numbers of students in need of special arrangements to require action on the part of professional educators. Failure to act will only exacerbate the problem and lead to solutions which are not desirable for school personnel or the students they serve.

3. For many adolescents, school does not provide a social or academic learning climate. Instead, it evokes escape and avoidance behaviors which are detrimental for both adolescents and school personnel.

4. Teacher preparation programs have only recently recognized the need for alternative educational programs for troubled adolescents. Therefore, programs for preparing teachers of this group are in their infancy and groping for appropriate solutions.

Perhaps the search for potential program options should begin with the alternatives not stressed by peers, teachers, and principals. The rationale for this point is, as stated previously, that these are alternatives over which school personnel can exert some control.

The first alternative is to improve teaching. Who can disagree with this? Everybody is for improved teaching, but how does one go about it? The study by Edwards (1978) on individualizing instruction provides one example. It also illustrates the relationship between expectations and avoidance or escape behaviors. When a student can obtain success through completion of an appropriate task, approach behaviors are stimulated (Whelan, 1977). Individualizing instruction is not easy, but it can be done and its positive effects are known. It does not necessarily mean tutoring or require multiple grouping. It does, however, require changing the task content and its presentation to the extent that a student can earn success through reasonable effort. For the emotionally disturbed adolescent with deficiencies in math, it requires arrangements of materials and presentation which do not provoke fear and panic. For a good reader, it can open up new vistas for understanding of self and others.

A second alternative is course changes. Again, who can argue with this need? Bruner (1960), for example, asserts that if one wants to learn about chemistry, one must act as a chemist. There is no substitute for mixing two chemicals, observing a reaction, and recording it—not even the most inspired lecture ever given. There is also merit in the "watch one, do one, teach one" approach. To be proficient in tuning a car engine requires just such an approach. The examples are endless. Present course offerings could be reorganized internally to foster motivation and pride in accomplishment as contrasted to the hear-recite-test approach. In addition, courses which more accurately reflect and address the needs of adolescents in an ever-changing world may be necessary. Stretching course changes to include program content modification opens other avenues. For example, rather than having a teacher attempt to teach content across and within content subjects, a learning strategies approach could be used (Alley & Deshler, 1979). This approach emphasizes the imparting of skills in organizing what is to be learned, rules for study, techniques for recall; in other words, teaching students how to learn and think.

A third alternative is individual counseling. This, of course, is a good idea, but how many secondary counselors can find the time when faced with enrollment, tracking absences, advertising college entrance tests, and other sundry duties not related to counseling? Then, too, do the counselors have the skills needed to conduct individual and group awareness sessions? However, whether undertaken by a special educator or counselor or provided by a community mental health center, this is an option which should be implemented. There is no way to separate the affective and cognitive elements when considering appropriate educational programs (Fagen, Long, & Stevens, 1975). Both must be recognized in the classroom as well as in counseling sessions which may focus on the affective element. Indeed, the opportunity to explore one's feelings with a good listener and responder and to hear others explore theirs is good practice, be it called therapy, counseling, or special education.

A fourth consideration is student rights and responsibilities. Certainty as to where one stands in terms of expectations and consequences for actions, realistic or not, does provide some comfort for a system's participants. The way in which rights and responsibilities are developed and communicated is also important. How often have these documents been written in a negative fashion? They abound with "*nos*" and "*don't*s" but very few "*yes*es" and "*do*s." Most adolescents, including the emotionally disturbed, respond to positive approaches in formulating rights and responsibilities. They get turned-off, however, when there is a mismatch between the written document and actual practice. Adults are trusted only when it is demonstrated that they are worthy of it.

Understanding behavior variance or differences and mutual respect are the fifth and sixth alternatives. These two are not separated, because understanding and respect are interrelated, though not necessarily covariant. Understanding can lead to rejection, and respect need not be dependent upon understanding. Nevertheless, understanding the basis for an emotionally disturbed adolescent's behavior can foster respect for the feelings if not the actions. Understanding and respect should not be confused with condoning behaviors which are destructive to self and others, but they can provide the foundation for positive environmental practices as contrasted with negative ones (Long, 1974). Positive environmental practices include listening to expressions of anger, grief, or joy. The negative side includes cutting off expression or responding as if the expressed anger were evil or a personal attack. Until educators come to understand the importance of interpersonal communication, its manifest and latent content, and recognize the phenomena of transference and countertransference, neither understanding nor respect will occur. In fact, the best of program changes will be to no avail until understanding and respect are practiced diligently from the heart as well as the intellect.

Participation in decisions by those affected by them, the seventh alternative, is closely related to student rights and responsibilities. The commonsense notion that people may gripe about what they do to themselves but at least can't realistically blame others is probably a good policy. Obviously, students should participate in formulating their rights and responsibilities. In essence, this alternative reflects due process procedures (Turnbull & Turnbull, 1978), notification, participation, and the right to a hearing. Participation does not imply veto power. It is recognized that many adolescents, especially emotionally disturbed ones, may not know what is best for them. Indeed, many are searching for realistic limits and guidelines and can often find them with supportive adult involvement. In any event, participation is a necessity, not a luxury, for school systems. Not to involve students is running the risk of sabotaging the best-laid plans for alternative ways of serving the emotionally disturbed.

WHAT NOW?

There is no doubt that professional educators are confronted with a problem of national significance: the provision of appropriate educational services for emotionally disturbed children. Federal and state mandates for the education of the handicapped do not exclude adolescents. Of course, in practice it is possible to exclude by not identifying them. Such denial occurs, but it is a tactic that is sure to backfire. The old three "L"s—leverage, litigation, and legislation (Whelan & Sontag, 1974)—will be brought to bear eventually. Parents will start to use leverage on school boards, legislators, and policy-formulating agencies. There is no question that educational programs for adolescents will be provided. The question is one of strategy. What is the proper use of prevention and services?

As noted previously, this book represents the combined effort of many special educators who are actively concerned with the education of emotionally disturbed adolescents. It does not provide all of the answers. Indeed, it may not even address all of the questions. But it is a start, a good one at that, and it meets a critical need. Nelson and Kauffman (1976) have stated the goal clearly: "Hopefully, the near future will bring a growth in innovative secondary educational programming, a reversal of educational conditions which help spawn and maintain adolescent maladjustment . . ., and subsequent . . . developments in secondary programming which will report a great number of positive accomplishments" (p. 37). This is the goal. Will we be able to accomplish it?

References

Alley, G., & Deshler, D. *Teaching the learning disabled adolescent: Strategies and methods.* Denver: Love, 1979.

Bower, E. M. *Early identification of emotionally handicapped children in school.* Springfield: Charles C Thomas, 1960.

Bruner, J. S. *The process of education.* New York: Vintage, 1960.

Edwards, L. L. *The effects of modifying curriculum materials on the social and academic performance of behavior disordered students in the regular classroom.* Unpublished doctoral dissertation, University of Kansas, 1977.

Fagen, S. A., Long, N. J., & Stevens, D. J. *Teaching children self-control.* Columbus: Charles E. Merrill, 1975.

Kelly, T. J., Bullock, L. M., & Dykes, M. K. Behavioral disorders: Teachers' perceptions. *Exceptional Children*, 1977, *43*, 316–318.

Long, N. J. Personal perspectives. In J. M. Kauffman & C. D. Lewis (Eds.), *Teaching children with behavior disorders.* Columbus: Charles E. Merrill, 1974.

National Institute of Education. *Violent schools—safe schools* (Vol. I). Washington, D. C.: U.S. Government Printing Office, 1978.

Nelson, C. M., & Kauffman, J. M. Educational programming for secondary school age delinquent and maladjusted pupils. *Behavioral Disorders*, 1976, *2*, 29–37.

Rhodes, W. C. The illusion of normality. *Behavioral Disorders*, 1977, *2*, 122–129.

Ruben, R. A., & Balow, B. Prevalence of teacher identified behavior problems: A longitudinal study. *Exceptional Children*, 1978, *45*, 102–110.

Turnbull, H. R., & Turnbull, A. *Free appropriate public education, law and implementation.* Denver: Love, 1978.

Ullmann, C. A. *Identification of maladjusted school children* (Monograph No. 7, U.S. Public Health Service). Washington, D.C.: U.S. Government Printing Office, 1952.

Whelan, R. J., & Sontag, E. Prologue: special education and the cities. In P. Mann (Ed.), *Mainstream special education.* Reston, Va.: Council for Exceptional Children, 1974.

Whelan, R. J. Human understanding of human behavior. In A. J. Pappanikou and J. L. Paul (Eds.), *Mainstreaming emotionally disturbed children.* Syracuse: Syracuse University Press, 1977.

Whelan, R. J. *Speed of learning evaluation (SOLE): Experimental edition.* Unpublished manuscript, 1979.

Adolescence

1

Richard L. McDowell

Adolescence is a label used to identify the developmental period between childhood and adulthood. It represents a time of change—a transition from the dependence of childhood to the maturity and independence of being an adult. This transition is such a major change in the individual's life that some cultures compare it to a new birth (Sommer, 1978). The individual leaves one form of life (childhood) behind to take on a new form of life (adulthood) with new modes of thinking, new roles in relationships, and new expectations for behavior. In some cultures a boy is sent out to live by himself in the wilderness. During that time he must fulfill certain requirements to demonstrate that he is worthy of membership in the adult society. In other similar cultures the boy is taken away and entrusted to selected males for training in specific skills. Only after the boy has demonstrated acceptable competencies in these skills is he allowed to return to society. Similar practices are also conducted with young girls and are usually related to menarche. The goal of these puberty ceremonies for girls is to explain sexual practices, childbirth, and role in the family. Each of these illustrations, regardless of the different methods used to demonstrate worthiness, has in common, after worthiness has been demonstrated, the total acceptance of the individual into the adult society. The rites that accompany these practices help to establish a very clear differentiation between the limitations of childhood and the privileges and responsibilities of adulthood. The individual has a clear-cut understanding of what is expected of him and what privileges he may expect.

Rituals or "rites of passage" such as these are disappearing from most cultures, and technological societies have all but eliminated them. Entry into adult society has been delayed, apparently in an effort to provide additional formal education and occupational training. This delay has created a rather extended period during which the individual is neither child nor adult. The individual is expected to give up the ways of a child and behave as an adult but is denied the rights and privileges of an adult. The inconsistency of this situation can create some rather complex problems so that adolescence is quite often described as a period of crisis or stress.

NORMAL DEVELOPMENTAL CRISIS IN ADOLESCENCE

The transition period referred to as adolescence is an experience common to all human beings. However it is defined, it represents the passage of the individual from a position of dependence to a position of independence. For some cultures it is marked by a specific event whereas in others it may be based on chronological age. For a majority of individuals today the parameters of this transition period have been established on a basis which takes into consideration a combination of physiological factors and chronological age. However, because of considerable variance among the population in physical development, it is considered less valid a criterion for adolescence. Social institutions such as schools and mental health facilities have come to rely primarily on chronological age to indicate the beginning as well as the end of adolescence, particularly with regard to eligibility for the services they provide. Although there is disagreement about what the ages involved should be, this chapter defines an adolescent as an individual between the ages of 13 and 21.

Crises that may occur during adolescence vary markedly in nature and degree from individual to individual, but generally involve elements common to all adolescents: physiological development (e.g., secondary sex characteristics) as well as psychological development (e.g., initial definition of or redefinition of such concepts as identity, relationships, and independence). Contrary to popular beliefs, adolescence is not a traumatic or stressful time for everyone who passes through it. For some the resolution of potential conflicts is a relatively simple matter. For others, however, adolescence is a time of turmoil in which problems seem to be insurmountable. Many of these adolescents exhibit exaggerated behavior patterns as they attempt to demonstrate their competence in stressful areas. The stereotype of the adolescent appears to have been taken from those individuals or groups which exhibit extremes in behavior, and certainly movies and television have done their part to popularize these stereotypes. In reality, these adolescents make up the minority (Horrocks, 1976). For example, there is a tremendous distance between the adolescent whose face breaks out just in time for an important social event and the adolescent who assaults someone in an attempt to establish an identity or position within a group. To the outsider, the adolescent whose face breaks out doesn't have a real problem, a little inconvenience maybe, but not a real problem. On the other hand, the adolescent who assaults someone is seen as having a major problem. Judgments of this type are not based upon whether the situation is a problem for the adolescent involved but whether the actions of the adolescent infringe upon the well-being of society. Either situation when viewed from that particular adolescent's perspective may be a crisis of gigantic proportions. The adolescent with the complexion problem may feel and believe that any chance for a meaningful social life has just been snatched away. The second adolescent may feel and believe the same thing if he is unable to establish an identity and position within his group. The situations are different but the feelings of stress experienced by the adolescents involved may be similar. The action taken by the adolescent to reduce the stress will determine the severity or importance of the issue involved. The adolescent with the complexion problem may feel a sense of embarrassment, but if a skin-colored cream or ointment is placed over the blemishes to cover or hide them, the adolescent, in all probability, will be able to function at the social event in a normal or near-normal way. This is not to say that the stress isn't real. The stress is very real and probably does involve feelings of embarrassment and inferiority. The solution, however, is one that both adult society and the peer group can understand and find acceptable. Another response to the same situation, such as withdrawing altogether from social activities, would be more difficult for some to understand and would not be as acceptable. In this instance the chosen behavior does little to resolve the problem. In the case of the adolescent who assaults another person, alternative actions sufficient to establish identity and position in the group may require even more of the adolescent. If the stress is great enough and the desire to belong strong enough, the adolescent may commit rape or murder in order to achieve the same end. The behavior that an adolescent chooses to reduce stress is probably the behavior perceived by the adolescent to be the most appropriate and effective in that particular situation.

Numerous theoretical positions have been postulated in an attempt to explain the psychology of adolescence. Muuss (1975) summarized the major theories of adolescence and their implications for education in a very clear and concise manner. It is beyond the scope of this chapter to include any discussion of the various theories here; however, it should be noted that in spite of the number of theories of adolescence in use today, there is very little *research* pertaining to adolescence. Yet, this period of development is seen as pivotal to the success of the individual as an adult. It is amazing how little we actually know about this period of development and how much we depend upon stereotypic descriptions of the adolescent for information which may not be accurate.

The one factor about which there is a consensus is that adolescence is a period of change. Adolescents must cope with and adjust to changes in their bodies brought about by increased hormone production. Adolescents must also respond to the expectations of society which challenge their status in that society.

Physiological Changes

Biologically, adolescence begins when the individual is capable of reproduction (Horrocks, 1976), a period called pubescence. Sommer (1978) has identified pubescence as a stage between childhood and adolescence. It begins when the hypothalamus produces and releases certain chemicals into the bloodstream to be carried to the pituitary gland. The pituitary gland is stimulated by these chemicals and in turn produces hormones which stimulate the gonads (ovaries in females and testes in males). The gonads produce sex hormones (estrogen and progesterone in females and testosterone in males) which are released into the bloodstream and are responsible for the development of sex characteristics. In the female these hormones are responsible for the maturation of the genitals as well as the increase in breast size, hip size and the growth of hair under the arms and in the pubic area. In the male the sex hormones are also responsible for the maturation of the genitals, growth of hair under the arms and in the pubic area, the growth of facial hair, and a deepening of the voice. The sex hormones also play a role in the alteration of body structure in both the female and the male. In the female there is a widening of the hips and in the male a broadening of the shoulders.

The biological clock which sets these processes into motion is not set the same for everyone. If fact, there is a great deal of variance with regard to developmental sexual characteristics. One child may begin to grow pubic hair at age 10 whereas another child might not begin until age 13. One girl might experience menarche at 10, another at 15. Not only is there considerable variance regarding the onset of sexual characteristics, there is also considerable variance with regard to maturational rate. These variances coupled with genetic variances such as height, weight, and body structure provide the potentially stressful situations. It is normal for pubescents to compare their development with that of others, and either early or late development of secondary characteristics may be a source of embarrassment. Considerable stress may be experienced if the pubescent begins to think there is something wrong with him which hasn't allowed him to develop at the same rate as a majority of his peers.

Peer response to the adolescent as an individual and to his behavior takes on a new meaning at about the same time that physiological changes occur. The primary feedback system switches from parents and family members to peers. In other words, what the peer group has to say becomes more important to the individual than what the parents or family members have to say on most issues. This shift in an accepted source of reference places the adolescent, in many instances, in conflict with the established values of society. The concerns of the adolescent and the responses from the peer group tend to emphasize the short-term view of an issue or situation, and little attention is paid to long-term consequences. Whether a problem does exist or not may depend upon the response or perceived response an adolescent receives from his peer group and in some cases from significant others. However, a majority of adolescents are able to handle physiological change without experiencing an inordinate amount of stress.

Both male and female adolescents are concerned with the overall appearance of their bodies. To be too tall or too short, or too skinny or too fat may evoke embarrassing remarks. One variable that frequently creates anxiety and concern is growth rate. The 15-year-old boy who has not started his growth spurt may feel left behind by his seemingly normal peers, who may even support this concept by calling him "Shorty" or by excluding him from certain activities. On the other hand, a 9-year-old girl who experiences rapid growth may find herself significantly taller than her age group with the prospect of waiting four or five years for them to catch up. To be four or six inches taller than the peer group may result in social isolation and all of the pains that accompany it.

Skin blemishes, such as acne, blackheads, and pimples, are a major source of stress for both male and female adolescents. The stress comes from the fact that the blemishes are visible to others and may serve as a signal that the adolescent is not "O.K." Many times adolescents are embarrassed by their skin blemishes because of myths that have been associated with them (for example, "pimples are the result of masturbation"). Many adolescents do not understand that there is an increase in the production of oil through the pores and they may not have learned proper hygiene techniques which might help reduce the number of blemishes.

Underarm hair doesn't seem to create many problems for adolescents. For males it's viewed as a sign of manhood and signals that it is time to begin bathing the area regularly and using a deodorant. For a female adolescent in most North American cultures it means not only bathing and using deodorant but also shaving the underarm area. The primary source of stress comes from not shaving (female) and from strong underarm odor (both sexes). For most individuals these are problems that can easily be resolved.

The growth of pubic hair can be both a badge of growth that one is proud of as well as a source of embarrassment. The embarrassment may be caused by either early or delayed growth. The teasing that may take place can affect how the adolescent interacts with peers. For example, in many public schools it is common practice for boys in gym classes to use a common shower following class. This allows all the boys the opportunity to compare themselves with the others. If a majority of the boys have started to grow pubic hair, they have a tendency to ridicule the boys who have not. Some boys become so self-conscious about the issue that they may refuse to shower or even dress for gym class. Most female facilities have been designed to provide more privacy; however, even with more privacy similar instances do occur. Eventually, for both male and female adolescents, pubic hair becomes a sign of physical maturity.

There are several changes that are unique to the female or the male. The following is a brief discussion of each by sex.

Female changes. Menstruation, increased breast size, and increased hip size are the three factors which indicate that the young female is maturing. Of the three, menstruation and breast size seem to be the source of most anxiety. It is unfortunate that not all mothers prepare their daughters for menarche and what it means. For the unsuspecting girl who first experiences menstruation away from home and who doesn't understand what is happening, it can be a frightening as well as an embarrassing experience. This trauma is usually short-lived although the memory of it may remain for some time. Public schools have had enough experiences of this nature to now keep the necessary supplies on hand, and school nurses have prepared materials to provide instruction on the subject for those who need it. Even for the adolescent who has been menstruating for several years, an accident (because her period starts earlier than expected and stains or soaks through her clothing) is tremendously embarrassing. It is embarrassing because it is a female thing from which males are excluded and because some regard it as "disgusting" and "dirty." It should be understood as a normal event.

Breast size is a source of great stress and anxiety, particularly for female adolescents with small breasts. Our society has overemphasized the female breast. Books, magazines, movies, and television present the image of an ideal woman with large breasts. Such propaganda has created feelings of inadequacy in many women who feel they don't measure up to the model. The concern of some female adolescents is, "Will they ever grow?" Others believe their popularity may hinge on the size of their breasts. Still others experience stress because their breast size is larger than that of their peers. Adolescents need to be made to feel comfortable with what they are, and understanding on the part of parents and others can go a long way to help.

Male changes. The changes in male adolescents do not seem to be so dramatic as those of the female. The male also has three basic changes which may be a source of some concern: growth of facial hair, a lowering of voice pitch, and an increase in penis size. Most male adolescents are very anxious to begin shaving, since the ability to grow a beard is seen as a sign of manhood. Anxiety develops in the adolescent who is late in growing facial hair; however, this anxiety is generally not that traumatic. Many adolescents start shaving anyway, just to go through the motions, hoping that the beard will grow faster, and also relishing the identity they can achieve by shaving.

The change in voice pitch is not of major concern except when the voice slips back to a higher range. A low voice pitch is associated with being a man; therefore, when the adolescent is trying to talk in a low pitch and his voice slips to a high pitch, it can be embarrassing.

The change in penis size probably creates the most anxiety for the male adolescent. Because of school (gym class) and sports he is placed in a situation which allows comparison with his peers. He also lives with the myth that penis size is an indicator of sexual functioning. For the adolescent with a small penis these myths create considerable anxiety and, additionally, he may receive ridicule from his peers. Also, during adolescence he may experience an increase in the frequency of situationally inappropriate erections. If he is at school, for example, and this occurs during class, he may be afraid to be called on and to have to stand up in front of the class. Most of the time these fears are unfounded but obviously that does not remove the concern.

In summary, it appears that most of the stress and anxiety pertaining to physiological changes in adolescence seems to revolve around three issues: (a) a general lack of understanding about what the adolescents can expect to happen; (b) an impatience with nature in the developmental process; and (c) the ridicule the adolescent might experience if for some reason certain standards are not met. If the adolescent were provided with appropriate information pertaining to physiology, including developmental sequence, and were to be given support and understanding, the degree of crisis might be reduced significantly. The adolescent eventually comes to recognize the variance that does exist among individuals on numerous characteristics and to accept those aspects of self which cannot be changed.

Psychological/Sociological Changes

The period of transition called adolescence extends beyond the physical changes brought about by hormones and maturation. The expectations for different modes of behavior and the desire of the adolescent to establish a separate identity and independence have the potential for creating psychological and sociological problems. It seems, to this author, a rather useless exercise to attempt to distinguish between psychological issues and sociological issues since to the adolescent they are so closely entwined. It is difficult to refer to a psychological issue without including the sociological ramifications and vice versa; therefore the issues will be presented as if they were one. The term *psychological change* will be used to encompass both.

Psychological stress in adolescence may be seen as the result of changes in the adolescent that require a revision of roles in adult relationships and of self-image (Levy, 1969). As the adolescent changes physically, new demands or expectations are made. Levy (1969) believes that these changes revolve around the adolescent's developing new perceptions of authority figures (including parents) and of self resulting from the physical maturation begun during pubescence. Seven issues that relate to this revision process have been identified. These issues are status, identity, independence, relationships, sex, values, and decision-making. This is not to imply that these are the only issues from which stress has a potential to evolve. They do represent the issues most commonly associated with psychological change. Although each is presented separately, it should be understood that each is closely interwoven with the others. When crises occur, it may be difficult to pinpoint the exact nature of the stress because of this close relationship. As the adolescent attempts to clarify or resolve these issues he finds himself in a position that requires that he choose among alternatives. For many adolescents crises occur when they are faced with the prospect of selecting one alternative over another.

Status. Of prime concern to every adolescent is personal status in a variety of groups as well as with selected individuals. Status is how one is perceived by others and how one is responded to by others. It includes not only one's reputation but the role or relative position taken by the individual within the group or, more than likely, assigned to the individual by the group. Status may change from group to group or from situation to situation but it must be established and clarified at all costs. This is a process through which the individual is able to identify expectations and establish criteria for behavior. Stress may develop if there is disagreement between the individual and the group as to what the individual's role should be or when the role accepted by the individual creates discomfort for either the individual or the group. For the adolescent attempting to revise relationships and self-image, determining status helps to define those relationships and to develop an estimate of self-worth. Status can be described by almost any set of adjectives pertinent to a particular group or activity. Within a school classroom the adolescent might be described as the smartest student in class, the hardest worker, the friendliest

student, the class clown, etc. The status of the adolescent so labeled will depend upon the value given that particular description by the class members.

The concept of an assigned value is an important factor to consider. For example, in one setting being a hard worker may be seen as a positive attribute and carry with it a certain amount of esteem or respect. The perception of the individual would be positive and the response of the group to the individual would be supportive of behavior that demonstrated that particular attribute. However, in another setting a hard worker might be viewed in a more negative manner. The group might interpret hard work, however demonstrated, as an attempt by the individual to show off or as a "put down" to demonstrate that the rest of the group is lazy or inferior. Such a perception by the group would probably result in low status for the individual in the classroom and the group in this instance would most likely punish the "hard worker" in some way.

Most adolescents are quick to learn that the value or worth of a behavior with regard to one's status may change from group to group or situation to situation. The ability to differentiate may increase the probability of functioning successfully in various settings. The recognition of this factor leads many adolescents to limit, when possible, the number of groups they actively become involved with. The adolescent will identify a significant group to whom to look for meaningful feedback. At times this sought-after feedback will be accepted from a single individual or from several individual members of the group. It is during adolescence that the individual shifts the need for recognition from parents and other adults to the peer group. Peer pressure becomes a powerful influence in the acquisition of new behavior patterns and the maintenance of old behavior patterns. The adolescent's status in the designated significant group may determine the quality and quantity of feedback the adolescent receives which in turn affects the adolescent's self-image and feelings of worthiness.

Identity. Some writers believe that the adolescent's search for identity is the primary source of crisis in adolescence. Erikson (1968) believes that the adolescent experiences an identity confusion to some degree. Glasser (1972) believes that adolescents today have restructured their priorities with regard to what they wish to accomplish as well as the time frame they have allowed themselves for obtaining it. He describes this change as a shift from a goal-oriented society which concerns itself with security to a role-oriented society concerned more with individual identity and human involvement. This shift in priorities (goal to role) has been made possible by the attainment of a relatively widespread affluence in society, an open concern for human rights supported in the political arena, government-supported security programs (for example, welfare, Medicare, social security, and so on), and an increased public awareness through communications (e.g., radio, television, magazines, etc.) that life should be enjoyed. By de-emphasizing the concern about security, energies that once were directed toward security (becoming a tradesperson, salesperson, teacher, or doctor) may now be free for determining and establishing one's own identity and for concern with the welfare of other human beings. To Glasser, the successful identity is achieved through involvement with others. The adolescent may make many awkward attempts to gain this involvement. The behaviors exhibited during these attempts, no matter how awkward they may appear, are the adolescent's efforts to gain that involvement based upon cumulative experiences up to that point. Eventually, through the support of peers and others, the adolescent will be able to gain involvement and to establish an identity.

A situation that adolescents frequently experience is that as children their identity was linked to that of someone else. Many times the child's identity was based on being someone's son or daughter or on being someone's brother or sister. The problem for the adolescent is to establish a personal identity, to be known and appreciated for one's own self. Many adolescents attempt to accomplish this through some type of action. For example, the adolescent who becomes an athlete is establishing credentials for being known through physical accomplishment. The same process may be in force with the adolescent who joins a gang and becomes known as "tough." In these instances the methods are different but the outcome is the same. Many adolescents initially establish their identity by associating themselves with a group. As they become able to differentiate self from group, they move toward more of an individual identification. Identity should help the adolescent know who he is, what he believes in, what he represents, and to be able to differentiate self from others. The ease with which this is accomplished depends upon such factors as opportunities to develop reasoning and decision-making skills, opportunities to develop responsibility, parental guidance, a willingness on the part of parents and others to allow for the selection of alternatives and to provide avenues for personal achievement. Most adolescents are able to resolve identity confusion and to appropriately manage the role/goal conflict.

Independence. Independence or autonomy represents the degree to which the individual is able to become self-sufficient. The adolescent in our society is expected to move from a state of dependence to a fairly high level of self-sufficiency by the time of high-school graduation. The adolescent is expected to become less dependent upon the family for material as well as psychological needs. The acquisition of independence is closely related to re-definition of relationships and the development of identity. The adolescent's assertion of independence helps to clarify identity. It is during this transition from dependence to independence that the adolescent discovers the need to learn about and to approximate the surrounding adult world. One of the more obvious issues confronting the adolescent at this time is what to do about sexual urges. The adolescent is physically capable of functioning sexually but society has established inhibiting standards. The limits placed on sexual functioning create the potential for considerable stress in the adolescent. Another aspect of learning to cope with the adult world is the dual standard: although adult behavior is expected of the adolescent, the adolescent will have to fight to receive adult privileges. The inconsistency of this situation leads to conflict with authority. Typically this is perceived as rebellion, characterized by a persistent disregard for authority. All adolescents exhibit some degree of rebellion, usually aimed at parental authority. There is a devaluation of parental ideas and values by the adolescent which generally creates as much stress in the parents as it does in the adolescent. This disregard for authority may take any number of forms but is usually geared toward redefining or reestablishing limits. Being late for dinner, growing long hair, growing a beard, staying out past curfew, and not keeping one's room clean are all examples of rebelling against limits. The adolescent behaves in these ways in an attempt to gain distance from parents and the ideas and values they represent. The adolescent will first shift to peer values. This is why during a time of rebellion against authority there is a considerable amount of conformity being practiced among adolescents. Conforming with the peer group provides the adolescent the necessary security needed to carry on the rebellion. Parents also need to provide some of this security by maintaining their own standards for the adolescent. Too much parental control as well as too much freedom for the adolescent are both conditions that can contribute to the development of psychological crises. The maintenance of reasonable behavior standards and the gradual increase of personal freedom as the adolescent learns to accept the responsibility which accompanies such freedom appear to be the most appropriate steps for parents to take. According to Sommer (1978) the ease with which the adolescent achieves independence depends upon three factors: the strength of the adolescent's attachment to parents, whether the adolescent receives training on how to be independent, and the degree of self-confidence the adolescent possesses. Psychological crises can be reduced if parents and others understand that a certain amount of rebellion in adolescence is normal and necessary to establish independence. Parents can be of great help to their child if they provide opportunities for self-determination and provide guidance and support in a constructive manner.

Relationships. To children, relationships are not something to be understood; rather, they are just there. The adolescent begins to question relationships particularly with regard to what is expected from him and what can be expected from others. In its simplest form a relationship is a consistent pattern of interaction between oneself and another person. A relationship is defined by the behaviors that make up this pattern of interaction. Individuals must establish some form of a relationship, be it a chance interaction or an intimate relationship, with all those with whom they have contact. Chance interactions may require a relatively strong self-confidence to manage the demands of the situation but demand little if anything in the form of personal investment. Casual relationships may require little more than an understanding of the other person's position and a predictable way of responding. Close personal relationships require a certain amount of intimacy. The individual is expected to enter into a reciprocal arrangement of giving and taking. Erikson (1968) believes that identity is a necessary prerequisite to intimacy. The adolescent cannot share until there is a sense of self.

During adolescence there is an increasing desire for closeness with others of the same sex. Gradually this expands to include the opposite sex. Feelings of aloneness may motivate the adolescent's attempts in establishing these relationships as a result of the rebellion against parental control and the self-enforced alienation from parents. The adolescent attempts to establish some security in relationships by developing a "best" friend. This "best" friend becomes a source of support and a confidant. There is a loyalty in these adolescent relationships which seems to be lost in most adult relationships. As identity is clarified, the adolescent develops the capacity for empathy and learns to share with others, and friendships become increasingly more stable.

During adolescence family relationships may become strained as a result of the adolescent's struggle for a separate identity and attempts to become independent. Difficulties arise in families when the members disagree with each other over roles, limits, and values. The potential for crisis is always present. The manner in which parents respond to the adolescent may serve to enhance a relationship or to damage it. Horrocks (1976) believes that certain factors, involving the concepts of dominance/submission and acceptance/rejection, must be recognized if one is to understand parent-child relationships. Each of these concepts is a continuum from one extreme to the other and must be jointly considered when attempting to identify and understand the roles played by both the parent and the child in a relationship. Many factors influence the establishment and maintenance of relationships in adolescence, and although most adolescents experience periodic stress over them (e.g., early opposite-sex relationships), most are ultimately successful in finding appropriate alternatives to resolve it.

Sex. Adolescents become acutely aware of their maleness or femaleness. This sexual identity plays a major role in their interactions with others and helps the adolescent to define the parameters of behavior. Even with the changes in thinking about sex-role stereotypes, the vast majority of boys wish to be identified as male and girls as female. Each exhibits the behaviors typically associated with their sex role. Sexuality is an extension of one's identity. Situations or events that interfere with the establishment of that sexuality can bring about psychological crisis. Most adolescents experience a rather sudden awareness of themselves and their bodies, an awareness so pronounced to them that they assume that everyone is as acutely aware of the changes that have taken place as they are. This newfound image may create some anxious moments and may lead to self-consciousness. Another concern for a majority of adolescents revolves around a lack of understanding about the sexual parts of their bodies and how they function. The attitudes adolescents develop toward menstruation in girls and ejaculation in boys may affect how they relate to others at given times. Training should be provided in sexual anatomy and functioning. The most appropriate place for this training is in the home, but unfortunately many parents are as misinformed as their children are. Also, many parents who are informed are nevertheless uncomfortable discussing these matters with their child. This task may, therefore, need to be conducted by an outside agency such as the public schools with input from and approval by parents. Everyone has a right to know how the body functions. Misinformation and myths have created considerable stress in the sex lives of many individuals and caused considerable anxiety about, for example, masturbation, homosexuality, petting, sexual intercourse, pregnancy, and venereal disease. Moral and religious teaching also has a tremendous impact on the adolescent's thinking about these issues and the alternatives available. The sense of guilt that might develop over a misunderstanding of what is normal or deviant might have life-long effects. Fadely and Hosler (1979) have included an excellent discussion of these issues in their book *Confrontation In Adolescence.*

Values. Each new generation of adolescents is accused of rejecting the values of their elders. The search for identity and independence places the adolescent in conflict with established authority and is usually perceived as a rejection of accepted standards of behavior. In an attempt to establish independence, the adolescent may alienate himself from the ideas and values of his parents which represent their control over him. If parents become overly concerned with the adolescent's rejection of their values, the potential for psychological stress in both the adolescent and the parents is greatly increased. During adolescence the individual may invest considerable energy searching for what Erikson (1968) refers to as "ideological commitment." Adolescents tend to search for someone or for some cause greater than themselves to believe in and become very emotional about the ideas they commit themselves to. Issues such as music, ecology, politics, and social service have provided popular causes in the past. During the 1970s the Vietnam War and concern for the environment served as forums from which many adolescents formalized many of their personal values and challenged and redefined older values such as patriotism.

Values are very much a part of an individual's identity and are one of the major criteria by which others know us. Values serve to guide individuals in their actions and toward establishing goals. Parents can help their children by teaching them the process for establishing values (see Simon, Howe, & Kirschenbaum, 1972) and by not leaving such important skills to chance. It should be comforting for parents to know that as adolescents become adults, they reflect many of the basic values their parents taught them.

Decision-making. The ability to choose one alternative over another for a desired outcome is a skill our society considers valuable for adult living. As adolescents strive for independence, they begin to demand the right to decide things for themselves. Matters such as curfew, where one is allowed to go, what clothes one is allowed to wear where, etc., are all matters that adolescents believe should be their prerogative to decide. Many parents allow adolescents these decisions only after they have demonstrated in other areas that they are capable of doing so.

Glasser (1969) believes that both parents and schools should teach children the fundamentals of how to make decisions and to give them an opportunity to practice those skills. He suggests that important decisions require that the individual have the strength to decide and to follow through on the selected response, to be responsible for the alternative selected, and to exercise good judgment in making that selection. The individual needs to have the self-confidence to make the appropriate decision. Sprinthall and Sprinthall (1974) indicate that there is a certain amount of risk involved in making a decision. Confidence in one's own ability helps to overcome the fear of failure associated with taking such risks. Glasser (1969) indicates that there are three steps the individual must learn to become an effective decision-maker: (a) identify the problem, (b) develop possible alternatives to resolve the problem, and (c) select the best possible alternative (keeping the situation open for possible revision if necessary).

Horrocks (1976) suggests that during adolescence the ability to see alternatives to various situations expands. This is particularly noticeable when parents or teachers give directions and the adolescent comes up with alternatives. Horrocks goes on to indicate that many times adolescents have a difficult time making decisions because of their expanded awareness of possible alternatives.

Psychological crises in decision-making occur most frequently among those who are not taught or who are given limited opportunity to exercise decision-making skills in childhood and adolescence. The adolescent must learn to become an effective decision maker. To do this, opportunities to make decisions must be available and adults must provide the necessary support and encouragement as the skill is acquired.

The psychological changes that occur during adolescence provide the conditions necessary for crises to develop. Factors such as a lack of understanding and/or information pertaining to development, a rejection of established values, and the acquisition of new roles are examples of potential points of stress between the adolescent and adult society. A majority of adolescents are able to cope with these and other potentially dangerous factors in a manner that results in little or no discomfort either to themselves or others. The remaining minority are faced with problems of adjustment which are painful to themselves and those around them. With understanding and support from peers and adults these individuals can be helped to overcome their problems. An encouraging fact is that many of these individuals will resolve many of their crises by themselves over time. But given an understanding and supporting hand that time might be reduced.

SPECIAL PROBLEMS IN ADOLESCENCE

Normal adolescent development is full of pitfalls which can bring about conflict, stress, and anxiety to the individual attempting to negotiate it. A majority are able to make it to adulthood with a minimal amount of distress. There are, however, a sizeable number of adolescents who find themselves with special or different problems which extend beyond the normal developmental crises, such as alcohol and drug abuse, crime, suicide, pregnancy, and teenage marriage. It is not the author's intent to provide detailed coverage of these areas but rather to describe the problem. A more detailed review of the possible etiology of these problems is provided by Nelson and Polsgrove in another article in this book. Some general considerations of these problems are presented here.

There are any number of possible reasons that an adolescent may become involved in or confronted with any of these special problems. In some cases the behavior is an exaggerated reaction to stress, a form of escape from some painful situation. The situation or stimuli may be aversive enough that the adolescent through deviant behavior is trying to remove the stimulus or separate himself from the situation so as not to be affected by it. Normal rebellion might be expanded to all areas of the adolescent's life either in an effort to escape punishing consequences or as a result of consequences the adolescent perceives as positive or reinforcing. This latter possibility might occur in situations where a peer group, such as in a delinquent gang, approves and supports the behavior. Another possibility might be that the adolescent is a victim of an unfortunate decision, that is, the situation is the consequence of a poor or reckless decision. One example of an unfortunate decision might be the adolescent boy who is dared by his buddies to race his car against that of a friend on a state highway. He knows that racing on a public highway is wrong but finally bows to the pressure and agrees to the race, only to lose control of his car and go over a 30-foot embankment. He survives the crash but one of his buddies who was riding with him is killed. He is brought to trial on charges of involuntary manslaughter with an automobile. The court finds him guilty and sentences him to one year in the county jail. Another example of an unfortunate decision might be an adolescent girl who feels pressure from her peer group and her boyfriend to become sexually active. She has been taught that sex before marriage is wrong but is afraid of being different or being rejected by her friends. She doesn't have all the facts about pregnancy; in fact, she is extremely naive about sexual matters altogether. One evening her boyfriend pushes her to "go all the way" with him and threatens not to go with her anymore if she doesn't. She is afraid of becoming pregnant but friends have told her not to worry because she can't get pregnant the first time she has sexual intercourse. With this misinformation and the threat of losing her boyfriend she gives in only to become pregnant. The consequences of each of these unfortunate decisions are drastic and will affect these two young people for the rest of their lives.

Regardless of how the special problem arises, the adolescent must deal with systems not really designed to meet the needs of adolescents. Service agencies in our society are designed for children and adults. Most of those that do exist for adolescents were adapted from either child services or adult services. The three major agencies the adolescents with special problems will most likely come in contact with are the public schools, mental health facilities, and the legal system. Secondary programs in the public schools are just beginning to develop program alternatives for adolescents with special problems. Most mental health agencies are still trying to adapt known child and adult interventions to fit the adolescent. The legal system or juvenile justice system can't decide if the adolescent should be treated as a child or as an adult. The problems involved in each of these areas are complex and will probably take some time to resolve. In the meantime, the adolescent with the special problem will be the one to suffer.

Alcohol and Drug Abuse

The use of alcohol or drugs by adolescents has been a concern of societies for the last 20 years. It has only been during the last 10 to 15 years that efforts have been made to do something about what has been perceived as a national problem. The concern has been centered on the use of hallucinogens, primarily LSD, and marijuana which were popularized by the youth subculture in the late 1960s. Descriptions of drug use and stories of their effects were communicated through songs and stories and eventually through television and the movies. Words such as *high* and *trip* took on new meanings. Drug education programs were developed to treat the drug abuser. Randall and Wong (1976) reviewed a number of studies about the effects of these programs and found that short-term programs are not effective in changing attitudes toward drug use and that although long-term programs do increase the clients' knowledge of drugs, it is not clear whether attitudes toward drugs and drug use were changed. Akers (1970) identified five major categories of drugs: (a) opiates (heroin, morphine, Demerol, and Dolophine), (b) hallucinogens (marijuana and LSD), (c) depressants (barbiturates), (d) stimulants (amphetamines and cocaine), and (e) deliriants (airplane glue and aerosol sprays). Alcohol is a depressant and is considered a drug. Of the drugs listed here, alcohol is the most widely used. A relatively small number of adolescents use alcohol; and of those who do, a majority use alcohol only on a social level, just as their adult counterparts.

The adolescent who becomes an abuser of alcohol or other drugs may be bewildered by the wide variation in reactions from the law enforcement agencies. Although it is against the law for adolescents to drink alcoholic beverages, those who are arrested for doing so will most likely be charged with a delinquent act. This is because the adolescent has been caught doing something that if he were an adult would be legal. Drug use, on the other hand, is illegal for everyone and if caught, the adolescent can be tried on a felony charge. Adolescents when they get into trouble because of alcohol or drug use get into trouble not so much because they have used a drug but because of where they used it. Aside from being against the law, the abuse and side effects of these substances can lead to emotional and physical problems as well as disrupt the adolescent's academic work. Many adolescents experiment with a drug upon occasion, but the regular abuser may be trying to avoid or escape some unpleasant aspect of life.

If the motivation for alcohol and drug use is social acceptance, intimacy, and status, as Fadely and Hosler (1979) have stated, and society is concerned about the harmful effects of these substances, then we need to find alternatives for helping the adolescent meet these needs.

Adolescent Crime

The majority of offenses for which adolescents are arrested and brought before the juvenile justice system are referred to as *status* offenses, that is, offenses that if committed by an adult would not be considered a criminal act. They include such offenses as running away from home, truancy, violating curfew, being incorrigible, having sex, and drinking in public (Gibbons, 1976). The response of the court to these offenses varies from a lecture to probation to placement in a detention facility. Many of these cases can be related to independence and relationship crises. The adolescent commits these acts in an effort to resolve some conflict.

Only a minority of adolescents are brought to court for truly criminal acts (theft, assault, rape, murder, etc.). The legal system is unsure as to what to do with the juvenile (below 17 years of age) who commits an offense of this type. It is possible for a juvenile to be tried as an adult but only after the court has ruled to do so. Regardless of the seriousness of the offense, the courts have been inconsistent in handling juvenile offenders. There have been cases in which a juvenile who has committed rape or murder has been given probation whereas others, convicted of breaking and entering, have been given sentences in a detention facility. Adolescents make up the last population to be protected under the due process provisions of the U.S. Constitution. Many states are now revising their juvenile codes to be more consistent and to meet the needs of the individuals with whom they come in contact.

Adolescent Suicide

Suicide, particularly adolescent suicide, is a phenomenon that is not well understood by society. Fadely and Hosler (1979) suggest that the incidence of adolescent suicide has been overstated, probably because we react so strongly when a young person takes his own life. Most suicide is seen as a result of severe depression and alienation from other people, a loss of the motivation to live. Suicide appears to be an alternative in dealing with problems and the individual who contemplates suicide may not be able to see any other way out of a situation.

Suicide in adolescents as with adults is closely related to relationship problems. The adolescent may believe that he has lost all involvement with the significant others in his life and without this involvement there may appear to be no reason for living. Suicide threats should be taken seriously and professional counseling should be provided to help the adolescent work through the crisis.

Teenage Pregnancy and Marriage

The effects of an unwanted pregnancy in an unmarried teenage girl can be devastating to both the girl and her family. Neither is prepared for it. Discussions about sex and birth control have become so common that most adults believe that adolescents have ready access to the same information. The publicity about the recent sexual revolution gives the impression that most individuals, including adolescents, are sophisticated when it comes to sexual matters. The advent of the Pill made it possible for all women to be free from the fear of pregnancy, or so it seemed. Contrary to the publicity and the Pill, many individuals are still quite naive, particularly adolescents. Very few adolescents will admit their lack of knowledge about sex because of their need to seem "in the know."

The consequences of sexual activity, pregnancy, venereal disease, and a bad reputation can be quite drastic for the adolescent. Adolescents who have yet to establish their own identities may possibly develop serious emotional problems. In an unwanted pregnancy, even if the couple marries, they are ill prepared to provide for a family either emotionally or financially. It is too much to expect such responsibilities of a teenage mother or father if they are still resolving the psychological changes of adolescence. Marriage is an adjustment even for people who are equipped to handle it, but it can become a critically stressful situation if husband and wife don't get to know each other prior to starting a family. A common result of teenage marriages is resentment on the part of either the husband or the wife or both that they were trapped into marriage and that they missed out on many of the things their friends experience. The divorce rate is higher for teenage marriages than for those married at later times in life.

THE BEHAVIORALLY DISORDERED ADOLESCENT

Some individuals experience sufficient stress and conflict during adolescence to cause them to exhibit behaviors which deviate from an accepted norm. Behavior outside the established limits calls attention to the individual; if this deviant response occurs frequently or to an exaggerated degree, the individual is identified as different. All behavior must be considered in light of the individual's age, expected growth patterns, the situation in which the behavior occurs, as well as who is judging the behavior to be acceptable or normal. For example, a 9 year old is not expected to behave in the same manner as a 15 year old, behavior that is appropriate for the gymnasium may not be appropriate for the library, or the peer group may approve of shoplifting although it remains unacceptable to the rest of society. Normal or accepted behavior is defined by limits established by a group, society, or culture. For example, many states have identified 21 as the age when an individual may legally purchase and consume alcoholic beverages. Adolescents who engage in this activity fall outside of the accepted age variance and may be punished by the law if caught. Most behaviors can be viewed on a continuum ranging from an extreme of overconformity to the opposite of excessive rebellion. Somewhere between the two extremes limits are established, and as long as the behavior remains within the limits it is seen as acceptable.

Adolescents are allowed, at times, to exhibit behavior which exceeds established limits. Such behavioral variance may be perceived as attempts to adjust to the changes in adolescence and the tolerance level of adults may increase with regard to certain behaviors. "Back talk" which most likely would have been punished in childhood may be ignored or excused on the grounds that it's just a phase. However, many adolescents become confused when limits are not clearly defined. This is particularly true when the adolescent exhibits behavior that is tolerated one time and at other times is severely punished. The inconsistency may create a great deal of stress within the adolescent. The ability to predict the consequences of one's behavior is important in the selection of alternatives (decision-making) and in one's overall adjustment.

Inconsistency on the part of parents may reflect a lack of understanding of normal adolescent development. They may recognize that previous responses to certain behaviors are no longer appropriate but they don't know what new appropriate responses to substitute. Some parents in this situation commit a most grievous error by withdrawing from the situation altogether and allowing the adolescent to behave in any way he chooses. Known limits and the consequences associated with them provide security, and consistency helps to clarify the relationship between the limit and its consequence.

Parents should be trained to recognize developmental change, to provide subtl guidance, to maintain open communication, and to support or reinforce behavioral alternatives they believe to be appropriate and beneficial to the adolescent. Parents may recognize that an adolescent's striving for independence is normal but may not know how to respond to specific adolescent acts geared toward achieving independence. They may not know how to give the adolescent room to grow up. The extremes of letting go too much or overcontrolling the situation may create problems for the adolescent, who may respond with behaviors which exceed the established limits. No matter how deviant an adolescent's behavior might be, it is that person's attempt to select the best alternative to meet the situation. It represents an effort to resolve some conflict or to bring about certain consequences.

Definition

A universally accepted definition of behavior disorders has yet to be developed. There are several problems to be resolved before this task can be achieved. One of the most serious of these problems concerns behavior variance, not only as it applies to an accepted norm, but to the amount of variance found within any particular behavior. That is, not only what behavior an individual perceives as normal or deviant but how extreme the deviation is from an accepted limit.

Most existing definitions evolved from work with children in elementary schools. Bower (1960) and Kauffman (1977) have each proposed definitions which can be easily adapted for use with an adolescent population. Bower developed a list of behavior characteristics which he believed identified the emotionally disturbed child. Display of one or more of the following characteristics either to a marked degree or over a period of time indicates emotional disturbance in a child:

> 1. An inability to learn which cannot be explained by intellectual, sensory, or health factors.
> 2. An inability to build or maintain satisfactory interpersonal relationships with peers and teachers.
> 3. Inappropriate types of behavior or feelings under normal conditions.
> 4. A general, pervasive mood of unhappiness or depression.
> 5. A tendency to develop physical symptoms, pains, or fears associated with personal or school problems.   (pp. 9–10)

Kauffman included statements pertaining to both the degrees of severity and possible differences in educational programming:

> Children with behavior disorders are those who chronically and markedly respond to their environment in socially unacceptable and/or personally unsatisfying ways but who can be taught more socially acceptable and personally gratifying behavior. Children with mild and moderate behavior disorders can be taught effectively with their normal peers (if their teachers receive appropriate consultive help) or in special resource or self-contained classes with reasonable hope of quiet reintegration with their normal peers. Children with severe and profound behavior disorders require intensive and prolonged intervention and must be taught at home, in special classes, special schools, or residential institutions.   (p. 23)

These definitions revolve around two major issues: the inability to establish appropriate, satisfying relationships with others, and demonstration of behavior which either fails to meet or exceeds the expectations of those with whom the individual comes in contact (McDowell & Brown, 1978). Since both of these conditions are found to a certain extent in normal adolescent development, it is important that one consider the fine line between normal adolescent behavior and disordered behavior. The distinction may lie in the frequency of the behavior or the degree of severity of the behavior.

Prevalence

Prevalence refers to the frequency with which a particular factor is distributed within a given population. One of the necessary prerequisites for determining prevalence is the ability to define the population concerned and the factor being identified. The major problems in trying to establish the prevalence of behavior disorders is the lack of an accepted definition and the lack of standardized measures for identification purposes (Kauffman, 1977). Schultz, Hirshoren, Manton, and Henderson (1971) reviewed the procedures used by the different states to identify children as emotionally disturbed and found a lack of consensus among states as to terminology and definition. Schultz et al. found estimates of prevalence ranging from 0.05% to 15%. The prevalence estimate presently used by the U.S. Office of Education (1975) is 2%. There is no particular reason to expect that the percentage reported here would be any different for an adolescent population.

Description of Population

Behavior disorders in adolescence can run the full range of disorders found in adults. For those who work with the disordered adolescent in an educational setting, the traditional classification of disorders is of little value on a day-to-day basis. The traditional classification system (see *Diagnostic and Statistical Manual of Mental Disorders* DSM-II of the American Psychiatric Association, 1968) is a diagnostic system resulting in specific labels. The system provides no assistance in the way of developing an appropriate educational program or of managing specific behaviors. (Although the system of labels provided in the DSM-II is widely used, the manual was not designed to be used in development of educational intervention programs.) This population might better be described by the degree of behavior variance exhibited and by the type of program that best serves its needs. Mild behavior disorders are characteristic of those adolescents who are involved in some type of crisis but are still able to function within the regular school system with a minimum of support help from a crisis teacher, counselor, or itinerant resource teacher. Disorders that fall within the "mild" category tend to be transient and may disappear without specific intervention. Moderate behavior disorders are those that require special class placement. They tend to be longer lasting, the disorder is more debilitating, and it does interfere with functioning. The severe level is based on the adolescent's inability to function and the necessity of providing a special environment. The severely disordered adolescent may have difficulty maintaining contact with reality. The behavior exhibited is more exaggerated and bizarre in nature. The severely disordered adolescent will need a self-contained classroom or possibly residential placement.

Educational intervention is an appropriate strategy to use with behaviorally disordered adolescents. However, the curriculum must be expanded (see McDowell

& Brown, 1978) to meet the unique needs of the disturbed population and new programs designed. The "special class" concept of remedial instruction does little to help the disordered adolescent. Teaching techniques need to be as up to date as possible and materials and tasks need to be functional. Secondary programs should prepare the adolescent to enter a world of work and to assist the adolescent in acquiring as many skills as possible so that the adolescent will be able to function outside the school environment.

Summary

Normal adolescent development allows ample opportunity for stress and conflict to occur. Physiological changes require the adolescent to learn about and cope with a mature body and its new functions. Psychological/sociological changes present the adolescent with new modes of thinking and new problems with regard to status, identity, identification, relationships, sex, values, and decision-making. Many of these changes put the adolescent in direct conflict with adult society. The ease with which the adolescent is able to resolve these conflicts appears to be related to prior teaching and support by parents and other adults. A number of adolescents find themselves with special problems, including alcohol and drug abuse, crime, suicide, teenage pregnancy, and marriage.

A majority of school programs for behavior disorders have been designed and exist primarily in the elementary schools. Secondary programs have been an adaptation of those programs into the high schools. A major problem in developing programs for the behaviorally disordered adolescent has been the inability to develop an accepted definition of the population. The common factors found in most definitions that are pertinent to the adolescent population are an inability to establish appropriate, satisfying relationships with others, and a demonstration of behavior which either fails to meet or exceeds the expectations of those with whom he comes in contact. Recognition of behavior variance and the establishment of limits helps to differentiate between normal developmental crisis and behavior disorders in adolescence. Educational intervention is seen as an appropriate approach to working with the behaviorally disordered adolescent. New alternatives need to be designed and the curriculum made functional if we are to provide the best possible chance for survival in the adult world.

References

Akers, R. L. Teenage drinking and drug use. In E. D. Evans, *Adolescents: Readings in behavior and development*. Hinsdale, Ill.: Dryden Press, 1970.

American Psychiatric Association. *Diagnostic and statistical manual of mental disorders* (2nd ed., DSM-II). Washington, D.C.: American Psychiatric Association, 1968.

Bower, E. M. *Early identification of emotionally handicapped children in school*. Springfield, Ill.: Charles C Thomas, 1960.

Erikson, E. H. *Identity, youth and crisis*. New York: W. W. Norton, 1968.

Evans, E. D. *Adolescents: Readings in behavior and development*. Hinsdale, Ill.: Dryden Press, 1970.

Fadely, J. L., & Hosler, V. N. *Confrontation in adolescence*. St. Louis: C. V. Mosby, 1979.

Gibbons, D. C. *Delinquent behavior*. Englewood Cliffs, N.J.: Prentice-Hall, 1976.

Glasser, W. *Schools without failure*. New York: Harper & Row, 1969.

Glasser, W. *The identity society*. New York: Harper & Row, 1972.

Horrocks, J. E. *The psychology of adolescence*. Boston: Houghton Mifflin, 1976.

Kauffman, J. M. *Characteristics of children's behavior disorders*. Columbus, Ohio: Charles E. Merrill, 1977.

Levy, E. Toward understanding the adolescent. *Menninger Quarterly*, 1969, *23*, 14–21.

McDowell, R. L., & Brown, G. B. The emotionally disturbed adolescent: Development of program alternatives in secondary education. *Focus on Exceptional Children*, 1978, *10* (4), 1–15.

Muuss, R. E. *Theories of adolescence*. New York: Random House, 1975.

Randall, D., & Wong, M. R. Drug education to date: A review. *Journal of Drug Education*, 1976, *6* (1), 1–21.

Schultz, E. W., Hirshoren, A., Manton, A. B., & Henderson, R. A. Special education for the emotionally disturbed. *Exceptional Children*, 1971, *38*, 313–319.

Simon, S. B., Howe, L. W., & Kirschenbaum, H. *Values clarification*. New York: Hart, 1972.

Sommer, B. B. *Puberty and adolescence*. New York: Oxford University Press, 1978.

Sprinthall, R. C., & Sprinthall, N. A. *Educational psychology: A developmental approach*. Reading, Mass.: Addison-Wesley, 1974.

U.S. Office of Education. *Estimated number of handicapped children in the United States, 1974–75*. Washington, D.C.: U.S. Office of Education, 1975.

The Etiology of Adolescent Behavior Disorders

2

C. Michael Nelson
Lewis Polsgrove

Anyone who reads newspapers or listens to news broadcasts is familiar with the problems the youth of the world pose to the older generation. We seem to have a fascination for adolescents, particularly in North American cultures. The effects of social and cultural change appear to show up most dramatically in persons between puberty and adulthood. Porter (1978) contended that an unparalleled social revolution occurred in the United States between 1950 and 1975 and that the effects of this revolution on our youth include increased rates of suicide and homicide, greater consumption of drugs and alcohol, and more sexual promiscuity. But what are the causes of these and other adolescent behavior disorders? Are youth responding to general sociocultural influences or are the antecedents of behavior disorders to be found in genetically determined predispositions, home environments, schools, or peer groups? The purpose of this chapter is to examine research into the etiology of behavior disorders, particularly that pertaining to adolescents, to discover what, if any, causal agents can be identified.

The difficulty of this task is compounded by several problems, not the least of which is that the etiology of behavior disorders, at any age, is highly speculative (Kauffman, 1977). Tracing the historical antecedents of a particular behavior

The authors are indebted to Ann Bucalos and Mark Posluszny for their assistance with the research for this chapter.

pattern involves sorting through an incredible tangle of variables. As Ross (1974, pp. 6–7) indicated:

> Any specific behavior, taking place at any one point, represents the end point of the interaction of genetic-constitutional factors, the current physiological state of the individual, his current environmental conditions and past learning which, in turn, was a function of a similar interaction.

In addition, relatively little etiological research has focused on adolescents as a separate group. Partly, this is because of the tradition of examining early life experiences and biological influences in explaining behavior disorders and partly because most etiological agents are assumed to have acted by the time a child reaches adolescence.

Another complicating factor in isolating the etiology of adolescent behavior disorders is the broad range of problems reported: from gang delinquency to anorexia nervosa, from rebellion against parental authority to schizophrenia. Such an extensive array of problems allows few generalizations regarding causal agents. Related to this difficulty is the way in which etiological research concerning adolescents is conducted. Generally speaking, research efforts have concentrated upon an easily identified population (for example, adjudicated delinquents) or a specific problem behavior (alcohol or drug abuse). Because subjects in either category are extremely heterogeneous, it is difficult to extend research findings beyond the immediate sample. As a result of this fact, plus the sparsity of research on adolescent behavior disorders, the literature contains many gaps.

Finally, the literature on adolescence reflects the prevalent assumptions and theoretical biases regarding the dynamics of adolescence. Many studies have proceeded from an analytic-interpretative frame of reference, in which underlying personality constructs are the focus. This problem is compounded by the correlational and speculative nature of most etiological studies. Only recently has social learning theory begun to influence etiological research, resulting in more reliable dependent measures and more tightly controlled experimental designs. We will elaborate on these problems and issues throughout our discussion.

PRELIMINARY CONSIDERATIONS

Because the literature reviewed herein is so varied and unwieldy, an initial discussion of several concepts and personal biases is in order. The purpose of this discussion is to give the reader a frame of reference, for evaluating both the research and the author's interpretations of it.

The Concept of Disordered Behavior

Until recently it was believed that behavior disorders are surface indicators of underlying pathology or disease processes. Problem behaviors, therefore, were (and, among many professionals, still are) seen as symptomatic manifestations of disease, much as the symptoms of pneumonia are manifestations of a viral infection. Critics of this "medical model" (Skinner, 1967; Szasz, 1960; Ullmann & Krasner, 1965) have argued against its relevance in the area of human social behavior. An alternative view—and one subscribed to here—explains behavior disorder as a label applied when a significant discrepancy exists between an individual's behavior and moral, legal, cultural, or personal expectations (Kauffman, 1977; Ross, 1974). The label thus reflects a judgment applied by persons or agencies in the immediate environment. Such judgments are, of course, subjective and vary as a function of many factors, including subcultural standards or the expectations held by a particular agency (e.g., the school). It is possible that the standards themselves, rather than the individual's behavior, may be inappropriate.

Standards applied to adolescents' behavior and the expectations made of them are markedly different from those applied to younger children and adults. The onset of adolescence signals the beginning of social expectations for "adult" forms of behavior: self-control, responsibility, an orientation to work, etc. At the same time, the adolescent is not accorded the behavioral freedom commensurate with adult responsibilities. The frequency of "status" offenses (i.e., behaviors which are not considered deviant or illegal in adults, such as drinking, sex, truancy) among adolescents is indicative of this double standard. The relatively abrupt change in environmental expectations may heighten an existing discrepancy between the demands of the environment and the child's behavior, or it may create a discrepancy where none existed previously. Regardless of where or when the discrepancy originated, it can result in a label being applied to the adolescent. Thus, disordered adolescent behavior is defined by subjective value judgments rather than disease processes or entities and it is not likely to have a simple or direct cause.

Views of Adolescence

Musgrove (1964) observed that the emergence of the concept of adolescence as a unique age category in the helping professions was associated with the development of spatially segregated programs and services, such as schools and children's quarters. The most objective perception of adolescence relates to a growth period between the age of puberty (roughly 12 or 13 years) and the attainment of legal adult status (age 21). Beyond this point, however, authorities disagree. The view of adolescence espoused by psychoanalytically inclined writers (Ackerman, 1962; Freud, 1958; Spiegel, 1961) is that it is a "normally" disturbed state, i.e., characterized by turbulent, distressing, and unpredictable thoughts, feelings, and actions. As a result of this turmoil, adolescents normally display symptoms that would indicate psychopathology in adults. Despite the popularity of this view, it has not received empirical support. To the contrary, recent studies indicate that adolescence may be characterized as more a period of stability than of turmoil (Bachman, O'Malley, & Johnston, 1978; Weiner, 1970).

A sounder view of adolescence, in our opinion, characterizes it as a developmental period requiring new behavior. The adolescent is undergoing rapid physical and physiological changes, with concomitant alterations in his/her social environment. Whereas parents have been the major socializing influence in earlier years, in adolescence they become distinctly less important than peers as social models (Muuss, 1976). Ferster, Culbertson, and Boren (1975) also conceptualized adolescence as a period of transition from continuous to intermittent schedules of reinforcement. Whereas much of the preadolescent's behavior has a direct effect on the environment (i.e., has received continuous reinforcement), the adolescent is expected to emit increasingly larger amounts of behavior prior to reinforcement.

The Question of Etiology

Physicians look for the causes of disease in order to treat afflicted patients more effectively. Unfortunately, here too, the disease analogy fails to meet the needs of the behavioral sciences. For one thing, the causes of adolescent behavior disorders may exist in the past, which makes them difficult to find or to treat. In the second place, it may not be helpful, or even necessary, for the treatment planner to have knowledge of specific etiological agents in order to generate an effective intervention (Kauffman, 1977; Worell & Nelson, 1974). Finally, since the causes of behavior problems are multiple, complex, and interacting, searching for etiological agents is likely to take time that could be better spent administering treatment.

Why, then, are behavioral scientists concerned with identifying causal factors? One reason is our curiosity about cause-effect relationships. Another is that in identifying etiological agents and factors, we acquire information important for preventing many behavior disorders from occurring in the first place. Then, too, there is the possibility that some behavior disorders do have specific and treatable causes. For example, the behavior disorders associated with phenylketonuria (PKU) may be treated and/or completely prevented by appropriate dietary regulation.

Research techniques for studying etiology have much to do with our present confusion regarding the antecedents of disordered behavior. The ideal strategy is to conduct research in a laboratory where dependent variables (behavior) can be reliably measured and confounding variables controlled while independent variables are systematically manipulated. This degree of control allows the researcher to clearly examine the effects of one variable upon another. These conditions are, of course, impossible to attain outside of laboratory settings. The natural environments of people are full of confounding variables and multiple interactions among potential independent variables. The behavioral scientist attempts to reduce this unwanted variance through research designs and strategies developed for the natural environment.

In general, the best alternative to laboratory research for etiological investigations is the *longitudinal study*. In this procedure, a group of subjects (or, ideally, an experimental group which has certain "characteristics" and a control group which does not) are followed for a period of time. The researcher assesses the group(s) periodically in order to identify the effects of variables selected as potentially influential on subjects' behavior. Probably the best-known study of this type is Terman's (1959) longitudinal investigation of gifted persons who were identified in childhood and followed into middle age. Because of the expense, few longitudinal studies have been done in the area of behavior disorders (the 10-year study of aggression by Lefkowitz, Eron, Walder, and Huesmann [1977] is a recent example and will be discussed in some detail later). To generalize the findings of such research to a meaningful extent, large numbers of subjects are required, and they must be followed for a period of years.

Another alternative strategy is the anthropological *field study*. In this approach, researchers collect copious amounts of data in the natural environment via interviews, questionnaires, and direct observation. This type of research also takes a great deal of time (usually several years) and involves a well-trained research team. In addition, the mass of data collected in such studies make clear interpretation difficult, and hypotheses are often made after data are collected, rather than beforehand. Nevertheless, field studies are a rich source of data; much has been learned about the problem of juvenile delinquency, for example, from this strategy (Miller, 1968; Stumphauzer, Aiken, & Veloz, 1977).

A less reliable, but also less expensive, research strategy is the *retrospective study*. This approach involves probing the case histories of adult subjects to identify common factors in their background. Retrospective studies of behavior disorders have been relatively popular. The histories of adult mental patients have been examined to determine whether they had behavior problems as children and, in some cases, to identify potential causal factors (Lewis, 1965). Aside from the questionable reliability of the data obtained by this method, researchers are limited by the necessity of making a priori decisions about which variables are important. This sets up potential biases which can affect the findings. Despite these shortcomings, most of the information we have about the continuity of child and adult behavior disorders is derived from retrospective studies.

The least satisfactory strategy for conducting etiological research also is the most popular. This tactic involves conducting one-time assessments of a sample of individuals who may or may not represent a specific population (Campbell & Stanley, 1963). Frequently, a large amount of data is collected, and interpretations of the results are based upon the intercorrelations among the variables studied. Sometimes an experimental group, which shares a common characteristic, is compared with a control group matched on variables the researcher thinks might confound the results. Confounding variables also may be controlled as covariates (that is, their effects held constant through statistical procedures) while the dependent variables are analyzed. This strategy is by far the least expensive or time-consuming.

Regardless of the type of design employed, all etiological research is plagued by methodological problems which need to be explained before we discuss the research itself. Chief among these is the use of the statistical method of correlation, which is employed in virtually all etiological studies. Correlation is an expression of the way in which two things vary together: it demonstrates the extent to which they are related but *it does not demonstrate that one thing causes the other.* Research has shown that behavior disorders are correlated with poor home environments, inappropriate parental disciplinary techniques, low intelligence, poor school performance, and a host of other variables. However, a relationship between these variables and behavior problems does not prove causality, no matter how many times the same finding is replicated. Neither, for that matter, does the relationship establish that a behavior disorder causes a poor home environment, inadequate discipline, and so on. Etiological speculations based on correlational methods are vulnerable to competing explanations, the chief one being that the relationship between two variables may be accounted for by their mutual relationship with a third, untapped variable.

Even complex multiple regression techniques fail to account for competing explanations. In such procedures, a number of variables are used to "predict" variance in a criterion measure. The term "prediction" is statistical and in no way implies causation. Which variables predict which criterion measures are largely determined by the researcher prior to the study. For example, Friedman, Mann, and Friedman (1975) tested the ability of a number of variables to statistically predict gang membership. The best predictor was self-reported violence. Had the experimenters decided upon self-reported violence as the criterion measure, they might have found that gang membership was the best predictor. The coefficient of determination, R^2, a measure of the amount of criterion variance accounted for by another variable, also fails to establish causation, despite the connotation of its name.

The problem of confounding variables continues to thwart efforts to identify causal factors in the natural environments of children and adults. For each independent variable selected, there are many more variables the researcher may choose not to measure which conceivably could explain the phenomenon as well as, or better than, those studied. While the scientist wishes to make functional predictive statements about the effects of an independent on a dependent variable (i.e., if X happens, Y will occur), the actual prediction of behavior involves a complex network of independent variables (Warner & De Fleur, 1969), many of which are uncontrolled in any given study. As Ross (1974) observed, "The only causal question science can investigate takes the form, 'Under what conditions does this phenomenon occur?' " (p. 6).

Our inclination to explain behavior in terms of internal variables and events gives rise to other significant methodological problems. In the past, psychology has offered numerous theoretical constructions of what "causes" an individual to behave: needs, traits, drives, wishes, habits, attitudes, and so on. Since these constructs have no physical properties, they are hypothetical and their existence cannot be proven. Nevertheless, they have provided many convenient explanations for problem behavior, and the research on etiology is full of instruments created to measure them.

Skinner (1972) noted that if psychology is to embrace mentalistic constructs, it needs to develop a valid and special methodology—which it has failed to do. On the other hand, the experimental analysis of behavior has such a methodology, which also conforms to the principle of parsimony. Skinner (1967) stated the behaviorist's objections to mentalistic explanations of human behavior:

1. The constructs are vague (and many, if not all, are probably invalid).
2. The constructs are not subject to scientific scrutiny, and therefore cannot be proven, disproven, or revised.
3. There isn't a one-to-one correspondence between inner and outer (observable) events.
4. The inner system isn't the best explanation of overt behavior.
5. Explaining outer events (i.e. behavior) by reference to inner states isn't complete (e.g. he struck out because he was angry. But what made him angry?).

Skinner (1967) argued 'that, given the present state of behavioral science, the best that can be done is to attempt to account for behavior without reference to inner states. This is not to say the behaviorist denies the existence of internal acts or mental behavior; rather, the objection is to their use as "mental way stations" in causal sequences (Skinner, 1972). Mental constructs frequently are interposed between environmental events and behavior and the causal explanation is stopped there. How the attitude, habit, or trait developed must also be explained (Skinner, 1972). Such explanations, when offered, often are tautological—for example, one may reason that minimal brain dysfunction (MBD) "causes" hyperactivity and, therefore, that a child's observed hyperactivity is an indication of MBD.

The reliability and validity of instruments used to measure hypothetical constructs is a significant problem in itself (Hersen & Barlow, 1976; Ysseldyke & Salvia, 1974). While the question of whether or not such constructs are valid is one of almost personal belief, the question of whether and how well instruments measure these constructs is one of scientific concern and, at present, our only way of approaching the matter of whether such constructs do exist. Thus, ratings of "ego strength," "utterance," "achievement motivation," etc. derived from questionnaires, interviews, or projective techniques are valid only insofar as they correlate with external measures of these same variables, whose reliability and validity have already been established. In etiological research, this requirement appears to be met infrequently (Hersen & Barlow, 1976); often items or instruments intended to assess a particular construct have only face validity. Even for overt behavior, we found relatively little use of standardized questionnaires or scales in the literature and almost no reliability studies of the instruments employed with a particular sample. Therefore, both the stability of the data reported as well as the extent to which assessment instruments measure what they purport to measure must be questioned.

An individual's response to the manipulation of an environmental variable tempts researchers to make causal inferences. For instance, consider the case in which parental attention is systematically removed whenever the child has a tantrum, which is followed by a decrease in tantrums; but, when the parents resume attending to tantrums (i.e., a reversal design), the frequency of tantrums increases. The conclusion could be drawn, from observation of its effects, that parental attention "caused" the production of tantrums. However, because parental attention can be manipulated to alter behavior does not mean that it necessarily contributed to its development (Ross, 1974). This kind of causal reasoning involves the fallacy of *post hoc, ergo propter hoc* (after the fact, therefore because of the fact). One may hypothesize from such an effect that parent attention caused the problem, but all that has been demonstrated is that parental attention was responsible for its maintenance.

Since anything short of laboratory research cannot identify, with a comfortable degree of certainty, events or agents which cause behavior disorders, we prefer the term *correlates* to *causes*. Hallahan and Kauffman (1978) described etiological factors as *predisposing* (those which establish conditions which increase the likelihood of problem behavior occurring), *precipitating* (those which may trigger a behavior), and *contributing* (events consistently associated with behavior disorders which may have some influence). Thus, a neurological dysfunction may predispose a child to exhibit hyperactivity, excessive environmental stimulation may precipitate it, and social attention may contribute to its maintenance. Given our knowledge about the causes of adolescent behavior disorders, the majority of factors described in this review should be regarded as contributing.

In addition to the major questions of what variables are consistently associated with adolescent behavior disorders, our review of the literature was guided by the following questions:

1. What disorders or problems are more common among adolescents than among children or adults?
2. What is the relationship of childhood disorders and adult problems to adolescent disorders?
3. How do changes in environmental expectations affect adolescents' behavior?
4. Is the identification of etiological factors useful or important?
   A. Will it lead to more effective interventions?
   B. Can etiological agents ever be singled out?
5. Can etiological research be improved?

The literature pertaining to these questions is scattered among the journals of several disciplines: psychiatry, social work, cultural anthropology, psychology, and education. In reviewing the literature for this chapter, we found a disappointing paucity of good data on adolescents as a separate population and a tendency of authors to speculate regarding the causes of behavior disorders. Because of this, we were limited in the conclusions we could make concerning the causes of behavior disorders in adolescence. In attempting to organize the extremely diverse, often contradictory findings which characterize this area, we have centered our review around three main topics. First, we will examine general correlates of behavior disorders. These are grouped into two main categories, biophysical and environmental. Next, we will briefly discuss the continuity between adolescent disorders and problems at other developmental levels. Finally, we will look at a sample of the specific problems of adolescents and their etiological correlates.

CORRELATES OF BEHAVIOR DISORDERS

Biophysical Factors

> In *nearly all* cases of "mental illness" (including psychosis), no reliable direct evidence of biological disease or disorder can be found and it must be *presumed* that there is a physical basis for the disorder if one wishes to implicate biological factors. (Kauffman, 1977, p. 99)

Biophysical correlates include genetic, neurological, or biochemical agents or conditions. There is more evidence for biophysical origins of severe and profound behavior disorders than for milder disorders but, as indicated in Kauffman's statement, interpretations of causal relationship cannot be made with any degree of certainty.

Genetic factors. One way of testing the contribution of genetic endowment to the development of behavior disorders is to study the rates of mental illness in the relatives of identified mental patients. This has been done rather extensively in the case of schizophrenia. Buss (1966) summarized the data from studies of the genetics of schizophrenia and found the rate of schizophrenia among the general population to be less than 1%. If one has a blood relative with the disorder, however, the risk increases at a rate proportionate to the closeness of the relationship. For example, the rate of schizophrenia among children who have one schizophrenic parent is 16%, and having two schizophrenic parents increases the rate to between 39 and 68%. The rate observed among fraternal twins is between 3 and 17%, whereas in 67 to 86% of the cases in which one of a set of identical twins has the disorder, the other will also display symptoms. A confounding factor in such studies is, of course, the effects of home environments containing a schizophrenic relative. Studies comparing children raised by schizophrenic mothers with children raised apart from their schizophrenic mothers report contradictory findings (Sagor, 1972). Nevertheless, research indicates a possible genetic component in schizophrenia, although environmental factors must also be considered in accounting for this disorder (Buss, 1966).

Another genetic factor linked to behavior disorders involves the karyotype XYY syndrome. Approximately 0.2% of males are born with an extra Y chromosome (Kauffman, 1977), a genetic anomaly thought to produce hyperaggressive characteristics. This conclusion is based on the observation that the XYY karyotype is 15 times greater among patients in mental-penal institutions (Lefkowitz et al., 1977). However, faulty research designs and sampling methods characterize these studies, as well as the failure to control for nongenetic factors (Kauffman, 1977; Lefkowitz et al., 1977).

Bender's (1969) theory of developmental lag incorporates the concept of a physiological crisis with an inherited predisposition to schizophrenia. She hypothesized that a physiological crisis, such as anoxia during birth, accident, or severe illness, activates the disorder. Neurologically, the child fails to develop beyond the embryonic level and maintains primitive or infantile patterns of behavior. Ritvo, Ornitz, Tanguay, and Lee (1970) observed developmental patterns in psychotic children characterized by unevenness, interruptions, and regressions, which also led Ritvo and his colleagues to formulate a developmental lag theory. Research concerning developmental lag in psychotic children, however, thus far has failed to produce conclusive evidence (Kauffman, 1977; Sagor, 1972).

Neuropathological Factors

Some researchers also consider the presence of central nervous system pathology, occasioned by genetic misfortune or trauma, to underlie behavior disorders, particularly those of a severe nature (e.g., Bender, 1969; Rimland, 1964). Brain damage or dysfunctioning often is inferred from such behavior manifestations as hyperactivity and distractibility, or from abnormal electroencephalogram recordings. However, unless obvious cerebral insult has occurred, a reliable diagnosis of brain injury cannot be made. Werry (1972) indicated that such inferences are extremely hazardous and that "studies on the effect of carefully established brain damage or a history of events which purportedly carry a strong risk of brain damage show that any increased frequency of childhood psychopathological disorder as compared with a properly matched control group is at least small and difficult to detect" (p. 97).

Studies of psychiatric populations tend to reveal higher frequencies of "soft" neurological signs and abnormal EEGs, but the evidence is not strong enough to rule out competing explanations based on environmental factors. Klinge and Vaziri (1975) compared the EEGs of 64 drug abusers with 64 adolescents who were hospitalized for nondrug-related problems. No relationship was observed between drug abuse and EEG diagnosis, but 31 % of the total sample had abnormal EEGs. In general, because of problems of instrumentation, experimental control, etc., research has failed to identify specific brain mechanisms responsible for psychotic disorders (Werry, 1972).

Biochemical Factors

The discovery of a biochemical irregularity as a causal agent in the behavior anomaly now known as PKU, which formerly was thought to be a functional disorder, emphasizes the potential of similiar biochemical causes for other disorders. Increased levels of certain neurochemical substances (e.g., bufoteine, serotonin) in the blood serum and urine of psychotic patients has led medical researchers to postulate complex causal theories (Kameya, 1974). The success, in some cases, of orthomolecular therapy also has caused speculation regarding the presence of toxic substances in the blood or abnormal concentrations of enzymes and vitamins in mental patients (Sagor, 1972). However, research concerning the effects of biochemical agents has been characterized by poor experimental design, inadequate controls, and contradictory findings (Kameya, 1974). Also, physiological changes may be secondary to psychological changes in psychotic individuals and the effects of such environmental factors as diet and long-term hospitalization cannot be ruled out (Sagor, 1972).

Developmental changes occurring in adolescence include alterations in body chemistry. The effects of hormones on behavior are poorly understood, but testosterone has been linked to aggressive behavior in males (Lefkowitz et al., 1977). Increased levels of sex and growth hormones in adolescence are popularly used to "explain" teenagers' moodiness, etc., but their relationship to severe behavior problems in adolescence is unknown to these reviewers.

Nutritional Factors

Just as diet may affect biochemical functioning in adults, so too it may influence neurological development and functioning in children. Malnutrition is known to have pernicious effects on mental development and performance, and severe caloric malnutrition, if it occurs shortly after birth, reduces cell proliferation and myelinization of the central nervous system. If it occurs after the period of rapid neurological growth, slower growth and increased susceptibility to infection result. Fortunately, these effects are reversible. Severe protein deficiency, on the other hand, produces irreversible effects at any stage of development: cessation of growth, wasting of muscles, edema, and, often, loss of appetite and apathy (Kameya, 1974);

other behavioral effects may include withdrawal and school failure (Cravioto, Gaona, & Birch, 1967). Recently, food additives have been implicated as a causal factor in children's hyperactivity (Rose, 1978).

Interaction of Biophysical and Environmental Factors

Chess, Thomas, and Birch (1967) followed 136 children for 10 years. Thirty-nine of their sample developed behavior disorders of various types and degrees of severity. On the basis of extensive interviews with the mothers of all 136 children, the researchers advanced the concept of temperament. Temperament refers to an inborn behavioral style, which Chess and co-workers divided into nine categories of reactivity: activity level, rhythmicity, adaptability, approach-withdrawal, intensity of reaction, quality of mood, sensory threshold, distractibility, persistence, and attention span. Three basic temperamental profiles identified in the sample were the "easy" child, the "slow to warm up" child, and the "difficult" child. The temperamental pattern associated with the greatest risk of developing behavior problems included a combination of irregularity in biological functions, a predominance of withdrawal responses to new stimuli, nonadaptability or slow adaptability to change, frequent negative moods, and predominately negative reactions. However, the response of the parents to the child's behavior pattern determined whether a behavior disorder developed. Chess and co-workers' findings indicate that while temperament may be a necessary condition for the development of a behavior disorder, it is not sufficient: interaction with parental behavior must also be considered.

Frisk, Tenhunen, Widholm, and Hortling (1969) looked at deviations in physical development to determine whether these were more frequent among adolescents who showed various symptoms of mental disorders. They did find more deviations among adolescents with various "psychic" problems, but observed that problems were more likely to result if external social conditions were unsatisfactory.

Virtually all reviewers of biophysical causes of behavior problems concur that biological variables do not act alone but interact with other variables found in the environments of children (Kauffman, 1977; Ross, 1974; Werry, 1972). As Kameya (1974, pp. 150–151) put it:

> To regard psychological factors and sociological agents as important in the etiology of an illness does not necessarily preclude a recognition of the role of the biological substrates of behavior, just as recognition of the biological agents does not obviate consideration of ecological, psychological, and sociological variables.

Environmental Factors

The environmental correlates of behavior disorders examined here include factors in the family, the school, the peer group, as well as inadequate or inappropriate social skills and personal behavior patterns which lead to, or exacerbate, problems. In all of these categories, however, general processes and conditions operate which seem to have consistent relationships to the acquisition and maintenance of behavior. We will discuss these first.

General factors. Modeling has been shown to be a significant factor in the acquisition of behavior (Bandura, 1969). Children and adolescents are particularly likely to imitate the behavior of a prestigious adult or peer. Modeling also may be vicarious. Recently, public concern regarding the effects of television violence on children's aggressive behavior has followed studies demonstrating increased aggression among children watching violent T.V. shows (Bandura, 1973; Lefkowitz et al., 1977). Modeling is particularly important to understanding adolescent behavior, as during this phase of development parents and teachers become distinctly less important than peers as models. "Some of the problems that arise during adolescence may be the result of an individual modeling the behavior of his peers who are no more knowledgeable, intelligent, mature and wise than he himself" (Muuss, 1976, p. 66). Inappropriate forms of behavior also may be acquired and/or maintained through intentional or unintentional environmental reinforcement (Bandura, 1973; Ullmann & Krasner, 1965; Worrell & Nelson, 1974) provided by peers or adults.

We previously mentioned the changes in environmental expectations that seem to accompany a child's transition into adolescence and concomitant shifts from continuous to intermittent schedules of reinforcement (Ferster et al., 1975). Sudden changes in expectations may result in some breakdown in behavior (abulia) as well as emotional side effects (Ferster et al., 1975). The effects of labels on expectations and environmental reactions to the labeled individual have been studied for several years. Research on these effects has yielded mixed results, but " . . . most people tend to view a labeled person differently from a nonlabeled one" (Hallahan & Kauffman, 1978, p. 38). Thus, adolescents who become known as behavior problems or as emotionally disturbed may very likely be responded to on the basis of their label, irrespective of their behavior in a given situation (Clarizio & McCoy, 1976).

Cultural anthropologists and sociologists have also pointed out that factors in the social milieu affect deviant behavior, particularly delinquency. Higher rates of psychopathology are found in urban as compared to rural areas (Dohrenwend & Dohrenwend, 1974); low economic status, in general, has been stated to be influential in the development and maintenance of delinquency (Miller, 1968). Hollingshead and Redlich (1971) found higher rates of psychotic disorders among the lower class whereas neurotic disorders were more common at higher socioeconomic levels. We will discuss these general factors in greater detail later in connection with specific behavior disorders of adolescents. They also contribute to the influence of variables in home, school, and peer group environments, which we take up next.

Family factors. Coleman (1978) voiced the concern that changes in the structure and function of family life are making this basic socialization unit significantly less able to meet the needs of youth. Psychoanalytic writers have seen the role of the family, especially parents, as central to the genesis of behavior disorders. The assumed dynamics of this influence are illustrated by Johnson and Szurek (1969, p. 16):

> The unwitting employment of the child to act out for the parent his own poorly integrated and forbidden impulses was observed by us in parents of all economic and educational levels with the frequency, regularity, and predictability of a well-defined psychological mechanism determining human behavior.

Although the frequent allusion to "mental way stations" in such statements reduces their usefulness for heuristic purposes, this point of view has dominated popular thinking for many years.

On a more empirical level, quite a number of demographic variables have been examined as they relate to behavior disorders in children and youth: family structure, which includes the number of parents in the home, extended families, stepparents, and birth order; parenting techniques, such as methods of discipline, maternal or paternal domination, and nurturance or rejection; and parental personality. However, these variables, by themselves, have not predicted adjustment. Rather, they appear to interact in complex ways with such factors as socioeconomic status, ethnic origin, the child's age, sex, and temperament (Kauffman, 1977). A good deal of research indicates that the presence or absence of a functioning father in the home strongly affects the adjustment of the son(s) (Smith & Walters, 1978), and broken or chaotic family environments in general seem to have negative effects on children. Socioeconomic level may be a confounding variable, however (Kauffman, 1977).

Patterson, Reid, Jones, and Conger (1975) observed that families containing aggressive children interacted wtih more hostility and negativism than did families of normal children. However, they pointed out that it is impossible to determine from their results whether such parental practices as punitive control *cause* aggression in the offspring or whether parents are reacting to the aggressive behavior displayed by their children. The imitation of the behavior of aggressive models nevertheless has been observed with sufficient regularity to suspect it as a causal factor (Lefkowitz et al., 1977), and parental punitiveness toward aggressive behavior appears to be associated with more, rather than less, childhood aggression (Muuss, 1976).

One consistent empirical finding complicates both genetic and environmental theories regarding the origins of schizophrenia: the presence of normal siblings in "schizogenic" families. A common explanation for this observation is that parents interact differently with the schizophrenic child than with his/her normal siblings. Waxler and Mishler (1972) tested this assumption by a direct observation study of parent-child interactions. Parents of adolescent or young adult schizophrenics were observed in two structured situations: one with their schizophrenic offspring and one with a sibling of the same sex and close to the same age. There was no evidence that overall family climate changed according to which child was present. Differences in interaction which were observed could be explained on the basis of parental response to schizophrenic behavior rather than as an antecedent to it.

School factors. Kauffman (1977) described five ways in which schools can contribute to the development and maintenance of behavior disorders: (a) by being insensitive to children's individuality; (b) by holding inappropriate expectations for achievement and behavior; (c) by practicing inconsistent management techniques; (d) by providing instruction in nonfunctional skills; and (e) by setting inappropriate contingencies of reinforcement. Schools tend to act against youth who violate standards of order and discipline and who are perceived as not fitting the monolithic pattern (Nelson, 1977). Rutherford (1976) observed that public schools often place too little demand on the adolescent's academic behavior while at the same time demanding near-perfect social behavior and following minor rule infractions with severe penalties. Such practices, coupled with the attitude of "I teach subject matter" reinforced in many schools, makes secondary school environments inhospitable for many adolescents.

The alarming increase in school violence, particularly at the secondary level, has led several authorities to raise serious questions about the operations of public schools and to call for reform. Neil (1978), for example, saw depersonalization, large buildings, large student populations, excessive use of corporal punishment, suspension, expulsion, and doing too little too late to help many children as ways in which the schools have contributed to the problem. However, Bayh (1978) pointed out that other factors, such as home problems, severe unemployment among young people, and lack of recreational activities, help create the problems schools must face.

School failure has itself been studied as a potential antecedent of disordered behavior. The interaction of this variable with intelligence, parental expectations, and other factors makes causal inferences risky and moreover leaves unanswered the question of whether school failure causes behavior disorders or vice versa. Kauffman (1977) indicated that the relationship is likely to be reciprocal. Swift and Spivack (1973) identified 13 factors, derived from teachers' ratings of overt behavior, which related to the school achievement of junior and senior high-school students. High achievers scored high on the factors of *reasoning ability, originality, verbal interaction, rapport with the teacher,* and *anxious producer,* whereas low achievers were high on *general anxiety, quiet-withdrawn, poor work habits, lack of intellectual independence, dogmatic-inflexible, verbal negativism, disturbance-restlessness,* and *expressed inability.* Lower measured intelligence has been observed more frequently among children identified as behaviorally disordered. The more severe the child's disorder, the lower his/her intelligence is likely to be (Kauffman, 1977).

Peer factors. We already have mentioned the primary role of the peer group in the lives of adolescents. Not only do peers serve as models but they also provide direct reinforcement and punishment for various forms of behavior. If the behavior modeled and reinforced by peers is antisocial or inappropriate, the results can be unfortunate for the individual or for society. The potential of direct peer reinforcement for maintaining maladaptive behavior was explored in a series of studies by Buehler et al. (1966) of the reinforcement patterns among staff and inmates in institutions for delinquent girls. Approximately 75% of the girls' delinquent behavior was followed by peer approval whereas compliance with social norms was consistently punished by the peer group. On the other hand, staff members were inconsistent in their responses to delinquent behavior, sometimes reinforcing and sometimes punishing it. Furthermore, staff remained in their offices or on the periphery of the group and therefore transactions between the staff and the girls were not so frequent as those among the girls.

Intrapersonal correlates. The frequent association of social competence factors with behavior and adjustment tempts one to postulate causal relationships. The failure to develop or employ appropriate personal skills is especially likely to negatively affect adjustment among adolescents, for these skills are crucial to success with the peer group and in increasing interactions with the adult world. In addition to faulty social skills, adolescents may be deficient in self-regulation, i.e., in self-monitoring, self-evaluation, and self-reinforcement (Kanfer & Karloy, 1972). Kanfer and Grimm (1977) developed an analytical framework for categorizing client compliants. Their categories included inappropriate self-generated stimulus control, which encompasses inappropriate self-labeling, inappropriate covert behaviors, and inappropriate discrimination of internal stimuli. Adolescents may also exercise inadequate control over their affective responses or engage in excessive self-criticism. Although the existence of these covert behavior patterns begs the question of how they were originally generated, such factors can act as independent variables in determining immediate behavior (Skinner, 1972). Another skill deficit may exist in the area of identifying contingencies of reinforcement and discriminative stimuli. For example, the youth who repeatedly fails to get to work on time or to meet assignment deadlines is exhibiting a behavior pattern that is sure to create negative environmental reactions.

Behavioral factors. Related to the previous discussion is the potential for the child's behavior itself to function as an antecedent to adjustment problems. The use of drugs, for instance, may produce affective or emotional changes. These may cause the individual to (a) attribute his/her feelings to external situations or interpersonal relationships and act accordingly or (b) resort to the further use of drugs to allay depression or to avoid withdrawal reactions. Similarly, involvement in antisocial gang activities may initiate a cycle of such behavior and at the same time lead to other forms of maladaptive behavior. While theorists and researchers with a dynamic/cognitive bent are prone to see intrapersonal variables as the instigators of such behavior patterns, we find it more parsimonious to view these covert behaviors as concomitants of overt antisocial or maladaptive acts.

CONTINUITY OF ADOLESCENT BEHAVIOR DISORDERS

Continuity involves the question of whether a behavior disorder at one stage of development is associated with maladjustment at a later stage. The typical method of studying this question is by reviewing the histories of adult mental patients and comparing the incidence of their childhood disorders with that of a behaviorally normal adult control group (Lewis, 1965). While such studies rarely have singled out adolescents, their results provide a rough indication of the extent to which a behavior disorder in youth can be said to "cause" problems in later life.

O'Neal and Robins (1971) conducted personal follow-up interviews with adults who had been referred to the Municipal Psychiatric Clinic in St. Louis between 1924 and 1929. All subjects in this group were no more than 17 years old at the time of their first clinic contact. Compared with a normal control group, subjects who had been patients over 30 years before were significantly more likely to be psychiatrically ill adults. Differences were especially pronounced in terms of the more serious problems: schizophrenia, alcoholism, and chronic brain syndrome. The childhood problems of normal adults were more likely to involve "neurotic" behavior, sociopathic adults were more likely to have been delinquents as children, and adult psychosis was associated with a history of childhood antisocial behavior which did not result in adjudication.

Lewis (1965) made an extensive review of the continuity literature up to that date and concluded that the question of whether childhood disorders produced maladaptive adult behavior patterns depends upon the criterion used for diagnosing adult psychiatric disorder. If the criterion is a diagnosed psychiatric disorder, research tends to support a continuity hypothesis. However, if the more stringent criterion of admission to a psychiatric hospital is used, the hypothesis is not supported. Nevertheless, Lewis's (1965) observation that the acting-out or conduct problem child is more likely to exhibit adjustment problems as an adult has been consistently supported (Clarizio & McCoy, 1976; Kauffman, 1977).

Studies of adult patients also reveal higher rates of school failure and lower measured intelligence during childhood, although these factors alone cannot account for adult maladjustment (Kauffman, 1977). For severely disordered children, however, later adjustment and behavior are rather well predicted by intelligence test scores. Lockyer and Rutter (1970), for example, followed up 63 children with infantile psychosis 5–15 years later. This group was matched with a group of nonpsychotic controls. Results from a battery of assessment instruments indicated that a lack of functional speech at the time of the first evaluation and a stay in a long-term institution during the interim between assessments were associated wtih lower social competence at the second testing.

Thus the combination of low intelligence, school failure, and severe acting-out behavior bode ill for adult adjustment (Kauffman, 1977). It seems possible that this constellation of characteristics reflects a general social incompetence factor which affects adjustment throughout life (see also Lefkowitz et al., 1977).

ADOLESCENT BEHAVIOR DISORDERS AND SUSPECTED ETIOLOGICAL AGENTS

Whereas the previous sections examined etiological factors and issues in general, in this section we turn to studies which have focused specifically on adolescents. We will sample research representing five areas of behavior disorder in adolescents: conduct disorders, delinquency, alcohol and drug abuse, suicide, and anorexia nervosa. Our approach to specific problems was motivated partly by the absence of literature on disturbed or disordered adolescents as a population and partly by our conviction that to attempt to summarize adolescents as a "population" representing homogeneous behavioral or etiological characteristics is counterproductive. The notion of such a population implies the existence of underlying pathology which we regard as an unnecessary concept and as an impediment to the clear analysis of functional relationships.

Unfortunately, some of the investigators whose research we summarize here do not share our view and thus, for these individuals, etiological agents are presumed to act upon or establish personality constructs. Nevertheless, we will review only external agents and factors that have been measured with some degree of objectivity. In contrast to previous sections, here we concentrate more upon data-based studies than upon clinical reports or theoretical speculation. The antecedents of aggressive behavior and delinquency receive disproportionate attention because they have been more thoroughly researched and sounder methods have been employed in their study.

Conduct Disorders

Quay and Quay (1965) obtained teacher ratings on Peterson's Problem Behavior Checklist of 518 seventh- and eighth -grade children. The majority of the variance in problematic behavior was accounted for by two factors: conduct problem (aggressive, acting-out behavior) and personality problem (inferiority, shyness, withdrawal). As used here, conduct disorders range from rebellion against parents or other adult authority figures to overt aggression against persons or property. Conduct disorders differ from delinquency in that the former behaviors are not "socialized," i.e., the individual is not behaving in specific accordance with the norms of a deviant subcultural group. This is not to say, however, that a peer group may not support aggressive behavior (Stumphauzer et al., 1977).

Rebellion is a relatively mild form of aggressive behavior. Balswick and Macrides (1975) asked a sample of college students to respond to a questionnaire which looked at parental variables in relationship to self-reported adolescent rebellion. Of their 417 subjects, 21% of the males and 23% of the females reported being very or extremely rebellious; 65% of the males and 56% of the females indicated that they experienced slight rebelliousness; while those reporting that they did not go through a period of rebellion amounted to only 14% of the males and 21% of the females. Correlations between these self-ratings and familial variables assessed on the questionnaire led the investigators to form several tentative hypotheses: (a) greater rebellion is associated with lower perceived parental marital happiness, with greater parental restrictiveness or permissiveness, and with greater paternal authority in the presence of general restrictiveness or permissiveness on the part of the parents; (b) lesser rebellion is associated with greater parental happiness and with less restrictiveness or permissiveness when associated with greater paternal authority. The results were interpreted as supporting the frustration-aggression hypothesis (i.e., that aggression is the inevitable result of frustration), in that parental restrictiveness or permissiveness produces frustration. However, this conclusion may be questioned on the basis of the methods employed in the study (self-reported data, correlational data analysis) as well as the fact that research has generally failed to confirm the frustration-aggression hypothesis (Bandura, 1973; Lefkowitz et al. 1977).

Since the 1960s, the problem of adolescent runaways has received extensive media coverage. This type of conduct problem can be regarded as a form of rebellion or perhaps as an outcome of it. Wolk and Brandon (1977) compared adolescents' perceptions of parental treatment and self-perceptions between a group of runaways and a control group. The groups were matched on sex, age, and race, and came from the same neighborhood. Runaways perceived their parents to be less supportive and more restrictive, and self-concept measures depicted them as more defensive, self-doubting, and less trusting. The authors felt that female runaways reacted to parental restrictiveness whereas this behavior among boys could be indicative of relative normlessness, resulting from parental failure to exert sufficient control over male aggressive behavior. However, they correctly pointed out the difficulty in establishing cause-effect relationships from their data: "what may be taken as antecedent conditions to the act of running away may, in fact, be a consequence of the need to justify an extreme act, i.e., establish some fault with parents" (p. 185).

Aggression is a form of adolescent conduct disorder which has received more research attention. Bandura and Walters (1959) in a well-controlled study investigated antecedents to aggressive and antisocial behavior in parent-child relationships. The subjects, 26 pairs of adolescent males, were carefully matched on age, intelligence, areas of residence, and father's occupation. All subjects came from intact homes, did not live in a high delinquency neighborhood, and were at least average in intelligence. One member of each matched pair had a history of antisocial, aggressive behavior but was not designated as delinquent. A variety of measures was used, including direct observation, interviews, and questionnaires. The findings indicated that relatively harsh and punitive discipline, particularly by the father, and encouragement of aggression outside the home, coupled with feelings of rejection by and less dependency toward fathers, typified aggressive subjects. On the other hand, parents of nonaggressive adolescents more often used reasoning as a means of discipline and parents in this group had higher achievement expectations for their sons.

The most ambitious study of aggression to date is that of Lefkowitz et al. (1977). Lefkowitz and his colleagues studied the entire third-grade population ($N = 875$) of Columbia County, New York, in 1959–60. Ten years later, 735 of the original sample were located and interviews were held with 427 subjects. Aggression was measured by peer ratings, parent ratings, self-reports, a personality test (the MMPI), and, in the case of male subjects, arrest records for violent crimes. The independent variables studied were: (a) instigators—stimuli which usually elicited aggression; (b) contingent responses to aggression, such as parental punishment of aggression; (c) identification—modeling and observational learning; and (d) socio-cultural variables, such as father's occupation, parents' educational level, and family ethnic background. Correlational analyses were performed to determine which variables statistically predicated aggression immediately as well as in the long run. The authors concluded that

> aggression at age eight is the best predictor we have of aggression at age 19 irre-spective of IQ, social class, or parent's aggressiveness. This suggests that aggressive-ness may be largely maintained by such learning factors as external reinforcement, vicarious reinforcement and self-reinforcement. (p. 192)

The best predictors of immediate aggression were instigators (parental rejection, low nurturance, and low IQ for boys), identification variables (low identification with both parents, which was positively correlated with aggression, and parents' reports of children's confessions of misdeeds and children's guilt, both of which were negatively correlated with aggression), and sociocultural variables (father's occupation and parental upward mobility). The best longitudinal predictors of adolescent aggression, aside from the child's aggressiveness at the age of eight, were identification and sociocultural variables. The effect of punishment (contingent responses to aggression) were complicated and mediated by other variables.

Another predictor of aggression was exposure to violence in the media. In fact, the relationship between viewing violence on television and aggression among boys was so strong that investigators termed the former "causal." In conjunction with evidence from other studies, Lefkowitz et al. (1977) concluded that "the pernicious effect of this kind of identification is rather overwhelming" (p. 195). Research by Bandura (1973) and by Liebert and Baron (1973) confirms that viewing aggressive behavior on TV or film increases the immediate aggressiveness of the child viewer.

Lefkowitz et al. (1977) also observed that aggression in their subjects was stable across time and situations. They further concluded that lower intelligence may exert a constricting effect on the behavioral repertoire, making aggression the child's most convenient response to instigators. The authors rejected the notion of inner causes, taking the position that the genotype for aggression is not a constitutional predisposition to aggression but rather a predisposition to learn certain response modes. Although they did find more aggression among their male subjects, these researchers did not support a biological difference in aggressiveness between the sexes.

The findings of Lefkowitz et al. generally corroborate those of other social-learning researchers, summarized by Kauffman (1977):

> 1. Viewing televised aggression will increase aggressive behavior in children, especially in males and in children who have a history of aggressiveness.

2. Delinquent subcultures, such as street gangs, will maintain aggressive behavior in their members by modeling and reinforcement of aggression.

3. Families of aggressive children will be characterized by high rates of aggression on the part of all family members and by inconsistent punitive control techniques on the part of the parents.

4. Aggression will beget aggression, i.e., when one person presents an aversive stimulus . . . the affronted individual is likely to reply by presenting a negative stimulus of his own, and a coercive interaction will be the result.   (pp. 184–185)

Juvenile Delinquency

The social significance of juvenile delinquency is reflected in the number of studies made of this phenomenon over the years.

Delinquent behavior has been attributed to spiritual degeneration or malevolence, to biological disorders (including genetic, morphologic, neurologic, and metabolic imbalances), to experiential deficiencies (including inappropriate learning, stimulus deprivation, and psychopathogenic factors), and to social inadequacies (including cultural, sociological, economic, and political inequities). (Wirt & Briggs, 1965, p. 12)

Recent investigations of the origins of delinquency have tended to focus on environmental factors. One prominent view during the first half of the twentieth century was Durkheim's theory of *anomie*. This theory held that delinquency represents normless or lawless behavior which develops when avenues toward, and forms of identification with, the values and goals of the larger society are not available. Therefore, these values and goals lose their ability to control the behavior of the group and of the individual (Wirt & Briggs, 1965).

The anthropological studies of Miller (1968) and the recent behavior analysis studies of Stumphauzer and his colleagues (Aiken, Stumphauzer, & Veloz, 1977; Stumphauzer et al., 1977) question this theory. Miller's team of seven social workers maintained contact, over a 10–30-month period, with 21 street corner groups in slum areas. These trained observers collected over 8,000 pages of direct observation data which indicated that the delinquent acts in accordance with the community's standards and values as he sees them. According to Miller, therefore, delinquent behavior is spawned by a host of variables in the lower-class culture and does not represent a reaction against middle-class values. Miller identified the one-sex peer group as a significant variable which he saw as a direct outgrowth of the female-dominated family. The lower-class youth's concerns for belonging and status govern his conformity to the group. Whether or not the gang becomes delinquent depends upon a host of environmental and dynamic circumstances.

Stumphauzer et al. (1977) also identified potential etiological agents in the social milieu of the delinquent. Using interview and observational techniques in the East Los Angeles barrio, these researchers focused on the influence of modeling and reinforcement. Their preliminary findings indicated that delinquent gang behavior is overtly reinforced by peers and often indirectly reinforced by parents, family members, police, community members, and agencies. Indirect reinforcement takes the form of sensationalized media accounts of gang activities, police contacts (which gang members reinforce), family support stemming from a familial history of gang membership, and community fear of reprisals for reporting gang behavior. Buehler et al.'s (1966) analysis of institutional reinforcement patterns also revealed high levels of peer reinforcement contingent upon delinquent behavior.

The analysis of nondelinquent youth from the East Los Angeles barrio is informative because it indicates how these adolescents learn, teach, and use alternate, incompatible, noncriminal behavior, even though they live in the same environment as their delinquent siblings and peers. Aiken et al. (1977) studied two brothers who were accepted by the local gang, yet openly disavowed any participation in delinquent behavior. Through interviews and direct observations it was found that these boys had learned a series of effective trouble-avoiding behaviors. The elder brother acquired these behaviors through trial and error and by imitating an adult model in the community. He, in turn, taught these skills to his brother, through modeling and direct reinforcement. Nondelinquent behaviors were maintained through successful experience and by social and self-reinforcement.

The family is one aspect of the delinquent's cultural milieu which has received much attention. It is consistently reported that delinquency is more prevalent in children from broken, disorganized homes, in which parents themselves are likely to have arrest records, are lax in discipline, but also use harsh, cruel, and punitive disciplinary methods (Kauffman, 1977). Differential association theory maintains that such unfavorable home conditions are related to delinquency only if the adolescent has associates outside the home who provide delinquent models (Sutherland & Cressey, 1966). However, this theory has received substantial opposition. For example, Jensen's (1972) study of junior and senior high-school students revealed that the relationships of such independent variables as parental supervision and support and father-son affection to delinquent involvement were equally strong regardless of whether subjects had three or more delinquent friends or none.

Smith and Walters (1978) compared the responses of 118 incarcerated delinquents with those of 212 nondelinquents to a questionnaire probing their perceptions of their fathers. Delinquency was associated with the absence of a loving, supportive, and warm relationship with the father, minimal paternal involvement with the son, high maternal involvement, and a broken home. While this study suffers from the methodological problems discussed earlier in conjunction with single assessment correlational procedures, it replicates the consistent finding that the presence or absence of a functioning father in the home strongly affects the adjustment of boys (Barker & Adams, 1962; Gordon, 1962).

Observed sex differences in types of delinquent activities have led some writers to speculate that male delinquency, which involves more crimes of violence and property offenses, is related to the assertion of masculinity, rebellion against female authority (i.e., a maternally dominated home), and a lack of opportunity to pursue legitimate goals. Female delinquency, on the other hand, more often involves "ungovernable" behavior which is associated with specific life problems, such as broken homes, school failure, and sexual involvement. Kratcoski and Kratcoski (1975) employed a self-report questionnaire in conjunction with a delinquency checklist to investigate sex differences in delinquent acts among 104 male and 144 female eleventh and twelfth graders from three public high schools. More boys reported acts involving aggression, property destruction, and acts designed to "prove" their masculinity (e.g., gambling and sex relations), but the reported delinquencies of males and females were more similar than indicated by official statistics, especially for less serious offenses. Particularly with respect to delinquent acts regarded as "fashionable" by the adolescent culture, such as drug use, few sex differences or socioeconomic class distinctions were found. Girls also reported engaging in acts traditionally considered masculine. The authors concluded that the view of female delinquency as mainly resulting from family disorganization must be questioned.

As in the case with aggressive behavior, school failure is closely associated with delinquent behavior patterns. For example, Burke and Simmons (1965) reported that 90% of their sample of institutionalized delinquents had made poor adaptations to school or were truants. Almost 75% had either dropped out of school before the age of 16 or had repeated two or more grades and 67% achieved below the sixth-grade level in reading. Stumphauzer et al. (1977) observed that few members of barrio gangs attended school or had any incentive to do so. While observations such as these undoubtedly reflect the low value placed on school by the delinquent's social milieu, schools too must take some responsibility.

> Schools along with other agencies are catalysts in the final categorization of the youngster into the "delinquent syndrome. . . ." The schools emphasize eradication of truancy, pressuring the miscreant to conform, and fail to keep the juvenile in the mainstream of education. (Jones & Swain, 1977, p. 568)

In summary, a constellation of sociocultural variables have been related to delinquent behavior in adolescents. Many of these variables are more often found in that strata of society traditionally referred to as "lower class": disorganized, father-absent homes; unsupervised, single-sex peer groups; school failure; the availability of delinquent models; and reinforcement of delinquent activity. Operating together, as they seem to do, these factors contribute, if not predispose, to seemingly intractable patterns of delinquent behavior.

Alcohol and Drug Abuse

To some degree at least, behavior problems in this category represent status offenses. While drug use is not legally sanctioned, it is a prevalent form of adult behavior in North American cultures. The consumption of alcohol, on the other hand, is normative social behavior among adults (Barnes, 1977). Three areas have been studied in the search for causal agents: the family, the peer group, and individual psychopathology.

Barnes (1977) reviewed the literature on adolescent drinking behavior and reported that the best predictors of adolescent drinking are the behaviors and attitudes of parents with regard to alcohol. While surveys indicated that most adolescents drink, they do so moderately and responsibly. Alcoholic parents are more likely to have children with drinking problems concomitant to other social maladjustment, attributable to the instability of the family structure. Heavy adolescent drinkers are more likely to report greater parental sanction of drinking in general and by adolescents in particular. Excessive drinkers also don't feel close to their families. Retrospective studies of alcoholics suggest that inadequate parents produce a higher rate of alcoholic offspring. No differences among teenage drinkers have been observed as a function of sex, race (black-white), or social class (Barnes, 1977).

Parental factors have also been implicated in drug use. Albrecht (1977) interviewed 59 college students and found that their self-reported use of marijuana was predicted for 69.5% of the sample by their reported attitude toward it. When the attitudes of the subjects were supported by "significant others" (usually identified as a parent or family member), the prediction was increased to 87.8%. On the other hand, if these attitudes were not supported by significant others, correct prediction dropped to 27.7%.

Evidence for supporting peer modeling as a causal factor in either drinking or drug abuse does not appear to be strong. Barnes (1977) reported only weak relationships between peer pressure and individual drinking levels. He observed that the peer group may only provide a social context for drinking and reinforce drinking behavior already learned in the home. While peers may encourage marijuana use and experimentation with other drugs, Amini, Salasnek, and Burke's (1976) review of this literature concluded that psychopathology predates the habitual use of "harder" drugs. Jessor and Jessor (1973), in a longitudinal study, reported more deviant behavior and tolerance for it among subjects who became problem drinkers as compared with those who did not. Achievement expectations also were significantly lower for those who later became problem drinkers. Retrospective studies of alcoholics have related antisocial behavior in childhood to adult drinking and have indicated that the antecedent personality correlates of alcoholics include rebelliousness, hostility, and aggression (Barnes, 1977).

While heavy adolescent drinkers display more signs of socially deviant behavior, drinking doesn't *cause* deviant and antisocial behavior. Rather, drinking appears to be one of several deviant acts and related problem behaviors often occur when the child is sober (Barnes, 1977). Thus, adolescent drug and alcohol abuse both appear to involve individual behavior problems, which again may originate in familial variables and parental practices.

Barnes's (1977) recommendations for research needed in the area of adolescent alcohol abuse apply equally well to drug use: (a) studies should not rely on only a single administration of a questionnaire; (b) the relationships of adolescents within the family should be intensively investigated; (c) independent information should be obtained from mothers and fathers; (d) the development of normal drinking and drug use patterns should be studied; and (e) more longitudinal research is needed.

Suicide

It is estimated that, in the United States, suicide is the third leading cause of death in the 15-to-19 year age group. Indeed some accidents, the leading cause of death among this group, may be unreported suicides. Among the correlates of adolescent suicide discussed in a recent review by Miller are the following:

Environmental conditions. The presence of a "death trend" among suicide cases is striking. Suicide, or attempted suicide, often is associated with the death of a loved one. The death frequently occurs several years before the attempt (which Miller attributes to the length of time required for the individual to work through his/her feelings about the death) but in most cases it takes place before the individual has completed adolescence. The number of "anniversary suicides" (suicide or suicide attempts occurring on the anniversary of the loved one's death) suggests that the individual may identify closely with the deceased. Stress from poor home conditions or school pressure also may be a factor.

Psychological states. Studies have identified depression as the most common emotion in suicidal adolescents. According to Miller, the adolescent may also believe that his or her suicide will transform the world. Whereas adult suicide threats or attempts outnumber actual suicides 5 to 1, among adolescents the ratio reported in studies ranges from 50 to 120 to 1. For this reason, Miller considers suicide attempts among teenagers to be a cry for help. In any event, studies have reported frequent evidence of pre-existing problem behavior.

Individual constitution. Miller cited adolescent suggestibility, hypersensitivity, and developmental changes attendant to the sex drive as variables potentially contributing to adolescent suicide. However, while it seems irrefutable that suicidal adolescents are unhappy persons, attributions of this behavioral pattern to constitutional factors are much more tenuous and based upon substantial interpretation.

Anorexia Nervosa

A self-imposed restriction of food intake with an accompanying severe weight loss is a problem which occurs primarily among adolescent and adult females (Kauffman, 1977). Psychoanalytic explanations involving symbolic conflicts (such as, conflict over sexuality, fear of impregnation, or conflict over aggression) are typical causal statements (Bachrach, Erwin, & Mohr, 1965). Several descriptive studies of anorexics have documented a number of associated problems. Hamli's (1974) survey of 94 cases seen in an Iowa hospital between 1920 and 1972 is illustrative. Among this group there were high rates of menstrual difficulties, feeding problems prior to the onset of the disorder, concomitant psychiatric symptoms (primarily anxiety and obsessive-compulsive traits) as well as indications of apathy toward the opposite sex and a high percentage of excellent academic records. The age of the parents at the time of the anorexic child's birth was significantly older than the national average and the percentage of broken homes was lower among Hamli's study group than that reported in previous surveys of anorexics. While most of the patients for whom weight records were available had been of normal weight prior to the disorder, over 30% had been overweight and around 10% had been underweight. Although 13% reported that dieting was precipitated by humiliating comments about their physique, 37% of the group began dieting with no external provocation.

Kauffman (1977) offered the opinion that fear of getting fat is a more parsimonious explanation for the genesis of anorexia nervosa than psychoanalytic formulations, especially since many anorexics deny their emaciated condition. The origins of this fear are more difficult to explain, however. While behavioral treatments, involving desensitization of the fear of becoming overweight and/or direct reinforcement of eating behavior or weight gain, have been successful, modeling and reinforcement are not sufficient explanations of such grossly inappropriate eating habits (Kauffman, 1977). One psychoanalytic writer (Levenkron, 1978) blamed the fashion world's emphasis on a slender figure, which is reinforced by the parents. The frequency of concomitant menstrual disorders invites speculation regarding biophysical agents, but most of Hamli's (1974) group experienced such problems subsequent to their refusal to eat. The prevalence of premorbid weight and feeding problems suggests that, in some cases, anorexia nervosa may be the outcome of a consistent pattern of feeding difficulties.

Conclusions

Our review of research on the etiology of adolescent behavior disorders supports the conclusion of others (Kauffman, 1977; Quay, 1965; Ross, 1974): the question of etiology is largely open. In particular, the specific causes of disordered adolescent behavior, as distinct from any other age group, are unknown. One fact that does stand out, however, is that etiological agents appear to be multiple, complex, and interacting. It is doubtful that present research techniques will untangle the etiological jungle. Nevertheless, the consistency of certain findings across studies does lead us to propose several *possible* causal factors, or correlates.

1. Although the specific actions of *biophysical agents*, such as genetic endowment, metabolic disorder, brain injury, etc., on behavior are unknown, it appears certain that they exert some influence. Their role is more firmly established in the etiology of severe behavior disorders (Kauffman, 1977) just as organic factors seem to be more important causal factors behind severe and profound mental retardation and multiple physical handicaps (Carter, 1975). That the effects of these variables generally are felt before a child reaches puberty does not lessen their importance; it only makes the problems of their study more imposing. The interaction of endocrine and metabolic changes accompanying the transition into adulthood with adolescent behavior disorders is poorly understood.

2. The consistency with which a history of *childhood conduct disorder*, such as antisocial, aggressive behavior, is associated with psychopathology in adolescence and adulthood leads us to postulate that this is a major antecedent. This conclusion is in substantial agreement with the etiological literature (see Kauffman, 1977). However, the interaction of conduct problems with a host of other variables suggests caution in concluding that later maladjustment is an inevitable outcome of a childhood proclivity to aggressive and antisocial behavior. In addition, this finding does little to answer the question of what creates conduct problems in the first place. We are distinctly uncomfortable with the notion of pathology as a cause of disordered behavior because the explanation does not indicate how the pathology originally developed (Skinner, 1972).

3. The presence of a *general incompetence* factor behind adolescent behavior disorders also represents a distinct possibility. Lower measured intelligence, school failure, and a lack of particular skills frequently appear in descriptions of the histories and current functioning of adolescents who exhibit problem behavior patterns (Kauffman, 1977; Lefkowitz et al., 1977; Stumphauzer et al., 1977). Once again, this finding begs the question of how such incompetence originated, and its influence is confounded by the presence of a number of other sociocultural variables.

4. The *social milieu* presents a confusing array of variables: economic, cultural, and familial. Yet, the identification of common elements in the environments of gang delinquents strongly suggests that practices in lower-class cultures contribute to this social phenomenon. Since many of these studies occurred in ethnic ghettoes in different geographical areas (Miller, 1968; Stumphauzer et al., 1977), it seems likely that environmental rather than racial factors are at play.

5. The consistent relationship of family disorganization and harsh disciplinary practices, combined with restrictive or permissive parental behaviors, to delinquency, alcohol or drug abuse, and aggression leads us to speculate that the role of *family structure* and *parental practices* may be causal (Bandura & Walters, 1959; Barnes, 1977; Muuss, 1976; Smith & Walters, 1978). The word *may* is important here, as studies fail to demonstrate whether family cohesion and parental behavior are antecedents to, or a consequence of, aberrant child behavior patterns, or whether all of these variables are spawned by other factors.

6. The influence of *modeling* in the genesis of maladaptive adolescent behavior cannot be ignored (Bandura, 1973; Muuss, 1976). The tendency of children and

youth to imitate the behavior of prestigious models is well established. Within a deviant peer culture, such as a street gang, modeling must be regarded as a major influence on behavior. Likewise, modeling of parental behavior appears to be a significant factor in the acquisition of aggressive and drinking behavior among adolescents (Bandura, 1973; Barnes, 1977). Its role in adolescent drug abuse is less clear, but it might be presumed that peer modeling influences experimentation with drugs. The frequency of "anniversary suicides" among adolescents (Miller, 1975) is suggestive of modeling, although it is doubtful that modeling by itself constitutes an adequate explanation of this problem. There are clear indications that vicarious modeling, e.g., the viewing of televised violence, is an antecedent of adolescent aggression.

7. Direct and indirect *social reinforcement* also appears to enhance the development and maintenance of disordered adolescent behavior. Aggressive behavior tends to provide its own reinforcement to the extent that the aggressor achieves his or her ends (Worrell & Nelson, 1974). Reinforcement has been shown to maintain delinquent behavior (Buehler et al., 1966), and it has even been suggested that social reinforcement contributes to anorexia nervosa (Kauffman, 1977), although the anorexic adolescent may misconstrue the actual contingencies of reinforcement.

8. Inappropriate *school practices*, while perhaps not adequate causal factors in and of themselves, may contribute to the maintenance or exacerbation of behavior problems (Jones & Swain, 1977; Kauffman, 1977; Rutherford, 1976). It is unfortunate that an institution so central to the lives of our youth can display such insensitivity to their needs and individuality.

Although we have been able to identify potential antecedents among the variables studied in the investigations we reviewed, our failure to uncover specific causes once again raises the question of whether etiological research is necessary or worthwhile. It is unlikely that research will produce any dramatic breakthrough in our understanding of the etiology of adolescent behavior problems in the near future. Recall, too, that knowing the cause of a behavior disorder is not critical to designing an effective intervention (Worell & Nelson, 1974).

We mentioned previously that the study of etiology has the potential for leading to effective prevention of behavior disorders. Moreover, the alteration of a functional antecedent may constitute a more effective intervention for an existing behavior disorder. For example, if certain parental behaviors do precipitate and maintain deviant adolescent behavior, perhaps teaching parents alternative behaviors will ameliorate behavior problems in their children. Parent education and training has, in fact, proven to be an effective procedure for improving a child's behavior (O'Dell, 1974; Patterson, Ray, & Shaw, 1968; Rinn, Vernon, & Wise, 1975).

To these arguments in favor of etiological research we must add two philosophical statements. First, we believe that such research contributes to our understanding of human behavior. Second, we believe that the study of society's young people, and of their behavior problems, tells us many things we need to know about our world, how it is changing, and how it needs to change to accommodate the evolution of our species in concert with the other inhabitants of the earth. Perhaps we will find that the causes of the problems of our youth are, ultimately, rooted in the causes of many of our social ills. To an extent, then, adolescents are a barometer of the progress, or lack of progress, of our civilization. We dare not ignore the signs.

To conclude this chapter on a more practical note, we see several ways in which etiological research might be improved. First, greater emphasis should be placed on longitudinal research. The studies of Chess et al. (1967), Lefkowitz et al. (1977), Lockyer and Rutter (1970), and O'Neal and Robins (1971), although certainly not methodologically perfect, are examples of a genre of research that presently is our best alternative to laboratory investigations. However, single-subject research methodology also shows promise for identifying causal factors (Rose, 1978).

Second, we would encourage etiological researchers to attend more to the reliable and valid measurement of behavior. Self-reports and subjective ratings should be balanced against the direct observation of behavior. It almost goes without saying that the reliability of all measures of behavior, whether previously standardized or not, should be demonstrated for each sample of subjects. Furthermore, instruments designed to assess traits, attitudes, or other constructs should be validated against external criteria. In this vein it would be wise to heed Skinner's (1972) admonition not to stop etiological explanations at such mental way stations.

The research strategy of the future, in our opinion, should incorporate the field studies of cultural anthropology with the direct measurement techniques of applied behavior analysis into longitudinal research designs. If suspected current antecedent variables can be identified in such designs, their specific influence could be controlled and tested in single-subject research designs (Hersen & Barlow, 1976). This does not negate the study of mediating intrasubject variables. As Skinner (1972) emphasized:

> behaviorism means more than a commitment to objective measurement. No entity or process which has any useful explanatory force is to be rejected, on the ground that it is subjective or mental. The data which have made it important must, however, be studied and formulated in effective ways.   (p. 98)

The general approach we advocate, therefore, falls within the framework of social learning theory, which incorporates sound research designs with the direct measurement of behavior and carefully limited (and data-based) inferences regarding mental processes.

Finally, given our current state of knowledge, we believe that greater priority should be placed on investigating the functional antecedents of behavior in the immediate environment. This is not to denigrate efforts to identify etiological factors in the remote biological or social history of individuals; it is only to say that, at present, we understand very little about the world of behaviorally disordered adolescents, and perhaps greater benefits can be realized on behalf of these children from the study of those variables in their contemporary environments which contribute to patterns of disordered behavior.

References

Ackerman, N. W. Adolescent problems: A symptom of family disorder. *Family Process*, 1962, *1*, 202–213.

Aiken, T. W., Stumphauzer, J. S., & Veloz, E. V. Behavioral analysis of nondelinquent brothers in a high juvenile crime community. *Behavioral Disorders*, 1977, *2*, 212–224.

Albrecht, S. L. Adolescent attitude-behavior inconsistency: Some empirical evidence. *Adolescence*, 1977, *12*, 433–442.

Amini, F., Salasnek, S., & Burke, E. L. Adolescent drug abuse: Etiological and treatment considerations. *Adolescence*, 1976, *11*, 281–299.

Bachman, J. G., O'Malley, P. M., & Johnston, J. *Adolescence to adulthood. Youth in transition*, Vol. VI. Ann Arbor: University of Michigan Press, 1978.

Bachrach, A. J., Erwin, W. J., & Mohr, J. P. The control of eating behavior in an anorexic by operant conditioning techniques. In L. P. Ullmann & L. Krasner (Eds.), *Case studies in behavior modification*. New York: Holt, Rinehart & Winston, 1965.

Balswick, J. O., & Macrides, C. Parental stimulus for adolescent rebellion. *Adolescence*, 1975, *10*, 253–266.

Bandura, A. *Principles of behavior modification*. New York: Holt, Rinehart & Winston, 1969.

Bandura, A. *Aggression: A social learning analysis*. Englewood Cliffs, N. J.: Prentice-Hall, 1973.

Bandura, A., & Walters, R. H. *Adolescent aggression*. New York: Ronald Press, 1959.

Barker, G. H., & Adams, W. T. Comparison of the delinquency of boys and girls. *Journal of Criminal Law, Criminology, and Police Science*, 1962, *53*, 470–477.

Barnes, G. M. The development of adolescent drinking behavior: An evaluative review of the impact of the socialization process within the family. *Adolescence*, 1977, *12*, 571–591.

Bayh, B. Seeking solutions to school violence and vandalism. *Phi Delta Kappan*, 1978, *59*, 299–302.

Bender, L. The nature of childhood psychosis. In J. G. Howells (Ed.), *Modern perspectives in international child psychiatry*. New York: Brunner/Mazel, 1969.

Buehler, R. E., Patterson, G. R., & Furniss, J. M. The reinforcement of behavior in institutional settings. *Behavior Research and Therapy*, 1966, *4*, 157–167.

Burke, N. S., & Simons, A. E. Factors which precipitate dropouts and delinquency. *Federal Probation*, 1965, *29*, 28–32.

Buss, A. H. *Psychopathology*. New York: Wiley, 1966.

Campbell, D. T., & Stanley, J. C. *Experimental and quasi-experimental designs for research*. Chicago: Rand McNally, 1963.

Carter, C. H. *Handbook of mental retardation syndromes* (3rd ed.). Springfield, Ill.: Charles C Thomas, 1975.

Chess, S., Thomas, A., & Birch, H. G. Behavior problems revisited. Findings of an anterospective study. *Journal of the American Academy of Child Psychiatry*, 1967, *6*, 321–331.

Clarizio, H. F., & McCoy, G. F. *Behavior disorders in children* (2nd ed.). New York: Crowell, 1976.

Coleman, J. S. Changing the environment for youth. *Phi Delta Kappan*, 1978, *59*, 318–319.

Cravioto, J., Gaona, C. E., & Birch, H. G. Early malnutrition and auditory-visual integration in school-age children. *Journal of Special Education*, 1967, *2*, 75–91.

Dohrenwend, B. P., & Dohrenwend, B. S. Social and cultural influences on psychopathology. In M. Rosenweig & L. Porter (Eds.), *Annual review of psychology* (Vol. 25). Palo Alto, Calif.: Annual Reviews, 1974.

Ferster, C. B., Culbertson, S., & Boren, M. C. P. *Behavior principles* (2nd ed.) Englewood Cliffs, N.J.: Prentice-Hall, 1975.

Freud, A. Adolescence. *Psychoanalytic Study of the Child*, 1958, *13*, 255–278.

Friedman, C. J., Mann, F., & Friedman, A. S. A profile of juvenile street gang members. *Adolescence*, 1975, *10*, 563–607.

Frisk, M., Tenhunnen, T., Widholm, O., & Hortling, H. Psychological problems in adolescents showing advanced or delayed physical maturation. In D. Rogers (Ed.), *Issues in adolescent psychology*. New York: Appleton-Century-Crofts, 1969.

Gordon, I. J. *Human development from birth to adolescence*. New York: Harper & Row, 1962.

Hallahan, D. P., & Kauffman, J. M. *Exceptional children: Introduction to special education*. Englewood Cliffs, N.J.: Prentice-Hall, 1978.

Halmi, K. A. Anorexia nervosa: Demographic and clinical features in 94 cases. *Psychosomatic Medicine*, 1974, *36*, 18–26.

Hersen, M., & Barlow, D. H. *Single case experimental designs*. New York: Pergamon, 1976.

Hollingshead, A. B., & Redlich, F. C. Social stratification and psychotic disorders. In R. Harth (Ed.), *Issues in behavior disorders*. Springfield, Ill.: Charles C Thomas, 1971.

Jensen, G. F. Parents, peers and delinquent action: A test of the differential association perspective. *American Journal of Sociology*, 1972, *78*, 562–575.

Jessor, R., & Jessor, S. L. Problem drinking in youth: Personality, social and behavioral antecedents and correlates. *Proceedings of the Second Annual Alcoholism Conference of the National Institute on Alcohol Abuse and Alcoholism*. Washington, D. C.: Department of Health, Education and Welfare, 1973.

Johnson, A. M., & Szurek, S. A. The agencies of antisocial acting-out in children and adults. In S. A. Szurek & I. N. Berlin (Eds.), *The antisocial child: His family and his community*. Palo Alto, Calif.: Science and Behavior Books, 1969.

Jones, F. R., & Swain, M. T. Self-concept and delinquency proneness. *Adolescence*, 1977, *12*, 559–569.

Kameya, L. I. Biophysical interventions in emotional disturbance. In W. C. Rhodes & M. L. Tracy (Eds.), *A study of children variance*. Volume 2. *Interventions*. Ann Arbor: Institute for the Study of Mental Retardation and Related Disabilities, University of Michigan, 1974.

Kanfer, F. H., & Grimm, L. G. Behavioral analysis: Selecting target behaviors in the interview. *Behavior Modification*, 1977, *1*, 7–28.

Kanfer, F. H., & Karloy, P. Self-control: A behavioristic excursion into the lion's den. *Behavior Therapy*, 1972, *3*, 398–416.

Kauffman, J. M. *Characteristics of children's behavior disorders*. Columbus, Ohio: Charles E. Merrill, 1977.

Klinge, V., & Vaziri, H. EEG abnormalities in adolescent drug abusers. *Adolescence*, 1975, *10*, 1–10.

Kratcoski, P. C., & Kratcoski, J. E. Changing patterns in the delinquent activities of boys and girls: A self-reported delinquency analysis. *Adolescence*, 1975, *10*, 83–91.

Lefkowitz, M. M., Eron, L. D., Walder, L. O., & Huesmann, L. R. *Growing up to be violent*. New York: Pergamon, 1977.

Levenkron, S. *The best little girl in the world*. Chicago: Contemporary Books, 1978.

Lewis, W. W. Continuity and intervention in emotional disturbance: A review. *Exceptional Children*, 1965, *31*, 465–474.

Liebert, R. M., & Baron, R. A. Some immediate effects of televised violence on children's behavior. In F. Rebelsky & L. Dorman (Eds.), *Child development and behavior*. New York: Alfred A. Knopf, 1973.

Lockyer, L. & Rutter, M. A five-to-fifteen year follow-up study of infantile psychosis. In S. Chess & A. Thomas (Eds.), *Annual progress in child psychiatry and child development, 1970*. New York: Brunner/Mazel, 1970.

Miller, J. P. Suicide and adolescence. *Adolescence*, 1975, *10*, 11–24.

Miller, W. B. Lower class culture as a generating milieu of gang delinquency. In H. C. Quay (Ed.), *Children's behavior disorders: Selected readings*. Princeton, N.J.: Van Nostrand, 1968.

Musgrove, F. *Youth and the social order*. London: Routledge & Kegan Paul, 1964.

Muuss, R. E. The implications of social learning theory for an understanding of adolescent development. *Adolescence*, 1976, *11*, 61–85.

Neil, S. Violence and vandalism: Dimensions and correctives. *Phi Delta Kappan*, 1978, *59*, 302–305.

Nelson, C. M. Alternative education for the mildly and moderately handicapped. In R. D. Kneedler & S. G. Tarver (Eds.), *Changing perspectives in special education*. Columbus, Ohio: Charles E. Merrill, 1977.

O'Dell, S. Training parents in behavior modification: A review. *Psychological Bulletin*. 1974, *81*, 418–433.

O'Neal, P. & Robins, L. N. The relation of childhood behavior problems to adult psychiatric status: A thirty-year follow up study of 150 subjects. In R. Harth (Ed.), *Issues in behavior disorders*. Springfield, Ill.: Charles C Thomas, 1971.

Patterson, G. R., Ray, R. S., & Shaw, D. A. Direct intervention in families of deviant children. *Oregon Research Bulletin*, 1968, *8* (9).

Patterson, G. R., Reid, J. B., Jones, R. R., & Conger, R. E. *A social learning approach to family intervention*. Volume 1: *Families with aggressive children*. Eugene, Ore.: Castalia, 1975.

Porter, J. W. The limits of school power. *Phi Delta Kappan*. 1978, *59*, 319–320.

Quay, H. C., & Quay, L. C., Behavior problems in early adolescence. *Child Development*, 1965, *36*, 215–220.

Rimland, B. *Infantile autism*. New York: Meredith, 1964.

Rinn, R. C., Vernon, J. C., & Wise, M. J. Training parents of behaviorally disordered children in groups: A three years' program evaluation. *Behavior Therapy*, 1975, *6*, 378–387.

Ritvo, E. R., Ornitz, E. M., Tanguay, P., & Lee, J. C. M. *Neurophysiologic and biochemical abnormalities in infantile autism and childhood schizophrenia*. Paper presented at the meeting of the American Orthopsychiatric Association, San Francisco, March 1970.

Rose, T. L. The functional relationship between artificial food colors and hyperactivity. *Journal of Applied Behavior Analysis*, 1978, *11*, 439–446.

Ross, A. O. *Psychological disorders of children*. New York: McGraw-Hill, 1974.

Rutherford, R. B. Behavioral decision model for delinquent and predelinquent adolescents. *Adolescence*, 1976, *11*, 97–106.

Sagor, M. Biological bases of childhood behavior disorders. In W. C. Rhodes & M. L. Tracy (Eds.), *A study of child variance*. Volume 1: *Conceptual models*. Ann Arbor: Institute for the Study of Mental Retardation and Related Disabilities, University of Michigan, 1972.

Skinner, B. F. What is psychotic behavior? In T. Millon (Ed.), *Theories of psychopathology*. Philadelphia: W. B. Saunders, 1967.

Skinner, B. F. Behaviorism at fifty. In J. F. Rosenblith, W. Allinsmith, & J. P. Williams (Eds.), *The causes of behavior* (3rd ed.). Boston: Allyn & Bacon, 1972.

Smith, R. M. & Walters, J. Delinquent and non-delinquent males' perceptions of their fathers. *Adolescence*, 1978, *13*, 21–28.

Spiegel, L. A. Disorder and consolidation in adolescence. *Journal of the American Psychoanalytic Association*, 1961, *9*, 406–417.

Stumphauzer, J. S., Aiken, T. W., & Veloz, E. V. East side story: Behavioral analysis of a high juvenile crime community. *Behavioral Disorders*, 1977, *2*, 76–84.

Sutherland, E. H., & Cressey, D. R. *Principles of criminology* (7th ed.). Philadelphia: Lippincott, 1966.

Swift, M. S., & Spivack, G. Academic success and classroom behavior in secondary schools. *Exceptional Children*, 1973, *39*, 392–399.

Szasz, T. S. The myth of mental illness. *American Psychologist*, 1960, *15*, 113–118.

Terman, L. M. The gifted group of mid-life: Thirty-five year follow-up of the superior child. *Genetic studies of genius, Volume 5*. Stanford, Calif.: Stanford University Press, 1959.

Ullmann, L. P., & Krasner, L. (Eds.) *Case studies in behavior modification.* New York: Holt, Rinehart & Winston, 1965.

Warner, L. G., & DeFleur, M. L. Attitude as an interactional concept: Social constraint and social distance as intervening variables between attitudes and action. *American Sociological Review*, 1969, *34*, 153–169.

Waxler, N. E., & Mishler, E. G. Parental interaction with schizophrenic children and well siblings: An experimental test of some etiological theories. In S. Chess & A. Thomas (Eds.), *Annual progress in child psychiatry and child development 1972*. New York: Brunner/Mazel, 1972.

Weiner, I. B. *Psychological disturbance in adolescence.* New York: Wiley-Interscience, 1970.

Werry, J. S. Organic factors in childhood psychopathology. In H. C. Quay & J. S. Werry (Eds.), *Psychopathological disorders of childhood*. New York: Wiley, 1972.

Wolk, S., & Brandon, J. Runaway adolescents' perceptions of parents and self. *Adolescence*, 1977, *12*, 175–187.

Worell, J., & Nelson, C. M. *Managing instructional problems*. New York: McGraw-Hill, 1974.

Ysseldyke, J. E., & Salvia, J. Diagnostic-prescriptive teaching: Two models. *Exceptional Children*, 1974, *41*, 181–185.

Sociology Looks at Modern Adolescents

3

Edward A. Wynne

There is a popular impression that contemporary American adolescents are displaying more signs of emotional stress than adolescents, say, 50 years ago, and various statistics tend to support this impression. However, before considering these statistics, it will be useful to develop an appropriate intellectual framework for looking at modern adolescence, a framework with implications for anyone concerned with adolescent behavior disorders and one which places heavy emphasis on a sociological perspective on adolescence.

We can appreciate what is meant by a biological perspective on adolescence. It means looking at adolescence as a biological phenomenon: paying attention to the spurt in the child's physical growth, the onset of puberty, and the development of secondary sex characteristics. These occurrences affect the status of the child, and so we can analyze these changes and their effect on adolescents. There is also, obviously, a psychological perspective that views adolescence in terms of the emotional patterns displayed by persons undergoing biological adolescence. We also realize that we may prescribe different solutions to adolescent problems, depending on the perspective we apply.

A sociological perspective on adolescence examines adolescents in the light of the institutions and public expectations that shape their conduct. In other words, sociology does not see adolescence as something that springs principally from inside the body or mind of the child. Instead, it looks at the society that causes adolescent youths to tend to have certain patterns of feelings and conduct. To offer a concrete example, there is a widely recognized "youth market" in America, comprised of millions of young people who have significant amounts of spending money and who are interested in comparatively non-utilitarian products. These products are merchandised through systems which especially cater to their age group and which subject this audience to a number of historically unique influences. The adolescents may term the feelings and concepts promoted by this marketing "natural," but, to a sociologist, such a conclusion confuses a temporal, culture- and class-bound event with the universality of true naturalness. However, the youth market is not a universal phenomenon. In earlier periods in American history, as in many contemporary cultures, there was no youth market. Adolescents, like everyone else, had less money and they essentially bought what adults bought. Thus, because there was no youth market, many contemporary "natural" adolescent feelings were less frequent or nonexistent.

A sociological approach tries to identify the relationship between patterns of adolescent conduct and emotions and numerous external variables. Understandably, this approach provides prescriptions for many adolescent dysfunctions that are different from the biological and psychological approaches. For instance, when it appears that a number of adolescents are in "trouble" or are exhibiting disordered behavior, the sociologist looks to see how their external environment may be manipulated to deal with the problem rather than considering medication or focusing on the psyche of the particular youths.

We cannot ignore the fact that the choice of approach will have philosophical implications for the selection of methods. Psychology, for example, when treating the problems of adolescence, tends to emphasize choice and deliberation by the subjects. If one wants to change the way a particular person feels, it is necessary to discuss the situation with the person and such discussion implies some process of consent. But sociology is not immediately interested in the feelings of particular individuals. It deals with groups and with *patterns* of conduct and feelings. It recognizes that the subjects of research may not even realize how their environment has structured their attitudes and those of their peers. Indeed, the most profound structuring typically occurs at a subconscious level. The corrective measures a sociologist might prescribe may occur outside the perception of the adolescent involved, or, if they are apparent, they may seem irrelevant or inappropriate to the persons affected. In essence, the psychological approach, vis-a-vis particular adolescents, is more direct and consensual, while the sociological approach tends to be more remote and manipulative.

SOCIOLOGICAL VARIABLES

Now let us consider exactly what perspectives should be applied by a sociology of adolescence and how they are justified. We can then test these perspectives against the data and finally consider corrective steps.

Much of the important information underlying the sociology of adolescence is derived from anthropology and social history (see Aries, 1962; Coleman, 1974; Eisenstadt, 1956; Handlin & Handlin, 1971). These disciplines enable us to see how people we now call adolescents were treated—and how they acted—in other cultures and earlier periods. The information shows us that adolescence is largely a *social* phenomenon. In other words, children always pass through puberty to adulthood, but how they feel about, and react to, that passage is essentially determined by the norms and institutions of their class, society, and era. In the past, there was little conscious awareness of the state we call *adolescence*. In modern American culture—as we will see—it is increasingly likely that children passing through puberty will feel "adolescent." Ultimately, the diffusion and intensification of this feeling of adolescence among our young has important policy implications.

If, in the past, youths did not feel like adolescents, how did they feel? Apparently, they tended often to feel like the adults three to ten years older than they were. (Incidentally, those adults probably felt younger—more playful, more overtly demonstrative—than do many adults today.) Specifically, young people in other cultures, in contrast to contemporary young Americans at about the time of puberty, felt less emotional uncertainty about their status, were more at ease in accepting and exercising authority, were more disposed to conduct themselves responsibly, and had easier relationships with people in all age groups (see the writings about adolescence by Horatio Alger, a late nineteenth-century American novelist). These particular feelings—or responses—had been *taught* them by the social structures around them. Most of this teaching occurred long before the period of puberty; and thus, at puberty, young people simply acted and felt the way they had been taught to respond.

The social structures in earlier societies taught these non-adolescent feelings because (long before puberty occurred) they treated young people more like adults than we do today. Young people were more likely to work beside adults in farming, hunting, or manufacturing, as compared to being isolated in schools. They were given significant—and maturing—responsibilities to take care of infants and young children in families and other community groups. They handled adult-like chores about the house. In many societies, ceremonial activities played an important role in the lives of all community members, and these activities often integrated adults and young people in collective activities. Because of these diverse structures, young people did not feel so different from adults since they were doing many of the things adults did and living their day-to-day lives in the presence of adults.

The puberty rituals in many societies also affected the nature of adolescence. Though not all non-Western societies have such rituals, they are a widespread form of social structuring and they are used to train feelings (van Gennep, 1960). While the rites of passage vary in content, they essentially demarcate the moment of passage from childhood to adulthood. Before the ritual, initiates are usually regarded, under the norms of their culture, as children. This does not mean they cannot do some forms of adult work or otherwise act like adults; however, in some essential ways, the pre-initiates were regarded as less than adults. For instance, in the Kikuyu tribe in Africa, boys—regardless of age—who have not completed their puberty ritual cannot associate with girls who have completed the equivalent rite (Gatheru, 1964). In other words, completion of the rite is a condition for being treated as a full-fledged adult. Conversely, once the rite is successfully completed, initiates are admitted to full adulthood. Often puberty rites are associated with ritual scarification of the initiate and with other forms of physical or emotional testing; for example, male Kikuyus are publicly circumcised, without anesthetic, and show no fear. The outcomes of such rites often result in actual, or symbolic, signs that demonstrate that adulthood had been attained. The effect of such rites is to reorient the emotional life of successful candidates, so that, on one side of the passage, they feel like—and hence are—children, but after the rite they feel as if they have attained adulthood, and hence they are adults. In effect puberty rites suppress or extinguish the emotions we associate with adolescence since there is no significant status between childhood and adulthood; the "in-betweenness" is only during the middle of the ritual, and that is a brief, painful moment and then over.

Modern American society organizes the life of its young in ways that sharply contrast with other cultures and earlier times. Essentially, our society tends to isolate youth from many adult activities and thus attentuates their in-betweenness. The major cause of this isolation has been the incremental but steady extension of formal education. We have increased the proportion of our young people attending school and stretched the average length of school attendance. While formal education has been practised in many societies, it has usually been restricted to much smaller fractions of the population than is the American pattern. The educational arrangements of other eras and cultures were less isolating than those in our times. Other factors, identified by researchers such as Wynne (1977), which tend to segregate the young from adult-like experiences have been the spread of urbanization and suburbanization, a decline in the number of rural families, the growth of comparative affluence, the decline in family size (which has diminished the child-care responsibilities of older children), and the diffusion of technological progress.

The long-term increase in prosperity has also had a significant biological effect, an effect with emotional repercussions. Essentially, between 1840 and 1960, the age of the female menarche has dropped from 17 to 13 years. Equivalent shifts have occurred in the area of male puberty. These incremental changes, resulting from steadily rising standards of living, have raised energy levels and hormonal activity in young people. Consequently, it has become more important that 13 year olds in our era be emotionally stable than was the case 100 years ago: sexually potent persons can cause great harm to themselves and others by unstable conduct.

Another American pattern that disrupts the transition from youth to adulthood is the segmentation of the process of transition. Such segmentation contrasts with the all-at-once impact of a puberty ritual. In our society, entrance to adulthood is marked by a number of checkpoints at indeterminate and uncoordinated times in the life of any particular adolescent. These checkpoints include: graduating from high school (or college), passing a driver's test, serving in the armed services, being eligible to vote or to buy beer or liquor, earning all or a good proportion of one's own living, living away from home and getting married (or having a child). Many adolescents have passed some of these points; others may be years ahead. During this interregnum, they may properly see themselves as still captivated in adolescence.

The effects of these contemporary patterns have been to isolate young people from diverse contact with adults as well as with younger and older children, and to narrow the forms of responsibilities and authority adolescents may carry. As a result, childhood has become more childish and extended, and adolescence has become more prevalent and prolonged. Indeed, conceptual questions have inevitably arisen, as more persons in their late teens and early twenties accept or pursue roles traditionally assumed by adolescents. To deal with this extension of adolescence, some writers such as Keniston (1968, p. 263) have invented a new age status: youth. They define youth as the period between the end of adolescence and the beginning of adulthood. A typical example of a person who might technically be termed a youth is someone in his mid-twenties who is still in graduate school and supported by parents or a fellowship.

It is understandable that such a person might not really qualify as an adult: he has not yet begun to earn his own living in a traditional job. However, it might be appropriate to call this an instance of prolonged adolescence—although graduate students might feel more at ease being called youths than adolescents. But this apparently trivial matter of semantics actually touches on an important element of social policy. When we decide to call persons (who might arguably be called adolescents) youths, we make it easier for them to choose to stay in their status. If we decide to call such people adolescents (when calling a 22 year old an adolescent is an insult) we may discourage them from remaining in their status; they may leave school and go on to work. Thus, our values shape our terminology, our terminology shapes the feeling of people, and those feelings then shape their conduct.

Neither can we ignore the effects of other adult values and attitudes on the spread of adolescence. In particular, it is probably safe to say that, over the past 25–30 years, there has been an intensifying sympathy for protecting and enlarging the rights of individuals; this sympathy has naturally affected opinions about what sorts of structured and planned emotional demands should be placed on adolescents. For example, many contemporary students and teachers might be critical of restrictions on male and female student couples displaying affection in a high-school building or on campus (e.g., holding hands; lying side-by-side on the lawn?). Such restrictions really constitute emotional demands since they prohibit the display of certain feelings, and, by prohibiting that display, they also inhibit the development of such feelings and encourage students to feel "businesslike" about their time in school. Some people might see such restrictions as intrusions on students' rights, but maturity is ultimately determined by our ability to satisfy many demands for emotional restraint—in work, marriage, parenthood, and community membership. Thus, in the end, this increase in philosophical individualism may make it harder for young people to learn to act in a typically adult fashion, and excessive immaturity may be evinced as conduct we call behavior disorders.

Another intellectual force that has assisted the spread of adolescence has been the disposition of segments of our society to give great emphasis to formal cognitive knowledge—and prolonged schooling is an important means of attaining such knowledge. In contrast, in other societies, character or physical strength or courage were given primacy over book-learning (Meyers, 1964).

These various developments have caused adults to support patterns of conduct and organization which discourage young persons from feeling like secure adults. This is not to suggest that no young person ever felt like an adolescent until the mid-twentieth century. Some transitory moments of adolescent feeling have probably occurred to young people in many cultures, but such moments were generally dissipated by the many maturing demands that were necessarily around them. Such moments were also probably more frequent among youths from more prosperous families, who could afford to escape involvement in adultlike work activities and thus might be provided with more time for introspection. However, adolescence, as we currently conceive it, was probably still quite rare. In addition, our perception of the frequency of adolescence in the past is probably distorted because writers such as Kiell (1964) have necessarily relied on diaries and literature for much of their evidence; such forms of evidence give undue weight to the values and conduct of a relatively elite literary class.

The more routine appearance of modern adolescent attitudes was heralded by the development of the fictional literary form the Germans called the *Bildungsroman* ("the novel of education"). Goethe's *Werther*, written in 1787, is the first prominent example of such a work. Goethe's central character was described as a young man, "gifted with deep, pure sentiment and penetrating intelligence, who loses himself in fantastic dreams and undermines himself with speculative thought until finally, torn by hopeless passions, especially by infinite love, he shoots himself in the head." *Werther* served as a model for many later successors, down to Holden Caulfield in *Catcher in the Rye*.

A sociologist would say that the *Bildungsroman* became more frequent because adolescence was spreading. In other words, changing social and institutional patterns taught successive waves of young people to feel differently from their predecessors. As a result, increasing proportions of young people did really tend to feel like Werther—or at least to identify with him. But, imagine that, by some magic, we could transform the institutions around contemporary young people into forms much more like those in traditional societies. If this happened, then later waves of young people would think Werther's feelings absurd or grotesque. They might say, "The very idea! Some healthy young man killing himself just because a woman rejected him!"

None of this discussion is to say that all, or even most, American adolescents are afflicted with severe adolescent feelings. Indeed, writers such as Offer (1969) have even contended that such feelings are extremely rare. American youths are raised in many different milieus: on farms, in suburbs, in central cities; they come from different sized families; they have different amounts of contact with paid work or other demanding collective responsibilities; their families and schools have varied patterns which also affect the structure of their psyche. Essentially, these variations mean that these youths are surrounded by environments with different degrees of modernity. These differences are related to social class and urban/rural variables. The greater the degree of modernity that pervades youths' environments, the more likely they are to undergo a stressful adolescence. The stress will be likely because more modern environments will tend to cause youth to undergo a prolonged adolescence—an isolation from adulthood when they are chronologically adults—during which time the rules for appropriate conduct will be ambiguous and conflicting. It is that ambiguity that leads to stress.

Another sociological variable to be considered is the difference in the adolescent stresses faced by lower- and upper middle-class youths. Typically, stress for lower-class youths is most intense in urban areas. Such comparatively modern environments often have large, bureaucratic schools. Compulsory attendance (another relatively modern innovation) requires these youths to attend school, although it often appears to them to have no relevance to their life plans. This mandatory scholarization is seen by many students as treating them as children when they believe they should be acting like and being treated as adults. The matter is further aggravated since they may not possess important academic skills. (For, if they possessed such skills, they might sublimate their energies into striving for academic achievement.) In any event, lower-class youths are sometimes likely to use violence and disorder—which dramatically demonstrate their physical strength, one characteristic of adults—to try to act like adults. Now, of course, most lower-class *adults* do not give great emphasis to violence and disorder in their day-to-day lives, but the young can only learn non-violent and more adaptive modes of adult conduct by first-hand experience with adult environments, and this cannot occur in schools.

Upper middle-class youths may more typically live in suburban environments which are quite modern. This modernity, by constricting them to particular patterns of interaction, necessarily makes them more prone to certain types of adolescent stress. However, unlike students from lower-class families, upper middle-class adolescents are likely to respond to stress by acts of self-destruction and withdrawal rather than overt aggression. Perhaps these suburban youth patterns are partly due to the types of role models they sense around them: upper middle-class adults are less likely to be *perceived* as releasing their hostilities through direct physical aggression. Another outlet more available to upper middle-class children (than to children from lower-class families) is the pursuit of academic excellence. This pursuit may enable them to attain some sense of competence and mastery, despite the confusion engendered by still being in school or college. One danger in this sublimated pursuit of formal education is that students (because they are successful students) may be stimulated to continue in school or college or graduate school, even though they feel that their schooling is irrelevant to true adulthood. Under such circumstances, they may resent school but remain enrolled because "being in the world" may subject them to emotional demands they are reluctant to meet.

STATISTICAL PERSPECTIVES

The preceding discussion has implied that there should be many signs of increasing emotional distress among American adolescents, and we will consider statistics dealing with this issue. First, there must be one final qualification regarding the evaluation of this distress.

As Rubel (1977) and others have observed, it is not easy to develop simple, consistent measures of emotional distress. It would be hard to determine exactly how much emotional distress typical students in any one school or community are experiencing. The matter would be even harder if we tried to compare that measurement with the level of distress experienced by other students ten years earlier at the same school. Such comparisons are, however, necessary to determine the trends. Without such information, it is impossible to say whether things are getting better or worse. If we are trying to develop such trend information, we must compare relatively common phenomena. For example, if school enrollment has doubled, then the fact that twice as many students are reported absent may mean only that the intensity of absence has not changed. Or, if the costs of vandalism have risen, we must be sure to allow for the effects of inflation or of more expensive school equipment. Despite these qualifications, there are some statistics that provide relatively accurate, long-range measures that are apparently highly related to emotional distress in youth.

The most significant of these statistics is derived from data collected by the federal government about changes in causes of death and rates of illegitimacy. Durkheim (1951) first recognized that these statistics measure phenomena which can be defined with relative precision: whether someone is dead and the identifiable cause of death and whether a baby is legitimate. For many years, almost all deaths and births in America have been registered by local authorities who judge the cause of death or whether a child is legitimate. There are consistent criteria which have been routinely applied in making these decisions, and there is no reason to believe the thousands of local officials involved in these decisions are conspiring to distort the statistics. While any one decision by an official may be possibly wrong, that possibility is a random one—if 2% of all these decisions are wrong in 1965, then there should be about 2% error in 1970, and thus the mistakes should average out. The statistics are also tabulated in a fashion that allows for changes in the size of age groups from year to year; in other words, the statistics compare the proportion of all adolescents dying from a particular cause in one year to the proportion in another year.

The first statistics to be presented concern white adolescents since one popular impression in this country is that behavioral disorder is primarily a problem for minority group members. Between 1950 and 1976 the annual suicide rate of white males between the ages of 15 and 19 increased 260% from 3.3 deaths for each 100,000 to 11.9, with a high point of 13.2 in 1975 (U.S.D.H.E.W., 1974a; 1978a). No other age group had so high a rate of increase. During these same years, the overall white male suicide rate increased by only 6%. The adolescent increase was relatively steady and incremental, and its gradualness suggests that it was not directly related to the major political and social upheavals of the period.

The absolute number of youths involved in the suicide increase is, fortunately, comparatively small—perhaps 3,000 to 4,000 reported suicides a year among whites aged 15 to 19. While this is a minute fraction of our youth population, the problem has immense symbolic and indicative significance. For each identified adolescent suicide, there are undoubtedly other suicides not identified as such, attempted suicides that are not tabulated, and youths who suffer from serious anxiety or depression but who do not attempt suicide. Hence, the 260% increase represents a concurrent 260% increase in general depression among our young people. This increase has occurred at a time when naive observers would infer that American youth, especially those from white families, "never had it so good."

There have also been increases in the rate of death by homicide among white males aged 15 to 19. In 1959 there were 2.7 such deaths per 100,000 members of the group (U.S.D.H.E.W., 1974a; 1978a). That rate increased to 4.9 by 1969; by 1976 it was 7.5. This represents a 170% increase over 17 years, with a high point of 8.2 in

1975. During the same period, no other age group had a comparable increase in its homicide rate. The highest previous homicide rate for white males aged 15 to 19 during the twentieth century was 5.2 in 1919.

Like the suicide rate, the homicide death rate probably measures other incidents of disorder, albeit indirectly, e.g., woundings, beatings, threats, and the stimulation of profound fear. There is every reason to believe that such an increase in crimes against white young have generally been committed by their peers, i.e., other white male adolescents.

There have also been significant changes in the statistics about sexual conduct. Between 1950 and 1976, the number of illegitimate births for unmarried white females, aged 15 to 19, went from 5.1 per 1,000 to the high point of 12.4 in 1976 (U.S.D.H.E.W., 1976; 1987a; U.S. Census, 1975, p.52). These statistics represent a change in the conduct of successive groups of young males and females. This increase in illegitimacy has occurred during a period characterized by increasing availability of contraceptives, abortion, and sexual information. Presumably, the increase means that young males are more willing to get females pregnant, that young females are more willing to risk (and accept) pregnancy, and that both females and males feel less responsibility for burdening infants with the handicaps of being born into a one-parent family consisting of a young and vulnerable mother.

Another pertinent sex-related change has been the spread of venereal disease among the young. Between 1956 and 1974, reported cases of gonorrhea (per 100,000 members of the 15–19 age group) rose more than 200%, while syphilis increased 100% (U.S.D.H.E.W., 1975, p. 12). These increases were associated with an increased availability of medicines, treatment centers, and appropriate preventive information. Obviously, the increases reflect a growth in casual (or promiscuous) sexual relations and in irresponsible attitudes among sex partners, who feel little concern for protecting one another.

It is also important to consider statistics about the conduct of black adolescents since our general analysis suggested that adolescents from lower economic classes (and blacks generally have lower family income levels than whites) would have different patterns of misconduct than adolescents from other economic classes. Between 1959 and 1976, the rate of death by homicide for black males aged 15 to 19, rose from 23.3 per 100,000 members of that group to 46.8; the high point of that rise was 60.2 in 1971 (U.S.D.H.E.W., 1974a; 1978a). As for suicide, the rate of death for black males, aged 15 to 19, rose from 1.7 in 1954 to the high point of 7.1 in 1976 (U.S.D.H.E.W., 1974a; 1978a). The figures on illegitimacy are also significant. Between 1950 and 1975, the estimated number of illegitimate births for unmarried black females, aged 15 to 19, went from 68.5 to 91.6 per 1,000. The high point of that rise was 95.1 in 1975 (U.S.D.H.E.W., 1976; U.S. Census, 1975, p. 52).

We do not have statistics about the national level of youth drug use before the late 1960s. Thus, the issue of long-term trends in drug use is complicated. However, the most recent national data show no sign of decline in general youth drug use from the recent historically high levels. Also, there continues to be a steady increase in marijuana use: 27.1% of a national sample of the 1975 high-school graduating class reported using marijuana one or more times, while the comparable figure for the 1977 class is 35.4% (U.S.D.H.E.W.), 1977, p. 41). The most thorough statistics on long-term drug use cover San Mateo County (California) students for every year from 1968 to 1976 (San Mateo, 1976). San Mateo, an affluent suburban county, is recognized as having relatively intense drug use and is, therefore, not typical. Still, there is evidence that trends originating in California tend to spread. For example, the 1968 San Mateo levels represent current rates of adolescent marijuana use in many communities. The San Mateo statistics on marijuana use among certain high-school grades are shown in Table 1.

Other data from San Mateo reveal steady increases in student use of a variety of harmful substances. Nationally, it is also significant to recall that arrests of males under age 18 for narcotics law violations increased 1,288% between 1960 and 1972 (U.S. Department of Justice, 1972, p. 124).

There are also statistics of increased use of alcohol by youths. The San Mateo survey reported that the percentage of seventh-grade boys who had begun drinking during the previous year increased from 52% in 1969 to 72% in 1973. This increase is consistent with equivalent increases reported in other surveys in Duval County, Florida, and Toronto, Ontario. This adolescent drinking is not simply tasting. In 1974, 23% of a national sample of youths between the ages of 13 and 18 reported being drunk four or more times during the previous year (U.S.D.H.E.W., 1974b, p. 128). The increase in drinking levels among high-school-age youths evidently was preceded by an earlier increase in the level of drinking among college-age youths. Blane's summary of long-term research on levels of drinking among college students concluded that between 1950 and 1970, the proportion of college students who would describe themselves as drinkers increased from 74% to 87% (1978). There were also increases in the proportion of students with drinking problems. Since 1970, college student drinking has remained stabilized at the new high level.

Some national trend statistics are available on delinquency. Between 1957 and 1974 the number of delinquency cases per 1,000 persons aged 10 to 17 disposed of by American juvenile courts rose from 19.1 to 37.5 (U.S. Department of Justice, 1976, p. 572). Throughout the period, the proportion of status offenses (e.g., running away from home and other noncriminal conduct) compared to criminal acts (e.g., shoplifting, robbery), both of which are added together to calculate total delinquency, remained relatively constant. Drug cases were a significant but not central element in the increase.

There are also statistics for increased antisocial conduct in schools. One survey

TABLE 1 Percentage of Marijuana Use among Male San Mateo County, California, High-School Students for the Period 1968 to 1976

Year	1 or more uses in past year		10 or more uses in past year		50 or more uses in past year	
	Grade 9	Grade 12	Grade 9	Grade 12	Grade 9	Grade 12
1968	27	12	14	26	na	na
1969	35	50	20	34	na	na
1970	34	51	20	34	11	22
1971	44	59	26	43	17	32
1972	44	61	27	45	16	32
1973	51	61	32	45	20	32
1974	49	62	30	47	20	34
1975	49	64	30	45	20	31
1976	48	61	27	42	17	30

SOURCE: San Mateo County, Department of Public Health and Welfare, *Summary report, 1976: surveys of student drug use* (San Mateo, Calif.: Department of Public Health, 1976).

reported that, in the national sample of schools studied, assaults on teachers increased 85% between 1970 and 1973. The survey also showed that the number of weapons confiscated from students by authorities in the schools rose by 54% (U.S. Senate, 1975). Another careful study on the patterns of school crime concluded that "the frequency of crimes in schools has increased since the 1950's, and the character of that crime has undergone drastic changes. Much of what we now take for granted would have been shocking twenty years ago" (Rubel, 1977, p. 1).

Interestingly enough, the available statistics on school crime show significant patterns of difference between the nature of misconduct in central city and suburban schools. For example, the rate of certain reported offenses in a national sample of high schools between September 1, 1974, and January 1, 1975, was compared for central city and suburban schools (for every 1000 pupils enrolled in a school). The assault rates were 1.9 per 1000 students in the central city and 1.0 per 1000 in the suburbs, whereas the equivalent drug abuse rates were 1.5 and 1.9 (U.S.D.H.E.W., 1978b, p. B–4).

We should also consider the student unrest, building takeovers, and other youth disorders of the late 1960s and early 1970s. Occasional student disorder has always been a fact of American history, but the most recent wave involved a higher proportion of youth and took more destructive forms. For example, during 1969 and 1970 more than 8,000 bomb threats, attempted bombings, and bombings were attributed to student unrest (President's Commission, 1970, p. 347). In 1970, 9 of the top 16 FBI most-wanted persons were youth activists and their crimes included murder, bank robbery, and bombing (*N.Y. Times*, 1970, p. 13).

Not surprisingly, changes in youth conduct have been accompanied by changes in youth attitudes. Some trend data are available. Between 1948 and 1968 successive freshman classes at Haverford College in Philadelphia took the Minnesota Multiphasic Inventory (MMPI), a short-answer test that measures attitudes (Heath, 1968, p. 67). Table 2 reports a sample of statistics derived from the student answers. The numbers listed for each item represent the proportion of students who answered "yes." Clearly, these data are not current, but they do help us to understand shifts in youth attitudes over a considerable part of the last quarter century and constitute the most complete longitudinal study available. (When we consider more recent data, a consistent relationship between the changes that occurred among the Haverford students and those revealed in current polls will become apparent.) It is easy to recognize an overall attitudinal trend in the shifting answers of these students. Essentially, the successive classes became less sympathetic to cooperative and group activities; more and more, they evinced attitudes consonant with withdrawal from contact or cooperation with others.

This increase in withdrawn attitudes among students was coupled with an apparent simultaneous increase in their self-centeredness. Between 1948 and 1968, the proportion of Haverford students who thought they could work great benefit to the world if given a chance rose from 40% to 66%, while the proportion of 17 year olds who thought they knew more than experts rose from 20% to 38%. It is not clear how these increasingly withdrawn and introverted students could render such benefit without human interaction or acquire the experiences incident to becoming so knowledgeable.

Other statistics about youth attitudinal trends show that the Haverford patterns are representative of trends displayed by successive groups of late adolescents on other college campuses. Attitudinal tests were administered to students at Dartmouth College in 1952 and 1968 and at the University of Michigan

TABLE 2 Haverford College, Sample MMPI Items for the Classes of 1948 Through 1968

Item	Percent "Yes"							
	1948-49	1952	1956	1960	1961	1965	1967	1968
When I was a child I didn't care to be a member of a crowd or gang	33	35	35	38	49	58	19	47
I could be happy living all alone in a cabin in the woods or mountains	23	28	34	38	33	35	42	45
I am a good mixer	77	49	48	63	60	58	38	43
I like to go to parties and other affairs where there is lots of loud fun	65	56	55	53	44	40	38	40
At parties I am more likely to sit by myself than to join in with the crowd	23	35	40	27	44	38	47	50
My worries seem to disappear when I get into a crowd of lively friends	71	69	73	68	58	65	56	55
If I were in trouble with several friends who were equally to blame, I would rather take the whole blame than to give them away	63	56	50	57	47	43	33	45
When a man is with a woman he is usually thinking about things related to her sex	29	37	15	27	35	28	36	43
I enjoy reading love stories	55	49	35	25	44	30	18	25
I like dramatics	80	74	73	75	60	73	67	65
I would like to be a singer	51	47	37	36	33	38	31	23

Source: Heath (1968), p. 67. Reprinted by permission.

in 1952 and 1969 (Hogue, 1974). Several similar questions were asked of all students queried at both colleges. For example, they were asked whether "human nature is fundamentally more cooperative." Agreement declined from 66% and 70% at Dartmouth and Michigan, respectively, to 51% and 55%. Another question was, "most of what I am learning in college is very worthwhile." Agreement declined from 67% and 74%, respectively, to 58% and 57%. Again, these students were asked to identify the private and public institutions (e.g., school, church, family) to which they felt related. The number and intensity of summed identifications declined from 296 and 259, respectively, to 269 and 206. In other words, successive groups of students have felt less and less relationship to the world. They have become increasingly alienated.

The 1969 and 1973 Yankelovich youth surveys (1973; 1974), while not replicating questions asked in the Haverford, Michigan, and Dartmouth studies, nor covering precisely equivalent groups of adolescents, do show a continuation of the trends toward egoism and withdrawal. Among the college students surveyed in Yankelovich's national samples, the importance of "privacy" as a value increased from 61% in 1969 to 71% in 1973. At the same time, the respective importance of "religion" and "patriotism," two values that stress the individual's obligation to extrapersonal concerns, declined from 38% and 35% to 28% and 19%. The two surveys also showed a continuing pattern of gradual dissemination and acceptance of the views of college youths among non-college youths.

There are also interesting cross-cultural statistics about the attitudes of American children. The statistics were developed by Whiting and Whiting (1973, p.

56) in an international study of youth interaction patterns in six cultures. Five of the cultures represented underdeveloped or primitive environments; the sixth group consisted of children in a New England community. A common rating scale was used by observers in all locations to evaluate youth conduct on the dimension of altruism versus egoism. A total of 134 children between ages 3 and 6 and between 7 and 11 were observed in the entire study. Approximately 9,500 interacts were identified. When the median level of altruistic conduct was treated as 50%, the American children, with a level of 8%, scored as the most egoistic. The next lowest group was a tribe in India, with a level of 25%. The number of children involved was small, but still, the dramatically high level of egoism among the American children, compared with children in non-Western cultures, suggests that the data may justify comparative generalizations about the overall level of egoistic conduct among American youths or youths from industrial societies.

The preceding statistics should be interpreted in light of the sociological perspective outlined at the beginning of this paper. That perspective contends that the social institutions and popular attitudes of a society play a significant role in shaping the feelings and conduct of its young people. It seems that a growing proportion of young people is displaying unease, loneliness, and a propensity to engage in acts that are self-destructive, other-destructive, or socially irresponsible. The disorderly acts and feelings described are consonant with those that are popularly associated with aggravated adolescent distress. It is easy to understand how the actions might logically arise from the patterns of underlying feeling described and how people who commit such acts may likewise possess the feelings attributed to them. The statistics support the main proposition of this paper: *the feelings we popularly attribute to adolescence are being intensified in America because of the institutional and attitudinal patterns that surround our young.*

Of course, adolescence, per se, even as described here, is not necessarily a form of emotional disorder; the issue involved is essentially one of degree. Thus, it is true that there have always been young persons whose home environments or psychological characteristics have predisposed them to emotional disorder. However, the "spread" of adolescence increases the likelihood that such youths will exhibit disorderly characteristics. They will be more prone to disorder in modern environments because (A) the adult institutions about them will provide them with fewer incentives or support for orderly conduct and (B) they will be more profoundly affected by peer influences and those influences will be less healthful than in other environments.

These conclusions about the spread of adolescence lead to another question. If we believe that an excessive spread of adolescent attitudes and conduct is negative, either for the young, or for society as a whole, what can be done about it? Obviously, we must strive to change the institutional and attitudinal patterns that surround our young people.

A SOCIOLOGICAL APPROACH TO PROBLEM BEHAVIOR

A sociological approach to adolescence argues that changing destructive adolescent conduct should aim not so much at changing the mind or opinion of adolescents, but at changing the environment around them. These changes in the environment will gradually produce the necessary changes in attitudes and conduct. Indeed, in an ideal case, the environmental changes may cause the adolescent to stop altogether being an "adolescent" or disorderly person and to be transformed into a mature adult.

Understandably, our power over the social and institutional environments around other human beings is usually quite limited. And so the preceding concepts must be greatly moderated in practice. Still, the concept of changing the events, processes, and attitudes impinging on the child or adolescent is an important key. Furthermore, the more long-range our vision, the more elaborate we can make our environmental changes: if we have some ambitious environmental change in mind, it may be more practicable if we gradually move toward it over a 5–15 year period. It might be worth that effort, for example, to reduce the homicide and suicide rates.

At this point, some of the general characteristics of appropriate environmental changes in and around school might be considered. The following list does not include the mechanics of implementation in any useful detail since these matters are complex and often vary considerably from one institution or location to the next. Furthermore, the ideas on the list are not original: many schools are now applying some of these approaches and other authors, such as Coleman (1974) and Heath (1968), have made equivalent suggestions; in some other countries, approaches of this sort are routinely applied (e.g., Bronfenbrenner, 1970). Still, the presentation of a list can help us think of the principles that should govern constructive transformation.

1. Children and adolescents (including disorderly youths) should be generally expected to display wholesome, maturing attitudes and conduct. To give specific examples, they should be held responsible for their acts and instances of inappropriate or disruptive conduct should not be ignored or excused because of adolescent "immaturity" or because limitations in their backgrounds make such conduct understandable. This is not to say that no charity nor tolerance should ever be displayed in relation to misconduct. However, as Coleman (1974) argued, our society has probably erred in failing to apply standards of responsibility to the young that roughly duplicate those applied to adults. This discrepancy between adolescent and adult standards has tended to increase the gap between childhood and adulthood and encouraged young persons to retain young attitudes and to fear the attainment of real adult status. After all, if adolescents are perpetually freed of demands and responsibilities, why should they want to grow up?

2. Children and adolescents should acquire more of the authority associated with adulthood. For example, they should have increased authority over other students in and about school (and be expected to exercise that authority in a responsible fashion). This school authority can occur in tutoring situations, service projects, school duties and responsibilities, and other situations where the "authoritative" adolescent is faced with a peculiarly maturing challenge: to get other persons to do what is expected of them, or to face the consequences of failure in this charge.

3. Children and adolescents should have a greater diversity of responsibilities assigned to them in school. Essentially, these responsibilities should tend to mirror the patterns of adult life. Such mirroring would mean that the responsibilities bring together students of different grade levels and ability levels, that the students are asked to work together to produce some product or service rather than isolated individual projects, and that many different awards—as well as grades—are offered

to stimulate success. The responsibilities might include school maintenance, area beautification, preparing and serving food, entertaining other students and parents, tutoring other students, fund-raising, and various extracurricular activities (For an example of a tutorially oriented school program, see Newmark, 1976.)

4. Students must be brought in touch with different types of adults in and around school (compared to interaction exclusively with college-trained education majors). The adults might be parents, community volunteers, or paid aides. In addition, students can be assigned to do school-related internships with various adults at their job sites or to interview them for class assignments.

5. Many steps can be taken to increase school spirit so that students may be stimulated to develop helpful and supportive feelings toward one another. Such feelings are a common and important attribute of vital adult work environments.

6. Discipline codes and punishment systems must be analyzed to determine whether they are effective, widely publicized, and consistently and effectively enforced so students are stimulated to deal with and sublimate antisocial feelings and conduct.

7. As has often been suggested (e.g., U.S.D.H.E.W., 1978a, p. 132), students should have more prolonged relationships with particular teachers and with small, identifiable groups of other students rather than being shuffled around among subject specialists and in computer-grouped modules. Such persisting relationships are typical of important social and work environments in adult life. Thus, a within-the-school shift to prolonged relationships will help students learn the modes of interaction that are appropriate to adult life. Of course, such a shift will require extensive planning and reorganizing in the operation of larger schools.

8. Teachers and administrators must carefully plan and coordinate the revised demands they propose to make on students and the new systems of support that will be required. Without such organization, students will be subject to incoherent structures, which will only intensify their current problems.

9. Individual teachers, working in self-contained classrooms, can take small-scale steps to apply these principles to their own students. Such steps might include maintaining a well-structured curriculum, grading system, and discipline code (appropriate to the students' age level); assigning appropriately designed and graded group projects (Wynne, 1976); giving students classroom maintenance and tutoring responsibilities; providing a variety of effective rewards and consequences for individuals and groups; bringing in nonteaching adults as resource people; and stimulating class spirit.

A SOCIOLOGICAL APPROACH TO CONSEQUENCES FOR PROBLEM BEHAVIOR

Some of the preceding proposals give greater emphasis to punishment-related or consequence-related approaches than is common in contemporary educational practice. Given current conceptual norms, even a moderate discussion of punishment (or consequences as a result of behavior that is destructive to self or others) may seem excessive. Timidity in dealing with these issues is an example of another contemporary adult attitude that fosters the prolongation of adolescent behaviors in young adults.

Some thoughtful writers, such as van den Haag (1975) are beginning to question these attitudes. The vital threat of consequences for antisocial or self-defeating behavior can significantly change human conduct and such methods are applied on a widespread basis. How else would anyone teach a 3 year old not to run into the street? What is going on when speeders slow down as a police car enters the stream of auto traffic? Why do some homes and stores in unsafe neighborhoods display notices that they have burglar alarms? Indeed, when we consider the following sociological definition of consequences, we will become even more conscious of the frequency with which it is practiced.

Punishment is any act—and we must realize that words and gestures are also acts—which is intended to change the conduct of other persons, and either provokes unpleasant feelings in them or makes them aware of consequences that will stimulate such feelings. This definition does not say that punishment must be the intent of the authority figure; *the definition describes punishment from the eyes of the recipient.*

This matter of definitional perspective is important; all too often, we mistakenly define punishment from the viewpoint of the potential "punisher." Thus, A. S. Neill, in his popular book *Summerhill*, emphasized that he never punished the pupils in his private residential school; however, he did face them with the consequences of their conduct. For instance, if a student made a mess in the dining room, the person would either clean it up or be expelled from the school. It is evident that the pupils coerced into such clean-up did not enjoy it and so they were punished (or threatened with punishment) if they engaged in certain conduct. As another example, a teacher in a relatively permissive school emphasized that pupils were never compelled to do classwork; it was all voluntary. To demonstrate this policy, the teacher pointed out one 8 year old who had voluntarily decided to do classwork after having been reminded 37 times in 3 days.

Whether Neill and the permissive teacher believe they were not establishing and effecting punishment is difficult to say. We can be sure, however, that these adults do not want to admit they engage in punishment and that they do not examine the character of their conduct from the viewpoint of their subjects. In such instances, pupils who feel themselves punished are then given the message that they should not become angry or guilty because they have only been advised, redirected, confronted with the consequences of their conduct, or some other confusing euphemism.

Punishment and the threat of punishment are common in schools. Pupils are punished if they do not study or apply themselves; they are punished if they are truant; they are punished if they conspicuously misbehave, are disrespectful or disobedient, use foul language, or steal. They are punished every time teachers give them harsh looks, warn them to change their conduct, call their parents with a complaint, give them less than a perfect grade, or otherwise make them feel uncomfortable in an effort to change their conduct.

Emotionally healthy adults should treat the establishment and delivery of consequences as one part of their repertoire for changing human behavior. While it is not so powerful a tool as approval or affection, there are circumstances in which its use is indicated. Essentially, consequences and threats of consequences are often useful to deter sporadic inappropriate conduct. The reality is that no teacher or adult can ever provide any child with a constantly enlarging supply of love and support since the adult can never have such a vast reservoir of time and positive emotions. Thus, there will be moments of temptation for the child when the appeal of bad conduct is greater than the reward for good conduct. There may also be occasion when the consequences of student misconduct are extremely serious, and the adult in charge must strive to prevent such acts and such occasions. At such times, punishment or the threat of punishment becomes useful; it warns the potential offender that pursuing a negative course will lead to harmful ends. In actuality, this describes the practices followed by Neill and the permissive teacher in the foregoing example: when rewards no longer worked, and it was important to change a pupil's conduct, they applied punishment. At the same time they refused to define their conduct as punishment. As a result, in an important sense, the actions of these adults were irresponsible; they did not have to justify their punishing acts— because, by their definition, no punishment occurred. Ultimately, such adult conduct probably teaches students to hurt others without carefully assessing their own conduct since proponents of this ambiguous application of consequences say they did not intend to hurt their pupils. In sum, punishment that adults do not have the courage to call punishment is probably the most harmful punishment of all.

The aim of establishing consequences and of maintaining honesty and responsibility in this regard is not to ignore warm human relationships but to establish conditions which permit such relationships to flourish. Essentially, a sociological perspective leads us to conclude that the quality of human relations between adults and young people in our contemporary society is declining. The decline is not so much because adults are ill-disposed to the young but because certain structures and attitudes frustrate the maintenance of good relations. If we change those structures and attitudes, then better human relations become possible. Without such changes, we may be defeated, regardless of our good will, and accomplish very little. Changes in structure and attitudes cannot guarantee that all tensions will be dissolved; some differences and frustration are inevitable, and there will be a continuous need for intimate, engaged human concern. Without structural change, however, in classrooms, schools, and society in general, that concern may be frustrated. A sociological perspective may help to stimulate such change.

References

Aries, P. *Centuries of childhood.* New York: Alfred Knopf, 1962.

Baumrinol, D. Utopian fantasy and sound social innovation. *School Review,* 1974, *83* (November), 69–84.

Blane, M. T. Drinking among college students: The scope of the problem. Mimeo, 1968.

Bronfenbrenner, U. *Two worlds of childhood.* New York: Russell Sage Foundation, 1970.

Coleman, J. S., Chairman, Panel on Youth, President's Science Advisory Committee, *Youth: Transition to adulthood.* Chicago: University of Chicago Press, 1974.

Durkheim, E. *Suicide.* New York: Free Press, 1951.

Eisenstadt, S. N. *From generation to generation.* New York: Free Press, 1956.

Gatheru, R. M. *Child of two worlds.* Garden City, N.Y.: Doubleday/Anchor, 1964.

Handlin, O., & Handlin, M. F. *Facing life.* Boston: Atlantic-Little, Brown, 1971.

Heath, D. *Growing up in college.* San Francisco: Jossey-Bass, 1968.

Hogue, D. R. *Commitment on campus.* Philadelphia: Westminster Press, 1974.

Keniston, K. *Young radicals.* New York: Harcourt, Brace & World, 1968.

Kiell, N. *The universal experience of adolescence*. New York: International Publishers, 1964.

Meyers, E. D. *Education in the perspective of history*. New York: Holt, Rinehart & Winston, 1964.

Neill, A. S. *Summerhill*. New York: Hart, 1960.

New York Times, "Nine radicals on most wanted list," November 28, 1970.

Newmark, G. *This school belongs to you and me.*. New York: Hart, 1976.

Offer, D. *The psychological world of the teen-ager*. New York: Basic Books, 1969.

President's Commission on Campus Unrest. *Report*. Washington, D.C.: Government Printing Office, 1970.

Rubel, R. J. *The unruly school*. Lexington, Mass.: D. C. Heath, 1977.

San Mateo County, Department of Public Health and Welfare. *Summary report, 1976: Surveys of student drug use*. San Mateo, Calif.: Department of Public Health, 1976.

U.S. Department of Commerce, Bureau of the Census. *Historical statistics of the United States from colonial times to 1970*. Washington, D.C.: Government Printing Office, 1975.

U.S. Department of Health, Education and Welfare, Public Health Service. *Mortality trends for leading causes of death, 1950–1969*. Washington, D.C.: Government Printing Office, 1974 (a).

U. S. Department of Health, Education and Welfare, Public Health Service. *Second special Report on alcohol and health*. Preprint edition. Rockville, Md.: National Institute on Alcohol Abuse and Alcoholism, 1974(b).

U. S. Department of Health, Education and Welfare, Health Services Administration. *Approaches to adolescent health care in the 1970's*. Washington, D. C.: Government Printing Office, 1975.

U. S. Department of Health, Education and Welfare, National Center for Health, Education and Welfare, National Center for Health Statistics. *Monthly vital statistics report*, 25, No. 10, Supplement, December 30, 1976.

U. S. Department of Health, Education and Welfare, Public Health Service, Alcohol, Drug Abuse and Mental Health Administration. *Drug use among American high school students, 1975–1977*. Washington, D.C.: Department of Health, Education and Welfare, 1977.

U. S. Department of Health, Education and Welfare, Public Health Service. Personal communication, 1978(a).

U. S. Department of Health, Education and Welfare, National Institute of Education. *The safe school study report to Congress, V. I*. Washington, D.C.: Government Printing Office, 1978(b).

U. S. Department of Justice. *Crime in the United States, 1972*. Washington, D. C.: Government Printing Office, 1972.

U. S. Senate, Ninety Fourth Congress, First Session, Preliminary Report, Committee to Investigate Juvenile Delinquency. *Our nation's schools*. Washington, D.C.: Government Printing Office, 1975.

van den Haag, E. *Punishing criminals*. New York: Basic Books, 1975.

van Genep, A. *The rites of passage*. Chicago: University of Chicago Press, 1960.

Whiting, J. W. M., & Whiting, B. B. & Altruistic and egoistic behavior in six cultures. In L. Nader & T. W. Maretzki (Eds.), *Cultural illness and health*. Washington, D.C.: American Anthropological Association, 1973.

Wynne, E. A. Learning about cooperation and competition. *Education Forum*, March, 1976, *40* (3), 279–288.

Wynne, E. A. *Growing up suburban*. Austin: University of Texas Press, 1977.

Yankelovitch, D. *Changing youth values in the 70's*. New York: John D. Rockefeller 3rd Fund, 1974.

Yankelovitch, D., Inc. *The changing values on campus*. New York: Pocket Books, 1973.

Screening and Assessment Strategies for Behaviorally Disordered Adolescents

4

Richard L. Simpson

Identification and diagnostic procedures are the initial steps in the sequence leading to the eventual delivery of appropriate services to behaviorally disordered students. The screening, identification, and evaluation process is designed not only to select for further investigation those students whose behavior is considered to be sufficiently aberrant to interfere with normal education and social functioning but also to isolate the problems and to identify realistic objectives and remediation strategies. When used skillfully and as a means of identifying individualized treatment alternatives, the assessment process can provide the educator with at least a preliminary blueprint for effective intervention.

Even though a number of identification and assessment procedures have been developed for behaviorally disordered students, most are designed for or most frequently used with pre-adolescents. However, with the passage of Public Law 94–142 and the recognition that secondary students can no longer be denied appropriate services, greater emphasis has been focused on adolescent populations. Nonetheless, there is currently a significant paucity of standardized identification and diagnostic procedures appropriate for secondary level students.

Because of the lack of appropriate standardized diagnostic instruments available for adolescent populations, much attention has been focused on informal evaluation tools and techniques. These procedures are being used with ever-increasing frequency to obtain information not available through standardized measures. Even though these informal procedures are not designed to compare a student's performance to that of a norm group, their value frequently exceeds that of standardized measures. These informal techniques are highly amenable for use by teachers, as opposed to norm referenced measures which are frequently designed exclusively for noneducational personnel, and thus provide a means of obtaining relevant and specific diagnostic and progress data not always available through formal testing. Thus, even though informal measures do not allow the diagnostician to compare a student with an "average" adolescent of the same age, they can be individually designed to provide information on the absolute level of performance, including strengths and weaknesses, in educationally relevant areas. When used skillfully in conjunction with formal measures, criterion-referenced procedures can yield highly functional diagnostic information.

THE ROLE OF THE TEACHER IN THE SCREENING AND EVALUATION PROCESS

Historically, evaluation efforts have been designed to accomplish three major goals: to identify and label a particular condition or set of behaviors, thus offering an explanation for a pupil's problems; to justify and facilitate the placement of a pupil in a particular program or learning environment; and to enable the educational system to plan for each student on the basis of individual strengths and weaknesses. Unfortunately, however, evaluations of handicapped children and youth, including the behaviorally disordered, have tended to accentuate identification and placement procedures and to minimize the production of data useful in planning an appropriate remediation strategy. Although this pattern is obviously a function of a number of factors, there does seem to be a correlation between this phenomenon and the relative importance given psychological and other formal standardized test data in the assessment process and the frequent assignment of individuals representing noneducational disciplines (e.g., psychologists) to leadership roles for coordinating evaluation activities. However, the time-honored practice of relying on formal and standardized procedures with little proven educational significance and which yield only minimal remedial information and on noneducationally trained personnel has been recently challenged and in many instances modified. Specifically, informal assessment techniques, classroom observation data, and other teacher-oriented procedures have been employed to yield not only functional diagnostic data but also information directly related to the development of a remediation program. In addition, the use of informal assessment procedures, extensive observation opportunities, and the accentuation of information related to the planning of specific teaching and intervention programs, all of which typically characterize evaluations conducted by educators, have at least enabled teachers to circumvent partially the problems of discriminatory testing and capricious labeling. Since teacher-conducted screenings and evaluations are most frequently designed to provide pragmatic program-planning information, they have tended to give at least some basic attention to language, culture, and other organismic variables and to de-emphasize the importance of IQ and exact grade level scores. Although these ingredients are basic to obtaining accurate assessment information, they have been routinely absent from the procedures employed by many other diagnostic groups.

Nonetheless, appropriate attention must also be given the role of personnel other than the teacher in the evaluation process. Although historically the input from these related disciplines has been exaggerated, certain relevant and salient information can only be generated via procedures available to these persons. In addition, PL 94–142 specifies that evaluations must be comprehensive in nature and must include input from individuals representing a number of different areas of expertise. Thus, since evaluations must include information relative to a pupil's school, home, and community and consist of physical, psychological, and educational data, it is essential that individuals other than the classroom teacher be involved in the assessment.

As a function of the intricate nature of the diagnostic process and the myriad of individuals and roles involved in conducting a comprehensive evaluation, screening and assessment procedures by their very nature are relatively complex. Although teachers must play a basic role in the assessment process, appropriate attention must also be given the contributions of other qualified personnel (e.g., nurses, physicians, psychologists, psychiatrists, speech therapists, counselors, administrators, parents, social workers, etc.). Consequently, the present chapter will address the process and issues of screening and assessing behaviorally disordered and socially maladjusted adolescents from the perspective of the classroom teacher while at the same time focusing appropriate attention on conducting a complete and thorough multidisciplinary evaluation.

SCREENING

The screening process, or those procedures employed to select individuals appearing to need more comprehensive assessment attention, is the initial evaluation step. According to Long, Morse, and Newman (1976):

> Screening consists of securing a roster of pupils who, at least on the basis of first-level scrutiny, deserve further study. Further study should result in clarification: the youngster has no problems; the problem is transitory; the problem is a response to a situational complex of overdemanding social or academic stresses in school which could or should be altered; or the problem is evident in school, home and neighborhood and will necessitate careful analysis and specialized assistance. (p. 88)

Although frequently underestimated in overall significance, accurate screening is an absolute necessity. Procedures which incorrectly select students for further evaluation (false positives) may not only create emotional crises for students, parents, and schools but can also produce cumbersome caseloads for individuals charged with conducting comprehensive evaluations. Screening techniques which fail to accurately identify appropriate students (false negatives) can also produce significant and obvious problems for diagnosticians and educators. Therefore, any screening process must differentiate appropriate potential students in relatively accurate yet parsimonious fashion.

As noted by Bower and Lambert (1961) and Lambert, Bower, and Hartsough (1979), screening procedures are designed to accomplish the following:

1. To ensure early in their school careers a more adequate identification of pupils with defects;
2. To help pupils with defects to receive more intensive individual study and, if necessary, remedial services;

3. To help teachers become aware of such disabilities and to help teachers to cope with disabilities educationally;

4. To provide necessary educational adjustments for groups of pupils in the school who can profit from such programs.

In addition, Bower and Lambert and Lambert et al. identified seven necessary elements of any screening process:

1. It should be possible to complete the screening procedure with only such information as the teacher could obtain without outside technical or professional assistance;

2. The procedure should be sufficiently simple and straightforward for the average teacher to undertake without long training or adult supervision;

3. The results of the procedure should be tentative identification of children with emotional problems—leading the teacher to refer to competent specialists those children who could benefit most from thorough diagnosis;

4. As a corollary to 3 above, the procedure should not encourage the teacher to diagnose emotional problems, nor to draw conclusions about their causes, nor to label or categorize children; in fact, the procedure should actively discourage the teacher from undertaking any of these highly technical interpretations;

5. The procedure should be one which neither invades the privacy of individuals nor violates good taste;

6. The procedure should be one which does not offer a threat to any child;

7. The procedure should be inexpensive to use.

Although screening by its very nature is a relatively indelicate process not designed for definitive inferences and conclusions, the process becomes even more tenuous when applied to adolescent students. Specifically, screening potential secondary students for a more intensive evaluation is further complicated by the very nature of normal pubescent development. Not only does adolescence involve dramatic physical development, it also encompasses a time of increased psychological upheaval that is significantly different from the relatively smooth course of development and adaptation that is typical of middle to late childhood. With tremendous intensity, adolescents experience and manifest the effects of attempting to retain their strong drives within previously established behavioral control boundaries. Thus, the selection of adolescent students for further evaluation from a population characterized by change and upheaval is at the least an arduous task requiring more than "gut-level intuition" and limited samples of behavior.

In addition, screening procedures used to identify adolescents considered worthy of further analysis should be carefully selected on the basis of their objectivity and appropriateness of language and culture. Again, because pubescent behavior is characterized by lability of mood and acute emotional responses in even the most typical situations and because students from minority cultures have historically been overidentified as exceptional on the basis of their failure to perform well on biased tests, care must be taken to guard against the detrimental effects of discriminatory assessment techniques and measures which reflect only transient patterns.

Because of these complicating factors, it is necessary that a number of individuals who are in contact with the adolescent under scrutiny participate in the screening process, although the educator must play a primary role in this process. Specifically, effective screening programs must provide for input from parents, the student, the peer group, and, of course, the teacher. In addition, input from other professionals and lay persons in the adolescent's environment may be considered.

A review of selected screening procedures considered appropriate for each of the groups described above is presented in the following section. Although several of the procedures reviewed are not exclusively limited to use with behaviorally disordered adolescents, each includes a consideration of emotional adjustment.

Teacher Screening Procedures

In general, the literature tends to support the position that classroom teachers, either independently or as part of a team composed of other professionals, lay persons, or student peers, are able to identify students who are behaviorally disordered or socially maladjusted (Lessing, Oberlander, & Barbera, 1974; Scarpetti, 1964). In fact, it has been noted on numerous occasions that the classroom teacher is the most likely person to identify a social or emotional problem (Bower, 1960; Shea, 1978). The following are considered appropriate screening devices for teachers attempting to identify behaviorally disordered adolescents. It should be again noted that these procedures are not diagnostic but rather tools designed to aid the teacher in referring select students to specialists for further assessment. Because of space limitations, an in-depth description of the various procedures and the interpretation of their results will not be provided.

Consequently, the various manuals and directions for usage should be consulted by individuals desiring to employ the techniques described.

Hahnemann High School Behavior Rating Scale. The Hahnemann High School Behavior Rating Scale (Spivak & Swift, 1972) was developed as a means of evaluating behaviors manifested by students in grades 7–12. The overt behaviors selected for assessment through the procedure are designed to indicate the academic and social adjustment made by selected students to classroom demands. The development of the Hahnemann scale followed the same methodology used in the development of the Devereux Elementary School Behavior Rating Scale (Spivak & Swift, 1967). The scale consists of 45 items, relating to 13 behavioral and academic factors. These factors were developed through a process of comparing ratings of teachers of public school students and similar emotionally disturbed students in residential treatment. The factors include: (1) reasoning ability; (2) originality; (3) verbal interaction; (4) teacher rapport; (5) anxious producer (characterizing the student who establishes extremely high expectations for his own academic performance), (6) general anxiety; (7) withdrawal; (8) poor work habits; (9) intellectual dependence; (10) rigidity; (11) verbal negativism; (12) disturbance and restlessness; and (13) verbalized inability to complete assignments. Although the Hahnemann High School Behavior Rating Scale has been shown to have good validity, no reliability data are available. Nonetheless, it appears to be a practical and efficient measure of classroom adjustment. As is the case with the Devereux Elementary School Behavior Rating Scale, major attention is given academic achievement.

Behavior Problem Checklist. Although the Behavior Problem Checklist (Quay & Peterson, 1967) was developed primarily as a means of defining clinical variables in elementary-age children rather than as a classroom measurement procedure, it does have classroom screening applicability and can be employed with students through the eighth grade. The measure requires that a rating judgment, using a 3-point scale, be made for 55 frequently observed deviant behavioral traits in children and adolescents. The scale was developed through factor-analytic studies involving students in public schools, residentially placed juvenile delinquents, students enrolled in classes for the emotionally disturbed, and children followed in a child guidance clinic.

The Behavior Problem Checklist is designed to measure four dimensions of deviant behavior: (1) conduct disorders (patterns of unsocialized aggression and poor interpersonal relationship); (2) personality disorders (patterns of anxiety, neurosis, and withdrawal); (3) immaturity (patterns of social immaturity, inattention, and daydreaming); (4) socialized delinquency (patterns of delinquent behavior developed as a response to environmental circumstances).

Reliability data suggest that the Behavior Problem Checklist can be accurately employed in a variety of environments and that the yielded results are relatively stable over short periods of time.

The checklist is reasonably simple to learn and use. In addition, the system is accompanied by functional norms. Finally, the checklist can be used by teachers, parents, and most professionals.

Pupil Classroom Behavior Scale. The Pupil Classroom Behavior Scale (Dayton, 1967) consists of 24 overt behavior items. Teachers are required to rate the frequency of occurrence for each of the items, using a subjective normative system. The scale, developed for both elementary and high-school students, is said to tap three primary factors. Achievement orientation refers to the perseverance of students in completing assignments and in successfully handling school subjects. Socio-academically creative, the second factor, pertains to a student's ability to participate in class activities, attempt novel pursuits, and undertake challenges. Sociocooperative, the third factor, refers to a student's willingness to obey rules and cooperate with teachers. Although the scale is reported to correlate highly with teacher grades and is very quickly administered (approximately 5 minutes), it is most appropriately employed as a measure of group changes rather than as a measurement device for individual students.

Pupil Behavior Inventory. The Pupil Behavior Inventory (Vinter, Sarri, Vorwaller, & Schafer, 1966) was designed as a measure of "behavioral and attitudinal factors which affect the degree of success a pupil will have in accomplishing his educational objectives" (p. 1). This device, consisting of 34 behavioral items, was developed as a means of obtaining information from teachers about students referred because of behavior disturbances. For each item, teachers are instructed to rate the frequency of the behavior, using a 5-point scale. The scale items were developed through a process of asking teachers and other professionals to generate behavioral descriptions of adjusted and maladjusted and achieving and nonachieving students.

The scale is said to measure five factors: (1) classroom conduct; (2) academic motivation and performance; (3) social-emotional adjustment; (4) teacher dependence; and (5) personal behavior.

Although the Pupil Behavior Inventory is deficient in reliability, validity, and normative data, it does appear to be a functional and easily administered scale. As noted by Spivack and Swift (1973), "The scale needs a great deal of work but is one of the few designed for high school aged youngsters" (p. 84).

Werry-Quay Direct Observational System. The Werry-Quay Direct Observational System (Werry & Quay, 1969) was developed as a classroom observational procedure for elementary-age students. However, the procedure has been shown to have applicability with postelementary populations.

The procedure is basically a structured means for obtaining behavioral frequency counts on specific students. The procedure provides for an analysis of attention to task and the type of teacher contact that occurs in the classroom. In addition, the system structures the observation of several deviant behaviors, including inappropriate vocalizations, physical contact, out of seat, and other deviant classroom behaviors. Observations are made during independent task situations where rules are clearly defined.

Although reliability and validity data are limited, the procedure appears to be an excellent screening technique, especially when used to compare select students against the norm for a given class environment. The Werry-Quay procedure, because of its objective dimensional approach, seems to offer an empirical screening alternative to the rating scale.

Bower-Lambert Screening Procedure. The Bower and Lambert method (1961) is probably the most widely employed screening process, and in spite of reliability problems and relatively lengthy time requirements for administering and scoring, it has served the screening needs of educators for a number of years. The procedure, designed for students from kindergarten through grade 12, consists of not only teacher ratings but also the student's self-perception and the perception of the peer group.

The teacher rating portion of the screening process involves use of the Pupil Behavior Rating Scale. Teachers rate and rank each of the students in their class on eight variables. These variables parallel Bower's (1969) definition of emotionally disturbed children: students who chronically and acutely display one or more of the following:

> (1) An inability to learn which cannot be explained by intellectual, sensory, or health factors; (2) An inability to build or maintain satisfactory interpersonal relationships with peers and teachers; (3) Inappropriate types of behavior or feelings under normal conditions; (4) A general, pervasive mood of unhappiness or depression; and (5) A tendency to develop physical symptoms, pains, or fears associated with personal or school problems. (pp. 8–10)

The remainder of the Bower and Lambert screening procedure will be discussed within the categories of peer ratings and self-evaluation, respectively.

Peer Evaluation Procedures

The attitudes not only of teachers but also of a student's peer group appear to be closely correlated with classroom adjustment. In addition, it appears that few groups are better able to identify the behavior-problem student than his own peer group. Nonetheless, aside from informal evaluations and overt behavior counts for specific types of social interactions, few procedures have been developed for allowing peer groups to participate in the screening process.

Bower-Lambert Student Survey. The Bower-Lambert Student Survey (1961) is a peer measurement procedure designed for students in grades 7 through 12. Specifically, this portion of the Bower-Lambert Screening Procedure is designed to disclose how a student is perceived by his peer group.

The survey consists of two sections. The first portion requires the student to match peers with descriptions of negative, neutral, and positive behavior. The second part of the survey uses the same behavior statements, although the statements are randomly grouped in sets of four. Each student is required to select one of the four behavioral statements in each group that he believes others in the class would apply to him or that he would apply to himself. The second part of the Student Survey is used to compare the student's self-perception with that of the peer group. The survey is designed to reveal the quantity and quality of visibility of each student in the class and to allow for a comparison of this data with the student's self-perception.

Although the scale is relatively time-consuming to give and score, it exists as one of the few structured means for obtaining input from a student's peer group.

Self-Evaluation Procedures

Numerous studies have suggested that a relationship exists between a student's self-concept, school achievement, and overall adjustment (Borislow, 1962; Gartner, Kohler & Riessman, 1971). It has also been suggested that a student's perception of self, especially when compared with peer and teacher ratings, can serve as valuable diagnostic information. However, just as in the area of peer evaluations, few structured techniques and procedures are available.

Bower-Lambert: A Self Test. The Self Test (1961) rating scale was designed as a measure of the discrepancy between a student's "real" and "ideal" self. The scale is based on the assumption that emotional adjustment is closely correlated with the differences between the real and ideal self, although it was noted that this assumption may not apply to seriously disturbed students. The scale involves two separate parts. In the first, students are asked to indicate how strongly they would like to be (or not like to be) a described individual. The second part of the procedure employs the same items as in section one except that students are asked to what extent they are actually similar to the described individuals. The Bower-Lambert Self Test appears to be a useful screening procedure only when used in conjunction with the other screening devices.

Behavioral Q-Sort. The Behavioral Q-Sort, developed by Stephenson (1953) and refined by Kroth (1973), has been employed in a variety of ways, although most notably as a measure of self-concept. According to Stephenson, the "Q technique provides a systematic way to handle a person's retrospections, his reflections about himself and others, his introjections and projections, and much else of an apparent 'subjective nature' " (p. 86). Others (Cronbach, 1953) have noted that the Q-Sort procedure provides for a qualitative self-evaluation that is a compromise between a clinical impression and data yielded through formal testing measures. Just as with the Bower-Lambert Self Test, an evaluation is made of the discrepancy between an individual's real and ideal self. In addition, the Q-Sort procedure can be employed as a measure of the discrepancy between a student's perception and that of his parents or teachers. Finally, the procedure can be used to identify targets for behavioral intervention.

The Role of Parents in the Screening Process

In addition to the screening procedures undertaken by the educator, the student, and the peer group is the information provided by the parents. Certainly, no single group will have as much intimate contact, relevant history, and the potential for generating as much information as the adolescent's parents or guardians. In addition, this group as a rule will have more motivation to be involved in the process than any other. However, it must be recalled that the process of screening is designed to identify individuals for further evaluation and not to solicit broad, in-depth diagnostic data. Consequently, it is imperative that parental contacts be initiated for the purpose of sharing the concerns of the educator with the parents and for solidifying the cooperative relationship between the home and school. In particular, attention should be focused on whether the behaviors of concern occur in more than the school environment, whether the problems appear to be transient and the possible reaction to some particular crisis situation such as a divorce or death, and the perception by the parents of the problem and its solution.

If the parent component of the screening process is to operate effectively and do more than cause the parents to become alarmed or defensive, it is necessary that the screening contact be based upon a pre-existing relationship and upon at least some degree of pre-established rapport. As noted by Kroth (1975), "holding conferences early during the academic year provides the teacher with an opportunity to receive information from parents and to get acquainted in a non-threatening situation" (p. 14). In addition, initial contacts between parents and teachers have been reported both to enhance academic and social productivity (Duncan & Fitzgerald, 1969) and to establish the basis for future problem-solving activities. Therefore, it is imperative that the screening contact be based on a firmly established relationship of trust. Without such a relationship, the parent screening process will have numerous potential difficulties. Although the establishment of such relationships in secondary level public school settings is considered difficult by some, its importance cannot be overestimated.

In addition to apprising the parents of the concerns of the teacher and securing an analysis of the adolescent and the problem by his parents, other screening techniques can be utilized. For example, parents can be instructed in evaluating their adolescent's behavior by means of certain behavior rating scales and with the Q-Sort technique. Not only may this information be salient in the screening process but it can also have the effect of sensitizing the parents to the classroom problems and to the importance of securing parental input in arriving at potential solutions.

Although the specific battery to be employed in the screening process will be dictated by the circumstances, environment, age, and behavior of the adolescent under scrutiny, certain basic procedures must routinely be utilized in order to assure an effective evaluation. Because of the necessity for accurate and complete information, a thorough screening process must be undertaken. Each screening should include (a) an interview with the parent(s) or legal guardian; (b) the use of at least one rating scale (Hahnemann High School Behavior Rating Scale, Behavior Problem Checklist, Pupil Behavior Inventory, or the Bower-Lambert Screening Procedure); (c) a direct classroom observation system (e.g., Werry-Quay technique) capable of yielding objective, empirical observational data; (d) a peer evaluation method (e.g., Bower-Lambert Student Survey); and (e) a self-evaluation procedure (e.g., Bower-Lambert: a Self Test and/or the Behavioral Q-Sort).

The following is a summary of a screening evaluation conducted by three teachers of a 16-year-old male. This student was being screened because of below average academic performance and social withdrawal. The procedures were designed to determine whether this adolescent was appropriate for further evaluation.

Although only the mother attended the parent-teacher conference, she reported that both she and her husband were concerned about PG, their only child. The mother described her son's problems as consisting of a lack of interest in attending school and completing assignments and an unwillingness to initiate social contacts. PG's mother also indicated that he had few friends and generally preferred to stay in his own room and watch TV or read. It was also reported that PG "pouts and sulks" a good deal of the time and "will go for days without speaking to his father and me." Although the mother described PG as being somewhat withdrawn since early childhood and as "only an average student," she reported these patterns to have heightened during the past year. Mrs. G was unable to offer any explanations for her son's change in behavior.

The Hahnemann High School Behavior Rating Scale, completed by each of the three teachers, indicated problems in the following factor areas: general anxiety, withdrawal, poor work habits, and verbalized inability to complete assignments. The Werry-Quay Direct Observational System, also completed by each teacher, yielded the following composite data: attention-to-task, 18% (average attention-to-task for the three classrooms, 69%); daydreaming, 81%; and other deviant behaviors, 26%. Physically aggressive behaviors, audible noises, vocalizations, and out-of-seat were not observed during the 7 days the recordings were made.

The Bower-Lambert Student Survey generally revealed that PG was perceived, if at all, in a neutral manner, while both the Bower-Lambert self-evaluation procedure and the Behavioral Q-Sort suggested a significant discrepancy between his real and ideal self, especially in the area of academic productivity.

Finally, the teachers involved in the screening were able to share anecdotal information and subjective observations. On the basis of their shared findings, it was decided to schedule PG for a comprehensive evaluation.

DIAGNOSTIC EVALUATION

Although the screening process is an integral and basic component of the diagnostic model, the actual analysis of a student's abilities, skills, and behaviors can only be accomplished through an accurate and thorough evaluation. Therefore, whereas screening consists of "securing a roster of pupils who, at least on the basis of first-level scrutiny, deserve further study" (Long et al., 1976, p. 88), the assessment process is designed to yield both diagnostic classification data and, more importantly, those specific instructional goals and curricula best suited for each student's individual needs.

There is a variety of standardized and nonstandardized evaluation systems that have varying degrees of applicability in assessing behavior-problem adolescents. These procedures vary from interview techniques, personality and intellectual measures to specialized academic tests designed to identify and aid in the remediation of specific learning problems. Although the diagnostician will have a number of assessment procedures from which to choose, each measure or procedure should provide information within one of the following areas: environmental (social), physical, intellectual, emotional (personality), or academic. Although there are obviously a number of other areas that may legitimately be appropriate for assessment, the foregoing are considered most salient and relevant. Since the evaluation process must consist of input from educators and other psychoeducational diagnosticians, the present discussion will consist of tests and procedures appropriate for both groups.

Environmental

Not only is it apparent that each school, agency, and system is a subculture of our society, it is equally evident that each individual is also a member of a subsystem, the family. In addition to having their own traditions, objectives, components, and organizational structure, family variables will also determine, at least in part, a child's or adolescent's classroom behavior. Thus, if the diagnostic evaluation is expected to provide a comprehensive analysis of a student, provisions must be made for gaining understanding of the student's family and environment. Opler (1965) suggested that considering the family along with the individual under evaluation "leads to a more accurate diagnosis, a better chance for successful treatment, less pressure for repeated clinical visits, and faster progress toward sound solutions" (p. 235). In addition, since PL 94–142 clearly specifies that parents must be involved in the identification, evaluation, and selection of an appropriate educational program for offspring, it is only logical that the diagnostic process include the parents. Not only will this strategy serve to facilitate compliance with the Education for All Handicapped Children Act of 1975, but it will also aid in gaining a more comprehensive understanding of the adolescent under scrutiny. Moreover, since educators frequently assume that a child's or adolescent's behavior problems are a function of environmental factors which are responsive to environmental changes, it is necessary that information relative to this area be generated. Without this information, a major source of hypotheses may go unchecked.

Psychoeducational diagnostician procedures. Although each parent contact will have its own special emphasis and purposes, certain basic procedures will typically result in the most productive results. Initially, the diagnostic interview should allow the parents or guardians an opportunity to share their perceptions of the adolescent's behavior and the degree to which (if any) the behavior is of concern. Although it will be necessary for the educational diagnostician to structure the purpose of the interview with the parents and to apprise them of the concern of the school community, every attempt should be made to avoid contaminating the responses of parents with an educator's in-depth analysis of a student's school behavior. This, of course, is a difficult task. The interviewer must attempt to secure the diagnostic and clinical viewpoints of parents in as pure a fashion as possible, without giving the impression that the school personnel are avoiding responsibility for the problem or that proper preliminary attention has not been given the situation. In addition, it must be remembered that PL 94–142 requires parental permission to conduct evaluations. Thus, at least in some instances, the diagnostic interview is also the session in which parents are initially apprised of their son's or daughter's suspected problems and at which permission to evaluate is solicited. Although these situations can be potentially incompatible with a purely clinical interview, the diagnostician is nonetheless charged with securing a statement from the parents concerning their perception of the problem and their attitude regarding the proposed evaluation and possible remediation services that might be available. Beginning the diagnostic interview in terms of the suspected problems will both start the session in a productive manner and also specifically provide information about the degree to which the parents' perception of their adolescent's problem (if any) correlates with the chief complaint of the educators who have observed and screened the student.

As part of the environmental evaluation, information should also be obtained on the adolescent's developmental history. However, the diagnostician conducting the parent interview should in most instances be able to secure the necessary developmental history from school or professional records, thus negating the need for direct solicitation of developmental information from the parents or guardians. Only in instances where an identified student's history is not available from other sources should this information be directly sought. As noted by Kroth and Simpson (1977, p. 109),

> developmental information in the majority of situations should not be solicited by the educator unless it is believed that no other professional person has obtained it. Thus in instances where it can be demonstrated that other professionals, such as a physician, social worker, school psychologist or health worker have previously obtained significant developmental data, the educator can concentrate on other areas. However, in instances where it is believed by the educator that the salient features of a child's developmental history have not been previously obtained, efforts should be made to secure this information. Since educators are frequently the only professionals to come into contact with all school age children, it is necessary for the one professional with whom the child will have sustained contact to have sufficient developmental data to guard against a child being denied appropriate services because of a lack of information.

The parent interview should also be designed to obtain information on the personality of the adolescent and his or her attitude toward school, friends, family, and leisure time activities. Special attention should be focused on atypical behavior patterns and interactions (or lack of interactions) with peers and adults. Although parents may frequently dismiss the significance of observed problems or changes as only a function of adolescence, the overall importance of this information, especially when paired with other observations, cannot be overlooked.

Among the most significant areas of interest in the parent interview will be the adolescent's school history as perceived by the parents. Specifically, discussions involving school history should be designed to reveal patterns of acute or chronic behavioral excesses and deficits, academic patterns, and previous professional procedures undertaken to diagnose or remediate home or school problems. Since the psychoeducational diagnostician should have well-documented school records (although with increasing regularity this is not the case), the information generated through the interview may be compared with school records.

The interview should also be designed to evaluate the goals and expectations of the parents or guardians of adolescents screened for further evaluation. Again, discrepancies between the expectations of the parents and those of the student and his teacher should be noted, as should discrepancies between these expectations and the student's actual abilities.

Finally, the parent interview should be designed to reveal aspects of the adolescent's sociocultural environment. However, this information may most readily be obtained through school records or from nondirect discussion. As noted by Kroth and Simpson (1977, p. 113),

> Practitioners almost universally agree that the interviewer should not ask personal questions frequently associated with soliciting sociological information. Thus, for example, although it is probably valuable to know the makeup of the family, the marital and educational status of the parents and the family's general financial situation, it is necessary to tactfully solicit this data. In most cases, personal, family and sociological information can be subtly obtained from parents simply by establishing a warm, supportive relationship and then by asking general questions followed by reinforcing comments relating to the family.

Specific sociological information that the teacher or psychoeducational diagnostician should focus on include: the composition of the family and its cultural and ethnic make-up; the occupation of the parents; the physical and mental health of the family; languages other than English spoken by the parents or others in the family; the child-rearing practices of the parents; agencies which may be involved with the adolescent or family; supervision provided the youth; and the emphasis the parents place on educational endeavors. The cultural and language factors, in addition to providing environmental information, will also be useful in selecting appropriate psychometric procedures.

Profound importance during the parent contact should be placed on confronting the observed problems and encouraging the parents or guardians to participate in the evaluation. It is also important to indicate to the parents that there are effective solutions to adolescent behavior problems, most of which do not consist of placing a student in a self-contained class or residential facility for the emotionally disturbed. Finally, parents and guardians should be dissuaded from rationalizing their offspring's behavior as a normal extension of adolescence.

Physical

Of course, it goes without saying that a student's classroom behavior can be correlated with physical and sensory factors. In addition, even though teachers and psychoeducational diagnosticians may consider themselves inept within this area, it is essential that proper attention be focused on physical variables during the evaluation. Even though the psychoeducational diagnostician or educator may play no more than a screening and referral role, the importance of these activities cannot be overestimated. Not only are many educational diagnosticians quite adept at identifying possible physical factors related to classroom behavior, they are frequently the professional group in the most advantageous position to make this identification.

Psychoeducational diagnostician procedures. The burdens and conflicts of adolescence along with the demands of junior and senior high school can be seriously aggravated by malnutrition, poor health, drug or alcohol dependence or abuse, and sensory impairments. In addition, behavioral disturbances may be manifested through physical symptoms. However, regardless of whether these physical factors are part of the cause for the behavioral excess or deficit or a manifestation of the emotional problem, they are of extreme importance in the development of accurate diagnostic inferences and individualized remediation and treatment programs.

Although the following list is far from comprehensive, it does suggest those areas to which the diagnostician should be most sensitive:

1. Frequent school absence.
2. Fatigue and lack of physical stamina.
3. Lack of attention, restlessness, and evidence of boredom.
4. Poor motor control.
5. Evidence of visual limitations, including facial contortions, chronic rubbing of eyes, excessive blinking, excessive head movements, and inflammation, tearing, and reddening of the eyes.
6. Evidence of auditory deficiency, including frequent colds or sinus infection, ears that discharge, frequent request for repeating directions or questions, turning one ear toward a speaker, and frequent faulty word pronunciation.
7. Stuttering and stammering.
8. Frequent episodes of crying, uncontrolled laughter, or other strong emotional responses, especially when associated with a relatively mild eliciting stimulus.
9. Signs of extreme excitability or anxiety, including nail biting, hair twisting, hyperactivity, masturbation, and increased bodily movements.
10. Depression.
11. Unpredictable mood changes.
12. Enuresis or encopresis.
13. Exceptional sensitivity to noises, lights, heat, or cold.
14. Sloppy physical appearance.
15. Frequent headaches, stomach aches, or other physical complaints.
16. Self-stimulatory responses, such as rocking, hand flapping, or light filtering.
17. Signs of alcohol or drug abuse or dependence. Because of the reported frequency of drug and alcohol abuse by adolescents, it is important that educators have a basic knowledge of the signs of each.

Even though the diagnostic process should include an analysis of physical factors, it is essential to note that data generated within this area are frequently derived from observational or interview procedures or from instruments designed to assess other than physically associated emotional variables. Thus, there are few formal tests or procedures available to the diagnostician for the express purpose of evaluating the physical status of adolescents. The exceptions to this rule are in the speech and language, auditory discrimination, and perceptual motor areas. Formal evaluations within these areas should, of course, be undertaken only by individuals with formal training and experience and familiarity with the specific procedure being used. Speech and language measures appropriate for adolescents are the Utah Test of Language Development and the Peabody Picture Vocabulary Test. For evaluating auditory discrimination, the Goldman-Fristoe-Woodcock Test of Auditory Discrimination and the Goldman-Fristoe-Woodcock Auditory Skills Test Battery have been found to be useful. The evaluation of perceptual-motor deficits can be accomplished by means of the Bender Visual-Motor Gestalt Test, Developmental Test of Visual Motor Integration, Memory for Designs Test, and the Purdue Perceptual Motor Survey.

Finally, it is not uncommon for data and observations within the "physical" area to be of significance only after all other diagnostic procedures have been completed. Specifically, this information is frequently found to be of greatest value when integrated with other findings or as supportive evidence for hypotheses generated from other formal tests and procedures. Nonetheless, even though the physical evaluation process may rely on more informal procedures, it is necessary for a thorough evaluation.

Intellectual

That intelligence tests yield reasonably reliable indexes of ability is being disputed less and less. However, controversy continues over the educational utility of intellectual test scores and the value of these measures in diagnosing and remediating behaviorally disordered and socially maladjusted students. In spite of this controversy, intellectual ability appears to be among the best predictors of academic achievement and overall prognosis (Garmezy, 1974; Robbins, 1966, 1972, 1974). In addition, a discrepancy between a student's intellectual ability and academic achievement remains among the most significant diagnostic indicators for behavioral disturbance (Rabin, 1965). Thus, since the goal of each psycho-educational evaluation is both accurate diagnosis and a suitable intervention plan, it behooves individuals charged with this duty to consider this variable thoroughly. Since the accurate measurement of intelligence requires specialized training, this component of the evaluation should be undertaken only by appropriately trained diagnostic personnel.

Psychoeducational diagnostician procedures. In general, research findings tend to indicate that emotionally disturbed students produce lower intelligence test scores than normal students, albeit usually within the normal range (Bower, 1969). In addition, data suggest that the more severe the emotional disturbance, the lower the intellectual abilities, with most psychotic individuals functioning at a retarded level (DeMyer, Barton, Alpern, Kimberlin, Allen, Yang, & Steele, 1974).

Although there is a variety of intellectual measures available, designed for either group or individual administration, most well-trained psychoeducational diagnosticians prefer the individual scales. Specifically, the most widely employed measures are the Revised Wechsler Intelligence Scale for Children (WISC-R) and the Wechsler Adult Intelligence Scale (WAIS). The two tests are similar, with the choice of instrument determined by the age of the individual being evaluated. Both measures provide an overall IQ along with verbal and performance IQ scores and clinical information (Pope & Scott, 1967). The Wechsler IQs are statistically derived from a deviation of obtained scores from the mean of a standardization group. The Wechsler Adult Scale has six verbal subtests: Information, Comprehension, Similarities, Digit Span, Arithmetic, and Vocabulary. The performance scales include Digit Symbol, Picture Completion, Block Design, Picture Arrangement, and Object Assembly. The Revised Wechsler children's scale follows much the same arrangement of subtests but with content designed for children and younger adolescents.

Wechsler diagnosticians have historically relied heavily on patterns of subtest strength and weakness and scatter profiles (differences between the verbal and performance IQ) as diagnostic indicators (Rapaport, 1945). However, contradictory findings have shown test patterns and scatter profiles to be poor diagnostic prognosticators, at least when employed in the absence of other information. Consequently, most scatter profiles and subtest patterns are considered significant diagnostic indicators only when combined with additional diagnostic data.

Although there is some evidence that many emotional disorders are associated with impairment more in performance than in verbal abilities, except in adolescent delinquents and psychopaths (Wechsler, 1958), there is a trend away from rigid intelligence test interpretation. Rather, because of equivocal findings and numerous inconsistencies, greater emphasis is being placed on the combined approach of evaluating responses on a series of measures, including the Wechsler Scale, along with more conservative rule and pattern interpretation. However, diagnosticians and consumers of diagnostic data would be wise to remember that test results in isolation have extremely limited utility. The manner in which the various procedures and measures combine to form consistent patterns will produce the most accurate diagnosis and efficient remediation plans.

Emotional

Without question, the evaluation of an adolescent who manifests classroom excesses or deficits will involve an analysis of specific behavioral responses and personality. Although assessment within this area will vary widely, depending on the training and orientation of the educator or diagnostician and the adolescent under study, the process will consist of tests, observational procedures, and interview techniques designed to assess clinically significant personality qualities and overt behavioral patterns. The following is a selected list of procedures and tests employed in the diagnosis of behaviorally disordered adolescents.

Psychoeducational diagnostician procedures. Rorschach Test: The Rorschach Test (Rorschach, 1942), the first of the projective techniques, has been a basic, although somewhat obsolete, personality assessment procedure for several decades. This device is employed in the assessment of thought disorders, motivational dynamics, adaptiveness, and other personality variables. The Rorschach, like other projective instruments, consists of ambiguous stimuli which the individual under evaluation supposedly interprets according to his own personality and emotional needs. The Rorschach consists of 10 inkblots; the individual being examined is instructed to indicate what the blots look like, what they might be, or what they make the individual think of. These spontaneous free association responses are followed by inquiries by the examiner regarding the location of each response and the properties of the stimuli which evoke each.

In spite of its traditional acceptance and wide usage, the utility of the Rorschach technique, especially with regard to school-related problems, is seriously questioned. As noted by O'Leary (1972), "the Rorschach appears to qualify as an instrument for research, but it has not met requirements which demonstrate its utility in the decision-making process of diagnosis or treatment" (p. 239).

Thematic Apperception Test: Murray's Thematic Apperception Test (1943) is also a widely employed projective instrument, although it was originally developed as a technique for studying fantasy in normal individuals. The test consists of 31 drawings and photographs, such as a child staring reflectively at a violin. Certain stimulus items are designed for specific age and sex groups. Individuals being administered the test are asked to make up a story about each stimulus card. Subjects are specifically instructed to indicate what is happening, what led up to it, how the individuals involved feel, and how the story will turn out.

As is true of the Rorschach, the TAT is an assessment procedure whose time requirements for administration, scoring, and interpretation and relatively poor reliability and validity make it a questionable technique. In addition, the relevant information that it yields would appear to be more available through simpler and less expensive procedures.

Human Figure Drawing: This easily administered projective procedure (Machover, 1949) consists of instructing the examinee to draw a picture of a man and woman on a blank sheet of paper. Most diagnosticians usually assume that the drawings reflect the individual's perception of himself. However, as with other projective techniques, this assumption has little empirical support, and more importantly, only dubious utility.

Bender Visual Motor Gestalt Test: Although developed as a test of organic brain damage, the Bender-Gestalt (Bender, 1946) has become a basic clinical instrument. The test consists of nine designs which individuals are asked to copy on a blank sheet of paper. Although this technique appears to have some validity in the assessment of certain types of physical and intellectual deviations, it appears to have only limited utility as a clinical measure with behaviorally disordered adolescents.

Psychoeducational diagnostician procedures. Observational procedures and rating scales: Essentially, alternatives to projective measures and other traditional diagnostic procedures, these procedures allow for a more direct analysis of classroom responses most frequently associated with adolescent behavior disorders. Specifically, techniques applicable for screening can also be employed as diagnostic tools and as measures of improvement. The previously discussed Hahnemann High School Behavior Rating Scale, Behavior Problem Checklist, Pupil Classroom Behavior Scale, Pupil Behavior Inventory, and the Werry-Quay Direct Observational System—each has varying degrees of efficacy in the diagnostic process. In addition, the direct assessment of specific target behaviors has been found to have excellent diagnostic utility. Barr and McDowell (1972), for example, using a direct observation technique, discovered significant differences in the frequency of three deviant classroom behaviors for emotionally disturbed and learning disabled students. Whether the direct observation encompasses only an analysis of the target behavior or a description of the behavior, along with the contingencies and environmental variables associated with it, this type of assessment appears to have good utility relative to the identification and control of behavior-problem children and adolescents. This type of procedure is less expensive, more valid, and more often within the repertoire of the psychoeducational diagnostician and is also typically based on larger samples of behavior within the classroom environment.

Interview procedures: No matter what the philosophical or theoretical orientation of the diagnostician, the interview is undoubtedly a major source of information in the assessment of behavior-problem adolescents. The interview process involves a purposeful pattern of verbal and nonverbal interactions between the adolescent and psychoeducational diagnostician, designed to generate information which will, it is hoped, facilitate an accurate diagnosis and remediation strategy. Even though the content and strategy involved in the interview will vary as a function of the system employed (e.g., nondirective, directive, etc.) and the personalities of the participants, it is necessary that certain basic guidelines be followed. Paramount is the need to make the adolescent a participant in the diagnostic process rather than a passive recipient of the various procedures. This should involve a candid statement regarding the purpose of the interview and evaluation, the role of each participant in the process, and the possible alternatives that might result. The adolescent should be apprised of his need to be involved during the assessment.

The exact content of the interview will vary as a function of the numerous variables involved. However, frequently the session will focus on many of the same areas as the parent interview. Specifically, the student should be asked to describe the problem (if any), its cause, his feelings and those of his parents with regard to the problem, and other specifics about the nature and development of the behaviors of concern. The adolescent should also be encouraged to discuss his developmental and personality history. The latter should focus on the individual's perception of his personality traits, attitude toward home, friends, family, school, leisure time activities, and marked likes and dislikes. The interviewee should also be encouraged to describe his school-related history. Special attention should be directed to descriptions of academic functioning and to previous relationships with teachers and peers. Finally, the adolescent should be encouraged to describe his personal goals and expectations and those of his parents for him and to describe the environmental and social factors involved in his family. Although the analysis of information generated through the diagnostic interview is beyond the scope of this work, the diagnostician should attempt to focus on discrepancies between the responses of the subject and those of teachers and parents, and the relationship of the interview data to other diagnostic information.

Academic Achievement

Psychoeducational diagnostician procedures. As previously reported, discrepancies between a student's intellectual abilities and academic achievement are among the most significant indicators of a behavioral disturbance. Consequently, it is imperative that an examination of academic productivity and abilities be included in the diagnostic evaluation. Not only is this data useful in the formulation of an overall diagnostic impression but it many times is the most significant data resulting from the evaluation. This information should consist of classroom records and grades, standardized academic group test results, and standardized individual measures. A review of individual, standardized academic tests frequently employed with behaviorally disordered adolescents is included below. Although this review examines only general academic skills, it should be noted that diagnostic questions relating to specific academic areas will require either teacher-made procedures or specific tests, if they are available. The review does not focus on the vocational area, since this is considered to be primarily a remediation area rather than an integral part of diagnosing behaviorally disordered adolescents.

Gates-McKillop Reading Diagnostic Tests: The Gates-McKillop Reading Diagnostic Tests (Gates & McKillop, 1962) include a battery of reading skill tests in two forms. Each form of the test is designed to evaluate oral reading, word and phrase knowledge, and knowledge of word parts. In spite of the lengthy time requirements of the test, it is recognized as an excellent diagnostic reading scale.

Durrell Analysis of Reading Difficulty: Although the Durrell Scale (1955) is designed for students at the nonreading through sixth-grade reading levels, it is obviously appropriate for many behaviorally disordered adolescents. The scale consists of tests in oral and silent reading ability, listening comprehension, word recognition, word analysis, and a series of supplementary scales. Although the scale lacks reliability, validity, and standardization data, it is recognized as an excellent diagnostic test.

Diagnostic Reading Scales: The Diagnostic Reading Scale (Spache, 1972) consists of word recognition, comprehension, and phonics tests. The scale is designed for both elementary-age children and adolescents with reading problems. Although the scale lacks normative information, detailed reliability and validity data are provided. As with the Gates-McKillop and Durrell Scales, this instrument is a thorough and well-respected test of reading ability.

Classroom Reading Inventory: The Classroom Reading Inventory (Silvaroli, 1973) consists of word lists, paragraphs for oral reading, and a spelling test. This graded scale, designed for students in grades 1–8, yields data on a student's independent, instructional, frustration, and hearing capacity reading levels. Since this scale is not standardized, it must be used informally. Although valuable for instructional purposes, the Classroom Reading Inventory is not a diagnostic scale.

Peabody Individual Achievement Test: The Peabody Individual Achievement Test (Dunn & Markwardt, 1970) consists of two reading subtests (recognition and comprehension) and tests of mathematics, spelling, and general information. The scale allows for a conversion of raw scores into age equivalents, grade equivalents, percentile ranks, and standard scores. A major benefit of the scale is the comprehensive nature of the subtests and the K–12 grade-level sample employed in its standardization.

Stanford Diagnostic Arithmetic Test: The Stanford Diagnostic Arithmetic Test (Beatty, Madden, & Gardner, 1966), Level II, is designed for students in grades 4–8 and with lower-achieving students in upper grades. The subtests of the scale include Concepts of Numbers and Numerals, Computation with Whole Numbers, Common Fractions, Decimal Fractions, and Percent and Number Facts. This diagnostic scale involves only minimal reading for students. In general, this standardized measure is considered to be an excellent diagnostic scale.

A summary of a diagnostic evaluation conducted with a 16-year-old male is provided below.

Environmental: Developmental information offered by Mrs. T revealed that R was the older of two children. The mother indicated that RT was born in the fourth year of the T's marriage and that the pregnancy was planned. Mrs. T reported "normal" prenatal events, although she experienced some toxemia and intermittent high blood pressure during the pregnancy. These conditions were not judged to be significant by her physician, and he also reported that prenatal events were normal. Birth was breech after a labor period of 10 hours; the birth weight was 6 1/2 pounds.

R was breast fed for three months. Mrs. T described him as an "active child." She stated he was not really "colicky" but cried a lot. Formula feeding was initiated the fourth month. Bilateral crawling was reported at 6 months. Cross pattern crawling followed. R began to walk at 11 1/2 months. Vocalization—"bye-bye, da-da"—occurred at 11 1/2 months. Sentence use was initiated at age 2 and speech development from that point appears to be within normal limits.

The T's began toilet training R at age 2 1/2. They experienced some difficulty. Daytime bowel and bladder control was established by age 3 1/2, but nighttime control could not be maintained. A medical examination initiated by the parents resulted in a report that R had a small bladder and it would be difficult for him to control this function at night. From this time the parents have apparently withdrawn pressure in training behavior, although he occasionally wet the bed until he was 12.

R attended a university-supported nursery school at age 4. Mrs. T reported adjustment to this environment was accomplished with a minimum of difficulty. During the following year R attended public school kindergarten, again with satisfactory performance. R transferred to a different elementary school following his kindergarten year because of a school boundary change. First through fifth grade instruction in the new school followed an "open area organizational design," and the mother reported that she and her husband were extremely dissatisfied with the school. Specifically, she related that R "learned almost nothing during that time, although his school records revealed adequate performance. In spite of mostly C grades, however, there were frequent comments such as "doesn't follow directions," "is distractable" and "experiences difficulty in relating to peers and adults." This same pattern continued through the 9th grade. However, during the current year (grade 10) RT has made poor academic progress (Ds and Fs) and has withdrawn even more than previously.

As was the case during the screening interivew, Mrs. T indicated that she and her husband were most concerned with R's poor social relationships and his failure to progress adequately in school. Their goals for R are to develop his social interests and skills and to make him more academically productive. Their specific goals are to have R graduate from high school and to "find a vocation and get a good job."

R's family includes his father, age 46; mother, age 43; and a younger brother, J, age 12. Mr. and Mrs. T have been married for 20 years and report a very satisfactory marriage. Both parents completed high school and both are employed. Mrs. T's job is "part time," allowing her to be in the home whenever her sons are not in school. The family generally appears to be "middle class" in values and behaviors. No other significant social or environmental information was obtained in the interview or from previous records.

Physical: R experienced some difficulty with visual processes during childhood. When he was 5, surgery was performed on the muscles of his left eye to correct muscle imbalance contributing to difficulty in fusion or use of the eyes in binocular vision. Following surgery, training was initiated at an orthoptic clinic. Two 3-month training sessions reportedly produced measurable progress and R currently appears to process visual information adequately.

R appears to be in relatively good physical health and no indications or reports revealed other physical factors of significance.

Intellectual: Intellectual measures indicated RT to be functioning in the average range of mental abilities with some indication of bright normal ability. The high degree of reliability between this measure and previous samples suggest this intellectual inference to be accurate. The Wechsler scale did not provide a convincing pattern of specific strengths and weaknesses of cognitive processes. In addition, test scatter was limited.

Emotional: Structured classroom observations and teacher ratings generally revealed patterns similar to those discovered during the screening process.

Specifically, direct observation data generated via the Werry-Quay Direct Observational System indicated an extremely low rate of attention to task and a high percentage of daydreaming. In addition, a daily frequency count of appropriate conversation between RT and his peers revealed that almost no interactions took place during the 7 days of observation. The teacher rating scales employed in the evaluation also revealed poor social skills and high levels of anxiety.

Although RT was both distant and anxious during a series of interviews with diagnostic personnel, his affect was appropriate and he revealed no disorganization in his thinking process. He described his relationships with his teachers and peers as satisfactory, although he did volunteer that he had "no real friends." Although RT indicated that he was unhappy over his poor academic performance and limited social contacts, he did not feel he had a "problem."

It was the clinical impression of the psychoeducational diagnosticians that RT demonstrated pronounced and pervasive dependency needs which are not being met. In addition, it was felt that his unmet needs have instilled a paranoid perception of the world.

Academic Achievement: Educational measures revealed RT to be functioning approximately 2 years below grade level in all areas measured. Relative prowess was noted in his quantitative abilities and comprehension when materials were delivered via the auditory channel. His most notable deficit areas included reading recognition and comprehension. A general language retrieval deficit with some indication of weakness in the associative process was also discovered. However, it appeared that RT's performance was a direct function of his interest or the amount of attention he received for attempting a task. Specifically, on those tasks which he found interesting or when contingent social reinforcement was utilized, his performance improved significantly.

Recommendations: On the basis of the information summarized above, it was recommended that RT be provided academic remediation and social training through a resource room program in the school. In addition to the 1 1/2 hour daily session in the resource room, RT was also scheduled for individual and group counseling through the Guidance and Counseling Department at the school. Finally, the entire family was referred for family counseling at the county mental health center.

Summary

Perhaps the most obvious issues that emerge from a discussion of screening and diagnostic procedures for behaviorally disordered adolescents are the complexity of the factors involved, the paucity of proven diagnostic procedures, and the lack of clearcut and easily recognizable diagnostic patterns. These problems highlight the need for the diagnostician to be thoroughly aware and sensitive to the normal problems of adolescence and the typical responses of this age group. Only with this baseline information will the diagnostician be able to draw valid inferences from the samples of behavior generated from the assessment process. In addition, the present discussion suggests the need to interpret the various diagnostic sources of information in an integrated manner rather than as independent units of data. Without a pattern analysis strategy, the diagnostic process is much less of a scientific endeavor.

References

Barr, K. L., & McDowell, R. L. Comparison of learning disabled and emotionally disturbed children on three deviant classroom behaviors. *Exceptional Children*, 1972, *39*, 60–62.

Beatty, L., Madden, R., & Gardner, E. *Stanford diagnostic arithmetic test.* New York: Harcourt Brace Jovanovich, 1966.

Bender, L. *Instructions for the use of the Visual Motor Gestalt Test.* New York: American Orthopsychiatric Association, 1946.

Borislow, B. Self-evaluation and academic achievement. *Journal of Counseling Psychology*, 1962, *9*, 199–205.

Bower, E. *Early identification of emotionally handicapped children in school.* Springfield, Ill.: Charles C Thomas, 1960.

Bower, E. *Early identification of emotionally handicapped children in school.* 2nd ed. Springfield, Ill.: Charles C Thomas, 1969.

Bower, E., & Lambert, N. M. *A process for in-school screening of children with emotional handicaps.* Princeton: Educational Testing Service, 1961.

Cronbach, L. J. Correlations between persons as a research tool. In O. H. Mowrer (Ed.), *Psychotherapy theory and research.* New York: Ronald Press, 1953.

Dayton, C. M. *Technical manual: Pupil Classroom Behavior Scale.* College Park, Md.: University of Maryland Research Center of the Interprofessional Research Commission on Pupil Personnel Services, 1967.

DeMyer, M., Barton, S., Alpern, G., Kimberlin, C., Allen, J., Yang, E., & Steele, R. The measured intelligence of autistic children. *Journal of Autism and Childhood Schizophrenia*, 1974, *4*, 42–60.

Duncan, L. W., & Fitzgerald, P. W. Increasing the parent-child communication through counselor-parent conferences. *Personnel and Guidance Journal*, 1969, 514–517.

Dunn, L. & Markwardt, F. *Peabody individual achievement test.* Circle Pines, Minn.: American Guidance Service, 1970.

Durrell, D. *Durrell Analysis of reading difficulty.* New York: Harcourt Brace, 1955.

Garmezy, N. The study of competence in children at risk for severe psychopathology. In E. J. Anthony & C. Koupernik (Eds.) *The child in his family: Children at psychiatric risk.* New York: Wiley, 1974.

Gartner, A., Kohler, M., & Riessman, F. Every child a teacher. *Childhood Education.* 1971, *48*, 12–16.

Gates, A., & McKillop, A. *Gates-McKillop Reading Diagnostic Tests.* New York: Columbia University Press, 1962.

Glidewell, J., Domke, W., & Kantor, L. Screening in schools for behavior disorders: Use of mothers reports of symptoms. *Journal of Educational Research*, 1963, *66*, 508–515.

Hollister, W., & Goldston, S. Classes for the emotionally handicapped. *National Education Association.* 1962, 6–15.

Kroth, R. The behavioral Q-sort as a diagnostic tool. *Academic Therapy*, 1973, *8*, 317–330.

Kroth, R. *Communicating with parents of exceptional children.* Denver: Love, 1975.

Kroth, R., & Simpson, R. *Parent conferences as a teaching strategy.* Denver: Love, 1977.

Lambert, N. M., Bower, E. M., & Hartsough, C. S. *A process for the assessment of effective student functioning.* Monterey: CTB/McGraw-Hill, 1979.

Lessing, E. E., Oberlander, M. I., & Barbera, L. Convergent validity of the IPAT Children's Personality Questionnaire and Teachers' rating of the adjustment of elementary school children. *Social Behavior and Personality*, 1974, *2*, 222–229.

Long, N., Morse, W., & Newman, R. (Eds.) *Conflict in the classroom: The education of emotionally disturbed children.* (3rd ed.). Belmont, Calif.: Wadsworth, 1976.

Machover, K. *Personality projection in the drawings of a human figure.* Springfield, Ill.: Charles C Thomas, 1949.

Murray, H. *Thematic Apperception Test Manual.* Cambridge, Mass.: Harvard University Press, 1943.

O'Leary, K. D. The assessment of psychopathology in children. In H. C. Quay & J. S. Werry (Eds.) *Psychopathological disorders of childhood.* New York: John Wiley, 1972.

Opler, M. K. Cultural determinants of mental disorders. In B. B. Wolman (Ed.) *Handbook of clinical psychology.* New York: McGraw-Hill, 1965.

Pope, B., & Scott, W. *Psychological diagnosis in clinical practice.* New York: Oxford Press, 1967.

Quay, H. C., & Peterson, D. R. *Manual for the Behavioral Problem Checklist.* Champaign, Ill.: Children's Research Center, University of Illinois, 1967.

Rabin, A. I. Diagnostic use of intelligence tests. In B. B. Wolman (Ed.) *Handbook of clinical psychology.* New York: McGraw-Hill, 1965.

Rapaport, D. *Diagnostic psychological testing* (Volume I). Chicago: Year Book Medical Publishers, 1945.

Robbins, L. N. *Deviant children grow up.* Baltimore: Williams & Wilkins, 1966.

Robbins, L. N. Follow-up studies of behavior disorders in children. In H. C. Quay & J. S. Werry (Eds.) *Psychopathological disorders of childhood.* New York: Wiley, 1972.

Robbins, L. N. Antisocial behavior disturbances of childhood. Prevalence, prognosis and prospects. In E. J. Anthony & C. Koupernik (Eds.) *The child in his family: Children at psychiatric risk.* New York: Wiley, 1974.

Rorschach, H. *Psychodiagnostics.* Berne, Switzerland: Verlag Hans Huber, 1942.

Scarpetti, F. R. Can teachers predict delinquency? *Elementary School Journal.* 1964, *65,* 130–136.

Schultz, E., Manton, A., & Salvia, J. Screening emotionally disturbed children in a rural setting: FIRO and behavior problem checklist. *Exceptional Children,* 1972, *39,* 134–137.

Shea, T. M. *Teaching children and youth with behavioral disorders.* St. Louis: Mosby, 1978.

Silvaroli, N. *Classroom reading inventory.* Dubuque, Iowa: William C. Brown, 1973.

Spache, G. *Diagnostic reading scales.* Monterey, Calif.: California Test Bureau, 1972.

Spivack, G., & Swift, M. *Devereux Elementary School Behavior Rating Scale Manual.* Devon, Pa.: Devereux Foundation, 1967.

Spivack, G., & Swift, M. *Hahnemann high school behavior rating scale manual.* Philadelphia: Departmental Health Sciences, Hahnemann Medical College and Hospital, 1972.

Spivack, G., & Swift, M. The classroom behavior of children: A critical review of teacher administered rating scales. *Journal of Special Education,* 1973, *7,* 55–89.

Stephenson, W. *The study of behavior: Q-technique and its methodology.* Chicago: University of Chicago Press, 1953.

Vinter, R. D., Sarri, R. C., Vorwaller, D. J., & Schafer, W. E. *Pupil Behavior Inventory: A manual for administration and scoring.* Ann Arbor, Mich.: Campus Publishers, 1966.

Wechsler, D. *The measurement and appraisal of adult intelligence.* 14th ed. Baltimore: Williams & Wilkins, 1958.

Werry, J. S., & Quay, H. C. Observing the classroom behavior of elementary school children. *Exceptional Children,* 1969, *35,* 461–470.

Strong Educational Programs: Laying the Foundation

5

Gwen Blacklock Brown

In the early days of a school year, teachers make decisions which profoundly affect the tone and success of their classrooms for the entire year. Among the most important and often most difficult decisions teachers confront are those involving classroom structure and the level of parent involvement. So much remains to be learned about adolescence that to make good decisions in these areas, teachers must take full advantage of what has been learned in other contexts. Until more meaningful research is available, educators can begin to develop sound educational programs by examining the theoretical models found effective with elementary-age children with behavior disorders, studying new directions in psychology, and involving parents in early decision-making.

This chapter examines theoretical issues which have long divided educators committed to the educational well being of students with behavior disorders, discusses classroom applications of psychology's cathartic approaches, and introduces the topic of parent involvement. It is hoped that the chapter will help teachers during the beginning phases of their planning, when questions regarding theoretical issues and level of parent involvement must be resolved. While these are distinct topics, they are included together in this chapter because they provide the foundation upon which all other instructional decisions are made. Chapters 6 and 7 of this book continue the discussion of parent involvement and Chapters 8 and 10 extend the discussion of classroom structure.

THEORETICAL CONTROVERSY

The most consistent questions asked by new teachers of young people with behavior disorders are theoretical in orientation: "How much freedom should I give the student who refuses to try to learn to read?" or "What shall I do when a student gets frustrated with arithmetic and throws his book at another student?" Answers to these questions differ according to the theoretical orientation of the consultant and, in most cases, the college or university at which the consultant was educated. There is a fundamental conflict over the proper theoretical orientation for teaching students who exhibit self-defeating behavior patterns. To understand this conflict, an examination of the literature which addresses the behavior-disordered elementary-age child is essential.

Although individual classroom models vary, educational theorists concerned with the subject of students with behavior disorders generally align themselves with either a behavioral or a psychoeducational approach. Typically, graduate schools rush teachers through a one-year program, inculcating them with only one point of view or bewildering them with the diversity in theoretical positions. Inevitably, at least some students are left with an inadequate conception of the theories and the school practices propounded by each. This inadequacy is carried into the classroom as new teachers confront the reality that no single method is so well developed that it can satisfy the needs of all students.

Finding a single theory insufficient, many new teachers resort to a "grab bag" approach to teaching. Morse, Cutler, and Fink (1964), in their national survey of classes for emotionally disturbed students, found "an amazing lack of specific patterns and uniformity of approach" (p. 130). They interpret this as an indication of conceptual uncertainty among educators as to how the needs of emotionally disturbed students should be met. The majority of the teachers in the classrooms surveyed were trained either in regular elementary and secondary education or in aspects of special education not directly related to emotional difficulties. Although today's classes are staffed by a new breed, conflicts and uncertainties concerning theories and techniques still exist.

Behavioral and psychoeducational theories are markedly different; yet similarities exist in some of the school practices advocated by each. Morse has challenged special educators to "discover how we can cultivate the intensity and variety of programs needed to meet the individual differences we find in these children" (Morse, 1971c, p. 578). The first step toward such a goal at the secondary level is to examine similarities and differences in existing techniques.

The Psychoeducational Model

Although the psychoeducational model is historically linked to Freudian psychodynamic theory, it became evident early on that one or two hours of therapy per week was neither adequate nor affordable for most behaviorally disordered students; thus clinicians shifted their emphasis to "milieu" therapy which involves the student's total living situation. Lewin's (1942) cognitive field theory and Redl's (1957) residential work with predelinquents encouraged wide acceptance of "milieu" therapy.

Caplan's theory of crisis intervention (1961), which assumes that during a time of stress a student is "more apt to search for cues from some aspect of his inner and outer environment to solve his dilemma" (Morse, 1971a, p. 295), influenced the formulation by Redl (1959) and Morse (1963) of life space interview techniques for exploiting the meaning of behavior episodes that occur outside of the therapeutic hour. During a life space interview the teacher and student discuss the crisis, using the opportunity to strengthen the student's ego so that he can successfully cope with a wider variety of reality-oriented demands. The life space interview now occupies a central role in psychoeducational programming.

When the concept of milieu therapy is applied to schools, it becomes the psychoeducational model. An important component of the milieu, the classroom, is increasingly recognized as offering considerable potential for effecting behavioral changes. Berkowitz and Rothman (1960) were early advocates of psychoeducational therapy, but today the psychoeducational approach is commonly identified with the more educational and less permissive ideas of Morse (1971b), Fenichel (1966), and Long (1974).

Briefly stated, Morse, Fenichel, and Long believe that educational decisions should be based on the consideration of unconscious motives and underlying conflicts; that learning should be pleasant and relevant to the student; that group processes and crisis situations should be utilized to develop insights; that the teacher should establish an empathic relationship with the student; and that, although the teacher must enforce necessary limits, flexibility is important.

While Knoblock and Johnson (1967) and Trippe (1966) plead for "humanism" and Rhodes (1963) supports a social competence model, each parallels the psychoeducational approach. Their common interests in interpersonal relationships and in classrooms where the teacher and students work together for mutually accepted goals cast them as allies in opposition to strict behaviorists.

The Behavior Modification Approach

The behavioral approach to educating students with behavior disorders was born of the methodologies that employed structured environments for teaching brain-injured and hyperactive children (Cruickshank, Bentzen, Ralzeburg, & Tannhausen, 1961; Strauss & Lehtinen, 1947) and of the S-R-S operant conditioning model (Skinner, 1938; Spence, 1951; Thorndike, 1903; Watson, 1914). Advocates of behavior modification concern themselves "with the relationship between changes in the environment and changes in the subject's responses" (Ullmann & Krasner, 1965, p.1).

Hewett (1971), Haring and Phillips (1962), Whelan (1966), and Kauffman (1977) lead the crusade to extend the use of behavior modification techniques in the classroom. Teachers, they argue, must focus on observable behavior as it is manifested in the classroom rather than on internal conflicts and unconscious motivations. The teacher should: "(1) select a terminal goal: (2) prepare a series of tasks involving reasonable increments which lead up to such a goal; and (3) through careful selection and presentation of stimuli and consequences, modify the child's behavior and bring it in line with the goal" (Hewett, 1971, p. 360).

Common Ground

Psychoeducational and behavioral educators both recognize the primary importance of ensuring that the student learns to relate behavior to its consequences. Haring and Phillips's (1962) interference theory assumes that individuals live by their expectations of how events will occur. According to this theory, the expectations of students with behavior disorders have a high probability of being disconfirmed. These students are unable to assess the probable environmental response to their behavior. "Disordered or pathological or disturbed behavior represents a condition wherein the results of action (feedback) are different from what is anticipated" (Phillips, 1967, p. 153).

Because the student cannot structure and organize his world, behaviorists urge the teacher to structure it for him. A behavioristic teacher seeks to provide a consistent environment in which the student can learn to predict accurately the outcomes of behavior. Rewards follow appropriate behaviors and decelerating consequences follow inappropriate behaviors. In a behavior modification classroom the rewards provide immediate positive feedback to the student and increase the likelihood of that behavior recurring under similar conditions at a later time.

Psychoeducational theory also concentrates on helping the student develop "insights" into the relationship of behavior to its consequences. But it rejects the inflexible structure of the behaviorist, insisting that "at times, daily routines which were established to give security go by the board to capture the emotion of the moment" (Morse, 1971b, p. 331).

Rather than relying on structure and extrinsic reinforcement, the psychoeducational teacher utilizes verbal discussion of behavior to help the student develop insights. One of the major goals of the life space interview is to lead the student to the discovery that his behavior has led to many of the difficulties in which he finds himself. When a student cannot discern the meaning of an event in which he becomes involved, the teacher must administer what Redl (1957) calls the reality "rub-in interview" (p. 497). If the problem has not resolved itself by the resolution phase of the interview, "the adult at this stage begins to inject reality factors in an objective way: implications of behavior, standards, expectations. Reality limits are explained in a non-moralistic way. Why some attention must be given to the behavior is covered, but not vindictively" (Morse, 1971d, p. 488). Thus the teacher makes it very clear that the child must change some inappropriate behavior to avoid negative consequences.

Whereas the behavioral teacher employs structure and extrinsic rewards to provide feedback, the psychoeducational teacher uses verbal discussion. Both of these techniques help the student change behavior to increase the gratification received from the environment. With either method the final decision to change rests with the student. Good teachers of either persuasion avoid embarrassing the student, and in a nonjudgmental manner provide support and an environment which allows the student to recognize his power to avoid negative consequences and increase positive ones. As Rhodes (1963) says, the student should be "heedful of his own resources and potentialities for the beauty of well being" (p. 61).

Advocates of either technique insist that theirs is the superior means of helping a student learn the relationship of behavior to consequences. Perplexed by the pressure to choose one theory to the exclusion of the other, teachers sometimes ask if it is not possible to employ both techniques selectively in a single classroom to achieve better results.

Whelan (1966), a proponent of behavior modification, maintains that the life space interview "is a powerful mode of therapeutic intervention if correctly applied but it can also produce negative effects if utilized without cognizance of important behavioral and environmental variables" (p. 39). The increased attention given by the teacher during the interview may actually reinforce maladaptive behavior. Thus, if a student is acting out to evoke a response from the teacher, the interview would increase the frequency of such behavior. Psychoeducators agree that the life space interview should not be used indiscriminately. Morse (1971) warns that "many events which are crisis to adults are often satisfying, ego-building, and gratifying to pupils" (p. 295).

The interview technique, then, could be employed even by behaviorists when the teacher is reasonably sure that the student is not acting out to receive teacher attention. Teachers can use the life space interview more effectively by recording on graph paper the effects of their attention on the behavior of each student. For students whose inappropriate behavior increases when the teacher attends to it, a delay interview technique may be in order; that is, the teacher can wait until the inappropriate behavior has ceased before sitting down to discuss the student's earlier difficulties. Verbal techniques can help the student by showing him that the teacher is an ally and by increasing the ability to identify feelings and control behavior. However, if the student is nonverbal or does not respond to the discussion technique, the behavioral alternative may be more appropriate; the student may need structure and extrinsic reinforcement to help him begin to make accurate assertions about his environment and to develop self-control.

Just as the behaviorist can find ways to use the life space interview, the psychoeducator can use structure and external rewards without compromising the ideal of joint teacher-student goal-setting. During the last step of the interview, the adult typically offers to assist the student and suggests plans for helping the student avoid a recurrence of the difficulty. Many students not yet able to control their behavior without a reminder find a behavior modification plan appealing and helpful. For some adolescents, peer reinforcers are often effective. For instance, the class clown who does not complete his academic work might readily accept a plan in which the other members of the class agree to support him by ignoring his clowning behavior until he finishes his math problems. When the work is completed, the group can cheer for his success. The point is that teachers and students can discuss the problem, come to an agreement, and work together to make their classroom a gratifying and productive place. So palatable a form of behavior modification is not incompatible with the ideals of psychoeducators who emphasize the "need to articulate a new humanism for children and teachers that would allow them to function in schools with the feeling that it is their school and their responsibility to create a partnership for living and learning" (Knoblock, 1970, p. 69).

A second concern common to the behaviorist and the psychoeducator is that the student not be exposed to stimulation and environmental demands with which he is unable to cope successfully. Cruickshank et al.'s (1961) stripped-down classroom with bare walls and blank study carrels represents the paradigmatic classroom in which stimulation is controlled so that students can attend to academics. The techniques of Cruickshank and the structure of the behaviorist are sometimes shunned by teachers who believe that "manipulation of stimuli and consequences in the classroom dehumanizes the teacher and provides a 'technician' rather than a 'teaching artist' role" (Hewett, 1971, p. 360). Although the issue of environmental control evokes controversy among special educators today, it is essential that stimuli in the classroom be controlled to some extent.

Even those in the psychoeducational camp must sometimes resort to extreme environmental controls when dealing with young people with severe behavior disorders. Redl (1957) emphasizes the need for "limitation of space and tools." The environment should be controlled so that there is little "appeal to impulses the gratification of which would lead to danger or guilt" (p. 83). Redl arranges those tempting elements in students' lives which "bring out the worst in them" into three categories: (a) situational lure; (b) gadgetorial seduction; and (c) contagibility. Even to a "normal" student, a large, open space proclaims "run," a ball suggests "bounce me" and the sight of other students acting out says "join us!" Thus, psychoeducators also agree that to avoid disasters and an "overload on the ego," the teacher of young people with behavior disorders must control the environment for stimuli that are too tempting for the students to handle.

Teachers should ask themselves several questions regarding environmental stimuli: How much control? For which students? and, For how long? To answer these questions the behaviorists and the psychoeducators both start at the student's level of ability and very gradually move forward. "A disturbed child's self-image, like that of any other child, is enhanced by experiencing success and diminished by frequent failure. It is imperative, therefore, therapeutically and educationally, that we organize a highly individualized program of teaching and a learning procedure and pace for each child to meet his own capacities and needs" (Fenichel, 1966, p. 303). The important consideration for both behaviorists and psychoeducators is that the classroom be carefully arranged to provide each student with success and challenge.

With a structured environment and a shaping technique, the behaviorists communicate to the student, "We will not let you fail" (Hewett, 1971, p. 364). In shaping, successive approximations of the desired behavior are reinforced. The teacher asks from a student only what he or she is capable of producing so that, for example, the student who is overwhelmed by a whole page of arithmetic may be given only one or two problems to complete. Very gradually, as the student experiences success with arithmetic, more problems are added to each page. The technique of shaping is also useful for developing social skills. The student too shy to talk in a large group is first asked to work with only one other student, then after experiencing success with one person, the student begins working with two classmates. By reinforcing successive approximations, the teacher provides the student with challenge and success. If the student's work is threateningly difficult, the teacher is misusing the shaping procedure.

The psychoeducational group also controls environmental stimuli to provide challenge and success. Redl (1957) calls his technique "widening the experiential range." He assumes that the teacher helps the student gain a feeling of mastery by "offering ego-challenging life situations but ones which are not far away from the scope of ego control" (p. 383).

Psychoeducators and behaviorists control stimulation only when a student cannot function in a more distracting or demanding situation. Neither model advocates leaving a student in such a controlled environment indefinitely. Appropriate use of shaping or "widening the experiential range" means that gradually environmental demands are added to help the student develop responsible behaviors that bring success in the regular classroom and in natural living situations. No matter which theoretical orientation a teacher chooses, careful attention to stimulation levels is essential for educating adolescents with behavior disorders.

Even within classrooms carefully planned to provide stimulation and demands appropriate to the student's level of development, teachers of young people with

behavior disorders confront acting out, defiance, and testing of limits. In these situations behaviorists advocate giving the disruptive student "time out," that is, "removing a child from a situation in which he has been receiving accelerating consequences for appropriate behavior whenever he exhibits behavior which is inappropriate" (Whelan, 1966, p. 69). The "time out" may involve placing the student in a small room next to the classroom for a specified time interval or may be limited simply to ignoring the student's behavior (time out from teacher attention).

Historically, psychoeducators have condemned behaviorists for using these impersonal control techniques. Trippe (1966) fears that "assembly line organization and extensive use of surplus repression foster conforming behaviors and depletes children of their creative resources" (p. 25). For the management of disruptive surface behavior psychoeducators suggest "planned ignoring" when "ignoring makes it easier for it to stop" (Redl, 1957, p. 401) and "antiseptic bouncing." A student is "bounced," that is, asked to leave the room for a few minutes when his behavior reaches a point where he will not respond to verbal controls. A substitute activity such as getting a drink or delivering a message could be provided.

In spite of the similarity of "bouncing" to "time out," psychoeducators insist that their technique is quite different because "there is no intent of punishing the child but simply to protect and help him and/or the group to get over their feelings of anger, disappointment, uncontrollable laughter, hiccups, etc." (Long & Newman, 1971, p. 450). However, in looking at the "behaviors received" by each child in a day's time, Redl (1971) emphasizes that "what people really 'do' to each other counts as much as how they feel" (p. 248). This notion applied to "bouncing" suggests that if a student who is receiving gratification is cut off against his or her will from the source of that gratification, the impact may be the same regardless of whether the teacher calls it planned ignoring, antiseptic bouncing, or time out.

These common features in classroom models should be clearly recognized by teachers because they represent the essentials of classroom management about which no significant disagreement exists in the profession. As to those points on which there are real differences between the behavioral and psychoeducational approaches, the teacher should selectively choose techniques based on personal beliefs, classroom experience, and the needs of the particular students.

Divergent Paths

Behaviorists and psychoeducators find little in common regarding the practice of withdrawing privileges for inappropriate behavior. Speaking for psychoeducators, Redl (1957) insists that art, games, free time, and other enjoyable activities are important for developing a student's ego strength and should never be deleted from the program. Although behaviorists agree that these activities are essential in the therapeutic process, they believe that pleasurable behaviors should be made contingent upon appropriate behavior.

The behaviorists follow the Premack (1959) Principle which holds essentially that a behavior may be accelerated when it is followed by a behavior which normally occurs at a high rate. In practice this means that the behaviorist looks for activities that the student enjoys and makes these contingent upon appropriate behavior. For instance, the student may be asked to complete 10 multiplication problems before being allowed 10 minutes of free time.

Psychoeducators believe that pleasurable activities are the student's right and not a privilege which can be taken away. They point disapprovingly at practices such as keeping a student in at lunch time for extended periods because difficult math assignments are not completed. Most behaviorists, however, also shudder at such inappropriate use of the technique. The withdrawal of privileges is essentially a shaping technique that insures the student's success by rewarding successive approximations to the desired behavior. To apply the technique appropriately, the teacher must begin by giving the student a relatively simple assignment to complete in order to earn a little free time. The amount of work required is geared to the student's level of development so that he is successful in earning pleasurable activities in almost all cases. Thus, the behaviorist attempts to get double mileage out of those things in the school that students enjoy and makes sure that the student does, in most cases, participate in pleasurable activities, but these activities are also used to reinforce appropriate behaviors.

Motivation is perhaps the most significant issue dividing educational theorists today. Psychoeducators castigate behaviorists not only for utilizing the Premack Principle but, more importantly, for using trinkets, candy, and other extrinsic reinforcement to motivate students. Psychoeducators stress the importance of using joint teacher-student planning and of making learning relevant and pleasurable. The teacher-pupil relationship is considered valuable "not only as an interpersonal feeling, but as a mode of helping the pupil with his motivational defects" (Morse, 1971b, p. 333). The teacher is seen as a facilitator of learning and one of her primary goals is to "develop pupil-teacher rapport and to restore the sense of pleasure in learning" (Morse, 1971b, p. 332). Accordingly, the curriculum is built around the students' interests.

Behaviorists believe that acquiring some types of appropriate behavior "is probably not intrinsically fun or pleasurable" and that when a student is left to plan his own learning experiences, "many learning gaps will exist because learning that needs to be accomplished may never fall within the realm of expressed interest" (Whelan, 1966, p. 65). The use of external reinforcement is a behavioral technique for motivating the student to acquire new behaviors. "Once behavior is acquired, it may result in feelings of self-satisfaction because difficult tasks have been accomplished" (p. 65). The goal is to move the student gradually from dependence on extrinsic rewards to the development of intrinsic motivation.

Behaviorists and psychoeducators both hope to help the student become a self-directed and self-motivated learner who as an adult will possess the social and academic skills necessary for independent functioning in a complex society. Psychoeducators fear that reinforcing students extrinsically robs them of their creativity and of the opportunity to become self-directing and "self-actualized" (Maslow, 1971, p. 169). Behaviorists, on the other hand, fear that giving a student the freedom to choose not to learn appropriate behavior or academic skills denies that individual the opportunity to become all that he or she can, thereby restricting the freedom to choose from a wide variety of life styles in adulthood. The teacher must assess each student's academic and social abilities and decide which techniques will be most successful in helping the student become an independent and self-fulfilled adult.

Toward an Integration of Approaches

It is premature to proclaim either that all behavior is learned or that all behavior results from unconscious motivations. There is not enough empirical evidence to establish that one set of procedures is superior in every situation and with every student. Special educators still lack the evidence to build a comprehensive system; yet there is something to be learned from each of our theories and each theory has uncovered phenomena which move us forward in our knowledge about learning and behavior.

> Science ought to be systematic, not eclectic, but a premature systematic position is likely to be dogmatic and bigoted just as an enduring eclecticism is likely to be superficial and opportunistic. It is possible for a system to blind the seeker after it to the truths unearthed by those with views unlike his own. (Hilgard & Bower, 1966, p. 13)

Until there is comprehensive empirical data supporting the superiority of one theory, teachers should seek to integrate the two approaches. This does not mean that an educator must compromise educational ideals, but rather seek ways to use techniques of alternative theories in order to advance personal educational goals and values. A few ideas for harmoniously combining the behavioral and psychoeducational approaches have been suggested. Others, no doubt, can be found.

Debates that stem from semantic differences or from misapplication of techniques should be abandoned. Such arguments only impede our progress. Well-informed advocates of both the psychoeducational and the behavioral views already agree that certain practices are inappropriate: using the life space interview immediately following teacher attention-seeking behavior; continuing extrinsic reinforcement after a student has developed internal control and motivation for the behavior; using a shaping program that requires large steps rather than successive approximations; the use of verbal techniques on nonverbal children; withdrawing privileges for long periods of time; embarrassing or frightening the student with a hostile, judgmental attitude; and waiting until the student solves his emotional problems before providing a sound educational program.

Psychoeducators and behaviorists also agree that the following practices are essential in an appropriate program: being honest and respectful with students; providing students with frequent fun activities to serve as breaks from difficult or tension-producing learning periods; giving students large amounts of positive teacher attention; making learning activities enjoyable and relevant whenever possible; controlling stimulation that is beyond the student's ability to handle; setting firm but fair limits; facilitating joint teacher-student goal setting; accepting the student as a worthy person without condoning self-defeating behavior; and establishing learning environments that provide challenge and insure considerable success. Whether behavioral or psychoeducational, programs that include these elements should significantly enhance the adolescent's chances for satisfying relationships and successful life functioning.

TOUCHING BASE WITH PSYCHOLOGY AGAIN

Educators of young people with deviant behavior patterns have a long history of borrowing and adapting techniques from the field of psychology. Progressive educators keep their eyes on developments in clinical and experimental psychology, adapting promising new theories and techniques whenever possible to further their educational goals. Both the psychoeducational and the behavioral models were adaptations of the avant-garde psychology movements of their day.

Currently a new force appears to be having a major impact in the field of psychology and must be reckoned with by educators. This new approach emphasizes the role of emotional arousal and expression in treatment programs. Increasingly, therapists are stressing emotional catharsis as a necessary component of effective therapeutic programs (Nichols & Zax, 1977). Many therapists maintain that the human organism tends toward homeostasis in emotional as well as physical ways. Just as the body sneezes to expel foreign elements in the respiratory tract, regurgitates to rid itself of harmful substances in the digestive tract, and blinks to wash out foreign particles in the eye, so the body attempts to rid itself of tension by crying, laughing, and shaking. A young child, not socialized to inhibit the tension-release process, cries when hurt (either physically or emotionally), laughs or shakes when nervous, frightened, or embarrassed, and throws a tantrum when angry. According to the new theorists, crying, laughing, and throwing tantrums may be seen as the human organism's attempt to free itself of unnecessary tension and distress and regain emotional health. However, young children are generally socialized to inhibit this natural healing process. They are belittled when they cry or show other signs of emotional expression, rather than being taught appropriate times and places to release their distress. The theory asserts that because most adults in our society have lost the ability to take advantage of this natural process, they carry an unnecessary store of emotional distress that inhibits their ability to think clearly, to function effectively, to give and receive love freely, and generally to enjoy life fully.

Therapists who accept this logic believe that emotional catharsis is essential to full human functioning. They insist, for instance, that to adjust fully to the loss of a loved one, an individual must release grief through tears. The stoic, they argue, who shuts off the grieving process before crying out the hurt, may never come to terms with the loss. Nichols and Zax (1977) in a review of a few of the innovative approaches based on emotional catharsis in treatment discuss primal therapy, gestalt therapy, Re-Evaluation Counseling, bio-energetics, and psychodrama. Each of these approaches enjoys a fast growing number of supporters who report an increase in the quality of their lives because of their cathartic experiences. To date, very little scientific research has been reported to support these claims.

While teachers are not therapists, they do need a clear understanding of the therapeutic practices on which their educational procedures are based. Just as psychiatry students often undergo psychoanalysis as a part of their training, teachers committed to establishing the best possible educational program for young people with behavioral disorders should try to experience various therapeutic approaches employed in education. Becoming a "client" in both a psychoanalytic and a behavioral program offers unique insight into the impact of those approaches on the student with behavior problems. With the growing acceptance of the cathartic approach, teachers should consider the value of experiencing firsthand one or more of the new therapies that employ catharsis in order to determine the relevance of tension-release techniques in the education of adolescents with behavior disorders. Re-Evaluation Counseling is highly recommended for teachers because its techniques were developed for use by nonprofessionals, have high educational applicability, and offer individuals a positive and practical approach to problem-solving.

At the very least, special educators should take time to reconsider what may be happening for the adolescent who bursts into tears at minor criticism or who acts out by expressing rage at classmates. The exhibition of tears and anger may be an attempt to get rid of an overload of tension that has accumulated from repeated stressful experiences. If this is the case, a teacher might view the student as doing his best to take care of himself, but having chosen an inappropriate time and place. By labelling the time and place rather than the student's behaviors as inappropriate, educators might begin to see the student's available strength and determination to work out the problems.

The notion of permitting the release of tension is not new for special educators. According to Redl (1959) the trouble with many young people with behavior disorders is not only that they "have more feelings of anxiety, panic, shame, guilt, fury than they should or than the normal child would experience, but also that they don't know what to do with such states of mind when they get into them" (p. 332). To provide support when students reach such states, Morse (1976) suggests that teachers "permit catharsis and ventilation (p. 338)" during the first step of the life space interview.

Recently a few educators have begun, not only to permit catharsis, but to encourage it at an appropriate time and place in an attempt to free students of pent-up emotions that interfere with the learning process. This approach seems rational. Learning requires attention and, if all of the student's attention is focused on a distressing experience, one logical solution is to facilitate the release of tension associated with that experience so that attention can be redirected toward learning activities. In fact, it appears that, given an uninterrupted period of time to focus attention on the stressful experience, many students find that afterward they can turn their attention away from the experience and attend to school tasks. Teachers who give students an opportunity to release tension report not only that students are better able to attend to learning tasks but that "acting out" and withdrawn behaviors diminish in frequency.

Clearly, encouraging tension release has many limitations as a classroom procedure. First, to listen with awareness and to deal warmly and objectively with emotional outpourings requires a patience that not all teachers have. Second, encouraging catharsis would be inappropriate for the most severely disturbed young people who might be overwhelmed by the depth of their feelings. Certainly mild to moderately involved students could benefit the most from catharsis. However, the process takes time and usually must be undertaken in a separate room or area to avoid interrupting the learning of other students. Consequently, to keep the attention of students on the task of learning rather than on painful experiences, other techniques better suited to the classroom can be used in conjunction with a limited use of catharsis. Some activities for freeing students' attention for learning tasks are listed below. The tension-release activities should not be attempted by teachers who feel uncomfortable or impatient with the emotional outpourings of others.

Refocusing Attention with Light and Playful Activities

In general, human beings work and learn more efficiently when they feel happy about themselves and when they focus on the positive side of life. This principle applies as well to young people with behavior disorders. Since they often have difficulty attending to anything other than their negative feelings, they tend to be inefficient learners. In most cases, if a student can be helped to develop the habit of attending to the bright side of his life, rather than the dark, he will be a better learner. Pleasant thoughts at the beginning of the day help to rid students of negative thoughts so that they can focus on educational tasks. Listed below are some examples of ways in which the attention of young persons can be focused in positive directions.

1. Students can share in turn experiences that are going well in their lives. For example, ask, "What good news about yourself do you have to share today?" Simple pleasures such as watching the morning sun rise or enjoying a drink of cold juice can serve as appropriate answers. Encourage each student to mention at least one positive experience. Let students know that a sense of well-being can be fostered in part by focusing attention on positive aspects of their lives. Such good thinking habits require practice.

2. Students can be encouraged to focus on positive features of the world around them. For example, ask, "What are three bright colors you see in this room?" or, "What's your favorite picture on the wall?" or, "What do you see that you like outside of the window?"

3. Nonsense and fantasy questions can be asked. For example, ask, "If an elephant wore polka dots, what colors do you think they'd be?" or, "If you were to fly away on a magic carpet, where would you go?" (These questions would not be appropriate, of course, for a student who has difficulty in maintaining contact with reality.)

4. Playful childhood games such as Duck, Duck, Goose and Eraser Tag can be helpful to many young people once they understand that the purpose of the activity

is to be as carefree as possible. Even though the purpose is carefully explained, some adolescents may still reject these games as too childish, in which case the teacher would have to devise more popular but equally frivolous games.

5. Dance, music, songs, exercise, relaxation techniques (Maltz, 1971; Walker, 1975) centering activities (Hendricks & Wills, 1975), and light self-control activities (Fagen, Long & Stevens, 1975) can also be used.

Creative teachers, of course, can invent countless other ways to refocus attention so that students are at their best for the learning experience. Many students who initially resist attempts to refocus their attention soon begin to cooperate as they relax. They come to appreciate the teacher who uses these activities to communicate the expectations that they will learn and assurances that the teacher will help them enjoy what is good in their lives rather than abandoning them to their feelings of hopelessness and negativity. The activities can be used to brighten the mood of the class first thing in the morning and any time during the day when the atmosphere seems to get heavy.

Refocusing Attention with Appreciation

Recent investigations suggest that negative self-evaluations are a prime determinant of self-defeating behavior (Auxter, Zahar, & Ferrini, 1967; Johnson, Fretz, & Johnson, 1968; Noland & Gruber, 1978). It seems reasonable to assume that a student's inappropriate behavior will diminish as self-evaluations improve. Because self-esteem, at least in young persons, is largely a function of what they hear about themselves from others, a program to improve self-esteem and learning should expose students to frequent compliments about their good qualities and achievements. A negative, deeply ingrained self-evaluation is generally not easy to reverse and requires a firm and consistent refusal by others to accept verbal and behavioral assertions of unworthiness.

Students with behavior disorders become so accustomed to hearing unpleasant comments about themselves that they focus on these remarks much of the time and cannot accept objectively accurate compliments. Appreciation for achievement is essential, but teachers should not overlook laudable personal qualities. For example, to the class bully the teacher might say, "I saw you listening to Sara this morning and noticed your kindness, John." To the student who has experienced considerable school failure, a teacher might comment, "When you speak, you express yourself very clearly. It shows how well you can think." In many cases, appreciative comments will have a stronger impact if accompanied by a reassuring arm around the shoulder or an understanding touch on the hand. To appreciate students effectively teachers often need to develop the habit of refocusing their own attention from inappropriate behaviors to the many positive qualities of their students. Throughout the day teachers should refocus their attention in a positive direction so their feelings of anger or despair do not occlude their vision of the potential for effective learning and healthy development within each of their students.

To help counter the habit many students have of focusing on negative comments, students can be encouraged to repeat the good comments they hear from the teacher and fellow students. In addition, students can proudly share what they like about themselves.

Refocusing Attention with Tension-Release Time

Despite the efforts of teachers to reinforce achievement, to enliven learning activities, and to direct the attention of their students toward the positive, young people with behavior disorders may be overwhelmed by their feelings of distress. The result may take the form of "acting out" behavior or despondency which brings the learning process to a screeching halt. When this occurs, it is important that the teacher view the behavior, not as a personal affront or a challenge to her authority, but as a cry for help. What the student needs is the teacher's full support and, if possible, the opportunity to release the tension and emotional build-up that is responsible for the inappropriate behavior so that the student's attention can be refocused on learning. Below are several suggested methods which teachers can use to prevent or respond to disruptive classroom behavior.

1. Times for student/teacher sharing. The teacher can schedule a daily or weekly meeting—depending on the number of students in the class and the availability of classroom assistance—of 20 minutes or so to meet with each student individually in a separate room or area. These periods would provide an opportunity for the teacher to give each individual attention and for the student to express feelings and to share with the teacher any personal concerns or problems. Used regularly, they should significantly reduce disruptive behavior during learning time.

In order for the student to express feelings openly in these periods, the student must trust the teacher. How to build this kind of trust is largely an intuitive matter and cannot be prescribed by a rigid formula. However, it is clear that a student is most likely to trust someone who listens, shows genuine understanding, affection, and interest, and who treats the student as a peer in terms of his or her inherent worthiness as a human being. Teachers, however, should never push the student to disclose problems. Initially, it may be a good idea simply to let the student choose a game to play during these periods so that the time is felt to be truly for the student's benefit and enjoyment. The student may even want to discuss a school assignment or describe a movie.

Once trust is established, the student will begin to share feelings. As this occurs, the teacher's role should not be seen as one of "analyzing" the student psychologically, solving his or her problems, or directing behavior. What is most helpful is simply listening attentively and exhibiting confidence that the student is fully capable of finding solutions to problems if given appropriate support. If emotions surface as the student talks, the teacher can encourage the release of the emotion by having the student repeat the phrase or the part of the story that brought it on. For instance, if the student's voice begins to waver and tears begin to flow while saying, "I wish I could read better," the teacher should encourage the student to focus on the feeling until the tension associated with those words is dissipated. An attitude which says "I care about where you hurt and I want to help you through it" is important to most students.

The emotional release in student/teacher meetings may involve displays of anger or fear as well as tears. Release of anger can be encouraged by permitting the student to, for example, hit a pillow or stomp on the floor. He or she should be told that it is helpful to express feelings of anger in ways that will not hurt others. In instances during which fear surfaces, a teacher's reassuring embrace may offer the safety that will bring on bodily shaking and give the student the sense that there really is someone to hold on to from time to time.

Whatever emotion is released, it is important for the student to know that what is being expressed is a feeling only and that although the feeling may seem very real, it is not necessarily in harmony with reality. For instance, an intelligent student may feel "dumb" because of repeated failures. But feelings, it should be explained, are to be felt and released, not necessarily believed or acted upon. That is, a student who feels unlovable should be encouraged to believe and act as if he is lovable. This concept may be difficult for the student with self-defeating behavior to comprehend because the only known "reality" is the one seen through a history of distressing experiences and apparent failures. Reminding the student frequently of his or her talents and positive qualities can help contradict a false sense of reality.

The student should be reassured that a show of emotions is healthy. It is also important that the student be permitted to say whatever brings the emotional release even if the statement is not objectively accurate. If a student begins to cry because "I never get a turn with the basketball," for instance, that is not the time for the teacher to state that he or she had three turns yesterday. The release of emotion is more important. (Indeed, the student in the foregoing example is probably conveying something quite accurate: that he or she "feels" left out.)

Toward the end of a period in which the student has been in touch with his or her feelings of distress, the teacher should begin redirecting attention outward from the feelings to the world going on outside. The light activities discussed previously can be used for this purpose.

2. Work-it-out corner. Fagen et al. (1975) recommend that a corner of the room or another room be set aside to give students a motoric means of working out destructive feelings. "The corner could contain, for example, nails to be hammered, paper to be torn, pencils and crayons to be broken, chalk to be stamped, and clay or foam rubber to be squeezed and jabbed. Once the child has worked out his feelings in this corner, he may return to his seat" (p. 174).

3. Modifying the life space interview. When using the life space interview after a student crisis, the teacher can help the student release tension by repeatedly asking, "What happened? Start from the beginning and tell me again." As long as the student seems to be releasing tension by talking in an animated manner, crying, throwing a tantrum, laughing, or shaking, it is appropriate to remain at the initial phase of the interview. As the tension level subsides, the student can go to the remainder of the interview. The teacher should avoid hurrying students to the resolution phase when feelings are on the surface and likely to block clear thinking.

Although encouraging students to give attention to their disturbing feelings can be an effective means of freeing student attention for on-task behavior, if used inappropriately the technique can achieve the opposite effect. That is, after tension-release time the student may have less rather than more attention available for learning. Essential to the technique's success is spending the time necessary to refocus the student's attention onto the environment once the tension-release time is over. Again, the light activities mentioned earlier are useful for this purpose. The goal should be for each student to realize that he or she has the power to feel and behave better by directing his attention toward the positive whenever attention to the distress is inappropriate. As a student begins to learn this, he is better able to exercise self-control over his behavior. In addition, he starts to appreciate himself more fully as he stops identifying negative feelings with the person that he is.

The same concepts that enable students with self-defeating behavior to feel better about themselves and operate more effectively in the world can be used by teachers through the use of support groups. Teachers of such students, it goes without saying, have very difficult jobs. The frustrations are many and the praise from others for their work is discouragingly scant. By joining together in support groups, teachers can share their successes, their difficulties, and their goals. They can provide one another with ideas and with encouragement, listen attentively to one another, encourage the release of stored-up emotion, and, when the emotional release is over, help one another to refocus his or her attention on the positive. They can also provide one another with the positive feedback that each deserves and gets too little of in the classroom. Teachers can operate even more effectively if they are given these things and if they have the support and understanding of others— particularly of other teachers who share similar experiences. To maximize the effectiveness of these groups, negative feedback should be discouraged; teachers hear enough of that all day long in their classrooms. Like their students, teachers function most effectively when they are supported by caring people who help them attend to the positive aspects of themselves and their lives.

PARENT INVOLVEMENT

Although teachers have wide latitude in selecting the teaching techniques and theoretical approaches suitable to their beliefs and the needs of their students, parents must play a role in decision-making. Although parent involvement was not emphasized in the programs of the last decade, Public Law 94–142 revolutionizes the role of parents in the educational process. Recognizing that it is impossible to provide appropriate educational services without focusing on the needs of individual students, Congress requires that each student enrolled in a program be given a written statement outlining the educational plan. The plan must be jointly developed by a qualified school official, the student's teacher, and a parent or guardian. When possible and appropriate the student should be involved in the planning. Thus, as local education agencies implement the law, special and regular educators find themselves in closer contact with families of students with behavior disorders than ever before.

Parents sometimes find their new roles as joint educational planners confusing. Although the list of parental rights provided in Public Law 94–142 is extensive, most of the provisions are meaningless unless parents are relatively sophisticated in their understanding of educational theories and programming techniques. To insure the full promise of the law for each student with behavior disorders, programs must be developed to help parents prepare for their new educational responsibilities. The following section of this chapter introduces the topic of parent education programs. More detailed information on parent involvement is provided in Chapters 6 and 7.

Parent Programs

Parents of young people with self-defeating behavior patterns are a diverse group, but most share fear, frustration, and disappointment in child-rearing beyond that typically experienced by parents of nonhandicapped students. Unfortunately, except for parents of autistic children, parents of young people with behavior disorders have not organized themselves for mutual support and social action as effectively as have parents of other types of exceptional children.

Guilt, a sense of personal failure, and family disorganization have kept many parents from reaching out successfully for understanding and support from others. Especially in cases for which a biological basis for the exceptionality is not evident, parents are often too overwhelmed with feelings of inadequacy and embarrassment to ask for help from others. In some cases the parents have self-defeating behavior patterns from their own distressful childhood experiences and these patterns are repeatedly played out against the school as well as the child. When interacting with such parents, teachers should be firm but patient, recognizing, as they would when dealing with a student, that any negativity or hostility probably results from the parents' distress rather than a rational perception of what the teacher is trying to do. Teachers should never, of course, make the mistake of predicting the parents' behavior on the basis of a child's inappropriate and self-defeating behavior. Parents of children with behavior disorders most often are well adjusted and very capable of discussing their child's problems rationally and intelligently.

Parent education programs will not realize their potential unless teachers take advantage of skills and information that parents have and can share with the schools and each other. These programs are least likely to be effective where teachers do all the teaching. Parent involvement can take many forms, ranging from an annual or semiannual individual education plan (IEP) conference to extensive parent education groups and classroom participation. At a minimum, teachers should conduct early IEP conferences for all students receiving special education services. After considering available time and resources, teachers can determine whether they will stop at the IEP conference or develop a more extensive parent involvement program. In developing successful parent programs, the teacher must consider the characteristics and interests of the families involved. Following are three lists which may be helpful in stimulating teachers to think about programs appropriate for their students' parents.

Typical informational questions parents may have
1. What happens at an IEP conference?
2. What are my rights and responsibilities under the law?
3. How do you see my adolescent's problem in relation to normal development?
4. How is my child progressing?
5. How can I support my child's development?
6. What other community resources are available to my child? Library materials? Medical services? Recreational activities? Career experiences? Part-time jobs? Counselors?
7. Are there other parents in the community who can be of help? Parent organizations? Civil groups? Legal advisors?
8. How do I handle siblings' reactions to my child's behavior?
9. How do I talk to neighbors and relatives about my child's behavior?
10. How can I use the home environment and resources to their best advantage for my child and family unit? Budgeting? Nutrition? Inexpensive materials to stimulate learning? Family support?

Skills with which parents may need help
1. Attentively listening to their adolescent.

2. Communicating warmth, acceptance, and appreciation to their adolescent.

3. Accepting the adolescent's feelings, but not necessarily his or her behaviors. Saying "no" firmly, but with positive regard. Assisting the adolescent in releasing emotions at appropriate times, not acting them out inappropriately against others.

4. Acquiring behavior management skills, including observation, joint goal setting, pinpointing target behavior, charting, reinforcing, and time out.

5. Developing techniques for involving other family members in the student's programs.

6. Developing techniques and strategies for working with professionals, including school personnel, to get services for their children.

7. Tutoring their child academically. Advising their child in social areas such as drugs, sex, dating, etc.

8. Using strategies for stepping out of the stress cycle (see Chapter 8).

9. Communicating their own feelings and needs to others, including their children.

10. Appropriately handling their own frustrations, anger, and despair.

Typical personal and social needs parents may have

1. To be listened to.

2. To have both positive and negative feelings accepted.

3. To be respected as competent individuals who can take a strong role in helping the student.

4. To hear from other parents going through similar kinds of experiences.

5. To get occasional time away from their child.

6. To be appreciated for what is going well with their child and in their own lives.

7. To feel free of guilt and the accusatory attitudes of others.

8. To feel a sense of optimism and hopefulness about the future.

9. To have supportive relationships and recognition for their successes and their attempts to implement new strategies in the home for their child.

10. To have a major role in the decision-making process that affects their own program as well as their child's.

Once the particular needs and interests of the families involved are established, teachers can set up parent programs in much the same way they set up programs for their students. Good educational programming strategies work for young people and adults alike. The following recommendations are designed to help develop parent involvement programs that really work:

1. Meet during times of success rather than simply at times of crisis. Help parents see what is going well. Avoid blaming parents for the student's difficulties.

2. Involve parents as much as possible in the decision-making. Offer options as to what will be covered in the parent program.

3. Identify and take advantage of the skills and information of parents, relatives, neighbors, and siblings.

4. Accept the existence of feelings without condoning inappropriate or irrational behaviors that may stem from such feelings. Firm direction may be needed at times.

5. When involving parents in projects to change student behavior or in tutoring: (a) be specific about what they are to do, (b) limit the number of activities they try to do at any one time, (c) check frequently to assess how they are doing, (d) adjust plans when necessary, (e) reinforce parents' behavior frequently.

6. When holding conferences or meetings with parents, have information ready to share, be receptive to parent comments. Expect to develop a sharing, cooperative relationship.

7. When holding conferences with parents, keep meetings small; do not overwhelm parents with the presence of large numbers of professionals.

8. Be flexible in program planning.

9. Maintain the realistic optimism and positive attitudes that are essential to a successful program.

10. Take advantage of mistakes. Learn from them and never let them stand in the way of trying again. It may seem difficult at times, but it can be done. Have fun with the challenge.

Public Law 94–142 outlines only the minimum requirements for parent/teacher interactions. A new and rapidly developing federal emphasis on parent involvement strongly suggests that in both the elementary and secondary years parents will play an increasingly important role in their child's formal education.

Conclusion

To set up strong educational programs for adolescents with behavior disorders, teachers must begin by thinking about theoretical orientation and level of parent involvement. While much remains to be learned about programming for adolescents, it seems clear that the best programs will develop where teachers understand theoretical issues and can use a variety of management techniques to provide students with daily success and challenge. The cathartic approaches currently popular in clinical treatment programs have much to contribute to our understanding of deviant behavior, our theory development, and our success in teaching. When these techniques are intelligently combined with behavioral and psychoeducational techniques, in programs offering strong academic or vocational instruction, adolescents with behavior disorders can make great progress.

By involving parents in early decisions and plans, student opportunities for growth both at home and at school are maximized. As school personnel become more skilled and confident in working with parents, the home/school relationship should become increasingly successful. Once teachers have resolved their theoretical questions and have shared information and planned extensively with parents, they will have established a strong foundation upon which to build their daily instructional program.

References

Auxter, D. M., Zahar, E., & Ferrini, L. Body image development of emotionally disturbed children. *American Corrective Therapy Journal*, 1967, *21*, 154–155.

Berkowitz, P., & Rothman, E. *The disturbed child: Recognition and therapy in the classroom.* New York: New York University Press, 1960.

Berry, K. E. Comprehensive research, evaluation, and assistance for exceptional children. *Exceptional Children*, 1968, 223–228.

Brown, G. B., & Palmer, D. J. A review of BEH funded personnel preparation programs in emotional disturbance. *Exceptional Children*, 1977, *44*, (3), 168–174.

Caplan, G. (Ed.) *Prevention of mental disorders in children.* Sacramento: California State Department of Education, 1961. N. Y.: Basic Books, 1961.

Cruickshank, W., Bentzen, F., Ralzeburg, F., & Tannhauser, N. *A teaching method for brain injured and hyperactive children.* Syracuse, N.Y.: Syracuse University Press, 1961.

Fagen, S., Long, N. J. & Stevens, D. J. *Teaching children self-control.* Columbus, Ohio: Charles E. Merrill, 1975.

Fenichel, C. Psycho-educational approaches for seriously disturbed children in the classroom. In P. Knoblock (Ed.), *Intervention approaches in educating emotionally disturbed children.* Syracuse, N.Y.: Syracuse University, 1966.

Haring, N., & Phillips, E. *Educating emotionally disturbed children.* New York: McGraw-Hill, 1962.

Hendricks, G., & Wills, R. *The centering book.* Englewood Cliffs, N.J.: Prentice-Hall, 1975.

Hewett, F. M. Introduction of the behavior modification approach to special education: A shaping procedure. In N.J. Long, W. C. Morse, & G. Newman (Eds.), *Conflict in the classroom: The education of children with problems.* Belmont, Calif.: Wadsworth, 1971.

Hilgard, E. R., & Bower, G. H. *Theories of learning.* New York: Appleton-Century-Crofts, 1966.

Johnson, W. R., Fretz, B. R., & Johnson, J. A. Changes in self-concepts during a physical development program. *Research Quarterly,* 1968, *39,* 560–565.

Kauffman, J. M. *Characteristics of children's behavior disorders.* Columbus, Ohio: Charles E. Merrill, 1977.

Knoblock, P. A new humanism for special education: the concept of the open classroom for emotionally disturbed children. In P. A. Gallagher & L. Edwards (Eds.), *Educating the emotionally disturbed: Theory to practice.* Report of a symposium, Topeka, Kansas, 1970.

Knoblock, P., & Johnson, J. L. (Eds.) *The teaching-learning process in educating emotionally disturbed children.* Syracuse, N.Y.: Syracuse University Press, 1967.

Lewin, K. Field theory and learning. *The psychology of learning.* National Society for the Study of Education, 41st Yearbook, 1942, 215–242.

Long, N. J. Early experiences: A kite flies against the wind. In J. M. Kauffman & C. D. Lewis (Eds.), *Teaching children with behavior disorders.* Columbus, Ohio: Charles E. Merrill, 1974.

Long, N. J., & Newman, R. G. Managing surface behavior of children in school. In N. J. Long, W. C. Morse, & R. G. Newman (Eds.), *Conflict in the classroom: The education of children with problems.* Belmont, Calif. Wadsworth, 1971.

Maltz, M. *Psycho-cybernetics.* North Hollywood, Calif.: Wilshire, 1971.

Maslow, A. H. *The farther reaches of human nature.* New York: Viking Press, 1971.

Morse, W. C. Working paper; training teachers in life space interviewing. *American Journal of Orthopsychiatry,* 1963, *33,* 727–730.

Morse, W. C. Public schools and the disturbed child. In P. Knoblock (Ed.), *Intervention approaches in educating emotionally disturbed children.* Syracuse, N.Y.: Syracuse University Press, 1966.

Morse, W. C. The crisis of helping teacher. In N. J. Long, W. C. Morse & R. G. Newman (Eds.), *Conflict in the classroom: The education of children with problems.* Belmont, Calif.: Wadsworth, 1971a.

Morse, W. C. Education of maladjusted and disturbed children. In N. J. Long, W. C. Morse, & R. G. Newman (Eds.), *Conflict in the classroom: The education of children with problems.* Belmont, Calif.: Wadsworth, 1971b.

Morse, W. C. Fact and fancy regarding the mental health revolution and its implications for educational programs for the disturbed child. In N. J. Long, W. C. Morse, & R. G. Newman (Eds.), *Conflict in the classroom: The education of children with problems.* Belmont, Calif.: Wadsworth, 1971c.

Morse, W. C. Worksheet on life space interviewing for teachers. In N. J. Long, W. C. Morse, & R. G. Newman (Eds.), *Conflict in the classroom: The education of children with problems.* Belmont, Calif.: Wadsworth, 1971d.

Morse, W. C., Cutler, R. L., & Fink, A. H. *Public school classes for the emotionally handicapped: A research analysis.* Washington, D.C.: Council for Exceptional Children, National Education Association, 1964.

Nelson, C. M., & Kauffman, J. M. Educational programming for secondary school age delinquent and maladjusted pupils. *Behavior Disorders*, 1977, 2(2), 102–113.

Nichols, M. P., & Zax, M. *Catharsis in psychotherapy.* New York: Gardner Press, 1977.

Noland, M., & Gruber, J. J. Self-perception, personality, and behavior in emotionally disturbed children. *Behavior Disorders*, 1978, *4*, 6–12.

Phillips, L. E. Problems in educating emotionally disturbed children. In N. G. Haring & R. L. Scheefelbusch, (Eds.), *Methods in special education*, New York: McGraw-Hill, 1967.

Premack, D. Toward empirical behavior laws: I. Positive reinforcement. *Psychological Review*, 1959, *66*, 219–233.

Redl, F. Strategy and techniques of the life space interview. *American Journal of Orthopsychiatry*, 1959, *29*, 1–18.

Redl, F. The concept of a therapeutic milieu. In N. J. Long, W. C. Morse, & R. G. Newman (Eds.), *Conflict in the classroom: The education of children with problems.* Belmont, Calif.: Wadsworth, 1971.

Redl, F., & Wineman, D. *The aggressive child.* New York: Free Press, 1957.

Rhodes, W. C. Curriculum and disordered behavior. *Exceptional Children*, 1963, *30*, 61–66.

Skinner, B. F. *The behavior of organisms.* New York: Appleton-Century Crofts, 1938.

Spence, K. W. Theoretical interpretations of learning. In S. S. Stevens (Ed.), *Handbook of experimental psychology.* New York: John Wiley & Sons, 1951.

Spivack, G. *The Devereux school behavior (DSB) rating scale: A study of symptom behaviors that appear in the classroom.* Devon, Pa.: Devereux Foundation, 1964.

Strauss, A. & Lehtinen, L. *Psychopathology and education of the brain injured child.* New York: Grune & Stratton, 1947.

Thorndike, E. L. *Educational psychology.* New York: Lemeke & Buechner, 1903.

Trippe, M. J. Educational dimensions of emotional disturbance—past and forecast. In P. Knoblock (Ed.). *Intervention approaches in educating emotionally disturbed children.* Syracuse, N.Y.: Syracuse University Press, 1966.

Ullmann, L., & Krasner, L. (Eds.) *Research in behavior modifications.* New York: Holt, Rinehart and Winston, 1965.

Walker, C. E. *Learn to relax.* Englewood Cliffs, N.J.: Prentice-Hall, 1975.

Watson, J. B. *Behavior, an introduction to comparative psychology.* New York: Holt, Rinehart & Winston, 1914.

Whelan, R. J. The relevance of behavior modification procedures for teaching emotionally disturbed children. In P. Knoblock (Ed.), *Intervention approaches in educating emotionally disturbed children.* Syracuse, N.Y.: Syracuse University Press, 1966.

Involvement with Parents of Behaviorally Disordered Adolescents

Roger Kroth

Within the last few years, parental involvement at the secondary levels in all areas of exceptionality, including the parents of behaviorally disordered adolescents, has accelerated. The movement may be somewhat surprising to special educators, many of whom assume that parents of secondary-level students either never were interested or over the years have lost interest in working with the schools.

As with many social changes, a number of factors contribute to this trend toward parental involvement; particularly Section 504 of the Rehabilitation Act of 1973 and the subsequent passage of Public Law 94-142. These pieces of legislation and the interpretations of them clearly point to parental involvement in providing consent for testing and placement decisions as well as assistance from parents in developing their sons' and daughters' educational plans. While educators have received these laws with mixed reactions, these events have, nevertheless, increased parent/teacher interaction. Perhaps equally important has been the right of parents to review the school records of their children. The Family Educational Rights and Privacy Act caused many school system personnel to reevaluate the information that was being maintained on children, as a number of parents and older students began to review their folders. Of course, as Weintraub (1972) points out, the parents' "right to know" was established in the courts a number of years earlier, and more recent legislation has outlined some of the rights and responsibilities of parents in the education of their own children.

A second factor prompting greater parent involvement seems somewhat more subtle. Almost all early childhood education efforts have had some sort of parent component, varying from programs in which parents learn to teach their own children at home to programs that involve parents in support groups. As the children moved forward in the educational system, many of the parent groups continued and parents became accustomed to keeping in contact with the school personnel. Elementary-school special education teachers have a long history of participation in regularly scheduled conferences and parent meetings. It is not uncommon today to see these same activities being carried on at the middle-school or junior-high-school level. Many teachers of behaviorally disordered children at the middle-school level use daily or weekly reporting systems, hold conferences, send home class handouts and news, make frequent phone calls to parents, and hold informational parent meetings. These patterns of accessibility between parents and teachers have begun to carry over into the high-school levels.

Perhaps a third factor that has increased parental participation is the changing nature of parent organizations such as the Association for Children with Learning Disabilities (ACLD), the Association for Retarded Citizens (ARC), and the Society for Autistic Children. Often the initial struggle of these groups was to obtain programs for younger children. Now that these children are older, the organizations have become interested in providing secondary academic, remedial, and vocational programs. It is significant that the ARC changed its name from the Association for Retarded Children to the Association for Retarded Citizens. It is perhaps only a matter of time until the Council for Exceptional Children becomes the Council for Exceptional *Citizens* and the Association for Children with Learning Disabilities becomes the Association for *Citizens* with Learning Disabilities. These parents have become used to advocating for children and interacting with school personnel. Since a great deal of the involvement has been productive and mutually satisfying, it is only natural that secondary programs will begin to receive more attention.

A fourth factor contributing to the parent involvement movement may be the decreasing size of families. During the 1940s and 50s, it was not uncommon for parents to have 3, 4, or 5 children, but in the 1960s *families began to decrease in size*. Fewer children in the family has meant fewer PTA meetings for parents to attend, fewer conferences, and an increased opportunity to attend to the needs of troubled children. Also, by the time children are of high-school age, there are often not so many younger children at home to keep parents from attending meetings.

Finally, professionals have grown somewhat more receptive to becoming involved with parents. Earlier assumptions that parents of secondary-level students do not care, are not interested, will not come to school, or that the students do not want their parents to come to school are in question. As professionals and parents tentatively extend their hands and find acceptance, the possibility of meaningful interactions is enhanced. Some credit may also be attributed to teacher-training programs, which are offering more and more courses and in-service training sessions on working with parents.

Deterrents to Parental Involvement

1. *Family structure.* By the time a child has reached secondary school, there may have been many alterations in the family structure. Given the rate of divorce in the United States, it is likely that one-fourth to one-third of all adolescents will not be living with their original parents. In the case of exceptional children and their

families, the percentage is likely to be higher. It is also not uncommon to see the behaviorally disordered child living with other relatives on a part-time basis. Grandparents, aunts and uncles, and even brothers and sisters sometimes attend parent conferences or meetings. Because of difficulties and disagreements in the home, children may move in with friends for extended periods of time.

2. *School size.* Another deterrent to parental involvement at the secondary level is the size and complexity of secondary schools. In designing comprehensive high schools with a multiplicity of offerings, school districts have aggregated larger numbers of children and faculty members in large institutional settings. Many secondary schools today have enrollments and course offerings greater than those at many colleges. A request to visit such a school is an adventure that most parents do not relish. The challenge of trying to locate the right room or person among over a hundred can be awesome. In some schools, even the faculty members do not know one another nor where many of the classes are located.

3. *Types of contacts.* At the secondary level, contacts between school personnel and parents, particularly parents of behaviorally disordered students, concern negative events. Because parents of troubled students usually have a long history of contacts with educators over problem situations, a call from school can elicit negative reactions. Recently it was suggested to a high-school teacher that she call one of her students' parents regarding some positive progress by the student. She was at first apprehensive. A week later, she reported that she had made the call, and that the conversation went something like this:

> "Hello Mrs. Smith, This is Bill's teacher."
> "What did he do now?"
> "I just wanted to tell you that he did very well on his last science test."
> "Are you sure you have the right number?"

Because of long-standing histories of problem-laden communications most parents would probably react as Mrs. Smith did. Few parents indicate that their interactions with school personnel are more positive than negative. While school personnel say that they do not have time to make these positive contacts, the payoff is potentially great in that many parents appear willing to be involved in positive programs.

Cautions and Considerations

It may seem inappropriate to explain precautions relative to parent involvement before describing or justifying a variety of programs and activities. The purpose of these preliminary cautions is not to discourage involvement but to highlight the need to educationally analyze parents and families just as an educator would analyze a group of children. Parents of behaviorally disordered adolescents are not a homogeneous group; they represent a wide variety of life styles and resources. Some parents may only have one child, others may have several; some may be wealthy, others may be on welfare; some may be the original biological parents, others may be guardians; some may be well educated, others may have little formal education; some may have strong internal resources, some may be fragile; some may be assertive, others may be submissive. And, of course, there are numerous combinations of these characteristics. It would be a mistake to assume therefore, that all parents of behaviorally disordered youth will respond to a common service strategy.

An excellent article by Doernberg (1978) deals with the negative effect on family integration of even the suitable services which parents are provided. Although the population Doernberg discusses represents families of young physically handicapped children, the concerns expressed apply to parents of handicapped children in all categories and at all levels. She points out that the time and energy devoted to home-treatment programs may erode the family support system. The treatment regime may cause stress in marital relationships and sibling relationships; an inability to carry out the plans may cause feelings of guilt, frustration, and anger. Her thesis is that it is necessary to consider the total family unit in designing parent involvement activities.

Any service that is provided to the family of a behaviorally disordered student is going to have an effect on all family members—for better or for worse. While it may be argued that instructing parents in Gordon's (1970) "no-lose" methods of problem-solving or in a variety of behavioral management techniques may provide the parents with tools that will enrich their lives and assist them during crises, the training does take time—time away from the rest of the family members. For instance, Guerney (1969) presents a number of parent-involvement programs. One, designed by Walder, Cohen, Breiter, Datson, Hirsch, and Leibowitz, teaches parents of behaviorally disordered children behavioral principles, but the program is approximately 16 weeks long. Another program is Guerney's (1965) Filial Therapy program, which is designed to teach parents the techniques of play therapy. It, also, is approximately 16 weeks long. In addition to each group session, which may take from one to two hours, there are homework assignments. Concentrating this amount of time and effort on the behaviorally disordered student may make other family members resentful. One mother confided that she had spent a tremendous amount of time getting appropriate programs for her child, attending due process hearings, and becoming a spokesperson in her community and that now, while her handicapped child was progressing, one of the other children was having a great deal of trouble. Another mother related that, "I've spent so much time providing for my exceptional child that I forgot I had a husband—and then one day I found I didn't have one."

A second problem is that parents are sometimes made to feel guilty if they do not participate as the professionals think they should. A frequent comment around schools is that parents do not care about their children because they do not attend conferences or meetings. The message conveyed to parents is that they are not good parents if they do not participate in special programs designed by the professionals. Thus, if a mother decides to stay home with her children instead of attending a meeting, she is damned; on the other hand, if she comes to the meeting, she is damned for not spending time with her children. A student once reported to the teacher that the reason he had not done well on a particular assignment was because his mother had attended some "dumb" meeting and, therefore, had not been home to help him. The meeting the mother attended was on "how to help your child at home." Important questions that professionals should ask themselves is whether they could afford the time from their own busy schedules to attend the series of meetings that they ask parents to attend and whether the content of those meetings is more important than being at home with their families.

A related problem is that parents of behaviorally disordered adolescents are frequently requested to be involved with a number of different professionals whose services are not coordinated. The professionals may include a school administrator, a special education teacher, a school psychologist, a social worker, a welfare worker, a physician, a probation officer, or assorted other professionals. Trying to cooperate with such a variety of people with different treatment plans and expectations may become overwhelming. Each professional will judge the quality of the parents' participation and some will deem it inadequate. It is entirely possible that the parents of a secondary student may become involved with a professional who wants them to learn behavioral techniques and with another professional who feels strongly that the use of behavior modification with any children, especially adolescents, is inappropriate. Professionals have a propensity toward "tunnel vision" about treatment requirements without considering the values, knowledge, and skills of the parents who are to be involved or other treatments that are simultaneously being recommended.

Educators or service providers working with parents tend to operate from a deficit model rather than a strength model. The reasoning is that since the emotionally disturbed youth is deviant and inadequate socially, emotionally, or academically, then the parents must be inadequate. With this perspective, the educator feels a necessity to teach the parents better parenting skills. While it may be true that all of us could use training in parenting, some parents of the emotionally disturbed demonstrate excellent parenting skills. They may be well read and they may have raised a number of other children quite successfully. Even successful parents can be made to feel inadequate if they are continually put through training programs and placed in groups of inadequate parents. Exclusive use of a deficit model can lower the self-esteem and confidence of a mother and father rather quickly.

One set of parents with four children (three of whom are very successful by almost any set of standards and one of whom is rather unsuccessful by the same standards) continually punish themselves with guilt feelings and statements about their child-rearing practices. They have attended a number of workshops on communication skills, behavioral skills, and so on—some at the suggestion of the professionals in their child's life and some of their own volition. Even though they have successfully raised three children, no one has suggested that they lead groups nor have they volunteered to lead groups, even though they could offer a great deal to other parents. Their strengths and successes have never been appreciated. They have been made to feel like failures because of the problems of one of their offspring.

It is often difficult for conscientious parents to understand or accept the wide variety of influences in an adolescent's life that may affect behavior. Among other things, successful older siblings, strong peer pressure, family relocation, death, sudden shifts in financial conditions, job changes of the parents, poor teaching, and not getting a prized position are all things that individually or together can have significant effects on adolescents' behavior and yet be out of the parents' control. Behaviorally disordered adolescents demand and receive a great deal of adult attention, particularly at times of heightened stress. At this point, one can only guess how deviant behavior may be affected by increased efforts on the part of significant adults during crises.

This section on concerns and considerations in working with parents is not meant to dampen the enthusiasm for professional/parental involvement but to set a tone for much that follows. It is hoped that professionals will carefully analyze the family structure and the demands that are placed on parents. Are we compounding the problem? Are we operating from a deficit model? These and other questions should be foremost in our minds as we plan parent involvement activities.

THE MIRROR MODEL OF PARENTAL INVOLVEMENT

The Mirror Model of Parental Involvement was developed at the Parent Involvement Center in Albuquerque, New Mexico. It is proposed as a guide for involving professionals with parents and parents with professionals and other parents in public school settings. It is meant to be both a deficit and strength model, thereby assuming that parents have a great deal to offer as well as a need to receive. It also assumes that not all parents need everything or that all parents should be expected to provide everything.

Parents have often been the scapegoat for unsuccessful treatment strategies and have seldom been seen as the vital force that makes treatment work. This is particularly common in terms of behaviorally disordered students. Hobbs (1978), taking a rather extreme position that many professionals will find hard to accept, states, "We have to reconceptualize the role of parents . . . . Professional specialists and public school people have deplorably neglected parents in the past. Schools often treat parents as nuisances, but actually they have to be central in any kind of intelligent programming for children . . . . Parents have to be recognized as special educators, the true experts on their children and professional people . . . . Teachers, pediatricians, psychologists, and others . . . have to learn how to be consultants to parents" (pp. 495–496). The first part of Hobbs's statement will probably be agreeable to most professionals, but the last sentence will undoubtedly raise eyebrows.

In our present value system it seems that most professionals have forgotten whom we work for, and we as professionals seem to say to parents, "Put yourself or your children in our hands and we'll take care of the situation." Most people have been conditioned not to question the doctor's advice, the lawyer's legal advice, the psychologist's treatment plan, or the teacher's educational program. The request for a second or third opinion is a recent development to which many professionals have had a difficult time adjusting.

The Mirror Model of Parental Involvement attempts to put the parent back in the driver's seat. The top half of the model assumes that professionals—educators, psychologists, physicians, and others—have information, knowledge, and skills that should be shared with parents to help them be the "special educators" that Hobbs talks about. The lower half of the model assumes that parents have information, knowledge, and skills that can help professionals or other parents be more effective in the roles assigned to them in the growth of children.

The following discussion of the model begins in the middle and works up. The middle strand is labeled Level 1, the second strand Level 2, and so forth. Moving down, the middle strand is labeled 2.1, the second strand 2.2, and so forth.

FIGURE 1   Mirror Model for Parental Involvement in Public Schools

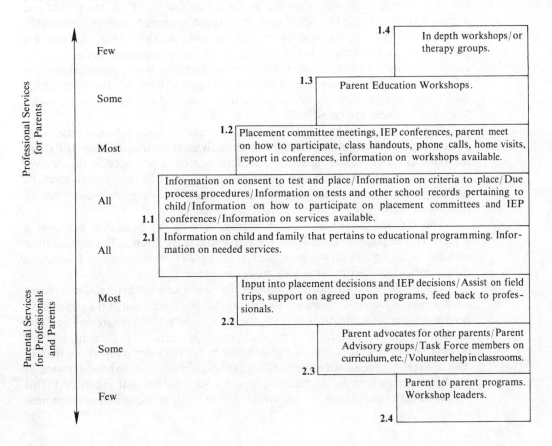

Level 1.1

Level 1.1 is basically an informational strand. In some respects, it may be viewed as a parental or child rights strand. The model assumes that all parents of exceptional children should be provided with this information in a clear and understandable form if their children are to receive services. This is often a neglected area for parents of behaviorally disordered adolescents who have been in special programs or residential centers of some kind. Quite often this information is provided to parents in a throw-away statement during a conference; for example, "By the way, you will need to sign this form so that we can continue Arnold in the program for another year," or "Here's a handbook which you can take home to look over; it explains the rules and regulations. If you have any questions, give me a call." This is not to imply that the professional is trying to mislead the parent intentionally. It may mean that, at that time and in that situation, other issues are more important. It could come back to haunt the professional at a later time if these housekeeping chores are not carefully attended to, at some point, with the parents.

Recently a parent called the Parent Involvement Center. He was the father of a child in a middle-school program for behaviorally disordered students and was concerned about something that had been reported to him by his son in regard to classroom procedure. The father had been unable to reach the teacher and wanted someone to talk to. It was suggested to the father that he phone the school and request a team meeting to discuss how the prescribed procedure fit into his child's plan. He said that he did not know that he could do that. Then he asked for information on the criteria for placing children in the program. Because of the conscientiousness of personnel in the school in question, it was probable that the information had been provided to the parents upon placement. However, at the time it must not have seemed important to the father, and so this question surfaced when the problem presented itself.

It is difficult to make sure that parents understand consent-to-test criteria for placement, consent to place, the right to an Individual Education Plan (IEP), and the right to a due process hearing. This information is provided in the *Federal Register*, each state's rules and regulations, and usually in each school district's handbook for parents. The problem is that legalistic writing is usually boring reading to everybody but lawyers and irate parents.

The Council for Exceptional Children, Reston, Virginia, has prepared a number of one-page handouts that are useful to give to parents. The organization also has a very good filmstrip entitled *P. L. 94–142: Implementing Procedural Safeguards* which can be shown to groups of parents.

The professional cannot assume that the parent of a behaviorally disordered adolescent has received this basic information before. Even though the pupils have been in programs for a number of years, there is no guarantee that parents know and understand the implications of testing, placement, criteria for placement, and due process procedures. It is usually much better to tell the story many times than to wait until the parent is under stress and seeks the information elsewhere. The second challenge is to present the information in such a way that it is well understood. This may involve the use of interpreters, visual aids, or audio tapes, as well as the printed word.

Level 1.2

In addition to the information they have received at Level 1.1, most parents of exceptional students become involved with professionals at Level 1.2. The information obtained and the knowledge gained at Level 1.2 becomes much more personalized. In large school systems the development of "rights, rules, and regulations" information and plans for its dissemination will most likely occur at the district level. The center of activity for Level 1.1 will usually be at the building or classroom level and the teacher will be the major contact with the parent.

The contacts may vary from the formalized, required meetings (such as placement committee meetings and IEP conferences) to notes and phone calls on a random basis. For parents of behaviorally disordered adolescents and their teachers, this becomes a critical and sensitive contact point. Unfortunately, teachers have received very little, if any, training in these very matters. In a survey of two rather large school districts, it was found that fewer than half of the special education teachers had any formalized course work in communicating with parents. Even with in-service training, there are still a substantial number of teachers who have not received any instruction in this area.

The training scene is, however, changing. At the University of New Mexico, one section of one course on parental conferences was offered in the 1972–73 academic year; in 1978–79, seven sections of the course were offered, along with two sections of an advanced course. Heward, Dardig, and Rossett (1979) noted that at the 1972 Council for Exceptional Children Convention 14% of all the presentations contained words such as "parent," "family," etc., but at the 1978 CEC Convention, 28% of the presentations contained these terms. A few years ago, a teacher trainer found it difficult to find a text for a basic course on parent conferences. Publishers considered it a "thin" market and only a few were available (Kelly, 1974; Kroth 1975; Ross, 1964). Within the last year, a number of text books have been published (Coletta, 1977; Croft, 1979; Heward et al., 1979; Kroth & Simpson, 1977; Kroth & Scholl, 1978; Rutherford & Edgar, 1979), providing the teacher trainer with a wider selection.

Just how crucial good parent/teacher interaction may be is difficult to assess. The number of due process hearings and Section 504 complaints that have emerged because of poor teacher/parent communications and professional defensiveness will probably never be determined. It is difficult for teachers to see themselves as consultants to parents and parents as "special educators," as Hobbs suggests. Therefore, many placement committee decisions are made in advance and parents are asked to approve the decisions at a formal meeting. Many parents are beginning to oppose this unilateral decision-making process. For instance, the father mentioned in the previous section, who called the Parent Involvement Center regarding procedural decisions and criteria for placement information, would probably have been satisfied if he had been consulted on the procedural decision made by the teacher. Most parents realize that teaching behaviorally disordered adolescents is a difficult task. The youngster has probably frustrated the parents' attempts at educating him/her for many years.

It is often difficult for the secondary-level teacher to persist in sending home daily or weekly reports or in making positive phone calls because initially there may be little feedback. It is natural for parents to be cautious and slow to establish a relationship with an institution which they have grown to dislike or mistrust. Parents often take a "wait and see" attitude.

It has been found that for teachers of behaviorally disordered students in a large school system there is a sharp decline in frequency of contact with parents from the elementary and secondary level to the high-school level. Whether this is because of training, philosophy, or some other factors is difficult to determine. In special education, the pupil/teacher ratio is similar at both levels.

The teacher is the main source of contact in Level 1.1. Parental involvement may occur in placement meetings, IEP conferences, scheduled or unscheduled conferences, a variety of progress reporting systems, or through informational materials sent home. If these interactions are well done, the parent will be able to gain a great deal of information for decision-making. If the conferences are usually called only to control behavior or to confront crisis situations, then the probability of meaningful interaction is greatly reduced (Kroth, 1979).

Level 1.3

While most parents of behaviorally disordered adolescents will have their information and knowledge needs met by the activities in Levels 1.1 and 1.2, there will probably be some who will need or request further skill training. It should not be assumed that all or most of the parents need to have skill training just because their children are assigned to a behavior disorders or any other special education program. There are many reasons why not all parents should be expected to be involved: they may already have the skill; they may not be ready; they may have other, more pressing concerns; or they may not be available.

Parent education workshops take considerable time to design and implement properly. Some of the procedures for doing this are described in *Getting Schools Involved with Parents* (Kroth & Scholl, 1978). The population of parents should be carefully considered to determine whether the training design is appropriate. In addition, the objectives for the sessions should be identified and obtainable. Many professionals have sat through staff meetings whose only purpose seemed to be that they were scheduled for 3:30 P.M. on Tuesday afternoons. This same mistake should not be perpetrated with parents.

In designing parent education workshops at the Parent Involvement Center, a usual condition is that both teachers and parents involved in the training also function in the planning and implementation of such programs. There are several reasons for this. First, the teacher, through activities carried out at Levels 1.1 and 1.2, may often have a good idea of the needs of the identified parents. Second, the teacher usually has established a trusting relationship so the parents feel comfortable in participating. This also reduces the amount of time needed to establish rapport. Third, it is intended that the teacher will be able to carry on the program with other parents, as needed, at a later date.

There are a number of commercial materials available which the parent group leader can use. These kits, usually requiring a filmstrip projector and tape recorder, provide the leader with a manual and workbooks. For example, the following kits address various phases of parent education: *Systematic Training for Effective Parenting* by Don Dinkmeyer and Gary D. McKay (American Guidance Service,

Inc., Circle Pines, MN 55014, 1976); *Managing Behavior: A Parent Involvement Program* by Richard L. McDowell (B. L. Winch and Associates, P. O. Box 1185, Torrance, CA 90505, 1974; also distributed by Research Press, Champaign, IL); *The Art of Parenting* by Bill R. Wagonseller, Mary Burnett, Bernard Salzburg, and Joe Burnett (Research Press, Champaign, IL, 1977); *Even Love is Not Enough: Children with Handicaps* (Parent Magazine Films, Inc., 52 Vanderbilt Ave., New York, NY 10017, 1975); *Keeping in Touch with Parents: The Teachers Best Friends* by Leatha Mae Bennett and Ferris O. Henson (Learning Concepts, 2501 N. Lamar, Austin TX 78705, 1977).

The first three kits have been used at the Parent Involvement Center with parents of secondary-level behaviorally disordered students. Usually, only part of the kit is used or the training package is used as part of the total program. For instance, in a group whose major objective is developing skills in managing behavior, McDowell's kit on *Managing Behavior* may be used, but it usually is not introduced until the second or third session. A first session activity might include using *Target Behavior* (Kroth, 1972) to identify discrepancies in the perceptions the parents have about their child's real and ideal behavior, or between the teacher's perception and the parents' perception. Discussion of the youngsters' strengths and needs will highlight areas of concern. The first week's assignment may be to observe the child at home for a week, using a format developed at the Center. The second week, the data that parents bring from their observations are discussed. The first filmstrip from the kit may be introduced at this time if it appears that the parents are ready. Throughout the sessions, additional materials are used to supplement the kit and one or more activities from one of the other kits may be used when deemed appropriate.

A basic problem in parent training seems to be that a group leader will select a program such as Parent Effectiveness Training (PET), Systematic Training for Effective Parenting (STEP), or a behavior management program and then want every parent to complete it, regardless of their philosophies or needs. Just as a skilled teacher adjusts the curriculum to meet the needs of students, groups and regroups students for various learning activities, the skilled group leader will adjust the offerings to the needs of the parents. This does not negate the value of kits and programs; rather it is suggested that they be modified when necessary and that they be offered selectively to parents. For example, many parents of behaviorally disordered adolescents will seek to learn more effective communication methods and management and assertive techniques.

A number of texts and other reading materials may be helpful to a group leader. The STEP manual is particularly helpful. *Parent Effectiveness Training* (1970) by Gordon is useful and texts by Cooper and Edge (1968), Kroth and Scholl (1978), and Rutherford and Edgar (1979) have sections on working with parents in groups.

Parent education workshops can be very useful to parents in building skills. Usually they should be kept small (under 10 people) to maximize involvement, should have specific objectives or goals, and should be of relatively short duration (3 to 5 sessions). Stated objectives help to keep the group on task. Parents of secondary-level students often tend to intellectualize by discussing whether children are more troublesome today or reviewing the problems of society as a way of avoiding the hard work of building skill. The value of having a small number of sessions is that parents will see a conclusion to workshop activities.

Level 1.4

A few parents may need therapy sessions or in-depth workshops in addition to the activities outlined for the first three levels. Their physical, emotional, and social resources may be depleted and their coping skills may be at a low ebb. If information, knowledge, and skill building have been provided adequately (Levels 1.1, 1.2, and 1.3) for parents, there would probably be only a few who needed additional help.

In general, therapy is not provided to parents by the school system and this is probably the way it should be. Most communities have mental health centers, guidance clinics, and other agencies with specially trained personnel whose major responsibility is to provide these services. While it may be argued that teaching is treatment and that education is therapeutic, it does not follow that therapy is necessarily educational. Education is the school's responsibility and parents who need therapeutic services should be referred to appropriate agencies.

Level 2.1

Starting at the middle of the Mirror Model of Parental Involvement (Figure 1) and working down, there are a number of levels of information, knowledge, and skills that parents can impart to professionals and other parents. All parents may be expected to provide information that will be helpful in educational planning. The completeness and comprehensiveness of this information will depend upon the enthusiasm, ingenuity, and skill of school personnel. It is probably safe to say that no behaviorally disordered adolescent should be placed in special public school programs unless family history data have been gathered. Two basic questions center on the kinds of information to be collected and the personnel who should collect it.

Typically, in the public schools, there are a number of people who collect information from parents: the diagnostician or school psychologist, the school social worker, the classroom teacher, the special education coordinator or director, and the secretarial staff. There are legitimate reasons for each of these people to be involved in the process of gathering this information; on the other hand, it can be overwhelming for parents to be interviewed repeatedly, especially if the same information is being elicited by different staff members. Conceivably a parent may have to make a number of trips to school or accommodate a number of visits to the home. Data collection activities should be coordinated so that the necessary information is available to the professionals who need it at the least expense to the system and to the parents and without unnecessary invasion of family privacy.

Since they work directly with the child, the two people that have the greatest need for information are the diagnostician or psychologist and the teacher. Unfortunately, these people are often not specifically trained in interviewing techniques with parents. To do an adequate job of evaluating the adolescent, the diagnostician needs to know what the primary language in the home is; whether there are hearing or vision problems that might affect testing; how much, what kind, and how recently testing has been done; whether the child is on medication; what the attention span is; and what is reinforcing to the child. Since many of the tests that a diagnostician uses are based on chronological age, it will also be important to check the date of birth.

In addition to these facts, the teacher will want to know something about the different schools that the student has attended, how the student and parents get along with the school personnel, what the parental expectations are, and other educational insights that the parent can provide.

It would seem desirable for the people who need family, education, and/or social history to develop a form that includes sets of questions. Each person could fill out the information obtained from the family during the total intake procedure. If the form were printed on NCR paper, various members of the team as well as the parents could have a copy, and it should reduce duplication of effort on the part of parents and professionals. In addition, the parents would have a copy upon which to note changes.

Level 2.2

Most parents can provide a great deal of assistance in the placement and IEP decisions. Parents of secondary behaviorally disordered students have usually learned, in a very immediate way, what works and does not work with their children. Unfortunately, many times parents have not been encouraged to be active participants in the process.

In recent years, the Parent Involvement Center staff and public school teachers have been conducting short, one-evening workshops on being an active participant in school planning meetings (Kroth, in press). This activity seems to fit more naturally into Level 2 (what professionals provide for parents) because it helps parents prepare to provide services and information for professionals.

The mini-workshop has the advantage of being an activity for parents of children with any type of handicap. Parents of behaviorally disordered, learning disabled, and mentally retarded secondary-level students have been brought together for evening meetings. They receive a hand-out on ways to be an active participant, with some demonstration and time for discussion. During the session, they are requested to fill out three sheets: one lists issues on which they would like more clarification; one, information they would like to share with school personnel prior to decision-making; and one, suggestions they have for their child's education program. By filling out these sheets before the meeting, they come prepared to interact with professionals. It is also helpful to professionals to know in advance some of the questions and suggestions parents may have.

Many parents of behaviorally disordered secondary pupils can be expected to help in some ways with classroom activities. This may be on a one-time-only basis (helping with a field trip or talking to classes about their jobs and career opportunities). One father, for instance, speaks regularly on an informal basis about his job as an auto mechanic to a high-school class of behaviorally disordered students.

Many parents have successfully reinforced their children's classroom behavior on the basis of daily or weekly report card systems. This works well at the secondary as well as the elementary level if parents are involved in the design and implementation of the program; parents can give important feedback about the effectiveness of this program. When parents and teachers arrange systems for frequent two-way interactions, the possibilities increase for parents to show professionals ways to teach their children.

Parents can also be written into the IEP. Many educators have assumed the responsibility for writing and implementing the IEP, but, since the intent of the law is that this should be a shared procedure, parents should not only assist in the writing of the program but in its implementation. To date, this seems to be done only rarely, but if parents and teachers agree that certain activities should be home-based (such as regular study times, limited TV time, contingent allowance, selected field trips), then parents can provide support for these activities. As true partnerships emerge, it is likely that parents will be more involved in the delivery of services than they have been in the past.

Level 2.3

Some parents can become actively involved in providing even further service to professionals and other parents. If one remembers that parents of behaviorally disordered adolescents are not a homogeneous group, it follows that some parents will have the time, energy, commitment, and knowledge to assist in the improvement of educational programs.

A program in Arizona, designed to train parents to be advocates for other parents, is operated in conjunction with the state's child-find program. Parents or other persons who are interested participate in an eight-hour training program to familiarize themselves with the law and techniques for assisting another parent in interacting with school personnel. These parent advocates are available to other parents whenever needed.

Many school districts have formed parent advisory groups for special education. Much of the precedent for this activity comes from child service projects funded by the federal government which mandated parent advisory groups. Some of these groups have been quite effective, others have been mere formalities; their potential for change depends upon their purpose (Kroth & Scholes, 1978). It would seem reasonable to establish such groups for secondary behavior-disorders programs in large school systems, particularly since many programs at this level are still in the formative stages.

Another important role for parents of behaviorally disordered adolescents is curriculum task force membership. Recently parents at the secondary level have pointed out a need for sex education, special classes in driver education, and vocational and career education, and some parents have community contacts that would be quite helpful in the placement of students in jobs. Parents have been a neglected resource in the area of curriculum development, yet, in some cases, especially with severely behaviorally disordered students, parents will be taking over total care when their child has completed formalized education. Perhaps by starting early with parents on curriculum committees a further liaison can be established with sheltered workshops or vocational-technical schools for furthering the child's education.

A number of parents have become quite active politically. It is unfortunate that groups of parents of behaviorally disordered children and youth have not found the acceptance that parent groups for other exceptionalities have found. Since parents are a diversified group, it is possible that some who find it uncomfortable to work with their own children or school personnel might effectively work for legislation and funds at the state and national levels.

In a recent survey of teachers of behaviorally disordered students at the high-school level (Albuquerque Public Schools, 1978), only about 8% reported that they used parent volunteers in the classroom and only about 30% indicated an interest in using parent volunteers. Although there was a higher interest at the middle-school level, the inclusion of parent volunteers in the classroom remains a question for many teachers.

This is interesting in that "Teacher Mom" appeared to be very successful in an experimental program at the elementary level (Donahue & Nichten, 1964). Part of the problem may be that teacher education programs seldom address the techniques of working with aides or volunteers in the classroom.

Level 2.4

A few parents can provide a significant service to parents and professionals by conducting workshops for other parents. Recently staff members of the Parent Involvement Center conducted a two-day workshop for parents in North Dakota. The purpose was to teach them to conduct workshops for other parents in their respective districts. The parents were nominated by the directors of special education from various districts. The content of the workshops was basically the IEP.

Since the parents were expected to return to their school districts to conduct workshops, it seemed important to present techniques for leading groups. Parents were encouraged to keep the size of groups to 10 or fewer people and were given ideas on warm-up activities that would enable group members to become acquainted. They were also taught how to reflect questions back to the group for group discussion and solution. Then the parents role-played brief sessions, each member alternating as group leader. In addition, they participated in a session on being active listeners (Kroth, 1975) and had an opportunity to role-play this activity, using appropriate body language and questioning techniques.

The general on-site procedure used by the Parent Involvement Center staff for teaching parents to be group leaders is somewhat extensive. After parents have been identified by a teacher or through self-selection, they go through the designed program as participants. They then assist one of the staff members with a group, after which they conduct a group session with staff assistance. The procedure gives the parent an opportunity to build a repertoire of skills and experiences to draw from. If one does not provide a parent with a variety of experiences before he or she takes on a group, the parent tends to draw on experiences with his or her own child. After having been a participant and a co-leader for a few groups, the parent will have had an opportunity to see a number of different situations and a variety of ways in which parents have coped with them. This makes it possible for parent leaders to say, "I knew a parent who tried using . . ." or "One parent, who had a similar problem . . ." rather than having to say, "I tried this with my son." One's own experience is often the most meaningful, but being involved with many parents' experiences also becomes a part of one's own and, therefore, adds a wider range of knowledge and skills for the parent as a group leader.

Educators often resist the idea of parents as group leaders, perhaps because they assume that the emotional disturbance is caused by the home environment and that the parents are not capable of teaching other parents. This is an unfortunate assumption as there are a number of parents who have demonstrated excellent parenting skills with their children, who are knowledgeable and skillful and, with some training, could conduct workshops even though they have a child who is behaviorally disordered. These parents are an untapped resource. Because of their own child's handicap, they often have a high level of interest and commitment. In some cases, they may need to be encouraged to become involved at this level because their self-esteem may have been undermined by professionals who concentrated on their deficiencies as parents rather than on their strengths.

Summary

Within the past few years there has been an upsurge in parental involvement at the secondary level in all areas of exceptionality. Contributing factors to the trend might include mandated parent participation in IEP conferences and placement team meetings, successful programs at the elementary levels which parents want to see continued at the secondary levels, and public awareness programs in the media which may help parents feel more comfortable in acknowledging that they have a behaviorally disordered child.

In their search for meaningful involvement, parents are often faced with large public schools, educators without adequate training in parent conferencing skills, and suspicious attitudes toward parents on the part of professionals. Although there is still minimal training in the teacher training institutions, professionals are becoming more responsive, as witnessed by the numbers of textbooks that have been published in the past few years.

A comprehensive model for parental involvement proposed for public schools gives attention to the parents of the secondary behaviorally disordered student. The Mirror Model of Parental Involvement is meant to be a *strength* model as well as a *needs* model. A basic premise is that parents are the major teachers of their children and that professionals are consultants, as Hobbs (1978) suggests. It also assumes that the greatest part of parental involvement should be at the teacher level rather than elsewhere. Parents need information, knowledge, and skills from professionals—the top half of the model—but not all parents need everything. Moreover, parents can provide information, knowledge, and skills to professionals and other parents—the bottom half of the model—but not all parents can provide everything.

One cannot help but be optimistic about the future of parental involvement at the secondary level. The creative minds of parents and professionals will be put to the test during the next few years to develop innovative ways of fostering and maintaining cooperative relationships. Some old attitudes will die hard. The idea of blaming parents for children's problems and the concept that parents do not care need to be put to rest. There are many benefits to be gained for the student by concentrating on the strengths that parents and professionals possess.

References

Albuquerque Public Schools. Special education task force on parent involvement (behavior disorders). Unpublished report. Albuquerque: Albuquerque Public Schools, May, 1978.

Coletta, A. J. *Working together: A guide to parent involvement.* Atlanta: Humanics Limited, 1977.

Cooper, J. O., & Edge, D. *Parenting strategies and educational methods.* Columbus, Ohio: Charles E. Merrill, 1978.

Croft, D. J. *Parents and teachers: A resource book for home, school, and community relations.* Belmont, Calif.: Wadsworth, 1979.

Doernberg, N. L. Some negative effects on family integration of health and educational services for young handicapped children. *Rehabilitation Literature,* 1978, *39(4),* 107–110.

Donahue, A. T., & Nichten, S. *Teaching the troubled child.* New York: Grune & Stratton, 1964.

Gordon, T. *Parent effectiveness training.* New York: New American Library, 1970.

Guerney, B. G., Jr. *Psychotherapeutic agents: New roles for non-professionals, parents, and teachers.* New York: Holt, Rinehart, & Winston, 1969.

Heward, W. L., Dardig, J. C., & Rossett, A. *Working with parents of handicapped children.* Columbus, Ohio: Charles E. Merrill, 1979.

Hobbs, N. *A conversation on exceptional child education.* Reston, Va.: Exceptional Children, 1978.

Kelly, E. J. *Parent-teacher interaction: A special education perspective.* Seattle: Special Child Publication, 1974.

Kroth, R. L. *Target behavior.* Bellevue, Wash.: Edmark, 1973.

Kroth, R. L. *Communicating with parents of exceptional children.* Denver: Love, 1975.

Kroth, R. L. *Counseling and human development.* Denver: Love, In press.

Kroth, R. L., & Scholl, G. *Getting schools involved with parents.* Reston, Va.: Council for Exceptional Children, 1978.

Kroth, R. L., & Simpson, R. L. *Parent conferences as a teaching strategy.* Denver: Love, 1977.

Ross, A. O. *The exceptional child in the family.* New York: Grune & Stratton, 1964.

Rutherford, R. B., Jr., & Edgar, E. *Teachers and parents: A guide to interaction and cooperation.* Boston: Allyn & Bacon, 1979.

Weintraub, F. I. Recent influences of law regarding the identification and educational placement of children. *Focus on Exceptional Children,* 1972, *4(2),* pp. 1–10.

Individualized Education Programs for Seriously Emotionally Disturbed Adolescents

7

Frank H. Wood

Public Law 94–142, the Education for All Handicapped Children Act, requires that an individualized education program (IEP) be developed for each student receiving special education services. This program, or plan as it is more commonly called by parents and teachers, must include:

(a) A statement of the child's present levels of educational performance;

(b) A statement of annual goals, including short term educational objectives;

(c) A statement of the specific special education and related services to be provided to the child, and the extent to which the child will be able to participate in regular educaional programs;

(d) The projected dates for initiation of services and the anticipated duration of the services; and

(e) Appropriate objective criteria and evaluation procedures and schedules for determining, on at least an annual basis, whether the short term instructional objectives are being achieved. (U.S. Department of Health, Education, and Welfare, 1977, p. 42491.)

Speaking before a large audience of special educators in the fall of 1977, Thomas Irvin, of the Bureau of Education for the Handicapped, reported that more questions and comments had been received about the IEP requirements than any other part of the new law. Some of these questions related to the content of the IEP and others to the due process procedures through which the IEP is to be developed and approved by the student's parents and representatives of the school system.

Why so much concern? The concept of individualized education programs is certainly not new to special educators, therefore reasons for concern must be sought elsewhere. Some complaints stress the administrative burden of implementing the due process aspects of the law which require meeting with parents to explain program plans and secure their signed consent to them. Other complaints focus on the possible liability of teachers to legal sanctions because of a failure to implement some requirement of the law satisfactorily or emphasize the paperwork required to document the implementation of the law's provisions. Beneath all of these concerns, one senses a general anxiety about our competence as special educators; a fear that our areas of inadequacy will now be more exposed to public scrutiny particularly to the scrutiny of parents. Rather than viewing the IEP procedure as an opportunity to show off our professional skills as genuinely exceptional teachers, many of us drag our feet as we approach the preparation and implementation of individualized education programs.

To respond to these concerns, we must become thoroughly familiar with the requirements of the law and the implementing rules and regulations that define the IEP procedure. But, beyond clarifying what the law requires, we should also consider the IEP process from a positive viewpoint: How can IEPs facilitate appropriate instruction for students with special needs? How can teachers and students receive the benefits of individualized educational programming as efficiently as possible? The purpose of this chapter is to suggest to special teachers of seriously emotionally disturbed students ways to use their knowledge and skills to develop useful individualized programs for their students while meeting the requirements of P.L. 94–142.

THE RIGHT TO FREE APPROPRIATE PUBLIC EDUCATION FOR ALL HANDICAPPED STUDENTS

The fundamental purpose of P. L. 94–142 is to assure that all handicapped students "have available to them a free appropriate public education" (U.S.D.H.E.W., 1977, p. 42474). This mandate is not exclusive to this particular legislation. The same right is guaranteed through the broader language of Section 504 of P. L. 93–112, the Vocational Rehabilitation Act Amendments of 1973, which provides that:

> No otherwise qualified handicapped individual in the United States 7(6) shall, solely by reason of his handicap, be excluded from the participation in, be denied the benefits of, or be subjected to discrimination under any program or activity receiving federal financial assistance. (Ballard, 1977, p. 1)

P. L. 94–142 and the implementing rules and regulations contain guidelines to ensure that the rights of parents and their children with special needs to appropriate special education are protected and that the effectiveness of special education programs will be evaluated. In addition, financial assistance is provided to state education agencies and local school districts to offset some of the costs of special education programming. It was not the intent of the Congress that this financial aid would necessarily cover all additional costs of complying with the other provisions of P. L. 94–142, a point that has sometimes been misunderstood. Even without funding, the basic right to education assured through these two acts has been clearly established, and the rules and regulations implementing P. L. 94–142 constitute the standard for judging the adequacy and appropriateness of special education programs being provided.

Since the primary purpose of the present chapter is to provide information useful to special teachers, our review of the specifics of P. L. 94–142 will be selective. A reference to the basic rules and regulations (U.S.D.H.E.W.; 1977) is given in the bibliography. A briefer summary of key provisions has been provided by Ballard (1977). Information about state and local responsibilities can be sought for one's own area. Through them the concept of the individualized education program is established as the foundation stone of an appropriate special education for students with special needs.

The Seriously Emotionally Disturbed as Defined by P. L. 94–142

Because of the additional costs of special education, the definitions of eligibility for reimbursed special services have been the focus of much attention. Under P. L. 94–142, "seriously emotionally disturbed" is defined as follows:

> The term means a condition exhibiting one or more of the following characteristics over a long period of time and to a marked degree, which adversely affects educational performance:
> (A) An inability to learn which cannot be explained by intellectual, sensory, or health factors;
> (B) An inability to build or maintain satisfactory interpersonal relationships with peers and teachers;
> (C) Inappropriate types of behavior or feelings under normal circumstances;
> (D) A general pervasive mood of unhappiness or depression; or
> (E) A tendency to develop physical symptoms or fears associated with personal or school problems.
> The term includes children who are schizophrenic or autistic. The term does not include children who are socially maladjusted, unless it is determined that they are seriously emotionally disturbed.   (U.S.D.H.E.W., 1977, p. 42478)

The referral of a student as a candidate for special education because of serious emotional disturbance should be based on evidence that the student displays one or more of these five characteristics. Are teachers in a position to collect such evidence?

Generally speaking, no. Teachers are not usually licensed to perform several functions required by this definition—the exclusion of intellectual, sensory, or health factors as primary causes; the definition of inferred psychopathology such as a "pervasive mood of unhappiness or depression;" or the linking of physical symptoms or fears to personal or school problems. Although teachers may be asked to document the frequency and intensity of classroom problem behavior typical of the "disturbed" student, the actual assignment of the label on the basis of the criteria in the definition appears to be the prerogative of psychiatrists or psychologists. Thus, in deciding to refer a student for severe emotional disturbance, the teacher is assuming that these other professionals will agree that the student's behavior is indicative of the problems listed in the definition. As mentioned later, there is evidence that teachers view disturbance from a different perspective than these mental health professionals and do not always agree with them about who should have priority for special services or what the nature of such services should be.

Whereas children with the developmentally disabling conditions of childhood schizophrenia and autism come under the provisions of the eligibility definition, a large group of students whose behavior seriously interferes with the educational process, the "socially maladjusted," appear to be denied special services under this act unless they are also certified to be emotionally disturbed. No federal agency has yet defined "socially maladjusted but not emotionally disturbed," so we cannot be certain who is being excluded. In point of fact, it is not likely that many students who are the source of truly serious disturbance in schools will be excluded as "maladjusted but not disturbed" because the numerical limitation on the total percentage of students with all disabilities eligible for special education set in P. L. 94–142 is only 12%. The much larger number of students with milder or more transient problems, for whom the differentiation between emotional disturbance and nondisturbed social maladjustment may be much more difficult, make up 10%–30% of the school population at any given time. They are more appropriately served in the regular classroom than in special programs.

The major limitation of the P. L. 94–142 eligibility definition from the point of view of the teacher charged with individualized educational planning is its lack of educational relevance. When a student comes back from those whom Ullman and Krasner (1969, p. 21) call the "professional labelers" certified as disabled for learning because of inappropriate feelings, moods, psychosomatic symptoms, or fears, the teacher is no further ahead in planning a special education program than when the referral was made. Teachers cannot teach to these characteristics directly without departing in major ways from their traditional classroom role.

Although there will be exceptions in some special settings, the teacher's traditional role as arranger of conditions in the classroom that facilitate the learning and maintenance of academic and social behavior appropriate to the developmental level of the individual student provides a unique therapeutic potential for helping seriously emotionally disturbed students. The therapeutic potential of the teacher's role is more readily realized when an educationally relevant definition of emotional disturbance is used to structure assessment and intervention. Many of the therapeutic interventions practiced by mental health professionals fit with a model of emotional disturbance based on a psychodynamic model of human personality and behavior—the type of model implicit in the P. L. 94–142 definition—but the special teacher will find it more useful to work with a definition based on a behavioral or social learning model (Wood & Lakin, 1978). Thus, while special educators need to be familiar with the P. L. 94–142 definition of emotional disturbance for eligibility reasons, another definition will be suggested as more appropriate for guiding educational assessment and planning.

An Educational Definition of the Seriously Emotionally Disturbed Student

Surveys have shown that teachers tend to define students as needing therapeutic attention more frequently because their behavior is disturbing than because teachers infer disturbance from their behavior. The differences between teachers' judgments of the "seriousness" of problem behavior and those of mental health clinicians that have been reported in the research literature since the time of the Wickman study (1928) are of this type. They probably result more from differences in role requirements and setting factors than from the lack of sensitivity to the significance of feelings with which teachers have been charged (Beilin, 1959).

In crowded classroom settings, teachers find it difficult to accept behavior that is disruptive or disturbing. They tend to project blame onto individual students despite the warning of Rhodes (1967) that problem behavior is systemic in nature and most adequately conceptualized in ecological terms. They can, and frequently do, change their own behavior, however, to facilitate student functioning and cooperate with more far-reaching environmental changes conceptualized and initiated by school administrators and others. Their perspective reflects certain realities of their daily experience. Rather than seeking to restructure the way teachers think about behavior, the definition to guide referral offered here reflects the behavior bias and the student focus of most teachers' views of disturbed and disturbing behavior as the most appropriate place to begin. Acknowledgment is made to definitions previously offered by others, particularly those of Graubard (Dunn, 1973, p. 246) and Ullman and Krasner (1969, p. 11). For educational purposes, we suggest that *the student who is potentially eligible for special educational service as seriously emotionally disturbed is one whose social (and academic) behavior in school settings is judged by teachers and other school personnel to be inappropriate for his/her chronological age and/or grade placement so frequently and excessively that school personnel wish to stop or change it, or to teach new behavior to replace it.*

Let us assume that mental health professionals concur with teacher judgments that students defined by these criteria are indeed "seriously emotionally disturbed." If they do, we are then prepared to initiate educational planning that has a good probability of success.

Steps in the Development of the IEP

The content of the IEP as specified by P. L. 94–142 has already been noted. The steps to be followed in the development and implementation of an IEP can be outlined as follows: (a) informal identification and referral; (b) referral review; (c) formal educational assessment following prior parental approval; (d) development of statement of educational alternatives; (e) meeting with parents to develop the IEP; (f) approval of the IEP by parents; (g) implementation of the IEP; (h) periodic review of the IEP by parents and school personnel with possible reassessment and modification.

Since the language specifying the due process rights of parents is scattered through the rules and regulations implementing P.L. 94–142 and is somewhat technical, it will not be repeated here in detail. All state agencies and many local school districts should be able to provide teachers with guidelines and checklists to facilitate adherence to the proper procedures. For a readable discussion with some illustrative forms, see Reynolds and Birch (1977). A detailed, comprehensive discussion is available in Turnbull, Strickland, and Brantley (1978).

Step 1: Informal identification and referral. Anyone, including parents and students themselves as well as school personnel, may initiate a referral. If the referral is initiated by school personnel or the student, parents should be notified informally early in the process, well before a request is made for consent to a formal evaluation. Parents should be reassured that they have the right to decide whether to proceed with the referral later on, but the early contact prevents surprise and promotes trust. Since the typical organization of the secondary school has the student interacting with several teachers during the day, some plan for coordinating referrals must be established in advance so that this contact will occur. The teacher or other school person taking responsibility for coordination of the referral should record the date and nature of the parent contact. Formal parental consent is not necessary at this point and lack of parental approval does not stop the initial referral.

However, the requirement for informed parental consent prior to formal assessment makes the use of most standardized assessment procedures during the referral process inappropriate. The teacher(s) in whose classroom(s) the student is placed would certainly not be expected to observe a moratorium on educational planning for the student during this period, and data relevant to such planning and related instruction will form part of the justification for the referral and be shared with the referral review committee. Information collected can include anecdotal records of typical behavioral incidents illustrating strengths as well as weaknesses in the student's performance, pupil products, and informal tallies of the frequency of occurrence of significant behavior. Differences in behavior in different settings or when relating to different teachers can be important data. One of the checklists of problem behavior, such as the Quay-Peterson (1967) or the Walker (1968), may be used to provide general descriptions of student behavior and facilitate comparisons of how the student is observed by different teachers.

Step 2: Referral review. While special teachers play a key role in initiating and formulating the IEP, P.L. 94-142 requires that "a representative of the public agency, other than the child's teacher, who is qualified to provide, or supervise the provision of, special education" U.S.D.H.E.W., 1977, p. 42490) be included in the process. Thus, the referral should be reviewed by a school person other than the teacher(s) who initiated the referral or received the parents' or student's request prior to requesting parental permission for formal assessment. The review serves as a check on the informal identification that has been made and often serves to alert school personnel to the needs of mildly or moderately handicapped students for whom adjustments in regular programming should be made even though they do not require special education services.

A decision by the reviewers to begin a formal assessment sets in motion a time clock for the rest of the IEP procedure. If a student has not previously been receiving special services, a meeting to develop and confirm an IEP "must be held within thirty calendar days of a determination that the child needs special education and related services" (U.S.D.H.E.W., 1977, p. 42490). During this time, formal parental consent to the assessment must be obtained, the assessment must be completed, educational programming alternatives must be developed and discussed with the parents, and formal approval must be obtained for the written IEP. Careful advance planning is required to complete these four important steps of the IEP process in the time allotted. Teachers will find it helpful to develop a checklist of important activities with timelines indicated.

The need for such self-regulation by school personnel is illustrated by the fact that in most cases the meeting with parents to develop the IEP must be scheduled before the assessment is completed. The outline of steps at the beginning of this section might serve as the basis for such a checklist, although useful forms are available from state or local sources in most instances.

Step 3: Formal assessment following parental approval. Before beginning the formal assessment, written parental approval must be obtained. It is best that approval be obtained on a prepared, dated form. Parents must be given a reasonable period of time to consider the request and return the form (perhaps a maximum of 10 days); therefore, the need to promptly send or deliver the form to them is obvious.

Since *informed* parental consent is a keystone of the due process procedure, the form sent for their signatures should specify the kinds of assessment to be done, the dates on which they will be done, and by whom. The law requires that all information collected in the student file be made available to parents upon request.

(The issues of personal and institutional liability will be discussed more fully later in this chapter, but in general it can be said that the interests of all involved will be best served by openness and a concern to provide mutual support.) Parents will respond positively to school personnel who take time to educate them about their rights and responsibilities. If they sense that they are being deceived or manipulated, they may withhold cooperation or seek support from external advocate groups—as they should. In spite of the inconvenience of the due process procedures, as professionals we must understand and accept that such procedures exist to protect the rights of parents and students to be served appropriately by a system of tax-supported public schools.

Since many parents do not understand the significance of a written request for approval of the assessment plan, the teacher or some other member of the school staff—preferably one with whom the parents are already acquainted—should contact them by phone to tell them that the form is being sent and to offer to answer any questions about it then or after it is received. In some cases, home visits may be appropriate. Personal experience suggests that parental misunderstanding of the purpose of the procedure and anxiety about what rights they may be "signing away" is a much more common source of parental resistance than deliberate opposition. Thus, we may wish to encourage parents to discuss the request with relatives or friends if we sense a mistrust of the school. The process of obtaining parental consent can be very time-consuming, and in districts or neighborhoods where considerable parental education and follow-up is necessary teachers should have the assistance of school social workers or other appropriately trained professionals. Assistance from such school support personnel is especially needed when the referral suggests serious emotional disturbance in the student since in these cases the disturbance in social relationships will usually be as acute at home as at school.

The assessment should be guided by stated objectives. Given the nature of the P.L. 94–142 definition, assessment in the social/emotional area can be seen as having two components: (a) the determination, in quantitative as well as qualitative terms, of the nature, frequency, and intensity of socially maladaptive or disruptive behavior; and (b) the determination of whether the observed social maladjustment is associated with emotional disturbance. The first type of assessment is the particular responsibility of the special educator, perhaps working in close cooperation with the student's regular class teacher. The second will usually be primarily the responsibility of a psychiatrist or psychologist. Here again, cooperation between the teacher and these other professionals is necessary. (Note: The focus here is on social maladjustment and emotional disturbance. Our discussion deals primarily with the kinds of assessment that should be undertaken by the special teacher. A comprehensive assessment requires the gathering of information on intellectual and perceptual-motor functioning and physical health as well. Such information is needed to test alternative hypotheses about the causes of the problem behavior.)

The educational definition of serious emotional disturbance given above stresses deviance from chronological and grade placement norms as critical factors in the judgment of student social behavior. Educators will find it more useful to assess in the context of a developmental model which contrasts behaviors as more or less "mature" than a sickness model that sees them as more or less "sick," or a moralistic model that sees them as more or less "bad." Reference to some kind of "sequence" or "hierarchy" in the development of social behavior is critical for educational assessment or planning purposes. Although there are important

theoretical differences between the developmental stage-based sequences suggested by developmentally oriented special educators and the sequentially organized hierarchies of tasks developed by those who are behaviorally oriented, they will be found to share many of the same characteristics when used for assessment purposes. Both types of sequences will be mentioned here.

The behavior checklists useful as part of the description of the student's behavior preceding the formal assessment are of little value in the development of educational plans. Like a snapshot, they are static, telling us little about the reciprocal patterns in the student's social interactions with others. However, for many years, such checklists and the similar personality tests were the only instruments available for assessing social behavior, with perhaps the exception of the Vineland Scales of Social Maturity (Doll, 1953) which were developed with reference to the social skills of mentally retarded persons and therefore lack depth and detail when applied to seriously maladjusted and disturbed populations. Fortunately, better procedures are being developed, and if those available do not meet the unique needs of a particular school system or age group, they do provide useful models to guide us in developing our own procedures.

One of the first special educators to present an argument for the usefulness of a sequential or hierarchical perspective on assessment was Frank M. Hewett. In a paper published in 1967, he presented a procedure which he later elaborated in his book, *The Emotionally Disturbed Child in the Classroom* (1968). Hewett suggested that the school performance of socially and academically disabled students would be facilitated if teachers assessed student performance against a series of skill descriptions clustered at seven levels, beginning from the lowest, *attention*, and advancing through the *response, order, exploratory, social,* and *mastery* levels to the highest in the hierarchy, the *achievement* level. He described typical student skills at each level and a procedure for determining the student's functioning level. Hewett has continued to refine and expand the skill descriptions placed at each level of the hierarchy, working in close collaboration with Frank D. Taylor of the Santa Monica Public Schools. The expanded hierarchy and instructions for its use will soon be available (Hewett & Taylor, in press). The new sequence contains many more skills relating to the life situations of chronologically older students and accordingly should be more useful to teachers of older seriously emotionally disturbed students.

The Hewett hierarchy and the others mentioned in this section are basically refined checklists. However, rather than being lists of adjectives describing behavior as "moody," "aggressive," or "hyperactive," they are brief descriptions of skills. Two taken at random from the Hewett sequence are: "Does not pay attention to learning tasks (Attention level)" and "Does not respond to learning tasks (Response level)" (Hewett, 1967). The assessment must be completed by teachers familiar with the student's social and academic performance in particular settings. Beginning at the lowest levels of skills, the teacher moves up through the sequence marking those the student has mastered, those not mastered, and those not observed. At some point in the sequence, the number of unmastered skills increases rapidly. This is the level of special need—and looking ahead, the level for beginning instruction. Thus, the mastered skills become the basis of a description of the student's strengths, skills that must be maintained in the future, and the unmastered skills become the objectives for the instructional program. The student is viewed as a learner whose present level of functioning provides a basis for future achievement.

Mary Margaret Wood has also developed an assessment procedure that places the current behavior of the student with special needs in the context of a series of developmental levels. Working with a team of colleagues at the Rutland Center in Athens, Georgia, and at the University of Georgia, Wood developed a model that drew, like Hewett's, from various theories of child development but stressed personality constructs in its major categories in contrast to Hewett's stress on skills needed for task learning. Wood's procedure has been described in two publications (1972, 1975).

Wood developed a hierarchy of five stages (levels). These are:

Stage I: Responding to the environment with pleasure.
Stage II: Responding to the environment with success.
Stage III: Learning skills for successful group participation.
Stage IV: Investing in group processes.
Stage V: Applying individual and group skills in new situations.

At each stage, representative behavior descriptions have been categorized under four headings: behavior, communication, socialization, and academic skills. Like Hewett, Wood developed an assessment procedure and form. Her general name for her educational treatment program is "developmental therapy," and the form is called the Developmental Therapy Objectives Rating Form, or DTORF for short. Like Hewett's, the DTORF assessment procedure undergoes continual refinement on the basis of field experience, and attention is currently being given to expanding its coverage at the higher levels. The 1975 version has sufficient coverage to be useful in many secondary-level programs with seriously disturbed students, particularly those with autistic or schizophrenic characteristics. However, like Hewett's procedure, the description of skills specific to different secondary-level course content is limited.

Developmental psychologists continue to debate the truth of developmental theories, seeking to establish that normal children do or do not pass through the hypothesized levels or stages. Thus, special educators may encounter those who question the conceptual validity of skill sequences or hierarchies such as those developed by Hewett and Wood. Such criticisms do not diminish the usefulness of these approaches, which propose assessment of performance in terms of a series of skills, covering both academic and social areas, arranged in a sequence that seems to facilitate progressive mastery. Whether normal children master these skills in the same order is a matter for study by developmental psychologists but not a critical issue for special educators. For us, the question is whether such sequences help teachers to assess the present functioning level of individual students and to plan for their continued learning. It seems clear that they do.

Hewett's and Wood's assessment procedures are relatively generalized, but inevitably they reflect to some extent the specific characteristics of the student populations on which they were developed. Whereas some special educators will find them quite adequate for their assessment needs, others may find that their students have performance deficits in areas not well enough represented in the Hewett or DTORF sequences. In such cases teachers can take these assessment systems as a model or use them as a beginning system and proceed to develop lists that better fit their own students. Two examples of such "tailor-made" procedures will be discussed here.

Sheldon Braaten first learned of the Developmental Therapy program in 1973 when he was coordinator of a special school program for elementary-level seriously emotionally disturbed students in Minneapolis, Minnesota. At that time, with consultation from the Rutland Center staff, he introduced elements of the program in his school. A few years later he assumed responsibility for developing a special school program for seriously emotionally disturbed adolescents ranging in age from 13 to 17. Many of these students showed aggressive, acting-out behavior, resembling as a group the "conduct disorder" type described by Quay, Morse, and Cutler (1966). However, most also showed characteristics that suggested underlying severe emotional disturbance.

Braaten and his staff found that the 1972 version of the DTORF scale lacked the range necessary to assess their students. Convinced of the usefulness of the skill sequence model, they set to work to "fill in blanks" with behavior descriptions that fit their student population and setting. The result is the Behavioral Objectives Sequence, excerpts from one section of which are shown in Chart 1. The general format and procedure is similar to that of the DTORF, but instead of five "stages" the BOS has three "levels." To be eligible for admission to this special program, students must have shown an inability to function consistently at Level III, the lowest of the three levels. The behaviors described at that level are those of secondary students who do not relate or work well with fellow students or teachers and whose verbalizations about their behavior are characterized by projections of blame and denial of responsibility. An initial assessment provides the basis for the IEP; as mastery of the lower level behavior is demonstrated, the focus of instruction shifts to the upper levels. When a student performs consistently at Level I in all areas, he or she is considered ready to return full or part time to the regular program. The procedure provides for specification of setting, curriculum, and people factors that may be related to observed differences in student functioning.

CHART 1   Selected Items from the Behavioral Objectives Sequence: Behavior Area (Braaten, 1977)

(LEVEL III)

1. To physically or verbally *demonstrate* awareness of environmental events by looking in the direction of the event or responding to it (appropriate behavior not necessary).
3. To appear alert and able to focus on activities (not excessively tired, under the influence of drugs, or excessively hyper).
4. To attend school 75% of the school days.
9. To bring *NO* weapons or potential weapons to school *100%* of the time.
13. To accept positive or friendly physical contact from others such as a pat on the back or a handshake.
15. To respond when angry without hitting, kicking, spitting, or pushing people (verbal abuse is not included).
18. To *participate* in *non-academic* activities from beginning to end of class period 50% of the time.
23. To accept cue from adult for counseling and/or removal from the situation when angry.
24. To respond when angry *without verbal* threats showing intent to harm someone.

(LEVEL II)

27. Plays or works without interfering with or disrupting work of others.
28. To *spontaneously* participate in *routine* class activities (verbal cues may be used but student displays some personal initiative to comply).
30. To change activity without emotional outburst when change is announced.
34. To respond when angry by *initiating* self-removal from the situation and/or seeking counseling in an appropriate manner.
35. To *complete* individual and/or group tasks *assigned* by *teacher* (includes putting away materials being used and cleaning up).

(LEVEL I)

39. To speak appropriately to others with no cues from adults (includes swearing, use of Mrs., Ms., Miss, or Mr., name calling, etc.).
40. Maintains self-control when faced with failure, problems, or disappointments.
44. To begin, attend, and participate regularly in part-time mainstream classes including vocational programs when appropriate with support from Level I staff.
45. To accept and use support from mainstream resources (demonstrate ability to function successfully independent of support from the outreach staff).

A second example of refinement of an assessment system based on the concept of a sequence of skills is the material published by the Cajon Valley Union School District (California) with the title, *BCP's: Behavioral Characteristics Progression organized as the STEP (Sequential Tasks for Educational Planning) system* (1976). Sets of objectives are arranged sequentially under a number of headings covering a range of social and academic behavior. For example, there are 32 objectives in STEP sequence #5501, "Responsible Behaviors." Here are a few to illustrate the range, which is intended to permit application with students from approximately age 4 into early adolescence: Objective 1: Claims ownership of items and defends possessions physically; Objective 7: Conforms to group decisions despite personal disappointment or disagreement; Objective 32: Conforms to stated and implied rules of conduct for school, play, home, and work situations. As with the other procedures already described, assessment consists of determining the lowest level at which the student consistently performs with success and establishing the immediately "higher" level as that where instruction should begin. Other sequences in the STEP material focus on academic content.

Most of the objectives and sequences in the *BCP* material appear to have been either developed by Cajon Valley teachers or adapted by them from material developed by others. Like the other systems of assessment that have been described, this one is undergoing continuous development and refinement. In 1977, after five years of development, W. D. Stainbeck, Cajon Valley Director of Special Education, commented that it was "still embryonic and evolving. It is hoped that by the time you receive this document, many of the STEP's and the system itself will be outdated through improvement and growth." For a commercially published example of material similar in format to that developed by Cajon Valley but with more ideas about related interventions, see Stephens (1978).

One of the great strengths of the general approach to assessment illustrated in the work of Hewett, Wood, Stephens, and the staffs of the Minneapolis and Cajon Valley schools is its clear relationship to the development of objectives for instruction that form the heart of the IEP. Indeed, in the case of the Cajon Valley material, the assessment process is fitted into a sequenced plan for the development of IEPs. In all cases, the behavior descriptions that form the basis of the assessment translate easily into instructional objectives and related interventions that can be carried out by teachers. The collaborative assessments being undertaken by other professionals (psychiatrists, psychologists, speech clinicians, social workers, and physicians or nurses) to assist in the development of an appropriate educational plan will produce information that may help the teacher to modify or better "individualize" the educational plan that he or she begins to develop as the assessment proceeds, but much of their assessment data will also relate to objectives/interventions that are not in the teacher's area of responsibility. The teacher must never lose sight of the primary question guiding the educational assessment: Does this student have special needs that must be met through special modification of the instructional process? Are these specific to certain classes or settings, or are they apparent across a wide spectrum of school environments? The procedures described will help maintain this educational focus.

Step 4: Development of a statement of educational alternatives. On completing an assessment of the type described, the special educator has an overall picture of the seriously emotionally disturbed student's social and academic performance in school settings and is ready with tentative statements of annual goals and short-term objectives. Now it is time to think about two other questions: What is the best instructional strategy for making progress toward these objectives and goals? What is the least restrictive environment in which such a strategy can be implemented? To answer these questions requires that special teachers assess their own resources and those of the schools in which they teach. The attitude to maintain as one undertakes this phase of program development is that of the responsible, competent professional: These are the resources I can bring to bear that should prove helpful in facilitating this student's learning. Educators should avoid the negative, resistant, "can't do" attitude sometimes encountered.

American high schools are usually organized on a departmental model in which teachers are responsible for specific subject matter and students move from room to room during the school day, studying first one subject and then another according to their schedule. This arrangement makes it necessary for students to adjust to numerous adult, setting, subject matter patterns during the day. Adult expectations and teaching styles will inevitably vary greatly. Secondary schools also often house a number of building-based support personnel such as assistant principals and counselors who will have certain effects on the school experience of students with special emotional needs. From one point of view, this variety makes the adjustment of such students more difficult; from another, the possibilities for special programming are made greater by the range of options. In some systems they are extended by the existence of alternative schools, work-study programs, vocational training programs, and others (Jordan, 1978).

But if the range of placement opportunities is often greater at the secondary than at the elementary level, the logistics of arranging appropriate placements are usually quite difficult. Committed to a narrow specialization and already responding to large numbers of students each day, secondary-school personnel may resist making accommodation to the needs of an individual special student. To actualize a plan that taps the potential of the total secondary-school program, the special educator must often be a persuasive advocate as well as a skillful assessor and planner. When out-of-the-building placements are required, the assistance of the special education supervisor or coordinator will also be needed.

Whenever possible, several alternative educational plans should be developed to bring into the IEP planning meeting with the parents. Often it will be helpful if the special teachers and supportive staff can share their thinking about the alternatives they see developing in advance of the formal IEP conference, but premature decisions must be resisted. The goal is to develop possibilities and involve the parents in planning rather than to "sell" them a predetermined plan.

Step 5: Meeting with parents to develop the IEP. The contents of the IEP required by P. L. 94-142 were stated at the beginning of this chapter. It is further stipulated that the participants at the conference where the IEP is drawn up include the teacher, another representative of the school who is qualified to supervise the provision of special education services to the student, one or both of the student's parents, other school personnel if their presence is considered by the school to be helpful to the planning process, and, if appropriate, the student. As already mentioned, it is the responsibility of the school to inform the parents of the time and place of the proposed meeting sufficiently in advance so that undue hardship in attending is avoided. Records should be kept of contacts and efforts to contact the parents so that full documentation is available should the good faith of the school's efforts be questioned.

The special teacher should take an active role in the negotiation of the IEP. Often we educators are too passive in such conferences. Having played a major role in the assessment process and preparing for one in the implementation of the IEP, we need to clarify for ourselves and the other participants our responsibilities and expectations (Wood, 1968).

The purpose of the meeting is to inform the parents of the results of the assessment, discuss with them the alternative special service options available, and agree on a final plan to guide the student's education for the following year. The plan should be formulated in final form at the meeting, if possible. Given the range of alternative placements sometimes available, final parent approval may depend on their visit to an alternative setting. Parents do not have to sign the form at the meeting and should certainly not be asked to sign a blank form to be filled in later. Some very legitimate grievances have developed when these procedures were attempted.

The special teacher responsible for providing services to the child will often be asked to coordinate the writing of the formal IEP and, in any case, should be familiar with its typical contents. Expanded from the minimal essentials of our earlier list, these include: (a) names and identification of the participants at the meeting; (b) a list of areas of student functioning assessed, the assessment procedure used and the person responsible for the assessment, and the date when the assessment took place; (c) a summary of the strengths and weaknesses revealed by the assessment; (d) a statement of the annual goals and short-term objectives to be achieved by the special educational program; (e) the services to be provided to achieve the goals and objectives and the persons who will provide them; (f) a justification of the plan as the least restrictive environment; (g) the date of meeting(s) to review the student's progress and the continuing appropriateness of the IEP. In most cases, local education agencies have prepared forms that provide space for the necessary information so that the main responsibility of the teacher is the compilation and condensation of information for the purposes of the form.

The amount of time and work that goes into the preparation of a formal IEP must not be minimized. In many cases, the work is passed on to the special education teacher who is given forms and instruction manuals intended to make the process as simple as possible while ensuring compliance with the law. Because of the heavy connotations of legal liability, the actual limits of which will be noted later, teachers have compared the experience to that of completing one's annual income tax statement. Although the preparation of an IEP is a hard but necessary chore, we need to remember that the concept of the written IEP, developed with careful attention to due process procedures, was introduced into the legislation at the urging of parents and child advocates; its purpose is to improve the educational opportunities provided children with special needs rather than to make the job of the professional teacher easier.

Some special issues make the preparation of formal IEPs for seriously emotionally disturbed students even more difficult than it is for other types of disabilities. Despite our fondness for assigning the "blame" for disturbance to individuals, disturbance is pervasive in the systems in which the disturbed and disturbing interact. Negative thought patterns such as projection and denial and negative emotions such as fear, anger, and hostility often influence the interactions when parents, students, and school personnel meet. It has been noted that the rules for developing the IEP state that the student may be present at the planning meeting "where appropriate" (U.S.D.H.E.W., 1977; p. 42490). Some special developmental considerations make this a critical question where secondary-level emotionally disturbed students are concerned.

As children mature socially, their efforts to establish their autonomy as individuals become more intense (Erikson, 1963, 1968). Adolescence is a stormy period in the relationships between many young people and their parents. It is usually acutely so in the case of seriously disturbed students. Instances of "abnormal" social and emotional attachment or alienation (abnormal in the sense of being extremely atypical for those of the same age) occur frequently. Often it is traumatizing for parents and students to sit down with authority figures such as school personnel to talk about goals and objectives for the student that imply changes in present behavior. Efforts should be made to avoid causing unnecessary pain. Unless we are very certain that the student's presence will facilitate constructive interaction, the best rule is that he or she not be present at the same IEP meeting as the parents.

But what about the student's need to develop a sense of personal autonomy and identity as an individual? There seems to be no question that many special educational plans for disturbed adolescents are not successfully implemented or have only superficial effects because the students feel that the plans have been "laid on" by others. Lefcourt (1973) has reviewed research on the effects of a sense of freedom in contrast to a sense of control by others on the behavior of the individual and concluded that the loss of what he calls the "illusion of freedom" is harmful.

The best solution is to discuss goals and objectives with the student both during the assessment period and following the meeting where the IEP is developed. The word *discuss* is used here with the recognition that each student must be approached in a way that he or she can best understand. With some students a negotiation of objectives or methods for reaching them may be appropriate. The IEP may even become the basis of a formal contract in which the student agrees to make specified changes in his or her behavior in return for specified rewards or recognition by parents and teachers (Polsgrove, 1979). For others a respectful stating of the objectives together with an assurance of careful monitoring of the student's responses to instruction and necessary adaptations to facilitate learning may be sufficient. The key point is the involvement of the student in the manner that is most appropriate.

There are some special issues that must sometimes be negotiated with the parents of seriously emotionally disturbed students during the formulation of the IEP. If tangible rewards are to be used, parents should understand how they are earned. On occasion the author has known parents to forbid the giving of tangible rewards because they objected in principle to their use and felt that an example was being set with their son or daughter at school that produced conflict at home. In another case a student was beaten by his father when he brought home a model kit because the father did not believe his story about earning it at school and assumed it had been stolen.

The use of time-out periods or isolation rooms can also be a source of later conflict if they are not fully explained to parents as part of the IEP. While their aversiveness must be recognized and their abuse guarded against, such measures may be justifiable in certain situations (Wood & Lakin, 1978). However, any use of such procedures must be open and well regulated, with parents regularly informed of the nature and frequency of use.

Another topic to be addressed at the IEP conference is the possible prescription of medication for the student or concurrent involvement in psychotherapy. These services are not among those for which the student is eligible at public expense under the provisions of P.L. 94–142. However, in many cases, students may be receiving them through another public agency or at parental expense. If information about such services is not available to school personnel during the assessment period, it is still appropriate to ask the parent about them during the conference. Parental disclosure of such information is not required and, since the school does not provide them, their availability to the student may not be made a condition for the receipt of other services. However, the predicted relationship between concurrent noneducational therapeutic treatment and success of the school program can be noted in the written IEP.

Some secondary-level emotionally disturbed students will be known to the police or may even be on probation for past offenses. It is appropriate to discuss the nature of such involvements with parents at the conference. School policies related to permitting students to be interviewed on school premises by police or probation officers should be discussed at the meeting. Again, such contacts cannot be made a condition of the IEP because these services are not under the control of the school.

Occasionally certain secondary-level emotionally disturbed students lose control and become so aggressive toward persons or property that they cannot be managed in the school environment. School policy in handling such situations should be explained to parents at the time of the IEP conference. They should be assured that efforts will be made to contact them and to cooperate with their wishes prior to the involvement of police or nonschool mental health personnel. However, it is important for both parents and students to know that school personnel have a prearranged plan of action for such extreme situations.

Another conference issue involve transportation. Does the proposed program require transportation of the student? If so, who has the responsibility for providing it? Is transportation provided by the school on the condition that acceptable behavior is maintained by the student? These fundamental issues regarding transportation may need to be discussed at the IEP conference if they are important conditions of the school's ability to carry out the proposed program.

While some of these special issues are awkward to discuss with parents, it is in the best interests of all parties that they be brought into the open at the IEP meeting and that any special parental consent necessary be obtained. It is true that, in most cases, the issue will remain moot; however, too many serious situations develop suddenly and unexpectedly to believe that it is possible to get the necessary understandings worked out "later on if they are needed." Sound professional programs are characterized by good advance planning.

The largest number of unresolvable disagreements between parents and school personnel arising during the IEP negotiation process seem to center on two issues: the amount of time students are to spend in the regular mainstream program and the extent and quality of special supportive services to be provided as part of the educational program. Often these involve the commitment of resources that the special teacher does not control and, therefore, they are best left to administrative personnel. The special teacher's obligation is to develop a program based on what he or she has to offer that will meet the students' needs. If parents insist on more (a residential school) or less (full-time in the regular classroom) or on the provision of services which the teacher is not trained to provide (daily sessions of neuromuscular patterning), the initiative in the further negotiation of the IEP will have to be taken by others. The regulations implementing P.L. 94–142 describe the hearing and appeals process to be followed in resolving such disputes. The special teacher's formal responsibility probably ends with the obligation to inform dissatisfied parents about the existence of such procedures.

Step 6: Approval of the IEP by the parents. In almost all cases parents will be ready to sign the form indicating their approval of the individualized education program worked out for their child. They have the right under law to consider the plan for a reasonable period of time before signing and may in the interim consult with advisers of their choosing if they wish. As a matter of fact, even after they have signed, they have the right to withdraw their consent if they see fit to do so. Teachers need not become anxious reflecting on such possibilities for they will seldom occur.

Step 7: Implementation of the IEP. Once the IEP is approved by parents, its provisions must be translated into action as soon as possible. Thus, if there is to be a delay in the provision of any service, the length of the delay should be specified and agreed to by the parents in the signed IEP.

Much work is required to translate the general goals and short-term objectives of the IEP into daily instructional plans. One of the strengths of the type of assessment which has been recommended in this chapter is the direction it gives to the preparation of such plans. The sequences of skills also make useful checklists to guide monitoring of student progress. Hewett and Taylor (in press), Wood (1975), and Stephens (1978) all provide suggestions for instructional activities related to their respective sequences, but these should be regarded only as suggestive. Other chapters in this volume describe a variety of instructional strategies, both psychoeducational and behavioral, that will prove useful.

Regular evaluation of student performance and recording of the results is an important part of ongoing instruction. Written anecdotes, sequentially arranged behavior checklists, charts and graphs—the procedure used can be chosen to fit the style of the individual teacher. The important thing is to form the habit of keeping a regular daily or, at most, weekly record. It is sensible to use shortcuts, such as summary forms and standardized procedures, and to involve others such as aides or students themselves, but there is no way to avoid this task if you wish to have a quality program. Try to obtain the same kind of information about the student's performance in other school settings. Plan—implement—observe what happens—record your observations—plan and repeat. This remains the pattern for efficient instruction.

Step 8: Periodic review of the IEP by parents and school personnel. The individualized education program is a statement of intent. When it is implemented, things change—or they do not change. In any case, regular review of student progress and comparison with the goals and objectives of the IEP is necessary. P.L. 94-142 requires that the IEP and student progress be reviewed at least once each year (U.S.D.H.E.W., 1977, p. 42490). State or local policy may require more frequent reviews. In a sense, each review involves a repeat of Steps 3 through 6, although, since the student is now receiving special education services, the effects of such services will now be known. This review provides educators an opportunity to summarize and share the results of the ongoing assessment.

While the author's experience makes him cautious about predicting the number of students who progress sufficiently to be able to return full time to the regular classroom without some supportive services, the need for continued placement in special settings must always be addressed at review conferences. After experiences that desensitize them to large groups and enable them to master some basic social skills, severely disturbed students with psychotic and autistic characteristics can often be placed with benefit in regular classrooms for at least part of the day if supplemental support from an aide is available as needed. The opportunity to teach regular students to accept the variability of human behavior through such experiences should encourage us to make the trial. Except in rare cases, students should spend some part of each day in the company of typical peers.

A record should be made of the date and content of any review meeting. Any major changes in the original IEP should be written out and approved in writing by the parents.

The Issue of Professional Responsibility

Conscientious teachers provide their students with the best instruction of which they are capable. The results are not always pleasing to parents, students, or the teachers. The disparity between effort and results exists in most professions. Despite the best efforts of doctors, some patients are not cured, and despite the best efforts of lawyers, some clients are found guilty. The issue of professional responsibility, then, is only partly one of accountability for outcome. It is primarily an issue of accountability for good professional practice. The rules and regulations implementing P.L. 94-142 make this clear:

> Each public agency must provide special education and related services to a handicapped child in accordance with an individualized education program . . . .

However, . . . the Act does not require that any agency, teacher, or other person be held accountable if a child does not achieve the growth projected in the annual goals and objectives. (U.S. D.H.E.W., 1977, p. 42491)

What *are required* are "good faith efforts to assist the child in achieving the objectives and goals listed in the individualized education program" (U.S. D.H.E.W., 1977, p. 42491).

Special teachers who carry out their professional duties as suggested in this chapter will be making good faith efforts and, more importantly, will be facilitating the growth of most seriously emotionally disturbed students.

Conclusion

The responsibility of special educators to prepare, implement, and review individualized education programs for their emotionally disturbed students has always been recognized as good professional practice. With the passage of P.L. 94–142, the Education for All Handicapped Children Act, and the rules and regulations which implement it, the preparation of IEPs is now required. Fortunately, since the IEP concept was already in practice, educationally relevant definitions of emotional disturbance and related assessment procedures and intervention strategies are available. As conscientious and competent educators, our task is to use these resources.

References

Ballard, J. *Public law 94–142 and Section 504—Understanding what they are and are not.* Reston, Va.: Council for Exceptional Children, 1977.

BCP's: Behaviorial Characteristics Progression organized as the STEP (Sequential Tasks for Educational Planning) system. Cajon Valley, Calif.: Cajon Valley Union School District, 1976.

Beilin, H. Teachers' and clinicians' attitudes toward the behavior problems of children: A reappraisal. *Child Development*, 1959, *30*, 9–12.

Braaten, S. *Madison School Behavioral Objectives Sequence.* Minneapolis, Minn.: Minneapolis Public Schools, 1977.

Doll, E. A. *A manual for the Vineland Social Maturity Scale.* Minneapolis: Educational Test Bureau, 1953.

Dunn, L. M. (Ed.) *Exceptional children in the schools: Special education in transition* (2nd ed.). New York: Holt, Rinehart & Winston, 1973.

Erikson, E. *Childhood and society* (2nd rev. ed.). New York: Norton, 1963.

Erikson, E. *Identity: Youth and crisis.* New York: Norton, 1968.

Hewett, M. Educational engineering with emotionally disturbed children. *Exceptional Children*, 1967, *33*, 459–467.

Hewett, M. *The emotionally disturbed child in the classroom.* Boston: Allyn & Bacon, 1968.

Hewett, F. M., & Taylor, F. D. *The emotionally disturbed child in the classroom* (2nd Ed.). Boston: Allyn & Bacon, in press.

Irvin, I. The Education for All Handicapped Children Act of 1975: Public Law 94–142 regulations. In J. Smith (Ed.), *Personnel preparation and Public Law 94–142: The map, the mission and the mandate.*

Jordan, J. B. (Ed.). *Exceptional students in secondary schools.* Reston, Va.: Council for Exceptional Children, 1978.

Lefcourt, H. M. The function of the illusions of control and freedom, *American Psychologist*, 1973, *28*, 417–425.

Polsgrove, L. Self control: Methods for child training. *Behavioral Disorders*, 1979, *4*(2), in press.

Quay, H. C., Morse, W. C., & Cutler, R. L. Personality patterns of pupils in special classes for the emotionally disturbed. *Exceptional Children*, 1966, *32*, 297–301.

Quay, H. C., & Peterson, D. R. *Behavior problem checklist.* Champaign, Ill.: Children's Research Center, University of Illinois, 1967.

Reynolds, M. C., & Birch, J. W. *Teaching exceptional children in all America's schools: A first course for teachers and principals.* Reston, Va.: Council for Exceptional Children, 1977.

Rhodes, W. C. The disturbing child: A problem of ecological management. *Exceptional Children*, 1967, *33*, 449–455.

Stephens, T. M. *Social skills in the classroom.* Columbus, Ohio: Cedars Press, 1978.

Turnbull, A. P., Strickland, B. B., & Brantley, J. C. *Developing and implementing individualized education programs.* Columbus, Ohio: Charles E. Merrill, 1978.

Ullman, L. P., & Krasner, L. *A psychological approach to abnormal behavior.* Englewood Cliffs, N.J.: Prentice-Hall, 1969.

U.S. Department of Health, Education, and Welfare, Office of Education. Education of Handicapped Children: Implementation of Part B of the Education of the Handicapped Act. *Federal Register*, *42*(163), Tuesday, August 23, 1977, Part II, 42474–42518.

Walker, H. M. *Walker problem behavior identification checklist: Manual.* Los Angeles: Western Psychological Services, 1968.

Wickman, E. K. *Children's behavior and teacher's attitudes.* New York: The commonwealth Fund, Division of Publications, 1928. (Quoted and discussed in various periodicals reviewed.)

Wood, F. H. The educator's role in team planning of therapeutic education placements. *Exceptional Children*, 1968, *34*, 337–340.

Wood, F. H., & Lakin, K. C. (Eds.) *Punishment and aversive stimulation in special education: Legal, theoretical, and practical issues in their use with emotionally disturbed children and youth.* Minneapolis, Minn.: Department of Psychoeducational Studies, 1978.

Wood, M. M. (Ed.) *The Rutland Center model for treating emotionally disturbed children* (2nd ed.). Rutland, Ga.: Georgia Psychoeducational Center Network, 1972.

Wood, M. M. (Ed.) *Developmental therapy.* Baltimore, Md.: University Park Press, 1975.

Therapeutic Management: A Psychoeducational Approach

Nicholas J. Long
Stanley A. Fagen

The therapeutic management of emotionally disturbed adolescents requires a complex set of teacher behaviors which need clarification and elaboration. Therapeutic management is the most demanding, difficult, complex, and challenging part of being a special educator and a prerequisite to effective classroom instruction. With specific training and supervision, therapeutic management can be learned and internalized as a way of life rather than a bag of tricks. Therapeutic management involves the dynamic understanding of the psychosocial forces coming from the pupil, the groups, the social atmosphere, the physical setting, the learning task, the instructional method, and the school, family, and community norms. All of these forces are processed through the teacher who has the responsibility for developing, maintaining, and enforcing minimal behavioral values, standards, and limits. The first problem is: Whose standards and what limits? Many an adolescent is justified in voicing a concern about how he is treated and what code he is expected to accept. Often, when these rules are examined, they support adult comfort, convenience, and a host of arbitrary issues. Yet the basis of therapeutic management must reflect the basic human values in our society, such as fair play, the protection of nonexploitive interpersonal behavior, the right to individual self-esteem, and respect for property and the community. Therapeutic management means teaching, modeling, and respecting these values in all interpersonal relationships, although these values are rarely put into full practice in our society.

Of course there can be no therapeutic management in a punitive, suppressive setting. Unfortunately most teachers want to punish adolescents when adults "have had it." Frequently the intervention is not done to teach but to relieve adult anger, rage, or confusion. Morse (1976) and Redl (1959) have made it clear that reality should be the basis of intervention rather than adult authoritarianism, whims, or righteousness over a given state of order.

One of the most important and least understood aspects of therapeutic management is that it is based more on the nature of the relationship between teacher and pupil than on the specific management technique a teacher may use. This is why we say that all significant learning, including control of behavior, evolves and revolves around the teacher. This relationship is extremely demanding and complex because each teacher must struggle with his history to understand how certain feelings and conditions lead him to respond differentially to various adolescents: that is, to experience empathy with certain pupils, tolerance toward others, and disgust, anger, and rejection toward still others. No teacher has a symptom-free history or the capacity and the skills to work therapeutically with all of the pupils assigned to the classroom. All teachers carry their history with them including some unfinished psychological problems, attitudes, and prejudices toward authority, peers, learning, rules, and self. This is why some teachers are more comfortable relating to aggressive pupils and others to dependent, anxious pupils; still other teachers can accept the confusion and infantile behavior of an autistic pupil whereas others will react to this same pupil with irritation and disgust. As a result, the same management techniques used by these two teachers on the same autistic pupil could have significantly different outcomes. This is why we accept Behavior Modification as *a* technique and not as *the* technique and why we believe the "Great Teacher Syndrome" is an educational myth since the nature of the teacher-pupil relationship is the vital part of learning.

Once a teacher understands why his mental health is an important part of therapeutic management, he can focus on what the pupil is doing to him that causes him to perpetuate or intensify the pupil's emotional problems. In plain language, the teacher's task is to make sure the adolescent's belief that the teacher is there to hurt, deprecate, and fail him is not fulfilled. This concept is expressed as one of our training principles: *A pupil in stress can arouse in you his feelings and, if not trained, also his behavior.* This is why many untrained, basically unaggressive high-school teachers can end up being counter-aggressive and tell a defiant pupil, "You said you won't do it and I'm telling you, *You will* do it!" It is fascinating and alarming to know how emotionally disturbed adolescents can get teachers to take on their personalities and behaviors during emotional conflicts and why many of the behavior modification techniques are not used during moments of interpersonal conflict. To prevent this from happening, this chapter will focus first on the teacher's reactions to the pupil's stress cycle and second on specific classroom management strategies.

THE STRESS CYCLE

For years teachers have been reporting that many emotionally disturbed adolescents can get them to behave in irrational ways. One mild-mannered English teacher expressed this problem with feeling, "Each night I promise myself I will not lose my temper with Peter, but by 11 A.M., after he has done all his passive-aggressive tricks on me, i.e., not remembering what I said, not hearing the instructions, always diddling around with a smirk on his face, I want to kill the little bastard!"

To understand this painful interaction, Long has developed a paradigm called the Stress Cycle. This model describes how the transaction between pupil and teacher follows a circular process in which the attitudes, feelings, and behaviors of the teacher are influenced by the attitudes, feelings, and behaviors of the pupil. During a stressful incident, this circular process becomes a stress cycle, creating additional problems for the pupil and the teacher. Once in operation, this negative interplay between pupil and teacher is extremely difficult to interrupt. For example, we know that adolescents under stress behave more emotionally than rationally. They protect themselves from physical and psychological pain by becoming defensive, primitive, and regressive. If the teacher reacts to these inappropriate behaviors impulsively or with righteous indignation, a "power struggle" develops in which understanding and helping disappear and "winning" becomes the only acceptable outcome for the teacher. To understand the dynamics of the stress cycle and the power struggle and what the teacher can do not only to prevent them but also to change the stress cycle to a coping cycle, the following questions will be answered: (a) What is stress? (b) How does stress manifest itself? (c) What are the various types of stress? (d) How does stress lead to the pupil-teacher stress cycle? (e) What can teachers do to promote coping with stress?

What is Stress?

Stress is defined as a personal and subjective reaction to a specific life event, causing the individual to experience physiological discomfort. Stress can be experienced not only in response to real situations but also to anticipated and imagined ones.

Stress is not intrinsically good or bad. As educators we must help pupils view stress as a normal, natural, and accepted fact of life. The usefulness of stress, however, depends on its *frequency*, *intensity*, and *duration*. If all stress were eliminated, pupils would become lackadaisical and passive. Too much stress overwhelms them, causing psychological panic and thinking disorders. However, the right combination of stress motivates pupils to new levels of creative and problem-solving activities. The ability to master stress becomes the primary source of building pupils' feelings of competence, success, and positive self-esteem.

How Does Stress Manifest Itself?

Although stress was first studied as a medical problem in the early twenties, researchers are just beginning to understand how it functions and what impact it has on the mental health of individuals. First, there is a single basic biological response to a stressful incident. This response is automatic, unconscious, and very predictable. Stress prepares the body for action by releasing a series of hormones into the bloodstream which activate the autonomic nervous system. This system controls the involuntary muscles, altering the blood pressure, respiration, and digestive system. Anthropologically, stress functioned as a personal alarm system enabling a person to survive an attack. During this stress state, all bodily senses are intensified. The person has an abundance of energy, with increased levels of strength, agility, and endurance. The person may either attack a foe with new ferocity or escape by running great distances without tiring. In either case, stress served a very useful, specific, and important purpose for primitive man and may have formed the basis of his survival.

However, in today's complex society there are many rules against attacking or running away. Pupils must learn to control what their bodies are urging them to express, and to cope with this state of stress instead of acting it out. Since self-control takes considerable skill and maturity and is a difficult task even for adults, we can expect that even "normal" adolescents will break down and act inappropriately at times.

If this interpretation of human behavior is true for the average pupil who has been protected from chronic life stresses, what about the few pupils who have been flooded by stress and have emotional problems? For these adolescents even the normal life stresses can become difficult and overwhelming. Many of these pupils are woefully lacking in coping skills. In fact, they perceive themselves as incapable, defective, or victimized by stress. They feel the only solution for them is to escape from the situation as quickly as possible. The behaviors they choose may include aggressive outbursts, such as throwing objects, cursing, threatening another; or they may follow withdrawal-defeat behaviors such as giving up, sobbing, staring into space, refusing to talk, inattention, and passivity. Eitherway, such classroom behaviors take their toll on the emotional energies of both pupil and teacher. For this reason teachers who are responsible for helping troubled adolescents during times of stress need to know about its sources.

What Are the Various Types of Stress?

Pupil stress has been organized around the following four categories: (a) developmental stress, (b) economic stress, (c) psychological stress, (d) reality stress.

A.   *Developmental stress.* This refers to all the normal developmental crises from birth to death. For example, to be born is stressful; to be weaned from the breast or bottle is stressful; to be toilet-trained is stressful; to leave mother and home for teacher and school is stressful; learning to read is stressful; learning to understand basic sex differences is stressful; learning to be part of a group is stressful. For adolescents, there are numerous developmental stresses such as watching one's body change, becoming independent, developing personal values as opposed to group values, understanding the excitement and confusion of one's own and others' sexuality, developing career courses, graduating from high school, and so forth. Each of these developmental events is stressful and predictable. They are the same for all pupils, regardless of race, color, creed, or socioeconomic level.

B.   *Economic stress.* Millions of families in our society are living on the brink of economic disaster. Not all of these families come from the slums, ghettoes, or disadvantaged groups; many are striving middle-class families, living beyond their financial resources and with over-extended credit.

For the chronically poor, economic stress shows itself in: poor diet and food; poor health habits; greater susceptibility to illness; lack of acceptable clothing; lack of privacy; lack of sleep; limited opportunity to participate in social and school-related activities; greater parent exhaustion and conflict; parent models of joblessness and helplessness; social isolation from the mainstream of society; a sense of being different from the "norm."

C.   *Psychological stress.* This consists of conscious and deliberate attempts by individuals, groups, and institutions to systematically and consistently destroy the worth of the individual. For example, many adolescents are told that they are unwanted, that they are the source of their parent's problems, that life would be better if they were not around, that they spoil the family and neighborhood because of their demands and behaviors. They are told they are stupid, dumb, infantile, inconsiderate, ungrateful, and totally useless to themselves and others. For some pupils the stress does not come from open rejection but from trying to meet unrealistic standards. Pupils are told they must be perfect to be loved. They must be smarter, more responsible, socially mature, and more loving than they are capable of being. For others, the psychological stress is related to specific adults who are socially maladjusted. For example, the seductive, pleasure-seeking parent who frequently stimulates the adolescent's sexual awareness and fantasy by showing excessive attention and interest in sexual topics and fun. A psychotic parent, who is suffering from a major mental illness, is not capable of carrying out his adult responsibilities. In these homes, simple issues become distorted, creating a tense atmosphere for everyone in the family. An alcoholic or drug-abusing parent, who creates a home where there is little consistency, causes the pupil to feel confused, guilty, and ambivalent about life. The pupil never knows if the parent will be available to care for him or her, or whether the parent will expose him/her to everything from exhibitionism, physical and sexual abuse to desertion and/or suicide.

Other pupils must deal with the overprotective parent, the retarded parent, the moralistic parent, and the depressed parent. Also, any sibling, relative, or significant friend who is emotionally disturbed will have a profound effect on the pupil's ability to focus on classroom learning.

D.   *Reality stress.* This consists of all those unplanned events which frustrate the personal goals of an adolescent. These frustrations happen spontaneously with no organized attempt to defeat the pupil, but they happen with such frequency for a few adolescents that they begin to believe the world and all the people in the world are against them. Some examples: A pupil looks forward to wearing his favorite sweater only to discover that his brother wore it yesterday and spilled syrup on it. A pupil lends his algebra book to a friend who forgets to bring it to school the next day. Two classmates are fooling around in class. One pushes the other into the pupil's desk tearing his English composition which is due in a few minutes. A teacher warns the class that the next pupil who talks will be given a detention. A student whispers to a friend and the teacher points to an innocent pupil as the offender. The pupil's dad lets him use the car for a basketball game. He arranges to pick up his friends only to discover that the battery is dead. In other words, things go wrong that should not go wrong. It is not anyone's fault, but the stress is very real, frequent, and intense.

How Does Stress Lead to the Pupil-Teacher Stress Cycle?

For some pupils stress does not come from one but from multiple sources. For example, a pupil may have the normal developmental stress of a final exam. That evening his parents have a violent argument and he is unable to study or sleep. On the way to school he is scapegoated by a hostile group who call him various racial and ethnic names. As he enters the classroom, a friend greets him by slapping him on the back, causing his glasses to fall and break. Finally the teacher announces a new school policy that no exam can be taken over, regardless of the circumstances.

When teachers understand these multiple cycles of stress, they are more willing to help pupils develop new coping skills rather than *blame them for their misfortunes.*

This is a major change in thinking for most pupils and teachers. Our personal history has taught us that when goals are frustrated or something goes wrong, someone is to blame. For example, teachers find it easier to criticize pupils and parents for not trying, being careless and/or irresponsible than to understand what is blocking or interfering with a pupil's ability to learn in the classroom. Simultaneously, adolescents find it easier to attack the educational system, teachers, parents, peers, and rules for their failure than to understand what is overwhelming them.

Our goal is to develop a no fault stress program in which the focus of attention is on understanding, supporting, and teaching new skills to the injured party. To accomplish this, the stress cycle can be used to help teachers understand how the negative cycle of stress functions and how adolescents under stress frequently create in teachers their feelings and, at times, their behavior. The stress cycle is illustrated in Figure 1.

The Four Stages of the Stress Cycle

A. *Stressful incident.* The cycle begins with a pupil experiencing a stressful incident from a developmental, economic, psychological, and/or reality source.

B. *Feelings.* Many pupils, unfortunately, are taught that certain feelings are bad and unacceptable and that "healthy" adolescents should not have these feelings. When this occurs, pupils who have these unacceptable feelings either deny them, project or give them to others, or reorganize them so that they are acted out in disguised forms. Since feelings are a natural and an intrinsic part of being a human

FIGURE 1   The Pupil's Stress Cycle

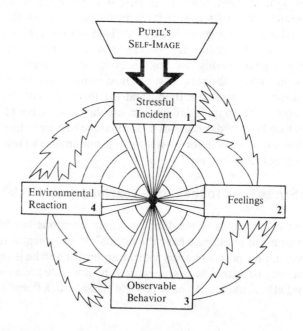

being, *it is our goal that everyone should learn to recognize one's own feelings.* While feelings give meaning and excitement to life, there is a difference between having feelings and being had by the feelings. Pupils need to distinguish between their feelings and their behavior. For example, it is healthy to feel anger when one has been psychologically depreciated or cruelly discriminated against, but it is not acceptable to assault the offender. It is very healthy to experience intense feelings of sadness when someone you love dies or moves away, but it is not healthy to withdraw from all relationships. It is healthy to feel guilty when you behave in a way that you know is unacceptable, but not to act so that others will punish you. It is normal to experience anxiety when you are anticipating a new experience or new relationship, but it is not healthy to handle this anxiety by drinking or drug abuse. It is normal to feel happiness when you are in love, but it is not helpful to express blatant sexual feelings in front of others. The existence and importance of accepting these feelings is incontestable. The question is, how are they expressed in behavior?

C. *Observable behavior.* When pupils react to feelings of stress by expressing them directly or by defending against them, they usually create additional problems for themselves in their school environment. For example, behaviors such as hitting, running away, psychogenic illness, stealing, teasing, lying, hyperactivity, fighting, using drugs, inattentiveness, and withdrawal cause pupils to have difficulty with teachers, peers, learning, and school rules. For example, when an adolescent dumps his feelings of hostility he has for his father on his teacher, an inevitable teacher-pupil problem develops. When a pupil becomes depressed because his mother is having a baby, the pupil may not be able to complete assignments and a learning problem emerges. Accepting this interpretation of behavior, *the problems pupils cause in school do not necessarily reflect the causes of their problems.* More accurately, the problems pupils cause in school result from the ways they have learned to cope with stress.

D. *Environmental reaction.* One of the amazing concepts of interpersonal relationships is that a pupil in stress can actually evoke in others his feelings and, at times, his behavior. For example, an aggressive pupil can quickly bring out hostile feelings and counter-aggressive behaviors in others. A hyperactive pupil can make others feel anxious and act in impulsive, irrational ways. A detached pupil frequently gets others to feel depressed and to ignore him. If teachers are unaware of this natural reaction, the inappropriate pupil behavior will become automatically reinforced and perpetuated by the teacher's reaction. The phrase, "Do unto others as others do unto you" is an accurate but unfortunate psychological consequence of this negative stress cycle.

The negative feedback a pupil receives from a teacher simply supports his original view of himself and his world, increasing intense feelings which the pupil shows in a more unacceptable and primitive way. When this happens, the teacher becomes even more angry and disgusted by the pupil and consequently, intensifies the pupil's stress, negative feelings, and behavior. The stress cycle continues until an intense *power struggle* develops between the teacher and the pupil. When this happens, logic, caring, and compassion are lost and the only goal is to win the power struggle. For teachers the pupil is seen as the source of the problem and is told to "shape up" and to improve his attitude and behavior. If he doesn't, the teacher labels him as disturbed, delinquent, dangerous, and/or disgusting. The pupil is usually suspended, transferred, or referred to special education.

What is important to remember is that there are no winners when the stress cycle reaches the level of a power struggle. This cycle cannot be broken by asking

immature adolescents during intense states of stress to act maturely. If change is going to happen, the adult must accept responsibility for acting in a mature, professional manner. This means understanding how adolescents in stress can incite concerned, reasonable, and dedicated educators to act in impulsive, emotional, and/or rejecting ways. This problem becomes more complex when the source of the stress takes place in the adolescent's home environment, frequently outside the teacher's awareness and knowledge. In these cases, the teacher will need to have an even greater diagnostic awareness. The following example illustrates how the stress cycle operates and after five cycles ends up as a power struggle between the pupil and teacher.

> Joe is in grade 10, of average intelligence, and is not a chronic behavior problem in the classroom.
> STRESS 1—Joe's girlfriend, Mary, tells him she does not want to see him anymore.
> *Feelings*—Anger and inadequacy.
> *Behavior*—Joes does not turn in English assignment. Instead he says it is a stupid assignment.
> *Teacher Reaction*—Surprised by his attitude, the teacher tells him he knows better than to act like this.
> STRESS 2—Feels psychological stress: Joe believes the teacher is picking on him.
> *Feelings*—More anger.
> *Behavior*—Joe tells the teacher, "Why do you always pick on the boys in this class and not the girls?"

Teacher Reaction—"I do not. Besides, that is not the issue."
STRESS 3—Continued psychological stress.
Feelings—Anger, with pleasure.
Behavior—"Yes, you do, and you don't even know you do it. Ask the class."
Teacher Reaction—"What I do know is that you are going to get yourself into serious trouble if you don't settle down."
STRESS 4—More psychological stress.
Feelings—More anger.
Behavior—"I don't care what you do, it means nothing to me."
Teacher Reaction—"If you don't care, then you better not stay in class and mess it up for the other students who do care!"
STRESS 5—More psychological stress.
Feelings—Intense anger.
Behavior—"It's a pleasure to get out of this damn class." Walks out of the class and slams the door.
Teacher Reaction—Yells, "Don't you slam that door!"

In this example you can see how the pupil escalated the problem into a power struggle and how he was successful in getting his teacher to reject him as his girlfriend had. In this example Joe was never aware that the source of his difficulty was rejection by his girlfriend. Instead, he projected these feelings onto the teacher and ended up blaming her for his school troubles.

What Can Teachers Do to Promote Coping With Stress?

The dynamics of the stress cycle illustrate how students in stress evoke their feelings and behaviors in others and how the student's hope for help from the school environment frequently ends up in an intense and destructive power struggle with authority. Once teachers understand these concepts and no longer react to the student's defensive and defeating behaviors, teachers become psychologically ready to help their students cope with stress. The next steps require (a) positive concepts for helping and (b) practical teaching strategies.

Positive helping concepts. Any degree of help is useful to a student in stress. Some teachers feel that some adolescents' problems are so severe, complicated, and long-standing that their efforts to help seem useless and hopeless. One teacher expressed this concern openly: "I am willing to help Carl but I feel it's like building sand castles that are washed away by the nightly tide of home/community struggles. What I do doesn't seem to make a difference. He needs much more than the schools or I can provide. After all, I have only a limited amount of time and skill."

Though this attitude is understandable, it overlooks several significant factors that are intrinsic to any helping relationship. A student under stress needs to believe that there is some hope for the life situation. Even if the hope is marginal and temporary, the student needs some personal acceptance from an adult who does not blame him for his circumstances or magnify the severity of the problem.

Every successful experience a student has with an adult, no matter how small, is important. While a teacher's help may not be enough to "turn the student around" or make a significant difference in his life, it does lead to a basic trust of adults. It is an experience that cannot be taken away. Perhaps next semester or next year another adult will be able to build on this foundation, making it possible for the adolescent to make significant changes and to compensate for his life problems. Psychological conditions at home and in the community change with time. Nothing remains static or fixed. Crises in the family/community do become resolved or at least tolerable. If a student can be helped *not* to complicate his life by creating new problems, then he can be helped when the stress in this "other environment" diminishes.

Practical teaching strategies. Strategy One: Reducing Stress by Forming a Helping Adult Relationship. In helping adolescents cope with stress, teachers need to look beyond the surface explanation of behavior and to focus on the feelings causing the behavior. How a student feels often determines the way he perceives and behaves in school. Many pupils under stress try to hide their feelings by withdrawing from activities, by becoming hyperactive, or by exploding in anger. If a teacher is to help these children, she or he must begin the initial contact by reaching out and decoding the student's behavior. This is not always a simple or easy task. Many students who need help and support begin by refusing or ignoring the teacher's effort to help. However, we know that if a student can share thoughts and experiences with someone and have that adult understand and accept his or her problem, the exchange will result in a new feeling of emotional support and direction. In this kind of relationship, the student and teacher move toward each other. They talk and listen to each other. They open up. The student begins to share concerns and fears. To make this helping process happen, the teacher must be able to empathize with the student, to enter the student's world in such a way as to encourage the student to trust the adult. The teacher must develop the skill to see beyond what the student is saying and to decode how the student's verbal and nonverbal ways of communicating can provide cues to the real source of pain and stress. To do this, the teacher must understand the psychology of nonverbal communication, verbal communication, and labeling and accepting feelings.

Nonverbal communication. The more we observe students in stress, the more we listen to what they tell us without words. We learn to respond to their body language. We become acutely aware of the messages they send with their eyes, muscles, skin temperature, breathing pattern, and body movement. Many students learn early in life that if they express negative feelings and words, adults will react in anger. They also learn that the spoken word can be held against them as self-incriminating evidence. To avoid this problem, they learn to say one thing with words, while their bodies express a different sentiment.

Verbal communication. When a student is under stress, language is often used to mislead, hide, and protect real feelings. Consequently, teachers must learn to pay as much attention to *how* a student is speaking as to *what* is being said. By listening to the flow and tone of words, a teacher can "hear" them in terms of feelings, such as anger, fear, sadness, ambivalence, or happiness. For example, a student may say, "Get out of here and leave me alone!" while trying to communicate the sentiment, "Please don't go; I need your help, but I'm afraid to ask since you might reject me or tell me I'm acting silly or immature."

Labeling and accepting feelings. As a teacher listens to an adolescent and learns to trust the authenticity of nonverbal communication, the teacher is ready to label the student's feelings. Based upon what the teacher perceives and feels, he or she can say to a student in stress, "You look sad today, can I help you?" or "You look really upset, can you talk to me about it?" or "I have a feeling that you are worried about something. Did anything happen on the way to school today?" As a teacher reaches out and shares the student's inner life with honesty, reflecting the unspoken feelings and words, a meaningful relationship develops. The next step, accepting the feeling, is far more complex than labeling the student's feelings. The teacher needs to support the student's feelings as a genuine and healthy expression of interpersonal struggles. The teacher must indicate that the feelings the student has toward school, home, society, and the world are legitimate and should not be argued about. For example, the teacher can say, "It's okay to feel sad when you flunk an exam" or "I know you're angry with Larry but I can't let you hit him back." In many cases, the teacher can drain off the student's feelings by allowing expression of them through words as in the following exchange between a student and teacher. Billy: "I would like to punch him out!" Teacher: "I know you're really angry. You really hate his teasing." Billy: "Boy, he makes me mad." The student needs the chance to run through all the complaints of injustice or disappointment that he is feeling without fear of adult retaliation or rejection.

Offering a helping relationship to pupils means developing these skills of listening, labeling, and accepting feelings. During this process the student can discharge pent-up feelings in a safe, nondestructive manner. As these feelings are expressed the student is in a better position to evaluate his situation and to put his life in proper perspective.

Some serious problems involved in helping students need to be emphasized. The teacher must not rush to the student's rescue, take over responsibilities, and plan a logical solution. The helping relationship is based upon the following four ethical considerations:

1. The helping teacher is sympathetic but insists that the pupil has some responsibility for improving his own situation. The helping adult does not convey the message of "poor, poor pupil." This inappropriate feedback only reinforces the pupil's feeling of being gypped and it encourages him to act-out and take what he feels he should have in any manner available to him. Instead, the teacher should help the adolescent focus on his behavior: What can you do to make the situation better? What did you do to make the situation worse?

2. The helping teacher accepts the student's problem in a matter-of-fact way indicating that the student is neither dumb nor deviant for having this problem. The teacher accepts the problem as part of the normal process of becoming an adult.

3. The helping teacher positively reinforces all attempts by the pupil to improve his situation even though his efforts were not successful.

4. The helping teacher can be trusted to keep all conversations confidential. The teacher must serve as his advocate and protect his rights.

Strategy Two: Reducing Stress by Lowering School Pressure. While teachers cannot control what happens to the student in home and community, he or she can control what happens to the student in the classroom. One significant way teachers can reduce student stress is by lowering academic requirements, standards, and deadlines temporarily. The student may be told, "You have enough on your mind right now and do not have to worry about the term paper, book report, or exam next Friday. Of course once the crisis is over, I will help you catch up, but right now it is important for you to understand your feelings and situation." This strategy is like providing the student with an academic aspirin that will temporarily take away some of the aches and pains. However, it is important not to take away the student's total responsibility for learning or classroom assignments. The student is expected to turn in what assignments he can complete during the crisis but not to feel that he will fail if the assignment is late or at a lower level of competence. This strategy is an obvious one, but is used all too infrequently by classroom teachers.

Strategy Three: Reducing Stress by Redirecting Feelings into Acceptable

Behavior. Just as it is possible to channel the potentially destructive force of a rapidly flowing river into electrical power, an adolescent can be taught new and diverse ways of transforming intense, explosive thoughts and feelings into socially approved behavior. This strategy for coping with stress not only relieves physical and psychological tensions but also develops personal and social skills. Aggressive, sexual, fearful, and sad feelings can be directed into school activities such as art, sports, dance, manual arts, literature, drama, and creative writing.

Unlike other strategies, this does not *deny* or *block* the feelings, but uses them as a source of motivation and power. For example, a football coach might say, "Okay team, now that you are mad, let's get one for the Gipper!" "Let's go out and give them hell!"

For teachers, there are many ways of redirecting feelings into acceptable behaviors; for example, "You know, Cathy, maybe it would help you to spend some time in the art room on the kickwheel. You might feel better if you could put some of your energy into throwing a pot rather than smoking some." Or, "I think Mr. Donnelli needs some help in the auditorium with the light fixtures. Maybe if you would work with him for some time this morning you'd feel like you've accomplished something. I know when I feel upset, helping someone else always makes me feel like I have a little more control over things."

Teacher Strategy Four: Reducing Stress by Accepting Disappointment and Failure. Disappointment and failure are a natural and inevitable condition of interpersonal and family life and little can be done to prevent students from experiencing frustration. However, it is important for teachers to help students learn that their stress is not due to *badness* or *inadequacy*. The goal is to help students develop a greater capacity for enduring upsetting or disappointing life events without falling apart. This can be promoted by teaching students to accept a normal amount of hostility from others.

Unfortunately, many middle class students have unrealistic expectations of people. They feel people should be nice, kind, sympathetic, courteous, and fair. When adolescents experience adult rejection, peer criticism, and/or a blast of verbal abuse, they too often perceive it as a personal attack instead of the usual amount of hostility we learn to accept from one another. If the student does not overract to this behavior, the stress cycle can be stopped. As teachers we can teach our students to expect some negative feelings from all relationships, beginning with their closest friends.

Another meaningful way of coping with stress is to accept defeat since it is impossible to maintain one's infantile wish to always be first, best, and strongest. "I know it was really hard to lose the contest after you've worked so hard for it. You've been practicing that speech every afternoon and we all thought you were excellent at the contest on Saturday. But I also know how much you wanted to win. I know you feel bad. But I also know you learned a lot about contests and you'll never have to go through your 'first one' again. Next time you'll be a veteran and not so afraid of the unknown. You really did get something from that experience." The teacher might say, "You have done everything possible to improve your situation but right now you are going to have to live with it. You are a fine person and need to be proud of your skills. It will be difficult at times but I believe you have the strength to tolerate it." Sometimes it is helpful to refer to adults who have some meaning to an adolescent. For example, "Matt, I know you are unhappy about your batting average but you need to remember Babe Ruth struck out over 3000 times in his career before setting his home-run record."

Teacher Strategy Five: Reducing Stress by Completing One Task At A Time. When too many stresses and responsibilities build up, the collective view becomes gigantic and many students panic into a state of helplessness and frozen behavior. The experience is like being handed a ball of string tangled in a hundred knots and told to straighten it out in sixty seconds. The task seems impossible! After a few attempts, it changes from impossible to total hopelessness. A helpful strategy is to help the student to reduce the task to a manageable unit of work. Just as a thousand-mile trip must begin with one small step, the skill of coping involves selecting one concrete task and completing it within a day. This single action generates new energy, hope, and productivity. It reflects a basic law of nature: A body in motion stays in motion while a body at rest stays at rest. For example, a teacher could say, "Right now it seems like you have a lot of problems on your mind. Sometimes when you have so many things to think about it's hard to know where to start. Or perhaps you feel that it's just too much and they all can't be solved at once. You're right! It helps to start with one task and work on it until it's completed. Let's begin by having you select one task that you can complete today."

This stress reduction technique is important to teach since it brings order and a sense of control over your life.

Teacher Strategy Six: Reducing Stress by Helping Less Fortunate Students. The opportunity to wallow in feelings of self-pity, grief, and anger is available to everyone. Many middle-class students have little appreciation of the multiple pains of life and can overreact to normal developmental stress, that is, failing an exam, being rejected by a girl/boyfriend, or not being selected to a team, as though it were a disaster and not a disappointment. For these students there are many benefits in helping less fortunate and younger students. The helping experience forces the students to realize there are other students whose problems are more complex and stressful than their own. When they observe the coping skills of these students, our target student may see his own problem diminish in size and importance. The process of helping others enhances the helper's feelings of self-worth while concurrently diminishing the need for self-depreciation. The process of helping pushes the helper to focus on the present and future rather than on the past. "You know, Richard, I think its sort of hard for you to understand that life isn't always exactly the way you'd like it to be. I know you'd like everything to work out and be pleasant. I think it would be an interesting experience for you to get to know Peter in Mrs. Kellogg's classroom. He's younger than you and needs real help in reading. Because of his illness, he is a month behind in his English assignment. Maybe you could spend a half hour a couple of times a week with him. I know that he will appreciate it. Maybe you can help him catch up while I teach you a few teaching techniques."

Teacher Strategy Seven: Reducing Stress by Separating from the Setting. One of man's basic survival mechanisms is flight. Under stress, one way of coping is to leave the stressful environment temporarily. To withdraw to a more supportive environment to rest, play, and think by one's self or with others is a useful technique. The phrase "too close to the trees to see the forest" is applicable. It is our belief that physical distance between the stressful setting and the student frequently provides the needed psychological conditions for problem-solving. Free from the pressures of the situation, the student is better able to think through his situation. For example, "Sometimes, Sherry, it makes good sense to get away from a problem to regain a little strength. Didn't you tell me your teen group was planning a back-packing trip? Maybe a few days away from everyone would give you a needed break.

You might even have a better picture of the situation at home when you come back", or "You know, Andy, maybe it's a good time for you to visit your grandfather for the weekend. You've been talking about how long it's been since you two visited together. I bet a few days at the lake would not only give you a chance to visit with him but also would give you some energy to deal with these problems here. I think everyone needs time away from what seems like overwhelming problems to restore themselves a little."

It has been our experience that a little distance from the problem can bring you closer to a solution.

Teacher Strategy Eight: Reducing Stress by Helping the Student Seek Professional Help. When stress becomes chronic and overwhelming, teachers are in the right position to refer a student for psychological services or to encourage parents to seek professional mental health assistance for their adolescent. All too often, parents and adolescents who are unhappy and dissatisfied with life perceive asking for professional help as an obvious sign of personal weakness and inferiority. They become ashamed and spend their time denying and avoiding the reality of the situation. Special educators can be helpful by reflecting the importance and difficulty of making the initial appointment with the local or private mental health worker. Parents need to be told that while seeking professional help is painful, it takes personal courage, maturity, and insight. Most of all, it takes a conviction that their adolescent should feel more comfortable with himself and the world around him.

Initially, students are anxious about going to therapy, but once they learn the therapy sessions are confidential, the fear subsides and the student begins the process of discovering the value of therapeutic support, catharsis, and the power of therapy. It is one of the most loving gifts parents can give their adolescent and that a teacher can support.

Conclusion

This chapter reviewed the psychoeducational approach to helping disturbed adolescents cope with stress. We described how stressful school and community experiences can influence the pupil's ability to learn and behave in the classroom and how teachers can use stress to teach coping skills. The essentials for therapeutic management were presented in terms of the following principles: (a) stress should be viewed as a natural and accepted part of life; (b) stress is not good or bad but its frequency, intensity and duration is significant; (c) some pupils experience multiple stresses—developmental, economic, psychological, and reality; (d) during stress some pupils become flooded by their feelings and behave inappropriately; (e) during stress some pupils are unable to help themselves and will respond negatively to adult help and support; (f) during stress pupils can generate their own feelings in teachers and, if the teachers are not well trained, also their behavior patterns; (g) if the stress cycle follows its normal pattern, the stressful incident will end up as an intensive power struggle between teachers and pupils; (h) when a power struggle develops, neither pupil or teacher is a winner.

To change this stress cycle to a coping cycle, the teacher must have the skills to: (a) be in touch with her or his feelings; (b) be aware that these feelings originally came from the pupil; (c) be able to verbalize personal feelings; (d) be able to decode the pupil's feelings; (e) be able to support the pupil's feelings but not the inappropriate behavior; (f) be able to show how coping with a difficult situation leads to feelings of competence, success, and pride; (g) be able to demonstrate a feeling of hope and not hopelessness; (h) be able to reduce stress by lowering school standards; (i) be able to reduce stress by redirecting feelings into acceptable behavior; (j) be able to reduce stress by accepting disappointment and failure; (k) be able to reduce stress by completing one task at a time; (l) be able to reduce stress by helping less fortunate students; (m) be able to reduce stress by separating from the setting; and (n) be able to reduce stress by seeking professional help.

There are many additional psychoeducational concepts and techniques special educators need to learn, such as Surface Management (Long & Newman, 1976), Life Space Interviewing (Long, Morse, & Newman, 1976; Fagen & Hill, 1977), the Self-Control Curriculum (Fagen, Long & Stevens, 1975), and the three stages of Psychoeducational Programming for Adolescents (Fagen, 1978): stage 1, renew hope and motivation for learning; stage 2, develop caring and ownership for own efforts; and stage 3, strengthen self-control and internalization of responsibility. All these concepts and techniques are based on the importance of the teacher's relationship in helping disturbed adolescents find a sense of comfort and competence in themselves and the psychological world in which they live.

References

Armstrong, D. G. Alternative schools: Implications for secondary school curriculum workers. *High School Journal*, 1973, *56*, 267–275.

Bandura, A. *Aggression: A social learning analysis.* Englewood Cliffs, N.J.: Prentice-Hall, 1973.

Bayh, B. Our nation's schools—A report card: *"A" in school violence and vandalism.* Preliminary report of the subcommittee to investigate juvenile delinquency.

Bloomer, R., & Ducharme, R. A model instructional program for the emotionally disturbed, learning disabled child. In B. T. Saunders (Ed.), *Approaches with emotionally disturbed children.* Hicksville, N.Y.: Exposition, 1974.

Cheney, C., & Morse, W. C. Psychodynamic interventions in emotional disturbance. In W. C. Rhodes & M. L. Tracey (Eds.), *A study of child variance.* Volume 2: *Interventions.* Ann Arbor: Univ. of Michigan Press, 1972.

Colella, H. V. Career development center: A modified high school for the handicapped. *Teaching Exceptional Children*, 1973, *5*, 110–118.

Ditullio, W. M. Program planning for children with emotional disturbance and multiple disabilities. In B. T. Saunders (Ed.), *Approaches with emotionally disturbed children.* Hicksville, N.Y.: Exposition, 1974.

Dreikurs, R., Grunwald, B., & Perrer, F. *Maintaining sanity in the classroom: Illustrated teaching techniques.* New York: Harper & Row, 1971.

Fagen, S. A. Minimizing emotional wear and tear through adaptive frustration management. *Proceedings of a Conference on Preparing Teachers to Foster Personal Growth in Emotionally Disturbed Students.* Advanced Institute for Trainers of Teachers for Seriously Emotionally Disturbed Children. University of Minnesota, May 29–31, 1977, 67–68.

Fagen, S. A. Psychoeducational management and self-control. In D. Cullinan & M. H. Epstein (Eds.), *Special education for adolescents.* Columbus, Ohio: Charles E. Merrill, 1978.

Fagen, S. A., & Guedalia, L. J. *Individual and group counseling: A competency-based manual for in-service training.* Washington, D.C.: Psychoeducational Resources, 1977.

Fagen, S. A., & Hill, J. M. *Behavior management: A competency-based manual for in-service training.* Washington, D.C.: Psychoeducational Resources, 1977.

Fagen, S. A., & Long, N. J. Teaching children self-control: A new responsibility for teachers. *Focus on Exceptional Children,* 1976, *7* (8), 1–12.

Fagen, S. A., Long, N.J., & Stevens, D. J. *Teaching children self-control.* Columbus, Ohio: Charles E. Merrill, 1975.

Felker, D. W. Building positive self-concepts. Minneapolis: Burgess, 1974.

Gearheart, B. R., & Weishahn, M. W. *The handicapped child in the regular classroom.* St. Louis: Mosby, 1976.

Glasser, W. A new look at discipline. *Learning,* 1974, *3* (4), 6–11.

Gordon, S. Reversing a negative self-image. In L. Anderson (Ed.), *Helping the adolescent with the hidden handicap.* Los Angeles: California Association for Neurologically Handicapped Children, 1970.

Gray, J. *The teacher's survival guide.* Belmont, Calif: Fearon, 1974.

Hammill, D. D., & Bartel, N. R. *Teaching children with learning and behavior problems.* Boston: Allyn & Bacon, 1975.

Josselyn, I. M. The adolescent today. In W. C. Sze (Ed.), *Human life cycle.* New York: Aronson, 1975.

Kanfer, F. H. The many facets of self-control. In R. B. Stuart (Ed.), *Behavioral self-management: Strategies, techniques and outcome.* New York: Bruner/Mazel, 1977.

Kanfer, F. H., & Goldstein, A. P. (Eds.) *Helping people change: A textbook of methods.* New York: Pergamon, 1975.

Kauffman, J. M. *Characteristics of children's behavior disorders.* Columbus, Ohio: Charles E. Merrill, 1977.

Kounin, J. S. *Discipline and group management in classrooms.* New York: Holt, Rinehart & Winston, 1970.

Lazarus, A., & Fay, A. *I can if I want to.* New York: Morrow, 1975.

Long, N. J., Morse, W. C., & Newman, R. G. (Eds.) *Conflict in the classroom: The education of children with problems* (3rd ed.). Belmont, Calif.: Wadsworth, 1976.

Long, N. J., & Newman, R. G. Managing surface behavior of children in schools. In N. J. Long, W. C. Morse, & R. G. Newman (Eds.), *Conflict in the classroom: The education of children with problems.* Belmont, Calif.: Wadsworth, 1976.

Madsen, C. H., & Madsen, C. K. *Teaching discipline: A positive approach for education development.* Boston: Allyn & Bacon, 1974.

Martin, R., & Lauridsen, D. *Developing student discipline and motiviation.* Champaign, Ill.: Research Press, 1974.

Morse, W. C. The helping teacher/crisis teacher concept. *Focus on Exceptional Children,* 1976, *8* (4), 1–11.

National Commission on Resources for Youth. *New roles for youth in the school and the community.* New York: Citation, 1974.

National School Public Relations Association. *Suspensions and expulsions: Current trends in school policies and programs.* Arlington, Va.: National School Public Relations Association, 1976.

Newman, R. *Groups in schools: A book about teachers, parents and children.* New York: Simon & Schuster, 1974.

Polsgrove, L. Self-control: An overview of concepts and methods for child training. *Proceedings of a Conference on Preparing Teachers to Foster Personal Growth in Emotionally Disturbed Students.* Advanced Institute for Trainers of Teachers for

Seriously Emotionally Disturbed Children. University of Minnesota, May 29–31, 1977, 29–55.

Redl, F. The concept of the life space interview. *American Journal of Orthopsychiatry*, 1959, *29*, 1–18.

Reinert, H. R. *Children in conflict: Educational strategies for the emotionally disturbed and behaviorally disordered.* St. Louis: Mosby, 1976.

Samuels, M. S., & Moriarty, P. H. *The concept of classroom crisis control.* Schiller Park, Ill.: Motorola Teleprograms, 1975.

Sarason, I., & Sarason, B. *Constructive classroom behavior: A teacher's guide to modelling and role-playing techniques.* New York: Behavioral Publications, 1974.

Sherry, M., & Franzen, M. Zapped by ZING: Students and teachers develop successful problem solving strategies. *Teaching Exceptional Children*, 1977, *9*, 46–47.

Volkmor, C. B., Langstaff, A. L. & Higgins, M. *Structuring the classroom for success.* Columbus, Ohio: Charles E. Merrill, 1974.

Wood, M. M. (Ed.). *Developmental therapy: A textbook for teachers as therapists for emotionally disturbed young children.* Baltimore: University Park, 1975.

Affective Education: The Teacher, the Student, and the Process

9

Marian Shelton

The problems encountered by teachers working with behavior disordered adolescents are, in a more concentrated and dramatic form, the problems each of us encounters in our daily lives. The feeling of not being in control of the events in one's own life is perhaps one of the most frightening of experiences and one that people of all ages grapple with in a variety of ways: total withdrawal, helplessness, denial, blame, aggression, and so forth. As our environment and our relationships become more complex and transient, more and more people find themselves unable to cope with their particular circumstances (Toffler, 1971).

Because of our complex social structures, individuals now have less control over their lives and instead of being taught problem-solving skills and independence are taught to be more dependent on other people. This presents an organizational task, a need to learn to use the specialized expertise of many others in lieu of "hands on" personal control of one's life. This delegation of decisions to specialized others often promotes insecurity in one's self and creates the feeling that others are one's caretakers. The difficulty of constantly changing environments and the loss of significant others demands that we develop inner security, a positive self-concept, and flexibility. These qualities are difficult for anyone to attain and maintain, especially the adolescent.

As a "result of interaction with others, the structure of self is formed, an organized, fluid, but consistent conceptual pattern of perceptions of characteristics and relationships of the 'I' and 'me' together with values attached to these concepts" (Rogers, 1973, p. 498). For the adolescent who is continually responding to peer pressures, personal interactions are difficult at best. The behavior disordered adolescent has distorted self-perceptions so that the ability to choose when and how to allow interactions and interdependencies is extremely limited. This ability is directly dependent upon the development of a positive self-concept. Each person processes all behavior and information through his/her self-concept, which acts as a filtering system, "a screen through which everything else is seen, heard, evaluated and understood" (Combs, 1973, p. 43). As this filtering process develops, attitudes toward all learning and toward the self are shaped in small units. These units shape the adolescent's feelings toward all aspects of personal life relationships, school, and cognitive learning. The attitudes developed control not only the amount, quality, and retention of learning after the experience or teaching process is completed, but the willingness to learn more about what he/she has been taught as well. Consequently, affective skills are basic to the attainment of academic goals and crucial to the adjustment of the behavior disordered adolescent (Shelton, 1977).

AFFECTIVE DEVELOPMENT

Affect has been defined to include four essential elements: "(1) the production of some alteration of an internal physiological state; (2) a correlated change in surface expressive behavior; (3) the individual's perception of these changes in himself; and (4) the individual's interpretation of these changes" (Lewis & Rosenblum, 1978, p. 2).

In this chapter these affective components will be used to define affective development. Affective education is defined as those teacher skills, student interactive behaviors, and classroom environments that may participate in the affective development of the adolescent.

To help the behavior disordered student to unravel his/her self-perception, an environment and curriculum must be implemented in the public school or institutional setting which provides a milieu for growth. This affective environment must, of necessity, include four qualities: (a) a positive unqualified acceptance of the person as a valuable human being; (b) a model (teacher, counselor, cottage director, or the like) willing to share his/her own growth process; (c) an environment which helps students demonstrate to themselves their ability to control the various aspects of their lives; (d) an environment which affirms the reality of situations.

Positive Unqualified Acceptance

To find the energy and effort to change life patterns, defense mechanisms, habits, and attitudes, there must be an environment where individuals feel they are trusted and competent. It should be a place in which they can demonstrate and feel that they are interesting, likable, and responsible and where encouragement is given and the students' abilities (however well hidden) nourished.

The expectations teachers have of their students can be a helpful and productive shaping procedure. These expectations need to be explicit, carefully thought out, and based on the students' value systems as well as the teacher's.

Teacher Modeling

In order to work most effectively in the demanding situations set up by behavior disordered adolescents, teachers must model, that is, stay continually aware of their own process. Teachers must be in tune with their own psychological needs and areas of growth and excitement. Everyone tires of doing things at times and becomes weary with constant effort; it is essential to be aware of this human factor in order to maintain a self-nourishing situation. The teacher's willingness and ability to do this will reflect in all his/her interactions with students. Redl and Wineman (1965) show us that behavior disordered youngsters test their teacher, counselor, and others in their environment on a day-to-day basis. Redl and Wineman discuss the difference between love and identification and point out that teachers believe they are communicating with the young person when in fact they are not. They also state that if the student only likes or loves us ("this affectionate tie reserved for people who are nice, pleasant to be with, or whom it is nice to know," p. 224), positive affective growth, essential to change, will not occur. Being liked and popular with the students is a more gratifying daily experience than the difficult task of working with them through the growth and change process for long-term rewards. The most difficult adolescents are well aware of the "like, love" strategy and use it to avoid the risks involved in positive affective growth. They avoid teachers with "tough love," the willingness to say "no," who insist on the constructive behavior that leads the students to change.

To avoid change from the "like, love" to "tough love" interaction, the adolescent may use a variety of defenses, beginning with a barrage of hatred and hostile warfare, sometimes in the form of withdrawal. If hostility doesn't work, the adolescent offers "like or love," a "cooperative deal," as long as no intimacy occurs. The love relationship can be used by the adolescent as a manipulation to get what is wanted. If adults are willing to keep their place in the "like, love" relationship and not expect change, secrets are exchanged.

This is the point at which many teachers stop, fooled by the situation. It is imperative to measure change in behavior, not professed affection and shared secrets. If adults do not know themselves, there is a return to warfare. Redl and Wineman state that when the adolescent and significant others allow their relationship to stay in the "like, love" stage, the youngster may remain a friend of the teacher through adulthood, from one trouble to another, one failure to another. Since we have not helped to bring about change, the person retains the self-destructive behaviors. Without the identification process, teachers are "friends without influence." Being a friend has its rewards but one has to choose either that or the role of change agent. Teachers cannot have it both ways.

When an adolescent shares secrets with a teacher, it could be a move toward intimacy or a subtle form of manipulation that is avoiding rather than establishing real communication. Teachers must develop the ability to assess motivations. If they do not, then once again they have modeled poor communication and exacerbated the life patterns many of these students have experienced. It is another demonstration that miscommunication and lack of understanding is all that exists.

Student Control of Environment

The teacher can help students learn to control even minute parts of their lives. Emotional disturbance is often a dependency problem; the emotionally disturbed person is not asked to take responsibility for him/her self. In an experiment done with about 30 of my students (freshmen and sophomores) in an introductory class in special education, I asked each student to participate in an activity to simulate each particular exceptionality (for example, the trust walk, deaf experience, etc.).

After the students had completed all eight exceptionalities, we discussed their experiences. With few exceptions they had enjoyed the experience of simulating emotionally disturbed behavior. Each student was paired with another; one student was told to demonstrate whatever form of emotional disturbance they wanted to emulate—total withdrawal, acting out behaviors, inappropriate acts, etc. The couple was to go to a public place—for example, grocery store, shopping center, restaurant; one of the two was asked to be the companion who was not disturbed. When discussing the emotional disturbance experiment, with few exceptions all students stated they "enjoyed this the most," "didn't want to go back to their usual behavior," "didn't find it difficult." Upon further questioning as to why, they stated that they didn't have to take responsibility for anything; they left all responsibility to the other companion or to others in the environment.

Cultural influence on the individual. Bruner (1973) speaks of his theory that "collective orientation does not arise simply as a by-product of individual powerlessness vis-á-vis the inanimate world, but is systematically encouraged as socialization progresses" (p. 377) and discusses the study of two cultures, the Tiv culture (Price-Williams, 1961, p. 302) in Nigeria which promotes an active manipulation of the physical, inanimate world and the Wolof culture (Rabain-Zempléni, 1965, p. 17) in which manipulation of the inanimate world is not encouraged. He postulates that perhaps "a collective, rather than individual, value orientation develops where the individual lacks power over the physical world. Lacking personal power, he has no notion of personal importance" (p. 376). Rabain-Zempléni in studies of the Wolof culture and child-training practices finds that the "child's manipulation of the physical, inanimate world fails to be encouraged in isolation from social relations, the personal desires and intentions which would isolate him from the group are also discouraged" (p. 377). There may be parallels here to the "learned helplessness" of the emotionally disturbed person who feels a lack of power over the physical and emotional world. The behavior disordered adolescent may choose not to accept responsibility for care of his or her body or immediate physical environment (no power over the physical world). This lack of responsibility for simple maintenance needs gives the power or control to others in the environment but the adolescent may require the "others" to meet absolute demands for exactly what is wanted in terms of personal desire.

Bowers (Harshman, 1969, p. 15) discusses significant behavioral deviations demonstrated in the emotionally disturbed adolescent such as an inability to learn when all other possibilities for lack of learning (such as mental retardation, specific learning disabilities, physical impairment) have been ruled out; inability to establish positive interpersonal relationships; the demonstration of inappropriate behavior or feelings under normal conditions; a pervasive mood of unhappiness or depression; and a tendency to develop illness or fears associated with personal or school problems.

When looking at these characteristics one sees, of course, many things—but one common element in all is the sense of helplessness, a learned unwillingness to take responsibility for necessary survival (Seligman, 1975). Looking at our complex social structure makes us aware of how difficult it is to attain skills which give real power over the physical world. The complexity of the physical world necessitates learning to depend on others (for example, mechanics to fix cars, growers to provide food, and so on) and requires great organizational ability to identify and locate necessary people as well as sort out priorities, follow through, and meet one's own needs and desires.

We are far removed from the Tiv and Wolof cultures, but they have something important to say in helping to understand the behavior of disordered adolescents. They have neither the skill to take power over inanimate objects (at times giving control and power to these objects) nor the ability to become members of a collective society. If we examine the environment, we might come to know how individuals develop the feeling they have no power over the physical world or ability to be part of a group. It is possible to discover how they have become helpless, dependent, and deficient in self-control. As teachers we can begin in minute steps to help them gain personal power over small segments of their world and thus build to larger areas of their lives. It is useful to realize that teaching a process is much more difficult than helping achieve a goal, that helping students to learn the first steps in the process of learning a particular skill may be very time-consuming. Teachers often analyze a task and then teach it step-by-step; the students need to learn *how* to task analyze in order to be able to apply that step-by-step approach, and thus become more independent.

Once individuals have proved to themselves that they can control enough of their lives to be self-sufficient, they may become secure enough to allow others to participate in their lives. People protect their world carefully when they feel little control and survival is threatened; they can not allow others freedom and spontaneity because that means change and change might mean a loss of control again. Thus, a sense of mastery is crucial if youngsters are to be able to make realistic choices, hope for self-fulfillment, and strive toward nourishing interactions with others.

The classroom could be the most positive environment in the students' life, one where they can learn to attend to aloneness as well as to constructive communication and can learn the value of each. We cannot expect students to internalize controls without ever witnessing that process in another person. To learn to change destructive life patterns, individuals need to see others making positive alterations. Students can sense when the teacher is psychologically growing because there is a lack of pompousness and commanding behavior which distances people. Teachers' awareness of their own fallibility allows them to experience and sort among the feelings and consequences of behavior to find a result that is congruent with their value systems and understanding. This can produce an inner peacefulness which leads to behaviors that create a calming atmosphere in the classroom and makes controlling the students less necessary as they absorb the calmness for themselves.

Reality Environment

Perhaps the greatest consistent instructional help a teacher can offer is to teach the student to attend to the present situation and stimuli. Students who constantly withdraw, fantasize, or act out cannot attend to the present environment and cannot function within it. The teacher can help the students to stay in touch with their present reality by observing each student's nonverbal behavior (facial expression, body language, and so on) and determining whether, at that moment, a student is capable of attending to work or whether he needs to withdraw for a while. If teachers stay in touch with the student's verbal and nonverbal responses, they can act as a reminder and bring the student back to the task at hand without creating hostility.

It is useful to remember that behavior disordered adolescents want to be "all right" in the classroom, in their own eyes, and in the eyes of others. The teacher can help achieve this goal by finding ways to gently assist the student back into the reality of the classroom.

Affective education requires a curriculum in living skills and attitudes and occurs whether or not it is a conscious and deliberately chosen part of the curriculum. Young people learn how to feel about school from all their experiences so it becomes vital to look at how positive experiences are or can be deliberately included.

AFFECTIVE CURRICULUM

The organization and execution of a program in affective education needs consistency in its presentation and integration with the cognitive domain. A commitment to affective education requires that some time be set aside for instructional purposes. Six components are necessary for careful planning: (a) physical environment, (b) psychological climate, (c) curriculum, (d) materials, (e) assessment and evaluation, and (f) teacher facilitation (Shelton, 1977).

Physical Environment

Physical environment can create opportunities for interaction, self-exploration, and study. To facilitate interaction, space and furnishing can be arranged for students to communicate in twos or threes or with the entire group.

Territories can provide a place for each student to be alone to think or to accomplish assigned tasks. Designated areas where specific tasks can be completed help the behavior disordered adolescent handle impulsiveness and encourage self-discipline by determining what is appropriate at any given time in a given space. The classroom can provide a graphic example, a constant reminder that "This is where I talk" or "This is where I work quietly."

Helping the students to interact appropriately, to listen to others, and to verbalize can be encouraged by placing chairs in random patterns so that students can have eye contact with one another and with the teacher. When students are seated in rows, eye contact is made only with the teacher at the front of the room. Verbalization is directed toward the teacher rather than toward other students and tends to come from the center of each row. Participation decreases along all sides and toward the back of the room (Knapp, 1972).

Teachers should allow students to place barriers, such as a chair, a table, or desk between themselves and others in order for students to feel secure while communicating. Allowing students to create the space around themselves, either more open or more closed, gives students a sense of their ability to control the environment and make it responsive to their felt needs; it also allows teachers to perceive which students require more privacy and which are more available to communication at any given time.

Students need, just as teachers do, a space they can call their own, which is inviolate, which can be used as a personal retreat at any time. Frequently, behavior disordered adolescents have no such space at home, finding themselves always visible and interrupted. School can provide much needed privacy for such students; available, inviolable privacy is an indication of respect by others and this encourages respect toward others.

An attractive room creates feelings of pleasure, comfort, and enjoyment. Studies testing for recall and problem-solving skills found that the performance was more effective in a "beautiful" room (Knapp, 1972). "Beautiful" here must be defined in terms of what is beautiful to the students as well as to the teacher. The students need to be comfortable in surroundings that seem to belong to them and reflect their interests and life style.

Frequently, the life styles of behavior disordered adolescents will differ from that of the teacher. It is important to recognize this and not try to impose one's own value systems on students whose values may be equally valid but different. This notion requires sensitivity on the teacher's part, a willingness to stay open to the unfamiliar.

Lack of space seems to affect exceptional children more severely than normal children as demonstrated by Hutt and Vaizey (Knapp, 1972). Density of population was varied from less than 6 to a total of 12 in a hospital playroom. As the numbers increased, all groups demonstrated either aggressive or destructive behavior, withdrawal, or detrimental changes in social behavior. Skinner (1971) believes that lives are shaped by environment and all that is necessary to change behavior is to control the individual's environment, physical and psychological.

Psychological Climate

A healthy learning environment is one in which the participants are successful. Successful experiences control how much students learn, how rapidly they learn, and how they feel about learning. A classroom can provide experiences for children in thinking, creating, problem-solving, and sorting among alternatives, experiences which must be a part of both the cognitive and affective portions of the curriculum. These skills require an atmosphere that is positive, accepting, and encouraging. Students and the general population alike repress their new ideas or thoughts for fear of being wrong, looking foolish, or failing to come up to another's expectations. Feldhusen and Treffinger (1977) review many suggestions for creating an atmosphere conducive to creative thinking, questioning skills, critical thinking, brainstorming, and other skills helpful to teaching and learning. In a healthy psychological climate each person has the freedom to explore, the freedom to be wrong, and each can discover that curiosity is fun and problems frequently have answers (Shelton, 1977).

The psychological climate of the environment of behavior disordered adolescents is one of the most crucial areas for their education. The feelings we have about our "home base" or nest are a strong part of our security system. This nest is both a physical setting and a psychological one; each contributes to the productivity of the other. A person clings to and protects his/her psychological nest regardless of how uncomfortable it may be because behavior is based on what people have known and experienced, regardless of how terrifying. Familiar habits usually are preferred to the unknown or new, even when those habits are destructive or life-threatening (as in the case of the battered child, wife, or husband). The people who destroy their own or others' property or relationships will not give up that behavior without a new sense of security and a new set of reinforcing habits.

It is useful to realize that defense systems have significant value in a person's life and to recognize what those values are in order to be able to let go of defensive behavior when it is inappropriate to the situation. The past experiences of many behavior disordered adolescents have been harsh, usually from a series of damaging situations leading to distorted perceptions of life. To establish a new, more positive environment and to help develop a psychological basis for a future productive life, the available psychological environment needs to possess qualities which encourage success, availability to new ideas, communication with others, and comfort with ambiguity.

Psychological growth occurs in an uneven pattern. When the student is beyond Redl and Wineman's "like, love" and into the identification process, various stages of conflict, hostility, and immature patterns will emerge. It is important that the teacher recognize that the growth process sometimes produces hostile and strange behaviors.

It is difficult at best to define "psychological growth," for ourselves and for others. Here is a tentative definition:

> "Modeling psychological growth" means being able to respond flexibly and honestly to new situations, being open about one's expectations and desires, being able to choose when to make contact and when to withdraw, being available to the realities of a given situation, being willing to say, "I don't know"; "I am confused"; "I am afraid"; being able to celebrate achievement in one's self and in others.   (Howarth, 1979)

Ideally, teachers should be open about their own process, willing to share it with students without fearing loss of authority. It is especially useful for students to recognize that the teacher or authority figure in their lives also feels, at times, unsure and inadequate and that such feelings need cause no shame; as the teacher shares personal feelings, students learn that their sense of inadequacy is not unique but is indeed part of the human condition.

The "burnout rate" among teachers of the behavior disordered adolescent is significantly high partly because of a learned unwillingness to share feelings, partly because one has little opportunity to share with peers the inevitable frustrations of the work, and partly because teachers do not perceive their own students as a source of support. The only consistent source of reward for the teacher is enjoying the students as interesting, unique, and ever-changing individuals and observing their academic and affective growth. Teacher training needs to include a range of growth experiences, and ongoing support groups should be available to all teachers as a vital part of their continuing development.

Suggested Sequence of Affective Development

It is also difficult to task analyze an affective quality. A suggested sequence of steps for maximum affective development follows (Maslow, 1954; Krathwohl, Bloom, Masia, 1964; Raths, Harmin, & Simon, 1966). To maximize affective learning, the student must feel: (a) physiologically comfortable; (b) physically safe; (c) psychologically safe and (d) cared about and respected. Given the above, a possible sequence for developing psychological skills is as follows:

The student can	*The teacher can*
1. become aware of specific or selected (by teacher) affects,	arrange the environment to facilitate awareness (put chairs of possible "friends" closer together),
2. differentiate stimuli and begin to give attention to new affect,	point out frequency, desirability ("John has a new friend; you can have friends at home, in the neighborhood," etc.),
3. search for new stimuli and begin to appreciate new skills,	provide a range of stimulations and reinforce emerging appreciation ("You and Emily work well together." "You and your friends can play basketball during recess."),
4. begin to comply with imposed constraints,	point out appropriateness ("When it's quiet time to study, you and Bill mustn't disturb the other students."),
5. look for more ways to demonstrate their new abilities,	leave the student alone to explore; intervention here can undermine new found strengths,
6. begin to become emotionally involved,	offer personal experiences ("I used to have a friend who . . ."),
7. find self unable to generalize appropriately,	point out where behavior can be appropriately ("You might want to jump rope with Margaret as well."),
8. become aware of personal process and begin to apply this situation to others,	strengthen awareness of the process and revalidate the rewards the child is receiving,

9. fail in new situations, vacillate between old and new behavior,

understand that this is not failure but growth; be supportive, not punitive; point out the satisfaction of the new behavior,

10. question self, sometimes return to familiar and destructive patterns ("The new me isn't *really* me."),

share personal experience ("I sometimes feel inadequate"); point out that a single rejection is not a devaluation of self; encourage other students to share experiences; recognize the power of the sense of loss and frustration,

11. question self and proclaim new awareness ("I really like having friends."),

encourage verbal statement of new attitude and feeling,

12. choose new behavior for themselves, recognizing that one won't always be successful; be aware of alternative choices,

point out both positive and negative consequences of behavior; point out realistic alternative behavior choices,

13. generate possibilities on their own and choose between alternatives, recognizing possible consequences.

leave the student alone unless asked.

The teacher can only facilitate movement in a student by recognizing where that student is on the hierarchy and encouraging one step at a time.

Curriculum

Developing a curriculum for the affective domain must be approached from two perspectives. The first requires a hard look at desired outcomes for each child on completion of 12 years of schooling. On completion of this assessment, the teacher selects the skills that may be accomplished during the present school year and ranks them, taking into account the child's functioning ability. This is an important part of the Individual Educational Program (IEP) required for each special education student (Public Law 94–142). The aim is independence, self-direction, responsible behavior, and a useful and creative value system. Throughout the curriculum, communication skills, verbal and nonverbal, must be stressed (Shelton, 1977).

It would be valuable for all students to gain greater facility handling their own physical environments. Behavior disordered adolescents especially need a sense of their own power to influence and control their world. Manipulative skills, such as mechanics, cooking, carpentry, sewing, or gardening, should be taught as invaluable aids to mastery.

The skill of communicating with others, self-discipline, and determining personal values are crucial to productive living and economic independence. Simon and O'Rourke (1977) have outlined a first-rate sequenced program in value clarification for the exceptional child. They include ways to approach giving life meaning, replacement therapy for "love hunger," and methods in "fill, hold, release" techniques for feelings.

The second perspective in curriculum development includes adaptation and modification of the curriculum to meet the specific individual disability. Several adaptive techniques include:

1. helping the student to relate growth to himself and not comparing himself to others;

2. looking at all personal skills, not just focusing on cognitive or academic;

3. finding areas of success, encouraging participation, and emphasizing these strengths;

4. teaching other students recently acquired skills;

5. changing the environment to minimize the effect of the disability on the accomplishment of the task;

6. teaching the student to look for alternative solutions when one way is not workable;

7. identifying desired goals of students and modifying the process toward these goals so that the disability does not prevent attainment; and

8. helping the student having difficulty in self-control to know control can be maintained if taken minute-by-minute or in small time-frames.   (Shelton, 1977)

Materials

Many materials are available and more are being developed in affective education. Careful evaluation and selection of these materials is necessary to ensure that the content is handled in an appropriate manner and to determine whether they teach what they purport to teach. Many of these materials are carefully structured in step-by-step procedures; however, since this sequencing does not take into account the level of each student, individual adaptation of the materials is necessary. The materials must be presented and used with interest, authenticity, warmth, and much care to provide a safe and constructive environment for personal growth. Particularly useful materials include Simon, Howe, and Kirschenbaum's (1972) book of exercises on value clarification; Gordon's (1977) materials on listening, problem-solving, confronting, and nonverbal communication.

Assessment and Evaluation

One of the main reasons that affective education has been neglected is because of the difficulty in assessing student growth. Some teachers have a natural facility for teaching sound living skills; for others, systematic lesson plans are helpful. If the teacher begins by writing long-term goals, develops short-term behavioral objectives, and finally does a task-analysis of each objective, evaluation is much easier. Popham (undated) suggests a series of steps to develop affective objectives. First, goals for each child are defined. Second, the teacher writes a description of a child that has successfully accomplished each of the goals (what they do, how they act, how they feel about it). Finally, the teacher describes a child who is unable to accomplish any of these skills. Within this framework, the teacher can plan how best to help the child move step-by-step from the negative position to the positive.

Research has been done in developing hierarchies for teaching attitudes, feeling, and values. Krathwohl, Bloom, and Masia (1964) outline a sequence of steps to follow for internalizing feelings. The first two steps are extremely important to the behavior disordered student. The first step, introducing a student to a new idea or process, is called *receiving*. The process of receiving begins with an awareness of the stimuli, the fact that these experiences are present. Awareness is followed by a willingness to receive, not fight, the idea. The process of receiving is completed with controlled or selected attention, looking at the ideas as possible ways of feeling or behaving.

The second step is *responding*, which begins with acquiescence in response, then willingness to respond, and, finally, satisfaction in response. Bloom continues his hierarchy with valuing, organization, and value complex. Raths, Harmin, and Simon (1966) develop their hierarchy solely by choosing values through internalization; their hierarchy of affective development gives the teacher a sequence to follow in writing behavioral objectives. Metfessel, Michael, and Kirsner (1969) have listed infinitives and direct objects to help teachers translate the taxonomy of Krathwohl et al. into behavioral terms. Mager (1968) discusses student approach and avoidance behavior as a way of developing objectives as well as assessing attitude and change.

The teacher's accurate and consistent observation, empathy, sensitivity, and awareness of student needs, both spoken and unspoken, provide much data for assessment. If a teacher listens to remarks made by a student, notes nonverbal behavior, and attends to actions the student chooses, the teacher can assess growth (Shelton, 1977).

See the listing on pages 184 and 185 for possible assessment guidelines.

Teacher Facilitation

Some teachers are able to create an atmosphere of warmth, communication, curiosity, and creative problem-solving so naturally that the classroom radiates these qualities in all academic areas and social learning skills. These teachers need little assistance; others do. Some states require human relations training for all teachers as a requirement to certification. Gazda (1973) gives an extensive review of research relating to teachers' interpersonal characteristics and student performance. Carkhuff (1969) states the core conditions which receive the most impressive backing from the research: empathy, respect, warmth, genuineness, self-disclosure, concreteness, confrontation, and immediacy of relations. The students gain significantly with teachers who have these characteristics. Programs in teacher-training institutions need to stress the acquisition of these affective skills in their human relations training. We cannot teach qualities we do not know, understand, and practice.

Morgan (1979) discusses the importance of the empathy process in teacher education. Her study, based on interviews, describes this process with emotionally disturbed young people. She states that verbalization of understanding is not the complete process but includes four modalities and the subsequent behavior of the teacher for each:

MODALITIES AND BEHAVIORS

I. MANAGEMENT OF INSTRUCTION
   A. Devises legitimate reasons to change an activity when the child is frustrated.
   B. Begins with a guaranteed success.
   C. Personalizes lesson to teach concepts.
II. ORGANIZATION OF THE ENVIRONMENT
   A. Gives the child a time and a place to be alone and quiet.
   B. Does not send the child to someone else for punishment.

C. Room itself (space and furnishings) is organized and unclut-
tered.
III.   RESPONSES TO FEELING AND EMOTIONAL WELL-BEING
   A. Senses when the child is on the verge of trouble and offers help
      before it's requested or a blow-up occurs.
   B. Identifies for children feelings they are unable to verbalize.
   C. Stays physically close and lavishes assurances.
IV.   INTERPERSONAL QUALITIES
   A. Has a sense of humor.
   B. Is warm and can openly show affection to the child.
   C. Appears calm, relaxed, speaks softly and smiles frequently.

A teacher's verbal interaction and tone of voice convey pleasure, displeasure, or confidence, and set the mood for the classroom. Jackson and Lahaderne (1967) clarify the importance of verbal interaction. They looked at the number and kinds of teacher-student contacts in the classroom and found over 100 different teacher-student interactions per hour, excluding the small-group interactions or teacher addresses to the class as a whole. Frequently the quantity of negative interactions, even if accurate and in the form of teasing, damages an individual's self-concept (Shelton, 1977).

Some of the verbal barriers to clear communication include: *commands* ("Do this!") rather than discussing how to share the tasks at hand and distributing re-sponsibility; *diagnosis* and *interpretation* ("You're doing this because you're lazy.") rather than support for problem-solving; *reassurance* rather than allowing the student to struggle with a problem ("Oh, everybody does those sorts of things."); *joking*, being sarcastic, making light of rather than dealing directly with the issue; *always . . . . never* rather than dealing with the immediate circumstance ("You always make a mess; you never clean up . . . "); *praise* rather than speaking to the issue ("You're really wonderful to be dealing with this."); *criticism* ("You're no good; none of the kids in your family has ever been any good."); *distraction* by asking questions about details rather than attending to the central issue; *fogging* by changing the topic slightly from the central issue; *comparisons* ("Your brother could do this when he was fourteen, why can't you?"); *simplistic solutions*—often cliches ("Sleep on it, you'll feel better in the morning.").

Other examples are cited by Gordon (1977). The general principle behind this list is that it is more productive to share where *you* are at the time (the "I" approach) rather than telling the other person where or what he/she is at the time (the "you" approach).

It is also important for teachers to recognize the limits of their power. The teacher cannot, for example, insure that a student gets to school on time without cooperation in the home. It is fruitless to make unrealistic demands or rules which are impossible to enforce. Such rules and demands have no "consequence" which the teacher can impose and thus only undermine the student's sense of worth.

The process of working with the behavior disordered adolescent requires sensitivity and persistence. Tuning into the student's moods, feelings, and anxiety is much easier when the teacher has a knowledge and understanding of nonverbal communication. Nonverbal messages are communicated by gestures, clusters of gestures, touch, and spaces or territories used (Shelton, 1974). These cues express interest, concern, boredom, encouragement, and other emotions and may exclude or include group members. Each person reacts to this body language and picks up an awareness of the feelings in each situation. Students who demonstrate superior ability receive more positive nonverbal messages. Some authorities (Birdwhistell, 1970; Mehrabian, 1972) feel that 65% to 95% of all communication is nonverbal. If one has the basic information necessary for looking at nonverbal behavior, then individualizing students' personal nonverbal responses furnishes information to the teacher to use in many ways:

1. Establishing some consistent parameters for each student and for what the students usually can or cannot tolerate. For example, some students cannot tolerate touching or physical closeness.

2. Defining the *usual* classroom behavior of each student, such as their space or territory, touch behavior or aversion to it, and gestures or clusters of gestures that are consistent in their lives.

3. Being aware of when the usual behavior of an individual changes and understanding the usual meanings of these cues or the student's different nonverbal behaviors.

This information affords the teacher the opportunity to intervene, verbally or nonverbally (by touch, for example, or eye contact, or softening voice quality), if it appears that a student is losing control.

Individuals may change nonverbal behaviors to indicate a change in problems in their living environment, signaling the quantity of energy present for a particular day. The student's ability to handle more work may change; he/she may signal difficulty in handling any work, new competency and confidence in a task, or the necessity for a new challenge. A student may signal readiness to relate to another individual in the classroom or the teacher for the first time by voluntary physical closeness, by initiating touch, or by direct eye contact. Sometimes this readiness is shown with a certain amount of awkwardness: a hostile touch (a punch or mild slap) may indicate a desire for further contact or affection.

Each person has a personal space or territory which is defined variously in different circumstances. These spaces are very important to each of us. The usual spaces used in the United States are as follows (Hall, 1966): 12 feet or more, formal space for presentations, sermons, lectures; 12 to 4.5 feet, formal social or business use; 4.5 to 1.5 feet, friendly space; 1.5 to 0 feet, intimate space. Respect for an individual's personal space is crucial to a person's comfort.

How close does one get to the student? At what distance is the teacher's presence distracting? This is a matter for individual discretion, observation, and sensitivity. Some students have difficulty with others, they cannot tolerate the usual territories. Personal space changes with changes in relationships.

Teachers need to touch students with care, moving slowly toward the student with some pressure but no containment. Students attend to the way adults handle inanimate objects and other persons; a soft touch encourages caring. An uncaring touch encourages a hostile response. It is important to handle students' posessions gently, with the same concern one shows for one's own belongings.

For people to be at peace within themselves, they must be able to establish timing. The teacher needs to respect each student's internal time mechanism as well as his/her own. Some people are faster, some slower, some more productive in the morning, some in the afternoon. Almost everyone hates to be hurried and appreciates being told, "Take all the time you need." Attention to a student's timing often softens a critical home atmosphere where one person's timing is different from another's. Being explicit about variations in timing can help students respect their own rhythms and thus enhance their positive self-concepts.

The ability to listen is rarely considered when "communication" is discussed; however, the teacher's willingness and ability to listen to students is an important element in the development of a student's positive self-concept. Eye contact and body language tell the students if they are really being given full attention and thus being given a measure of respect. If the teacher has other priorities, it is useful to be explicit and to make another time to listen with full attention. If there is any possibility of a misunderstanding, the teacher can repeat what the student has just said to be certain that both speaker and listener understand the communication. When students recognize that they are really being heard, they are freer to express ideas and to share feelings. Without a listener communication cannot exist.

To work in an environment where students have a variety of value systems, teachers need to be clear about their own values and to allow themselves to hear, see, and come to appreciate the values of others. Teaching and learning involve tuning into a wide range of value systems, recognizing their uniqueness and their richness in order to enlarge the worlds of both teachers and students. The teacher's verbal and nonverbal behavior demonstrates to the students an openness to unfamiliar value systems and a willingness to show them respect and appreciation.

Summary

Affective education is the development of the total individual in the school setting, including feelings, attitudes, values, communication, and interpersonal skills. In order to execute a program successfully in affective education, it must be integrated with the cognitive domain. Sensitive, perceptive teachers who are in touch with their own values, attitudes, and developmental processes are crucial to the psychological growth of the behavior disordered adolescent.

References

Birdwhistell, R. L. *Kinesics and context*. Philadelphia: University of Pennsylvania Press, 1970.

Bruner, J. S. *Beyond the information given, studies in the psychology of knowing*. New York: W. W. Northon, 1973.

Carkhuff, R. R. *Helping and healing relations: A primer for lay and professional helpers*. Vol. 2: *Practice and research*. New York: Holt, Rinehart & Winston, 1969.

Combs, A. W., Avila, D. A., & Purkey, W. W. *Helping relationships: Basic concepts for the helping professions*. Boston: Allyn & Bacon, 1971.

Feldhusen, J. F., & Treffinger, D. J. *Teaching creative thinking and problem solving*. Dubuque: Kendall/Hunt, 1977.

Gazda, G. M. *Human relations development: A manual for educators*. Boston: Allyn & Bacon, 1973.

Gordon, T. *Leader effectiveness training, L.E.T.* New York: Wyden, 1977.

Hall, E. T. *The hidden dimension*. New York: Doubleday, Inc., 1969.

Harshman, H. *Educating the emotionally disturbed, a book of readings*. New York: Thomas Y. Crowell, 1969.

Howarth, E. Personal communication. January 19, 1979.

Jackson, P. W., & Lahaderne, H. M. Inequalities of teacher–pupil contacts. *Psychology in the Schools*, 1967, *4*, 204–211.

Knapp, M. L. *Nonverbal communication in human interaction.* New York: Holt, Rinehart & Winston, 1972.

Krathwohl, D. R., Bloom, B. S., & Masia, B. B. *Taxonomy of educational objectives, Handbook II: Affective domain.* New York: David McKay, 1964.

Lewis, M., & Rosenblum, L. A. *The development of affect.* New York and London: Plenum, 1978.

Mager, R. R. *Developing attitude toward learning.* Belmont, Calif.: Fearon, 1968.

Maslow, A. H. *Motivation and personality.* New York: Harper & Row, 1954.

Mehrabian, A. *Nonverbal communication.* Chicago: Aldine-Atherton, 1972.

Metfessel, W. S., Michael, W. B., & Kirsner, D. A. Instrumentation of Bloom's and Krathwohl's taxonomies for the writing of educational objectives. *Psychology in the School,* 1969, *6,* 227-231.

Morgan, S. R. A model of the empathic process for teachers of emotionally disturbed children. *American Journal of Orthopsychiatry,* 1979, *49,* 446-453.

Payne, D. A. *The assessment of learning: Cognitive and affective.* Lexington, Mass.: D. C. Heath, 1974.

Popham, W. J. *Affective behavioral objectives.* Los Angeles: Instructional Objectives Exchange, undated. (Film)

Price-William, D. R. A study concerning concepts of conservation of quantities among primitive children. *Acta psychologica,* 1961, *18,* 297-300.

Rabain-Zempléni, J. *Quelques réflexions sur les modes fondamenteaux de relations chez l'enfant wolof du sevrage à l'intégration dans la classe d'age.* Paris: Association Universitaire pour le Développement de l'Ensignement et de la Culture Afrique et à Madagascar, 1965.

Raths, L. E., Harmin, M., & Simon, S. B. Values and teaching: *Working with values in the classroom.* Columbus, Ohio: Charles E. Merrill, 1966.

Redl, F., & Wineman, D. *Children who hate.* New York: Free Press, 1965.

Rogers, D. R. *Client-centered therapy: Its current practice, implications, and theory.* Boston: Houghton-Mifflin, 1951.

Rosenfeld, L. B. *Human interaction in the small group setting.* Columbus, Ohio: Charles E. Merrill, 1973.

Seligman, M. E. P. *Helplessness.* San Francisco: W. H. Freeman, 1975.

Shelton, M. N. Body language in the classroom. *New Mexico School Review,* 1974, *50*(4), 24-25.

Shelton, M. N. Affective education and the learning disabled student. *Journal of Learning Disabilities,* 1977, *10,* 618-624.

Simon, S. B., Howe, L. W., & Kirschenbaum, H. *Values clarification, a handbook of practical strategies for teachers and students.* New York: Hart, 1972.

Simon, S. B., & O'Rourke, R. D. *Developing values with exceptional children.* Englewood Cliffs, N.J.: Prentice-Hall, 1977.

Skinner, B. F. *Beyond freedom and dignity.* New York: Knopf, 1971.

Toffler, A. *Future shock.* New York: Bantom Books, 1971.

Behavioral Approaches to Behavioral Management

10

Robert H. Zabel

Behaviorally disordered youth typically exhibit deficits of those behaviors considered desirable and/or excesses of those behaviors considered undesirable by teachers, parents, peers, and society in general. In other words, they engage in too many inappropriate, disruptive, disagreeable behaviors and too few appropriate, cooperative, agreeable behaviors.

Secondary teachers responsible for educating students with behavior problems are usually interested in modifying behaviors in three areas. First, like all teachers, they are interested in improving the academic performance of their students. Second, they are also interested in increasing behavior that contributes to academic performance by improving what might be called "the conditions for learning," such as the percentage of days in attendance and the amount of time spent working on tasks. The third area in which teachers frequently wish to modify behaviors is social: increasing cooperation, sharing, helping, and decreasing fighting, arguing, disputing. Social behaviors are often the primary concern for teachers of behaviorally disordered youth because of their importance to a smoothly running educational program as well as to a student's "successful interaction with others." This chapter focuses on behavioral approaches for the second and third areas—behaviors that contribute to learning and social adjustment.

Intervention strategies used with behavior-disordered youth are based upon specific theoretical models. The behavioral interventions discussed in this chapter have been developed largely from operant learning principles (Skinner, 1938), which view behavior as learned because of the reinforcing consequences that follow it. Behavior that is rewarded increases, whereas behavior that is not rewarded or is punished decreases. Other interventions presented in this chapter are based upon social learning theory (Bandura, 1969; 1977), which recognizes that behavior is learned by observing others and that observers are more likely to imitate the behavior of models who are rewarded than those who are not.

Behavioral interventions have a number of features that lend themselves to application with behavior-disordered youth. For example, behavior modification approaches can be used with subjects of any age, can be adapted to developmental level, and can be used in all kinds of settings where behavior-disordered adolescents are educated, schools as well as para- or nonschool settings. In addition, they can be employed by a variety of modifiers in the natural environments where the behavior is occurring. Teachers, paraprofessionals, peers, parents, and the students themselves can learn to use behavioral techniques.

Despite the flexibility and adaptability of behavioral approaches, they should not be viewed as magical methods for changing student behavior. Although they provide teachers with a theoretical framework for understanding disordered behavior and with some systematic means for modifying behavior, they do not relieve teachers of responsibility for deciding what behavior needs to be changed or how to change it. The framework of any behavioral intervention includes three major phases of decision-making: (a) determining behavioral goals and objectives, (b) selecting methods for modifying behavior, and (c) utilizing procedures to monitor the effectiveness of the intervention. In this chapter some of the considerations involved in each of these phases of planning and implementation will be discussed.

DETERMINING BEHAVIORAL GOALS AND OBJECTIVES

The selection of which behavior to modify is a crucial step in designing behavioral interventions; yet a major limitation in the application of these techniques is that they do not determine educational goals for students (Hewett, Taylor, & Artuso, 1969; MacMillan & Forness, 1970). Mager and Pipe (1970) proposed that, when faced with problem behavior, the teacher really has four choices: change the behavior, change expectations for the behavior, change the behavior and expectations, or do nothing. Most school interventions are biased in that they focus on the first of these choices—changing students' behavior. "Because of culturally defined social stratification patterns, teachers, parents, and other adults find it easier to make interventions requiring accommodative change in the lives of children rather than changes in their own lives" (Wood, 1973, p. 187). For this reason, Wood suggests an intervention model to help insure that special educational plans are guided by recognition of the rights of and benefits to pupils. Although his model is not limited to behavioral approaches, it provides helpful guidelines for defining behavioral goals.

During the initial assessment/diagnostic stage of the Wood model, measures of individual student performance along with descriptions of interactions within the classroom system are obtained. In behavioral interventions it is essential that teachers first analyze the functional (cause and effect) relationships between student behavior and the interpersonal or social conditions within the school or classroom that support or discourage those behaviors. A functional analysis of behavior requires what is called the "A-B-C" analysis of *A*ntecedent conditions, resulting *B*ehavior, and environmental *C*onsequences that encourage or discourage the behavior. As Rhodes has pointed out in his ecological analysis of emotional disturbance (1970), behavior often is highly disturbing or distressing in some settings but not in others. This situation necessitates an analysis of the contributions of all elements of the particular environment. In the environment of the school, the analysis must attend not only to the disturbing behavior of individual students but also to the preceding and subsequent behavior of teachers, other school authorities, fellow students, and to the ensuing transactions between the disturbing individual and others. Often certain conditions within the school or classroom encourage behavior that is not considered desirable and discourages behavior that is desired.

In addition to examining the context in which disturbed / disordered behavior occurs and the reactions it elicits from others, a behavioral analysis includes obtaining measures of the current status of the behavior of interest. These *baseline* or *baserate* data are often recorded in terms of the frequency of a particular behavior within a given period of time (number of profane words per hour), sometimes in terms of duration (minutes spent sitting in seat during an hour), or magnitude (loudness of finger drumming on a desk).

Wood also suggests that assessment/diagnosis include comparisons of the disturbing behavior with that of peers. The relative difference, *discrepancy*, between baselines for target student behavior and peer behavior or between target student behavior and desired behavior can help teachers determine the relative seriousness of the problem behavior. For instance, a different approach is needed for a student who is out of his seat 30% of the time as compared to only 3% for his fellow students than for a situation in which other students are out of their seats 25% of the time. Deno and Mirken (1977) advocate the actual computation of a *discrepancy ratio* between baseline behavior of a target student and randomly observed peers. In the above examples, the ratios would be 10:1 (30/3) and 6:5 (30/25), respectively. These ratios illustrate that the out-of-seat behavior is much more discrepant in the first than it is in the second situation.

The degree of behavioral discrepancy that indicates a need for intervention depends upon how important the behavior is in the school environment and to whom (student, teacher, peers) it is important. A question teachers can ask to help determine the importance of behavioral discrepancies is: "What would happen if nothing were done about it?" (Mager & Pipe, 1970). Since youth who are considered behavior disordered often present a number of behaviors that are troubling, the teacher must assess their relative importance to general educational goals for the student. Wood suggests that, based upon assessment of the discrepancy and resources available for remediation, initial goals and objectives of an intervention plan can be outlined.

The next stage of the intervention process proposed by Wood is a key to appropriate planning of behavior modification interventions. He advocates involving both pupils and their parents in either implicit or explicit *negotiation* concerning the objectives and procedures involved in an intervention plan, as well as a justification of goals and the means of accomplishing them to the educator's peers and, if necessary, to the personnel of child protection agencies. This justification, he says, "requires reference to knowledge of child development, the probable effects of given interventions, and the requirements of law as well as available educational resources" (p. 189). Many behavior-disordered adolescents can be actively involved in this negotiation/justification phase. In fact, several of the procedures discussed later in this chapter include this involvement as an integral aspect of the intervention.

It is not only necessary to define behavioral *goals* in terms of desired or valued competencies, states of being, or general levels of proficiency, the specific *objectives* required to accomplish these goals must also be clarified. Objectives specify the quantifiable and / or observable behavior to be performed under certain conditions. An objective contributing to a goal of "appropriate classroom behavior" for the student who was out-of-seat 30% of the time might be stated: "During English class, Bill will be seated at his desk at least 80% of the time." "Appropriate" behavior is not quantifiable, but being "seated at his desk" can be observed and measured. Behavioral goals are often broken down into their component parts and sequentially taught or *shaped* until the goal is accomplished. *Shaping* consists of teaching a complex behavior by reinforcing "successive approximations" of the desired terminal behavior. It is commonly employed to increase classroom behaviors such as duration and rate of working, paying attention, and staying in one's seat (Becker, Engelmann, & Thomas, 1971, p. 87) and can also be used to teach behavior that is not yet in an individual's repertoire. For example, if a goal for a withdrawn student is participation in small group discussions, the teacher could sequentially reinforce the following behaviors: (a) approaching the group; (b) sitting with the group; (c) attending to speakers; (d) responding to direct questions; (e) volunteering a single response; and (f) engaging in interactive discussion.

Individual Educational Programs (IEPs) and due process requirements mandated in federal legislation such as the Education of All Handicapped Children Act encourage the participation of students and their parents in the negotiation of goals, objectives, and methods; teachers are required to justify their interventions; yet to a certain extent, teachers may still operate fairly independently in both of these arenas. Also embodied in recent legislation is the requirement for education in the least restrictive environment that is appropriate to the needs of the student. This principle should be used as a guideline for determining goals, objectives, and the means of accomplishing them. To the greatest extent possible, less restrictive, less aversive methods for modifying behavior should be used, and teachers should take care that behavior modification interventions are employed with the long-range benefits to the student as the central concern.

METHODS OF MODIFYING BEHAVIOR

As discussed earlier, behavior may be considered disordered because it is excessive or deficit, and a major interest of teachers of behavior-disordered youth is to increase deficient behavior and to decrease the excessive behavior. If the behavior analysis has indicated a discrepancy between subject behavior and peer or expected behavior which, in the context of negotiated behavioral goals and objectives, is judged to require modification, a number of behavior modification procedures can be employed. These modifications can frequently be accomplished by careful management of the consequences of the behavior. What follows are descriptions of some of these methods for modifying behavior with examples, either hypothetical or drawn from the literature, that illustrate their application with behavior-disordered adolescents.

Increasing Behavior

Reinforcement refers to stimuli that increase the probability of a response. There are two kinds of reinforcement that can be used to increase desired behavior. Of these, *positive reinforcement* is the most commonly employed. It involves giving a student a reward or incentive for performing a specific behavior so that the behavior is strengthened—the future rate of the behavior increases. Forms of positive reinforcement vary from tangible rewards to compliments to attention. They can also be used to serve different purposes: "Positive incentives can be presented as supportive aids ('This is to help you do x'), as expressions of appreciation ('This is in recognition of your achieving x'), or they can convey evaluative reactions ('This is what we think your performance is worth')" (Bandura, 1977, p. 110). If positive reinforcement is to be effective, it is important that reinforcers are delivered immediately following performance of the desired behavior and that they be truly rewarding to the student. *Negative reinforcement* also strengthens or increases the frequency of target behavior, but does so by removing something aversive from the environment when a student performs the behavior. For example, a teacher who tells a student that he will not have to do a third row of math problems if he finishes the first two rows correctly in a ten-minute period is using negative reinforcement. Since negative reinforcement is essentially a coercive technique for modifying behavior, the teacher who uses it risks evoking oppositional behavior in students.

Three general categories of extrinsic reinforcers that can provide incentives for engaging in behavior that students would probably otherwise not engage in are primary, secondary, and token reinforcers. *Primary*, or unconditioned, reinforcers include rewards that have intrinsically reinforcing properties, for example, items that are edible or drinkable or toys, trinkets, and other hobby items. *Secondary*, or conditioned, reinforcers are rewards that have been learned and are primarily social in nature. For instance, attention and approval from peers and teachers can be very rewarding for many adolescents, as can a variety of activities and events. Among activities that have been found rewarding for secondary students are card games, dominos, checkers, tick-tac-toe, chess, jigsaw puzzles, and talking with friends (Homme, Csanyi, Gonzales, & Rechs, 1969).

For behavior-disordered youth, it is not always possible to determine the effectiveness of reinforcers based upon assumptions of what is age-appropriate. In some cases, it may make more sense to choose reinforcers based upon the *developmental* needs of the target student. Social approval and activity-oriented reinforcers may not be as motivating for some adolescents as primary reinforcers (candy or cigarettes) and these students may require primary reinforcement, at least initially. In such cases, it is important to pair secondary reinforcement with primary reinforcement until the two are associated, and the desired behavior can eventually be maintained by secondary reinforcement alone.

Probably the best way to select reinforcers for secondary students is to *observe* what they like to do and to *ask* them what would be rewarding for them. Even students who might be expected to demand goods and services that the teacher cannot deliver are often surprisingly reasonable when selecting and negotiating reinforcers. Recently one of my students was having difficulty determining something that might be rewarding for a student at a school for behavior-disordered youth. She was reluctant to ask for his suggestions but finally in desperation, she did. He surprised her by indicating that he would really like to help the school janitor with his work. Subsequently, they negotiated a daily work period with the janitor, contingent upon the student's appropriate behavior in class.

Token economies are a form of tangible secondary reinforcement that has been an effective means of modifying the behavior of groups or individuals with maladaptive behaviors (Kazdin & Bootzin, 1972). Tokens are symbolic rewards in the form of checkmarks, points, or poker chips that can be earned for performing certain predetermined behaviors and cashed-in later for a variety of primary and/or secondary reinforcers. Token economies are based upon the so-called "Premack Principle"—a higher frequency behavior may be used to reinforce a less probable behavior (Premack, 1965). In other words, activities that students like to engage in can often be used as reinforcers for other behaviors that they do not like and engage in less frequently. A major benefit of tokens is that they can provide immediate reinforcement of responses and they gain effectiveness by being paired with back-up primary or secondary reinforcers. In a review of token economies, Kazdin and Bootzin (1972, p. 343) outlined some of the advantages of generalized conditioned reinforcers and found that tokens:

(1) bridge the delay between the target response and back-up reinforcement; (2) permit the reinforcement of a response at any time; (3) may be used to maintain performance over extended periods of time when the back-up reinforcer cannot be parcelled out; (4) allow sequences of responses to be reinforced without interruption; (5) maintain their reinforcing properties because of their relative independence of deprivation states; (6) are less subject to satiation effects; (7)

provide the same reinforcement for individuals who have different preferences in back-up reinforcers; and (8) may take on greater incentive value than a single primary reinforcer since the effects resulting from association with each primary reinforcer may summate.

To insure success when employing token systems, it is important to specify how tokens may be earned (how many for what behaviors), how they must be spent (when and the exchange rates), and, if a response-cost procedure is used, how they may be lost. For further discussion of response cost, see the discussion of punishment below.

Token economies have been shown to be effective ways for teachers to manage naturally occurring contingencies within the environment in order to encourage desired behavior of individuals and groups. Meacham and Wiesen (1969, p. 51) reported on a successful token system with an adolescent girl:

> In a nearby school, a teen-age girl who was doing poorly academically and socially agreed to a point system which allowed her time out of class for relatively free play, reading, or whatever else she wanted to do. She started to accumulate points very rapidly but would not trade them in. At the end of several months, during which her academic and social behavior improved markedly, she accumulated enough points for several days out of class. However, she did not want to trade them in. She preferred accumulating and recording them to spending them. . . . She likes school much more than she previously did and probably the social reinforcement of teacher praise has taken over the task of maintaining her behavior.

The effectiveness of the token system with this girl points to additional benefits of token economies with adolescents. First, tokens can be accumulated for rewards of greater value in the eyes of the students. Some adolescents may be more motivated by a substantial reward, such as a day off from school, than a lesser reward, such as five minutes of free time. This example also illustrates the often reinforcing effect of earning tokens as evidence of social approval. In some programs for secondary behavior-disordered students, teachers award points to each student during each period of the school day. Students carry point cards with them from class to class and they are used as the basis for weekly behavioral reports that are provided to parents. Essentially, these points represent social approval in addition to serving as a behavioral record that provides feedback on performance for both students and teachers. The role of feedback for modifying behavior will be further discussed later. Examples of successful token economies to improve behavior and academic performance of *groups* or *classes* of behavior-disordered adolescents are also available in the literature (Broden, Hall, Dunlap, & Clark, 1970; Clark, Lachowicz, & Wolf, 1968; Heaton, Safer, Allen, Spinnato, & Prumo 1976; Kaufman & O'Leary, 1972).

Graubard (1969) showed how the group could be utilized in a token economy to teach disturbed delinquents to learn. Observing that reinforcement from peers in the form of approval for delinquent behavior is usually greater than that which teachers can provide for appropriate school behavior, Graubard determined that it was essential to get a group of eight delinquent teenage boys to "buy into" a token contingency system if it was to be effective. The group was told that they could earn points exchangeable for tangible rewards, such as baseball bats, kites, and money, and social rewards, such as free time for games and listening to records, when the *entire* group followed classroom rules and completed specified academic assignments. Rules involving attendance, destruction of property, and use of physical force were given to the group, while others dealing with talking out, discussion procedures and so forth were jointly agreed upon by the teacher and students. Bonus points could be earned if all members of the group were working and behaving appropriately when a bonus bell was randomly rung. The teacher assigned work, awarded points, and ignored inappropriate behavior but management of the token system was left to the group. When the group contingencies were found to be effective, individual self-selected prizes were also made available and could be earned by members of the group for additional academic points. In 20 morning sessions, inappropriate behavior of the group decreased from 24% to 10% of all behavior and academic gains of approximately two years in reading were recorded.

Token systems have also been effectively used with delinquent and predelinquent youth in nonschool, residential settings to improve school behavior. At Achievement Place, a community-based, family-style behavior modification program for predelinquent boys, a token system includes daily school performance (Phillips, 1968; Phillips, Phillips, Fixsen, & Wolf, 1971). Points can be earned or lost for a variety of social behaviors, homework, and grades earned in public school. Alexander, Corbett, and Smigel (1976) reported the use of both individual and group contingent lunch money for improving school attendance of behaviorally disordered males in residential treatment. The group contingency condition, where all members of a group had to attend school for any of them to receive lunch money, was found to be more effective than individual contingencies for increasing class attendance for the group as a whole as well as for two subjects who were unresponsive to individual contingencies.

Fading Reinforcement

If improvements in behavior accomplished through systematic use of reinforcement are to apply to other settings and situations, it is important for teachers to think in terms of moving from reliance on extrinsic to intrinsic forms of reinforcement—from "arbitrary," teacher-determined rewards to rewards that are more naturally related to the behavior of interest (MacMillan & Forness, 1970). Extrinsic reinforcement in the form of primary or token rewards is sometimes necessary for helping a student acquire some new behavior; but when the behavior needs to be maintained, it should be *faded* from primary to secondary (social) reinforcement and eventually to intrinsic rewards, such as feelings of self-worth and the satisfaction of assuming responsibility (Whelan & Haring, 1966). Fading can also be undertaken by varying schedules of reinforcement from continuous to intermittent.

Reinforcement Schedules

Teachers using reinforcement must determine an appropriate reinforcement schedule. There are no hard and fast rules for this, but a number of possibilities exist. *Continuous reinforcement*—rewarding desired behavior every time it occurs—can be used to help increase the rate of a behavior that seldom occurs independently. Once the behavior is established, *partial* or *intermittent reinforcement* of the desired behavior is used since there is evidence that behavior is most persistent when it is reinforced at a low, variable level (Bandura, 1977, p. 116). Some types of intermittent reinforcement are fixed-interval, variable-interval, fixed-ratio, and variable-ratio schedules. A *fixed-interval* schedule provides reinforcement for the first correct response following given time periods, such as every third or fifth minute; *variable-interval* schedules reinforcement at irregular intervals, such as the third, eighth, and twelfth minutes of a fifteen-minute period. *Fixed-ratio* reinforcement is provided for a given number of desired responses, such as every fourth or sixth response, and *variable-ratio*, for an irregular number of responses, such as after the second, fifth, seventh, and eighth responses. For additional discussion of the uses, relative advantages, and disadvantages of each of these schedules, see Axelrod (1977, pp. 13–15) or Meacham and Wiesen (1969, pp. 57–61).

It is not usually necessary for teachers to reinforce every desired behavior each time it occurs, except perhaps in the earliest stages of establishing the behavior. Once a desired behavior, like raising the hand before speaking, occurs, it is usually better to employ one of the intermittent reinforcement schedules to produce a stronger, more stable response and to avoid *satiation*—the decrease in the strength of a reinforcer because of the frequency with which it is used in a given period of time (Becker et al. 1971, p. 55). Alexander and Apfel (1976) reported how varying schedules of token reinforcement from fixed to variable intervals could increase the attending behavior and decrease the disruptive behavior of behavior-disordered students during classroom activities that were less structured and not amenable to programmed materials.

Methods for Decreasing Behavior

Since behavior-disordered youth sometimes engage in an excessive amount of undesirable behavior, it is important for teachers to reduce behaviors. Among behavior modification procedures that can be used to reduce behavior are the *incompatible behavior technique, extinction*, and other forms of *punishment*.

The *incompatible behavior technique* is a recommended procedure for reducing undesired behavior because it does not introduce aversive conditions. It involves decreasing undesired behavior by increasing behavior that is incompatible with that behavior. For instance, if a student leaves his seat so often that he is not finishing his work and is disrupting the rest of the class, the teacher may decide to provide rewards when he stays in his seat. The teacher is not directly working on the problem behavior, but if in-seat behavior is increased, out-of-seat behavior must also diminish. There are numerous situations for which the incompatible behavior technique can be used.

Some studies have reported the effectiveness of eliminating problem behavior by strengthening academic performance. Kirby and Shields (1972) used the technique with a 13-year-old boy who was easily distracted and did not attend to his arithmetic lessons. His teacher combined immediate correction of his work with reinforcement in the form of teacher praise for every two arithmetic problems completed in an attempt to reduce his inattentiveness. Not only did the subject's rate of correct answers triple, but percentage of time he spent paying attention to his work nearly doubled so that he was spending almost all of his time attending.

In another study (McAllister, Stachowiak, Baer, & Conderman, 1969), a teacher employed a combination of praise for appropriate behavior (being quiet, not talking) and disapproval for target behaviors (inappropriate talking and turning around) in a low track, high-school English class where she was having difficulty with disruptive classroom behavior. Observations of these behaviors indicate that the combination of praise and disapproval by the teacher decreased the two target behaviors.

Many academic behaviors desired by teachers seem to be incompatible with behavior that is disruptive or somehow interferes with the functioning of the classroom. There has been, however, some concern regarding the relationship between teaching a student to behave better in class and the student's academic performance (Ferritor, Buckholdt, Hamblin, & Smith, 1972; Winett & Winkler, 1972). While "appropriate" nondisruptive classroom behavior certainly does not insure learning, there is evidence that increasing completion of academic work can be associated with a decrease in disruption (Kaufman & O'Leary, 1972). The incompatible behavior technique is an especially appealing method for reducing problem behavior because it focuses teacher attention on the aspects of learning that may improve performance.

Attention from the teacher can sometimes unintentionally reinforce undesired behavior. Students who have been unable in the past to obtain recognition for academic achievement and appropriate behavior often elicit attention for undesired behavior. In some cases, punishment or disapproval from the teacher actually functions as positive reinforcement (Thomas, Becker, & Armstrong, 1968). A study conducted by Buckley and Walker (1971) showed how this "free operant attention" can maintain deviant behavior as well as occupy much of a teacher's time. In a special class that I recently visited, there was a dramatic example of this. The teacher was annoyed by the frequent dropping of a pencil by a boy, so she told him that every time he dropped his pencil, she would put a mark on the blackboard for which he would lose one minute of recess. Immediately, his rate of pencil dropping increased. The "punishment" in this case was clearly reinforcing to the student.

In cases where a teacher's attention seems to be maintaining or strengthening such undesired behavior, the teacher may try *extinction*—ignoring behavior. Various kinds of bothersome behaviors have been reduced through the systematic removal of attention. Hall, Fox, Willard, Goldsmith, Emerson, Owen, Davis, and Porcia (1971) presented several studies in which teachers modified disputing and talking-out behaviors by using combinations of extinction and reinforcement. In one of these, the arguing and disputing of a 15-year-old boy in a junior-high classroom for educable mentally retarded students was ignored by the teacher who turned and walked away every time he began to dispute with her. He received the teacher's attention and praise when he did not dispute her instructions. The boy's disputing decreased and eventually was no longer considered a problem.

Extinction is not effective in all situations. Some behavior cannot be ignored because it poses dangers to the student, to others, or to property. In addition, some behavior is especially resistant to extinction because it is maintained by other reinforcers such as fellow students' laughter or attention for disruptive behavior. Also, some behaviors are themselves reinforcing. Axelrod (1977) gives the example of a teacher's ignoring students who frequently converse with each other at inappropriate times. Use of extinction by the teacher for this behavior would undoubtedly fail since the conversation is itself reinforcing. A final caution concerning the use of extinction is that behaviors often initially increase in frequency or magnitude during extinction, making it difficult for the teacher to "stick it out" until the behavior diminishes.

Various forms of *punishment* can also reduce undesired behavior. Punishment consists of presenting a physically or psychologically aversive stimulus which reduces the future probability of the behavior (Azrin & Holz, 1966, p. 381). Corporal punishment is sometimes used by teachers and other school authorities. What might be termed "psychological" punishment in the form of shaming and scolding students or removing privileges is even more commonly employed. Although punishment has been shown to be sometimes effective in producing immediate, though often only temporary, reductions of undesired behavior, it should be used with caution. In addition to ethical concerns about the physical and psychological damage punishment may cause, punishment may also produce undesirable side effects in the form of anger and antagonism toward the punisher. Teachers should also consider the kind of model for solving conflicts that they provide if they use punishment. Finally, unlike reinforcement, punishment does not teach an alternative desired form of behavior, and the punished individual may merely try to avoid the punishing situation (Azrin & Holtz, 1966, p. 440). A substitute teacher in a junior-high recounted an example of avoidance behavior: A student in one of her classes had been sent to an in-school suspension room where disruptive, problem students are "sentenced" for specified periods of time for such behavior as fighting, belligerence, or truancy. Conditions in the suspension room are intended to be highly aversive. Students are closely supervised, not allowed to leave their seats or to talk, can only raise their hands when they need to sharpen their pencils, and are even accompanied to and from the bathroom. During the following school day, the teacher happened to see this young man leaving a movie theater and later, still during school hours, she saw him riding a bike. Ironically, he had been sent to the suspension room for truancy. Apparently making the school situation punishing was not an effective means for increasing this boy's attendance.

Response cost, a form of punishment used in some token economies, is the subtraction of previously earned rewards contingent upon engaging in specified undesired behaviors. In the previously cited Kaufman and O'Leary study (1972), the effectiveness of reward vs. response cost procedures to reduce disruptive behavior in two special tutorial reading classes on the adolescent unit of a psychiatric hospital was assessed. Both procedures produced marked reductions in disruptive behavior while significantly increasing educational output and reading achievement, but no significant differences between the two procedures were found. In this study, possible undesirable side effects of the response cost procedure were not observed.

Another variation of punishment used with behavior-disordered children and youth is *time out*. As a behavior modification intervention, time out is the contingent withdrawal of opportunities for reinforcement, such as access to teachers, peer interaction, and participation in school activities, that are thought to be maintaining the behavior of interest (Johnston, 1972). Time-out provisions vary from excluding a student from class activities to secluding the student in a specially designed time-out room supervised by an adult who monitors the student's behavior and determines readiness to return to the program. A prerequisite for successful time out is that the classroom environment must be rewarding since time out will obviously be ineffective if it provides reinforcement by permitting avoidance of aversive classroom conditions. For these reasons, time-out settings should be relatively free of reinforcing stimuli while the classroom situation should be made as desirable and reinforcing as possible. Gast and Nelson (1977) suggest a number of guidelines for the use of time out. These include systematic planning, careful supervision, and continuous evaluation. Among their recommendations are that milder forms of time out such as ignoring, contingent attention, and exclusion time out should be employed before resorting to seclusion time out. Gast and Nelson also recommend concise, written procedures specifying the behaviors that result in time out, the use of warnings, duration of time-out periods, and release contingencies (pp. 462-463).

Self-monitoring. There is evidence that feedback in the form of monitoring, recording, and graphing behavior can itself serve to both increase desired behavior and reduce undesired behavior of adolescents even in the absence of external contingencies. Gottman and McFall (1972), for example, found that disruptive adolescents increased their contributions to class discussions when they recorded instances when they spoke out in class; a comparison group which was asked to record the number of times they felt like speaking out, but did not, decreased their class discussion behavior. Broden, Hall, and Mitts (1971) illustrated the use of self-recording to reduce the disruptive talking-out of an eighth-grade boy during his math class. The boy was simply instructed to make a mark on a slip of paper each time he talked without teacher approval. This self-recording, even without praise or attention for decreased talking out, initially reduced the boy's unapproved talking and improved his overall study rate. However, without differential reinforcement for reduced talking out, the self-recording appeared to eventually lose its effectiveness. Present research suggests that the effects of feedback through self-monitoring has differential effects across different treatment conditions, different subjects, and different behaviors (Polsgrove, 1977).

Contingency contracting. A form of contingency management that may be especially applicable to adolescents is the teaching of self-management through the use of *contingency* or *performance contracting*. Contracts are defined as reciprocal agreements between two or more parties establishing conditions for an exchange of mutually beneficial behavior, goods, or services. They can be informal verbal contracts or formal and written. Much interpersonal interaction is probably based upon implicit contracts governing behavioral expectations and contingencies, yet behavior disordered children and youth frequently violate these implicit contracts. Explicit formal contracts are a means of helping individuals to modify their own behavior and thereby to handle interpersonal interaction more acceptably. There is evidence that self-control is not only a function of environmental contingencies but is also influenced by observational learning and cognitive variables. Furthermore, training individuals to control their own behavior involves teaching them to manipulate both intrapersonal (convert) and external (overt) antecedent and consequent events (Meichenbaum, 1975; Polsgrove, 1977; Thoreson & Mahoney, 1974).

Kanfer and Karoly (1972) view self-control as the final outcome of a three-stage self-regulatory process including self-monitoring, self-evaluation, and self-reinforcement. It may be that, as a group, behavior-disordered youth have not adequately assimilated these three stages. Performance contracting is a behavior modification procedure for teaching all three stages involved in self-control.

Homme, Csanyi, Gonzales, and Rechs (1969) suggested a step-by-step procedure for gradually moving students from externally or teacher-controlled contracts to student-controlled contracts. In the first phase the teacher determines the amount of a specific task required to receive a teacher-specified reinforcer. In intermediate phases the student may select the task to be modified and jointly select reinforcers and monitor progress with the teacher while the teacher still controls the amount of reinforcement. Finally, the student assumes total responsibility for all phases of the contracting procedure. The procedure described by Homme et al. includes:

> (1) specification of the behavior to be changed, (2) the performance criteria for the behavior, (3) the reinforcing events and the payoff ratio between the behavior to be performed and the consequences to be received, (4) the time of delivery of payoffs, (5) a bonus clause for near perfect performance, (6) a penalty clause specifying aversive consequences for breaking the contract, and (7) the method to be used to determine whether the behavior meets selected criteria. · . . . (p. 10)

Research on contracting in educational settings is limited, but some studies involving behavior-disordered youth have been reported. Brooks (1974) presented two case studies in which contracts were set up for truant high-school students and adolescents excluded from junior high schools because of severe behavior problems. For each student the program first used three-party contracts among the student, his parents, and school staff specifying that the student would attend school in return for free schooling, bus transportation, and hot lunches. Within two weeks of entry into the program, each student's basic contract was expanded to include additional behavioral and social objectives and a token system was established in which students could earn points exchangeable for recreational activities and privileges by completing school work and behaving appropriately. As the shaping of appropriate behavior progressed, this contractual procedure gradually faded to a merit system utilizing a numerical grading system. Based upon drop-out rates, attendance, re-entry into public school, and improved academic achievement scores, the authors judged the program a success.

Modeling and rehearsal. Another approach to teaching self-control techniques that has developed largely from social learning theory involves modeling and rehearsal of behavior. Imitative learning has been shown to be a major means for learning new, complex behaviors (Bandura, 1969; 1977). Furthermore, a distinction can be made between *learning* and *performing* behavior. For instance, a person may learn a new form of behavior by observing the behavior of another but performance is largely dependent upon whether the model was rewarded or punished for the behavior. Behavior-disordered youth may not engage in certain socially desirable behaviors because they have never learned these behaviors or have not seen others rewarded for engaging in them; *modeling* and *rehearsal* techniques have been suggested as a means for teaching some of these behaviors.

For example, Gittleman (1965) used modeling and rehearsal to successfully reduce the aggressive behavior of a group of adolescent boys. The boys were instructed to engage in provocative behaviors while individual subjects rehearsed nonaggressive responses to the provocations. Kifer, Lewis, Green, and Phillips (1974) taught predelinquent adolescents to negotiate conflict resolutions with their parents. First, the experimenters presented child-parent pairs with written conflict situations. Then the subjects selected various preferred options for resolving the conflicts along with their likely outcomes. Subjects rehearsed these and negotiated settlements, including each party's position statement, identification of important issues, and suggested resolutions and outcomes, for which they received feedback from the experimenters. According to the authors, this kind of training produced improved interpersonal negotiation skills between the parents and their children.

A series of interesting projects involving modeling and rehearsal to train special education students to modify the behavior of their peers, teachers, and parents have been reported (Gray, Graubard, & Rosenberg, 1974; Rosenberg & Graubard, 1975). In one of these projects (Rosenberg, 1973) students who were to be reintegrated from special classes into the regular junior-high program were first trained to count and record the number of snubs and hostile remarks directed toward themselves by peers. Then they were taught to modify those peer behaviors by walking away when teased and ignoring provocative remarks (extinction). They were also taught to reinforce positive interactions. Special-education teachers modeled these behaviors and the students rehearsed them in classroom games. Records kept by the students indicated that positive, friendly contacts with peers increased while hostile, unfriendly behavior was reduced. Similar procedures were also found successful in modifying the nature of behavioral interactions with teachers and parents of problem kids.

MEASURING BEHAVIOR

Precise, objective, and continuous monitoring of behavioral change is integral to behavioral interventions. Behavioral records enable the teacher to determine the current extent of a behavior and the effectiveness of the specific behavior modification procedures used. Hall, Hawkins, and Axelrod (1975) discussed some of the benefits that can grow out of the process of assessment.

A. Measurement forces the teacher to define target behaviors more precisely.

B. It results in a precise assessment of performance that is a more relevant form of diagnosis than most psychological testing.

C. It focuses the teacher's efforts on the specific behavior and, thus, is more likely to achieve the desired changes.

D. The frequent—usually daily—measurement and charting of data on a graphic record encourages the teacher to persist with the technique until its effect is adequately tested, rather than to give up when immediate and obvious results cannot be seen.

E. With frequent measurement, the teacher is stimulated to make small improvements in his technique and to note the effects; the final form of the technique achieved may be much more effective than the original.

F. Measurement increases the likelihood that a teacher will apply a planned technique consistently and exclusively; often teachers who do not measure behavior will contaminate a promising technique by introducing other procedures along with it or vacillating between it and one or more other techniques that counteract its effect. (pp. 195–196)

Data collection can require a good deal of teacher time, effort, and ingenuity; however, the benefits may also be great in terms of accurate assessment of the effectiveness of interventions. This information can help determine modifications of interventions that ultimately save the time of both teacher and student as well as the interventions employed. While the teacher may often be the observer and recorder of behavior, classroom aides, volunteers, and students themselves at the secondary level can be involved in data collection. Several basic procedures for behavioral analysis that can be used in school situations have been presented in the literature (Axelrod, 1977; Hall, 1971; Hall et al., 1975). These include the direct measurement of permanent effects as well as several forms of observational recording. The measurement of *permanent effects* or lasting products is a time-honored technique of data collection—usually of academic performance. It refers to tangible products that can be observed and measured. A student's answers to math problems, compositions, and scores on standardized achievement tests are examples of lasting products. Teachers can evaluate these at their convenience.

Observational Recording

Observational recording is usually more appropriate for the collection of data on transitory behaviors that are of interest to teachers of behavior-disordered youth. Several forms of observational recording have been developed. Each has certain applications, advantages, and limitations.

Frequency recording can be used when the observer is interested in *how many* times a specific behavior of short duration occurs over a specified period. For instance, if a teacher is interested in how often a student is absent from school, raises his hand, swears, or hits another student, the teacher may want to use frequency recording. This procedure involves recording a tally, such as checkmarks on a sheet of paper, each time the behavior of interest occurs within a set period of time.

For some types of behavior it is more important to know *how long* a student engages in a particular behavior. For instance, tardiness, being out of seat, and attending to school work are types of behaviors whose *duration* may be more important than their frequency. A student may only be out of his seat once, but it could be for the entire day. The duration of some behaviors can be relatively easily timed using a wrist watch or a wall clock. Others require continuous observation of the subject and the use of a stop watch.

Duration recording can sometimes place heavy burdens on a teacher's time, and *interval recording* is an alternative procedure that accounts for both frequency and duration. In interval recording, a period of time (an hour, for instance) is broken down into shorter units of time on a recording sheet as shown in Figure 1. The teacher can then simply indicate with a "+" or "-" whether or not the behavior of interest occurs or does not occur within each unit of time. According to Hall et al. (1975), "In general, teachers find it most convenient to use interval recording when sufficient assessment can be obtained by short sessions of constant observation, the behavior of interest occurs infrequently so that the intervals can be large, or the behavior is easily detectable without intensive observation" (p. 209).

A time sampling or momentary time sampling procedure can be even more convenient for teachers than the interval recording technique. Instead of continuous observation, the teacher can observe the student only at the *end* of regular intervals of time, such as the end of every second or fourth minute. Sometimes, it is helpful to vary the sampling intervals (that is, fourth, ninth, thirteenth, fifteenth minutes) if sampling at regular intervals affects a student's performance in such a way that he modifies his behavior only at predictable observation points. As shown in Figure 2, the time intervals do not have to be regular. The teacher decides the number of behavioral samples to be taken per session and observes the specified number of times.

FIGURE 1

					Minutes						
5	10	15	20	25	30	35	40	45	50	55	60
+	+	-	+	-	+	+	+	-	-	-	+

FIGURE 2

					Minutes						
4	9	13	15	19	26	31	39	42	47	53	59
+	−	−	+	+	−	+	−	−	+	−	−

The use of devices such as a kitchen timer, the "Memo Timer," and tape recorded signals can further relieve teachers from constantly watching the clock.

To obtain an accurate record of behavior, it is important to avoid bias when recording behavior. The *reliability* measurement for lasting products depends, of course, upon the type of behavior of interest. For example, a second person may be asked to grade an essay. To account for possible bias in observational procedures, a second observer is sometimes used to determine observer reliability. In event recording, reliability is determined by dividing the observer's record with the smaller number of recorded behaviors by the record with the larger number of recorded behaviors and multiplying by 100.

$$\frac{\text{smaller number of recorded behaviors}}{\text{larger number of recorded behaviors}} \times 100 = \text{percentage agreement}$$

For interval and time sampling measurements, the formula is:

$$\frac{\text{number of agreements}}{\text{total number of measurements}} \times 100 = \text{percentage agreement}$$

The acceptable level of reliability depends to a great extent upon the specificity with which the observed behavior is defined. Generally the more precise and objective the description of the behavior of interest, the higher the reliability. While 90% agreement or above is considered desirable, 80% or better is acceptable for many types of observational recording (Hall, 1971, p. 18).

Research Designs

In addition to selecting a procedure that is appropriate for observing the behavior of interest and that is feasible within setting and time constraints for the teacher, it is necessary to determine a behavioral research design that is compatible with the behavior of interest. Most behavior modifiers use either the *reversal* or *multiple baseline* design.

The typical *reversal design* consists of several phases. The first, called *Baseline*$_1$, or base rate, which was discussed earlier, is a measure of the target behavior under normal conditions. A teacher takes baseline measures to obtain a standard against which to measure the changes in target behavior should a modification procedure be implemented. It is also during baseline definition that the behavioral discrepancies are determined. Following the collection of baseline data, the *Experimental*$_1$ phase is implemented when the teacher applies the behavioral procedure to modify the target behavior. To determine if changes in behavior are due to the intervention rather than to other influences, the process is then reversed during the *Baseline*$_2$ phase, with a return to pre-experimental conditions. Next, during the *Experimental*$_2$ phase, the behavior modification intervention is reinstated to obtain additional data on the effectiveness of the intervention procedure. A final phase, *Postchecks*, is really an extension of *Experimental*$_2$ to determine the degree of generalization of experimental effects over time. During this "follow-up" phase, measurements are usually taken less frequently. Figure 3 shows a hypothetical chart of behavior using a reversal design to illustrate the effect of extinction on the number of talk-outs.

The dotted lines in Figure 3 show the *mean* (arithmetic average) number of talk-outs during each experimental phase. Mean is computed by adding the number of behaviors observed in each phase and dividing that figure by the total number of observations. Sometimes another measure of central tendency, the *median*, or middle score, is used. This is computed by ranking the behavior frequencies of each observation from lowest to highest and finding the middle number.

There are no absolute standards for determining the length of time or number of observations that should be involved in each phase. Axelrod (1977) recommends that *Baseline*₁ in the reversal design should be carried out for a minimum of five sessions and the length of each condition should be based upon an inspection of graphed data. If the rates of behavior in the *Baseline*₁ are fairly stable, a relatively short baseline may be sufficient. Data trends are also important in determining the length of each phase. In some cases, it may be essential to continue a phase, if marked ascending or descending slopes are indicated in the graphs, until the behavior has stabilized.

Although the reversal design is useful for charting many behaviors, for others a *multiple baseline* design is appropriate. There are situations, for instance, when it is dangerous or undesirable to return to baseline conditions and when an intervention procedure appears to be effective. If an intervention appears to be reducing self-abusive behavior, for example, a teacher probably would not want to reverse the procedure. Also, some target behaviors may be irreversible. For instance, the reading performance of students may not deteriorate when a behavior modification procedure used to improve reading performance is withdrawn. In situations such as these, one of three *multiple baseline* designs may be appropriate.

The *different behaviors multiple baseline* design obtains baseline measurements for several different behaviors of an individual or group over a period of time. During an experimental phase, the intervention can be applied first to one behavior and, if successful, sequentially applied to other behaviors of interest. In the study by McAllister et al. (1969) cited earlier, contingent teacher praise and disapproval were first employed to decrease the inappropriate talking behavior of students in a disruptive English class and then to decrease inappropriate

FIGURE 3

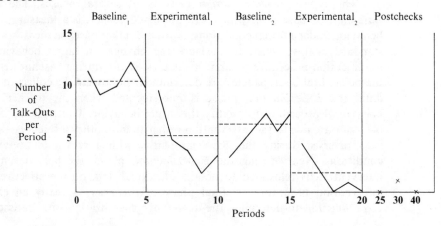

turning behavior. The *different settings multiple baseline* design consists of measuring the same behavior of an individual or group in different settings. Following a baseline phase, a behavioral intervention can be applied to a particular behavior in different situations. A student might receive reinforcement for positive interactions with peers in class. If positive interactions increase in this setting, the intervention could be extended to the lunchroom, the bus, and so on. A third multiple baseline design involves *different students*. Following the collection of a baseline for all students involved, an intervention is first applied to an individual student or subgroup of students. If the procedure is effective, it can be applied to a second, and then a third. Hall, Cristler, Cranston, and Tucker (1970) used this design in a study of the effect of negative reinforcement, in the form of contingent after-school tutoring for receiving a D or F on French quizzes, on high-school students. When the procedure improved the grades of one student, it was applied to a second, whose grades also improved, and then to a third, with similar results.

Graphing can be a valuable aspect of behavioral interventions because it provides a visual representation of the data. A conventional graph has a vertical axis (ordinate) consisting of a series of points and a horizontal axis (abscissa) with a series of points. Typically, the target behavior is charted on the vertical axis and the units of time involved in the experiment are charted on the horizontal axis. In Figure 3, the ordinates represent talk-outs per period; the abscissa represent periods of time.

Collection of data is integral to behavior modification efforts since classroom interventions are treated as experiments. As such, it is essential to determine both the current extent of a behavior and the effectiveness of an implemented intervention. Obviously observational data collection and graphing can be a time-consuming process for teachers, so it is helpful to have assistance in these activities whenever possible. Should assistance be unavailable, teachers should reserve charting for important behaviors. All behavior of every student cannot be studied; teachers must carefully select target behaviors and then carefully monitor those behaviors.

Summary

This chapter has provided an overview of approaches to behavioral management for secondary-aged students. For more detailed presentations and discussions outlined in this chapter, readers are referred to the following bibliography. Behavioral interventions do not provide all of the answers for dealing with behavior-disordered youth in our schools; however, they do offer educators a number of methods they can systematically employ to improve student behavior as well as procedures for assessing the efficacy of those interventions.

References

Alexander, R. N., & Apfel, C. Altering schedules of reinforcement for improved classroom behavior. *Exceptional Children,* 1976, *43,* 97-99.

Alexander, R. N., Corbett, T. F., & Smigel, J. The effects of individual and group consequences on school attendance and curfew violations with predelinquent adolescents. *Journal of Applied Behavior Analysis,* 1976, *9,* 221-226.

Axelrod, S. *Behavior modification for the classroom teacher*. New York: McGraw-Hill, 1977.

Azrin, N. H., & Holz, W. C. Punishment. In W. K. Honig (Ed.), *Operant behavior*. New York: Appleton-Century-Crofts, 1966.

Bandura, A. *Principles of behavior modification*. New York: Holt, Rinehart & Winston, 1969.

Bandura, A. *Social learning theory*. Englewood Cliffs, N.J.: Prentice-Hall, 1977.

Becker, W. C., Engelmann, S., & Thomas, D. R. *Teaching: A course in applied psychology*. Chicago: Science Research Associates, 1971.

Broden, M., Hall, R. V., Dunlop, A., & Clark, R. Effects of teacher attention and a token reinforcement system in a junior high school special education class. *Exceptional Children*, 1970, *36*, 341-349.

Broden, M., Hall, R. V., & Mitts, B. The effect of self-recording on the classroom behavior of two eighth-grade students. *Journal of Applied Behavior Analysis*, 1971, *4*, 191-199.

Brooks, B. D. Contingency contracts with truants. *Personnel and Guidance* Journal, 1974, *52*, 316-320.

Buckley, N. K., & Walker, H. M. Free operant teacher attention to deviant child behavior after treatment in a special class. *Psychology in the Schools*, 1971, *8*, 275-284.

Clark, M., Lachowicz, J., & Wolf, M. A pilot basic education program of school dropouts incorporating a token reinforcement system. *Behavior Research and Therapy*, 1968, *6*, 183-188.

Deno, S. L., & Mirken, P. K. *Data-based program modification: A manual*. Minneapolis, Minnesota: Leadership Training Institute/Special Education, University of Minnesota, 1977.

Ferritor, D. E., Buckholdt, D., Hamblin, R. L., & Smith, L. The noneffects of contingent reinforcement for attending behavior on work accomplished. *Journal of Applied Behavior Analysis*, 1969, *2*, 277-285.

Gast, D. L., & Nelson, C. M. Time out in the classroom: Implications for special education. *Exceptional Children*, 1977, *43*, 461-464.

Gittelman, M. Behavior rehearsal as a technique in child treatment. *Journal of Child Psychiatry*, 1965, *6*, 251-255.

Gottman, J., & McFall, R. Self-monitoring effects in a program for potential high school dropouts. *Journal of Consulting and Clinical Psychology*, 1972, *39*, 273-281.

Graubard, P. S. Utilizing the group in teaching disturbed delinquents to learn. *Exceptional Children*, 1969, *35*, 267-272.

Gray, F., Graubard, P. S., & Rosenberg, H. Little brother is changing you. *Psychology Today*, 1974 (March), 42-46.

Hall, R. V. *Managing behavior*. Part I. Lawrence, Kansas: H & H Enterprise, 1971.

Hall, R. V., Cristler, C., Cranston, S. S., & Tucker, B. Teachers and parents as researchers using multiple-baseline designs. *Journal of Applied Behavior Analysis*, 1970, *3*, 247-255.

Hall, R. V., Fox, R., Willard, D., Goldsmith, L., Emerson, M., Owen, M., Davis, F., & Porcia, E. The teacher as observer and experimenter in the modification of disputing and talking-out behaviors. *Journal of Applied Behavior Analysis*, 1971, *4*, 141-149.

Hall, R. V., Hawkins, R. P., & Axelrod, S. Measuring and recording student behavior: A behavior analysis approach. In R. A. Weinberg & F. H. Wood (Eds), *Observation of pupils and teachers in mainstream and special education: Alternative strategies*. Minneapolis, Minn.: Leadership Training Institute/Special Education, 1975.

Heaton, R. C., Safer, D. J., Allen, R. P., Spinnato, N. C., Sr., & Prumo, F. M. A motivational environment for behaviorally deviant junior high school students. *Journal of Abnormal Child Psychology*, 1976, *4*, 263-273.

Hewett, F. M., Taylor, F. D., & Artuso, A. A. The Santa Monica project: Evaluation of an engineered classroom design with emotionally disturbed children. *Exceptional Children*, 1969, *35*, 523-529.

Homme, L., Csanyi, A. P., Gonzales, M. A., & Rechs, J. R. *How to use contingency contracting in the classroom*. Champaign, Ill.: Research Press, 1969.

Johnston, J. M. Punishment of human behavior. *American Psychologist*, 1972, *27*, 1033-1054.

Kanfer, F. H., & Karoly, P. Self-control: A behavioristic excursion into the lion's den. *Behavior Therapy*, 1972, *3*, 398-416.

Kaufman, K. F., & O'Leary, K. D. Reward, cost, and self-evaluation procedures for disruptive adolescents in a psychiatric hospital school. *Journal of Applied Behavior Analysis*, 1972, *5*, 293-309.

Kazdin, A. E., & Bootzin, R. R. The token economy: An evaluative review. *Journal of Applied Behavior Analysis*, 1972, *5*, 343-372.

Kifer, R. E., Lewis, M. A., Green, D. R., & Phillips, E. L. Training predelinquent youths and their parents to negotiate conflict situations. *Journal of Applied Behavior Analysis*, 1974, *7*, 357-364.

Kirby, F. D., & Shields, F. Modification of arithmetic response rate and attending behavior in a seventh-grade student. *Journal of Applied Behavior Analysis*, 1972, *5*, 79-84.

MacMillan, D. L., & Forness, S. R. Behavior modification: Limits and liabilities. *Exceptional Children*, 1970, *37*, 291-297.

Mager, R. F., & Pipe, P. *Analyzing performance problems*. Belmont, Calif.: Fearon, 1970.

McAllister, L. W., Stachowiak, J. G., Baer, D. M., & Conderman, L. The application of operant conditioning techniques in a secondary classroom. *Journal of Applied Behavior Analysis*, 1969, *2*, 277-285.

Meacham, M. L., & Wiesen, A. E. *Changing classroom behavior: A manual for precision teaching*. Scranton, Penn.: International Textbook, 1969.

Meichenbaum, D. Toward a cognitive theory of self-control. In G. Schwartz & D. Shapiro (Eds.), *Consciousness and self-regulation: Advances in research*. New York: Plenum, 1975.

Phillips, E. L. Achievement Place: Token reinforcement procedures in a home-style rehabilitation setting for "pre-delinquent" boys. *Journal of Applied Behavior Analysis*, 1968, *1*, 213-223.

Phillips, E. L., Phillips, E. A., Fixsen, D. L. & Wolf, M. M. Achievement Place: Modification of the behaviors of pre-delinquent boys within a token economy. *Journal of Applied Behavior Analysis*, 1971, *4*, 45-59.

Polsgrove, L. Self-control: An overview of concepts and methods for child training. Paper delivered at Advanced Training Institute for Teacher Trainers of Seriously Emotionally Disturbed Children, Minneapolis, Minn., 1977.

Premack, D. Reinforcement theory. In D. Levine (Ed.), *Nebraska Symposium on Motivation*. Lincoln, Neb.: University of Nebraska Press, 1965.

Rhodes, W. C. A community-participation analysis of emotional disturbance. *Exceptional Children*, 1970, *36*, 309-314.

Rosenberg, H. E. On teaching the modification of employer and employee behavior. *Teaching Exceptional Children*, 1973, *5*, 140-142.

Rosenberg, H. E., & Graubard, P. Peer use of behavior modification. *Focus on Exceptional Children*, 1975, *7*, 1-10.

Skinner, B. F. *The behavior of organisms*. New York: Appleton-Century-Crofts, 1938.

Stein, E. M., Ball, H. E., Jr., Conn, G. T., Haran, J., & Strizver, G. L. A contingency management day program for adolescents excluded from public school. *Psychology in the Schools*, 1976, *13*, 185-191.

Thomas, D. R., Becker, W. C., & Armstrong, M. Production and elimination of disruptive classroom behavior by systematically varying teacher's behavior. *Journal of Applied Behavior Analysis*, 1968, *1*, 35-45.

Thoresen, C. E., & Mahoney, M. J. *Behavioral self-control*. New York: Holt, Rinehart, & Winston, 1974.

Whelan, R. J., & Haring, N. G. Modification and maintenance of behavior through application of consequences. *Exceptional Children*, 1966, *32*, 281-289.

Winett, R. A., & Winkler, R. C. Current behavior modification in the classroom: Be still, be quiet, be docile. *Journal of Applied Behavior Analysis*, 1972.

Wood, F. H. Negotiation and justification: An intervention model. *Exceptional Children*, 1973, *40*, 185-189.

Academic Programming for Behaviorally Disordered Adolescents: An Approach to Remediation

11

Terry L. Rose
Michael H. Epstein
Douglas Cullinan
John Lloyd

One of the major goals in educating adolescents with behavior disorders is to make certain that they are competent in fundamental academic skills, for example, decoding words, comprehending written and spoken material, computing numbers, spelling accurately, and producing legible writing. It is a major goal because incompetence in academic fundamentals, a serious handicap to almost any youth, characterizes a large proportion of behaviorally disordered adolescents. Evidence of these academic deficiencies comes from studies of the relationship of behavior problems to poor educational achievement in the general population of secondary students and among adolescents identified as behavior disordered.

For example, the findings of a national survey of the educational achievement and adjustment of noninstitutionalized 12- to 17-year-old pupils (Oliver, 1974) closely link poor school achievement to behavior disorders. Disregarding sex differences, age-related changes, and other features for the sake of brevity, pertinent results can be summarized as follows: (a) of secondary-school pupils requiring frequent discipline, more than 80% were behind in their academic achievement; (b) of those who were unpopular with their peers, more than 70% were academically behind; (c) 70% of pupils judged somewhat maladjusted and more than 80% of those judged seriously maladjusted were behind academically. Looked at another

Preparation of this manuscript was supported in part by a grant from the Bureau of Education for the Handicapped, U.S. Office of Education (grant no. G00–7700642) to the Department of Learning and Development, Northern Illinois University.

213

way, these teacher rating data showed that compared to pupils achieving at an average or better than average level academically, those who were behind academically were 3 times as likely to have poor school attendance records, 5 times as likely to be unpopular with peers, 5 times as likely to be judged somewhat maladjusted, 10 times as likely to be seen as seriously maladjusted, and 12 times as likely to require frequent discipline.

Swift and Spivak (1969) studied achievement and behavior patterns of disturbed and nondisturbed secondary-school pupils, finding that the poor achievers were significantly more likely to show dysfunctional and disruptive behavior. Educational failure has long been shown to be related to juvenile delinquency (for a review, see Silberberg & Silberberg, 1971), which certainly characterizes some fraction of disturbed secondary schoolers. Regarding the educational achievement of pupils identified as disturbed, Kauffman (1977) briefly reviewed available research and concluded that "most mildly and moderately disturbed children are academically deficient even when it is taken into account that their mental ages are typically slightly below those of their chronological age mates" (p. 122). There can be little question, then, that poor academic achievement is associated with school maladjustment among secondary-school pupils and is a major characteristic of disturbed adolescents. Therefore, important as other goals and activities for disturbed secondary pupils may be (self-understanding and acceptance, drug-abuse education, sexuality education, vocational preparation), major programming efforts must still be directed toward the goal of competence in fundamental academic skills.

APPROACHES TO ACADEMIC REMEDIATION

A number of frequently recommended teaching procedures, some of which are incompatible with one another, are available to guide efforts to strengthen academic competence (see Mann, Goodman, & Wiederholt, 1978). One possible approach to remediating academic deficits is the *process training* approach advocated by numerous authorities (for example, Bannatyne, 1969; Frostig, 1967; Minskoff, 1975) and implemented widely with the learning disabled. This approach calls for formal and informal assessment of perceptual, cognitive, language, and other psychological processes believed to underlie learning and school achievement. Patterns of functioning are noted within and among these processes and instruction is tailored to either strengthen or "teach around" deficient processes.

While process training appears logical, there is little empirical evidence that supports its efficacy in improving academic skills. Critics of the process training approaches (Hammill, 1972; Hammill & Larsen, 1974; Mann, 1971; Ysseldyke, 1973, 1978) have pointed out that the role of deficit processes in causing learning problems has not been established, the psychometric characteristics of instruments that assess psychological processes are poor, and the notion that children benefit from instruction adjusted on the basis of process strengths and weaknesses has been unsupported and even contradicted by research. Further reservations more specific to adolescents include the following: the processes to which process training approaches have attended may not be relevant for older children and adolescents; most commonly recommended process assessment instruments do not provide standardization data for adolescents; process training generally assumes an extended period of ability-building, an impractical requirement in light of the limited amount of schooling remaining for most poorly achieving adolescents. For these reasons, process training approaches are not recommended.

Another style of intervention for behaviorally disordered adolescents concentrates on building and utilizing *interpersonal relationships* to facilitate academic as well as social and personal growth (Ack, 1970; Berkowitz, 1974; Redl & Wineman, 1952; Rogers, 1969). The rationale for this approach is that because of a history of unsatisfactory dealings with teachers and other adults, unsuccessful experiences with academic tasks, dislike for schooling, and so on, the disturbed youth is unwilling and/or unable to become meaningfully involved in the educational situation. The teacher must avoid or at least play down direct instruction in deficient academic skills, instead attempting to improve the attitudes and feelings the adolescent holds toward himself or herself (Redl & Wineman, 1952; Rogers, 1969), toward the teacher (Ack, 1970), and toward the educational situation as a whole (Berkowitz, 1974). Only when these goals have been attained will the pupil spontaneously begin to learn necessary skills and/or be amenable to teacher-directed instructional procedures.

Although it is doubtless desirable that poorly achieving disturbed adolescents view themselves, their teachers, and their schools positively, it does not follow that favorable attitudes and relationships are a prerequisite to educational improvement. It may be that the better way to produce more favorable feelings about school

is to teach needed academic competencies successfully. In any case, those who insist that better relationships must precede academic remediation can point to little or no scientific evidence to support their position.

A third approach to the educational problems of adolescents with behavior disorders focuses on *direct modification* of specific unproductive behaviors. Applied research has clearly shown that on-task behavior can be increased and disruptive behavior reduced through behavior modification techniques applied to adolescents with behavior problems (Kaufman & O'Leary, 1972; McAllister, Stachowiak, Baer, & Conderman, 1969). Frequently, the major emphasis of these programs is on improving attention to task and disturbing behavior, without specific programming for academic skill improvement, perhaps on the assumption that academic gains will follow from on-task behavior. Direct evaluations of this assumption have not generally supported it, however (Ferritor, Buckholdt, Hamblin, & Smith, 1972). Conversely, behavioral interventions which have successfully modified academic functioning have also frequently brought about improved levels of pupil conduct as well (Allyon & Roberts, 1974; Kirby & Sheilds, 1972; Winett & Roach, 1973). Of course, gross physical activity, physical aggression, flagrant talking-out, and other extreme forms of classroom disruption may call for intervention directed at the conduct itself. Where milder disruption and inattention are involved, however, the bulk of available research indicates that programming efforts that encourage successful participation in learning are also likely to help solve classroom disturbance problems.

The foregoing material was intended to justify our recommended approach to planning and implementing academic remediation for disturbed adolescents. It is relatively simple to recommend a strategy and justify it on some basis; much more difficult, especially given the complex nature of adolescent disturbance, is providing detailed information on how to put such a recommendation into practice, which is the substance of the next sections.

APPLIED BEHAVIOR ANALYSIS APPROACH

Special educational applications of the technology of applied behavior analysis (ABA) have grown rapidly over the past few years. This technology is characterized by several basic tenets to which applied behavior analysts, including teachers, have adhered. Rather than attending to the improvement of hypothesized abilities or traits, behavioral practitioners have limited their teaching and investigations to specific, observable behaviors and to the measurement and evaluation of those behaviors or their products. The specification and definition of the observable aspects of teaching has become the cornerstone of a behavioral technology of teaching. The extent to which teaching procedures, curricular changes, and consequences applied to student behaviors (that is, independent variables) are defined in such a way as to allow other teachers to replicate those procedures is often the critical determining factor regarding the social impact of a teacher's efforts. Consequently, anecdotal accounts of teaching interventions are restricted in their usefulness because of their limited utility to the teaching profession.

Evaluation of the effects of any given independent variable, such as teaching intervention, is closely related to the research design employed. Numerous ABA research designs have been developed for this pupose, but because a discussion of these designs is not central to this chapter, they will not be explored further. (The interested reader is referred to Baer, Wolf, and Risley [1968], Hartmann and Hall [1976], and Hersen and Barlow [1976] for thorough explanations of the various ABA research designs.)

The accurate measurement of observable, well-defined phenomena is another fundamental tenet of ABA. The essential components of a measurement system for academic behaviors include direct measurement, daily measurement, continuous evaluation, and reliable measurement. These concepts are described below and compared to traditional methods of measuring and evaluating academic perform-ance. More detailed discussions and reviews of ABA measurement procedures are found in Baer et al. (1968), Hallahan and Kauffman (1976), Haring, Lovitt, Eaton, and Hansen (1978), Kauffman (1975), and Lovitt (1975a, 1975b).

ABA Measurement

Direct measurement refers to the assessment of specific academic behaviors and target skills of concern, or their direct products. Behavior analysts take great care to define the student's academic behaviors so that what will be measured is of direct interest in the remedial effort. For example, if the teacher is concerned with how well a student computes a specific type of addition problem (for example, mixed digits, two addends, with regrouping) the behavior that is defined and measured would be performance on an item such as $37 + 46 = \square$, rather than a grade equivalency score derived from an achievement test or subtest "scatter" on a test of psychological processing.

Daily measurement addresses the need to measure specific academic behavior on a frequent basis, if possible, daily. For example, if the specific target skill is solving addition problems of the class $37 + 46 = \square$, the teacher would collect samples of the student's responses over several consecutive days. This daily collection of performance samples contrasts with traditional methods of pupil assessment wherein evaluation is made on a monthly, quarterly, or yearly basis. An inherent advantage of daily measurement is that it allows teachers to become data-reactive because they have access to an ongoing source of data information upon which to base teaching decisions. Thus, teachers can react to facts rather than intuition and, as a consequence, can more adequately and immediately assess their own teaching strategies and/or the learner's progress.

Continuous evaluation means that with direct, daily measurement the teacher can continuously evaluate performance. As daily student performance is measured, these data can be plotted on a graph. Generally, the measure of student performance (for example, number or percentage of correct or incorrect responses) is plotted on the ordinate and time (sessions, days) is charted on the abscissa. When the data are represented graphically, the teacher can note day-to-day changes in student performance, observe the outcome of program and teacher efforts, compare student performance across difference program changes, and ultimately make accurate, data-based decisions on student progress.

Reliable measurement of student performance requires that the observation of student behavior is a true measure of the student's responses and is not confounded by extraneous variables. In applied behavior analysis, where direct observation of behavior is central, reliability is assessed by having two independent recordings of the same behavior or behavior products. To the degree that the independent records agree on the occurrence or nonoccurrence of that which is recorded, the reliability of a measurement system has been demonstrated.

From what little is known about human learning, it would appear that the acquisition of academic competence is a complex situation in which subskills and partial skills may be individually learned as the individual moves toward skillful performance of the higher level behavior. A logical way to organize efforts to teach a complex skill is to analyze its various components, arrange them in a systematic manner, and teach each of the component subskills. A recommended method for accomplishing this goal is discussed in the next section.

Curriculum and Task Analysis

In order to apply behavior analysis to academic learning, it is best to delineate the types of responses students must make and then to identify the skills learners have to be taught in order to make those responses. This requires a "top-down" analysis in which one begins by specifying terminal goals and then proceeds to work backwards from a goal through all of the components that go into the goal. The product of such a procedure is a hierarchy of tasks which, when the learners can perform them, allow us to say that the learners have attained the goal. Each task can be further analyzed in order to identify the subskills that students must have to insure adequate performance.

The procedure involving analysis of curriculum goals is called *curriculum analysis*. The goal areas that may be analyzed via curriculum analysis include oral language comprehension, written language decoding, mathematical computation, and writing. Combinations of these tool skills are essential for adequate performance in subject areas such as history, English, consumer survival, algebra, and any other area where students must understand lectures, read textbooks, write answers or essays, take multiple choice examinations, and so forth. The procedure involving analysis of curriculum subareas is commonly referred to as *task analysis*. Tasks that may be analyzed include computing answers to long-division problems, decoding words of a given type, composing topic outlines, answering questions about the economics of inflation, and so forth.

Curriculum analysis and task analysis share some characteristics: both processes break something down into its constituent parts and both are accomplished without reference to characteristics or types of learners—that is, the analyses are logical breakdowns. But they are different in two ways: (a) in curriculum analysis, *general goals* are analyzed, whereas in task analysis, *specific objectives* are analyzed; and (b) curriculum analysis identifies tasks but task analysis identifies subskills for a task.

Curriculum analysis. As an example of curriculum analysis, consider the area of arithmetic computation. The following description parallels Figure 1. The goal to be analyzed is "learners will be able to make arithmetical computations." (Notice that this is not a behavioral objective, but rather a description of a general area of competence.) The first slice in this analysis might be describing the types of numbers with which learners must work. Hence, beneath arithmetic computation one could list (a) problems involving only whole numbers, (b) problems involving only fractional numbers, and (c) problems involving mixed (whole and fractional) numbers.[1] Momentary reflection about problems involving fractional numbers

[1] For the sake of clarity in this discussion, we have omitted branches for imaginary numbers, indeterminate numbers, and so forth. Obviously, however, these lines can be considered as part of a goal of understanding mathematics.

(types b and c, above) reveals that these may be further divided into hierarchical sequences ("strands") based on decimal fractions expressed in numerator-denominator form. Under each of the types identified to this point, one should list the types of computational operations which may be applied. That is, there are whole-number-only problems requiring addition, whole-number-only problems involving subtraction, whole-number-only problems requiring multiplication, and whole-number-only problems requiring division. The same is true for decimal-fractions-only problems and the other types of numbers. Each of these types may be analyzed, as well, into subtypes: (a) whole-number addition problems which require regrouping; and (b) whole-number addition problems which do not require regrouping. Continuing, whole-number addition problems which do not require regrouping can be split into those that involve only two addends and those that involve more than two addends. Whole-number addition problems which do not require regrouping and involve only two addends can be further stratified on the basis of the number of digits in the addends. If considering only whole-number addition problems that do not require regrouping, involve only two addends, and in which each addend is a single digit, then the type of problem arrived at is commonly called a *basic math fact*.

The outcome of curriculum analysis is a hierarchy of increasingly more difficult tasks—in this case, addition tasks. At each level we could prepare an instructional objective describing the performance of a learner. Furthermore, we could construct a diagnostic inventory for determining on what tasks learners have adequate skills and on what tasks instruction is needed. By identifying the unmastered objective that is lowest on the hierarchy, we can identify where instruction must begin. When a learner has not mastered a particular objective, that objective can be directly inserted into an individual educational plan.

Task analysis. At this point one can analyze the types of problems involved in the task in order to identify the subskills which must be mastered in order to achieve a given objective. This is task analysis. Actually, it involves a preliminary decision: What is the most efficient strategy that can be taught to learners so that they can attack problems of a given sort and solve them? (In this sense, decoding in reading is seen as a problem to which learners can apply an attack strategy.) When this

FIGURE 1   Goal: Arithmetical Computation Competence

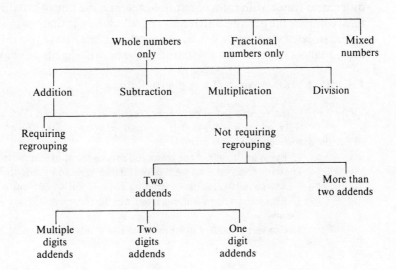

decision has been made, then it is possible to analyze the task and identify the skills that learners must have in order to master the task.

For an initial example, consider the task of decoding any real or nonsense regularly pronounced, consonant-vowel-consonant word. Clearly, one could undertake a rote memorization approach to this task and have learners master each word as a unique item; this would be equivalent to the traditional "look and say" approach to decoding. However, such an approach will require the learner to memorize over 2,000 items—a formidable task—and would have limited generality when pupils must learn another 10,000 words to acquire a reasonable reading vocabulary. As an alternative, students might be taught an attack strategy which would allow us to teach fewer items but to be assured of generalization. Such an approach would require that the learner (a) begin at the left of the word and move toward the right, (b) say sounds for the individual letters, (c) slide one sound into the next (blend), and (d), after completing the first three steps, say the word at a normal speech rate. The task analysis of this attack strategy (which borrows heavily from Bateman [1971] and Jeffrey and Samuels [1967]) is shown in Figure 2. The skills shown are the ones that must be taught.

It is important that adolescents with behavior disorders master all of these basic academic tool skills, which commonly they have not. There are, of course, other areas of academic work that are important, and tasks within these areas may also be analyzed. For example, suppose that learners are to decide which investment plan provides the best hedge against inflation, given five alternatives, a set amount of money to invest, and a projected annual rate of inflation. Clearly, it is essential that the learners have tool skills, as discussed above (that is, can calculate compound interest), in order to even begin such a task. Given those skills, however, they must simply go through a series of steps that will allow them to compare rates of return on investments with the projected inflation rate. That is, first, the pupils must determine which investment possibilities are available to them; for example, if one of the alternatives is a five-year $10,000 savings certificate, this option might be excluded from further consideration because of the amount of money they are given to invest. Second, they must determine the annual rate of return for each of the alternatives remaining after step one. Third, they must compare each alternative's rate of return with the inflation rate in order to determine the difference between inflation and earnings. Finally, after eliminating those alternatives with negative differences (those with rates of return lower than the rate of inflation), the learners must compare the positive differences and select the one that has the highest positive value. In later versions of similar tasks students may be requested to perform the same analysis when certain alternatives have been designated as having greater risk

FIGURE 2   Task Analysis of a Beginning Reading Task

Objective: Given printed list of any twenty regularly pronounced CVC words, the learner will read the words aloud at a normal speaking rate with no more than one error.
What the learner must be able to do:
   1. Begin at the left of the word and proceed to the right (note: does *not* include knowing "left" and "right"; only starting here and going that way: ⟶).
   2. Say sounds for letters including conditional sounds for c and g.
   3. Blend sounds by sliding from one to the next without stopping between sounds.
   4. Convert stretched out pronunciations into normal speaking rate pronunciations.

(stock investments in times of a highly variable market). Regardless of which task is chosen, logical analyses of tasks indicate what skills the learners must have before we can expect them to be able to perform the entire task. Each identified skill can be taught separately and then they all can be linked together into a chain that allows solution of the problem.

In summary, curriculum analysis and task analysis are tools that can be applied to academic areas and activities, tools that allow us to identify the tasks within an area and the necessary subskills within a given task. The results of these analyses can be developed into diagnostic instruments, teaching activities, and continuous monitoring systems. Additionally, the outcomes of the analyses simplify the preparation of individual education plans because sequenced goals and objectives are already specified.

Assessment

Once a curriculum analysis and a subsequent task analysis have been completed, the teacher is ready to begin the assessment procedures that are required for the successful implementation of a teaching program. Effective teaching of the educationally handicapped demands that the teacher determine where to begin instruction and monitor pupil performance once instruction has begun. The ABA approach permits accurate identification of a pupil's beginning skill level and ongoing evaluation of the effectiveness of an instructional program for that child. Assessment should lead directly to the identification of a skill or collection of skills that the student has not learned to perform correctly, either because it is a new skill or because it is performed in an unacceptable manner. Once this skill has been identified and an instructional procedure is employed, the student's performance must continue to be measured in ways that produce direct, daily, and reliable data, as discussed previously. In this section, several methods that allow a teacher to attain these objectives will be discussed.

Probes. Direct assessment of a student's performance on any given skill should address three issues. First, a student's initial proficiency on a particular academic skill needs to be determined ("Where do I begin teaching?"). Second, the breadth and consistency of any performance problem should be obtained. The student may only have problems with an individual subskill—for example, it may be that the pupil does not add correctly problems that have a 5 as the addend. On the other hand, he may have difficulty with a particular class of problems, for example, mixed digits without regrouping. Third, the strategies with which the child attacks a particular type of problem should be assessed. Informal experience indicates that educationally handicapped adolescents use strategies which may be logical and consistent but incorrect; such strategies will enable a student to answer only some problems correctly. Thus, the erroneous strategies may need to be identified and corrected.

The most effective method for assessing directly a student's beginning skill level, the extent or consistency of an academic problem, and the various strategies employed by that pupil to attack a problem involves the use of a series of *probes* (Haring & Gentry, 1976; White & Haring, 1976). An academic probe is a collection of specific examples of some class of academic tasks. Within each class the problems are arranged sequentially in order to determine specific levels of functioning within that class. Typically, each probe contains several problems that tap each skill.

Probes may be constructed along two dimensions. A *mixed probe* is designed to be a more general assessment instrument used to determine initial placement. Mixed probes contain problems or measurement opportunities for the various skills in a broad class of academic operations. For example, a mixed probe of addition will include samples of whole number problems, fractions, and decimals with and without regrouping. It will also present problems with varying column lengths and place values. After assessment with a mixed probe, the teacher has data that indicate the student's skill level and more specific assessment can take place.

Once the data from the mixed-probe have been analyzed, the teacher can then provide *probes of specific skills* that appear to warrant further analysis. For example, a student who, on the mixed probe, made frequent errors when presented with problems of the type "two digit + two digit, with regrouping in the hundreds place" may be given a probe of the type in Figure 3. The data from this probe will provide the answers to the major questions regarding the student's proficiency with this particular skill. If the student answers most problems incorrectly or answers them correctly but very slowly, then this skill may be the appropriate place to begin instruction. If, on the other hand, the student performs adequately, then further assessment must be undertaken in the form of probes that tap higher level skills.

Assessment strategy. The accumulation and analysis of accurate assessment data can best be achieved within a three-step approach which proceeds from more general to very specific information on skill levels. First, the teacher will probably receive or acquire a number of global measures of achievement early in the intervention process. These measures may include scores on standardized achievement tests, for example, the Wide Range Achievement Test (WRAT), or data from informal teacher-made inventories. These data are most useful for determining approximate performance levels and should be analyzed with that objective in mind.

The next step involves the administration of mixed probes that are based on the

FIGURE 3   Specific Skills Probe: Two-Column Addition—Regrouping in Hundreds Place

32 +87	55 +64	79 +30	45 +81	92 +23	71 +60
66 +50	75 +42	37 +90	13 +94	23 +85	44 +84
37 +71	40 +87	55 +54	41 +81	73 +65	48 +60
62 +57	46 +73	11 +94	54 +60	70 +54	91 +87
40 +60	25 +81	72 +46	55 +64	78 +40	37 +81
14 +92	81 +72	63 +94	51 +67	42 +73	61 +86
81 +43	72 +63	73 +74	54 +84	90 +91	50 +99

general information obtained from the above sources. At this level, the mixed probe should be used as a skill inventory from which more specific conclusions can be reached regarding a student's performance in particular skill areas. Consequently the student should be encouraged to attempt all problems on a mixed probe. The student's *attempts* should be emphasized rather than any performance standard; the mixed-probe sessions should not be timed and errors should not be discussed with the student.

Third, when all necessary mixed probes have been administered and scored, the teacher is in a position to select specific probes for a given subskill. Specific probes should be designed to thoroughly assess a child's performance on a particular subskill and will, therefore, offer the student a number of opportunities to demonstrate knowledge of that skill.

Probes can serve two functions: They complete the initial assessment and they provide the means for continuous monitoring of ongoing performance. A teacher need only provide daily probes in order to acquire direct, daily measures of the specific skill to be learned. The extra steps of noting beginning and ending times for each probe performance session will enable the teacher to express the child's performance in terms of rate of correct and incorrect responses.[2] An alternative solution is to simply hold the time constant for each probe, for example, one-minute timed probes.

Once a student has demonstrated mastery of the subskill, it is still necessary for the teacher to collect follow-up data to assess the retention and generality of the student's knowledge. *Retention* may be assessed by periodic assessment with specific probes, perhaps once or twice a month after mastery is demonstrated. Data from these follow-up sessions indicate whether the student is still performing a skill at the desired level of proficiency. *Transfer* of the correct problem-attack strategy to another response is assessed most economically by providing a revised version of the initial mixed probe of the same skill area. The "transfer" mixed probe should assess a more narrow band of subskills than did the initial mixed probe. For example, perhaps the initial mixed probe assessed the student's performance on all addition skills involving whole numbers and the specific probe and instruction focused on mixed digits with two addends and no regrouping (for example, $45 + 13 = \square\square$). Transfer could be assessed with a narrow-band mixed probe that includes new problems of the type learned as well as problems representative of skills at the next several higher levels on the hierarchy (for example, mixed digits, three addends, no regrouping [$16 + 52 + 21 = \square\square$]; mixed digits, two addends, with regrouping [$37 + 5 = \square\square$]). These data will allow the teacher to determine if the learned skill has generalized to related, but untaught, skills. Knowledge of any response generalizations that have occurred allow the teacher to remediate academic deficits more quickly and reduce the potential for student boredom that may be generated by teaching skills that the student has already acquired.[3]

---

[2] Rate, which is the number of occurrences of the behavior divided by the number of minutes spent responding, is the preferred measure because of its universal properties. All behavior occurs in two dimensions—count and time. Percentages may be inaccurate, especially when few items are to be calculated. For example, when 20 items are to be measured, a change of 1 response from correct to incorrect results in a change of 5%. Rate data are not subject to these whims of mathematics.

[3] Several educational programs have begun recently to employ the ABA procedures described in this section, although with populations that differ from the one discussed in this book. One of the most promising of these programs is Project ExCEL, a Title VI–G Child Service Demonstration Center for Children with Learning Disabilities located at Northern Illinois University. The purpose of the project is

Analysis of assessment data. The collection of precise assessment data is a prerequisite to implementation of ABA principles and technology. Subsequent analysis of the collected data will lead to teaching decisions regarding the efficacy of any selected intervention and will, in large part, determine the future course of many of the teacher's endeavors on behalf of a particular student.

Regardless of the selected intervention, the process of teacher scrutiny or analysis of the effects of that intervention is the cornerstone of any successful teaching endeavor. This analysis is a two-step process that will maximize the probability of a successful intervention. In step one the teacher specifies desired levels of student responses (*mastery levels*). These mastery levels are the rate or percentage of correct responses that will be accepted as evidence that the student has reached proficiency for the particular skill being taught and measured. For example, mastery for "two digit + one digit addition without regrouping" could be set at 30 correct per minute. While the establishment of mastery levels is by no means an exact science, there are several methods that can be useful as guides for the teacher (Lovitt, 1978). Briefly, these methods require data on the targeted skill from (a) peers of the student who have demonstrated superior ability, (b) peers who have demonstrated average ability, or (c) adults. The rationale for collecting these "local norms" is that the teacher may compare the rates or percentage scores of the instructed student to similar data of either his peers (to determine what performance levels are exhibited by good or at least adequate pupils) or of adults (to determine performance levels exhibited by those who compete in the larger society). The teacher can then set a level of expected performance (mastery) that the student must attain in order to demonstrate his or her competence in that skill.

The second step in the analytic process requires that the teacher formulate a *decision rule* that specifies the criteria with which a teacher will decide to (a) continue a given procedure or (b) choose to modify or change that procedure. This decision rule should allow the teacher to be data reactive, that is, the decision to continue an intervention should be based on the direct data collected regarding the student's performance on that skill. As with mastery levels, there is no exact science which allows the teacher to formulate these decision rules. An example of a successful decision rule is the "30% method" (Eaton, 1978). When using this rule, an improvement rate of at least 30%, for both correct and incorrect responses, is required in order for the teacher to continue using the current intervention. For each 3–5 day period throughout the instructional phase in which the intervention is used, the teacher calculates the medians for correct and incorrect responses on a monitored skill. If the median for either set of data shows less than 30% improvement over a given 3–5 day period, the teacher must consider selecting a new intervention. For example, the following median rates were computed from the data obtained in the first week of an intervention: corrects = 5.5 per minute, incorrects = 10.5 per minute. Medians for the second 3–5 day period of 7.0 correct/minute and 7.5 incorrect/minute were obtained. Thus, the comparison percentages between week 1 and week 2 showed that corrects increased 36.36% and incorrects decreased 33.33%. In both cases, the rate of improvement exceeds 30%;

to provide direct service to children via an applied behavior analysis model and to in-service teachers in applied behavior analysis procedures. Project ExCEL has adapted many of the features of precision teaching for use in self-contained classrooms for children with learning disabilities. The assessment and evaluation system within Project ExCEL has several essential components: it is focused on observable academic responses; it is concerned with individual student performance; it measures directly academic responses of individual children; it is used on a daily basis; and it has a specified set of materials.

therefore this intervention will continue to be employed (for at least another 3–5 day period).

It is important to remember that this process is offered as a guide for a data-based decision-making policy. It is not to be considered the definitive policy, but should serve to stimulate teachers to develop a range of sensible decision rules. In many cases, which decision rule is selected may be of less importance than the consistent adherence to a carefully formulated one.

INTERVENTIONS

Following establishment of mastery levels and decision rules, the teacher uses daily results of probes to determine the need for an intervention beyond that which is currently being applied. Teachers are given the important responsibility of providing conditions that encourage students to acquire knowledge and skills, and the responsibility includes ascertaining that interventions achieve the desired goals efficiently. The ABA measurement technology helps the teacher decide when additional intervention is called for, but how can interventions be selected?

There are several possible selection methods. First, teachers are understandably inclined to use teaching tactics that have previously been successful for them. Also, the interventions recommended by fellow educators are another source of possibilities. Further, the teaching professional consults appropriate journals and texts to locate potential methods for promoting student competence. These and other sources for possible interventions are legitimate, as long as the teacher evaluates the ideas logically and in practice; again, the ABA measurement strategy enables an empirical determination of the actual effectiveness of implemented teaching methods.

There is another method of selecting an intervention which has begun to receive attention: matching the intervention to the student's "learning stage" (Haring & Eaton, 1978; Lovitt, 1977; Smith & Lovitt, 1976). Three learning stages have been tentatively identified: (a) the acquisition stage, in which a student's percentage of correct responses to a new skill is near zero; (b) the proficiency stage, in which the new skill has been acquired but the student is not yet proficient in its use; and (c) the generalization stage, in which the student has achieved proficiency with the skill but now must learn to use this skill in new situations. Recent research with the learning disabled has indicated a possible need for matching procedures or interventions with the student's placement in one of these three learning stages (Blankenship & Lovitt, 1976; Lovitt & Curtiss, 1968; Smith & Lovitt, 1974, 1976).

The ABA research literature on remediation of academic disabilities provides ideas for teacher intervention. The advantage these ideas have over many other suggestions is that they have been tried in conjunction with ABA measurement of student academic performance, often within an ABA research design; thus there is documentation that the intervention can produce certain behavior changes. A common behavioral classification for interventions discriminates between those which focus on a change in the *antecedent events* (that is, those present before the student emits a response) and those which deal with changes in the *consequent events* (that is, those which occur subsequent to the student's response). Teaching procedures that are associated with antecedents and consequents are discussed in this section, with examples of several techniques provided along with guidelines for their use.

Antecedent Techniques

Antecedent techniques include interventions implemented prior to the occurrence of the student's targeted response. These may include (a) changes in the curricula, including curricular programs and the various stimulus dimensions of a particular curriculum; (b) changes in teacher presentation, for instance, demonstration procedures or modeling; or (c) requirements that students engage in various behaviors as a prerequisite to emitting the targeted response, for example, verbal rehearsal or mnemonic devices. Because curricular changes are discussed in another chapter, the following discussion of antecedent techniques will be limited to the latter two types of antecedent interventions: varying teacher presentation techniques and varying the "pre-target" responses of students.

Modeling refers to any of a wide variety of effects of a model's behavior upon an observer. Introspection as well as a large body of research evidence indicate that modeling can, for example, (a) promote the acquisition of novel response capabilities, (b) induce and eliminate emotional responses associated with particular situations, and (c) inhibit, facilitate, and otherwise regulate the expression of familiar behavior patterns (Bandura, 1977). Either alone or in combination with reinforcement and/or other techniques, modeling has been the basis for interventions into a wide range of behavior problems of concern to teachers of disturbed adolescents. These problems include aggressive classroom behavior (Csapo, 1972), ineffective job-seeking and interviewing skills (Prazak, 1969), failure to forego immediate gratification (Stumphauzer, 1972), and inability to accede to adult authority (Sarason & Ganzer, 1973).

In the area of academic remediation, Smith and Lovitt (1975) reported the beneficial effects of a modeling intervention on arithmetic performance. Students observed the teacher demonstrate the solution to a sample arithmetic problem; the teacher also concurrently verbalized each step of the solution, and the completed problem remained available to the student as a reference while other problems of that type were attempted.

The following illustration of modeling as an antecedent-type intervention into academic disability is compatible with Smith and Lovitt's (1975) report.

Anthony was unable to correctly solve multiplication problems which required carrying of tens-place digits. Probe results indicative of this problem are as follows:

		but	
32	70		46
×21	×17		× 23
32	490		1218
64	70		812
672	1190		9338

Anthony's teacher sought to remediate his failure to follow the carrying rule by demonstrating the convention for carrying the tens-place digit prior to assigning Anthony a worksheet of multiplication problems which required carrying. She made certain that he was attending carefully to a 3 × 5 index card on which she solved such a problem; then she exaggerated the operation in which only the ones-place digit of a two-digit product is written under the line, while the tens-place digit is placed above the next multiplier digit. Her demonstration produced, step-by-step, these products:

46	46	46	46
$\times 23$	$\times 23$	$\times 23$	$\times 23$
8	138	138	138
		2	92

Next Anthony was required to reproduce this strategy immediately while the teacher ascertained that he repeated each step as she had demonstrated. If there was an error, he had to correct it and start again from the beginning. When he could imitate the sequence perfectly, Anthony proceeded to complete the worksheet of multiplication-with-carrying problems while the example on the card remained available for review. On subsequent days, the card was turned face-down on Anthony's desk, but could be consulted if necessary; then it was placed on a nearby table to be retrieved only if Anthony needed a review. By the time multiplication-with-carrying problems were mixed with other types of problems on Anthony's worksheets, he did not find it necessary to utilize the example.

Self-verbalizing instructions. Self-verbalization training is based on the assumption that an individual's cognitions are automatic thoughts that may be part of an incorrect response chain (Meichenbaum, 1977). Therefore an initial teaching objective is that the student become aware of these cognitive response chains and the importance of each step (thought) in the successful completion of any task. Further it is theorized that habitual maladaptive behaviors should be preceded by deliberate cognitions (Premack, 1970). Self-verbalization of these cognitions will allow the individual to interrupt the sequence of behaviors that lead to an inappropriate target response. These self-verbalizations increase the probability of interrupting a maladaptive chain of events by providing appropriate instructions that are incompatible with incorrect responses.

A covert self-verbalization instructional sequence might include five steps (Meichenbaum, 1977; Meichenbaum & Goodman, 1971):

1. A model performs the targeted task while verbalizing each successive step in the problem-solving process.

2. With the model's direction, the student performs the task sequence while verbalizing the successive steps.

3. With no external directions, the student performs the task sequence while verbalizing the successive steps.

4. The student performs the task sequence while whispering key portions of the problem-solving process.

5. The student performs the task while using subvocal speech.

Within these steps, the student is required to perform several subskills that are performance relevant: (a) problem identification (what response is required), (b) attention focusing and response guiding (how and upon what is the response to be performed), and (c) feedback (self-reinforcement and error detection and correction). (For further discussions of self-verbalization, the reader is referred to Bergin [1967], Cullinan [1976], Meichenbaum [1977], and Premack [1970].)

Lovitt and Curtiss (1968) investigated the effects of self-verbalization of instructions with a behaviorally disordered pupil. Given an arithmetic task, the student was taught to verbalize a description of the task and the appropriate problem-solving sequence. In a series of three studies, Lovitt and Curtiss found that when self-verbalizations were employed by the student, the rate of correct responses increased and the incorrect response rate decreased sharply.

Other researchers have investigated the effects of self-verbalization on problem-solving (Robertson & Keeley, 1974), attending to the assigned task (Bornstein & Quevillon, 1976), reducing rule-breaking behavior (Monahan & O'Leary, 1971), and eliminating lunchroom disruptions (MacPherson, Candee, & Hohman, 1974).

> Steve has learned most of the basic addition facts and is able to compute these types of addition problems with a degree of accuracy and speed that indicates his mastery. Recently, he has begun to work on addition problems with decimal fractions and has encountered difficulty with the correct placement of the decimal point. Sample problems from one of Steve's probes reveal the following:

$$\begin{array}{ccc} .7 & .8 & .6 \\ +.7 & +.5 & +.8 \\ \hline \end{array}$$

> It is clear that Steve is adding these problems correctly except for the placement of the decimal point which is merely placed to the left of the sum.
>
> Steve's teacher sought to correct this problem by training him to verbalize an appropriate problem-solving strategy prior to his placement of the decimal point. In this case, Steve performed the addition process as he had done previously. Before placement of the decimal point, Steve said, "Find the number which has the most numerals after the decimal point. How many are there? Start at the right in my answer and count the same number of places. Put the decimal point there." In this example of a relatively easy skill, Steve verbalized these instructions to himself for a short period of time. Gradually, he internalized these instructions and could follow them when the active verbalizations were no longer required.

Consequent Techniques

Consequent techniques require the teacher to manage systematically those events that occur following the student's targeted response. Effective consequences may have one of three effects on a given response: (a) increasing the rate of responding, (b) maintaining the rate of responding, or (c) decreasing the rate of responding. One well-known example of a consequent event is reinforcement. Reinforcement is any environmental event, contingent upon a behavior, that increases or maintains the rate or duration of occurrence of that behavior (Holland & Skinner, 1961; Skinner, 1938, 1953). Reinforcement facilitates the learning and strengthening of new responses and is highly relevant to ABA intervention; thus, consequent procedures that allow the teacher to deliver reinforcement for appropriate behaviors will be discussed in this section.

Consequent procedures, unlike antecedent procedures, have been investigated extensively by researchers in a variety of fields. Various consequent events have received ample research support, including extinction (Wolf, Risley, & Mees, 1964), differential reinforcement of low rates of responding (Deitz & Repp, 1973), differential reinforcement of other behavior (Repp & Deitz, 1974), response cost (Iwata & Baily, 1974), and generalization training (Walker & Buckley, 1972). Because it is beyond the scope of this chapter to discuss all consequent events, two that appear to be among the most relevant for use with behaviorally disordered adolescents were selected for discussion.

Premack principle. An effective and efficient procedure for identifying and implementing reinforcing activities was investigated by Premack (1959). This procedure, subsequently known as the Premack principle, states that contingent access to preferred activities serves as a reinforcer for the performance on nonpreferred activities. For example, when a teacher schedules a trip to a football game contingent on the class's completion of a unit of work (if a trip to a football game is a preferred activity), the teacher is employing the Premack principle.

Although this procedure is not new, Premack's contribution was to investigate systematically the various dimensions of this phenomenon. One of the most important dimensions was found to be the need for objective verification that certain activities are, in fact, preferred. This is accomplished by observing the student as he or she engages in the activities available in the environment. By determining which activities the student engages in most frequently, one can identify preferred activities based on data rather than intuition.

The Premack principle is appealing to teachers of behaviorally disordered adolescents because potential reinforcers are already present in their programs. Adolescents always have some activities which, given unlimited opportunity, they engage in with greater frequency than others. In order to implement the Premack principle, the teacher must identify objectively the preferred activities and rearrange the program so that the preferred activities are contingent upon completion of a specified nonpreferred activity.

The Premack principle has been used with notable success in a variety of settings. Ayllon and Azrin (1965) implemented this principle with hospitalized, long-term psychiatric patients, and Homme and his colleagues (1963) were similarly successful with a group of nursery-school children. The accurate completion of assigned academic tasks was noted by Hopkins, Schutte, and Garton (1971) after they employed the Premack principle.

> Yvonne's teacher, Mrs. Olson, has noticed that, while Yvonne has been assigned reading materials well within her demonstrated ability range, she is often very slow in completing her reading assignments. Furthermore her accuracy in the reading assignments is highly variable. Yvonne reads her material with 100% accuracy several days a week but also commits numerous errors over comparable material on other days.
>
> Mrs. Olson has also observed that much of Yvonne's conversation with her friends revolves around the subject of clothes, including the latest fashions and, to a lesser degree, sewing her own clothes. The latter topic of conversation appears significant to Mrs. Olson because Yvonne has recently enrolled in an introductory sewing class offered through the Home Economics department of the high school.
>
> After collecting some preliminary information, including rate data on Yvonne's "sewing talk" and conversations with Yvonne's sewing teacher, which indicated a high rate of appropriate behavior for Yvonne during sewing class, Mrs. Olson decided to implement the Premack principle. Mrs. Olson explained to Yvonne that on those days when (a) Yvonne completed her assigned reading material during the specified reading time and (b) achieved a score of at least 100 words read correctly per minute on her daily "check-out" (probe), she could spend an extra 15 minutes with her sewing teacher. During the 15 minutes, Yvonne would receive individual attention as she worked on her sewing project.
>
> By the end of the first week, Yvonne was earning the extra 15 "sewing" minutes every day. Her reading assignments were completed on time and the data from her daily probes consistently demonstrated a high degree of accuracy. In addition, Yvonne was now proceeding through her reading materials at a rate that had heretofore been unprecedented.

Tokens are reinforcers exchangeable for objects or activities that are reinforcing for an individual. Money is a token system by which the behavior of most individuals is influenced. Likewise classroom token economies can produce desired (and undesired) changes in pupil behavior. Information on applying token economies in classrooms and cautions in their application are widely available (Ayllon & Azrin, 1968; Drabman & Tucker, 1974; Kazdin, 1977; Kazdin & Bootzin, 1972). To review briefly the use of a classroom token economy, (a) the token should be delivered with a minimum delay after the emission of the target behavior; (b) the tokens must be delivered consistently; (c) a careful balance must be maintained between the number of tokens available and the amount of back-up reinforcers that are available for exchange—too many tokens may allow the student access to reinforcers that is disproportionate to the amount of effort expended and too few tokens can lead to reduced access to reinforcers and a decrease in the rate of responding; and (d) all the conditions of the "agreement" between teacher and student need to be explicitly specified in the form of rules because when the student knows the conditions under which tokens are given and the benefits for which the tokens may be exchanged, the student will be more likely to meet those conditions. In general, token economies should be considered only when other, more natural methods have not proven effective. Tokens are a powerful and potentially intrusive intervention which are best implemented after easier to manage interventions have failed.

Many reports of the effective use of tokens have appeared in the literature. For example, tokens have been used to help adults develop coping strategies to deal with the problems of day-to-day living (Ayllon & Azrin, 1968; Schaeffer & Martin, 1969); to develop social and personal skills among predelinquents (Phillips, Phillips, Fixsen, & Wolf, 1972); and to improve academic responses for behaviorally disordered adolescents (Cohen & Filipczak, 1971; Main & Munro, 1977; McCarty, Griffin, Apolloni, & Shores, 1977; Rickard, Melvin, Creel, & Creel, 1973; Sloggett, 1971; Tyler & Brown, 1968).

George attended school in an impoverished area of Chicago. He and most of his friends were staunch fans of the White Sox, although George had never actually seen the White Sox play. Mr. Schultz, his teacher, decided to implement the Premack principle by providing access to a White Sox game at Comisky Park (preferred activity) contingent upon George's achievement of mastery levels of performance on the next three skills in his addition sequence [(a) mixed digits, two addends, no regrouping, (b) mixed digits, three addends, no regrouping, and (c) mixed digits, two addends, regrouping in ones]. It was obvious immediately to Mr. Schultz that he could not deliver this reinforcer as he had previous reinforcers because he was requiring a large amount of work and he would have to delay George's access to the game. For these reasons, Mr. Schultz implemented a token system with points being awarded. Together he and George decided that for each day that George answered at least one more problem correct on his daily probe than he had the previous day, George would receive one point. Through careful calculations, Mr. Schultz predicted that it would take George at least 20 performance sessions (days) to proceed through the targeted steps of addition skills. Consequently, Mr. Schultz and George agreed on a "price" of 20 points for his trip to the baseball game.

During the next two months, George surprised everyone, including himself, by his rapid acquisition of the skills necessary to solve the problems on his daily probes. Of course, there were days in which he did not earn his "White Sox point," but there were many more days in which he did. Additionally, Mr. Schultz always praised George's efforts, regardless of whether those efforts earned George a point or not. By the time George earned his trip to the baseball game, he was apparently working to please himself and Mr. Schultz as much as he was for the points. After their trip to the game, Mr. Schultz continued praising George's efforts, both verbally and in the glowing reports he sent regularly to George's parents and neglected to institute another token program for George. Because Mr. Schultz had been careful to "pair" his social praise of George's addition performance with the "White Sox points," the social praise served to maintain George's rate of performance even when the points were no longer available.

Procedural Steps for Solving Performance Problems

The thrust of this chapter had been to provide the teacher of the behaviorally disordered adolescent with a set of viable educational procedures. When implementing these procedures, there are eight basic procedural events to which the teacher must attend. These sequentially arranged steps are discussed briefly in the following sections and are represented in Figure 4.

1. *Pinpoint the behavior.* The teacher must operationally define the behavior of concern specifically enough for another observer to record the same behavior.

FIGURE 4

PROCEDURAL STEPS

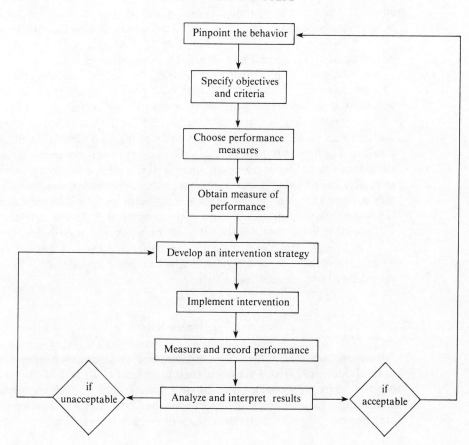

For example, "academic achievement" is *not* operationally defined because everyone will have a slightly different notion of "academic achievement." A pinpointed behavior which may be a truer reflection of the student's behavior may be the addition computation of the class two digits + one digit with regrouping. The descriptions of the specific, observable behavior to be taught is the essential ingredient of a pinpoint.

2. *Specify objectives and criteria.* The teacher must decide what is to be learned and how well it must be learned. As in driving a car we have a much better chance of arriving at a given destination if we know where we are going. A behavioral objective that specifies the student's response, the situation in which the behavior is to occur, and the acceptable criterion is the pathway to effective teaching.

3. *Choose performance measures.* Decisions must be made regarding the most appropriate data collection procedure (that is, observational or permanent product). For most academic responses, the use of permanent products is the recommended data source.

4. *Obtain a measure of actual performance.* Direct, daily measures are most useful for monitoring student performance. Probes which thoroughly sample the targeted skill are easily administered.

5. *Develop an intervention strategy.* The teacher may select either an antecedent procedure (for example, self-verbalization or modeling), a consequent procedure (the Premack principle or a token system), or some combination of antecedent and consequent intervention tactics. Precise teaching activities need to be described so carefully that the procedures are replicable by another teacher.

6. *Implement the intervention.* Explain the intervention to the student, including what you expect and what may be expected of you.

7. *Measure and record performance.* As in the preintervention phase, continue to collect direct and daily data during the intervention phase. These data will allow you to determine the effectiveness of your teaching procedure.

8. *Analyze and interpret the results.* After a sufficient period of time employ a decision rule to the recorded data. At this point, two alternative decisions are possible. The data may indicate that sufficient progress is not being made, thereby indicating a need for programmatic change. If this is the case, the teacher will have to recycle back to step 5 and develop a further intervention strategy. Or the data may indicate that adequate progress is being made and the intervention is, in fact, facilitating the student's acquisition of the targeted skill. In this case, the decision will probably be to continue the intervention and the data-recording process.

These eight steps and the attendant teacher responses are the essence of teaching from the viewpoint of ABA. The procedures discussed in this chapter allow the teacher to implement those steps.

Conclusions

Educational services for behaviorally disordered adolescents are meager in relation to need (Metz, 1973) for a variety of reasons, primarily the lack of emphasis on this population by most teacher-training programs, school districts, state and federal education agencies, and producers of educational "methods and materials." There are, however, signals that the pattern of neglect is changing, as evidenced by increased interest from the legislative and judicial branches of government, professional groups, and the like (Epstein & Cullinan, 1979).

Beneficial as these recent developments appear, adolescents with behavior disorders require not only more services but better services. Treatment efficacy studies in the area of behavior disorders (for example, Levitt, 1963) provide little reason for complacency in arranging services for the behaviorally disordered, and it is clear that special educational interventions need to be carefully examined through appropriate formative and summative research efforts. The inherent capacity for evaluation of pupil improvement is a major strength of the ABA approach.

The procedures outlined in this chapter, although founded upon a solid base of research, nevertheless require continued formal and informal investigations with the behaviorally disordered adolescent. There is a paucity of research on the efficacy of these techniques with the population in question. The research that is available has accrued across a number of settings with a number of different populations and, for those reasons, these techniques have been recommended. More important, the applied behavior analysis principles and techniques presented in this chapter provide teachers with a unique opportunity to conduct their own research in the most relevant settings—their own classrooms. These teacher-directed research efforts are highly compatible with instructional efforts and, moreover, will probably facilitate improved instructional practices. To this end, the individual teacher is heartily encouraged to engage in ABA investigative activities that will allow evaluation of the efficacy of any teaching method for the ultimate consumer of those instructional practices: the individual student.

A compelling argument for continued efforts to apply ABA principles and procedures can easily be made. These continued efforts will probably be most effective if pursued in a coordinated manner on three fronts. One, as mentioned above, the need for both summative and formative research efforts is evident. These research efforts must be undertaken without delay and should be supported by all levels of the educational establishment. Two, teacher preparation programs, both within and outside of special education, must begin to prepare teachers more adequately to educate the behaviorally disordered adolescent. Both preservice and in-service training in the procedures described in this chapter will allow teachers to provide exceptional education more adequately to their students as well as allow them to participate in the accumulation of solid data which will, in turn, lead to better education. Three, model demonstration centers should be established for behaviorally disordered youth that will incorporate present knowledge as well as extend our level of knowledge. These demonstration centers should be uniquely equipped to provide direct service to children through application of what is known, to demonstrate integrated ABA programs for possible adoption on wide spread basis, and to refine ABA procedures and techniques through evaluations.

References

Ack, M. Some principles of education for the emotionally disturbed. In P. A. Gallagher & L. L. Edwards (Eds.), *Educating the emotionally disturbed: Theory to practice*. Lawrence, Kans.: University of Kansas, 1970.

Ayllon, T., & Azrin, N. H. The measurement and reinforcement of behavior of psychotics. *Journal of the Experimental Analysis of Behavior*, 1965, *8*, 357-383.

Ayllon, T., & Azrin, N. H. *The token economy: A motivational system for therapy and rehabilitation.* New York: Appleton-Century-Crofts, 1968.

Ayllon, T., & Roberts, M. D. Eliminating discipline problems by strengthening academic performance. *Journal of Applied Behavior Analysis*, 1974, *7*, 71-76.

Baer, D. M., Wolf, M. M., & Risley, T. D. Some current dimensions of applied behavior analysis. *Journal of Applied Behavior Analysis*, 1968, *1*, 91-97.

Bandura, A. *Social learning theory.* Englewood Cliffs, N.J.: Prentice-Hall, 1977.

Bannatyne, A. Diagnosing learning disabilities and writing remedial prescriptions. *Journal of Learning Disabilities*, 1969, *1*, 242-249.

Bateman, B. D. *The essentials of teaching.* Sioux Falls, S. Dak.: Adapt Press, 1971.

Bergin, A. A self-regulation technique for impulse control disorders. *Psychotherapy: Theory, research, and practice*, 1967, *6*, 113-118.

Berkowitz, P. H. In J. M. Kauffman & C. D. Lewis (Eds.), *Teaching children with behavior disorders.* Columbus, Ohio : Charles E. Merrill, 1974.

Blankenship, C. S., & Lovitt, T. C. Story problems: Merely confusing or downright befuddling. *Journal for Research in Mathematics Education*, 1976, *7*, 290-298.

Bornstein, P., & Quevillon, R. The effects of a self-instructional package on overactive preschool boys. *Journal of Applied Behavior Analysis*, 1976, *9*, 179-188.

Cohen, H. L. & Filipczak, J. *A new learning environment.* San Francisco: Jossey-Bass, 1971.

Csapo, M. Peer models reverse the "one bad apple spoils the barrel" theory. *Teaching Exceptional Children*, 1972, *5*, 20-24.

Cullinan, D. Verbalization in EMR children's observational learning. *American Journal of Mental Deficiency*, 1976, *81*, 65-72.

Cullinan, D. Verbalization in EMR children's observational learning. *American Journal of Mental Deficiency*, 1976, *81*, 65-72.

Deitz, S. M., & Repp, A. C. Decreasing classroom misbehavior through the use of DRL schedules of reinforcement. *Journal of Applied Behavior Analysis*, 1973, *6*, 457-463.

Drabman, R. S., & Tucker, R. D. Why classroom token economies fail. *Journal of School Psychology*, 1974, *12*, 178-188.

Eaton, M. D. Data decisions and evaluation. In N. G. Haring, T. C. Lovitt, M. D. Eaton, & C. L. Hansen (Eds.), *The fourth R: Research in the classroom.* Columbus, Ohio: Charles E. Merrill, 1978.

Epstein, M. H., & Cullinan, D. Special education for adolescents: An overview. In D. Cullinan & M. H. Epstein (Eds.), *Special education for adolescents: Issues and perspectives.* Columbus, Ohio: Charles E. Merrill, 1979.

Ferritor, D. E., Buckholdt, D., Hamblin, R. L., & Smith, L. The noneffects of contingent reinforcement for attending behavior on work accomplished. *Journal of Applied Behavior Analysis*, 1972, *5*, 7-17.

Frostig, M. Testing as a basis for educational therapy. *Journal of Special Education*, 1967, *2*, 15-34.

Hallahan, D. P., & Kauffman, J. M. *Introduction to learning disabilities: A psychobehavioral approach.* Englewood Cliffs, N.J.: Prentice-Hall, 1976.

Hammill, D. D. Training visual perceptual processes. *Journal of Learning Disabilities*, 1972, *5*, 552-559.

Hammill, D. D., & Larsen, S. C. The effectiveness of psycholinguistic training. *Exceptional Children*, 1974, *41*, 5-14.

Haring, N. G., & Eaton, M. D. Systematic instructional procedures: An instructional hierarchy. In N. G. Haring, T. C. Lovitt, M. D. Eaton, & C. L. Hansen (Eds.), *The fourth R: Research in the classroom*. Columbus, Ohio: Charles E. Merrill, 1978.

Haring, N. G., & Gentry, N. D. Direct and individualized instructional procedures. In N. G. Haring & R. L. Schiefelbusch (Eds.), *Teaching special children*. New York: McGraw-Hill, 1976.

Haring, N. G., Lovitt, T. C., Eaton, M. D., & Hansen, C. L. *The fourth R: Research in the classroom*. Columbus, Ohio: Charles E. Merrill, 1978.

Hartmann, D. P., & Hall, R. V. The changing criterion design. *Journal of Applied Behavior Analysis*, 1976, *9*, 527-532.

Hersen, M., & Barlow, D. H. *Single case experimental designs: Strategies for studying behavior change*. New York: Pergamon, 1976.

Holland, J. G., & Skinner, B. F. *The analysis of behavior*. New York: McGraw-Hill, 1961.

Homme, L. E., DeBaca, P. C., Devine, J. V., Steinhorst, R., & Rickert, E. J. Use of the Premack principle in controlling the behavior of nursery school children. *Journal of the Experimental Analysis of Behavior*, 1963, *6*, 544.

Hopkins, B. L., Schutte, R. C., & Garton, K. L. The effects of access to a playroom on the rate and quality of printing and writing of first and second grade students. *Journal of Applied Behavior Analysis*, 1971, *4*, 77-87.

Iwata, B. A., & Bailey, J. S. Reward versus cost token systems: An analysis of the effects on students and teachers. *Journal of Applied Behavior Analysis*, 1974, *7*, 567-576.

Jeffrey, W. E., & Samuels, S. J. Effect of method of reading training on initial learning and transfer. *Journal of Verbal Learning and Verbal Behavior*, 1967, *6*, 354-358.

Kauffman, J. M. Behavior modification. In W. M. Cruickshank & D. P. Hallahan (Eds.), *Perceptual and learning disabilities in children* (Vol. 2). Syracuse, N.Y.: University of Syracuse Press, 1975.

Kauffman, J. M. *Characteristics of children's behavior disorders*. Columbus, Ohio: Charles E. Merrill, 1977.

Kaufman, K. F., & O'Leary, K. D. Reward, cost, and self-evaluation procedures for disruptive adolescents in a psychiatric hospital school. *Journal of Applied Behavior Analysis*, 1972, *5*, 293-309.

Kazdin, A. E. *The token economy: A review and evaluation*. New York: Plenum, 1977.

Kazdin, A. E., & Bootzin, R. R. The token economy: An evaluative review. *Journal of Applied Behavior Analysis*, 1972, *5*, 343-372.

Kirby, F. D., & Sheilds, F. Modification of arithmetic response rate and attending behavior in a seventh-grade student. *Journal of Applied Behavior Analysis*, 1972, *5*, 79-84.

Levitt, E. E. Psychotherapy with children: A further evaluation. *Behavior Research and Therapy*, 1963, *1*, 45-51.

Lovitt, T. C. Applied behavior analysis and learning disabilities. Part I: Characteristics of ABA, general recommendations, and methodological limitations. *Journal of Learning Disabilities*, 1975a, *8*, 432-443.

Lovitt, T. C. Applied behavior analysis in learning disabilities. Part II: Specific research recommendations and suggestions for practitioners. *Journal of Learning Disabilities*, 1975b, *8*, 504-518.

Lovitt, T. C. *In spite of my resistance I've learned from children*. Columbus, Ohio: Charles E. Merrill, 1977.

Lovitt, T. C. Arithmetic. In N. G. Haring, T. C. Lovitt, M. D. Eaton, & C. L. Hansen (Eds.), *The fourth R: Research in the classroom*. Columbus, Ohio: Charles E. Merrill, 1978.

Lovitt, T. C., & Curtiss, K. A. Effects of manipulating an antecedent event on mathematics response rate. *Journal of Applied Behavior Analysis*, 1968, *1*, 329-333.

McAllister, L. W., Stachowiak, J. G., Baer, D. M., & Conderman, L. The application of operant conditioning techniques in a secondary school classroom. *Journal of Applied Behavior Analysis*, 1969, *2*, 277-285.

McCarty, T., Griffin, S., Appoloni, T., & Shores, R. E. Increased peer teaching with group-oriented contingencies for arithmetic performance in behavior disordered adolescents. *Journal of Applied Behavior Analysis*, 1977, *10*, 313.

MacPherson, E. M., Candee, B. L., & Hohmen, R. J. A comparison of three methods for eliminating disruptive lunchroom behavior. *Journal of Applied Behavior Analysis*, 1974, *7*, 287-297.

Main, G. C., & Munro, B. C. A token reinforcement program in a public junior high school. *Journal of Applied Behavior Analysis*, 1977, *10*, 93-94.

Mann, L. Psychometric phrenology and the new faculty psychology: The case against ability assessment and training. *Journal of Special Education*, 1971, *5*, 3-14.

Mann, L. Goodman, L., & Wiederholt, J. L. (Eds.), *Teaching the learning disabled adolescent*. Boston: Houghton Mifflin, 1978.

Meichenbaum, D. *Cognitive-behavior modification: An integrative approach*. New York: Plenum, 1977.

Meichenbaum, D., & Goodman, J, Training impulsive children to talk to themselves: A means of developing self-control. *Journal of Abnormal Psychology*, 1971, *77*, 115-126.

Metz, A. S. *Statistics on education of the handicapped in local public school*. Washington, D.C.: U.S. Government Printing Office, 1973.

Minskoff, E. H. Research on psycholinguistic training: Critique and guidelines. *Exceptional Children*, 1975, *42*, 136-144.

Monahan, J., & O'Leary, K. D. Effects of self-instruction on rule-breaking behavior. *Psychological Reports*, 1971, *29*, 1059-1066.

Oliver, L. I. *Behavior patterns in school of youth 12-17 years*. (National Health Survey, Series 11, No. 139, U.S. Department of Health, Education, & Welfare). Washington, D.C.: U.S. Government Printing Office, 1974.

Phillips, E. L., Phillips, E. M., Fixsen, D., & Wolf, M. M. *The teaching family handbook*. Lawrence: University of Kansas, Department of Human Development, 1972.

Prazak, J. A. Learning job-seeking skills. In J. D. Krumboltz & C. E. Thoresen (Eds.), *Behavior counseling: Cases and techniques*. New York: Holt, 1969.

Premack, D. Toward empirical behavior laws: 1. Positive reinforcement. *Psychological Review*, 1959, *66*, 219-233.

Premack, D. Mechanisms of self-control. In W. Hunt (Ed.), *Learning and mechanisms of self-control in smoking*. Chicago: Aldine, 1970.

Redl, F., & Wineman, D. *Controls from within*. New York: Free Press, 1952.

Repp, A. C., & Deitz, S. M. Reducing aggressive and self-injurious behavior of institutionalized retarded children through reinforcement of other behaviors. *Journal of Applied Behavior Analysis*, 1974, *7*, 313-325.

Rickard, H. C., Melvin, K. B., Creel, J., & Creel, L. The effects of bonus tokens upon productivity in a remedial classroom for behaviorally disturbed children. *Behavior Therapy*, 1973, *4*, 378-385.

Robertson, D., & Keeley, S. Evaluation of a mediational training program for impulsive children by a multiple case study design. Paper presented at the meeting of the American Psychological Association, 1974.

Rogers, C. R. *Freedom to learn.* Columbus, Ohio: Charles E. Merrill, 1969.

Sarason, I. G., & Ganzer, V. J. Modeling and group discussion in the rehabilitation of juvenile delinquents. *Journal of Counseling Psychology,* 1973, *20,* 442-449.

Schaffer, H. H., & Martin, P. L. *Behavior therapy.* New York: McGraw-Hill, 1969.

Silberberg, N. E., & Silberberg, M. C. School achievement and delinquency. *Review of Educational Research,* 1971, *41,* 17-33.

Skinner, B. F. *The behavior of organisms.* New York: Appleton, 1938.

Skinner, B. F. *Science and human behavior.* New York: Free Press, 1953.

Sloggett, B. B. Use of group activities and team rewards to increase individual classroom productivity. *Teaching Exceptional Children,* 1971, *3,* 54-66.

Smith, D. D., & Lovitt, T. C. The influence of instructions and reinforcement contingencies on children's abilities to compute arithmetic problems. Paper presented at the Fifth Annual Conference on Behavior Analysis in Education, University of Kansas, October, 1974.

Smith, D. D., & Lovitt, T. C. The use of modeling techniques to influence the acquisition of computational arithmetic skills in learning-disabled children. In E. Ramp & G. Semb (Eds.), *Behavior analysis: Areas of research and application.* Englewood Cliffs, N.J.: Prentice-Hall, 1975.

Smith, D. D., & Lovitt, T. C. The differential effects of reinforcement contingencies on arithmetic performance. *Journal of Learning Disabilities,* 1976, *9,* 21-29.

Stumphauzer, J. S. Increased delay of gratification in young prison inmates through imitation of high-delay peer models. *Journal of Personality and Social Psychology,* 1972, *21,* 10-17.

Swift, M., & Spivack, G. Achievement related classroom behavior of secondary school normal and disturbed students. *Exceptional Children,* 1969, *35,* 677-684.

Tyler, V. O., & Brown, G. D. Token reinforcement of academic performance with institutionalized delinquent boys. *Journal of Educational Psychology,* 1968, *59,* 164-168.

Walker, H. M., & Buckley, N. K. Programming generalization and maintenance of treatment effects across time and settings. *Journal of Applied Behavior Analysis,* 1972, *5,* 209-224.

White, D. R., & Haring, N. G. *Exceptional teaching: A multimedia training package.* Columbus, Ohio: Charles E. Merrill, 1976.

Winett, R. A., & Roach, E. M. The effects of reinforcing academic performance on social behavior. *Psychological Record,* 1973, *23,* 391-396.

Wolf, M. M., Risley, T. R., & Mees, H. L. Application of operant conditioning procedures to the behavior problems of an autistic child. *Behavior Research and Therapy,* 1964, *1,* 303-312.

Ysseldyke, J. E. Diagnostic-prescriptive teaching. The search for aptitude-treatment interactions. In L. Mann & D. Sabatino (Eds.), *The first review of special education.* Philadelphia: Buttonwood Farms, 1973.

Ysseldyke, J. E. Remediation of ability deficits: Some major questions. In L. Mann, L. Goodman, & J. L. Wiederholt (Eds.), *Teaching the learning disabled adolescent.* Boston: Houghton Mifflin, 1978.

Teaching Subjects and Skills to Troubled Adolescents

12

Judy Smith
Susie R. Rice
Barbara I. Gantley

Devising relevant and effective instruction for troubled adolescents is a complex endeavor. Excellence in programming for these students requires a wide variety of teaching, management, and organizational techniques, applied intelligently according to the changing needs of the student and the group. It is not possible to establish standard educational, recreational, or vocational programs that benefit and interest adolescents at all age, grade, social, or achievement levels, and is less feasible still to presume such programs for behaviorally disordered adolescents who display an even wider range of emotional reactions and capabilities than do their peers (Eason, 1969). By the time these young men and women have entered secondary programs, they are often more difficult to deal with than they were at earlier ages, their behavior patterns may be deeply ingrained, they may have been removed from the mainstream of normal educational processes or placed with alternative agencies (Morse, Cutler, & Fink, 1964), and their problems are generally compounded by the turmoil of adolescent development. To the extent that these circumstances interfere with their scholastic achievement, these students exhibit wide divergence in the mastery of basic skills and content areas, both individually and as a group. Further, because the student with a history of difficulties in school anticipates similar difficulties in the future, attitudinal and motivational problems often need to be solved.

In consideration of these variables, this chapter argues that teachers of adolescents with behavior disorders must exercise an unusual degree of insight, versatility, and mastery of the facts and principles of academic subjects and basic skills and that they should apply these qualities to a repertoire of techniques for engaging the student in meaningful learning activities that correspond to special needs, sense of relevance, and progress toward independence and constructive maturity. The purposes of this chapter are, therefore, to delineate the multiple qualities and capabilities that the teacher should bring to the work of educating troubled adolescents, to describe some special considerations in the use of methods and materials with these students, and to suggest an approach for using the potentials of the group for adolescent education.

The chapter also presents a selection of activities that may be used to help these students master instructional tasks and integrate learning. As examples of what others have found useful with certain students and groups, these suggestions are intended as stimuli for creative planning and intervention, not as handy tools to be applied without assessing their relative benefit or impact in relation to specific students. In general, the activities represent teaching-learning situations that have relevance, a social context, clear objectives for learning, and intrinsic reinforcement for participants. Because the focus is on specific learning tasks and experiences, the presentation is eclectic in orientation and should be applicable in a number of settings and compatible with various educational philosophies. At the same time, the approaches to be presented rest upon the philosophy that:

> The adolescent who is disturbed needs not less but more of the "life stuff" that makes so-called normal kids normal. He needs to be made to face his life and the ultimate responsibility and accountability for its living. He must be moved through human and program challenges to address himself to skill and achievement. He can do this only if his treatment program plan is appropriate and if his education is reality bound, not tempered or watered (down). . . . By insisting upon and delivering an age appropriate and developmentally appropriate, fully accredited high school program, reality boundaries become more clearly discernible and then, in many cases, more bearable.   (Green, 1978, p. 13)

In addition to flexible and relevant programming for adolescents with behavior disorders, their individualized education also depends greatly upon the nature of the educational setting. "Many sensitive and ambitious plans in schools have been upset because the people engaging in them have failed to take account of what Schon (1973) called 'the theory of the institution.' By this he meant the unspoken aims of the institution, as opposed to its spoken aims. This can be true in a school, i.e., when the maintenance of the hierarchy is in fact more important than the spoken aim of educating the children" (Bruce, 1978, p. 51).

The current social philosophy of education, as well as legislation for the benefit of handicapped children and youth, supports not only equality of opportunity for all students but the concept of educating the handicapped in the least restrictive environment appropriate to their characteristics as learners as well. For handicapped adolescents, the environment that would appear to be least socially restrictive is the public secondary school. Thus, educational methods and activities suggested for the instruction of troubled adolescents must necessarily be applicable to practice in the high school and junior high school, which have been slow to respond to full programming for handicapped students. While this postponement stems in part from the traditional larger focus of special education on the younger child in the elementary school, it also relates to the current nature of education in the high school and junior high school. Because both teacher and student behaviors may be mediated by the impact of the environment in which they occur, the first objective of this chapter is to examine the characteristics of the American secondary school.

HIGH SCHOOL

The quality of public education in elementary, junior high, and high schools in the United States has been in question for more than a decade. In the context of rapid social change within the same period, it is not reasonable to charge the schools with the entire responsibility for this decline, nor to single out the secondary schools as its prime source. However, it is reasonable to examine secondary education's vulnerability to social and political forces and, consequently, the mutability of its own tradition.

The Factory School

In the 1970s, three major national panels were commissioned to study the public education of adolescents: the National Commission on the Reform of Secondary Education (Brown, 1973), the Panel on Youth of the President's Science Advisory Commission (Coleman, 1974), and the National Panel on High School and Adolescent Education (Martin, 1976).[1] The final reports of these groups, particularly the latter, set forth serious concerns. Central among these is the monumental growth of the high school itself. Whereas public secondary education was serving only 10% of the adolescent age group in 1900 and 50% as late as 1950, it serves today more than 90% of this population and graduates a full 75% (Martin, 1976). In extending educational opportunity, however, secondary education has generally not made requisite changes to accommodate expansion and social transition.

> The high school as it presently exists, regardless of its size or organization, is in most essentials the academic institution that emerged near the end of the 19th century. Over the years, it has expanded fitfully, but without much long-range planning, from an institution designed to train a small proportion of highly selected adolescents for scholarly or professional careers, into an all-purpose . . . agency for nearly all of this country's adolescents.
>
> In attempting to meet the needs of all American youth, the high school today is often failing to respond adequately to the needs of individual students. The traditional pattern of curriculum and administrative development attempts to fit changing populations . . . into an essentially static institution. [While most of the high school's academic values] deserve to be cherished, . . . their articulation and application in contemporary life seems alien to many students who acquire informal but powerful collateral education via television, the other media, their peers, and other groups with whom they associate in the community. The comprehensive high school, the most recent development of the institution, has left today's high school with its academic character weakened but still persisting and with its capacity to alter its structure to meet the needs of contemporary adolescents not significantly altered. (Martin, 1976, p. 1)

Multiple causes have been advanced for these problems. Among these is the

---

[1] The report of the National Panel on High School and Adolescent Education (Martin, 1976) is in the public domain. Portions of it quoted in this chapter remain in the public domain.

assumption that housing larger numbers of students in larger operational facilities is more cost-effective, an assumption countered by Turner and Thrasher (1976) with considerable evidence that educational effectiveness diminishes with increasing school size and numbers served, while the actual cost per pupil decreases very little. More pervasive has been the public and political philosophy that school should be the starting place for resolving social inequalities. This, in turn, has prompted some communities to enroll the entire adolescent population in a single school to circumvent segregation. Centralization has also made it easier to provide greater diversity in course offerings in an attempt to encompass the growing heterogeneity of the student body. Curricular diversity, which spawned the comprehensive high school, is now itself in question. One reason is because it frequently gives students choices that make possible the avoidance of fundamental academic and skill courses (as, for example, the choice between science fiction or grammar and composition to satisfy an English requirement). Second, academic standards are found wanting: "In high school textbooks, pictures have grown larger as words have gotten fewer; hours are shorter, instruction less rigorous, homework scarcer" (Reed, 1979). Third, the general direction and beneficiaries of the comprehensive high school's multiplicity of course offerings are questioned, inasmuch as the time, money, and substantive effort associated with such diversity often centers on the college preparatory program rather than on programs for special-needs students (Turner & Thrasher, 1976).

The "melting pot" character of expanded secondary education, coupled with the ever earlier sophistication of American youth, has also transformed high school into a microcosm of larger social dilemmas. In its efforts to stretch further its resources and extend its scope to address these symptoms, the large urban school struggles to become "a social surrogate parent for the children of the city," disciplining, feeding, clothing, counseling, financing sports activities, and trying to teach academics and culture; "all but the academics, however, are overlooked when measuring the school's success" (Woodson, 1979).

The measurement of academic achievement is an issue unto itself. Critics argue that standardized achievement and intelligence tests are academically invalid or biased against minority groups, and the 1.8 million member National Education Association advocates the abolishment of standardized testing in public schools (Sewall, Carey, Simons, & Lord, 1980). When coupled with the performance level of students entering college, however, the gradual decline of scholastic aptitude scores appears to represent some fundamental educational loss:

> Consider, for example, the steady drop in the average national score on the verbal section of the Scholastic Aptitude test; the fact that nearly half of the entering class at the University of California at Berkeley, a fairly selective school which takes only the top eighth of California high-school graduates, failed placement exams and had to be enrolled in remedial composition courses; the news that applicants to journalism programs at Wisconsin, Minnesota, Texas, and North Carolina flunk basic spelling, punctuation, and usage tests at rates that vary between 30 and 50 percent; a survey by the Association of American Publishers showing that college freshmen *really do* read on what used to be considered a high-school freshman level. (Lyons, 1976, p. 33)

The combined impact of all of these factors has made internal management in many secondary schools increasingly authoritarian, bureaucratic, repressive, and stereotyping toward students and personnel alike (Kraushaar, 1972). Moreover,

there is often a blatant contradiction, which students clearly perceive, between the public values the school espouses and the conditions that actually exist. For example, a Wisconsin modular high school publicly states that, "Our school philosophy commits us to the development of the inquiring creative mind and the self-directed individual," but the school's "self-directed individuals" are placed in detention if they chew gum, come late to class, or violate what the school calls its "Almighty Policy," which reads:

> No student should be in the corridors after the 4 minute passing time unless he has an approved pass. Students must plan their day in such a manner as to remain in each classroom or study area for the entire length of the mod. Once a student has 'alighted' he must remain in that room until the end of the mod. Violaters will be assigned detention make-up duty. Although some movement in the corridors will occur at the termination of each module, students are not to use the occasion to take a 4 minute rest every 20 minutes. During unscheduled time students are expected to stay in one area or room as much as possible. Students who have consecutive modules of unscheduled time should plan to spend at least 2 mods in a given location before moving to another area.   (Silberman, 1970, p. 342)

Such pressures and attitudes make it possible eventually for education to view students as "raw materials" and the faculty as "managers" who "design the manufacturing process (the curriculum to develop the educated student), manufacture the product (deliver lectures and seminars), evaluate the product (give grades to the students), and, if satisfied, recommend the product (student) for sale (for graduation . . .)"   (Arons, 1980, p. 18).

Teachers and Students

The National Panel on High School and Adolescent Education (Martin, 1976) pointed out that failure to plan multiple educational programs through other agencies and media had left the schools with more responsibilities than they can succeed in discharging. It was also the panel's judgment that schools housing upwards of a thousand students are not conducive to promoting intergroup and interpersonal relations. Indeed, in this atmosphere, the quality of interactions tends to deteriorate and a lack of humane concern for the individual tends to alienate students from one another, from their teachers, and from the purpose of attending school. Operating in such an emotional and intellectual vacuum can generate hostile feelings and behaviors on the part of staff and students alike, as witnessed by the published report of a former teacher:

> I could not face another demoralizing day of matching wits with a bunch of insolent and insubordinate 14-year-olds who have never been taught that it is not proper to swear at, interrupt or otherwise mock and insult a teacher. I could not bear another day of dispensing detentions, ordering kids to their proper seats (after asking them politely several times), throwing them out of my class because they failed to comply with ground rules, and otherwise dealing with rude and discourteous human beings. . . . What is most frightening about today's classroom goes well beyond the established lack of students' demonstrable skills. There seems to be a total disregard for and lack of knowledge about the proper way to treat one another as human beings. There is no such thing as respect. There is a violence and a lack of personal control that characterizes the way students relate to each other and, more noticeably, to those in authority.   (Mitric, 1980)

If educators feel powerless to evoke positive change in students and to deal with problems of the system, this sense of powerlessness is almost certain to be communicated to and experienced by students. The administrative reaction to this turmoil is to reward passivity, conformity, and obedience far more consistently than critical thinking or activism (Martin, 1976). That these values run counter to adolescent strivings is obvious. An active, rather than a passive, role is a human developmental need, and an individual's ability to exercise influence over the environment contributes importantly to a sense of identity and self-worth (Newmann, 1976). One study of secondary students (Witte, 1970) showed that the more a student was able to influence decisions in the educational setting, the greater his sense of control over his school life and the smaller the personal frustration that is a frequent cause of school disruption. It would appear that the educational experiences of many adolescents thwart their efforts toward self-definition through cognitive, as well as physiological and sexual, maturation, whereas "the proper kind of education gives meaning and direction to the search for identity, preventing it from being a mere exercise in narcissism" (Silberman, 1970, p. 336).

If it is true as Friedenberg says, that "what is learned in high school depends far less on what is taught than on what one actually experiences in the place" (Gross, 1976), then it becomes important to understand how students internalize the school milieu. One source of such information is the Pennsylvania Department of Education's Division of Quality Assessment, which has been mandated by the State Board of Education to measure annually and on a rotating basis the cognitive and affective behaviors of all fifth, eighth, and eleventh graders in one-third of the school districts in the state. Among the results reported in 1976 are these:

> Twenty-four percent of fifth graders do not like themselves very much, and nearly one-third of all fifth graders believe they can't do anything right by themselves. The

situation is even more severe for eighth graders where forty-nine percent often wish they were someone else. In addition, forty-five percent feel that, when planning to do something, it usually goes wrong. Perhaps the thirty-four percent of eighth graders "made to feel not good enough by their teachers" are a subset of this group.   (Guerriero, Coldiron, & Husband, 1976, p. 45)

The authors go on to report that 27% of eighth graders and 19% of eleventh graders would throw rocks at windows if others in a crowd were also throwing rocks, and only 40% of eighth graders and 54% of eleventh graders are certain that they would not throw rocks under the same conditions. Among the older group, only 47% are certain that they would not help to shout down a speaker, whereas 29% are certain that they would. Finally, "nearly half of the future work force believes that if money were not needed, nobody would work, and one-third of the eleventh graders believe in working only as hard as they have to" (Guerriero et al., 1976, p. 46).

More recent is a 1979 *Washington Post* report of conditions at a large public high school in one of the country's most affluent school districts, Montgomery County, Maryland:

Last year, a reporter for [the school's] award-winning newspaper, *The Tattler*, went around school with $75, hoping to write an investigative piece about the availability of drugs. He expected the money to last perhaps a week. But he was able to purchase $75 worth of marijuana . . . within four hours.

Generally, students smoke marijuana before school or during lunch, in select outdoor hideaways, in student automobiles or discreetly on outdoor bleachers. But students say they have also seen marijuana smoked in bathrooms, the library, the weightlifting room, the gymnasium, the stairwells, and the front steps outside the main office.   (Henry, 1979)

The same report details the activities of a student at the same high school who, with a group of other students, routinely pries open and burglarizes lockers—working at this before school or during classes with a foot-long pipe concealed under his coat sleeve. "Naw, I don't feel guilty," he says. "It's just too easy to pass." His father, he adds, "is a policeman" (Henry, 1979).

While the majority of adolescents do not manifest this kind of antisocial behavior, their stage of development is a transition that creates stress, problems, and/or confusion in nearly all of them at one time or another. Their education should take into consideration and address these characteristics, not aggravate them. The evidence suggests that many high schools are failing to provide a relevant and substantive educational experience and an atmosphere conducive to social learning. Adolescents are living in a society whose influences negate many traditional values; they experience considerable freedom to experiment, largely without experience or education in how to use this freedom.

While a subgroup of secondary students has been diagnosed as behaviorally disordered or emotionally disturbed and therefore eligible for special educational services, the extent and nature of adolescent behavior disorders is apparently far greater and more serious than might be extrapolated by means of incidence figures based on expectancies within the total population. More and more of these students will doubtless be referred for special services, and many others will at one time or another be vulnerable to the stresses of adolescence and society. Thus, all secondary personnel should perhaps re-examine their roles and responsibilities and, if a goal of education is to create the best learning environment, ask: "What are the best situations in which learning can take place?" (Martin, 1976, p. 8).

Less Restrictive Environments

In some schools and communities, people *are* making efforts to improve secondary education. Among the outcomes have been the creation of mini-schools, schools without walls, internships and action learning, independent study programs, open schools, apprenticeships, voucher systems, and alternative schools which emphasize small enrollments, innovative curricula, and cooperative planning by parents, students, and educational staffs. Some schools are also initiating programs that match instruction to individual needs through variation in methods, materials, content, setting, and grading systems.

For example, the students at Quincy II High School in Illinois may select from seven subschools, including a traditional model, career training, work study, and a school of fine arts, and a Burlington, Vermont, high-school program called "Aspire" permits students to spend a year away from the formal academic program in order to work alongside skilled adults in the community (Rockefeller, 1977). In Grant County, West Virginia, the Union High School week consists of four days of academic work and one day of credit-earning employment activity tailored to the goals of the individual student. In New Jersey, the State Board of Education has created an individualized plan of graduation credit on the basis of specific and measurable instructional objectives (Rockefeller, 1977).

Lakeview High School in Decatur, Illinois, encourages students to use out-of-class time for a variety of activities. If students are working on their own on assignments from teachers, the process cannot honestly be termed "independent," and so the faculty distinguishes four levels of unscheduled activity. Level 1 is conventional homework; Level 2 (project work) is homework in which students participate in selection of the topic and usually take a somewhat longer time to complete. Contract work at Level 3 allows the student to proceed through a course at his own rate, class attendance is optional, and the student indicates when he is ready for a test. Level 4 is independent study: the student initiates, plans, and evaluates his own work, asking for faculty advice or evaluation as he sees fit (Silberman, 1970, pp. 343–344).

The city of Milwaukee, Wisconsin, operates Liberty School (Eary, 1973; Haessly, 1973) as an alternative school for emotionally disturbed adolescents who had, before entry into the program, been variously described as disturbed, delinquent, disruptive, retarded, withdrawn, truant, schizophrenic, learning disabled, brain-damaged, and under-achieving. The Liberty School staff views high school as a rite of passage which transforms a child into an adult. If a person cannot successfully negotiate this transition, then there is a serious question about his ability to identify himself as an independent adult in society. Accordingly, the staff interprets its task to be:

> to produce the kind of adult who is mobile and swift to adapt to changing environments; that is, he must be able to evaluate his reality quickly and have a variety of behaviors ready to cope with changing landscapes of persons and places. Our problem is one of developing models of thinking and behaving which will serve to stabilize and organize disoriented children so that they may survive as adults. (Eary, 1973, p. 6)

Program design stresses daily structure, communication and mutual trust, and the willingness of staff members to reveal themselves and their patterns of living and, thereby, become meaningful role models. Although a psychologist is a member of the staff, there is no principal or administrative hierarchy; tasks and roles are shared, usually with students; nor is there a staff lounge or staff free period.

No student can be forced to enter Liberty School and none can be placed there by parents or referring schools. When a student applies, he is given a two-week trial period in which he must attend school every day and make some decisions about how the program can be helpful to him. On this basis, the staff decides whether or not a student will be formally admitted. (The subsequent attendance rate for admitted students is 85%.)

Education is based on long-range student goals and any behavior that interferes with these goals is considered inappropriate. A major strategy for dealing with inappropriate behavior is the creation of an environment where deviant behavior is not required. Thus, teachers do not ask students to do something that they themselves would not do and they realize that focusing attention on smoking or language, for example, can become a game used by students to challenge authority or disrupt situations that arouse emotional tension in them.

The first hour of each day is spent around a table where students and teachers talk, have coffee, discuss problems, plan futures. Staff and students also prepare meals together, sit together at the same table to eat, and clean up together. Thus, an environment is created that demands interaction. Scheduling is so flexible that on a given day there may be six classes, or none. The curriculum includes general math as well as algebra and geometry, reading, the standard academic subjects, driver education, and sports. During a twelve-month period, some students increased their reading abilities from a fourth-grade level to competence sufficient to pass the high-school equivalency examination or to enter college. Students and staff take an annual field trip to a university where they spend one night and two days visiting classes and exploring college life; camping trips are also a feature of the program. Students usually spend one year at Liberty and then return to regular high-school programs or move forward to employment, military service, or higher education.

The staff calls Liberty School a safe place where behavior problems and difficult emotions will be elicited and managed. Students must choose to come to the school and, in so doing, must commit time and energy to "growing themselves up"; students must gain control over their own lives and become responsible for their own behavior—they have to choose to survive.

The schools just described *stand for something*. All schools should stand for something that students can believe in and trust; to the extent that this is not the case in the American high school, change should take place. Buckminster Fuller (1962) pointed out that the twentieth century has witnessed the full-scale emergence of the theory that significant change can be made only by transforming the environment, as opposed to trying to change the people within it. The social history of the past few decades has revealed that this theory is fallacious and, indeed, has probably figured heavily in the current problems of the secondary school. In truth, change is made first by individuals, then by institutions (Hall, 1978), and is best facilitated by interpersonal interactions and involvements (Horvat, 1972).

Among those who should initiate change are teachers and administrators, and a way to begin might simply be to acknowledge to students the problems and conditions that exist. If there could be more genuine interaction among school personnel and students, understandings might be derived and mutuality might be generated that would make change possible. The feasibility of this approach to school-wide change is illustrated in the following example:

A large (3,000 students) comprehensive high school in a suburban city wracked by racial and ethnic conflict had posted uniformed guards throughout the school in a futile attempt to maintain order. A new principal removes the guards, telling the students, in a series of meetings on the first day of the school year, that he has done so out of respect for their maturity and confidence in their ability to maintain order. While conveying empathy and affection for them, his manner at the same time makes it clear that he is no sentimental pushover. The principal also goes to great pains to win the respect and confidence of the leaders of the black and dominant white ethnic student groups, asking them to report instances of racial and ethnic slurs and tension so that he can take prompt action. The self-fulfilling prophecy works: despite enormous tension in the adult community, the school remains calm. Over Easter vacation, the students return the compliment, deluging a local radio station with some two and a half million postcards to elect the principal "principal of the year" in an area-wide contest. (Silberman, 1970, p. 340)

There are also steps that classroom teachers can take to enhance and improve the quality of student-teacher interaction and, hence, the quality of the learning experience in the secondary school, not only for handicapped adolescents, but for all adolescents. The remainder of this chapter will address some of these steps.

METHODS AND MATERIALS

The preparation of teachers, whether for general or special education, places considerable emphasis on "methods" and "materials." Methods courses are intended to prepare teachers to plan, design, and present instruction to pupils, whereas materials courses are concerned with preparing trainees to select, construct, and incorporate learning materials into classroom instruction. This background helps the prospective teacher understand *how to teach*. In special education, additional emphasis is placed on preparing personnel to use methods and materials to remediate learning deficits and to individualize instruction. These skills are also developed through coursework and practice that present the nature, needs, behaviors, and characteristics of children with various handicapping conditions and cognitive styles. People who are preparing to work with behaviorally disordered or emotionally disturbed pupils spend a good deal of additional time learning how to interpret, manage, modify, ameliorate, respond to, and/or treat pupils' affective, behavioral, and social deficits. This is training in *how to help students to manage their behavior*, whether the model is behavioral, psychoeducational, ecological, developmental, or otherwise. For trainees whose goal is teaching in the secondary schools, a further requirement is concentration in a subject area, such as English, history, music, biology, business, foreign language, so that trainees become well informed on *what to teach*.

The actual expression of these competencies depends, in part, on the characteristics and training of the teacher and, in part, on the educational policies, traditions, and technologies that also shape teacher behavior. Notwithstanding formal coursework and experiences with various methods and techniques, most educators evolve a prevailing style of teaching that probably reflects individual temperament, response to the ambience of the school environment, focus of interest in what and whom they are teaching, the time and energy they elect to spend on the task, and the extent to which they themselves are still learners. It is possible to identify some of these teaching styles by generalizing from the work of Axelrod (1976), which specifies the most prevalent instructional attitudes in higher education.

Didactic and Evocative Methods

Axelrod (1976) first divides teachers into two groups on the basis of major contrasts in method. The first is characterized by an emphasis on didactic teaching modes which neither require nor encourage students to inquire, participate actively, weigh alternatives, or engage in other interactions with the instructor. The second, defined as practicing evocative teaching modes, does require and encourage student inquiry, participation, and interaction for successful completion of learning tasks. Axelrod describes didactic teachers as *craftsmen* and evocative teachers as *artists*.

Didactic and evocative teaching modes correspond, of course, to different kinds of learning tasks. The skills of the craftsman are paramount when students are "learning to do" (learning how to drive a car, for example), whereas artistry facilitates "learning about" (discovering universals expressed in Shakespeare's plays). Although the scope of secondary curricula suggests a balanced application of didactic and evocative methodologies, a combination of craftsmanship and artistry, in practice it appears that craftsmanship prevails.

By the time children have been introduced to reading, writing, and reciting, many educators seem to think that they should do most of their learning by these means. As students advance to higher grade placements, their teachers' methods become increasingly oriented toward lectures, assigned readings, paper-and-pencil exercises, and evaluation by means of written examination. Although language comes to the forefront as a medium of thought as the adolescent moves into the final stage of cognitive development or formal operations (Flavell, 1963), this does not mean that education should consist chiefly of listening, noting, memorizing, and repeating. On the contrary, genuine educational experiences provide opportunities for adolescents to test thoughts and ideas, use facts to discover principles, and apply acquired knowledge to new problems and situations.

It is questionable that genuine educational experiences occur when a teacher spends fifty minutes reading notes while students struggle to copy them down so as to commit them to memory at a later time. In fact, this particular didactic teaching method may elicit what are possibly the most prevalent questions asked by high-school students today: "Will this be on the test?" or "Are we responsible for this?" (Silberman, 1970) and similar attempts to separate the essential (to be memorized) from the nonessential (acquisition will not count toward a grade).

This is not to say that lecture can never lead to learning, nor that students should not note and remember things. Nor is it to suggest that methods used with young children in the elementary school should be transferred to the junior high and high school. It is, however, to suggest that authentic teaching is far more than the one-way casting out of facts and directives, that learning is not a spectator sport, and that the design of instruction should capitalize on students' emerging capacities to reason, question, and interact with the content, the materials, the teacher, and one another.

Teaching Styles, Behaviors, and Situations

In addition to contrasts in methodology, instruction may be described in terms of three general styles: the subject-centered, the instructor-centered, and the student-centered (Axelrod, 1976). Those whose orientation is subject-centered maintain that subject matter cannot or should not be reshaped for any reason (including accommodation to special-needs learners) and that teachers and students must adjust to the requirements of content which must be learned according to its own traditions. This attitude places responsibility for failure more on students than on teachers, and its expectations (as expressed by the bell-shaped curve) imply that a few will excel, most will achieve in acceptable moderation, and some will not achieve at all. Those on the downside of the curve may experience education as an adversarial relationship with the teacher, with the subject matter as the battleground.

The instructor-centered orientation requires that subject matter and students accommodate to the teacher who serves as a model for students and uses personality and point of view to shape learning. The philosophy that students should learn to approach tasks and problems in the same manner as the instructor does, inasmuch as this approach espouses the modeling of appropriate behaviors and problem-solving activities, has useful applications in the teaching of behaviorally disordered adolescents, particularly if expressed as mentorship that leads students eventually toward developing and internalizing their own models of thinking and behaving. If, however, student responses become symbiotically bound to highly personalized teacher behaviors, students may be not so much motivated as manipulated.

The student-centered approach arises from the belief that education should exist to meet the student's needs as a human being. The student-centered view stresses that the educational process will not succeed if students have to be vastly reshaped before the process can begin, and thus it advocates altering other variables, for example, the subject matter or the teaching method. This holistic philosophy of education as a means for student growth suggests the therapeutic value of successful learning experiences. It contradicts the view that problems and symptoms must be "treated" or "cured" before a troubled adolescent can profit from attending school, and it assumes that the student can learn subject matter, academic skills, interpersonal skills, and behavioral control in the educational setting.

Also suggested by the student-centered orientation is an acknowledgement that teacher behaviors can create reciprocal behaviors in students. Mour (1977) defines productive teacher behaviors as those that promote creativity and experimentation and, therefore, learning. The teacher behaviors that students perceive as positive and productive are: (a) ongoing efforts to understand each student, (b) fair treatment of and respect for each student, and (c) willingness to share with students—all of which require that the teacher listen to students rather than continually lecture or admonish them. Conversely, counterproductive teacher behaviors that inhibit creativity, experimentation, and learning are: (a) attempts to force students to submit to the will of the teacher, (b) attempts to control students by punishment or threat of punishment, (c) humiliating and belittling students, and (d) exercising authority in any form that suggests that teaching/learning is not a cooperative effort.

> The power to create a classroom climate conducive to learning, or the power to modify existing environments so they are supportive of learning belongs primarily to the teacher. Teachers can go from day to day disturbed by and despising the behavior of the children . . . and maybe even the children themselves. Or teachers can attempt a variety of intervention strategies. But until teachers are willing to examine their own behaviors as the possible causes/sources of unacceptable

behaviors on the part of children, and attempt to modify such behaviors, the chances for a balanced classroom ecology are remote. (Mour, 1977, p. 57)

In the particularly sensitive area of educating troubled adolescents, the teacher deals with multiple considerations and requirements. To simplify the task, one might define *any* learning situation as the successful interaction of the teacher, the student, the learning materials, and the environment (which includes other students). To these components, it is possible to apply the principles of situational analysis (McLoughlin & Kershman, 1978). Because this approach emphasizes interaction among these elements, it does not assign blame for failure to any one of them but, rather, helps to clarify the individuality of each student in the learning situation. Clearly student-centered, the model is based on the assumptions that: (a) teachers can set goals for what they are teaching, establish objectives for instruction, and gain the information necessary for individual programming; (b) teachers can make maximum use of what can be seen, heard, and understood in the instructional situation—as opposed to relying heavily or exclusively on results of formal testing outside the classroom; (c) teachers can plan tasks after analyzing the situation, can consider the many variables that may impede teaching and/or learning, and can make immediate changes in order to prevent students from practicing incorrect responses or maladaptive behavior; (d) teachers can collect evidence of other possible factors involved in the situation; and (e) teachers can refocus instruction by adjusting variables in the situation.

Teachers can analyze learning situations by determining answers to a short set of questions about key variables (McLoughlin & Kershman, 1978) which apply equally to interactions involving handicapped and nonhandicapped students.

1. *Input: What did the teacher assign the student to do?* The student must comprehend the assignment before he can be expected to perform it. Were directions clear or were they complex or confusing? Were the modeled responses sufficient or insufficient?

2. *Output: What did the student have to do?* Although the student may understand, he may have difficulty responding in the required manner because of limitations in requisite skills or inexperience with the kind of task involved.

3. *Sensory: What kind of information was involved?* For example, if the student performs best in a visual-motor mode but the task is auditory-receptive, how does this affect performance and behavior?

4. *Kind of learning: How complex was the task?* Labeling and naming, for instance, are relatively simple tasks, but classifying items according to different criteria is more complex. Since the former contributes to achieving the latter, the student who has not yet mastered the first will obviously fail at the second.

5. *Reinforcement: What encouragement was available?* The behavior of everyone in the learning situation is always being reinforced to continue or to change. When the need for change is clear, the teacher may modify the nature of the reinforcement.

6. *Distractors: What was going on around the student?* Distraction takes many forms, including stresses from outside the classroom.

As an exercise in analysis, the reader is invited to apply the foregoing questions to the following situations, derive situational variables, and consider whether change is indicated in any situational component. The reader might also evaluate the craftsmanship or artistry of the teaching methods depicted, the teacher styles and quality of teacher behaviors portrayed, and the degree to which each situation parallels the general situation in the secondary school.

> *Situation 1.*   To initiate a unit on poetry, a ninth-grade teacher gives a class a lecture on blank verse, free verse, rhyme, and meter, while students take notes. The teacher refers to two short poems written on the blackboard but uses no other visual or auditory aids. When a student interrupts to ask how to spell a word, the teacher does not disgress but responds: "Do the best you can; I won't count for spelling on this." At the conclusion of the class period, the teacher assigns as homework the reading of a short poem in the literature text and the answering of five questions concerning the poem which also appear in the text.
>
> *Situation 2.*   In a special class for behaviorally disordered adolescents, teacher and aide endeavor to provide individual attention to students. So that the teacher can work with one student and the aide with two others for a particular 30-minute period, the remaining five students are assigned individual work. Two are instructed to work individually on the identical task of mapping the various territories acquired during the expansion of the United States. One solves math problems presented in the math text. A fourth is assigned a self-drill of third-grade words on a Language-Master, by which a voice imprint on each vocabulary card repeats the printed word as the card passes through the machine. The last student waters the plants and rearranges the bulletin board.

Situational analysis can be applied to individual or group learning by handicapped or nonhandicapped individuals at any grade level. Because it can help the teacher to identify discrepancies in the teaching/learning situation, its application at the secondary level might reveal some sources of counterproductive behavior among adolescents and suggest some important changes that teachers might begin to make.

Materials

The fact that students work with materials does not automatically guarantee that they are learning something, albeit they are occupied. If they are to have any meaning or achieve any objective, such tasks as filling in workbooks should serve as a means toward some end that the teacher can define and the student can perceive. Students recognize busy work for what it is and can sense teacher disengagement from the instructional role, as observed by a boy enrolled in an educational program for delinquent adolescents: "Some teachers don't really teach. They have us play games, give us work to do by ourselves, or make us read; but they don't teach. Most of the time I go to sleep or pretend to read. Nobody seems to care" (Brown, 1975, p. 62).

In structuring remedial activities for adolescents, an interfering variable that teachers might discover in a situational analysis is the adolescent's need to preserve an idealized self-image and to save face in the presence of peers. Tasks should be presented in new ways, so that they do not appear to be watered-down repetitions of those things that represented failure in the past. Both methods and materials should be selected with consideration of the adolescent's need to save face. When a 16 year old is presented with materials very clearly borrowed from a third-grade classroom, there is a needless sense of humiliation. Through creative and sensitive planning, teachers can devise face-saving, yet effective, ways to help students begin to compensate for long-standing achievement deficits, as was the experience of the young man described below, who, through neglect and misplacement, had at the age of 20 spent the greater part of his life in a state institution for the mentally retarded.

He was, however, of normal intelligence but manifested long-standing behavior disorders and overall achievement at the elementary level. As part of his transition to a more normalized life style, he was part of a hospital's therapeutic milieu and was assigned to educational services.

He showed great vulnerability in relation to any kind of formal learning experience. His customary role was that of tough guy. He had enormous physical strength, stood well over six feel tall, and could and did punch holes in walls. It was difficult for him to reconcile his age, size, and preferred self-image with his educational deficits, which he tried to hide.

The very first thing his instructor did was teach him the rudiments of a slide rule and give him one to carry around. The next step was to work with him on selecting colorful and descriptive words, and then use these to tape record his efforts at dictating poetry. The poetry was typed and given to him in multiple copies, both for sight reading and for sharing. He used these initial accomplishments in his therapy group to regain the stature he felt he had lost by attending school, and thereafter continued to progress rapidly in arithmetic facts and reading.   (Smith, 1971-1974)

To students like this one, recognition and status may be more important in the teaching/learning process than any other variable. Individualization is not confined to planning for academic work and skill building; it also represents a priority of values in relation to each student and each curricular goal.

When instruction is individualized, many teachers find it convenient to establish routines whereby students learn to work more or less on their own for parts of each day with preplanned or programmed instructional materials and media. This practice can increase classroom efficiency, give students opportunities to structure and take responsibility for their own learning tasks, and free the teacher to spend more time in one-to-one instruction. When programming of this type becomes the teaching method of choice, however, it can drastically reduce teacher-student interaction.

This lack of interaction has made many students feel less personally involved with the teacher and with the instructional program. Consequently, many students who need external motivation to become more personally involved in the educational program are not receiving the personalized attention that is necessary to foster such involvement.

Before students can be expected to take full advantage of an . . . educational program, and before negative attitudes concerning education can be replaced with student interest, teacher involvement with students and with the educational program must be optimized. Without strong teacher-student interaction, there is too high a potential for complacency to evolve at both the teacher and student level.   (Brown, 1975, p. 63)

The quality and quantity of interaction in the classroom are particularly important in the large secondary school where sheer numbers and rotation from class to class often make faculty and students virtual strangers to one another. In these settings, psychologists report, one encounters the "completely left-out student," the student with an almost total lack of relationships (Glatthorn, 1976).

INTERACTION AND MOTIVATION

Because compulsory education guarantees neither motivation nor receptivity on the part of students, teachers should not despair when students are apathetic to pursuits which represent no particular relevance nor clear purpose to them. Rather, teachers should adopt one of the more successful strategies of planned change, for example, the practice of introducing new material by couching the unfamiliar in the familiar. People more readily integrate new information when it relates to current knowledge and experience. Where adolescents are concerned, relevance also becomes a matter of various environmental influences and interests.

> While children in informal infant schools work at what interests them, the teacher easily and decisively influences those interests through the environment she creates. Teenagers, on the other hand, arrive in school with their interests, their likes and dislikes, and their values much more clearly formed. They are far less susceptible to the teacher's influence; one of the characteristics of growth, as Jerome Bruner of Harvard emphasizes, is the "increasing independence of response from the immediate nature of the stimulus." Moreover, teenagers are subject to a far wider range of influences outside the classroom: influences from their own peer culture, as well as from the adult culture as transmitted by parents and the mass media. (Silberman, 1970, p. 324)

It makes sense, then, to introduce new areas of learning within contexts that relate not only to students' current performance levels but also to their interests and aspirations. The availability of this contextual information depends on the degree of relatedness or nonrelatedness between teacher and students.

Through communicating and interacting with students, teachers can gain first-hand insights and understandings that will supplement and humanize information from such traditional sources as permanent records. If the student can be known to the teacher as a composite person, this dynamic knowledge can be translated into increasingly relevant and meaningful learning activities for the student. If the teacher sees a student only as a 15 year old who has a low level of reading comprehension, a defiant attitude, and a record of truancy and disruption, there will be very little positive understanding to build on.

By scheduling activities for communicating and sharing concerns and interests, the teacher can simultaneously enhance rapport and generate new sets of student-centered starting points. When students are withdrawn or noncommunicative, interaction can be initiated in nonthreatening ways, as proposed by Vetter (1979). For example, they can complete open-ended questions and personal inventories ("I wish I_____," "My three wishes are _____," "Likes and dislikes_____"). Students can also express themselves by creating collages that represent feelings, attitudes, and/or interests, and can use a tape recorder to describe themselves individually, initially recording name, age, and address, and progressing to describe attitudes, interests, hopes, likes, dislikes, and so forth. Through such efforts, the teacher can use student information to tailor learning tasks that students will perceive as relevant, purposeful, and motivating.

Reward and Relevance

External sources of motivation are frequently introduced to elicit acceptable performances from students; for example, Eisenstein's (1975) use of contingent guitar lessons to improve the reading performance of a small group of inner-city students. When the contingent reward is clearly based on student interests, this practice can produce results. However, there is evidence that extrinsic rewards can have negative, rather than positive, effects (Greene & Lepper, 1974; Netick, 1977).

According to Netick, a student who is working at something that is enjoyable or intrinsically motivating may perceive as negative a reward that the teacher considers positive. When this is the case, the desired behavior may decrease rather than increase upon presentation of the reward. Similarly, Netick points out the deleterious effect of overrewarding for every small gain. The student learns quickly that very little work or very easy work is positively rewarded and, therefore, the operant conditioning program may neither promote extrinsic motivation nor develop intrinsic motivation. One alternative is to give the individual student the responsibility for daily plotting, graphing, or charting his progress so that he will have his own evidence of progress. Student-made charts can also be used to show improvement in group work or group behaviors associated with learning.

Rowell (1977) suggests a number of activities designed to develop in students an intrinsic motivation to read:

Students independently practice reading from a library book or basal reader until they achieve some measure of success. Then individual students tape the story on a cassette tape, play it back, and retape it until they are satisfied with the recording. In this process, students become concerned with correct pronunciation because the reward comes in the form of hearing themselves read well.

Students publish a class newspaper containing such features as an interview with the bookkeeper in the school, a joke section, a poetry column, a new student section, a word puzzle, and even a section on national news. Students have roles and titles such as Editor, Circulation Manager, Art Editor, Copy Editor, and so on. Even more important, many students who had long since tired of the materials used to teach them to read do in fact read the newspaper in its entirety.

In the writing and binding of peer-produced books, students write their own stories, examine library books to learn the various parts of a publication, illustrate, type, and bind their works.

Students use the community's daily newspaper to search for and cut out examples of word-building or writing principles, or to find the meaning of an unknown word in a headline from the context, then verifying the meaning of the word by referring to a dictionary.

Still more effective with adolescents is the practice of implanting student contexts and concerns directly into the material to be learned, as explained by Manzo (1977) in the Parallel Form Procedure. Manzo reports on the development of the procedure with students in a low-achieving eighth-grade American history class in a disadvantaged black community in 1961. Once a week the class was required to read and study current events and, on one such occasion, an unusual role-playing situation was established. Students were asked to pretend that they were sixth-graders at a very progressive elementary school where an annual prom was given for graduates (and there was in fact such a school nearby that the students knew of). A new and pretty girl had recently joined the class (as a new and pretty girl had recently joined the role-players' class), and the two most popular boys were competing for her attention (as they were in that real-life situation). The teacher wrote the names of the students who were to play the leading roles at points of a triangle on the blackboard, Alpha's name at the top and the names of the suitors (Donnie Ray and Osceola) at the two angles of the base, and then presented the following situation:

Donnie Ray's father owns a florist shop and Osceola's father is a candy maker. At recess time a few days before the prom, Donnie Ray and his friends gather and the friends demand to know how he will win a date with Alpha. Donnie Ray, Osceola, and Alpha then begin the role play.   (Manzo, 1977, p. 13)

Donnie Ray announced that first he had to let Alpha know he existed, then dashed past her several times to demonstrate his skill and speed. Observing this, Osceola began to chin himself as his friends counted aloud to announce his special strength. This stimulated Donnie Ray's decision to send Alpha a single rose, by emissary, the following morning, to which Osceola responded, "I will send candy." These enticements enlarged until Donnie Ray's plan was to send a bouquet and Osceola's was to bring a box of candy and a sack lunch for two. This vying continued, while the class cheered, until Alpha was asked to select her date. While she coyly held out for more time, her "suitors" took the decision away from her as they prepared to settle the question by a fist fight. While the students were still talking and laughing, the teacher slowly erased each name from the triangle and entered new names. The class became quiet and perplexed when they noticed these changes:

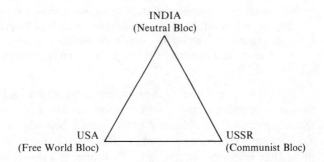

The students were told that if they read pages 29–36 in the current events book, they would find a story very much like the one that was just role played. This was true. At the time, the USA and USSR were "wining and dining" India and the neutral nations to get their support in the General Assembly of the United Nations. When the "give away" programs appeared to be faltering, we (the USA and USSR) exploded atomic bombs in various tests, shot up space missiles, and generally sang a macabre refrain like "My bomb's bigger (more megatons) than your bomb." In fact, the youngsters had anticipated, by a few months, the near catastrophe at the Berlin Wall where the world learned a new word . . . "brinksmanship."

What the class learned while they read and analyzed was mind expanding, if not uplifting. They discovered that the study of nations is the story of people, and that within themselves were the experiences and abilities to follow and understand seemingly complex and distant topics.   (Manzo, 1977, p. 14)

In further explaining the Parallel Form Procedure, Manzo points out that designing motivational activities can be a "hit or miss" situation. Teachers tend to "miss" when they project their own particular emotional needs beyond themselves, for example, when a teacher finds value in mathematics because it is orderly and exact and, therefore, suits his own emotional needs, not those of the students. On the other hand, teachers tend to "hit" or be accurate in understanding and motivating students when they reach deeper into the essentials of the human condition.

Using the Popular Culture

Teachers can find clues to adolescent questions, concerns, and interests by listening to what students say about such issues as nuclear disaster, abortion, capital punishment, air pollution, additives in food, the energy crisis, and international relations. Teachers should also take the popular culture seriously in terms of films and music and the reading adolescents do on their own. Respect for and creative uses of students' ideas, interests, and talents can encourage mutuality between student and teacher and greater motivation in both, as in the situation described below:

> A bright student in an adjustment class was resistant to learning literary forms and symbolism until narrative style was interpreted to him in terms of movie scenarios and poetic style was conveyed in terms of the lyrics of popular music. On the basis of these generalizations, many of his learning tasks were structured as and named "experiences," rather than assignments. One such experience involved interpreting and identifying symbolic language in Stephen Spender's poem, "Judas Iscariot," Edna St. Vincent Millay's "To Jesus on His Birthday," and the student's own recording of "Jesus Christ Superstar," followed up with his own illustrated poem.
>
> Another experience involved viewing a televised movie based on an Ernest Hemingway novel and preparing a character study of the protagonist, then reading a short novel by Hemingway and finally having a discussion with the teacher on a comparison and contrast of character development on film and in print.   (Smith, 1971-1974)

The issues surrounding the medium of television itself open vast opportunities for teaching and learning as well as many questions concerning the contribution of television in shaping disturbed or disordered behavior in children and youth. For example, in a CBS news special in 1973, Erich Fromm commented on the states of mind that television advertising encourages in viewers, as follows (CBS Special, 1973):

> Fearfulness.
> Belief in miracles, instead of human effort (gadgets and gimmicks will create a good life).
> Doubt about the value of rationality and independent thinking because of mass information and conflicting claims that the individual cannot cope with alone.
> A fantasy-like sense of existence and subsequent dislike for those who would impose the conditions and consequences of the real world.

In addition, critics make frequent reference to the violence and stereotyping that comprise much of television's content as well as the passivity thought to be induced by this communication medium.

An obvious curricular concern should be consumer education, which is intended to help adolescents understand the influences emanating from television, explore programming as a vehicle for organizing an audience that will buy things, become a critical audience, and understand the conflicting issues that television presents. Students can also be encouraged in the creation of their own media (on print, film, and videotape) in situations that combine instruction in the techniques of media with analysis of the social role of media and its possibilities (Martin, 1976). Students and teachers may also find videotaping a valuable means for pinpointing behaviors and understanding small group dynamics in the classroom.

The mass media and the educational system have been called the two great means of communication in contemporary society (Gitlin, 1969). The impact and availability of various media, most particularly television, may be partly responsible for the student's perception that the high-school curriculum lacks relevance. Particularly for troubled adolescents, schools should provide instruction and discussion that will help students sort out the messages they receive on film, television, records, and books. "Adolescents tend to organize their ideas according to certain societal expectations. . . . In our society, full of conflict and ambiguity, the adolescent has the terrifying task of identifying a coherent set of values in which to invest his energies and self-confidence and against which to test his own, meandering self" (Rockefeller, 1977, p. 93). Curricula and instruction that ignore these realities are not only irrelevant but negligent.

INTERPERSONAL AND EDUCATIONAL TRANSACTIONS

According to Bremer (1969), everything done in education should be judged in light of the search for the proper way to live.

> Everything that is done must itself be an appropriate way to live. This means placing greater emphasis on the quality of the relationships among students, teachers, and administrators, which means keeping the learning community small. Since learning is a human activity, . . . the problem of how to enter into the learning process or to be a learner can be restated in terms of group membership—how to be a member of the learning community. (Bremer, 1969, p. 353)

Behaviorally disordered adolescents are frequently rejected by their peers in the learning community by virtue of the disordered behaviors they present (Morgan, 1978). Their learning situations should therefore provide opportunities for improving interpersonal skills.

> Teachers need greater license in implementing specific and detailed programs for the development of socially appropriate behavior in children. We enter a hornet's nest here because we are requesting that teachers be allowed to implement training in behaviors which have important moral implications.
>
> It is striking to us that teachers by virtue of lack of action are underwriting and reinforcing a host of social behaviors which most people, including parents, would find objectionable across a wide variety of contexts. (Bryan & Bryan, 1977, p. 141)

The capacity of adolescents for objectionable behavior in interactions with teachers and other authority figures is demonstrable in many schools, homes, and communities. Many adolescents have previously developed a repertoire of polite behaviors but choose not to display their social skills for a variety of reasons: they desire to conform to certain ritual behaviors in their particular branch of the adolescent culture; in the process of testing independence, they engage in self-assertion by trial and error; they feel hostile when confronted with their own dependencies; they are frustrated when emerging needs and desires are thwarted; they react to the real or imagined irrationality of adult authority; they try to save face in situations that threaten their self-image or expose their weaknesses in the presence of their peers. They will also react rather reliably to adult challenges that they assert themselves as adversaries. And sometimes they have every right to be angry but are not sure how to handle it. Adults are vulnerable to many of these experiences, too.

Adolescents with behavior disorders are subject to these and other internal and external influences and have a lower tolerance for them. Their interpersonal behavior may be impolite, disruptive, or defiant with considerable frequency and intensity.

The overall management of behavior and the principles of affective education are well delineated elsewhere in this book; the intention here is to suggest a general precept that should enhance the teaching of socially appropriate behaviors—and anything else—to troubled adolescents. This precept is illustrated in selected situations in which the vehicle for improving interpersonal skills is embedded in other learning activities. Training in behaviors need not be a moral issue unless moral lessons and judgments become the content that is taught, nor do they need to be a "hornet's nest" unless those involved respond in arbitrary "either/or" terms. Whereas some troubled adolescents may evaluate stimuli in this manner, any high-school teacher needs to be much more subtle.

A PRECEPT FOR TEACHERS

The literature (for example, Hamachek, 1969; Herr, 1974) suggests many personal attributes that teachers of disturbed or behaviorally disordered students should possess; for example, flexibility, consistency, empathy, resourcefulness, objectivity, self-insight, tolerance. Although these and other positive characteristics are much to be desired of any teacher, specific personal qualities that contribute directly to achievement in troubled adolescents have not yet been uniformly identified on more than an intuitive basis. Nor can we suppose that there is a teacher alive who would describe himself as inflexible, inconsistent, unresourceful, nonobjective, intolerant, or lacking in empathy or self-insight. So, without disregarding the need for a strong set of positive human qualities, it is useful to consider one precept, or rule of conduct, that teachers can use to evaluate the impact of their own membership in the learning community. This precept is based on the assumption that teachers of adolescents should be *less authoritarian and more facilitative* in their dealings with students and in their organization of instruction. It is also based on the rationale that the concept of the group is a powerful force in the adolescent consciousness and that the adolescent group can function as a productive task force inside, as well as outside, the educational setting. To clarify this precept, it is first necessary to examine the issue of authority and the potentials of the adolescent group.

The issue of authority. In the not-too-distant past, teaching was not only a profession; it was a way of life that sometimes resembled a monastic vocation. Until well into this century, public-school teaching was largely a female profession, one of the few positions a woman might respectably take as a clear alternative to marriage. Teachers in many communities were frowned upon if they married and their private lives were scrutinized by the local citizenry. They were known by the parents of their pupils and held accountable on many levels. In addition, they often taught groups that were quite heterogeneous in age and grade level, necessitating multiple preparations, and they often taught several academic subjects, including Latin. Thirty or forty years ago, teachers did these things without the benefit of calculators, full lines of commercial materials, computers, video equipment, audio-visual aids, and other accoutrements that we take for granted. The current phenomena called burnout and teacher stress were not part of their vocabularies; they often taught for their entire adult lives. As far as we can tell, their pupils did not generally fail to learn.

Compared with a teaching career today, the professional lives of our fore-runners seem to have been repressive, frustrating, narrow, hard-working, repetitive, joyless, and nonactualizing. They would clearly appear to have had a much harder time of it, except for one thing—*they had authority*. They had a high degree of control over pupils, classroom, and curricula.

Today's teachers would appear to have a much easier time of it—except that *they lack a sense of authority*. A number of social, economic, educational, and political changes in the intervening years, such as those described at the beginning of this chapter, have diluted the teacher's real and perceived authority. At the same time burnout and teacher stress have become issues of real concern (Skinner, 1980; Warnat, 1980).It would be interesting to study how much teacher burnout, stress, and resistance might be attributed to the incipient loss of authority and control over pupils, classroom, and curricula, as opposed to the external conditions usually identified as sources of teacher discomfort. It would also be interesting to discover whether any correlation exists between an authoritarian drive and the selection of teaching as a profession.

Of much greater interest and immediate value, however, are the answers to these questions:

1. How extensively do teachers consciously or unconsciously model the authoritarian behaviors of those who taught them in another era?

2. How pervasive are the expectations in schools and society that teachers should properly behave in authoritarian ways toward students?

3. To what extent do loss of authority and diminished effects of authoritarian behavior create anxiety that stimulates some teachers to intensify their authoritarian responses until their efforts become counterproductive because they are out of joint with the realities of the situation?

4. To what extent does loss of authority create, in other teachers, abandonment of any attempt to control anything?

5. What sorts of preparation do teachers need and receive in the interpersonal dimensions of working in a large comprehensive high school?

These are questions that individual teachers can answer for themselves—and they should. Before they can model and teach appropriate interpersonal skills, particularly when their students are adolescents with behavior disorders, they first need to be sure that they are not inadvertently aggravating the very behaviors that they endeavor to extinguish.

The nature of groups. A teacher and his students are members of a group. Groups have dynamics, forces in motion, that fluctuate in accordance with the composition of the group and the interaction of its members. In the learning group, the teacher is the central figure and can derive considerable power or helplessness, according to the nature of his or her own contribution. The paradox in this or any other group situation is that those who exert authority to seek a power position may gain authority at the expense of group cooperation, while those whose control needs are not so great usually achieve more productive group interactions.

Changes in the quality or quantity of teacher assertions and responses will evoke changes in the group. The group may change more slowly than the teacher because, of course, the teacher is acting while the group is reacting. Changes in behaviors by students in the group can also create voluntary or involuntary changes in the teacher. However, the teacher is central because the teacher should be better able than the troubled adolescent to plan consistent assertions and resist automatic responses.

Teachers can draw a parallel by visualizing themselves playing baseball with their students, with the teacher at bat. Since the students know from past performance that the teacher always hits the ball into left field, they will tend to move in that direction even before the first pitch. If the teacher instead hits a high fly to right center field, the players will move from their positions and follow the other direction.

The teacher can similarly change the behavioral "positions" of other members of the learning community by changing his or her own position or the direction of his or her own behavior, but first the teacher has to be a geniune member of the group. One can draw another parallel by examining the following list to determine which items are most typical of personal teaching assertions, then trying the opposite response and watching for new responses among other members of the group.

Let's take a look at what your book has to say about the kind of weather we have here.	Read chapter 7.
Do you think we could finish this in 15 minutes so we could all go to the gym?	Those who don't finish on time will not attend the basketball game.
Who wants to guess the topic of the headline in tomorrow morning's newspaper? Why do you think that will be the headline?	Current events will be every Monday. Each person should bring in a news clipping to talk about.
We could use this book of *Bartlett's Quotations* to find cryptic messages to give to one another, but if the other person can't guess what it means, I guess we ought to explain it if we can. Some of them get pretty heavy and might even be in Latin.	The quotations I write at the top of the blackboard each morning are for you to copy down because they are famous lines that everyone should be familiar with.
By the end of the week, the two of you could get out of the Reconstruction Period if you want to. By Friday, I'd like to be able to talk with you about how you think the segregation problem was handled right from the beginning, and how you think both the North and South could have been more effective in the post-war reconstruction, and which side you would have been on at that point. You can take half an hour right now to plan how to move on this in the next five days, and then we can set a time for Friday.	On Friday I'll collect notebooks and workbooks. Your workbooks should be complete up to page 127, "Reconstruction," and your notes should be in order by dates. If they are not handed in Friday, they won't be accepted later and 5 points will come off the independent study part of your history grade.

Learning groups as task forces. The precept, or rule of conduct, presented here is that teachers of all adolescents, and most particularly those with behavior difficulties, can allay many of their own anxieties, can avert nonproductive confrontations with students, can arrange more situations conducive to learning, and can model more reasonable interactions—if they will simply treat students as viable members of a multipurpose learning group or task force whose accomplishments are not only gains by individuals but are also the glue that holds the group together as a functioning force. Through the use of indirect (facilitative) rather than direct (authoritative) assertions, the teacher can elicit greater responsiveness from members of the group and can use the content of these responses and the responsiveness itself to structure relevant tasks and choices for all members of the group, including the teacher. Leadership may reside temporarily among different segments of the group; the teacher's level of assertion may rise or wane. Moreover, although individuals within the group may not be ready to set directions of their own, the group as a whole eventually can and will begin to shape its own short-term and long-term destiny and each participant will begin to know that aspect of responsibility which is liberation. Underlying the precept that can help to bring this about is the assumption that today many adolescents are trapped in their own freedom and do not know how to get out and that they need things from their teachers that they know neither how to ask for nor accept. By maximizing the constructive dimensions of an influence adolescents use in identifying and evaluating themselves, their values, and their behaviors (the group) and by minimizing the nonproductive dimensions of an influence that stirs defiance or avoidance as they deal with dependence and independence (direct and arbitrary authority), teachers can make it possible for adolescents to receive what they need from their educational experience not by asking or accepting or taking but by helping to create it.

As a facilitator of the tasks of the group and its members, the teacher can regain a sense of autonomy in working with adolescents, a purposefulness that emanates from the power of the group, not the authority of the individual. When this precept works at top potential, the teacher will also discover that adolescents can create among themselves within this small community a subculture more satisfying and infinitely more positive than the one that beckons from the streets.

This precept also serves teachers well in displacing some of the motivations that prompt adolescents to behave objectionably and in neutralizing some of the stimuli that influence behaviorally disordered adolescents to lose or lack control. First of all, if adolescents are susceptible to the prevailing behaviors of the adolescent culture, it would behoove teachers to reduce the distance between themselves and the adolescent group so that "we/they" conflicts can be minimized and students find it less often necessary to bring forth in the classroom the behaviors they use to establish themselves among the larger body of their peers. For example, the adolescent who claims to love school, to love teachers, to love doing homework, to love doing extra work after school is going to find very few peers to identify with. As expressed in the peer culture, adolescents hate school, hate teachers, hate the work, hate the food. While a great many of these vehement statements represent little more than swaggering, they may be made manifest in learning situations that adolescents feel they have no real part in, situations that they perceive to go right on with them or without them. If teachers can relinquish authoritarian control and increase the quality and frequency of occasions when they are person to person with students, they might discover some of the things that rightly do bother students, rather than enduring generalized contempt in offensive language.

When offensive language is a problem, the experience reported earlier by the staff of Liberty School suggests that authoritarian approaches may fail to change behavior, may in fact perpetuate it, and may engage teacher and student in a fruitless power struggle over symptoms at the expense of substantial work they could be doing together. Power struggles are more likely to occur when students are presented routinely with arbitrary demands and requirements but are seldom presented with choices or with opportunities to express and assert themselves productively in school. That some students are themselves arbitrary in their demands and assert themselves long and loud does not mean that teaching personnel or any other adult should make automatic responses in kind. With normal insight and foresight (which good group leaders always have), a teacher can engage such a student in a learning group, as in the following example.

A 13-year-old boy had a habit of spending time filling many pages, even whole notebooks, with material he would copy from texts and other sources. He would routinely fail to hand in assigned work but would, instead, hand in his neat and orderly papers. On finding that this irrelevant effort was not acceptable and that he was still expected to complete the original assignment, he would rail loudly at the teacher and assume a victimized attitude. His resistance to following directions reflected his authority problems and his tendency to manipulate. He also appeared to get some gratification from compulsively producing neatly written pages.

The teacher and student met to discuss his immediate academic objectives from both viewpoints, and the teacher suggested that perhaps he might wish to devise his own lesson plan for a week and develop a list of the learning tasks and assignments he might complete to attain one of the objectives. He readily agreed and, when he had completed the plan and list, he and the teacher made some minor modifications and drew up a mutually agreeable contract for the completion of the work; the contract included a provision for teacher assistance. He executed his plan for the week. In subsequent weeks, the boy was teamed with another student for planning sessions with the teacher, and the two students devised many lesson plans for themselves individually and as collaborators, under the teacher's supervision. Feeling more in control of his own work, the boy was less resistant to completing tasks and became generally more cooperative.   (Rice & Gantley, 1973–1975)

Although authoritarian classrooms might have effectively discouraged the initial behaviors of that 13-year-old boy by virtue of their inhibiting ambience, in fact, by discouraging virtually all spontaneity, they would probably have elicited automatic negative responses that communicate flawed attitudes, not ideas.

On the other hand, the greater internal responsiveness of the facilitated task group may appear at first glance to encourage automatic interpersonal interactions. These behaviors, however, diminish because the opportunities are greater for genuine interaction and for spontaneity, as in a digression that occurred during the reading of a scene from *Julius Caesar* that represents a spontaneous identification with a universal idea.

STUDENT 1   "Why did Portia swallow fire?" (Moans, groans, shivers . . .)

STUDENT 2   "How do you swallow fire?"

TEACHER   "She swallowed hot coals."

STUDENT 2   "Hot coals?"

STUDENT 4   "Why would she have picked that way?"

STUDENT 5   "Maybe it felt good."

STUDENT 6   "Come on. How could it feel good to swallow hot coals?"

STUDENT 5   "Maybe it felt better than the other way she felt already?"

TEACHER   "What way was that?"

STUDENT 5   "Like really bad, man, in a knot. Everything was coming down and it was all over and she was losing her husband and everything. She

	knew it for a long time and she felt like that. I guess it really got to her."
TEACHER	"That is a kind of pain."
STUDENT 5	"Yeah, and another kind of pain can stop it. Like one time I got a toothache for a long time, not a real bad one but it was always kind of dull and it really brought me down because it was always there. Until one day I took a popsicle stick and jammed it right up between my teeth and stuck it in my gum where the toothache was. And it felt good. It bled and all but it really felt good. It was a bright red pain."
TEACHER	"And Portia?"
STUDENT 5	"Well, if she had this dull pain for a long time because of everything that was happening and nothing could change it, then maybe she needed a bright red pain."
TEACHER	"I imagine some of the rest of us could think of examples like that that we've heard about or read about or had. I'm thinking about sometimes when little children bang their heads on the wall. Could that be the same? . . . " (Smith, 1962–1965)

In groups of adolescents with behavior disorders, every member will have problems and deficits, but every member will also have strengths. When operating in an authoritarian mode, the teacher will be likely to evaluate the group as an aggregate of problems and deficits because the "we/they" positioning of group members will accentuate the negative for everyone concerned. When the attitude is facilitative, the teacher will be more likely to see the strengths that even the most troubled among them will indeed possess.

The following strengths belong to adolescents in general (Otto, 1964, p. 439). If teachers of troubled adolescents cannot sense any of these strengths in any of their students, they should return in their mind's eye to the baseball diamond and try to determine why they are striking out.

Strengths of Adolescents

Exhibit considerable energy, drive, and vitality	Have a sense of humor which often finds expression	Have above-average sense of loyalty to organizations, causes, etc.
Are idealistic, have a real concern for the future of the country and the world	Often think seriously and deeply	Have heightened sensory awareness and perceptivity
Are courageous, able to risk themselves or stick their necks out	Often exercise their ability to question contemporary values, philosophies, theologies, and institutions	Have optimistic and positive outlook on life more often than not
Are flexible, adapt to change readily	Possess a strong sense of fairness and dislike intolerance	Demonstrate greater sensitivity and awareness of other persons' feelings
Are usually open, frank, and honest	More often than not are responsible and can be relied on	Are engaged in a sincere and ongoing search for identity
Have a feeling of independence		

Reprinted by permission of the National Mental Health Association, Inc.

When unable to perceive any redeeming strengths in students, some teachers will grow to dislike them actively if their behavior produces conflict and disruption. These feelings in teachers will be expressed in excluding the student in tangible and intangible ways, limiting the student's role in the group and thereby limiting the potential of the group. With only a marginal role, the student may have only a marginal investment in improving behavior; the student may, instead, elect to play long-term showdown with the teacher and the group. When such a student presents so many outward imperfections and inadequacies that it is not clear at once where strength may lie, the teacher may have to begin by *believing* in just one strength and communicating this belief to the student gradually. Teachers very often get what they expect.

> The boy was over-aged for his eighth-grade class, was a slow learner and had been adjudicated for an incident of group theft of a car. His school behavior was troublesome and unproductive, he was frequently truant, and he paid little attention to rules and regulations. The teachers in his public school often discussed their difficulties with him in the teachers' lounge and most hoped out loud that he would never (or never again) be assigned to their classes.
>
> His English teacher would save money taken up in homeroom until his class period and would frequently select him to deliver it to the school office. The money always arrived intact. When the teacher sponsored the school literary magazine, she took him to a local printing plant so he could see various presses in operation and learn to operate a multilith. She placed him in charge of printing the magazine, using the school's multilith equipment. He tried his hand at writing short poems and vignettes. He joined the school's very popular writing club and began to change his image to that of "artist and writer." And he completed his work in English class because his extracurricular printing pursuits depended upon it.
>
> Near the end of the term, he was suspended from school because he repeatedly skipped other classes. But he had always been present for English class and would, in fact, often come to school to attend only this class.   (Smith, 1962–1965)

The helping strengths of adolescents in a learning group can contribute greatly to the task-orientation of the group, to teacher efficiency and effectiveness, and to students' sense of responsibility and autonomy. These strengths can also be valuable in peer teaching, in which students use their talents and skills to help one another. In so doing, pairs of students relate to one another in new roles and try new interpersonal skills.

Peer teaching can be used in Assisted Reading (Hoskisson & Krohm, 1974) or reading by immersion. The premise is that children learn to speak without formal instruction because they are simply immersed in the speaking world; therefore, they should likewise be able to learn to read by immersion in the world of written symbols. The Assisted Reading approach proceeds in three phases (Hoskisson, 1975). In the first stage, student (or teacher or aide or parent) reads to student, sentence by sentence, pausing after each sentence so that the listener can repeat it while visually following, word for word, in the text. In the second stage, the reader presents all words except those that the other student has learned to recognize. By the third stage, the learner reads independently while the reader supplies only unknown words. Although the process is not rapid and requires one-to-one attention, teacher-made tapes and student pairing works well to immerse the learner in written symbols. When used with special needs students, the developers claim that both reading and concept learning improve.

In peer teaching, the helping student often realizes that there are others whose problems may be more complex and stressful than his own. The process of helping enhances feelings of self-worth while minimizing the need for self-deprecation (Duffner, Long, & Fagen, 1979), and the student who is helped may begin to see peers as valuable resources. If the roles of helper and helped are frequently reversed, both students can expand their perceptions of and capacity for human interdependence.

> A particularly isolated 17-year-old was found to have excellent oral reading skills but very poor reading comprehension. She had at one time won several prizes for her forensic abilities but had gradually relinquished competitive activities and interaction in general as her behavior became more withdrawn.
>
> She was asked to make tape recordings of history lessons for another student whose poor word recognition skills were causing him problems with his history lessons. The history student would read the pages as he listened to the tape recordings. The relationship between the two students led to the positive inclusion of the reader into the adolescent group, partly because the history student was able to see her as a needed resource for his own success. Her greater involvement in the history lessons also led her to develop an improved comprehension of content.   (Rice & Gantley, 1973–1975)

Currencies of Words

Pairing works well to *clarify* what cooperation means and what it means to have consideration for other people. Students undertake a serious, mutual task and, to do it well, each must hold up his own end while taking into account personal factors involved in the enterprise. The successful interaction of students, learning materials, and environment enables the participants to recognize that they are demonstrating behaviors that before might have been only abstractions to them. More often than they know, adults say words that troubled adolescents might be able to define but do not understand in a personal way and therefore tend to disregard as platitudes. Many have had their negative behaviors reflected back to them so often (and their positive behaviors so seldom) that they are not very sure whether or when they have been "cooperative."

Verbally facile adolescents readily pick up and use specialized vocabularies without much real comprehension of the concepts involved. This is particularly striking among adolescents in short-term stays at residential facilities where treatment is based on milieu therapy with a psychiatric orientation. In these settings, where staff and client interaction is intense, the language can become quite clinical. As a result it is not uncommon to hear a 14 year old tell about his or her "separation anxiety" or "defenses" or "passive-aggressive tendencies" during group therapy after a stay of a few weeks. To the uninitiated, this might sound like insight. In truth, it represents immersion in clinical communication and identification with the psychiatrist. The speaker has no idea what he or she is talking about.

It is more common and less difficult for adolescents to deal in a currency of academic terms. When high-school students study together for a test, they often drill each other in one- or two-word answers, since they know the format of the test will be multiple choice, fill in the blanks, true or false, or all of the above. Possibly the second most asked question in today's high school is: "Will it be an objective test?" and teachers almost always answer this question specifically. (What this bandying of the term *objective* does to students' concepts of "to be objective" is not known.) Tying for second place is the question, "What will be on the test?"—to which many teachers respond rather fully. As to the tests, one individual honored as "Teacher of the Year" in his city made his tests "more interesting" to students by adding items like: "Who is the current head of the Chinese government? (a) Mao Tse Tung, (b) Ho Chi Minh, (c) Flip Top Box." Also interesting on some teacher-made tests administered to junior-high and high-school students are the spelling and punctuation errors (Smith, 1962–1965).

It is not at all difficult to coach a 5-year-old child to say, "Boethius," when asked, "Who wrote *The Consolation of Philosophy*?" In Nebraska, there once was a man who had a horse that could correctly answer a simple addition question by stamping its foot. "Supercalafragilisticexpialadocious" is a very long word that many people are able to articulate. Yet none of these responses means much to the initiator.

There are a few things, though, that should mean a great deal in secondary education:

1. Fluid intelligence is the ability to perceive complex relations and form concepts. It tends to peak in adolescence and then gradually decreases. The more concrete and culture-specific crystallized intelligence continues to develop into old age (Horn, 1970).

2. In cognitive development, the stage of "formal operations" takes place in adolescence—if it takes place at all (Inhelder & Piaget, 1958).

3. *Adolescents respect competence* (Schaeffer, 1967).

ACADEMIC ACHIEVEMENT

Nonhandicapped students in public secondary schools generally attend classes of 25 to 30 students conducted by one teacher who may use one or many methods and materials. Whatever the combination of procedures, instruction is in most cases delivered classwide: all of the students experience the same thing at the same time. With even the most seriously disturbed or behaviorally disordered students, however, it is suggested that the procedures used be as varied as the students themselves. Professionals involved in teaching hospitalized schizophrenics, depressives, and habitual drug users (who were nonreaders) found the following approach successful, inasmuch as 45% of those enrolled gained in excess of one grade level per twelve weeks of the class; one who could not read ten words on the Dolch 220 word list when the class began learned to read adequately enough to fill out papers and find a job.

> Materials and methods were considered valid only if they produced desired results. No material or method was an assumed teaching tool; it was used only when effective. Conversely, no technique or material was considered out of order if it brought desired results. Methods used in one class would vary from sophisticated reading machines to simple word recognition, to a walk on the hospital grounds. (Adams, 1973, p. 18)

This dichotomy between regular education and special education is not new, and it suggests that students enrolled in regular education tend to be a relatively homogeneous group and that those in special education tend to be heterogeneous. Yet White (1976), in reporting to the National Panel on High School and Adolescent Education, pointed out that differences in the rate of adolescent learning ability can be as startling as the variance in adolescent physiological development and that a whole segment of studies of intelligence testing treats adolescence as a period of differentiation of abilities. White also informed the panel that tests of regular, nonhandicapped students already in tenth grade showed reading and arithmetic scores ranging from the second-grade level to beyond the twelfth-grade level. In reading, 25% scored at or below the sixth-grade level and 44% scored at or below the sixth-grade level in arithmetic.

For the purposes of this chapter, it is assumed that the range of reading and arithmetic achievement scores of adolescents with behavior disorders corresponds roughly with the range given by White (1976) for nonhandicapped adolescents enrolled in regular classrooms nationally. Behaviorally disordered adolescents (and possibly some numbers of nonhandicapped adolescents) will also vary in achievement and ability level in academic content areas and in such other skills as written and oral expression.

Other variables that may influence the troubled adolescent's motivation and achievement and the design of learning tasks include the disordered behavior itself or in combination with specific learning disabilities which affect the learning styles of some of these students. Attempts have been made to determine whether adolescents diagnosed as emotionally disturbed have common difficulties in abstract concept formation and in maintaining conceptual boundaries. Subjects in at least two studies (Kates & Kates, 1964; Kennedy & Kates, 1964) produced evidence indicating that this might be so, but Boomer (1970), whose subjects were significantly behind in arithmetic achievement, found that intelligence and previous grade placement were associated with poor performance in arithmetic achievement and that "the factors associated with this deficiency have remained unclear and inconclusive" (Boomer, 1975, p. 3). While some behaviorally disordered students clearly have conceptual deficits, there is no reason to believe that all of them do, particularly in light of Inhelder and Piaget's (1958) proposition that difficulties in conceptual behavior might be a developmental feature of adolescent thinking.

In addition to a diversity of learning characteristics, strengths and deficits, and performance levels among individual students and within groups, the term *behavior disorders* denotes further diversity in a spectrum of conduct, including but certainly not limited to noncommunicative withdrawal, depression, antisocial behavior, aggression, rigidity, hyperactivity, hostile-dependency, and compulsiveness. Some of these students will be slow learners who require remedial and compensatory programming. Some will have sensory and/or perceptual problems that make necessary precise technologies, special materials, and equipment. Those whose education has been repeatedly disrupted may function on an inappropriately low achievement level, making it desirable to help them compensate for these deficits as rapidly as possible. When students are entering a less restrictive environment from an institution, a new set of learner variables may emerge. Students whose disorders are very serious, on the other hand, may be taught for some period of time in residential settings because they need highly structured, one-to-one instruction and other specialized services and cannot tolerate any but the most structured social situations. Still other adolescents will present disorders that can be called "reactive." These include, for example, individuals who have run away from a rejecting family; who have been beaten or sexually abused; who have been deeply shaken by a crisis or violent event; who are children of divorce; whose obesity and unhappiness are directly related. Though nothing in these situations suggests lowered intelligence, the conditions leading to the reactive behaviors can certainly interfere with achievement (Manifesto, 1979).

There are also a good number of behaviorally disordered adolescents who continue to function at grade level despite their difficulties. Nor is it extraordinary to find in this group students whose intelligence is superior or who possess special talents.

Learning groups composed of various of these students may seem so diverse as to make teaching and learning impossible. These students, however, regardless of their uniqueness and individuality, also have much in common. As an interacting task group, their behaviors over time will tend toward the middle ground as opposed to the extremes. As adolescent peers, they will share many interests and concerns, and in a facilitated task group they will pool their human resources. Most important, they want very much to leave the behavior disorder behind and lead normal lives.

These final pages present a sampler of teaching-learning activities that might be useful in helping troubled adolescents to integrate academic content and master related skills. Unless otherwise indicated, these activities were developed by the authors (and sometimes their students) for application in learning situations where teacher and students are viable members of a multipurpose learning group or task force whose accomplishments are not only gains by individuals but also define the group as a functioning whole. These activities are not specified for use with any particular student or group. All of them have been used to advantage with behaviorally disordered and emotionally disturbed pupils between the ages of 12 and 20 and/or with nonhandicapped junior-high-school students aged 12 to 15.

These activities do not represent continuous units of material leading to mastery of a subject or skill; they are examples of the sorts of tasks and interactions that might be used as part of larger, sequential plans. They imply a facilitative role for the teacher or group leader and usually engage the group or subsets of the group, although some activities are clearly individualized and many could be modified for individual use. The student-centered nature of these learning tasks is expressed as a list of objectives for their development, which might be useful as a stimulus for others who wish to develop student-centered curricular activities.

Objectives for Developing Student-Centered Academic and Skill-Related Tasks

1. Use student interests as vehicles for academic tasks to increase their relevance and meaning.

2. Install a face-saving quality in compensatory or remedial activities.

3. Stimulate student curiosity to go further with the activity and to repeat it on another occasion.

4. Plan group interaction to reduce, rather than heighten, tension.

5. Move the student into other, normal settings in the school and the community.

6. Move the content out of the book and into the open where it can be expressed and experienced in different ways. (Textbook activities and other tasks that are also part of a continuing program are not described here.)

7. Embed new or difficult material in an otherwise attractive activity. An effective change strategy is that of couching the unfamiliar in the familiar (or the otherwise "boring" in the stimulating). When activities are properly embedded, the student will be performing one activity while dealing with and attending to

academic content on another level. Repeating some of these activities over time will reinforce content learning.

A SAMPLER OF CURRICULAR TASKS

Curricula

There is no standard curriculum that is suitable for all time or for all students at a given time; "to insist that there is only one curriculum is to confuse the means of education with the end" (Silberman, 1970, p. 333). This is not to say that there need be no curriculum; rather, the curriculum should be adjusted to meet needs of individual students. Priestley (1978) has pointed out that some of the earlier work with behaviorally disordered students concentrated on "treatment" and the development of positive relationships in a restricted setting, sometimes with insufficient regard to their learning and wider social needs; others took a narrow emphasis on basic literacy and numeracy, which is as undesirable as a purely therapeutic regime that excludes normal educational considerations.

Specialized methods and materials, rather than the curriculum itself, can be the vehicles for therapy and remediation. For example, the student with a well-developed ability to ignore reality in favor of fantasies will need abbreviated, concise tasks with a minimum of pressure, as pressure to perform may prompt him or her to withdraw from the situation. Students who are depressed may need early consistent experiences of success in order to overcome their apathy. Others may need the sense of security that comes from outside controls and, therefore, require structure and pressure to perform (Adams, 1973).

In addition, students who are members of minority groups will have special interests, characteristics, and learning styles. For example, Chicano students may succeed better with process-oriented and relational, as opposed to purely analytic, tasks and in learning situations that are cooperative rather than competitive (Kagan & Buriel, 1977; Madsen & Shapira, 1973; Ramirez & Castenada, 1974; Smith, 1979). Further, since a greater number of males than females are classified as behaviorally disordered in student populations, a not unlikely phenomenon is a class in which only one or a few girls are enrolled, and this situation will present other sets of considerations.

Whereas a variety of specialized methods, materials, and interactions will be necessary, "special education for maladjusted pupils is not complete unless it affords educational opportunities of quality which subsequently enable the pupils to profit from education and training on relatively equal terms with their contemporaries" (Priestley, 1978, p. 297). Therapeutic, remedial, and cultural concerns should be incorporated, as much as possible, into curricula that approximate the fundamental pursuits of secondary education: English, social studies, mathematics, science, prevocational and vocational education, physical education, the arts, and electives related to students' special interests. Curricular objectives should include not only academic achievement and mastery of basic skills, but also the development of critical thinking, problem-solving skills, curiosity, critical thinking, social attitudes, appropriate uses of leisure time, concepts necessary for interpreting the environment, and preparation for the next higher grade. While all of these curricular areas and objectives will not apply to all students, nor will they apply to various individuals in the same ways or at the same levels, they should form the basis on which curricula are built.

Writing and Literature

Writing is thinking. Before students can write clearly, they must be able to organize information. Many organizational activities can proceed apart from the act of writing.

Students can organize information for bulletin board displays from the general (heading) to the specific (illustrative points).

Students can reduce one unit of information (one short section of a chapter) into sentences, expressed separately on 5 × 8 inch cards, shuffle the cards, then organize the information, going from general to specific, abstract to concrete, and so forth. They can transfer this activity to the content of songs and can be shown that presenting specific information without a proper general introduction can be likened to entering in the middle of a movie.

Students can task analyze their own activities to determine that certain sequences are necessary to prepare a meal, for example.

Students can tape record sets of ideas and order these individually, in pairs, or as a group.

Learning to write well is based on practicing writing in manageable segments and receiving rapid and helpful feedback. If a student's writing is characterized by incomplete sentences, punctuation errors, misspelling, and illogical ordering of information, the teacher and student should work with one thing at a time, moving from simple to complex. One way to help students focus on the difference between a complete sentence and an incomplete sentence is as follows:

> Have students take turns writing deliberately incomplete sentences on the blackboard in yellow chalk. As each writes an incomplete sentence, a different student completes the sentence in green chalk. (All sentence parts are the students' own creations.) Repeated practice helps the students to see and produce incomplete and complete thoughts and to get a better understanding of the difference between the two. It will also help them to begin to correct the incomplete sentences they produce in their own writing and eventually to extinguish this kind of error.

This same format is also useful in helping students see and integrate usage differences in adjectives and adverbs, for example, and in differentiating between simple, compound, and complex sentences for purposes of punctuation and structure.

Students might list the correct spellings of words they commonly misspell on a card or on a notebook page. When they have as many as 20, they can work together, with the teacher or on their own, to develop crossword puzzles based largely on these words. Making a crossword puzzle is an intricate task that forces students repeatedly to look at words as wholes and as sets of letters; as such, it is an activity that tends to reinforce the correct spelling of the words incorporated into the task.

When students have difficulty in writing correctly and clearly, their basic unit of written expression should be the paragraph. They should write a paragraph about something nearly every day and should receive immediate teacher feedback on the progress of this writing. They can compare complete and incomplete paragraphs in much the same way described for comparing complete and incomplete sentences. During these processes, they can also begin activities that will help them to write not only correctly but convincingly, and here they may begin to use comparisons from literature. One effective writing device is *contrast*, and one example of this is a series of long sentences followed by a very short one that contains the major and concluding idea of the paragraph. Another is *parallel construction*, or setting forth a variety of ideas in the same form. When presented with passages from literature and speech ("We shall fight on the beaches, we shall fight in the hills . . . we shall never surrender," "Ask not what your country can do for you; ask, rather, what you can do for your country."), students can begin to recognize and practice these devices in paragraphs. They may also begin to compare the styles of various authors and thereby begin to determine what comprises a good writing style. A good comparision is that between Faulkner, who wrote exceedingly long and involved sentences, and Hemingway, who wrote very short sentences in very simple words. When students are presented with the opening passages of literary works simply for the purpose of comparing how authors used words, they may also express interest in reading the remainder of the story.

Students should learn how to write a few things well, for example, letters and short reports. If teacher and students work on one kind of letter at a time (a friendly letter, a business letter, a letter of complaint, a letter of request), the teacher might ask that students who have special requests in the classroom prepare an appropriate type of letter. In this way, the writing of letters becomes more than mere practice and takes on an immediate purpose.

Students may report what others have discovered or they may do their own objective reporting of events as journalists.

> The teacher tells the group the story of *Rashomon*, in which a group of people all witness a crime but, at the trial, each describes the crime in a different way because each reflects his or her particular perspective, bias, and relationship to the event. Then students are assigned to observe an event at the school or in the community and prepare individual short reports in secret. When these reports are shared, students can determine whether they, too, see and interpret events according to various perspectives, biases, and relationships to events, and these may be examined.

As opposed to objective reporting, creative writing should perhaps not be subject initially to the same strictures of correctness. Some freedom in this direction helps to unlock students' imaginations and offers opportunities for success to those who might otherwise have great difficulty in producing a written product. The most manageable units for beginners are vignettes ("slices of life," rather than stories) and short poems. A device to start students in writing poetry is a teacher-made sheet of colorful, poetic, and useful words, in columns of adjectives, nouns, verbs, and adverbs. Students can choose among these words and add words of their own to create poems, the only requirement being that, in the end, they can explain the meaning of each poem.

For students whose writing and reading skills are fairly adequate, it is often useful to compare various kinds of objective writing as well as creative writing, for example, newspaper reporting vs. scientific writing. After making comparisons, students can write paragraphs or short papers in contrasting styles; companion activities might include visits to a newspaper office, science lab, television news-room, and possibly interviews with people who prepare information for these purposes.

Mathematics and Science

Mathematics offers unlimited practical applications and activities. The learning task force might open a bank account for some express group purpose, with certain group members keeping the books. The group might figuratively or literally invest in a stock and chart the progress of several stocks on logarithmic paper that shows relationships between one stock and the entire market and the relationships of stocks among themselves as they fluctuate. Or, as is typical of the Parkway Program in Philadelphia, students may take problem-solving into the community:

> The students meet . . . for formal instruction, then go about the city, trying out what they've learned. "We had one class in Logan Circle, where we tried to figure the diameter of the circle itself," a student reports. "That's something new—not just that you're told you have a circle of such and such a distance. You couldn't waste your time finding irrelevant facts, because you were going to get soaked by the big fountain there if you did. You actually learn by going out and doing what you're learning in theory, which is something I never did before." (Silberman, 1970, p. 351)

Activities that allow students to develop their own materials or create their own games create motivation while reinforcing content:

> Teacher and students devised a game concerned with teaching the equality of relationships between different rational numbers. The game involves hundreds of cards that show rational numbers and a more limited set of similar or equal numbers, patterned on a game board. Dice are thrown to determine steps on the board, which also includes free squares and penalties. The student draws cards until he makes a match of equality, and the person to reach the end of the board with the fewest cards is the winner.
>
> The teacher designed the playing board, and the class members made hundreds of cards, using pre-cut materials and a list of rational numbers. In working with the cards, students became familiar with the numbers and with the relationships among the numbers, while taking pride in the game as one of their own devices.

In addition to making their own games, students enjoy a number of commercially produced games that require math skills, notably *Monopoly*. Even though group members may be at various achievement levels, they can often function as a group in other sorts of game behavior:

> With a particularly rowdy group of ten acting-out adolescents in a self-contained classroom for behaviorally disordered and learning disabled students, the teacher found it difficult to provide immediate feedback during math instruction, as students were functioning at varying levels and each had an individualized assignment. Therefore, the teacher asked the class to form teams and line up their desks perpendicular to the blackboard. One at a time, students came to the board to represent their teams. The teacher gave each one a math problem based on his or her individually assigned lesson. Those who were able to succeed with their own board problems (some with teacher assistance and some on their own) earned a point for their team. The winning team received 15 minutes of free time. In this manner, the teacher was able to work individually with each student while maintaining a quiet atmosphere and initiating some group cooperation.

Students' curiosity about trends and issues in society may be useful in testing science facts. In polluted areas, it is possible to take small surveys in relation to the published air pollution index each day, then relating this index level to certain symptoms and discomforts among people the students know. If hamsters can be kept in separate cages, students can feed one pair a balanced diet and the other pair a diet of junk food, or one pair a high protein diet and the other pair a high carbohydrate diet, measuring changes in weight, activity level, and other variables. These activities can also lead students to form hypotheses, test them on these bases, and report results in scientific form.

Some students can start collections (for example, rocks, leaves, flowers, mineral samples) that reflect their scientific interests and/or individual programs, grow plants, and develop projects.

> Seven junior-high-school students in an Earth Science group were unable to cooperate well as a group after three weeks together. All work had been individualized, and efforts to impose a sharing situation had deteriorated whenever attempted. The teacher selected a project suggested in two texts and modified it to promote a group process involving secondary academic gains. Another teacher was asked to give time and assistance to the lesson, which concerned topography. The materials (butcher paper for protecting tables, clay, pieces of cardboard, plastic knives, grease pencils, and transparency acetate) were laid out before class for each student. But a rolling pin had to be shared.
>
> Students began by rolling clay to a prescribed thickness. Each student waited fairly patiently for a turn with the rolling pin because each was curious about what was being created. Both teachers moved about to give instructions as students completed the first task. These instructions involved cutting out shapes of decreasing size, outlining the shapes on the acetate with the grease pencil, and stacking the clay on cardboard to form miniature mountains. At this point, students were sharing not only their materials but also ideas on efficiency. It was also possible to observe their various cognitive approaches to the task and to see that each would frequently look around the room for hints from fellow students.
>
> The students were assisted individually in labeling contour lines on the map of their mountains; some named the mountains, others were more interested in the technical aspects of the work. Upon completion of the task, each student received his model after participating in clean-up activities. At the conclusion, they had experienced their first limited experience in working with one another as a group.

In *Broca's Brain* (1979), Carl Sagan, a writer who has done much to popularize science, presents simple and engrossing stories on, for example, Einstein's life as he progressed from "slow learner" to international prominence and describes his theories of relativity in easily understandable terms. Most students enjoy reading such stories or hearing about them from each other or from the teacher.

An interesting activity to start students thinking about evolution or about the interdependence of all life and matter is based on Aristotle's Chain of Being: simply stated, everything is both potentially something greater and more advanced than it currently is and the actuality of something lesser. In very concrete terms this means that grass, for example, is potentially the cow (if the cow eats the grass), and the cow is the actuality of the grass and other things it eats for, if it ate nothing, it would cease to exist. Once the concept has been explained and practiced, this discourse can be applied to evolution, interdependence, and many other topics and is very useful in expanding concepts.

History and Geography

If students are engaged in studying various culture areas, historical eras, or other diverse social studies topics, their activities may be opened to the group as follows:

> Start vertical rows of 5 × 8 inch index cards that can be permanently displayed. The

top card of each vertical row shows the name of the country (the reign of a monarch or dictator, the term of a president, or some other descriptor). When the cards are first displayed, members of the group present anything that is currently known about each country (era, reign, etc.), and these facts are listed in brief terms on the appropriate descending cards.

When current knowledge is exhausted, students can decide and discuss the country (era) they would prefer to live in among those presented, given current information. As time passes, students add more fact cards of their own, the activity is repeated, and further information is continuously aggregated for each topic. Again and again, students can evaluate countries (eras) on the basis of current information, changing preferences as the body of knowledge becomes greater, and discussing reasons for their changing opinions.

While many films are available for use in history and geography, and other subjects as well, some of them can be rather dull. Therefore, a film can be shown for an ostensibly new reason. Students are told that the film itself could be improved and that it will be presented to them so they can criticize it and suggest how it might have been improved visually, aurally, in content, and so forth. In so doing, they will probably absorb more of the film's content than otherwise. (This activity also works with high-quality films, whose effective features can be discovered.)

If the objective is to promote understanding of the location and proximity of physical features, countries, or regions, students can have a dart game, throwing plunger-tipped darts at a large map, with the bull's eye being a particular feature and a sliding scale of points for darts directed at other specified areas.

Historical and political concepts, such as "liberal" and "conservative," should be introduced and explored initially in relation to current political phenomena that students are likely to have heard about. How might we interpret changes in social and political views between 1600 and 1680 in England in light of some events today? How did views change, and what evidence do we have of this change? Who were the liberals and who were the conservatives and what were they called in that era?If, as has been suggested, the length of women's skirts goes up and down according to the liberalism or conservatism of the times, how can we check this? Would it apply to fashions in other areas and how can we check that?

Students might also be asked to view regularly the evening news on television or to listen to radio news once a day in school, developing a chronology of understanding on some basic issues, role-playing current events, and comparing them with broader political-social trends and earlier historical events.

Last, the teacher should be a story-teller, frequently presenting vignettes designed to illuminate a subject and to elicit student thinking and questioning.

At the end of his life, Leo Tolstoy turned away from his privileged life and embraced an existence of self-imposed deprivation. While his family continued to live lavishly at his estate, Yasnaya Polyana, he himself lived as one of the serfs he had freed. He gave up all worldly pleasures, including smoking. Yet when his friend Tchaikovsky would visit and play the piano for family and friends, Tolstoy would sit very near him, obviously breathing in the cigarette smoke that Tchaikovsky exhaled.

Toward the end of World War II in Europe, as the Russian army was advancing into Germany, the people of the city of Weimar were fleeing in advance of the troops. Roads were crowded with people, vehicles, carts, animals. The curator of the Weimar museum was most concerned about what to do to protect his museum's greatest treasures, the coffins of Goethe and Schiller. His efforts to contact Berlin for instructions were fruitless and so he set about removing these treasures which he did not wish to fall into enemy hands. The only transportation he could find was a taxicab, and so the coffins of Goethe and Schiller were tied to the top of this cab, which entered the masses thronging the road west. The curator followed but lost touch with the cab very soon. Months later, after the armistice, he continued to press for the recovery of Goethe and Schiller; American troops finally found them in a gully where the cab had gone off the side of the road, and they were restored to the Weimar museum.

Obviously, to stimulate students and supplement their activities in this manner, the teacher must also be a reader and a learner.

Feedback and Evaluation

The way a teacher provides feedback will directly influence the students' self-confidence and motivation. Students with behavior disorders need a generous amount of feedback, most appropriately growing out of activities that enable them to recognize their own successful participation in tasks, but they also need encouragement from teachers and peers. Feedback should occur as rapidly as possible and should be based on social as well as academic gains (Gallagher, 1979).

Evaluation of what goes on in the classroom should be a critical part of the teaching-learning situation. Student performance on various tasks, tests, papers, and projects should be useful to students, teachers, and administrators alike. These assessments should provide teachers with a means of determining whether they are meeting their objectives, of judging the effectiveness of their teaching in terms of student growth, and of examining the strengths and weaknesses of curricula to determine how the total program might continually be improved. Results of student work should provide administrators with a means of evaluating the effectiveness of the institution and the soundness of its assumptions (Silberman, 1970).

Equally important, evaluation should make it possible for students to see where they stand in relation to their own objectives. Examinations should enable them to test their knowledge and competencies by applying them in a new way or to new situations or problems. This kind of examination can help the student to discover what he has learned and what he has not yet fully understood.

> Since students will have to judge their own performance after they leave school, it is important to provide as much experience as possible in self-evaluation. . . . Schools rarely use tests for these purposes, either, except perhaps as a storm signal. It is a rare high school, for example, in which a student ever sees his final examination paper again, once he has handed it in; in most schools there is no feedback at all. (If evaluation were the goal, teachers would give their . . . exams well before the end of the semester, to allow time to return the exams to the students with detailed comments and suggestions.) The procedures make it clear to students that the purpose of testing is not evaluation but rating—to produce grades that enable the school to rank students and sort them in various ways for administrative purposes. The result is to destroy any interest in learning for its own sake; what is worth learning, the students quickly realize, is what will be asked on the exam. (Silberman, 1970, p. 348)

Test results and other evaluative data showing student change (or lack of it) can also be used to measure teacher effectiveness and the impact of the total learning situation. Teachers who are members of learning groups have the opportunity to make evaluation a process in which all members and the group as a whole share and benefit equally.

Conclusion

If educators seem to have lost control of what goes on in the large American high school, there are measures they might take to regain equilibrium, as this chapter has suggested. To the extent that students feel that they are being run by the system, they are not satisfied, and students across the country are asking that these conditions be changed (Koch & Koch, 1980). The traditional school was characterized by teacher authority, the contemporary school by student unrest. The need for a middle ground is obvious.

In terms of applying new and more equal teaching-learning roles to the education of students with behavior disorders, the experience and the fact of equality should be what their education is all about.

> The next great civil rights struggle is going to make the movements of the past look easy. The intellectual, emotional, financial, and spiritual demands of granting equality to blacks and women are going to seem like child's play compared to the full liberation of the handicapped. . . . The scandalous situation of the handicapped in our society is, like those other inequalities that only yesterday appeared to be laws of nature, basically a political problem. Disabled people are second-class citizens not because of the character of their bodily malfunctions, but because we able-bodied people will them so. By "will," I do not mean that we consciously wish them ill, but that our interpretation of their differentness imprisons them in subservience. Our culture believes that various abnormalities make otherwise perfectly able people unfit for full adulthood; unfit, indeed, for full humanity. (Benderly, 1980)

A purpose of this chapter has been to illustrate the need for across-the-board improvements in secondary education, for handicapped and nonhandicapped students alike. If genuine educational opportunities for all students might be advanced in a unified spirit, then intellectual, emotional, financial, and spiritual equality might indeed follow.

References

Adams, R. L. Teaching emotionally disturbed non-reading adolescents to read. *Newsletter: The Council for Children with Behavioral Disorders*, 1973, *11*(1), 16–20.

Arons, S. The teachers and the tyrant. *Saturday Review*, March 15, 1980, 16–19.

Axelrod, J. *The university teacher as artist.* San Francisco: Jossey-Bass, 1976.

Benderly, B. L. The handicapped: Making up for their losses. *Washington Post Book World*, March 30, 1980, 12.

Boomer, L. W. *The determination of the grade level for children in special education classes for the emotionally disturbed using the WISC, the WRAT, and previous grade placement.* Unpublished master's thesis, Lawrence, Kansas: University of Kansas, 1970.

Boomer, L. W. Factors associated with arithmetic achievement among emotionally disturbed adolescents. *Newsletter: The Council for Children with Behavioral Disorders*, 1975, *12*(2), 3–7.

Bremer, J. The good of the curriculum. *The Center Forum*, 1969, *3*(5). Cited in C. E. Silberman, *Crisis in the classroom.* New York: Random House, 1970.

Brown, B. F., Chairman, The National Commission on the Reform of Secondary Education, *The reform of secondary education: A report to the public and the profession.* New York: McGraw-Hill, 1973.

Brown, W. N. Delinquents comment about institutional educational programs. *Behavioral Disorders*, 1975, *1*(1), 54–56.

Bruce, T. Group work with adolescents. *Journal of Adolescence*, 1978, *1*(1), 47–54.

Bryan, T., & Bryan, J. H. The social-emotional side of learning disabilities. *Behavioral Disorders*, 1977, *2*(3), 141–45.

CBS Special. *Television and advertising*. New York: Columbia Broadcasting System, April 26, 1973.

Coleman, J. C., Chairman, Panel on Youth of the President's Science Advisory Committee. *Youth: Transition into adulthood*. Chicago: University of Chicago Press, 1974.

Duffner, E., Long, N. J., & Fagen, S. A. Reducing stress of students in conflict. *The Pointer*, 1979, *24*(1), 61–68.

Eary, W. H. Liberty School: An alternative public school for emotionally disturbed adolescents. The high school game—Its rituals and taboos. *Newsletter: The Council for Children with Behavioral Disorders*, 1973, *11*, (1), 6–9.

Eason, W. M. *The severely disturbed adolescent: Inpatient, residential, and hospital treatment*. New York: International Universities Press, 1969.

Eisenstein, S. R. The effect of contingent guitar lessons on reading behavior. *Journal of Music Therapy*, 1975, *2*, 138–146.

Flavell, J. H. *The developmental psychology of Jean Piaget*. Princeton, N.J.: Van Nostrand, 1963.

Fuller, R. B. *Educational automation*. Carbondale, Ill.: Southern Illinois University Press, 1962.

Gallagher, P. A. Hey, Teach, is this OK? *The Pointer*, 1979, *24*(1), 45–52.

Gitlin, T. The mass media. *Leviathon*, 1969, *1*(4), 58–60.

Glatthorn, A. A. The adolescent student as a social animal. Report presented to the National Panel on High Schools and Adolescent Education, 1973. In J. H. Martin, Chairman, The National Panel on High Schools and Adolescent Education, *The education of adolescents*. Washington: U.S. Government Printing Office, 1976.

Green, L. Facing two special fears. *Journal of the National Association of Private Psychiatric Hospitals*, 1978, *9*(3), 12–15.

Greene, D., & Lepper, M. R. Intrinsic motivation: How to turn play into work. *Psychology Today*, 1974, *8*(4), 49–54.

Gross, R. *Radical reform of high school education*. Report presented to the National Panel on High Schools and Adolescent Education, 1976. In J. H. Martin (Ed.), *The education of adolescents*. Washington: U.S. Government Printing Office, 1976.

Guerriero, C., Coldiron, J. R., & Husband, A. Educational quality assessment: A method of assessing educational profiles of institutionalized delinquents. *Behavioral Disorders*, 1976, *1*(1), 45–50.

Haessley, J. P. Liberty School program and follow-up evaluation. *Newsletter: Council for Children with Behavioral Disorders*, 1973, *11*(1), 9–16.

Hall, G. E. Facilitating institutional change using the individual as the frame of reference. In J. I. Grosenick & M. R. Reynolds (Eds.). *Teacher education: Renegotiating roles for mainstreaming*. Reston, Va.: Council for Exceptional Children, 1978.

Hamachek, D. Characteristics of good teachers and implications for teacher education. *Phi Delta Kappa*, 1969, *50*(2), 341–344.

Henry, N. Drugs, thefts signal decline in discipline. *Washington Post*, June 12, 1979, pp. 1, 16.

Herr, D. E. Competencies of teachers of the emotionally disturbed: A literature review. *Newsletter: Council for Children with Behavior Disorders*, 1974, *12*(1), 5–10.

Horn, J. L. Organization of data on life span development of human abilities. In L. R. Goulet & P. B. Boultes (Eds.), *Life span developmental psychology*. New York: Academic Press, 1970.

Horvat, J. J. Content and strategies of communication in current educational change efforts. In B. C. Porter (Ed.), *The Oregon studies: Research, development, diffusion, and evaluation*, vol. 2, pt. 2. Monmouth, Oregon: Teaching Research, 1972.

Hoskisson, K. The many facets of assisted reading. *Elementary English*, 1975, *52*, 312–315.

Hoskisson, K., & Krohm, J. Should parents teach their children to read? *Elementary English*, 1974, *51*, 295–299.

Inhelder, B., & Piaget, J. *The growth of logical thinking from childhood to adolescence*. New York: Basic Books, 1958.

Kagan, S., & Buriel, R. Field dependence-independence and Mexican-American culture and education. In J. L. Martinez (Ed.), *Chicano psychology*. New York: Academic Press, 1977.

Kates, W. W., & Kates, S. L. Conceptual behavior in psychotic and normal adolescents. *Journal of Abnormal and Social Psychology*, 1964, *69*, 659–663.

Kennedy, K., & Kates, S. L. Conceptual sorting and personality adjustment in children. *Journal of Abnormal and Social Psychology*, 1964, *68*, 211–214.

Koch, L., & Koch, J. Now teenagers want tougher schools: In Gallup poll, they ask for more discipline. *Washington Post Parade*, March 30, 1980, 24–26.

Kraushaar, O. *American nonpublic schools: Patterns of diversity*. Baltimore: Johns Hopkins University Press, 1972.

Lyons, G. The higher illiteracy. *Harper's*, 1976, *253*(1516), 33–40.

Madsen, M., & Shapira, A. Cooperative and competitive behavior of urban Afro-American, Anglo-American, Mexican-American, and Mexican village children. *Developmental Pyschology*, 1973, *3*, 16–20.

Manifesto, G. Personal communication. October 27, 1979.

Manzo, A. V. Motivation and reading: Personal reflections and lessons. *Behavioral Disorders*, 1977, *3*(1), 13–19.

Martin, J. H., Chairman, The National Panel on High Schools and Adolescent Education. *The education of adolescents*. Washington: U.S. Government Printing Office, 1976.

McLoughlin, J. A., & Kershman, S. Including the handicapped. *Behavioral Disorders*, 1978, *4*(1), 31–35.

Mitric, J. M. Diary of a fed-up teacher. *Washington Post*, January 26, 1980, 13.

Morgan, S. R. A descriptive analysis of maladjusted behavior in socially rejected children. *Behavioral Disorders*, 1978, *4*(1), 23–30.

Morse, W. C., Cutler, R. L., & Fink, A. H. *Public school classes for the emotionally handicapped: A research analysis*. Washington: Council for Exceptional Children, 1964.

Mour, S. I. Teacher behaviors and ecological balance. *Behavioral Disorders*, 1977, *3*(1), 55–57.

Netick, A. Extrinsic and intrinsic motivation: Bridging the gap. *Behavioral Disorders*, 1977, *3*(1), 27–29.

Newmann, F. M. Social action in social studies: Toward a rationale. Presentation to the National Council for the Social Studies Convention, 1976. Quoted in J. H. Martin, Chairman, The National Panel on High Schools and Adolescent Education, *The education of adolescents*. Washington: U.S. Government Printing Office, 1976.

Otto, H. A. The personal and family strength research projects: Some implications for the therapist. *Mental Hygiene*, 1964, *48*(3), 439–450.

Priestley, P. H. The implications of the Warnock Report for the education of the maladjusted. *Behavioral Disorders*, 1978, *3*(4), 294–299.

Ramirez, M., & Castenada, A. *Cultural democracy, bicognitive development, and education.* New York: Academic Press, 1974.

Reed, F. Half-educated generation. *Washington Post*, December 29, 1979, 11.

Rice, S. R., & Gantley, B. I. Anecdotal notes on Atlantic Academy. Unpublished. Norfolk, Virginia: Tidewater Psychiatric Institute, 1973–1975.

Rockefeller, D., Jr., Chairman, The Arts, Education, and Americans Panel. *Coming to our senses: The significance of the arts for American education.* New York: McGraw-Hill, 1977.

Rowell, C. G. Motivating students to learn to read through language arts. *Behavioral Disorders*, 1977, *3*(1), 20–26.

Sagan, C. *Broca's brain.* New York: Random House, 1979.

Schaeffer, R. J. *The school as a center of inquiry.* New York: Harper & Row, 1967.

Schon, D. A. *Beyond the stable state.* Harmondsworth, England: Penguin Books, 1973.

Sewall, G., Carey, J., Simons, P. E., & Lord, M. Tests: How good? How fair? *Newsweek*, February 18, 1980, 97–104.

Silberman, C. E. *Crisis in the classroom.* New York: Random House, 1970.

Skinner, M. G. Combating the effects of debilitating stress. *The Pointer*, 1980, *24*(2), 12–21.

Smith, J. Notes on teaching at Northside Junior High School. Unpublished. Norfolk, Virginia: Author, 1962–1965.

Smith, J. Anecdotal notes on Atlantic Academy. Unpublished. Norfolk and Virginia Beach, Virginia: Tidewater Psychiatric Institute, 1971–1974.

Smith, J. The education of Mexican-Americans: Bilingual, bicognitive, or biased? *Teacher Education and Special Education*, 1979, *2*(4), 37–48.

Turner, C. C. & Thrasher, J. M. *School size does make a difference.* San Diego: Institute for Educational Management, 1976.

Vetter, A. The withdrawn child. *The Pointer*, 1979, *24*(1), 21–23.

Warnat, W. I. Teacher stress in the middle years: Crisis vs change. *The Pointer*, 1980, *23*(2), 4–11.

White, S. The nature of the adolescent learning process and its implications for secondary school curriculum. Report presented to the National Panel on High Schools and Adolescent Education, 1973. In J. H. Martin, Chairman, The National Panel on High Schools and Adolescent Education, *The education of adolescents.* Washington: U.S. Government Printing Office, 1976.

Witte, S. *People and power: A study of crisis in secondary schools.* Ann Arbor: University of Michigan, Institute for Social Research, 1970.

Woodson, M. S. Burdens on the school. *Washington Post*, June 9, 1979, 15.

Mathematics Instruction for Behaviorally Disordered Adolescents

13

Robert B. Ashlock

The teacher of behaviorally disordered students often finds instruction in mathematics to be a special challenge. This chapter addresses and offers some suggestions for some of the difficult questions such a teacher faces, for example, what mathematical content is most appropriate for these students; should concepts or skills be emphasized; what teaching resources are available? These are just a few of the questions to be considered in an attempt to provide help for teachers.

What Math Content Is Appropriate?

Any math content for which a behaviorally disordered adolescent has prerequisite concepts and skills and for which the youth has a real interest is appropriate for instruction. Though some adolescents have the kinds of problems discussed in this book, it does *not* follow that there is an area of mathematical content which such students should necessarily focus upon, possibly to the exclusion of other areas. Adolescents, whether behaviorally disordered or not, need to be enabled to perceive mathematical regularity in the world around them, in the accuracy of planetary and stellar movements, in the vibrations of tones in the musical scale, and even in the order of the elements. The wonders of geometric designs in snowflakes, flowers, and crystals should not be hidden from them. The satisfaction of finding patterns in relationships among numbers should not be denied. There are explorations in number theory which are quite appropriate and may enhance a student's interest in the whole field of mathematics. This is especially true whenever the teacher joins the student in the search and shows genuine interest in the discoveries that are made.

However, for whatever reasons (and there are many), a large number of behaviorally disordered adolescents lack fundamental concepts and skills needed to explore mathematical ideas in the world around them and to use these ideas successfully in their daily lives. Such students have difficulty with much of the content usually associated with grades 1–8, including basic arithmetic. Establishing blame for misunderstandings, gaps in knowledge, and negative attitudes about mathematics is of little value. Instead, it is important to identify each student's strengths and build on these within the limitations of time and resources available. This, of course, is the difficulty. Though there are many areas of content which may be appropriate, instruction time is fixed. It is necessary to find those areas of content which are most needed by behaviorally disordered adolescents who, for whatever reason, are having considerable difficulty with mathematics.

Many teachers, and possibly most parents, assume that for the child struggling with mathematics, the most needed areas of content include the content associated with grades 1–8, especially arithmetic, and applications of those concepts and skills in everyday life. But mathematics educators are aware that other areas of content have applications as well, and students often find these areas intrinsically more interesting. Behaviorally disordered adolescents' feelings of self-worth increase as they become genuinely interested in a few areas of math content and learn to do a few things quite well. Most behaviorally disordered adolescents have experienced repeated failure in mathematics instruction and are fearful of trying new things. Daily successful experiences with numbers and mathematical concepts are essential in helping students overcome their fears so that they can move forward to new challenges.

My own view is that the most important areas of content include those associated with grades 1–8. These are the skills most essential for independent life functioning, and their mastery can positively affect feelings of self-worth and make

it increasingly possible for students to discover mathematical regularity in the world about them.

Two important topics within the content associated with grades 1–8 are the meanings of operations on numbers and the meanings of the numerals we use. Skill in computation and the use of such skill in problem-solving are also important. However, this content is not restricted to arithmetic; basic work in geometry and measurement is included as well.

Detailed descriptions of such mathematical content are available from a number of sources. Typically, a teacher's manual for a commercial text series will outline content for all of the grades, often in the form of behavioral objectives. A number of school systems have developed some form of curriculum guide which specifies math content for grades 1–8. Of the many taxonomies of content which have also been prepared one very helpful system has been developed by John Wilson, director of the Arithmetic Clinic at the University of Maryland (Wilson, 1969).

Diagnostic tests are another resource that specifies at least part of the math content of grades 1–8. Not only can we infer categories of content from such tests, but they can also be used to help us determine which categories of content are areas of strength or weakness for individuals, thereby providing a basis for planning instruction. One such test is the *Stanford Diagnostic Mathematics Test* (1976), a paper-and-pencil instrument which can be administered to groups of students. The four-level test covers both elementary and secondary grades. Another diagnostic test is the *KeyMath Diagnostic Arithmetic Test* (1971), designed to be administered to one student at a time. The flip-card format is especially effective, but there is only a limited number of items in any one category of content. The *Maryland Diagnostic Arithmetic Test* (Wilson & Sadowski, 1976) is unique in that it includes both paper-and-pencil tests for group administration (primary and intermediate forms) and individual interview protocols to be used for in-depth diagnosis in categories of content which appear to be weak on the paper-and-pencil test. This test has been used effectively at the University of Maryland Arithmetic Clinic with adolescents who are having difficulty learning basic mathematics. Another resource which could be consulted is the book *One Step at a Time* (Bitter, Engelhart, & Wiebe, 1977) which describes a diagnostic/prescriptive mathematics program containing much of the content of grades 1–8. Tests and instructional suggestions are included.

Instruction Should Focus on Concepts

When working with students who are not learning basic mathematics, it is sometimes tempting to focus instruction on skills and give less attention to concepts. It is important, however, to focus on concepts. If instruction in concepts is well done, it can help students learn skills and remember the basic facts of arithmetic and can help them know when to use the skills they do learn.

With the present emphasis on behavioral objectives, it is easy now to attend to what students actually understand. For example, do students know that certain numbers (powers of ten) are assigned a place instead of a symbol? Do they understand that the order of addends does not affect the sum? And do they know that a numeral to the left of a division sign is a product? The statements we call behavioral objectives *do* describe observable behavior, but such behaviors are merely indicators that a student may or may not understand a new concept or a cluster of concepts. (For a discussion of objectives and behavioral indicators, see Wilson, 1976.) The tasks or behaviors usually associated with concepts such as those listed above are, at best, weak indicators. For example, experience has shown that the following are weak indicators that a student understands the concepts involved: 207 = ___ hundreds + ___ tens + ___ ones or 36 + 85 = 85 + ___ . Too often the instructional goal is merely to have students succeed on such assessment tasks. However, not uncommonly students learn to complete many of the tasks correctly even though they do not understand the idea involved; they learn patterns of response which help them make responses on paper. The task behavior is not really the objective of instruction; it is only one indicator that the student understands. Of course, indicators are needed so we can infer that a student does or does not understand a concept. When they are weak indicators, we need a variety of tasks in order to have greater confidence that the student understands.

Children are continually acquiring concepts, even when we least expect it. They learn concepts as we attempt to teach them mathematical laws and skills; but we very frequently encounter two difficulties: students do not necessarily acquire the concepts a teacher is attempting to teach and students all too often learn one concept apart from others, failing to build them all into a conceptual schema which would enable them to remember newly acquired ideas more easily. Not uncommonly, the instruction that is provided fails to help a student tie ideas together so that concepts are reinforced in isolation, possibly with performance on a specific assessment task in mind.

An important thing to remember when planning instruction is that accurate math concept development requires the use of varied exemplars. When an idea is exemplified in only one way, students are apt to interpret the *specific* demonstration of symbolic statement as the idea that the teacher is attempting to convey, even giving it the label the teacher uses. For example, fractions are sometimes understood to be certain shapes. Exclusive use of circular regions for fraction concept development can produce the effect observed in Figure 1. If only wooden blocks are used to interpret numerals for whole numbers, the numerals may be perceived as describing relationships between pieces of wood rather than among numbers. If only one symbolic generalization is presented, students may come to think that a + b = b + a is commutativity but that x + y = y + x is not. Ideally instruction will incorporate examples which vary along a continuum from concrete to symbolic, and the exemplifications will vary sufficiently in attributes so that the only idea that can be observed as common across all settings is the underlying concept, pattern, or structure the teacher is attempting to teach. In recent years, this principle of instruction has led to the development of a number of very useful instructional aids for teaching math content.

Though it is true that instruction should focus on concepts, it is also true that the concepts associated with some areas of content are more critical than others. Clinical experiences with students having difficulty learning math suggest that two

FIGURE 1

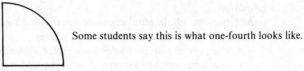

Some students say this is what one-fourth looks like.

such areas are the meaning of operations on numbers and the meanings of the numerals we use.

A mathematician may think of an operation on numbers (such as multiplication) as an arbitrary mapping of an ordered pair of numbers onto a unique number, but this is not the way such an operation should be introduced to students. Rather, such operations should be introduced as having meaning within the experience of students. If models for an operation are constructed from ideas with which students are familiar, the operation being introduced comes to have meaning in terms of learnings previously acquired. For example, multiplication can be introduced in terms of the following:

1. Union of disjoint but equivalent sets.

$3 \times 4 = ?$

2. A special addition situation.

$$3 \times 4 = ? \qquad \begin{array}{r} 4 \\ + \;\; 4 \\ \underline{ \;\; 4} \\ 12 \end{array}$$

3. An array.

$3 \times 4 = ?$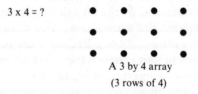

A 3 by 4 array
(3 rows of 4)

Such meanings are not to be confused with the computational procedures used for finding a missing sum, addend, product, or factor. These procedures, often called alogorithms, are ways of manipulating symbols to find the simplest name for a number shown with an expression, such as $876 + 498$, or 24×267. The procedures are not the operation itself, for students are often able to compute even though they do not understand the meaning of an operation. As a result, they experience great difficulty in solving open number sentences and do poorly with problem-solving.

If students are to become good problem-solvers, they must understand the meanings of the operations. Eventually they must comprehend operations in general terms. The following statements, selected from Wilson's content taxonomy (1969), illustrate the kind of ideas about operations which our students should come to understand.

> *Addition*
> Addition on whole numbers is an operation which associates a pair of whole numbers with a third unique whole number.
> - The pair of numbers added are called *addends*.
> - The third number associated with the addends
>   is called the *sum*

- Addition is used to find the sum when its
  addends are known.

The "+" (read plus) is a symbol which indicates addition.

An *addition phrase* consists of numerals or variables separated by the "+" sign,
e.g., "3 + 4"; 53 + ☐ "; "a + b".

- The numerals or variables on each side of the
  "+" in a phrase indicate addends.
- Addition phrases are like compound nouns. They
  name a single element—a number.
- The number named by an addition phrase is
  called an indicated sum.

Subtraction

Subtraction on whole numbers is an operation which associates a pair of whole
numbers with a third unique whole number.

- One of the pair of numbers is a sum (sometimes called a *minuend*) and the
  other number is one of the sum's addends (sometimes called a
  subtrahend).
- The third number associated with the sum and one of its addends is the
  sum's other addend (sometimes called the *remainder* or *difference*).
- Subtraction is an operation used to find one addend (remainder) when the
  sum (minuend) and its other addend (subtrahend) are known.

The "–" (read minus) is a symbol which indicates subtracton.

A *subtraction phrase* consists of numerals and variables separated by the "–"
sign, e.g., "7 – 2"; "52 – ☐"; "a – b".

- The numeral or variable to the left of the minus sign always indicates a
  sum (minuend).
- The numeral or variable to the right of the minus sign always indicates
  one of the addends (subtrahend) of the sum.
- Subtraction phrases are like compound nouns. They name one element—
  a number.
- The number named by a subtraction phrase is called an indicated addend
  (remainder, difference).

Subtraction is the inverse of addition. . . . Addition is used to find the sum
when its addends are known, whereas subtraction is used to find one of the
addends when the sum and its other addends are known.

Multiplication

Multiplication on whole numbers is an operation which associates a pair of
whole numbers with a third unique whole number.

- The pair of numbers multiplied are called *factors*.
- The third number associated with the factors is called the *product*.
- Multiplication is used to find a product when its factors are known.

The "✕" is a symbol which indicates multiplication.

A *multiplication phrase* consists of numerals or variables separated by the "✕"
sign, e.g., "3 ✕ 4"; 25 ✕ ☐"; "a ✕b"

- The numerals are variables on each side of the "✕" in a phrase indicate
  factors.
- Multiplication phrases are like compound nouns. They name a single
  element—a number.
- The number named by a multiplication phrase is called an *indicated
  product*.

Division

Division on whole numbers is an operation which associates a pair of whole numbers with a third unique whole number.

- One of the pair of numbers is a product (sometimes called *dividend*) and the other number is one of the product's factors (called a *divisor*).
- The third number associated with the product and one of its factors is the product's other factor (called *quotient*).
- Division is an operation used to find one factor (quotient) when the product (dividend) and its other factor (divisor) are known.

"÷" is a symbol which indicates division.

A division phrase consists of numerals or variables separated by the ÷ sign. e.g., $12 ÷ {}_\mid 3$; $\square ÷ 5$; $a ÷ b$.

- The numeral (or variable) to the left of a ÷ sign names a product (dividend).
- The numeral or variable to the right of a ÷ sign indicates a factor (divisor).
- The number named by a division phrase is called an *indicated factor* or an *indicated quotient*.

Division is the inverse of multiplication. . . . Multiplication is used to find a product when its factors are known, whereas division is used to find one of the factors when the product and its other factor are known.

Note that addition is not described as putting together; nor subtraction as taking away; and multiplication is not defined as a special kind of putting together, for in some instances the product is smaller than either of the factors. Suffice it to say that care must be taken to develop accurate ideas about what operations on numbers mean.

Another area of content upon which instruction should focus for students having difficulty with math is numeration. It is essential that students understand what numerals mean if they are to use them sensibly in computation, estimation, and problem-solving. Experience suggests that, frequently, adolescents having difficulty with math do not have an adequate understanding of the numerals we use, not even for whole numbers.

Understanding numerals for whole numbers is not just understanding place value, if that means naming the number of tens, hundreds, etc., for place value is but a small part. The following ideas are a few of the concepts which students need to understand if they are going to be able to use such numerals sensibly. (A more extensive list of such concepts can be found in Wilson, 1969.)

1. The face value of each of the ten digits tells how many things.
2. When telling or writing how many, we group objects into sets and into sets of sets.
3. A power of ten is assigned to each position and names the value of each place.
4. Only one digit can be placed in each position.
5. The product value of a digit is the product of its face and place values.
6. Each digit, including zero, designates a position and names a number.
7. The total value of a multidigit numeral is the sum of the product values for each digit.

The student who is learning what numerals mean must also have some understanding of the operations of addition and multiplication. Spatial orientation and imaging ability are also involved, as are aspects of verbal ability. For example, some students confuse "10 greater than" with "greater than 10," thinking they mean the same thing. To understand numerals for whole numbers, a student needs to understand the even more difficult concept of "10 times as great."

Perhaps even these brief references to key concepts associated with the meanings of operations and of numerals is sufficient to illustrate that there are many *ideas* for students to learn if they are going to be successful in learning skills, in remembering basic facts, and in knowing when to use the skills they do learn. It is important to focus instruction on concepts.

Skills Are Important

With the current emphasis on basic skills we hardly need to stress the importance of helping students learn mathematical skills. If anything, we probably need to stress the need for a more balanced and comprehensive program in mathematics. Even so, much instructional time devoted to mathematics focuses on skill development.

All too often skill instruction results only in a student's ability to do very specific tasks within a specific context. For example, a student may learn to subtract whole numbers whenever a row of examples with zeros in the ten's place of the minuends is presented or a student may learn to add mixed fractional numbers when they are presented vertically in a row. A student may learn to do such tasks successfully but still not acquire the needed skill. Skills need to be applied in varied contexts, and, until students can use them in varied contexts, it is hardly appropriate to say they are skillful. Students who can subtract whole numbers only when there is a zero in a certain position, students who can add mixed fractional numbers only when they have been conveniently arranged in vertical format, and students who can compute only in the context of in-school, paper-and-pencil exercises have not gained the skills they need. Instructionally what is required is *not* an exclusive focus on a specific task, possibly one which will be used to assess instruction; what is required is developmental instruction.

Developmental instruction in mathematical skills has continuity; the concepts involved are those a student needs in order to understand and use numerals sensibly. Teachers should make certain that students are proficient in those concepts and skills required for any process being introduced. Examples are varied, with the process itself often being introduced as a record of observations made. Such observations are made as students process physical materials or work out solutions in less efficient ways using concepts and skills they have learned previously.

Developmental instruction needs to *precede* practice activities as such. If practice in a skill is introduced too soon, students tend to become skillful in incorrect or inefficient procedures. At best their ability to remember the procedure and use it for estimating and problem-solving may be impaired. A student does not learn to do a procedure just by practicing it. A student must learn the procedure first, or there is nothing to practice. For the most part, practice reinforces and makes more efficient that which was actually learned previously.

Having noted that students should be involved in practice activities only after careful developmental instruction, it is also important to note that practice activities *are* essential. Students need successful practice in order to maintain skills. For maintenance, a given amount of instructional time is more fruitful when used in frequent brief periods than when used all at once. For example, 30 minutes of instruction is better used in five 6-minute practice sessions than in one 30-minute practice session. Providing for many short practice sessions is particularly important for those behaviorally disordered students who have experienced repeated failure with numbers. For these students, frequent reinforcement and light, tension-free activities between practice sessions will be helpful.

To the extent that practice activities involve paper-and-pencil computation procedures, teachers need to be very alert to possible patterns of errors. This points to another advantage of brief, frequent practice periods: the teacher is more apt to spot incorrect learnings before they are reinforced extensively. In order to observe such erroneous procedures, a teacher needs to go beyond simply scoring the papers and instead look at practice papers as puzzles and try to figure out what students are actually doing. Examples of error patterns common among students are shown in Ashlock (1976).

Not all practice activities need be paper-and-pencil exercises. For many skills, games can provide needed reinforcement. What is essential is that problem-solving settings be provided in which students can practice in a variety of situations those skills they have learned. A math program with a healthy emphasis on applications will provide many such opportunities for students. Problem-solving settings can be found within many games, within the study of other content areas, and within life situations generally. Designing appropriate problem-solving settings for a particular group of students is often hard work, but it can be very fruitful indeed.

Different Types of Instructional Activities

Because activities for instruction serve varied purposes, different types of activities are called for. Sometimes the process of instruction will consist simply of introducing a concept or process by explaining it to students (possibly providing a few illustrations) and then having students practice the new idea or process. Such an approach is an oversimplification which tends to ignore how students acquire, remember, and transfer concepts and skills. When activities for instruction in mathematics are considered carefully, it becomes clear that there is a sequence of different types of activities ranging from a student's initial contact with an idea or procedure to its application in novel situations or to a useful level of skill.

Different sequences of instructional activities have been described in the literature of mathematics education. For example, Marks, Purdy, and Kinney (1975) have developed a flow chart of the learning sequence which includes five steps. During *preparation* activities, the teacher makes sure that each student has prerequisite skills, concepts, vocabulary, and interest to study the content at hand. Activities for *exploration and discovery* involve students in problem situations where they begin to develop the concept or process. Then activities for *abstraction and organization* help students understand the concept or process and see its interrelationships with other mathematical content. These activities are followed by those which help students *fix skills* and provide for needed overlearning. Finally, *application* activities promote transfer by calling for the use of the concept or skill in varied contexts.

Another sequence, developed by Wilson, could be thought of as a refinement of the five steps described above. One way in which Wilson's (1976) Activity Type Cycle differs from the previously described steps is that abstracting/organizing activities are conceived of as two separate types: *abstracting* activities which help a student understand a concept and *schematizing* activities which focus specifically on interrelationships among different concepts and processes. There is an emphasis on building a rich conceptual schema in order to help a student remember and use more effectively what is learned. Wilson follows such activities with *consolidating* activities, thereby emphasizing practice for using ideas as well as fixing skills. *Transfer* activities complete the cycle. But it is a cycle, and transfer activities are often problem settings in which instances of a new, higher-level principle or process are first encountered. Another distinguishing feature of the Wilson cycle is the place given to *diagnostic* activities. These are not seen as just the first step in a sequence, but rather as activities appropriate between steps throughout the cycle. Diagnostic activities help determine whether the student is ready for the next type of activity in the cycle.

Cooney, Davis, and Henderson (1975) have also described types of activities, though their focus is on teaching a concept or principle. The sequence for such moves is sometimes implicit in the names given each type. For example, they list four moves for teaching a mathematical principle: *introduction, interpretation, justification,* and *application.* The introduction is a means of focusing on the lesson at hand, for it sets the objective and provides motivation for the lesson: interpretation is the attempt to help students understand the principle; justification helps students to supply reasons for the truth of the principle; and application focuses on student use of the principle.

It should be emphasized that diagnostic activities are appropriate at many points within the sequence of activity types for diagnostic-prescriptive teaching should involve continuous diagnosis and not only an initial diagnosis and prescription. Here the Wilson Activity Type Cycle is particularly helpful. Diagnostic activities are needed to determine whether the student (a) has knowledge and skills needed in order to improvise solutions in problem settings used to initiate a concept or skill, (b) has indeed come to understand the concept after appropriate instruction, (c) can relate the idea to other ideas, (d) has immediate recall of what has been learned, and (e) can use it in solving problems in varied settings.

Activities Involving Large Muscle Movement

Among the instructional activities that may prove useful are those that involve large muscle movement, such as games or other activities. In such activities students bounce balls, run, and throw. In the course of such activities, students get away from paper-and-pencil exercises with symbols crowded on a page. Instead, auditory, tactile, and kinesthetic sensory modes are involved.

It is important to ask how such activities can appropriately fit into a sequence of learning for learning activities serve different purposes. Most activities that involve large muscle movement are practice or consolidating activities. Typically they do not teach new material; instead they provide reinforcement for what was learned previously. Descriptions of such activities as part of the learning process are available in professional literature (Ashlock & Humphrey, 1976). One example is included here to illustrate what is meant by activities involving large muscle movement.

> For the game "Catch the Thief" students are divided into two teams, and for each team students are assigned numbers starting with 1. The two teams face each other as they line up on parallel lines about 25 feet apart. An object is placed between the two teams at a point equidistant from them. As a signal is called, those students from both teams whose numbers are called run to pick up the object and bring it back across their team's line-up before being tagged by a member of the other team.

If successful, a point is scored for the team. Appropriate signals vary depending upon the previous experience of the class. Possibilities include:

Less than 5
The sum of 6 and 7
The difference between 15 and 8
Multiples of 6
The product of 3 and 5
Factors of 30
Common factors of 18 and 24
Both greater than 9 and less than 12
Primes
The greatest common factor of 12 and 18
Both greater than 12 and less than 9

Resources Available

Regular textual material serves as a guide for planning instructional sequences as well as for some practice opportunities. But teachers are well advised to use a variety of other resources for planning and teaching. Mathematics specialists and supervisors are able to suggest many such resources, but a few are highlighted here to illustrate something of the diversity available. As textual material is more generally at hand, three other categories are illustrated: three-dimensional exemplars, two-dimensional exemplars, and games and kits.

There are many ways to exemplify mathematical ideas for students: both three-dimensional exemplars and two-dimensional exemplars can be used. For example, models for numerosity can involve some form of a set model or a measurement model. Important diagnostic feedback is gained as teachers have students use such exemplars to interpret the math content at hand or to work out solutions to problems.

1. *Three-dimensional exemplars.* (a) *A Math Balance* is useful for understanding the meanings of operations and for work with simple equations. (b) *The Dienes' Multibase Arithmetic Blocks* are useful for understanding the pattern of grouping inherent in our numeration system and for the meaning of powers. (c) *Cuisenaire Rods* have many uses including work with equations and fractions. (d) *The Cuisenaire Powers of Ten Kit* is color coded to the Cuisenaire Rods and is useful for understanding numeration and powers. (e) *The Fraction Blocks* kit is useful for understanding fractions, equivalent fractions, and some operations on fractions. (f) *Wooden Geometric Solids* help students with geometric relationships, particularly those students who have difficulty in relating two-dimensional drawings in textbooks to the three-dimensional objects which are modeled thereby.

Students need to be involved directly in measurement activity, and much of this should be with the metric instruments now available.

2. *Two-dimensional exemplars.* (a) *An Array* is useful for multiplication of whole numbers and fractions and for distributing multiplication over addition and subtraction. (b) *The Number Line* is useful for the meaning of operations, for signed numbers, and for equations. (c) *Drawings* are useful for a variety of topics. For example, the square of a binomial can be pictured as a square region with four sections.

3. *Games and kits* have become quite generally available from distributors in recent years. Though they need to be selected with care, many are very useful, especially for consolidating activities. The following are examples of games and kits

likely to be helpful to teachers of behaviorally disordered adolescents. (a) *Fraction Bars* is a program of games, activities, manipulative materials, workbooks, and tests for teaching fractions. (b) *Sportsmath* is a series of games involving practice with basic operations on numbers: football, basketball, baseball, etc. (c) *The Winning Touch* is a game which helps students master basic multiplication facts. (d) *TUF* can be adapted to many levels of mathematical development and helps students learn about equations while practicing operations on numbers. (e) *Prime Drag* is a game which provides practice with factors, multiples, primes, and composites.

Games and kits such as those listed above are usually available from commercial suppliers such as:

Creative Publications
3977 East Bayshore Road
P.O. Box 10328
Palo Alto, California 94303

LaPine Scientific Company
Dept. D4321
379 Chestnut Street
Norwood, New Jersey 07648

Selective Educational Equipment (SEE), Inc.
3 Bridge Street
Newton, MA 02195

Guidelines

In summary, a few rather specific *do's* are offered. These are intended as guidelines rather than as prescriptions for each teacher must make critical instructional decisions within the local context. The reader is urged to read them carefully to see if any of them point to things that might be done differently in his or her own instructional program.

1. *Enjoy the students.* Instead of focusing on those difficult moments, take time to know them and enjoy them as valued human beings.

2. *Show your own interest in mathematics.* Your own excitement in observing a relationship, testing a possible solution, or learning a novel computational procedure will do much to help students develop an interest in their own study of mathematics.

3. *Personalize your instruction.* It is not necessary or wise for students to work individually at all times, but you should personalize the curriculum so each student is successfully building on what he or she already knows and can do as new material is being learned. For some students this may require breaking the content into rather specific objectives.

4. *Help students master the mathematical content of grades 1–8.* Also give them many opportunities to apply these concepts and skills. Help them see how they will need these skills for independent functioning in the world.

5. *Involve students with a variety of topics.* Mathematics should not be just computation procedures.

6. *Focus instruction on concepts.* Help students understand ideas. Their behavior on tasks will indicate whether they do or do not understand such ideas.

7. *Emphasize the meanings of operations.* Understanding the meanings of the operations is the key to good sentence solving and successful problem-solving.

8. *Focus on skills*. Make sure students have opportunities to use the skills they learn in a variety of contexts.

9. *Focus on process as well as product*. Show special interest in *how* problems are solved. Value alternative solutions, but expect students to be able to show or explain why it always works—if it does.

10. *Include some projects in your instruction*. Let students do "research." For example, in order to reinforce the idea that a number has many names and to provide experience with equations and with basic operations on numbers, have them see if they can rename each of the whole numbers zero through ten using only the digit "4", and using it exactly four times. For example, $0 = 44 - 44$ and $2 = (4 \div 4) + (4 \div 4)$. Some numbers will have more than one name using 4 fours. Also see if names can be made using 5 fives and 6 sixes. For some projects, hand-held calculators may be appropriate.

11. *Use the discovery method as one of your methods*. Though it should not be your only method, interest in mathematics is enhanced by the discovery method. Structure the material at hand so students can more easily observe patterns and make generalizations without always being told. Make sure they test their generalizations on other examples and also seek some form of proof, either by appealing to physical representations or mathematical rules they already know.

12. *Use varied exemplars*. Demonstrate a concept or principle in more than one way and have students show you "what it means" or "why it works" in more than one way. In that way students will be able to use what they learn in more varied situations. If, in your effort to help a student focus on tasks, you eliminate such variety, the student may learn to do the task within the artificial context you create but not to use the concept or skill elsewhere.

13. *Use a sequence of activity types for the content being studied*. Make sure students understand a concept and can tie it in with other mathematical ideas before focusing on practice activities.

14. *Consider including activities which involve large muscle movement*. You may thereby involve some students more actively with mathematics.

15. *Look for patterns of error in practice papers rather than just scoring them*. Finding such patterns can lead to corrective instruction which is more focused and more fruitful.

16. *Make sure that students master prerequisite skills before proceeding to new skills*.

17. *Give students many opportunities for success with numbers and mathematical concepts*. Reinforce frequently with praise and other meaningful reinforcers.

18. *Provide many short instruction and practice sessions each day, rather than one long one*.

Teachers of behaviorally disordered adolescents are well aware that many of their students have experienced repeated failure in mathematics and have come to expect failure. It is not surprising, therefore, that it is difficult to get them to attend to instruction in math. Such youths desperately need successful experiences, and these can be provided only by beginning instruction within the less threatening context of concepts and skills the student already knows. A level of mastery must be attained before moving on to more complex concepts and skills. Successes, rather than failures, should be reinforced with whatever reinforcers work. Creative teaching is required, teaching which relates instructional activities to the students' interests and to the independent living of adults. Math can become, even for behaviorally disordered adolescents, less of an anxiety-ridden experience. Many such students will even come to enjoy math.

References

Ashlock, R. B. *Error patterns in computation.* 2nd ed. Columbus, Ohio: Charles E. Merrill, 1976.

Ashlock, R. B., & Humphrey, J. H. *Teaching elementary school mathematics through motor learning.* Springfield, Ill.: Charles C Thomas, 1976.

Bitter, G., Engelhardt, J, & Wiebe, J. *One step at a time.* St. Paul, Minn.: EMC, 1977.

Cooney, T. J., Davis, E. J., & Henderson, K. B. *Dynamics of teaching secondary school mathematics.* Boston: Houghton-Mifflin, 1975.

Keymath Diagnostic Arithmetic Test. New York: American Guidance Service, 1971.

Marks, J. L., Purdy, E. R., & Kinney, L. B. *Teaching elementary school mathematics for understanding* (4th ed.). Hyattstown, N.J.: McGraw-Hill, 1975.

Stanford Diagnostic Mathematics Test. New York: Harcourt, Brace, Jovanovich, 1976.

Wilson, John. *Some guides for elementary school mathematics.* College Park, Ma.: Author, 1969. (Available from the Emporium, University of Maryland, College Park, Maryland, 20742.)

Wilson, John. *Diagnosis and treatment in arithmetic: Beliefs, guiding models, and procedures.* College Park, Ma.: Author, 1976. (Available from the Emporium, University of Maryland, College Park, Maryland, 20742.)

Wilson, John, & Sadowski, Barbara (Eds.). *The Maryland Diagnostic Arithmetic Test and Interview Protocols.* College Park, Md.: Editors, 1976. (Available from the Emporium, University of Maryland, College Park, Maryland, 20742.)

Reading and Behavior Disorders

14

John F. Cawley
Raymond E. Webster

This chapter explores the relationship between reading and adolescent behavior disorders and suggests ways that teachers can consider instructional models in light of therapeutic approaches and student characteristics. Placement and teaching suggestions are included. This chapter is not intended to train personnel to teach reading to behaviorally disordered students; it is assumed that teachers will have some expertise in the area of reading instruction as well as in teaching strategies appropriate for students with behavior disorders.

An examination of the relationship between reading and behaviorally disordered adolescents must begin with a consideration of the terms *behaviorally disordered adolescents* and *reading* as concepts. As concepts, these terms subsume numerous attributes and varying degrees of manifestation. As concepts, *behaviorally disordered adolescents* and *reading* are pluralistic structures which can interrelate with and affect one another in a number of ways that have varying implications for teaching, for example:

1. Behavior disorders can contribute to the development of reading disabilities or to reduced reading proficiency and utilization of reading skills.
2. Reading problems can contribute to the development of behavior disorders.
3. Behavior disorders and specific disabilities can negatively affect the process of learning to read.
4. Behavior disorders can result in reading habits which, in spite of proficiency, are strange, bizarre, or unusual.

5. The behavior disorders of others may contribute to individual behavior disorders and/or reading problems.

6. Behavior disorders and reading performance may have no causal relationship.

When attempting to review the nature of the relationships between behavior disorders and reading, it is important to consider, at a minimum, the combinations just cited. It is important that the relationship is not overgeneralized, so that the reader does not automatically assume that: (a) all behavior disordered students have reading problems; or (b) all students with reading problems have behavior disorders.

Figure 1 depicts some of the combinations which could exist in the reading behavior-disorder interaction. The figure presents two degrees of behavior disorders—moderate and severe. Moderate disorders are intermittent, likely to occur under specific and predictable situations, do not maintain for extended periods of time, are under a fair degree of personal control, and are subject to modest efforts of intervention. Severe disorders are persistent, noticeable under nearly all conditions, likely to be beyond the personal control of the individual, and can be modified only after serious and extensive intervention.

The external disorder is associated with acting out, physical or verbal aggressiveness, and generalized behaviors that are distracting or disturbing to others. The internal disorder is associated with withdrawal, acceptable compensatory alternatives, and a set of behaviors that are more disturbing to the self than to others. For example, a moderately internally disordered youngster might be one who manifests behavior problems in one or two specific classroom or social situations, but not in others. This youngster may daydream, attempt to attend, but actually be inattentive; he or she might actually maintain considerable contact with the events and activities of the class but be unhappy and dissatisfied. A severely internally disordered youngster might be one who manifests specific or generalized sets of behaviors in all situations. The individual is detached from the communicative aspects of the environment and reality; there is no manifestation of social-cultural interaction; the individual operates within a restricted ecology without any conscious awareness of the reward-punishment domain.

FIGURE 1   Selected Depictions of Reading-Behavior Conditions

Degree and Type of Behavior Disorder		Degree and Type of Reading Characteristics			
		Proficient readers good habits; wide interests	Proficient readers strange or unusual interests; poor habits	Nonproficient readers	
				Mild handicap	Severe handicap
Moderate	External				
	Internal				
Severe	External				
	Internal				

Data obtained by the State of Florida on the functional literacy of adolescents with behavior disorders are presented in Table 1. The data are reported for eleventh-grade students referred to as emotionally disturbed (n = 114) and socially malad-justed (n = 79) and suggest that approximately 50% of each of these samples had proficiency in reading sufficient to meet the standards for a high-school diploma. (Comparable development was not observed in mathematics.) Further, these data indicate that there are varying degrees of reading proficiency among behaviorally disordered adolescents. This range of performance indicates that the tendency to equate *reading disability* and *behavior disorder* is inaccurate. Consideration must be given to those youngsters who are at least minimally proficient in reading, for they constitute some 50% of the sample shown in Table 1. The variations in patterns of reading proficiency and in type, degree, and character of a student's behavior disorders must be known in order to develop a sound placement and instructional plan.

Minimum proficiency in the skills shown on Table 1 is considered essential by many educators. The inclusion of basic life skills testing in the secondary schools is a matter that is sure to modify programming for students with behavior disorders. However, if one were to review the educational experiences and curricular programs for these youngsters, it is unlikely that one would find evidence that these areas are sufficiently covered and ably presented. Wherein does the responsibility for failure rest? If the youngster is excused or excluded from the proficiency test program, educators may be permitting handicapped students to leave school without the minimum set of competencies deemed appropriate for nonhandicapped students. As Table 1 suggests, far too few students with behavior problems are acquiring minimum literacy competencies.

If behaviorally disordered students are to have an equal chance to succeed, reading instruction for them must cover the same competencies as it does for other students. On a test of basic skills, Scott-Foresman Publishing Company includes a reading section with a short story of approximately 700 words.[1] This story is followed by 23 multiple-choice questions. Some of these questions require the student to return to certain paragraphs in the story and to answer the questions specific to that paragraph. The test situation requires considerable concentration, an element of speed because the test is timed, and a number of different tasks including reading the story, locating the designated paragraph, and answering multiple-choice questions. Reading instruction for the behaviorally disordered adolescent must include a number of activities similar to those listed above if the student is to have an opportunity to perform successfully on the test.

FROM BEHAVIOR DISORDERS TO READING PROBLEMS

The presence of a primary emotional disturbance often interferes with or complete-ly blocks attempts by the child to learn to read. Among his three major diagnostic categories of children with reading disabilities, Rabinovitch (1959) includes one group of children with normal reading potential which is impaired by such emotionally based factors as depression, anxiety, and emotional blocking. The two remaining categories relate to organic factors that interfere with reading success.

---

[1] Scott-Foresman Comprehensive Assessment Program, Scott-Foresman, Glenview, Illinois.

TABLE 1 Functional Literacy among Adolescents with Behavior Disorders: Percentage Passing

Communications	Emotionally disturbed	Social maladjusted	Mathematics	Emotionally disturbed	Social maladjusted
Identify main idea	52	44	Measure time between events	19	13
Correctly answer who, what type information questions	62	51	Calculate equivalent amounts	75	76
Understand cause/effect of an action or or event	61	47	Solve "real world" problems	36	44
Distinguish between facts and opinions	42	38	Compute decimal fractions/percentage	49	51
Identify unstated opinions	45	46	Do comparison shopping	14	14
Determine best source of information	50	52	Calculate simple interest	11	20
Use index to cross-reference	59	57	Figure sales tax	27	38
Read highway and city maps	56	44	Figure rate of discount	51	56
Write letters	61	54	Measure length, width with metrics	24	28
Complete a check and stub	53	57	Measure perimeter, area with metrics	14	15
Complete application form	73	63	Determine capacity with English/metric	30	39
			Determine weight with English/metric	12	15
			Read graphs	60	59
TOTAL	56	49	TOTAL	17	25

Professionals often rely upon psychoanalytic explanations that link these emotional problems to basic disruptions in the quality of the parent-child relationship, with particular reference to the child's psychosexual development (Blanchard, 1946). The emotional difficulty is thought to occur as the result of one significant traumatic experience, a continued series of negative emotional experiences, or a learned maladaptive behavior pattern (Scholfield & Balian, 1959). These experiences are thought to produce neurotic blocking, extreme narcissism, or other types of psychic conflicts which divert energy from the reading process (Pearson, 1952). This position maintains that reading disability is a symptom of underlying psychopathology and that the disability varies in form and intensity depending upon the specific symbolism associated with the disorder.

Family psychopathology as it relates to reading has been studied extensively. In an initial psychological study of 20 children with severe reading disabilities, Fabian (1959) demonstrated that family psychopathology may or may not be an influential factor precipitating the reading problem. Of the three general groups delineated within this sample on the basis of the climate within the familial environment, only one group evidenced severe family psychopathology. A follow-up study using a more varied population of reading-disabled students from public schools, child guidance clinics, and psychiatric wards revealed a very high incidence of severe reading problems in students from families rated high in psychopathology (Fabian, 1955). Wilderson (1967) obtained similar findings for 50 children seen in the Children's Psychiatric Hospital at the University of Michigan for evaluation of emotional and learning problems. However, the use of students from child guidance clinics and psychiatric wards does impose a sampling bias which limits the generalization of the finding.

Several studies have examined the personality patterns of reading-disabled students in an attempt to relate specific predisposing personality profiles to reading disabilities. Vorhaus (1952) distinguished four major personality types within a group of 309 disabled readers on the basis of responses to the Rorschach Inkblot Test. The first group was comprised of students who were emotionally inhibited, with a low energy level, and little motivation to perform well in school. The second group of students were described as self-preoccupied, egocentric, and with little active investment in the reading or learning process. Students in the third group exhibited basic difficulties with interpersonal relationships, and they appeared threatened by reading because of the relatively high degree of social participation generally required. The final group was characterized by feelings of personal inadequacy, inferiority, and a generalized chronic anticipation of failure.

Kunst (1959) suggested that reading failure seems to be a neurotic symptom associated with underlying personal conflict. Passive-aggressive reactions to parental demands and reliance upon ego defense mechanisms, such as avoidance and denial, appear to interfere with the acquisition and development of reading skills. This perspective views reading problems as a symptom of deeper, underlying emotional problems which emanate from within the reader. The reading problem occurs either because emotional energies are diverted in an attempt to deal with intrapsychic conflict or as a result of basic ego deficiencies. Clearly, emotional problems are seen as the cause of reading failure.

The impact that behavior disorders have upon reading performance is different from those situations in which reading disability precipitates behavior disorders. A primary difference is age at the onset of the reading problem. When reading disability is the designated cause, the reading disability may be identifiable as early as age 5, 6, or 7 years. This is not the case when behavior disorders lead to reading problems because behavior disorders can become manifest at any age. Thus, the young child who exhibits behavior disorders which interfere with learning to read (as well as the ability to perform other tasks) is quite different from the student whose emotional problems are not manifest until adolescence. In the latter case, when the tensions leading to the behavior disorder are reduced, it is probable that the adolescent will once again show reading proficiency, although he may need remedial programming to catch up on the learning time missed. The present authors doubt that it is possible for one to lose the cognitive ability to read, except in the case of psychoneurological insult that results in an aphasia-like disorder.

A frequent impact of behavior disorders upon reading is manifested in a diminished use of reading for dealing with school tasks. This tendency might be attributed to problems of attitude, attention, peer relationships, the sudden onset of emotional trauma, or to a change in values or interests. Various therapeutic interventions might be employed. The Life Space Interview (Morse, 1977) is one alternative intervention in which the teacher and student can relate in a mutual attempt to understand the situation and negotiate alternatives. The Problem

Solving Approach (Glasser, 1965) might be used to confront the problems more directly and set forth a course of action. The behavioral alternative of reinforcing successful completion of school tasks can also be employed. Certainly any abrupt or noticeable change in student characteristics and performance should be viewed within the totality of the ecology in which the individual functions.

No matter what reading program or management system that is chosen, it is essential that students experience daily reading success. Progress and success in learning to read often reduce stress, increase self-esteem, and lead to less maladaptive behavior in and out of school.

FROM READING PROBLEMS TO
BEHAVIOR DISORDERS

In many cases, behavior disorders result from continued failure experienced during the reading instructional process. The emotional problems gradually increase in intensity as the severity of the reading disability increases. Eventually, emotional problems perpetuate the reading problems. Research lends credence to this position. For example, the incidence of significant emotional problems in disabled readers is estimated to be 40% (Robinson, 1947) to 50% (Witty, 1950). Robinson reported that 9 of 22 disabled readers also exhibited severe emotional problems. In 7 of these 9 cases, the reading problem appeared to be the primary cause of the emotional problem.

A number of studies have indicated that emotional problems arise after the student experiences continued failure in reading. Fernald (1943) examined the preschool psychological histories of 78 severely reading disabled students to determine the relationship between reading failure and personal maladjustment. She found that only four of these students had a history of emotional problems before entering school. Yet all 78 were described by parents and/or teachers as having significant "emotional upset" after experiencing difficulty in the reading process.

More recent evidence collected by Glick (1972) supports Fernald's findings. Glick examined the relationship between early failure in reading and changes in (a) general and academic self-concept, (b) attitudes toward school, (c) the child's perceptions of parental behaviors, and (d) classroom peer attributes. Children were administered the Self-Concept of Ability Test, the Pupil Opinion Questionnaire (school attitudes), a reduced version of the Child Report of Parental Behavior, and the Syracuse Scales of Social Relations (peer relations) at the beginning and end of third grade. Male poor readers were found to show negative attitude changes toward teachers, peers, and parents. No changes in attitudes were observed for female poor readers or good readers. Apparently, there are patterns of sex differences in response to poor school performance which differ greatly between males and females.

Wright (1974) found that factors both within the family unit and external to it appear to be closely related to reading success. The feelings of frustration, personal inadequacy, and expectation of failure associated with reading failure may generate a substantial degree of stress within the student and for the parents. The need for the student to cope with these stresses and demands may necessitate the investment of personal energies into ego defense mechanisms which can range from social withdrawal to aggressive, erratic behavior.

The problem of clearly establishing a precise causal relationship between reading disability and emotional disturbance is complicated by the difficulty in conducting sound experimental research in this area. Those behaviors thought to be causes of reading disability are frequently mere symptoms of the reading problem. Furthermore, when studies are subject samples drawn from facilities that specialize in the treatment of disturbed young people, these samples are not representative of the typical reading-disabled student in school. It seems clear, however, that reading-disabled students demonstrate a higher incidence of personal adjustment problems, lower levels of peer group acceptance, and greater dislike for school than adequate readers.

Hake (1969) administered the reading subtest of the California Achievement Test and the Reading Apperception Test to 40 students of above-average intelligence, half of whom were below grade level in reading. The poor readers were significantly less well adjusted than the good readers on measures of attitudes toward their parents and home situation, school, reading, aggression, types of defense mechanisms used, and self-concept. Athey (1966) conducted a cross-validation study of personality factors which distinguished between the upper and lower quartiles in reading on the Stanford Achievement Test for two samples of 130 and 160 ninth graders. Using factor analysis, he found that the lower quartile of readers exhibited greater dislike of school, more dependency on their parents, and higher levels of feelings of personal inadequacy. Others obtaining similar findings include Ladd (1933) and Sheldon and Carrillo (1952).

Several studies have examined differences between good and poor readers along a variety of personality dimensions. Bell, Lewis, and Anderson (1972) specified five personality factors associated with reading disabilities for a sample of 100 average and poor readers. Three general personality characteristics were defined: aggressiveness, (irritability and impatience, assumed to be related to frustration with school), passivity and social withdrawal (tendency to avoid conflicts and low levels of motivation and energy), and negativism. Spache (1957) delineated five personality types for disabled readers which closely correspond with these groups. Similar results were found by Zimmerman and Allebrand (1965) for a sample of 71 reading disabled and 82 average readers. When Card 1 of the Thematic Apperception Test and the California Test of Personality was administered, results showed the disabled readers to be less self-reliant and to be characterized by social withdrawal and nervous symptoms. Glavin and Annesley (1971) administered the Behavior Problem Checklist to teachers and also administered to 130 elementary-school boys diagnosed as having behavior problems the Lorge-Thorndike or Slosson intelligence tests and the reading and arithmetic subtests of the California Achievement Tests. Within this group, 81.5% were found to be underachieving in reading and 72.3% underachieving in arithmetic. Stavrianos and Landsman (1969) administered the Rorschach to 150 good and 160 poor readers and concluded that the poor readers showed relatively few balanced and mature personality patterns.

The negative effects on personal adjustment of early reading disabilities seem to continue into later adulthood. Woolf (1965) administered the Barron Scale of the Minnesota Multiphasic Personality Inventory to 19 good and 20 poor readers who were college freshmen. The poor readers showed significantly higher levels of anxiety, scored lower on the ego scale, and were generally more immature than the good readers. Fennimore (1968) studied changes in self-concept related to the effects of an eight-week reading instruction program for 107 college students. Results of the Nelson Denny Reading Test and the Self-Concept Scale showed that the mean scores for ratings of the ideal self decreased, with no changes in the mean score for real self ratings as a measure of personal satisfaction (or dissatisfaction). Thus, it appears that these subjects showed a more realistic appraisal of self-worth after the reading program.

Disabled readers have been known to be less well accepted by their peers than adequate readers. Stevens (1971) administered the Ruth Cunningham (1951) Classroom Social Distance Scale to a sample of 886 fourth graders that included 25 male and 9 female poor readers. Both male and female poor readers were found to be socially isolated within their classes. Henderson and Long (1966) identified the top and bottom thirds of 81 fifth-grade good readers on the basis of self-social concepts. Each child was given a nonverbal measure of personal social orientation. High readers were shown to have significantly greater individualization and identification with peers. High readers saw themselves as more socially oriented and unique.

McGinley and McGinley (1970) analyzed the effects of psychological grouping on reading groups for six first-grade classes with three ability levels in each class. Each child was asked to name three other children in class whom they like to work with and the reason why. Teachers were also asked to provide the names of five children who were best in reading, arithmetic, sports, or most popular. It was found that children in the top reading group made more intragroup selections. Members of the middle reading group made more between-group choices in the top group and fewer in the lower reading group. Members of the bottom reading group made more choices in the top group. Further, among 21 children selected by teachers as most popular, 15 were members of the top reading group.

Reading problems among juvenile offenders are numerous. A report by the Comptroller General of the United States (1977) to the Congress states that about one-fourth of institutionalized delinquents tested in two states had learning problems. A study of 1,634 delinquent youths indicated that the one factor most predictive of delinquency was poor reading. Prior to either of these studies, Lunden (1964) noted that only 12% of delinquents demonstrated age-in-grade performance in contrast to 50% of nondelinquents. Slightly more than 25% of delinquent youth were two years educationally retarded and 21% were three years behind.

Many factors seem to be involved when reading problems are seen as precipitating behavior disorders. The relationship may be characterized by the fact that the behavior disorders do not manifest themselves immediately but rather are a long-term developmental phenomenon. Clearly, the experience of failure is a major contributor to the behavior disorder. No child can withstand a continuous, daily encounter with failure. Failure affects peer relationships; failure creates dissonance between individual and family expectancies and performance; failure may precipitate behavior disorders as a means of compensation. The interaction between reading and behavior disorders (Cawley, Goodstein, & Burrow, 1972) might be described as follows:

1. The individual lacks a tool (reading performance that is deemed satisfactory) and quickly learns that this tool is lacking.

2. Other individuals, teachers, peers, parents, conclude that the individual lacks the tool and they devalue the individual for lacking it.

3. The individual accepts this judgment of others that he/she is less worthy and devalues himself/herself accordingly.

4. The individual adjusts to this depiction and behaves in ways that will provide self-esteem, anxiety reduction, and some degree of self-worth.

The product of this sequence is an individual who demonstrates alternative behavior patterns to avoid failure, hurt, and embarrassment.

It is important to recognize the failure paradox. Failure is the daily lack of success and the production of unacceptable but tolerable rates of incorrect responses. The combination of being unacceptable but tolerable is paradoxical. The teacher tells the student that his/her performance is unacceptable; yet, by confronting the individual with situations in which failure regularly occurs, the teacher tolerates this failure. At some point the student asks, "Why are they doing this to me?" Such failure experiences can be reduced or eliminated entirely by determining where the student is functioning well and where he or she is making reading errors, and by planning instruction around this information and carefully pacing it to insure daily success and challenge.

Relating academic and vocational areas to one another is a means of making the educational experience more meaningful for the student and more cohesive in terms of inter-teacher planning. An illustration of this might be the case of a student who is enrolled in auto mechanics and who is also taking English and social studies. The student could use books on auto mechanics or racing as possible book reports or reading assignments. The student could prepare a report on some socially significant facet of the automobile. This might include its impact upon Americans, the OPEC countries, or the history of the automobile.

A teacher who is interested in creativity could include tasks such as:

(1) Write a short story in response to this statement: "You woke up this morning and found that all the wheels on automobiles have become square. What would you do?"

(2) Respond orally to this statement: "A clever friend has changed the interior of his car so that the steering wheel faces the rear and is now in what appears to be the back seat. He wants to know how people are going to react when they see this contraption on the road. What do you think their reactions will be?"

Torrance (1961) explored numerous ways of relating selected thinking and problem-solving abilities to coping with stress, of freeing one's mental abilities in order that they might function more effectively to meet individual needs and desires. Nearly all of the activities stressed by Torrance can be readily adapted for use in any subject-matter area. Thus, the teacher has the opportunity to include behaviorally oriented tasks without compromising the subject matter commitment.

Well-intentioned teachers sometimes assist students excessively or make great efforts to protect them. This is as aptly illustrated in reading as in any other area. Take the case of a student who is reading a set of material and, in doing so, making numerous errors. The teacher reads along with the student. It soon becomes evident that the teacher is doing more of the reading than the student. This is neither wise nor productive. Both would be better off if more appropriate reading material were assigned.

In another situation, the teacher may be aware that the student cannot read the material. This teacher, in order to protect the student from his/her peers, simply does not call upon the student. This contributes to the reinforcement of feelings of rejection and isolation. In these instances, the teacher should seek alternative tasks for the student. The student might listen to another student read and then be called upon to paraphrase the story. Most important, the student should not be allowed to experience repeated failure. Good instruction involves providing reading activities that are interesting and challenging, yet within the student's ability to complete successfully. For the student who has already experienced a long history of reading failure, insuring daily reading success is crucial in reversing a sense of self-identification as a reading failure.

The obvious way to prevent failure is to individualize instruction. In this context, individualization of instruction means simply that the tasks assigned to a student will be tasks he or she can perform at high levels of correctness. This does not imply that students will not be different; rather, it means that the teacher insures that students will not practice or perform a task incorrectly more times than they perform it correctly.

By the time the individual reaches the secondary level, the impact of reading failure upon behavior is well established. At this level, the school can concentrate on modifying the behavior disorders, reduce reading to the greatest possible extent in the content areas, and introduce the best possible reading support system to the individual. For example, science classes could be undertaken via multimedia instruction and reading instruction could relate to the reading demands of the science class. By adjusting the instruction to the student we place the change emphasis on education, not therapy. That is, rather than expecting the student to change through therapy, the educational system must change so that the student learns as much as possible and experiences as much success as possible in everyday life.

BEHAVIOR DISORDERS AND SPECIFIC LEARNING DYSFUNCTION

While the relationships between behavior disorders and reading are complex, complexity also exists in the relationship between behavior disorders and specific learning dysfunctions. The illustration below indicates that many dimensions must be dealt with before any generalized conclusions can be drawn.

Specific learning dysfunctions are defined in this context as those learning traits which characterize a group (less meaningful) or an individual (more meaningful). Traditionally, these have been categorized and described under headings such as perception (for example, visual or auditory discrimination), psycholinguistic or sociolinguistic skills, attention, cognition, or other comparable nomenclature (Lerner, 1976).

One has little difficulty in finding youngsters who manifest dysfunctions or in distinguishing samples of children from one another in terms of a variable such as reading and then finding differences in selected dysfunctions. The difficulty lies in determining the meaning to attribute to the dysfunctions once they have been identified. The question, "Do practice and experience in one area (such as psycholinguistic training or problem-solving) produce positive effects upon another area (reading)?" is difficult to answer (Cawley, 1977a; 1977b). The extent to which a behavior disorder produces deficits in attention which result in a reading problem is as obtuse an issue today as it was over a decade ago (Cawley, 1967). We would caution against an over-emphasis on remediating attentional dysfunction and suggest, instead, particularly at the upper grade levels, a direct approach to the problem. That is, if the student has attentional deficits, deal with them directly. This could be done by incorporating teaching strategies which reward on-task behavior or by using reading activities which require sustained and continuous attention such as that exemplified by the cloze technique. An example of a task fitting into this line of thinking is illustrated in the Early Assessment Program (Cawley, Cawley, Cherkes, & Fitzmaurice, in press). The task requires that individual to interpret picture-symbol associations into context, using a modified cloze technique (Figure 2). For adolescents, similar activities with higher interest value for this group can be devised.

Much has been written about the role of short-term memory (STM) and reading. Less definitive work has been done on the relationship between behavior disorders and short-term memory. This triad must ultimately be dealt with if we are to understand the comprehensiveness of the reading-behavior disorders relationship.

The important role of an effective and efficient short-term memory (STM) system in the learning process, particularly in reading, has been long recognized (Blankenship, 1938). Lashley (1959) suggested that deficits in reading, writing, and speaking are all related to a basic difficulty in the sequential organization of information within STM stores.

Short-term memory is a temporary storage mechanism which serves either to hold newly acquired information until it is processed for long-term storage or to hold previously acquired information retrieved from long-term storage for use in the present. It appears that STM capacity and processing efficiency are important

FIGURE 2   Cloze Technique Task

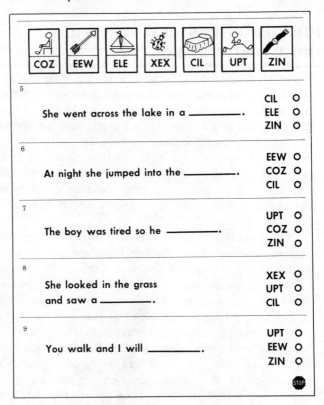

parameters which constrain the rapidity of new learning (Bjork, 1972; Miller, 1956), the ability to generate new ideas, and the capacity to integrate and conceptualize newly learned information with previously acquired knowledge (Baddeley, 1976). Deficits in any or all of these areas could impede the behavioral or cognitive (reading) development of the individual. The student who does not remember should be distinguished from the student who consciously uses "memory" problems as excuses to avoid responsibility ("I didn't remember to bring my paper in," when in fact the work was not completed). The effects of STM deficits can be minimized by reducing the mass and complexity of the task, by using a variety of modalities for input and output, and by finding appropriate amounts of practice in a variety of situations.

For example, in teaching the student to recognize the letters of the alphabet, the teacher's first step is to reduce the task's complexity by teaching discrimination between totally dissimilar letter pairs (b - x, d - n, a - y). This task could be further structured by using a contrasting color-coding system to maximize letter discrimination. The teacher must be sure that the student does not respond to letter color rather than letter name during the learning situation. The letter pairs are next presented in a multisensory manner, especially stressing the visual, tactile, and auditory components of each letter. The student is asked to respond to these inputs by either orally repeating the letter names or writing the letters, or both. This provides a further source of feedback to the student during learning. Massed practice sessions, where the student overlearns the letter names, are also given. As the visual similarity of letters increases (b - d, g - p, w - m), the teacher should emphasize color coding or essential parts which characterize the letters. This color coding is followed by multisensory input and output pairings involving massed practice and overlearning.

One of the primary issues to be resolved is that of "student change" or "teacher change," that is, when a student has a problem, can the problem be more readily dealt with by a modification of instructor style? Let us illustrate the point with the case of a behaviorally disordered student who seems to become confused and frustrated with lengthy assignments and who has difficulty remembering substantial parts of the learning activities. It might take considerable time for the student to develop a capacity to deal with these problems. Yet a teacher could make an instant adjustment. The length of the lesson could be shortened. The amount of material could be reduced. A greater number of repetitions could be included. As often as not, problems with "remembering" are often problems of original learning. If we expect the student to recall certain facts and concepts or to continue the use of specific skills on an independent basis, then it will be necessary to assure the student an ample opportunity to learn the task in the first place.

BEHAVIOR DISORDERS AND READING HABITS

One of the remarkable outgrowths of sociocultural variation and individual differences is the wide range of interests reflected in reading. There are countless books about innumerable topics and many books on a single topic. There is reading material at all levels of proficiency: comic books, magazines, newspapers, and letters, both business and personal. Printed media are everywhere, and learning to read is more important than ever before.

There are individuals, however, who spend an inordinate amount of their time reading or on a particular topic in reading. In such cases, the best interests of the student are served by limiting the behavior. For instance, the adolescent whose obsession with reading is so intense that peer relationships or other responsibilities are avoided should have some variation in total programming. The individual may have learned early in life that reading can be used as an avoidance mechanism. If the student continually refuses to participate in other activities because he is reading, intervention may be needed. This is sometimes difficult because our society has placed such a premium on reading that the last thing anyone wants to do is to interfere with it; yet with some behaviorally disordered adolescents it is necessary. Reading is only one of many behaviors necessary for successful life functioning.

The adolescent whose reading habits are confined to one or two topics may also present a problem. Such an individual may continually read literature while ignoring a science assignment. Some adolescents with behavior disorders become obsessed with a single topic, such as race cars or outer space, and try to impress their peers with their information in these areas. Others have bizarre or unusual reading habits. A continued, inordinate compulsion to read pornographic literature, for example, often is related to emotional problems. The reading habits and interests of the individual ought to be scrutinized, not for the purpose of censorship, but because they are pertinent to responsibility and human relationships. Consider the following case.

Warren was a well-behaved but quiet seventh grader, with a measured IQ of 138 on the Wechsler Intelligence Scale for Children—Revised. He was reading on a ninth-grade level with over 90% comprehension. His parents and teachers were very concerned about his total preoccupation and insistence upon reading about Nazi war crimes. Warren would complete his school assignments rapidly and accurately and begin reading either fictional or nonfictional accounts of war atrocities. He argued that he should have the right to select his own reading materials, especially if he completed his assignments and maintained an "A" average in his school work.

Warren is an example of a very bright young man with exceptional reading abilities who literally devoured every available book portraying a distorted side of human behaviors and relationships. Certainly his teachers were correct when they listened to and discussed his concerns about man's inhumanity to man and tried every means possible to encourage him to develop some other reading interests. Helping behaviorally disordered students attend to lighter, happier reading topics can result in positive behavior changes.

Quite often we encounter the student who expresses dissatisfaction with every task and with every set of material. In this type of case, a teacher might do well to change the assignment in such a way that the student becomes responsible for producing alternative materials and tasks to achieve the same goal. Such an approach can help sidestep authority struggles.

BEHAVIOR PROBLEMS OF OTHERS CREATE READING AND BEHAVIOR DISORDERS

Students of all ages are usually annoyed by the antics and disruptions of others. Older students may be openly critical, show their disgust with the individual, and even go so far as to question the capabilities of the teacher who fails to maintain an effective management system applicable to all. Younger students may offer their criticisms of the disruptive student without directly blaming the teacher.

The student who is on the brink of success or failure in reading is in a perilous situation when order is not maintained. Unless instruction is properly structured, the student may fail. Failure will not be a one-day event but will accrue day after day until the cumulative effects are devastating. The net result is not only reading failure but potential social-emotional failure as well. At the secondary level, the student who has learned minimal reading skills may fail to interpret content adequately. Since such a student has minimal reading skills, the actual source of this failure may be a distracting classroom environment. Teachers must maintain a classroom environment which fosters attention to task and good learning habits.

Secondary schools have a tendency to group youngsters according to achievement/ability combinations. The practice of placing ninth- and tenth-grade students into groups which function at the fourth-grade level must be questioned. Low reading level alone probably does not justify the group. A grouping system built around achievement/ability/behavior, so that students are grouped according to some standard of acceptable and productive behavior, may make more sense. If this is so, however, what are the implications of grouping students with disruptive behavior together? What are the effects of a bright, behaviorally disordered student upon the rest of the group? What happens when one student completes an act that is negatively received by the teacher while another gets away without rebuke? Careful thought about such issues must go into any grouping decision.

The impact of one person upon another at the adolescent level is likely to take effect in relationship to content, school marks, attitude, and motivation. In some cases, the behavior of others masks the incipient state of behavior disorders in a particular student, causing the problem to go unrecognized and preventive action to be neglected. This type of situation was evident in one seventh-grade class within a departmentalized junior high school.

> Fred was withdrawn and typically nonassertive in comparison to 5 other males in his class of 19 students. These 5 students were particularly disruptive toward one male teacher. Most of the disruptive behaviors involved verbal taunting of the teacher and throwing papers and chalk. Interviews with each student by the school pychologist indicated that these behaviors were related to the needs of these students for male attention and peer recognition rather than to serious underlying emotional problems. A behavioral intervention program was implemented which only slightly reduced the frequency of these behaviors. Fred's problem was that he occasionally (less than once a month) became verbally abusive toward the teacher. During these times Fred was removed from the room and sent to the office. Because of the infrequent nature of the outbursts, the vice-principal assumed Fred's problem was not so serious as that of the other boys. Therefore, he verbally reprimanded Fred and, once appropriate self-control had been regained, returned him to his next class. One afternoon after class, shortly before the end of the school year, Fred beat his teacher with a pipe and then attacked the vice-principal. Both adults were seriously injured. Subsequent psychiatric and psychological evaluations indicated that Fred was a severely emotionally disturbed boy who occasionally lost contact with reality. During these times he became highly suspicious of others and felt that he was being attacked. Unfortunately, because of the composition of his group, Fred's intermittent verbal outbursts were given little thought. Had the seriousness of his problems been recognized earlier, it might have been possible to prevent the beating of a teacher and vice-principal and to obtain the help Fred so urgently required.

This is one of many cases in which grouping together students with low reading levels and students with behavior problems led to more problems for both adults and students.

BEHAVIOR DISORDERS AND READING HAVE NO RELATIONSHIP

A final possible conclusion which must be examined pertinent to the relationship between reading and behavior disorders is that no causal relationship exists between the two. In the future, early screening and assessment practices may help determine the precise relationship between reading and behavior disorders. Early screening and assessment practices which take into account behavioral characteristics, developmental abilities, and achievement should help to keep track of the status of the child from approximately 4 years of age upward. One system currently being used includes assessment in the affective areas from age 4 through secondary school (Wick, 1980). An *Inventory of Teacher Concerns* (Cawley et al., in press) is used to assess prekindergarten through third grade affective development as well as other developmental qualities. The *Inventory* is a two-part strategy which contains both a classroom and individual component addressing 34 developmental factors. Each student can be rated on an equal number of strong and weak points, thereby providing some documentation of the range of attributes of that individual child.

The *Inventory of Teacher Concerns* is administered by having the teacher fill in the spaces with the names of students who are of immediate concern, as shown in Figure 3. The names to the left are those individuals who are not performing to expected levels in one or more areas. The names to the right are those of individuals who are the highest achievers in either the cognitive and affective areas or both. Once the classroom inventory has been completed, the teacher uses the individual inventory to delineate concerns about individuals. The student must be viewed in terms of both strengths and weaknesses. Those items coded to the left (Figure 4) represent weaknesses; those to the right, strengths. For example, it can be seen that the primary concerns the teacher has for Elena are the nonacceptance of her by her peers and her inability to stick up for herself. At the same time, Elena has an excellent attendance pattern and is willing to accept responsibility for her actions.

FIGURE 3   Classroom Inventory

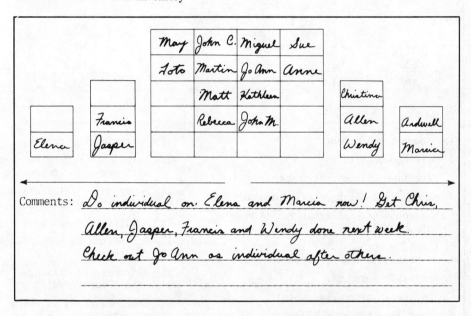

Each of the items in the individual inventory is accompanied by a set of descriptors scale as illustrated below for No. 4, memory/remembering characteristics.

| | EXAMPLES | |
Descriptors	*Weak*	*Strong*
4. Memory/remembering characteristics Remembrance of essential components of classroom routine; memory and application of things experienced in previous situations; short-term memory.	Seems not to have heard or to remember directions; seems to remember some things but not others.	Remembers classroom set up and arrangement; recalls previously learned material in appropriate context.
Teacher additions to list of descriptors	Poor recall for information and facts over short term memory	Good recall of facts and general information

FIGURE 4 Individual Inventory

Individual Inventory

Name of child: _____ Teacher: _____

Date: _____ School: _____

Age of child: _____ Grade: _____

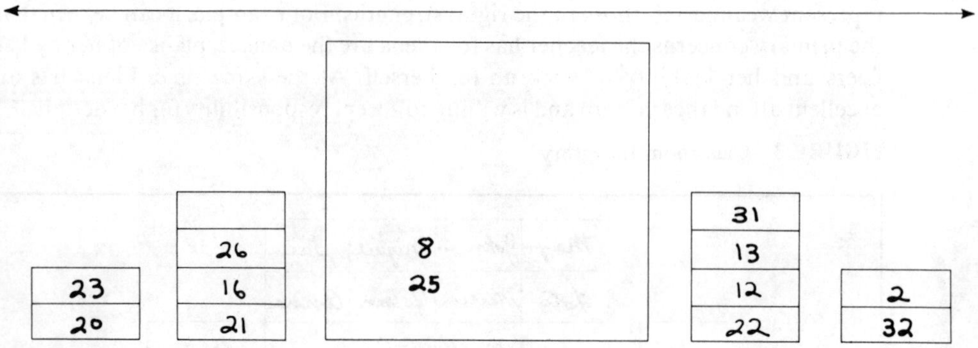

				31	
	26	8		13	
23	16	25		12	2
20	21			22	32

Comments _____

1. Academic performance
2. Attendance pattern
3. Receptive/expressive communication skills
4. Memory/remembering characteristics
5. Awareness of time-event relationships, responsibilities
6. Creative responses or interpretation of problems, tasks, situations
7. Quality of products
8. Physical/health development
9. Gross/fine motor development
10. Physical activity
11. Self help skills
12. Following specific directions
13. Completion of tasks and assignments
14. Need for supervision/instruction
15. Attitude toward directed play-work activities
16. Assisting others to complete tasks
17. Classroom behaviors
18. Use of excuses
19. Source of motivation

20. Acceptance by peers
21. Verbal and non-verbal exchanges with peers and authority
22. Concern for materials and belongings of others
23. Ability to stick up for self
24. Acceptance of ideas/suggestions of others
25. Awareness of attitudes of others toward self
26. Responsiveness to novel situations
27. Social amenities
28. Mood changes and range
29. Interpretation of or attention to situation or events
30. Phobias
31. Use of self-directed time
32. Acceptance of responsibility for actions
33. Attitude toward school, authority
34. Utilization of classroom/school surroundings and materials
35. Other

The teacher who places a 4 to the left is describing the student as *weak* in that area. When the 4 is to the right the student is described as *strong*.

From preschool through grade 2, four levels of cognitive tasks, with approximately 10 tasks to a level, are provided to assess cognitive development. From this point on, combinations of achievement, aptitude, basic life-function skills, and affective measures are provided up through the secondary levels. The Wick effort offers a means for developing an early data base on a youngster and for continuing longitudinal assessment through high school. Such a system should eventually clarify the behavior-reading relationship for each student.

A concern for individual assessment is an integral part of the Wick effort. This particular component provides for individual diagnosis in reading, language, and mathematics (Cawley et al., in press). Only the reading component will be described herein.

Diagnosis is a decision-making process. That is, once a given set of information has been obtained, it should be used to make a decision about the next step. The flow chart in Figure 5 illustrates decision-making diagnosis. The learner begins with the word list marked "A," where one of three decisions is made. If the learner attains a specified criterion, a decision is made to move upward to level B. If the student fails to meet that criterion but attains another, he/she is taken horizontally along row A and a sequence of A-level tasks are presented. Finally, if the student fails to attain the criterion for row A, the examiner makes a decision to continue the diagnosis by going to the skills section. The skills section provides for diagnosis within a set of skills that are largely at the prereading level. The examiner can decide to seek further information by going to the learning section. This section differs from the others in that the student is actually taught to perform a set of tasks. The examiner has the option to exit the flow chart and go to another component of the assessment program (Early Assessment Program) which contains some 40 different cognitive, language, and quantitatively related tasks. (See Figure 2 for one of the tasks at the six-year level.)

The specific etiology of reading disabilities appears to result from a variety of determinants. It is clear that emotional problems can lead to reading disability, especially for students with serious behavior problems. Nevertheless, a number of studies indicate that, for the general population of disabled readers, the reading problem leads to subsequent personal and interpersonal problems. These emotional problems serve to perpetuate the reading disability and to exacerbate personal feelings of inadequacy, social rejection, and failure. Although there is a high degree of interrelatedness between reading disabilities and behavior problems, this relationship is not now sufficiently robust to make the prediction of one from the other practical or realistic. Accordingly, the assessment program described above provides for assessment in a combination of affective and reading areas. Early attention to problems will lead to a more successful secondary school experience.

PLACEMENT AND PROGRAMMING

The design of an individualized educational program and the concurrent placement decisions vary with the type and degree of behavior disorder and reading characteristics. For instance, it is unlikely that the moderately behaviorally disordered adolescent with a severe reading disability will succeed in reading for content in his or her six or seven different content classes. By contrast, a more severely behavior-

FIGURE 5 Reading Diagnostic Flow Chart

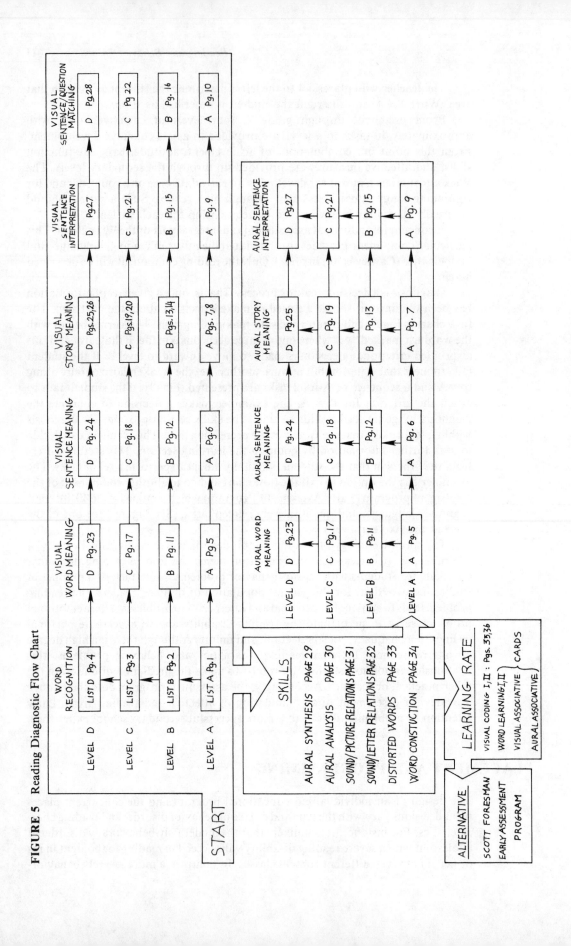

ally disordered student who is proficient in reading might be placed in a regular class program because reading skills are intact.

The total educational program should reflect a combination of therapeutic models and reading instructional designs. In the case of the behaviorally disordered youngster who is a proficient reader, the primary consideration would be to select an appropriate therapeutic intervention or behavior management model. However, for the poor reader, the therapeutic model and the reading instructional system should be matched. Work in mathematics among special education students (Cawley, Fitzmaurice, Goodstein, Lepore, Sedlak, & Althus, 1976–1977) identified the need to coordinate therapeutic and instructional elements. Using the Project MATH instructional model as a guide, Johnson and Schenck (1973) developed three short films and a study guide to illustrate how three different therapeutic models could be incorporated while teaching the concept of transitivity in a measurement activity. The three models illustrated were Redl's ego-supportive approach, Hewett's behavioral approach, and Glasser's problem-solving approach. The available literature has not indicated comparable endeavors related to reading. However, it is as important to provide appropriate instructional designs for reading as it is to provide appropriate therapeutic models. For instance, certain instructional strategies have a quantitative emphasis (for example, percentage correct over a specified time), whereas others have a qualitative emphasis (a group discussion as to which of three paragraphs has the greatest humanistic message, for example).

As an example of how instructional and therapeutic models might be combined, consider the reading design proposed by Fernald (1943) and the therapeutic model denoted as behavior modification. The Visual-Auditory-Kinesthetic-Tactile (VAKT) stage in the Fernald model is attentional and sequential in intent. The student traces a word while stating the component parts of the word (syllables or phonemes). During this activity the individual is attending to the stimulus dimensions of the reading material. On-task behavior is about 100%. When the individual is off-task (defined in this instance as not synchronizing the hand-eye-speech activity), the instructor notes this immediately. Behavior modification techniques may then be used to facilitate on-task behavior. The use of varying schedules and types of reinforcement would help to maintain the performance level of the individual over extended periods of time. This instructional-therapeutic combination might be quite effective with a severely handicapped reader who demonstrates attentional-sequential-synchronization problems.

Identification of the characteristics and commonalities of the various therapeutic and instructional models could become the basis for developing comprehensive systems of individual assessment in both the cognitive and behavioral domains. Specific student needs could then be related to program type rather than to program availability. The list of student needs compared with program types would become the basis for the establishment of criteria upon which placement decisions are made. It is necessary to operationally define sets of placement criteria in order to establish decision reliability. Sets of criteria, reliably interpreted, can also become the basis for program evaluation and research. Without established criteria the ability to predict and make proper placement recommendations will be limited. Moreover, without these criteria, the search for an appropriate education will remain chaotic.

The realities of the regular high-school education program are that the content is subject-matter controlled, taught by subject-matter specialists, and presented by five or more teachers for five hours per day over five days per week. These overriding factors make carrying out the decision to place the student in a public secondary school with a general education emphasis a most difficult and delicate procedure. Placing a student in regular secondary classes requires extensive negotiations with the receiving teachers, a clear description of the level of functioning and characteristics of the individual student, and precise commitments to supporting services and in-service training. It will also be necessary to delineate the instructional alternatives which the regular class teacher can use to meet the needs of the student who has limited reading skill.

If the behaviorally disordered student is enrolled in regular classes at the secondary level, the student is likely to have more than one teacher. There is a tendency for some students to play one teacher against another. For instance, a student may perform reasonably well in one class and not so well in another. The student may indicate that one teacher adapts to his reading level and another does not. It is important that each teacher have a clear picture of the actual status of the individual with regard to reading and maintain positive communication with colleagues.

Placement of the student in a self-contained public program is a somewhat less complicated decision in the sense that the receiving teacher, having been trained and certified in this area, should possess both the therapeutic and reading competencies necessary to meet the student's needs. The primary therapeutic consideration would be that of assuring that the models employed are tolerable, acceptable, and appropriate within a public environment.

Placement in a nonpublic day or residential setting may provide still greater means for meeting the needs of the student. Reading specialists with a commitment to behaviorally disordered youngsters are likely to be available and may be proficient in alternative reading approaches, thereby providing a more appropriate education. However, placement of behaviorally disordered students with low reading levels in regular classes in the secondary school requires the utmost thought and planning. Success for this student, who has already failed so often must be assured.

Certainly one aspect of an *appropriate education* should be that the providers delineate the relationship among curricular-instructional designs and the available therapeutic models. The placement decision should be made upon determination of the characteristics and needs of the individual when matched to the characteristics of the alternative educational programs. The critical element of appropriate placement is the extent to which the needs of the individual are met. Meeting the needs of the behaviorally disordered adolescent with low reading ability requires instruction and classroom management that will allow the student to experience daily success.

PLANNING FOR THE LIMITED READER AT THE SECONDARY LEVEL

How does a youngster with limited reading ability function in a secondary school experience where the subject-matter requirements focus heavily on reading? How do teachers adapt their instructional practices to provide for these youngsters? How do diagnosticians and other specialists convey information on these youngsters' needs to teachers and other involved personnel? How are meaningful roles given to the individual who cannot read and who has behavior disorders?

These questions lead to the main question: Do we all want to help this youngster? If we want to help, then as professionals it is necessary to adapt, both as individuals and as a total system. The skills lacking today are skills that must be acquired tomorrow. Workable school programs not currently available must be created in the future. Great creativity and determination will be required by educators at every level.

The first step in planning for the limited reader with behavior disorders is to distinguish among the respective roles of content, skill or task, and behavioral need or problem. Content is that which the student must know in order to succeed in the educational endeavor that is taking place or to meet imposed external demands. Skills or tasks involve performance by which an individual assimilates and expresses content. These skills are also the procedures used to develop meaningful roles and social interactions within the learning environment. Behavioral needs are individual characteristics which need to be accentuated (for example, more group participation for the withdrawn individual) or curtailed (less off-task behavior for a disruptive student).

We propose that the delineation of the different roles of content, skill, and behavior is restricted by the movement toward specifically written instructional objectives. In effect, we would argue that the format typically used to write and operationalize behavioral objectives is impeding program implementation. The behavioral objective, while necessarily precise if one is developing a criterion-referenced assessment item, is not at all efficient for curriculum or instructional purposes.

Specifically written objectives may in fact tend to focus the attention of the instructor upon measurement rather than upon teaching. An alternative is to write objectives which are both content and criterion free. This type of objective only stipulates the task that is to be performed. Each teacher can use the task in any content area and at different levels. This type of objective signals instructor input and learner output. The following are illustrative:

Teacher	*Learner*
states a word	states definition for word
states two words	states similarities between words
writes word	removes prefix/suffix and states word

Figure 6 (Carlisle, 1978) illustrates the use of the content-free objective. This illustration shows 4 of the nearly 700 tasks that have been developed. The advantages are twofold. First, any teacher, teaching any subject, can use the same set of objectives. Second, the number of tasks is so great that any teacher is bound to find a set of tasks with which the learner can be proficient. The opportunities for successful and meaningful classroom participation are extensive. The activities in Figure 6 are directly related to reading. Figure 7 describes a set of activities which provides for instruction in a specific subject area (spinal cord) while circumventing reading. Figures 6 and 7 provide a basis for including (Figure 6) or excluding reading (Figure 7) from the program. For the student with a reading problem, the negative effects of this problem can be minimized. For the student who is able to read, the assignment of reading tasks may be used as a positive reinforcer.

The following is excerpted from a story by Jack London, "To Build a Fire," from *Counterpoint in Literature* (Scott Foresman & Co., 1967), 7th grade.

Day had broken cold and gray, exceedingly cold and gray, when the man turned aside from the main Yukon trail and climbed the high earth bank, where a dim and little-traveled trail led eastward through the fat spruce timberland. It was a steep bank, and he paused for breath at the top, excusing the act to himself by looking at his watch. It was nine o'clock. There was no sun or hint of sun, though there was not a cloud in the sky. It was a clear day, and yet there seemed an intangible pall over the face of things, a subtle gloom that made the day dark and that was due to the absence of sun. This fact did not worry the man. He was used to the lack of sun. It had been days since he had seen the sun, and he knew that a few more days must pass before that cheerful orb, due south, would just peep above the skyline and dip immediately from view.

The man flung a look back along the way he had come. The Yukon lay a mile wide and hidden under three feet of ice. On top of this ice were as many feet of snow. It was all pure white, rolling in gentle undulations where the ice jams of the freeze-up had formed. North and south, as far as his eye could see, it was unbroken white, save for a dark hairline that curved and twisted away into the north, where it disappeared behind another spruce-covered island.

Visual Word Analysis

Teacher	Learner
Write words	State sound of underlined letters in word

cloud   south   around   thousand

Write the words	Remove prefix/suffix and state word
exceedingly (exceed)	intangible (tangible)
cheerful (cheer)	immediately (immediate)
unbroken (broken)	disappeared (appear)

Write word pairs	Write compound words
timber land	(timberland)
sky line	(skyline)
hair line	(hairline)

Visual Phrase-Sentence Meaning

Teacher	Learner
Write phrase/sentence	State meaning of underlined item

This exercise concerns the understanding of figurative language. Using the first item below, the teacher should discuss with the student(s) the idea that the author didn't mean to say that the day was really broken. The student(s) is asked to state what is literally meant.

1. "*Day had broken* cold and gray . . . "
2. "He knew that a few more days must pass before that *cheerful orb*, due south, *would just peep above the skyline* and dip immediately from view."

FIGURE 7 Visual Closure[2] Activities Related to Spinal Cord[3]

Visual Closure: *Input*: a sequence of letters   *Output*: completes dot-to-dot
or numerals   pictures and states
name of object repre-
sented by picture

VCL–4

Students will be given clues in sentences for completing their dot-to-dot pictures. For example, the sentence for the picture might read, "The spinal cord extends to the base of the FIRST SACRAL vertebra. All dot-to-dot pictures will be numbered, not to exceed 25 dots. Thus, the picture will be a simple dot drawing of the first sacral vertebra.

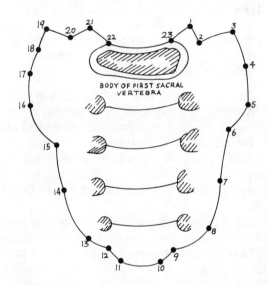

Let us assume now that a decision has been made to present content to the student without a reading emphasis and that there is a concurrent decision to attend to a specific behavior that has contributed to the student's being classified as behaviorally disordered. The specific behavior is classified as withdrawal and is observable in the student's avoidance of peer contact and, in turn, peers' avoidance of the student. The objective used as a basis for attacking this concern is as follows:

Teacher	*Learner*
States directions for learners to assemble a set of objects into a larger object or display	Assembles or participates in assembly of objects

The specific content to illustrate this procedure is the creation of a diorama illustrating two ecological displays, one pollution-free, the other polluted. Each scene is to include water, plants, animals, and varying degrees of light and shade. The teacher assigns the students in question the specific task of placing the animals

---

[2] From *Behavior Resource Guide*, Educational Development Corporation, Tulsa, Okla.

[3] By Cheryl Westerman, *A set of behavior related instructional activities: Spinal cord*. Storrs: University of Connecticut, 1978.

in their proper places within each scene. The animals are to be constructed by other participants, using clay and other materials. Two other students are assigned the task of creating the land-water-light conditions. Through the use of a specifically assigned academic responsibility the student in question becomes a focal point of the activity. The teacher, using appropriate techniques from a selected therapeutic model, responds to the student. Proximity control, a component of Redl's ego-supportive model, is incorporated into the therapeutic effort as the teacher approaches the student and touches him on the shoulder while talking about the display.

PLANNING FOR READING AND BEHAVIOR

The development of a plan to provide for the adolescent with behavior disorders who may or may not have a reading problem is a complex matter. Among the factors to be considered might be:

1. Staff competency with reading and therapeutic models.
2. Attitudes and values of staff, administrators, and community relative to range of services and alternatives that are desired and feasible.
3. Delineation of characteristics and qualities of reading and therapeutic models with which staff is proficient or in which they are willing to become proficient.
4. Establishment of criteria which will be used as the basis of the placement decision.
5. Selection of a comprehensive approach to assessment and diagnosis specific to curriculum and instructional materials for reading and therapeutic intervention.
6. Designation of components of system change necessary to accommodate the planned program.

Staff Competency

Professional staff vary in their interests and competencies as does any group of people. Each person on the staff is different, perhaps because of previous training, ability, and experience. These differences, while encouraged, should not be a mystery to others. Accordingly, each member of the staff should be requested to identify his/her own set of competencies with different models of reading and with various therapeutic models. This is essential if the placement decision is to serve as the basis for an appropriate education. If it is determined that a student has a set of needs which cannot be met by the staff, then an alternative placement must be sought. The unfortunate aspect of attempting to relate programming to staff competency and variability is the reality that most secondary schools have few staff members capable of identifying and appropriately carrying out their instructional and therapeutic models. Much work needs to be done to better prepare teachers for work with behaviorally disordered adolescents.

Attitudes and Values

What is it that the staff, administration, and community truly desire for the adolescent with behavior disorders and reading problems? Other than a desire to cure the problems, most would agree that there is the need to make firm commitments on behalf of the student. These commitments might require the development of skills, varying degrees of tolerance, and an understanding of the type of program being developed and the resources necessary to develop the program. The problems of the city will differ from those of the rural community. Nonetheless, the program should be developed in relation to the needs of the student and the attitudes and values of the community. The resolution of discrepancies between school and community should be undertaken in both private and public forums. The staff will have to know and understand the community and be able to relate to it on behalf of the learner.

Assessment and Diagnosis

If a school district undertakes an analysis of selected reading and therapeutic models and relates these to the proficiencies within the staff, the district has reached the point at which it can select a comprehensive approach to assessment and diagnosis. In this context, the term *assessment* relates to the measurement of individual growth for purposes of accountability. The term *diagnosis* refers to the measurement of individual characteristics and the specification of the intricacies and patterns among these characteristics. Diagnosis must constitute the basis for the development of an individualized educational program in that it determines the quality, character, and composition of the plan. The problem educators face is the limited knowledge of the interrelationships among reading, learning dysfunctions, and behavior disorders. In a better-safe-than-sorry approach, we suggest that the assessment be developed as comprehensively as possible. Diagnosis need not be centered upon grade equivalent data. Grade equivalent data constitute the basis for assessment in that they provide one standard of accountability. These data have more meaning for groups and for program accountability than for individualized educational planning. Diagnosis, on the other hand, is an individual matter in which the primary concern focuses upon patterns of learning, similarities and differences among tasks, and factors such as learning style and effort, or clusters of behaviors (for example, learning dysfunctions) to determine strengths and deficits. Accurate diagnostic assessment must systematically control potentially confounding variables or alternative explanations to delineate an individual's functioning levels, styles, and strategies. Cawley (1977b) has conceptualized this process along a behavior-by-content matrix. It may be argued that many standardized instruments, such as the WISC-R, ITPA, and the Detroit Tests of Learning Aptitude, really measure content deficiencies rather than behavioral deficits, and this is the basic reason that the so-called ability training versus task analysis argument lacks validity. The older and, presumably, more cognitively mature student is differentiated from the younger student on the basis of a greater number of items expected to be performed correctly. For example, on the WISC-R, an 8 year old may have to answer 9 questions of the information subtest correctly to function within the average range. A 12 year old may have to answer 16 questions to attain this level. The difference between the 12 year old and 8 year old is 7 questions based on the anticipated content of what each should know. There is no attention to qualitative factors in differentiating across mental age and chronological age levels. Clearly, these instruments are measuring content deficiencies rather than behavioral deficits. An alternative approach is to control content by using only those content areas within the individual's repertoire and to vary them across a variety of behaviors (visual perception, visual and auditory short-term memory, visual discrimination). In this manner, the role of cultural bias in assessment can be reduced substantively.

A basic proposition to be considered in planning for the youngster is to put the terms strengths and weaknesses within a task or content perspective. This will yield a proposition similar to the following: To conduct task-based activities, one should always use content with which the individual is familiar. To conduct content-based activities, one should always use tasks of which the individual is capable.

The above enables one to accentuate strengths by simultaneously using combinations of tasks the individual is capable of and content the individual knows. One can conduct task-based remedial activities based on known content. One can parcel out the effects of one disability upon performance in a given area by selecting objectives which indicate proficiency. This practice would relate to the concerns of Deshler (1978) who notes that long-term neglect of the areas of integrity may result in regression in these areas. On the other hand, the remedial emphasis may result in reducing strengths toward the level of weaknesses without any demonstrable growth in weak areas.

Some interesting experimental evidence on the nature of reading disabilities suggests attention to a third significant factor: information-processing styles. The first group of research is concerned with the role of language and linguistic functions in reading disabilities. Some (Goodman, 1968; Kolers, 1970; Smith, 1973) conceptualize reading as a "psycholinguistic" process which parallels spoken language. Reading and speech are related by syntactic and semantic cues (context clues, mnemonic devices) which produce efficient reading. Others argue that reading is a "parasitic" function of language (Elkonin, 1973; Mattingly, 1972; Shankweiler & Liberman, 1976). Mattingly (1972) suggests that the development of reading competency requires that the individual be explicitly aware of the internal structure of the language. "Linguistic awareness" refers to the individual's conscious knowledge of the elements (graphemes) comprising written language and their relationship to spoken language (phonemes). Both positions contrast sharply with traditional conceptualizations of the reading process, such as the perceptual-deficit hypothesis (Bender, 1957; Hermann, 1959; Orton, 1937), the intersensory integration deficit (Birch, 1962), and the temporal order deficit hypothesis (Bakker, 1972).

Another class of experiments has been concerned with short-term memory efficiency of disabled readers. Perfetti and Goldman (1976), Perfetti and Hogaboam (1975), and Waller (1976) have shown that students with reading comprehension problems have significantly longer response times in a rapid naming task than average comprehenders. Webster (in preparation a) has shown that disabled readers lose about 40% of newly acquired information after a 20-second time delay filled with meaningful verbal interference. Average readers lose only about 20% of the information during this same task. These experiments suggest a possible information-processing inefficiency, not deficiency, at the level of short-term memory for poor readers.

These findings have particular significance for the assessment of reading problems. First, the theoretical position supported by a test developer or examiner will dictate the specific focus of the evaluation. Those who advocate the perceptual deficit hypothesis may be searching for letter reversals, word transpositions, and other perceptually related deficits during an assessment.

A very different diagnostic approach would be undertaken by those who conceptualize reading as a parasitic function of speech. Efforts would be directed toward determination of the individual's linguistic awareness. Specific techniques could include testing for the individual's ability to segment words phonemically and syllabically in an accurate manner.

The aforementioned relates to the diagnostic process among youngsters who experience difficulty with beginning reading and related learning dysfunction. Consideration must be given to individuals who read at, for example, the fourth- to fifth-grade level but are significantly discrepant in relation to expected levels of performance (that is, fifth-grade performance but ninth-grade expectancy). Diagnosticians must respect the fact that reading at these upper levels reflects a different set of skills, strategies, and demands than does reading at lower levels. The present authors fail to understand why assessment practices fail to reflect this unless, of course, it is a function of the magnitude of the correlations between one reading behavior and others (for instance, word recognition and passage reading). Why would one continue to use a single task assessment device such as the WRAT (Jastak, Bijou, & Jastak, 1974) beyond the levels at which word recognition related deficits have instructional implications? Why not a strategy such as SOBAR (Science Research Associates, 1975) in which each level reflects a different set of reading skills. Diversity in skill assessment—that is, how many different tasks can the youngster perform satisfactorily—would seem to be a necessary component for the upper level. With the range of skills identified by the SOBAR, the teacher can select content that is stimulating and satisfying to the individual.

Summary

While a number of factors were addressed in this chapter, there are few, if any, definitive conclusions about any of them. The relationship between reading and behavior disorders, particularly in terms of cause and effect, is unclear in the cases of most students. Moreover, there is no definitive research that establishes the efficacy of various combinations of divergent models of reading and therapy. Thus, there is an element of uncertainty when attempts are made to design an appropriate education. However, the outlook need not be overly bleak. There are a variety of successful therapeutic models and many of their characteristics have been delineated. Further, there are a variety of successful reading models and, to a certain extent, their characteristics have been identified (Aukerman, 1971; Beck & McCaslin, 1978). It is possible, therefore, to bring about an amalgamation of what is available in reading and therapy or management. Current federal legislation stipulates a need for and commitment to in-service training. There is a cadre of people who are able and willing to conduct research on these important matters. Most important, there is reason for considerable motivation on the part of educators, for there are large numbers of students who still await an appropriate education.

References

Athey, I. Personality factors and the development of successful readers. In G. Schick and M. May (Eds.), *New frontiers in college adult reading*. Yearbook of the National Reading Conference, 1966.

Aukerman, R. .C. *Approaches to beginning reading.* New York: Wiley, 1971.

Baddeley, A. *The psychology of memory.* New York: Basic Books, 1976.

Bakker, D. *Temporal order in disturbed reading, developmental and neuropsychological aspects in normal and reading-retarded children.* Rotterdam: Rotterdam University Press, 1972.

Beck, I., & McCaslin, E. *An analysis of dimensions that affect the development of code-breaking ability in eight beginning reading programs.* Pittsburgh: University of Pittsburgh, 1978.

Bell, D., Lewis, F., & Anderson, R. Some personality and motivational factors in reading retardation. *Journal of Educational Research,* 1972, *65(5),* 229–233.

Bender, L. Specific reading disability as a maturational lag. *Bulletin of the Orton Society,* 1957, *7,* 9–18.

Birch, H. Dyslexia and maturation in visual function. In J. Money (Ed.), *Reading disability: Progress and research needs in dyslexia.* Baltimore: Johns Hopkins University Press, 1962.

Bjork, R. Theoretical implications of directed forgetting. In A. Melton & E. Martin (Eds.), *Coding processes in human memory.* Washington, D.C.: Winston, 1972.

Blanchard, P. Psychoanalytic contributions to the problem of reading disabilities. *Psychoanalytic Study Child,* 1946.

Blankenship. A. Memory span: A review of the literature. *Psychological Bulletin,* 1938, *35,* 1–25.

Carlisle, J. Reading tasks in subject-matter context. Unpublished manuscript. Storrs: University of Connecticut, 1978.

Cawley, J. F. Reading disability. In N. G. Haring & R. L. Schiefelbusch (Eds.), *Methods in special education.* New York: McGraw-Hill, 1967.

Cawley, J. F. Curriculum: one perspective. In R. Kneedler & S. Tarver (Eds.), *Changing perspectives in special education.* Columbus, Ohio: Charles E. Merrill, 1977a.

Cawley, J. F. Content or behavior: An issue in the assessment of specific learning disabilities. Paper presented at the Conference on Assessment in Learning Disabilities, Howard School, Inc., Atlanta, Ga. 1977b.

Cawley, J. F., Cawley, L., Cherkes, M., & Fitzmaurice, A. M. *Early childhood assessment program.* Glenview, Ill.: Scott-Foresman, in press.

Cawley, J. F., Fitzmaurice, A. M., Goodstein, H. A., Lepore, A. V., Sedlak, R., & Althaus, V. *Project MATH, Levels I-IV.* Educational Progress Corporation, Tulsa, Okla., 1976–1977.

Cawley, J., Goodstein, H., & Burrow, W. *The slow learner and the reading problem.* Springfield, Ill.: Charles C Thomas, 1972.

Comptroller General of the United States. Computer Printout, 1977. ERIC ED141731.

Cunningham, R. Classroom social distance scale. *Reading Teacher,* 1971, *25,* 52–55.

Deshler, D. Psychoeducational aspects of learning-disabled adolescents. In L. Mann, L. Goodman, & L. Wiederholt (Eds.), *Teaching the learning disabled adolescent.* Boston: Houghton-Mifflin, 1978.

Elkonin, D. U.S.S.R. in J. Downing (Ed.), *Comparative reading.* New York: Macmillan, 1973.

Fabian, A. Reading disability: An index of pathology. *American Journal of Ortho-psychiatry,* 1955, *25(2),* 319–329.

Fabian, A. Clinical and experimental studies of school children who are retarded in reading. *Quarterly Journal of Child Behavior,* 1959, *3,* 15–37.

Feldhusen, J., Thurston, J., & Benning, J. Longitudinal analyses of classroom behavior and school achievement. *Journal of Experimental Education*, 1970, *38(4)*, 4–10.

Fennimore, F. Reading and the self-concept. *Journal of Reading*, 1968, *6*, 447–451.

Fernald, G. *Remedial techniques in basic school subjects*. New York: McGraw-Hill, 1943.

Glasser, W. *Reality therapy*. New York: Harper & Row, 1965.

Glavin, J. P., & Annesley, F. R. Reading and arithmetic correlates of conduct-problem and withdrawn children. *Journal of Special Education*, 1971, *5(3)*, 213–219.

Glick, O. Some social-emotional consequences of early inadequate acquisition of reading skills. *Journal of Educational Psychology*, 1972, *63*, 253–257.

Goodman, K. The psycholinguistic nature of the reading process. In K. Goodman (Ed.), *The psycholingustic nature of the reading process*. Detroit: Wayne State University Press, 1968.

Hake, J. Covert motivations of good and poor readers. *The Reading Teacher*, 1969, *22*, 731–738.

Henderson, E., & Long, B. Self social concepts in relation to reading and arithmetic. In J. Figurel (Ed.), Vistas in reading: *Proceedings of the International Reading Association*, 1966, *11*, 576–581.

Hermann, K. *Reading disability*. Copenhagen: Munksgaard, 1959.

Jastak, J. F., Bijou, W. W., & Jastak, S. R. *Wide Range Achievement Test*. Wilmington, Delaware: Guidance Associates of Delaware, Inc., 1974.

Johnson, A., & Schenck, W. Instruction and management. Unpublished manuscript, Storrs: University of Connecticut, 1973.

Kolers, P. Three stages of reading. In H. Levin and J. Williams (Eds.), *Basic studies in reading*. New York: Basic Books, 1970.

Kunst, M. Learning disabilities: Their dynamics and treatment. *Social Work*, 1959, *4*, 95–101.

Ladd, M. *The relation of social, economic and personal characteristics to reading ability*. New York: Teachers College, Columbia, 1933.

Lashley, K. In L. Jeffress (Ed.), *Cerebral mechanisms in behavior*. New York: Wiley, 1959, 112–136.

Lerner, J. W. *Children with learning disabilities*. Boston: Houghton-Mifflin, 1976.

Lunden, W. A. *Statistics in delinquents and delinquency*. Springfield, Ill.: Charles C Thomas, 1964.

McGinley, P., & McGinley, H. Reading groups as psychological groups. *Journal of Experimental Education*, 1970, *39*, 35–42.

Mattingly, I. Reading, the linguistic process, and linguistic awareness. In J. Kavanaugh & I. Mattingly (Eds.), *Language by ear and by eye: The relationship between speech and reading*. Cambridge, Mass.: M.I.T. Press, 1972.

Mauser, A. J. Developing reading strategies for youths with educational handicaps. In S. Sabatino & A. J. Mauser (Eds.), *Intervention strategies for specialized secondary education*. Boston: Allyn & Bacon, 1978.

Miller, G. The magical number seven, plus or minus two! Some limits on our capacity for processing information. *Psychological Review*, 1956, *63*, 81–97.

Morse, W. The psychology of mainstreaming socio-emotionally disturbed children. In A. J. Pappanikou & J. Paul (Eds.), *Mainstreaming emotionally disturbed children*. Syracuse: Syracuse University Press, 1977.

Orton, S. *Reading, writing and speech problems in children*. London: Chapman & Hall, 1937.

Pappanikou, A. J., & Paul, J. (Eds.) *Mainstreaming emotionally disturbed youth.* Syracuse: Syracuse University Press, 1977.

Pearson, G. A Survey of learning disabilities in children. *Psychoanalytic Study Child*, 1952, 322–386.

Perfetti, C., & Goldman, S. Discourse memory and reading comprehension skill. *Journal of Verbal Learning and Verbal Behavior*, 1976, *14*, 33–42.

Perfetti, C., & Hogaboam, T. The relationship between single word decoding and reading comprehension skill. *Journal of Educational Psychology*, 1975, *67*, 461–469.

Rabinovitch, R. Reading and learning disabilities. In S. Arieti (Ed.), *American Handbook of Psychiatry. Vol. I.* New York: Basic Books, 1959.

Rhodes, W., & Tracy, M. A. A study of child variance. *Conceptual Models.* Vol. 1. Ann Arbor: University of Michigan Press, 1972.

Robinson, H. Causes of reading failure. *Education,* 1947, *47*, 422–426.

Ross, A. O. *Psychological disorders of children.* New York: McGraw-Hill, 1974.

Scholfield, W., & Balian, L. A comparative study of the personal histories of Schizophrenic and non-psychiatric patients. *Journal of Abnormal and Social Psychology*, 1959, 216.

Science Research Associates, *Criterion Referenced Measurement Program: SOBAR, Reading.* Chicago: Science Research Associates, 1975.

Shankweiler, D., & Liberman, I. Exploring the relations between reading and speech. In R. Knights & D. Bakker (Eds.), *Neuropsychology of learning disorders: Theoretical approaches.* Baltimore: University Park Press, 1976.

Sheldon, W., & Carrillo, L. Relation of parents, home, and certain developmental characteristics to children's reading ability. *Elementary School Journal*, 1952, *52*, 262–270.

Smith, F. *Psycholinguistics and reading.* New York: Holt, Rinehart & Winston, 1973.

Spache, G. Personality patterns of retarded readers. *Journal of Educational Research*, 1957, *50*, 461–469.

Stavrianos, B., & Landsman, S. Personality patterns of deficient readers with perceptual-motor problems. *Psychology in the Schools*, 1969, *6*, 109–123.

Stevens, D. Reading difficulty and classroom acceptance. *The Reading Teacher*, 1971, *25*, 52–55.

Torrance, P. *Constructive behavior: Stress, personality, and mental health.* New York: Teachers' College, Columbia University, 1961.

Vorhaus, P. Rorschach configurations associated with reading disability. *Journal of Projective Techniques*, 1952, *16*, 3–41.

Waller, T. Children's recognition memory for written sentences: A comparison of good and poor readers. *Child Development*, 1976, *47*, 90–95.

Webster, R. E. Loss of information during short-term shortage by atypical and average learners. In preparation.

Webster, R. E. Short-term memory processing efficiency of reading disabled students. In preparation.

Wick, J. *Comprehensive assessment program.* Glenview, Ill.: Scott-Foresman, 1980.

Wilderson, F. An exploratory study of reading skill deficiencies and psychiatric symptoms in emotionally disturbed children. *Reading Research Quarterly*, 1967, *2(3)*, 47–74.

Witty, P. Reading success and emotional adjustment. *Elementary English*, 1950, *27*, 281–296.

Woolf, M. Ego strengths and reading disability. In E. Thurston & L. Hafner (Eds.), *The philosophical and sociological bases of reading.* Yearbook of the National Reading Conference, 1965.

Wright, L. Conduct problem or learning disability? *Journal of Special Education*, 1974, *8(4)*, 331–336.

Zimmerman, I., & Allebrand, G. Personality characteristics and attitudes toward achievement of good and poor readers. *Journal of Educational Research*, 1965, *59*, 28–30.

Career and Vocational Education

15

Gary M. Clark

The career development needs of adolescents with behavioral disorders are frequently thought of by educators and parents in terms of occupational preparation and considerations for employment in the near or distant future. Typically, these needs are given little, if any, thought until these behaviorally disordered adolescents are into their mid- to late teens. Professionals and parents who respond to career development needs in this way are wrong in two ways.

First, career development must focus on the totality of a person's competencies if "career" is to be defined as "a person's course or progress through life" (Oxford English Dictionary, 1961). A restricted view of one's career as a lifetime occupation, or even a series of occupations, is not appropriate in educational planning for two reasons. The first is that the basic meaning of the word *career* is not restricted to occupational choices or experience at all, and the second is that, even if it were, there are other significant behavior areas that are critical to success in occupational adjustment. These areas are concealed by the obviously challenging tasks of choosing, seeking, obtaining, and maintaining a job. Such concealment leads to an emphasis in educational programming that neglects other important concerns.

Second, career development must be begun at developmental levels much earlier than adolescence. If it is not, significant gaps in adolescents' behavioral repertoires are probable. In many cases these gaps are at least as critical as any of the specific tasks of occupational adjustment. It is a questionable practice to assume that any youth, but more particularly one with behavior disorders, has the necessary prerequisites for occupational preparation and/or placement simply on the basis of chronological age or grade placement in school. It is also questionable that such skills are learned easily at this age.

This chapter begins, then, with an affirmation of the notion that career development is a developmental process. It is an aggregate of an individual's total development—cognitive, affective, and psychomotor. Significant deprivation in any aspect of human growth can affect career development which must be comprised of a myriad of specific competencies and based on over-riding skills in adaptability. This adaptability stems from a strong foundation in academic skills, a personally meaningful set of values, positive attitudes toward self and others, good work habits, satisfying and satisfactory human relationships, knowledge of occupational and leisure alternatives, knowledge of the nature and realities of the world of work, and skills for daily living as well as for a job.

The model presented in Figure 1 suggests a working model for conceptualizing career development through a career education approach for the handicapped. A more elaborated rationale for the model appears elsewhere (Clark, 1979) but it can be said here that a model of career education from this perspective focuses on career education for the handicapped through the mutually important domains of: (a) values, attitudes, and habits; (b) human relationships; (c) occupational information; and (d) acquisition of actual job and daily living skills.

These domains are clearly the foci of the elementary and junior high-school years, but also continue through the twelfth grade in the context of one of several curriculum options. From this perspective, the school should plan and provide a career education curriculum that includes more than just occupational information and skill training and begin it from the beginning of the school years.

The model proposed here is a curriculum model and the following sections provide a description of each of the major components.

When values, attitudes, and habits are cited as relevant curriculum areas of today's schools, many people agree wholeheartedly. Some people hedge. Others actively oppose such a position. Parents and educators are in each of the three camps because of their own values, habits, and attitudes.

One of the major reasons for concerns about the school's becoming involved in the process of developing and fostering values, attitudes, and habits is that there is a problem in determining *which* ones should be taught. Values, for example, can be associated with any number of things—money, religious beliefs, race, education, sex, responsibility, integrity, loyalty to country, work, leisure, and so forth. Many are controversial or sensitive areas as well.

There is no doubt that while our nation has historically maintained a sense of national identity concerning certain values, the pluralistic approach to our democratic form of government has created a nation of multiple values far different from the single-value system that we have idealized. This has led to internal problems, conflicts, and confrontation.

Recognition of this historical perspective suggests that Raths, Merrill, and Sidney (1966) offered a workable compromise, if not a solution, to the "teach values—do not teach values" dilemma when they suggested that educators should not be concerned with the *content* of people's values but rather with the process of valuing, that is, forming values.

Consideration of this view changes the focus from thinking about whether to teach students certain concepts that are value-laden to how to teach students to select, defend, and act on those concept areas so that they know *why* they think or

FIGURE 1   A School-Based Career Education Model For the Handicapped

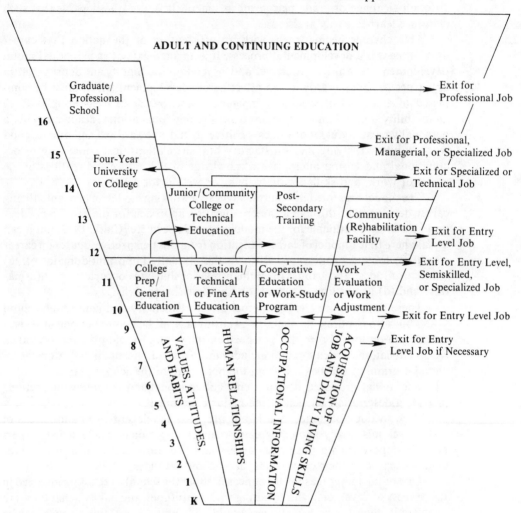

SOURCE: From G. Clark, *Career education for the handicapped child in the elementary classroom.* Denver: Love Publishing Co., 1979, p. 19. Reprinted by permission.

believe as they do, *how* their actions are related to those beliefs, and what the probable consequences of their actions would be.

A compromise in the area of values is not completely acceptable to many who believe the school should maintain and preserve certain moral and social values. To them a compromise that completely avoids value content begs the question. The valuing process is of great importance in career education for the adolescent with behavior disorders and it should be central to programming in this component of the model. Nevertheless, the valuing process should not be taught to the exclusion of, or apart from, certain critical content areas, such as *work* (as defined by Hoyt, 1975), *leisure*, *personal responsibility*, *learning*, and *equal opportunity*.

The rationale thus far for the need to have curricular provisions for developing values and the development of valuing has not specifically dealt with attitudes or habits. The reason for this is that values, attitudes, and habits are seen to be so interdependent that a rationale for one is a rationale for the other two. Values, or those beliefs which are cherished, lead persons to assume attitudes or positions that reflect those beliefs. These attitudes, in turn, are manifested in relatively consistent, predictable behaviors or habits. Instructional objectives in this area for adolescents whose behaviors are frequently in conflict with societal values and mores should reflect a consistent approach across all three areas in terms of awareness and clarification of *what* is believed, *why* it is believed, and *why* and *how* behavior is related to those beliefs. Glasser's (1965) approach is an example of a moral behavior approach which confronts a person's habits or patterns of behavior with the reality of right and wrong, acceptable and unacceptable, or legal and illegal.

Further rationale for the importance of programming for valuing, attitudes, and habits goes beyond an educational philosophy. Butler and Browning (1974), Cobb (1972), Goldstein (1964) and Henrich and Kriegel (1961) have all concluded from the research literature on adult adjustment of the handicapped and personal reports of handicapped persons that these human variables are of critical importance. In most cases they seem to be of greater importance for the handicapped than actual job skills in maintaining employment and successfully fulfilling roles in the home and community. The research of Stephens (1972) strongly suggests that moral judgment (based on values) and moral conduct (attitudes and habits) in children of normal intelligence and below are developmental traits and, as such, are amenable to change through education and training. Thus, the research literature supports the notion that values, attitudes, and habits are important and are subject to change through programming.

The following assumptions are proposed as considerations in programming for the behaviorally disturbed adolescent in the area of values, attitudes, and habits. They are adapted from the list of general programmatic assumptions for career education in the U.S. Office of Education's policy paper, *An Introduction to Career Education* (Hoyt, 1975).

1. A disturbed adolescent's personal value system is developed to a significant degree during the school years and is modifiable during those years.

2. If behaviorally disordered adolescents can see the relationships between what they are being asked to learn and do at school with their present and future worlds outside of school, they will be motivated to learn more in school.

3. An effective means of helping disturbed adolescents discover both who they are (in a self-concept sense) and why they are (in a personal awareness sense) is by helping them discover what they can accomplish in the work they do as learners, helpers at home and school, and by productive efforts for their own benefits.

4. The basis on which work of any kind can become a personally meaningful part of a disturbed person's life will vary greatly from one individual to another and from one stage of a life career to another. No single approach by educators can be expected to meet with universal success.

HUMAN RELATIONSHIPS

Historically, the American public school has concentrated its efforts in educating youth in the area of academic skills. Classroom discipline, behavior management, and meeting children's emotional needs have been integral parts of the instructional process but they have been taught almost exclusively through incidental meth-

330 *Chapter 15*

ods or behavior-specific events rather than clear-cut, purposeful objectives and procedures. Critics of public education have decried this approach and have advocated a humanistic philosophy that placed personal and social development alongside scholastic achievement as important aims for education (Illich, 1971; Phenix, 1964; Wilson, 1971).

The notion of specific, purposeful instruction in the area of personal/social behavior has been rejected by some who see it as the responsibility of the family, religious teachers, or even "everyone's" responsibility. Others have an attitude that "these are teenagers—just let them grow up—they'll learn." Those adults who take the latter view are either fortunate enough to have had a childhood environment that fostered personal and social growth without specific attention to it or they are insensitive to the ways some students (particularly disturbed students) learn and develop who have had different social environments and/or values than their own.

According to Campbell (1964), human relationships hinge on a person's acceptance or rejection. The criteria for acceptance or rejection are generally classified as pertaining either to personality and social characteristics or to skills and abilities. There is much research evidence which suggests that friendliness and sociability are associated with acceptance, and social indifference, withdrawal, rebelliousness, and hostility with rejection. In the area of skills and abilities, research findings indicate that more intelligent and creative children are more accepted by their peers, whereas slow learners and the retarded are less well accepted, if not rejected. Body size, muscular strength, maturational development, and athletic ability also appear as criteria for acceptance.

From these data, it can be seen that disturbed adolescents, who differ in personal-social characteristics as well as in their cognitive ability and psychomotor skill performance, need specific instruction to deal with those aspects of human relationships that affect their acceptance or rejection. Such instruction should come from every feasible source, particularly from the school.

Career education must include a deliberate effort to develop skills in creating and maintaining positive human relationships. Any career education effort specifically designed for disturbed adolescents must deal with those special and unique problems which involve communication with and understanding of others. Examples of these special and unique problems include such things as communicating with nonhandicapped persons about their ignorance, naivete, or attitudes, working through feelings of anger and hostility that are related to how others view their social or emotional problems, "suffering fools gladly," communicating feelings about excessive attention or therapy and denial of independence, and tendencies to withdraw from others.

Planning for this type of approach to career education programming with behaviorally disordered adolescents in the secondary school should be based on some underlying premises that give structure and direction to the programming. The following premises are based, in part, on the general programmatic assumptions for career education presented in Hoyt (1975):

1. One of the most critical skill areas for the behaviorally disordered in adjustment, from childhood through adulthood, is the area of human relationships. This stems from societal attitudes toward deviance and the phenomena of stigma and stereotyping, all of which affect society's acceptance or toleration of the handicapped in general and the emotionally disturbed in particular.

2. A handicapped person's skill in human relations is developed to a significant degree during the school years and is modifiable during those years.

3. Attainment of human relationships skills is a developmental process, beginning in the preschool years and continuing into the retirement years. Maturational level and patterns may differ from age to age and from individual to individual. There may be unique differences among types of emotional disorders.

4. Excessive deprivation in any aspect of human growth and development can retard career development. For persons suffering significant deprivation of positive human relationships, special variations in career development programming may be required.

Career education programming in the area of human relationships is not typically cited in the literature as a discrete, identifiable component. There is the tacit assumption that it is involved, but rarely is it emphasized as a distinct area of instruction parallel to attitudes and values, occupational information, and acquisition of job skills. The basic assumptions presented above, particularly the first and last ones, provide sufficient rationale for emphasizing this area as a separate element of career education programming for disturbed adolescents.

A case could probably be made for a similar emphasis in programming for the nonhandicapped, based on the literature that reports why people leave jobs, are fired from jobs, dissolve marriages, avoid personal and social interactions in leisure time, and seek anonymity in large urban environments. The nonhandicapped, however, are not the target population here. If you accept this area as a legitimate component of career education programming and if it gains more structure and visibility, other educators may also move to incorporate it into their future programming.

Given these basic assumptions and/or this rationale for career education programming for the emotionally disturbed in the area of human relations, what specifically might be incorporated into an instructional program? Fagen and Long (1976) have reported a curriculum approach for exceptional children in developing self-control. They define self-control as "one's capacity to direct and regulate personal action (behavior) flexibly and realistically in a given situation" (p. 3). From this perspective, skill in human relations can be viewed as self-control in *planning and carrying out positive interactions with others* and self-control in *planning and carrying out the elimination of negative interactions with others*. This type of conscious, planned relating to others is a process based on cognitive (intellectual) and affective (emotional) responses. An instructional program should be sure to include objectives of both kinds (Crosby, 1965; Fagen & Long, 1976).

OCCUPATIONAL INFORMATION

Occupational information programming within a career education curriculum includes several emphasis areas. Among these are occupational roles, occupational vocabulary, occupational alternatives, and basic information on some realities of the world of work. Each of these content areas for emphasis will be discussed below.

Occupational Roles as a Producer

Information concerning work in a producer occupational role begins very early in a child's life from what is observed in the home, the neighborhood, shopping trips, or other contacts with adults. At first the roles may seem rather grossly differentiated, such as "Daddy works, Mommy doesn't work" in the case where the father is remuneratively employed and the mother is a homemaker. The next level of awareness may be that "Dad gets paid for working, Mom doesn't." Depending upon the adult models children have for observation, information related to roles will vary from rather simple to very complex situations. The simple situations lead to concrete conclusions that either everybody works, nobody works, or adults work only sometimes. During early adolescence, the complex situations may lead young teens to the conclusion that some adults work all the time, some never work, some work without pay, some work seasonally, some work part-time, some work at home, and many change from one type of work to another. The junior high school's role in imparting occupational information in this area should be to present as accurately and objectively as possible a variety of existing producer occupational roles.

What are some of the existing occupational roles? Some of the examples cited above relate to temporal roles. That is, the roles are defined in terms of how much time a person spends in his job or on the time of day, month, or year that is spent in work. For example, some adolescents may conclude from what they have observed that working is good; therefore working all the time (steady work) must be better than working part of the time (part-time, periodic, or seasonal work). These values may be taught by parents or adult models who believe that a full-time worker role is better than a part-time worker role. From the point of view of the traditional work ethic, this simplistic interpretation is valid. However, when occupational roles are presented as equal, legitimate roles, depending upon the needs and purposes of the workers themselves and the supply and demand for labor, a simplistic interpretation is questioned.

One way of categorizing roles might be to place them in general categories which relate to the focus of the work, for example, workers with people, things, or ideas. Another would be the basic categories of paid and unpaid workers. Another way would be relating roles to location—indoor workers, outdoor workers, city workers, or rural workers. Another way might be to view worker roles in terms of producers, consumers, maintainers, disposers, and re-cyclers. Still another way might be to organize the roles into service categories, for example, health workers, transportation workers, construction workers, agriculture workers, manufacturing workers, entertainment workers, or government workers, similar to the U.S. Office of Education's occupational clusters (Clark, 1974; Weagraff, 1973).

However producer roles might be viewed, the important thing to remember is that disturbed adolescents need to establish an information base for their own roles in their career development and to be encouraged to try out those roles in classroom activities and work-related assignments. In this process, a deliberate effort should be made to have them be free from any stereotypic worker roles related to their disability, sex, or racial identity.

Occupational Roles as a Consumer

Everyone plays the role of consumer in the world of work at some time, and disturbed youth, depending upon the degree of severity of their handicap, may have experienced more as a consumer than as a producer thus far in their lives. Further, there may be the expectation by these youths and/or their parents that the consumer role may be the only one available. It is an individual value judgment that must be made for every person as to whether the producer role will be played at all. The consumer role, on the other hand, is one that is virtually inescapable in our society.

It is the responsibility of the school to provide occupational information for both roles. The career education movement has been conceptualized primarily as a systematic approach to educating children and youth for the producer or worker role. Again, the obvious implication of this is that being a worker/producer is good—for the individual and for society. What is not stated, but implied, is that being a consumer only is *not* good—for the individual and for society. Educators of students with behavior disorders must sort out their own philosophies at this point so that curricula will reflect opportunities for learning and career development which will not be restricted to just the role of producer, if the connotation of producer is only that of a *paid* worker.

Farber (1968) has theorized that the American work structure is based on a system of "slots" which need to be filled to keep in function. The number of slots varies according to the national economy and supply-demand factors for each of the types of slots available. Those persons most desirable for available slots are selected first on the basis of the many and varied criteria employers use for personnel selection. Farber describes those who are not selected to fill the slots as a "surplus population" which is comprised basically of the poor, the untrained, physically and mentally handicapped, elderly, convicted felons, and other "deviant" or "incompetent" persons. Although there are individuals who move in and out of the surplus population, the majority remain there or, at best, spend only a minor proportion of their time filling a slot. Individuals with mental health problems in this surplus population are particularly vulnerable since helping agencies (for instance, vocational rehabilitation services) try to differentiate between clients who are mentally ill or behavior disordered and those who are "mentally restored." The preferred clients are, of course, the latter.

This theory is somewhat pessimistic in terms of any immediate signs of change in favor of the handicapped and forces one to consider the question, "If the handicapped are going to be largely excluded from the work force, what will their roles be in our society?" Obviously, they will all continue to be consumers and may spend a majority of their time in that role. As Hoyt (1975) has stated: "The cosmopolitan nature of today's society demands that career education embrace a multiplicity of work values, rather than a single work ethic, as a means of helping each individual answer the question 'Why should I work?' " (p. 4).

In summary, an occupational information program should provide learning experiences which result in new or expanded awareness of possible roles for behaviorally disordered adolescents, now and in the future. In producer/worker roles there needs to be a stress on the possibility of productivity or work being inclusive of efforts which are unpaid, as well as paid, such as the work of the student as a learner, work as a volunteer, and the work activities or productivity in which one might be involved as a part of daily living or leisure time. In consumer roles, there needs to be a stress on an appreciation for those whose work and productivity have made possible the services, conveniences, or environments that are available. Further, adolescents need to begin learning how to use such services independently, efficiently, and effectively.

OCCUPATIONAL VOCABULARY

Vocabulary development in occupational information is necessary for understanding concepts about work roles, what occupations exist, and something about the characteristics of work and work settings.

Students who are learning about their present and future occupational roles must develop or expand their vocabularies to be able to acquire information basic to such learning. This is rather like the student who enters law or medical school. It is said that students in these professions must acquire up to 20,000 new words during their preparation. Students with behavioral disorders do not have such a monumental task but do have to establish those hearing vocabulary skills which are essential for any given occupational concept or fact. When possible, a reading vocabulary for those same concepts is desirable.

Educators of disturbed adolescents should have some perspective on occupational choice theory as it relates to normal growth and development before getting too deeply involved in any type of special programming for their students. There are a number of theories, but only one will be submitted in brief to serve as a general base. Ginzberg, Ginsburg, Axelrad, and Herma (1951) studied the occupational choice process and concluded that it is a developmental process. They believe that it is a series of decisions made over a period of years, and each step is meaningfully related to what has been decided before. They hold that the entire process ends in a compromise among many factors. Some people have to compromise little, others a great deal.

The Ginzberg et. al. (1951) theory suggests that the occupational decision-making process occurs in three basic stages or periods—fantasy, tentative choice, and realistic choice. The particular stage of interest for this discussion is the fantasy stage. Ginzberg and his associates conceptualize this stage as the first ten to twelve years of any individual's life. Their position is that children begin during this period to think of their desire to be adults. They believe that they can be anything that they want to be. Their choices of adult occupational roles are arbitrary, changeable, and ordinarily made without reference to reality. The nature of these choices will be limited by their environments and their own capacity for productive thinking. Teachers and parents of disturbed adolescents should not be overly concerned or alarmed at the persistence of the fantasy stage into the adolescent years. Developmentally, they are probably going to be behind their "normal" peers in this area by three or four years. The important thing is to provide opportunities to explore *why* certain occupations are chosen rather than expend large amounts of time exploring the occupation itself. Reality testing of the fantasies should begin to some degree during the junior high-school years and be fully utilized throughout the high-school years if fantasies persist.

Rinehart (1968) studied the relationship between mental illness and mobility aspiration-achievement discrepancies in two adult groups. One group was composed of outpatients from a mental health clinic, the other a carefully selected community sample who showed no tendencies nor history of mental illness. Information from both groups was obtained concerning the magnitude of their educational and occupational aspirations-achievement. Results indicated: (a) educational and occupational discrepancies were more prevalent among patients than among nonpatients and (b) the magnitude or extent of the patients' discrepancies exceeded those of nonpatients. These differences persisted even though significantly more patients than nonpatients perceived that their aspirations would not be realized.

All children and youth, but especially those who are mentally and physically handicapped, need to fantasize about their future roles or occupational identities because it is a normal expectation for everyone. Most of those who enter the professions do so after a period of years of trying to satisfy the most important personal needs (Crowne & Stephens, 1961; Englander, 1960; Super, 1963; Wylie, 1961). If one considers the hierarchy of needs suggested by Maslow (1954)— survival, safety or security, belonging or love, esteem, and self-actualization—the first three basic needs are usually met by someone else's efforts. The child who has had the first three met usually has further need for a positive self-esteem or self-concept. Statements about wanting to be a policeman, astronaut, pilot, or nurse in young children or pro-football player, rock musician, or movie star in teenagers relate to their needs to be esteemed for *who they are* or, at least, *who they are going to be*. When they assume occupational roles in play or daydreams, they see themselves as *being* adults in various roles right then. When they make statements of intent, they are compromising with the reality of age but still are seeking the positive feeling of esteem with that declaration of intent for the future. Super (1951, p. 91) stated: "In expressing a vocational preference, a person puts into occupational terminology his idea of the kind of person he is . . . ."

This is not to say that all adolescents with behavior disorders persist in fantasies. On the contrary, there is one study which suggests that they are fairly realistic, although their level of aspiration is low. Plata (1971) investigated the vocational interests and aspirations of two groups of emotionally disturbed high-school students and two groups of "normal" high-school students. He also compared the predicted levels of occupational attainment as judged by teachers and ward personnel with the students' self-ratings. His results indicated the following: (a) "normal" high-school students' occupational aspirations were significantly higher than those of the emotionally disturbed students; (b) occupations representing the interests of each of the groups were more prestigious for the "normal" students; and (c) emotionally disturbed students' aspirations were as realistic as those reported by the nondisturbed students.

Career education must include a component of occupational information that relates to occupational choice and awareness of occupational alternatives in a way that provides keen sensitivity to the need of emotionally disturbed youth for self-esteem. There is time later for personalizing the realities they must face in regard to who and what they will be. The crux of this position for the secondary teacher is to make students as aware as possible of occupational alternatives, while continually accepting their declarations (regardless of how seemingly bizarre or inappropriate) and affirming them as persons.

BASIC INFORMATION RELATED TO SOME REALITIES OF THE WORLD OF WORK

There is a point in providing occupational information to behaviorally disordered students that becomes problematic. That is, whereas on the one hand the teacher will encourage them to want to work and be a worker, there must be honesty in pointing out some of the negative realities of work. Attitudes, values, and habits that are important in career development are difficult to teach, however, without getting into some of the areas that may foster negative or unacceptable attitudes and behaviors. This section will deal with some of the realities that are especially important for handicapped youth to learn about. Positive or negative, they are the prevailing rules of the game that have been established by the people of influence and power in our society.

Reality #1

North American society in general is a work-oriented society. As such, it values work and those who are workers. No one can be directly compelled to work in our society, except those few who are ordered by the courts to labor as a punishment for some crime. Even so, there are many formal and informal elements of our society operating to "make" people into workers. For most of us, the system is so effective that unemployment produces high levels of anxiety, personal guilt, and feelings of worthlessness. For the mentally handicapped, these feelings are heightened, even though they may realize that factors beyond their control are responsible.

Even though the past ten years have shown even more indications of work alienation, rise of a "leisure ethic," and increasing numbers supported by welfare funds, the reality is that the traditional meaning of work is still held by the power structure and is still espoused by our major societal institutions. As long as that is the case, the reality should be communicated to youth in school.

Reality #2

Work, whether paid or unpaid, occurs in a particular locale: the factory, the store, the office, the construction site, the shop, the clinic, the home. Work can occur in the home for some occupations (artist, writer, telephone answering service), but, by and large, a person must go out to work. This reality has two important implications for handicapped individuals. First, one must be mobile in order to get to work. This requires a set of competencies regarding travel. Choices of work alternatives may be influenced by this reality alone. A second implication is that since work is most frequently away from home, it becomes a public place. A public place has limitations on privacy, usually has a set of expected behaviors, and formal or informal standards for dress and social amenities.

Reality #3

Work which is paid work is largely impersonal. Work for which there is no pay may or may not be impersonal, depending upon the nature of the work. This is to say that the personalized relationship one might associate with play, recreation, or a loving relationship are not expected on a job. In fact, they may be forbidden. This is one reality that youth may have already been exposed to indirectly at home when they detect a different set of expectations by a parent when the parent requests (or more frequently *tells*) the child to perform a household chore. The child learns that the parent becomes a "boss" and has certain expectations about *what* is accomplished, *how* well it was accomplished, and in some instances the *process* of accomplishing it. The parent temporarily becomes an impersonal work supervisor and acts out a role that is basically the norm in the work world.

The reality of impersonality and working with and for relative strangers who are "all business" may be discouraging to adolescents who have strong needs for more personal relationships. Although exposing them to this reality runs the risk of their being turned off to the notion of working, it is even more of an injustice to ignore or, worse, distort reality so that they build up unrealistic expectations.

Reality #4

Work has its reward systems. Paid work obviously has the reward of remuneration, but unpaid work may provide the reward of saving money—that is, not having to pay someone else to do the work. There are other rewards of work, however, that should be mentioned. Some people see work positively as a way of being of service, as an opportunity to pursue interests and abilities, a means of meeting and/or interacting with people, a way of avoiding boredom, or a change to gain or maintain self-respect or esteem.

Youth need to know that people work for money but that they work for other things also. The question "What's in it for me?" is not inappropriate as students begin to learn to sort out their values and establish a base for being able to verbalize, "I want to work because. . . ."

Reality #5

Work is bound by time. Most workers have starting times and ending times. Certain times are set aside for breaks, for eating, or for clean-up. Many jobs are based on payment for certain hours with extra payment for overtime. Even when pay is based on "piece rate," the individual is racing against time to produce or complete as many pieces as possible. There are job benefits that relate to time off and there are penalties or sanctions against being late. To waste time at work is always frowned upon and, if it is a chronic behavior, it may be grounds for removal from the job.

It is clear that an inability to discipline oneself to time demands or constraints is one of the most serious obstacles to adjustment to work. This is frequently an especially difficult area for some disturbed individuals who have trouble relating to time concepts. It may also be an obstacle to those disturbed youth who have a very rational view of time and believe that those who are slaves to time schedules are the "sick" ones. Nevertheless, although one might appreciate their resistance to the hectic time-oriented pace of American living, the reality is there and their understanding of the system and possible alternatives to it must be taught.

Reality #6

Work is seldom performed in complete isolation or independence. Most work involves two or more people who interact in various ways. One of the most important of these interactions is the worker to his/her supervisor. Another is the interaction with fellow workers or consumers (customers, patients, clients). Still another is the interaction of the worker with subordinates. Depending upon the size and complexity of the work setting, a number of interpersonal reactions are required which may be more critical to staying on that job than the ability to perform the work tasks.

There may not be a formal communication of expected behaviors in work interactions, but they are communicated, nevertheless, through modeling, worker "grapevine," and events which illustrate the rewards or penalties dealt to workers in the system. They need to learn these basic expectations so they can develop a response system that shows a balance between dependence and independence in job performance (worker-supervisor interactions) and between the intimate and the casual (employee-fellow worker and employee-consumer interactions).

Reality #7

Work settings, like individual workers, rarely exist in isolation. As societies have moved from primarily agrarian work to modern industrial work settings, there has been an increasing dependence and interdependence among workers and work groups. Producers of goods require the services of workers in raw materials, manufactured goods for tools and equipment, transportation workers, marketing and distribution workers, and business and office personnel on a continuous basis. Periodically, they may require the services of workers in the building trades, communication and media, health, and public service. Obviously any one of these work groups will have dependent or interdependent relationships with one or more of the others.

If adolescents have not already learned this, they should become aware of these relationships in order to understand the importance of all types of work groups and to combat some of the occupational stereotyping and status problems that inevitably arise in a study of the world of work and their own fantasies about being a part of it.

Reality #8

Not everyone who wants to work can obtain work nor can everyone who obtains work be employed in the job of first choice. This final reality is one that affects many workers, but particularly an individual with behavior disorders. At the junior high-school level, however, this reality should be presented as a general issue rather than a particular one. They should be allowed to have their fantasies about wanting to be various kinds of workers; too much reality at this stage would be inappropriate. Further, withholding some information from them on this topic is advisable because, although the facts show that the handicapped as a group may be adversely affected, it is not an accurate prediction for any one handicapped individual.

At the high-school level, however, the behaviorally disordered adolescent must begin to come to grips with the realities of the world of work so that coping with those realities will be easier later. The introduction of these realities must be gradual and include individual encouragement with cautious, but realistic, optimism.

Planning for some type of purposeful, systematic career education programming in the area of occupational information for disturbed adolescents should be based on a philosophy compatible to that of the programming for nonhandicapped students. A set of basic premises are offered here, based as in previous chapters in part on the general programmatic assumptions for career education presented in *An Introduction to Career Education* (Hoyt, 1975):

1. Occupational roles, occupational vocabulary, awareness of occupational alternatives, and basic information on some of the realities of work can be taught to and learned by disturbed adolescents. They can effectively use such skills, once learned, to enhance their career development.

2. Occupational roles for disturbed asolescents will vary over a lifetime. They need specific information on both producer and consumer roles.

3. Specific occupational choices represent only one of a number of kinds of choices involved in career development. They can be expected to increase in realism among disturbed teenage students as they move from adolescence to adulthood, but the rate may be slower. To some degree, choices can be modifiable during most of one's adult years.

4. Occupational decision-making is accomplished through the dynamic interaction of limiting and enhancing factors, both within the individual and in his present and proposed environment. It is not, in any sense, a simple matching of individuals with jobs, especially with the mentally handicapped.

5. Occupational stereotyping hinders full freedom of occupational choice for the handicapped and other minority groups. These restrictions can be reduced, to some extent, through programmatic intervention strategies begun in the early years.

6. The same general strategies used in reducing worker alienation in industry can be used to reduce worker alienation among pupils and teachers in the classroom.

ACQUISITION OF JOB AND DAILY
LIVING SKILLS

The literature in career education currently available focuses on occupational awareness, exploration, and preparation. Whatever mention is made of attitudes, values, and habits is usually directly related to work in paid employment. Similarly, whatever mention is made of the issue of human relationships usually relates to social interactions on a job. What is rarely mentioned is the importance of competence in daily living for one's career development and how daily living competencies relate to success in the world of work. These competencies in daily living should receive equal emphasis along with the acquisition of job skills or competencies.

Actually, job skills and daily living skills overlap in so many instances that there is little reason for debating the necessity of including daily living skills in a curriculum model. Just as the skills required for reading a recipe at home are the same as those needed for reading a recipe in a restaurant on a job, the skills required for driving a car or truck for personal reasons or for selecting and purchasing items for personal use can be basically the same skills required in the work world.

There are, obviously, scores of daily living demands that require skills or competencies that are not associated directly with occupational skills. These skills are still justifiable within a career education context because they are critical competencies that undergird all experiences. As has been demonstrated time and again in studies of handicapped adults and was recently shown to affect 20% of nonhandicapped adults in the United States (New Readers Press News, 1977), failure to acquire competencies in daily living cannot be isolated from success or failure in the world of work. If a person cannot maintain a healthy body, how can he/she work? If a person cannot abide by the laws of a community or state, how can he/she be expected to abide by the laws or rules of the work world? If a person does not know how to use leisure time at home, how can he/she be expected to use a work break effectively?

Any job performance, occupational or daily living skill, requires one or more basic skills. These are typically categorized under the domains of cognitive, affective, and psychomotor skills. The basic thrust of this section is that disturbed adolescents should have specific programming in basic cognitive and psychomotor skills which are useful in preparing them for (a) current and emerging work roles during adolescence, (b) assuming more complex work roles during young adulthood, (c) coping with current and emerging daily living demands, and (d) coping with the more complex demands to be made on them in daily living during adulthood. (Affective skills have been addressed for both occupational and daily living demands in a previous section of this chapter elsewhere in this book.)

Specific examples of the kinds of skills appropriate for this area include those advocated by Brolin (1974):

1. Managing family finances
2. Caring for personal needs
3. Raising children and family living
4. Buying and preparing food
5. Engaging in civic activities and responsibilities
6. Utilizing recreation and leisure resources
7. Getting around the community
8. Achieving problem-solving skills
9. Communicating adequately with others
10. Acquiring specific salable job skills

In addition to the usefulness of job and daily living skills, these skills are also important because of the expectations of our society for everyone to be able to demonstrate these kinds of competencies. There are certain social "penalties" people with handicaps have to pay if they cannot perform these competencies. Stares, comments of little children, embarrassed interactions, and well-meaning but ignorant questions are typical. Competence in as many skills as possible help the handicapped present themselves as more like the nonhandicapped than different.

The approach to instructional planning in this area should be based on an acceptance of the rationale presented above and some formalized assumptions to provide direction in planning and as a point from which to establish teaching objectives. The assumptions which follow are based, in part, on the general programmatic assumptions for career education presented in *An Introduction to Career Education* (Hoyt, 1975):

1. Basic academic, psychomotor, and daily living skills are survival and adaptability tools needed by the handicapped in today's rapidly changing society.

2. Increasingly, entry into today's work world demands that those who seek employment possess a specific set of occupational skills.

3. A positive relationship exists between education and level of occupational attainment, but the amount and kind of education required for competence at any level varies greatly from occupation to occupation and from life style to life style.

4. Academic, psychomotor, and daily living skills can be taught to and learned by most people. Individuals can effectively use such skills to enhance their career development.

5. Daily living skills are inextricably interwoven with the process of working and may be as significantly involved in success or failure for the handicapped as occupational skills.

6. While daily living skills are often considered the primary responsibility of the family, the school must assume a greater and more systematic responsibility in instructional programming in this area for handicapped pupils.

7. Many routine daily living skills can be taught for predictable situations. Others become obsolete because of our changing environment and technology. Consequently, problem-solving and decision-making skills should be taught as process skills.

IMPLICATIONS FOR PROGRAMMING

Nelson and Kauffman (1976) presented an excellent review of educational programming for secondary-school-age delinquent and maladjusted pupils which, while discouraging in terms of quantity and evidence of quality, did indicate some efforts at specific programming for the target population of this book. They cited seven basic approaches that have been taken:

1. Regular public school secondary programs.
2. Consultant teacher approaches.
3. Resource rooms and self-contained classes.
4. Work-study programs.
5. Special schools.
6. Alternative schools.
7. Residential programs.

The efficacy of these approaches vary from *apparent failure* (regular public-school programming) to *equivocal findings* (resource rooms and self-contained classes, work-study programs, special schools, and alternative schools) to *promising practices* (consultant teacher approach and residential programs).

Although few of the approaches reviewed focused clearly on curriculum content as the primary variable, it appears that the consultant teacher and residential program approach did the best job of specifying behavioral target areas that constituted the curriculum objectives. Those target areas cited were compatible with parts of the career education model discussed in this chapter. They included the following:

1. Academic and social objective (Tharp & Wetzel, 1969)—correlates with Acquisition of Job and Daily Living Skills and Human Relationships.

2. Classroom conduct, academic performance, and social behaviors (Phillips, 1968; Bailey, Wolf, & Phillips, 1970)—correlates with Acquisition of Job and Daily

Living Skills, Human Relationships, and Occupational Information (occupational roles).

3. Academic remediation (Cohen & Filipczak, 1971)—correlates with Acquisition of Job and Daily Living Skills.

4. Academic achievement in industrial arts shop (Krenter, 1967)—correlates with Acquisition of Job and Daily Living Skills and Occupational Information.

Despite the positive results and the appropriate content reported, it is apparent when one compares the content emphasized in current and past program efforts with the career education model presented in this chapter that there are still gaps. Systematic planning and programming in all four mutually important components of the model should be a basic programming principle. These can be presented in any instructional setting, whether in a traditional delivery system, an alternative school, a work-study model, or in a special school or residential program. The question is, "*Will* they be presented?" Whether they are or not depends upon the approach used in programming. It is interesting to note that the two types of programs which appear to be the most effective in the Nelson and Kauffman (1976) review were the two that make curriculum content or specific instructional objectives the primary variable, rather than the administrative arrangement or the "least restrictive environment." This approach has enough logical and empirical support behind it to use it as another basic programming principle.

Clark (1975) presented a case for viewing the secondary curriculum and the nature and needs of the adolescent educable mentally retarded as significantly different from the elementary level. The same arguments and assumptions can be made for the secondary curriculum and the nature and needs of adolescents with behavior disorders. If professionals can accept such differences and approach curriculum planning with pertinent assumptions in mind, they must be aware that a curriculum content approach as a commitment to programming may appear to be in conflict with the interpretation many people make regarding "mainstreaming" or the least restrictive environment concept. The real issue is, of course, determination of critical needs of students. There is no conflict or incompatibility in the use of the career education model presented in this chapter with the least restrictive environment if the content components of the model are critical needs for a student and the curriculum option (program, course of study, "track") best designed to address those needs is, in fact, the least restrictive environment. It is when "least restrictive" is interpreted solely as "most normal" that the problem arises.

The career education for the handicapped model presented in Figure 1 proposes four different curriculum options for high-school students. They are meant to represent different curricular content options that meet different occupational preparation goals. To a degree, they also suggest a hierarchy of options based on cognitive/academic skill prerequisites. This aspect is not one to be emphasized, however, as there should be free movement from one option to another as an individual is inclined or is encouraged to select a given curriculum. This decision should be based on career goals (occupational choice, life-style aspiration) and not on perceived (or reported) ability to succeed in a given curriculum.

Once a curriculum option has been selected by a student, there remains a concern for the degree to which the four components of the model are presented. A youth described as behaviorally disordered who wants to enter a college preparatory or general education curriculum and who has the academic record to support a prediction of success still needs some specific programming in the areas of attitudes, values, habits, human relationships, occupational information, and some skills in job and daily living. The current high-school curriculum for students planning to enter college or high-school curriculum that differentiates curricula only among academic, general, and vocational programs cannot be characterized at all as a "career education oriented" curriculum of any ilk, much less of the model presented here.

Similar kinds of concerns can be related to the other options in the model—vocational-technical education, fine arts education, cooperative and work-study programs, and work adjustment programs. Each of them certainly is directed toward programming for occupational information and acquisition of job skills and one or two of them also include some attention to the acquisition of daily living skills and human relationships. By and large, however, career education content, as described in this chapter, is not sequenced well (if at all), is not systematically programmed, and is still a secondary priority for actual instruction. This leaves the advocates for a comprehensive career development approach for disturbed adolescents with few, if any, very encouraging program alternatives at the present time.

What are some alternatives to this state of the art? The three most obvious are: (a) work within the current system to make changes that assure the inclusion of career education content, (b) program the content separately to assure its inclusion, or (c) compromise between *a* and *b* and have some content presented within the various subjects or courses in curriculum options and some presented separately. Each of these are briefly discussed below. (For a more elaborate description of these alternatives see Clark [1979].)

Infusion. The most frequently proposed approach for getting career education content into the traditional structure of secondary-school curricula is that of *infusion*. This approach introduces career education concepts and skills into subject matter areas (science, math, history, music) as a means of making the subject matter more relevant, more concrete, and more motivating. Essentially, it is an activities approach which enhances the primary instructional objectives of the subject matter. The career education concepts and skills are rarely emphasized as instructional goals and are viewed as the means to an end. If students learn the concepts and skills used in the activities in addition to the primary goals, so much the better. However, their inclusion even as activities may be a major breakthrough for many schools and their lower priority is understandable, given the secondary teacher's perspective.

Separate programming. Separate programming can be developed in several ways. Among the more common formats are unit teaching within subject matter areas, separate courses (full-unit courses, half-unit courses, mini-courses), or a total curriculum. In each of these formats, career education concepts and skills are the primary instructional goals and all other skills are incorporated as activities or means to the desired ends of the specified content.

Combination of infusion and separate programming. This approach attempts to use both infusion and separate programming to provide the most comprehensive coverage of career education concepts and skills possible. It draws on the advantages of each and minimizes their respective disadvantages.

As in many things in life, a compromise or moderate stance between extreme positions is frequently the happiest solution. The advantages of such an approach include:

1. A combination of infusion and some separate programming permits a balance between teaching critical academic skills (with career education content incorporated for application) and critical career education concepts and skills (with

basic skills incorporated as problem-solving tools or aids to making certain job or daily living demands go easier).

2. A combination approach avoids the issue of adding to an over-crowded curriculum and poses less of a threat to subject matter specialists.

3. Combining the two approaches permits the teacher to be involved in the total education process by retaining responsibility for covering all critical areas, but without having to take on certain instructional goals personally.

4. Infusion and separate programming combined provide a unique opportunity to tie together concepts and skills learned in both academic and career education instruction.

5. A combination of infusion and separate programming provides the handicapped pupil in the regular classroom the critical elements necessary for it to be a "responsive environment" and not a restrictive environment.

Although the combination approach has some potential disadvantages, the major disadvantage is that there is no way to control the infusion aspect. A school district or building principal can prescribe certain courses to be taught separately but they may not be monitored effectively. Infusion through unit teaching can be recommended or encouraged, but there is no really effective way of determining whether it has been done appropriately or at all. The issue rests completely with each teacher's commitment to career education and feelings of confidence in using the many instructional activities that are effective for infusing career development content and skills into basic academic subjects.

The determination of what types of separate programming should be used with disturbed adolescents is related primarily to the severity of the behavior disorders. If they are able to participate in a regular secondary school, then the separate subject format is the most flexible approach and has the greatest potential for adequate coverage. Keep in mind that this format allows for different durations of instruction and permits considerable control over the scope of subject matter in the career education courses offered.

If students are not able to participate in a regular secondary-school curriculum and require a special class, special day school, or residential program, then the severity of the behavior disorder should determine the type of delivery. Figure 2

FIGURE 2   Recommended Approaches to Delivery of Secondary Level Career Education Instruction Based on Grade Level, Degree of Disturbance, and Instructional Setting

	Mildly to moderately disturbed		Severely to profoundly disturbed	
	7–9	10–12	7–9	10–12
Regular class or resource room	Infusion and separate subject	Infusion and separate subject	*	*
Special class, day school, or residential program	Infusion and separate subject	Infusion and separate subject	Total curriculum	Total curriculum

* Severely or profoundly disturbed youth are not typically placed in regular classes or resource rooms.

summarizes recommended delivery approaches which can be used with disturbed adolescents at the secondary level.

Whelan (1978, p. 353) stated, "Emotionally disturbed children need experiences with external structure before they can develop the internal strengths to be successful as they function in a variety of environments." Paraphrased in the context of this chapter, the statement could be: *Emotionally disturbed adolescents need experiences with the rules of the game they are in and will be facing as adults before they can develop the inner resources (attitudes, values, habits, knowledge, and skills) they need to be successful in their life careers.* The model presented in this chapter is a working model, subject to change, which may provide a basis for planning and programming for disturbed adolescents from a perspective of career development.

References

Bailey, J. S., Wolf, M. M., & Phillips, E. L. Homebased reinforcement and the modification of pre-delinquents' classroom behavior. *Journal of Applied Behavior Analysis*, 1970, *3*, 223–233.

Brolin, D. Programming retarded in career education. Working Paper No. 1. University of Missouri-Columbia, Columbia, Mo., September, 1974.

Butler, A. J., & Browning, P. L. Predictive studies on rehabilitation outcome with the retarded. In P. L. Browning (Ed.), *Mental retardation: Rehabilitation and counseling.* Springfield, Ill.: Charles C Thomas, 1974.

Campbell, J. D. Peer relations in childhood. In M. L. and L. W. Hoffman (Eds.), *Review of child development research.* New York: Russell Sage Foundation, 1964.

Clark, G. M. Career education for the mildly handicapped. *Focus on Exceptional Children*, 1974, *5(9)*, 1–10.

Clark, G. M. Mainstreaming for the secondary educable mentally retarded: Is it defensible? *Focus on Exceptional Children*, 1975, *7* (2), 1–5.

Clark, G. M. *Career education for the handicapped in the elementary school.* Denver, Co.: Love, 1979

Cobb, H. V. *The forecast of fulfillment: A review of research on predictive assessment of the adult retarded for social and vocational adjustment.* New York: Teachers College Press, 1972.

Cohen, H. L., & Filipczak, J. *A new learning environment.* San Francisco: Jossey-Bass, 1971.

Crosby, M. *An adventure in human relations.* Chicago: Follette, 1965.

Crowne, D. P., & Stephens, M. W. Self acceptance and self-evaluation behavior: A critique of methodology. *Psychological Bulletin*, *58*, 1961, 104–121.

Englander, M. A psychological analysis of vocational choice: Teaching. *Journal of Consulting Psychology*, 1960, *7*, 257–264.

Fagen, S. A., & Long, N. J. Teaching children self-control: A new responsibility for teachers. *Focus on Exceptional Children*, 1976, *7(8)*, 1–11.

Farber, B. *Mental retardation: Its social context and social consequences.* Boston: Houghton Mifflin, 1968.

Ginzberg, E., Ginsburg, S. W., Axelrad, S., & Herma, J. L. *Occupational information: An approach to a general theory.* New York: Columbia University Press, 1951.

Glasser, W. *Reality therapy: A new approach to psychiatry.* New York: Harper & Row, 1965.

Goldstein, H. Social and occupational adjustment. In H. A. Stevens & R. F. Herber (Eds.), *Research in mental retardation*. Chicago: University of Chicago Press, 1964.

Henrich, E., & Kriegel, L. *Experiments in survival*. New York: Association for the Aid of Crippled Children, 1961.

Hoyt, K. B. *An introduction to career education: A policy paper of the U.S. Office of Education*. DHEW Publication No. (OE) 75-00504. Washington, D.C.: U.S. Government Printing Office, 1975.

Illich, I. Deschooling society. In R. N. Anshen (Ed.) *World perspectives*, Vol. 44. New York: Harper & Row, 1971.

Krenter, M. The prison school. In P. H. Berkowitz & E. P. Rothman (Eds.), *Public education for disturbed children in New York City*. Springfield, Ill.: Charles C Thomas, 1967.

Maslow, A. H. *Motivation and personality*. New York: Harper & Row, 1954.

Miller, D. C., & Form, W. H. *Industrial sociology*. New York: Harper & Row, 1951.

Nelson, C. M., & Kauffman, J. M. Educational programming for secondary school age delinquent and maladjusted pupils. *Behavioral Disorders*, 1976, *2* (2), 102–113.

New Readers Press News. Before APL there was NRP. *New Readers Press News*, 1977, *1*, 1.

Oxford English Dictionary, Vol. 2. London: Oxford University Press, 1961.

Phenix, P. *Realms of meaning: A philosophy of the curriculum for general education*. New York: McGraw-Hill, 1964.

Phillips, E. M. Achievement place: Token reinforcement procedures in a homestyle setting for predelinquent boys. *Journal of Applied Behavior Analysis*, 1968, *1*, 213–223.

Plata, M. A comparative study of the occupational aspirations and interests of high school age emotionally disturbed, vocational-technical and regular academic students. Unpublished doctoral dissertation, University of Kansas, Lawrence, Kans., 1971.

Raths, L., Merrill, H., & Sidney, S. *Values and teaching*. Columbus, Ohio: Charles E. Merrill, 1966.

Rinehart, J. W. Mobility aspiration—Achievement discrepancies of mental illness. *Social Problems*, 1968, *15* (4), 478–488.

Stephens, B. *The development of reasoning, moral judgment and moral conduct in retardates and normals, Phase II*. Philadelphia: Temple University, 1972.

Super, D. E. *Career development: Self concept theory*. New York: College Entrance Examination Board, Teachers College, Columbia University, 1963.

Super, D. E. Vocational adjustment: Implementing a self concept. *Occupations*, 1951, *30*, 88–91.

Tharp, R. G., & Wetzel, R. J. *Behavior modification in the natural environment*. New York: Academic Press, 1969.

Weagraff, P. J. Career education curriculum development using the cluster concept. *Educational Horizons*, 1973, *51, 149–156*.

Whelan, R. J. The emotionally disturbed. In E. L. Meyen (Ed.), *Exceptional children and youth: An introduction*. Denver, Col.: Love, 1978.

Wilson, L. C. *The open access curriculum*. Boston: Allyn & Bacon, 1971.

Wylie, R. C. *The self-concept*. Lincoln, Neb.: University of Nebraska Press, 1961.

An Experiential Method For Teaching Careers

16

Betty Delfs Bowling

If the last 20 years could be summed up in one word, that word would be *change*—change in attitudes toward involvement in war, toward civil rights, toward individual lifestyles. A midwest private hospital for emotionally disturbed children and its school, which serves the children in residence for treatment, was no less affected by these sweeping cultural changes.

Previously students in the school had been long-term patients from middle- and upper-class families; they were generally of average or higher intelligence and followed the traditional college preparatory program. With the sixties, this acceptance became passé. The students began to challenge authority, curriculum, and teaching methods. Relevance arose and tradition declined as values, and students sought earlier independence.

Accompanying these changes was a shift in the hospital population in general. More short-term patients were admitted. Greater divergence in race, socioeconomic background, and abilities necessitated a response to broader needs, and part of that response took shape in the creation of new curriculum courses, one which was entitled "careers." Another response was a less uniform and traditional approach to teaching. Teaching methods became eclectic, ranging from behavioral approaches to the incorporation of some of the innovative techniques of the human potential movement. This new freedom promoted the experiential method of teaching used in the careers class.

While the changes that have occurred have been difficult for adults to adapt to, they have been chaotic for the adolescent population. The task for the normal adolescent is change itself, the relinquishing of less mature behavior and, through intellectual, emotional, and physical growth, gradual assumption of adult behavior. Emotionally disturbed adolescents are poorly equipped to face this task, and the cultural changes which took place during the sixties have intensified the difficulties of this crucial adjustment. The careers class provides positive growth experiences through the building of skills, attitudes, and a healthier self-image. Its combination of academic content and experiential methods comprise one model useful in preparing students for vocational success.

STAGE ONE—ACADEMIC CONTENT

The careers class developed in two distinct stages over a period of several years. The first stage centered around content. The teacher located a textbook, surveyed the catalogues for materials, and called in the experts—the students in the class—who participated in deciding what was important to learn, how to go about the learning, and what materials would be most useful. A course syllabus was compiled, on which each succeeding class has left its imprint by continual evaluation, modification, and improvement of the original content.

Why Work?

The first unit of study is entitled "Why Work?" Alternatives need to be aired early in the course; otherwise, in times of difficulty, they become unresolved issues that impede solving current conflicts. For example, if a conflict arises over punctuality, a common response from students is, "I don't care if I get to work on time or not. So what if I get fired. I don't need a job anyway." This makes the problem of punctuality become more difficult to define and to resolve. Whether a student wants or needs a job must be established first. Generally students are aware of alternative ways to survive. At some point in their lives, most of them have tried such alternatives as begging, borrowing, stealing, the welfare system, living on the streets, pushing dope, crashing with friends, and getting money from home. Often the students are more aware than the teacher of the pitfalls in each of these alternatives to employment.

After exploring the alternatives, the positive aspects of working are introduced, and these vary in importance from student to student. However, two major aspects on which all agree are money and independence. The relationship between making money and being independent is a great motivation for the students. In *Succeeding in the World of Work* (1975), one of the resource materials used in the class, the authors state, "Based on the cost of living today and the outlook for the future, you will need at least half a million dollars to pay for the goods and services you will purchase during your lifetime." Students respond to this first with disbelief, next shock, then despair. Independence has a high price tag and this maxim is particularly frightening to emotionally disturbed youth. Their strengths make them want to struggle toward normal adulthood; their weaknesses make them fear they will fail. Failure means remaining emotionally as children. The teacher must support the students' strengths by showing them the means to make that $500,000. In this case, to divide is to conquer. Students not only need a life perspective but they also need to be helped to divide the means to the goal into successfully manageable segments, one day, one dollar, one step at a time.

What Kind of Work?

The next unit of study reassures the students that there *are* ways to make the half million dollars—in fact there are 20,000 ways! Most emotionally disturbed adolescents have poor self-images. A common complaint early in the course is, "I can't do anything." The task is to disprove and dispel such feelings of inadequacy. One of the most helpful tools is the Kuder Vocational Preference Test which crystalizes and categorizes interests. If a student can read, he can complete the Kuder test. If he cannot read well, the test can be read to him. Because it is not possible to fail a Kuder test, this tool is a useful means to begin to build self-confidence. After the test is scored, each student matches interests to corresponding vocations within his accomplishment range. Students also list potential careers and are encouraged to list some jobs beneath their potential that might be satisfactory for part-time or temporary positions as well as jobs which at the present seem above their reach. This process seems not to discourage them but rather expands their awareness that neither they nor their chosen areas are arbitrarily or permanently limited.

Next the students make lists of the things that they are capable of doing. At first, most of them respond negatively—"But I can't do anything." Of course, they can do many things, but they are not consciously aware of their abilities so the starting point encompasses everyday skills. "Can you read, write, add, bake a cake? Can you clean your room, change the tire on your bike? How about more sophisticated skills? Can you play a musical instrument, drive a car, paint a picture?" Personality traits, such as honesty and the ability to care for young children, are added to the list. The list grows long and encouraging. But how does one make money with these skills and abilities? A group brainstorm can help provide answers. For example, if they can tie their shoes, read the sizes on boxes, and add up a sales ticket, they could perhaps sell shoes. Of course, there are more tricks to the trade than that, but, with a willingness to learn on the job from those who are successful, these young people can be successful, too. The job possibilities which can be matched to the students' skills and abilities are numerous and can be explored until the students begin to feel confident that they have potential in the adult business world—one more step away from helplessness, another step toward a better self-image.

Job Analysis Forms

Supported now with the lists of interests, abilities, and skills, and the knowledge that these are applicable, students and teacher begin to explore specific careers in detail. To do so, they can use a job analysis form which covers duties, working conditions, requirements, remuneration, and evaluations.

Some students have completed as many as thirty job forms. Others do as few as fifteen. All prospective occupations are chosen by the individual students to match interests and abilities. A proportion of the forms, generally one-third, must be on semi-skilled jobs that students could consider for part-time or summer jobs. This can lend a sense of immediacy to the course.[1]

---

[1] Two good sources of information are the *Occupational Outlook Handbook* (1977) published by the U.S. Department of Labor, Bureau of Statistics, and the *Semi-Skilled Careers Kits* (1973). These are reasonably priced. The sources for materials in this area are vast. The state and federal agencies have many free materials as do many private organizations. Suppliers in the education field have a large selection. Some are specific and expensive, but they might be suitable depending on the school population and resources.

_____

JOB ANALYSIS FORM

1. Title of position: _____
2. In this job the most common tasks would be: _____
   _____
   _____
3. Physical surroundings: noisy, quiet, indoors, outdoors, hot, cold, air-conditioned, dirty, clean, other.
4. Working conditions: steady, loss of time because of weather, seasonal, dangerous, other.
5. Physical requirements: standing, sitting, tiring, heavy or light lifting, height _____, weight _____, other.
6. Mental abilities and aptitude: scholastic, mathematical, clerical, verbal, scientific, mechanical, musical, other.
7. Interest or personality requirements: working with ideas, machines, people, patience, good control, extroversion, others. (List at least two "others.")
   _____
8. Usual type of education: business school, technical or vocational school, apprenticeship, special school, high school, college, or on-the-job training.
9. Necessary subjects in high school or college. _____
   _____
10. Job outlook in next 10 years: poor, fair, good. Explain any unusual circumstances:
    _____
11. Opportunity for advancement: poor, fair, good.
12. Pay: _____ to _____ per hour, month, year.
13. Usual hours per week: _____.
    Overtime required: Yes or No.
    Extra pay for overtime: Yes or No
    Evenings, nights, holidays: Never, Always, A possibility
14. Money needed for the job: union dues, tools, uniforms, others. _____
    _____
15. For me, the advantages are: _____
    _____
16. For me, the disadvantages are: _____
    _____
17. The advantages, disadvantages seem to be greater.
18. Would you like to have this job: Yes or No.
    Explain: _____
    _____

The class generally works on the job forms several days a week throughout the entire semester, but to work on them continuously has proven too tedious. Students also ask adults whom they know to fill out job forms for them. Often they ask parents to do job forms on their particular occupations and, in some cases, doing so has helped the students establish a new respect for their parents and what they do for a living.

Business Forms

Once the job form procedure and schedule are established, a new unit is introduced concerning the annoying but necessary red tape that is a real part of all of our lives. An excellent workbook for this unit is *Fill in the Blanks* (1974) which contains a copy of an application for a social security card, a withholding exemption certificate, and many other business forms. Although, to most teachers, this may seem an overly simple task, the students have great tolerance for it. For example, one student remarked that it was one of the most helpful parts of the course. For all, it has seemed to alleviate the fear of the unknown, the fear of being embarrassed, and has increased confidence.

Finding a Job

By this time, the students are eager to get on with the real thing and so the unit on learning how to look for a job is introduced. The resource material for this phase of the course is abundant and often free. Copies of the local newspaper are obtained and we translate the jargon peculiar to journalism and vocations that appears in the classified ads: "Kitchen help, no ex., split shift, fringe benefits, ref. Write The Spastic Colon, Box 123" or "Girls wanted, attractive, night shift, $10 hr., call Fanny's Fox Trap Massage." (The latter generally requires a short lesson on the pitfalls of easy money.) A great deal of vocabulary and spelling can be incorporated to this unit of study, and students rarely recognize these activities as similar to what they have learned to dislike in English classes.

In addition to scanning and translating the classified ads, students make a field trip to the local state government Job Service Center (such a service exists in all states). This visit enables them to feel comfortable about returning to this source on their own later when they are job hunting. Sometimes the class also visits private employment agencies.

Who you know is as important in finding a job as what you know, and to emphasize this point students are asked to list those persons who can be helpful, such as relatives, teachers, and acquaintances. Suddenly authority figures become needed advocates instead of adversaries.

How to Get a Job

Following the unit on how to find a job, a useful section of study on how to get a job is introduced, and often students express the greatest concern about this phase. First, they are taught how to write a personal history and how to search for and collect names and dates. Many students need assistance with finding names of previous schools and dates of attendance. Often they do not know their mothers' maiden names. So the effort is to anticipate all the information that might be required by a potential employer. Next a past-work experience list is compiled. Most students recognize the irony of needing experience to get a job and needing a job to get experience, and they need help in searching for something that can be labeled work experience. Included here are babysitting, yard work, volunteer work, anything that has required effort and responsibility. This helps the students discover strengths that they may not have previously recognized. We add a list of names for references, with addresses and telephone numbers, and learning to use a telephone directory becomes a necessity rather than a workbook exercise. Next a list of school subjects the student has taken that are applicable to the kind of job that interests him is compiled. For example, if the job requires handling money, mathematics is included; if the job is for kitchen help, home economics can be listed. Physical education is applicable for construction work or any other kind of labor that requires strength or dexterity. And, of course, the careers class is listed on every application. For many students this exercise is the first recognition that what they are learning in school has any relationship to their lives in the real world. Thus armed with personal history material and the previously compiled list of skills and abilities, the students are ready to organize a data sheet, which has become a highly valued and convenient tool.

For jobs that require a letter of application, the data sheet greatly simplifies that task. When no letter of application is required, the data sheet is a

```
                    PERSONAL DATA SHEET



  Elizabeth Brown            Phone: 555-1234, x. 5678
  115 Main Street            Age:   17 years
  Topeka, Kansas 66601       Health:  excellent


  Skills
        Typing - 35 words per minute
        Mathematical aptitude
        Neat, organized

  Education
        Graduate of Topeka High School, 19--
        Subjects studied:
              Typing - 1 year
              Algebra - 2 years

  Experience
        Babysitter - 2 years
        Library assistant, volunteer - 1 semester
        Office work, part time - Radford Oil Company

  Outside Interests and Hobbies
        Art, photography and reading

  References
        Mr. Louis B. Boss
        Manager, Bradford Oil Company
        1726 Main Street
        Manhattan, Kansas  67231

        Phone:  234-5678

        Mr. I. M. Topps
        Counselor, Topeka High School
        1824 West 32nd Street
        Topeka, Kansas 66609

        Phone:  234-6199

        Rev. G. O. Dodd
        St. Simon's Church
        Gage & 21st Street
        Topeka, Kansas 66604

        Phone:  273-4987
```

convenient organizing tool. Several businessmen have said that they would be very impressed if a young person came to inquire about a job with a prepared data sheet to leave with the prospective employer. They stated that this kind of organization and preparation might tip the balance in favor of hiring the applicant, rather than someone else. Actually, most jobs that young people apply for are walk-in, informal, interview-type jobs. The data sheet is the most effective method the students have to deliver information and make certain that their names and phone numbers will not be forgotten. At least ten copies are made of the final draft of the data sheet and often students begin using them immediately to look for after-school or part-time jobs.

In conjunction with the data sheet, the students write a cover letter of application for jobs requiring a more formal approach. Getting these two documents into final form is a challenge. The spelling, punctuation, and grammar must be perfect. Those skills from English class now seem much more relevant and team teaching this unit with an English teacher is a viable possibility. The data sheet and letter of application must be typed. For those students who cannot type, it is required that they barter for this service. They may either use their own money to pay someone or they may exchange a service such as washing a car or lending a cherished record. Something for nothing is infantilizing; having something to offer for trade is a step toward adult independence.

```
                                       123 Main Street
                                       City, State 12345
                                       April 4, 19--




Mr. A. B. Mann
Administrative Assistant
Box 987
City, State 12345

Dear Mr. Mann:

(What is the job and how did you find out about the job opening.)
Please consider me an applicant for this position.

(A paragraph to interest the employer in you for the job.  Include
some skills and/or job experiences.) Enclosed is a personal data
sheet with more information.

May I have an interview?  I shall be glad to call at your
convenience.  You may reach me after 3 p.m. at 234-5678.  Thank
you.

                           Yours truly,

                           Signed Name
                           Typed name
```

Wallet Card

After the letter of application and data sheet are completed, a mini-copy of some of the information is made and this material is put on the "wallet card"—a 3×5-inch piece of paper which, when folded into quarters, is the size of a charge card and fits neatly into a billford. It is supportive to know that, when filling out an application blank, elusive telephone numbers, addresses of references, and other bits of information are readily available as a kind of "pocket security."

Now the students are requested to fill out a second application blank. The initial one was filled out on the first day of class with the assurance that it would not be graded, as completing it is usually a frustrating first-time experience. With more confidence, a Social Security card, and the wallet card, the second try is very rewarding. The students compare their first attempt with this latter one and can see for themselves the gains they have made.

Interview

Selling oneself on paper is one thing; face-to-face confrontation is something else. The interview is probably the most anxiety-provoking project of the careers course. A good beginning is the familiar and comfortable task of studying a text on the topic, after which students practice composing answers to typical interview questions. Members of the class write skits and students take turns playing interviewer and applicant. One class made a home movie showing the correct conduct for an interview and, much more entertaining, the wrong conduct.

The next step is to videotape a practice interview. It is best to use a setting and interviewer unfamiliar to the students, as this adds an atmosphere of reality to this practice run. The interviewer should ask difficult questions that might be asked by a potential employer and, at the same time, be supportive enough to help students use their strengths to cope successfully with the challenge. Later the video films are shown to the class which critique them together, discussing posture, voice, and mannerisms, as well as the verbal responses. The interviewer is most supportive in pointing out to the group the assets—qualities to be respected and emulated—of each student.

Following this dress rehearsal, students prepare for the main performance. A local business manager agrees to interview students who send his office a letter of application and a data sheet. These requests are answered by his secretary and an appoitment is made. Each student must make arrangements to attend this appointment alone—no teacher, no friends. This position is new and disequilibrating. One strategy that is supportive at this point is a discussion of what to wear. Scrapbook photographs of former students on their "big day" are available, wardrobes are perused for the appropriate attire. It is always amazing to see how willing adolescents (who depend on their blue jeans and T-shirts for identity) are to join the "establishment" in order to be successful at what they have come to deem important. Perhaps this is possible for them to do because they have begun to feel that the goal is within their reach.

The interview experience is not an easy one. Students have expressed the fear that they would faint, throw up, or back out; fortunately none of them have found it necessary to do any of these things. All of them have expressed relief when the interview is over and, more important, a sense of pride and accomplishment. Often these good feelings prompt students to begin looking for real jobs in the community and add motivation for the next unit of study on how to keep a job once it is secured.

Keeping a Job

Keeping a job is a skill most difficult to learn second-hand. The source material is limited and inadequate. A set of twenty cassette tapes entitled, "On the Job," based on research done under the direction of Dr. Stuart Margulies for the Office of Economic Opportunity, have proven useful. They dramatize the common reasons for which young people are fired from their first jobs. The most valuable learning in this area takes place in our day-to-day experiential approach, discussed in Stage Two.

Progress on the Job

A few class sessions on job satisfaction and upward mobility are held. Included is an investigation of the opening of some formerly all-male occupations to women. The key for emphasis here is that limitations are more often internal, within the individual, and modifiable than external and beyond the individual's control.

Money Management

The last unit of study is one of high interest to the students. Basically it involves matching lifestyles to career choices. Students formulate budgets based on the incomes of various careers which they have found interesting and obtainable. They price rooms and apartments, utilities, food, and transportation. Many students have the misconception that the minimum wage will provide the standard of living which their parents are currently enjoying, and their budget work quickly disproves that assumption. This hard fact of life is unpleasant to normal adolescents and more so to emotionally disturbed adolescents. One student commented after making out her budget, "I think I just won't grow up." It is necessary to divide dreams into realistically obtainable goals to help dispel feelings of helplessness and hopelessness. Students need to be encouraged by being told that they need not always remain at minimum wage. Although the need for immediate gratification is a common symptom, the delays can be tolerated if it can be shown that gratification comes with planning. Several students have changed their educational plans as a consequence. They decided that, since their lifestyles did not match their career choices, they would change their career choices to those that would generate greater remuneration. College education or vocational training have become viable alternatives which some have considered as a result of budget study. Further education then becomes not something decided by parents but something desired by students, an inwardly chosen control over their future lives.

Dispersed throughout the semester are three other useful activities: games, speakers, and field trips. Two of the games are "Steady Job" and "Managing Your Money," both good learning devices. Whenever possible, if students show strong interest in a particular occupation, someone who is involved in the field should come to school to speak informally to the class. A question-and-answer format is useful, including questions concerning the daily duties and the advantages and disadvantages of the particular job.

Better than speakers, but more difficult to arrange, are on-site observations of people at their work. At one time, several students were interested in becoming lawyers, and so it was arranged for them, through the local court, to attend a trial, an awesome experience. Another year, several law students put on a mock trial for a school assembly with students acting as jury. On another occasion arrangements were made to visit a local hospital. On mandatory excursions to a small factory and a heavy industry plant, students are able to see bench work and assembly-line work. The reactions of students to the repetitiveness in these kinds of jobs are varied: some react negatively and have consequently changed their career choices; others respond positively, feeling they would find security in the structured tasks. Also included is a visit to a local vocational training center where students visit classes that involve training for over forty different vocations. The semester's agenda for both speakers and field trips is designed by the students and dictated by their individual interests.

For several years this sequence comprised the entire course and it seemed successful. However, the ultimate test of most education is whether or not it helps the individual function in society. Our students summarize this as "makin' it in the real world." It is common for ex-students to come back to visit after their hospital treatment has been concluded. The alumni from the careers course always had gratifying reports to relay. "I just want you to know that Careers was the most useful class I ever had" or "The other day when I went for a job interview, I was nervous, but I thought about what we had done together, and it got me through"—music to a teacher's ears. However, one common problem became apparent. They knew how to find and get jobs, but they had not been able to keep them. They were not "makin' it in the real world." These young people had intelligence, skills, and the ability to learn, but they had been fired. What went wrong? As is often the case, they had the answer as well as the question. The problem appeared to be threefold: They had been unable to produce the quantity of work necessary; they had been inconsistent in getting to work regularly and punctually; or they had been unsuccessful in their relationships with fellow employees and supervisors. Sometimes all three problems occurred. These problems had been anticipated when the course content had been designed, as most emotionally disturbed adolescents display these difficulties in their work as students. The section on "Keeping a Job" was included for this reason, and these areas of potential difficulty had been studied and discussed. Still, it had not been enough. Thus, stage two of the development of the careers class began to emerge.

STAGE TWO—EXPERIENTIAL METHOD

Since the cognitive approach was not adequate by itself, it was decided to add an experiential approach. It was not enough to learn about keeping a job; it was essential to experience, feel, and practice the behavior conducive to keeping a job. The semester course about jobs became in itself an 18-week practical job experience. All of stage one, content matter, was retained, and an overlay of job experience, stage two, was added: Careers class became Careers, Inc. (sometimes referred to by the students as "The Company"). The students assume the role of employees, the teacher the role of boss, the class is seen a job, and the task is to learn about the world of work. As many aspects of real working conditions as possible are incorporated.

This experiential model is integrated into the class from the first day to the last. When the students are enrolled in Career, Inc., by their advisors, the unusual structure of the class is explained to them so that they are not totally surprised when they walk in on the first day, and, after a formal greeting, are requested to fill out an application blank for "the job." Then the Company rules and regulations are explained and a contract is negotiated.

The Contract

The contract covers wages, fringe benefits, responsibilities, and general working conditions. These must be clearly understood. Specifically, each employee works for the current minimum wage and each 50-minute class period is considered an eight-hour working day. For example, in 1978 the minimum wage of $2.65 an hour resulted in a day's pay of $21.20, a week's pay of $106; federal and state taxes, social security, and health insurance are deducted, leaving a net of $80. Thus students feel as well as learn the difference between gross and net. This exercise usually prompts the students to recount parents' stories of tax burdens and perhaps prompts a greater understanding of parents' problems. For the students, however, this is a paper game. The checks they receive once a week are not negotiable at local stores but the intensity of their involvement on payday is often as great as if the checks were real. The checks are deposited in a pseudosavings account with all the related practice of endorsing checks and filling out bank forms. The first few deposits seem meager but, as the weeks pass, the students are encouraged by the accumulating balance. They are required to buy their grade at the end of each grading period. A price is assigned to each letter grade. For example, a grade of *A* costs $820 and a *C* costs $640. If a student attends class regularly and does his work adequately, he can earn enough to purchase a *C*. Average job performance obtains average rewards.

Two fringe benefits are included in the contract: one for sick leave, one for vacation time. The students are told that they should not assume that these fringe benefits are available in all jobs, but we have found them useful incentives. A day of sick leave and of vacation are accrued following the completion of each month of work. Sick leave may be taken for physical illness and doctor or dentist appointments, nothing else. Requests for vacation days must be made 24 hours in advance, a practice which helps curb impulsive behavior.

The responsibilities of the job include getting to work regularly and punctually, completing all assigned tasks adequately, maintaining appropriate behavior, and cooperating with the employer and co-workers. Failure to meet acceptable standards results in being "fired." Obviously a goal of the class is to have a successful experience, but must be an honestly earned experience to be meaningful and there must be consequences for both negative and positive behavior. The consequences for negative behavior should be, if at all possible, seen as a constructive learning experience rather than as failure. So, when it becomes necessary to fire a student, instead of being dropped from the class (thereby losing the opportunity to recover the loss), he is required to forfeit $100 from his savings account. This amount was designated because it is realistic to assume that if a person loses a job in the real world it would take at least a week to get another, and the person would lose approximately a week's wages. A $100 withdrawal from the student's savings account diminishes buying power at grade time. The student can, if properly motivated, negotiate to be rehired and, with additional work in the form of overtime, recoup the loss. The contract lays the groundwork for providing students the experiences necessary to overcome the three problems being encountered by our ex-patients.

Attendance and Punctuality

Regular attendance and punctuality, which are accepted norms in our society both in school and in the working world, are not established patterns for most emotionally disturbed students. Students often express surprise when they are informed of the necessity to fulfill these expectations if they are to maintain their jobs. The direct relationship of attendance to the Friday paycheck has been a successful behavior motivation. Absence from class, other than for sick leave or vacation, means $21.20 less on payday. "No work—no pay" is a valuable lesson. Three absences from work within a nine-week period result in being fired. Another problem occurred because most students were unaware that they were responsible for calling the "boss" before starting time if they were unable to get to work. For the class, a student must personally call in and inform the teacher that he will be unable to attend class and appropriately explain the reasons. Failure to do so not only results in the loss of a day's pay but in the recording of an infraction. Three infractions and the student is fired. Being late for work also leads to loss of pay. Since our 50-minute class period is considered an eight-hour day, each minute late means being docked 43 cents. In addition to the loss in pay, being late is also recorded as an infraction.

Change does not come easily. Students may begin the semester by ignoring obligations and heated confrontations ensue, but, by the end of the term, they generally assume responsibility for their actions and the consequences. Students have arranged to have appointments changed so that they could attend the careers class. On occasion they have missed every other class during the day but have managed to get to "work." Some have cut short conversations with friends in the hallway so they can be in the room a few minutes early, just to be on the safe side. Behavioral change and growth does take place. This change is not initially motivated by a desire to keep a job in the fuzzy future; that message comes more slowly. The motivation comes from this Friday's check, an immediate and concrete reinforcement.

Productivity

One must not only get to work regularly and punctually but must also be productive on the job. This means the student must use all of the work period engaged in useful activity. Because activities and projects cannot always be accurately timed to last the entire fifty minutes and because not all students work at the same speed, we designed a "goof-off" prevention system. When a student has nothing to do and is tempted to get caught in the water cooler syndrome, he can always fill his time by reading something from the "goof-proof box" which contains magazine and newspaper articles and assorted short projects, all related to work. This "goof-off" prevention system has been particularly useful to students who have a tendency to rush through their work in a haphazard manner. They know there is always something they will be expected to do, so they become more careful with their work. It is also helpful for the students who work well and quickly. The material in the "goof-proof box" is interesting and, if they wish to summarize the material they read into a report, they may earn extra money on a piece-work basis.

Two other methods are available to increase productivity and provide additional pay. Some students are eager from the beginning of the semester to get enough additional money in the bank to buy a grade higher than a C. Others need to see their bank accounts grow more substantial before they realize that, with extra work, a better grade is within their reach also. As in most jobs, assuming additional responsibilities results in higher pay. "The Company" needs a timekeeper, two bookkeepers to do the payroll, and a banker. These positions can be changed weekly and are voluntarily assumed. The timekeeper and bookkeepers receive an

extra fifteen dollars a week; the banker whose job takes less time receives ten dollars. Even students who are having difficulty in mathematics will tackle one of these positions because the act of manipulating figures now has a new meaning to them. Surprisingly, they rarely make mistakes. If they do, the mistakes are quickly pointed out to them by their fellow employees. Money is serious mathematics. Contingent with these activities, they learn a great deal about adding machines, calculators, bookkeeping, and general business procedures.

The other method of adding to the weekly paycheck is overtime. Special projects are always made available for after-class hours. Overtime and homework, a word never used in Careers, Inc., are the same think in actuality, but the psychological difference to the students is immense. Overtime is a self-imposed, sought-after, rewarded activity, whereas homework is rarely seen to have these attributes. Pay is negotiated for these projects, sometimes in the form of a bonus for a particular task, at other times as a contract for time-and-a-half pay for a set period. These methods have not only increased the productivity of the students but have also helped them learn that rewards are commensurate to efforts.

Something needs to be said at this point about measuring the quality of students' work. Grading daily work is a part of a teacher's tasks and one which many will find hard to relinquish. There is always the fear that the quality of the work will deteriorate if it is not graded. In Careers Inc., students' work is monitored, but their activities are neither graded nor recorded. The quality has not deteriorated through this more realistic simulation of the business world.

Relationships

The third and most serious problem was in relationships with peers and with employers. This problem is obviously the most difficult to solve as it goes to the root of emotional illness. Inability to relate to family members in particular and society in general is the prime reason students attend a school for emotionally disturbed children. However, one must firmly believe that in all children, no matter how disturbed, there is a source of health and a potential for growth and must capitalize on this strength. For 50 minutes a day they are expected to act well, to behave normally. They may think or feel what they wish, but they are to act appropriately. They are expected to "hang up their symptoms in the hallway" and not to pick them up until the quitting whistle blows. They are to role-play healthy, productive employees and this is not an easy task.

Nor is it easy for the teacher to give up the role of a special educator who is concerned with the whole individual and assume the role of a boss who is interested primarily in an end product or service. To maintain these roles for 18 weeks is a formidable undertaking. One thing that makes it possible is that the roles need to be maintained for only 50 minutes each day. Adults often use the awareness of a limited time span to keep themselves functioning—10 more minutes until quiting time, 6 more months of car payments, 1 more semester of graduate school; hang on just a little longer and the goal will be achieved. The students learn that they, too, can use this system to their advantage.

A second structure is called "coffee break." The reality is that the students' strengths do have limits. The art is in pushing the limits to the growing point and stopping before the breaking point, a fine line. The students themselves are often the best judges of where the line is at a particular time. Each student is told that he may, within reasonable limits, ask for a coffee break when he needs it. It may consist of a trip to the drinking fountain, a jog around the building, or whatever is appropriate to relieve tension. Occasionally it may, under excessive stress, mean that the employee and employer need to step out in the hallway together and agree to shed their roles. We then relate as student and special educator and try to talk through, as much as the student is willing, the difficulty. For example, the teacher needs to empathize with the trauma evolving from a family visit or a painful therapy session. In a different kind of class, the teacher could change the lesson plans for the day and select a task that is more supportive to the student or suspend the school assignment for the day and reschedule it for a later time. In careers class, the teacher can drop the employer role temporarily and discuss the problem but the goal is to resume the work assignment, if at all possible.

A more concrete example of role changing is a situation that occurred one day before class. A student called in to say she would not be able to come to work because she was physically ill, an appropriate message from employee to the boss. The teacher suggested the foregoing role change and then asked her if she were physically ill or if she were depressed. As it turned out, she had had an argument with her mother and was depressed. She was reminded that she had been absent several times and that, if this were a real job, she would be in jeopardy of being fired. She was also told that many normal adults were occasionally depressed but went to work anyway and that some even found their work supportive. She agreed to come to work and try to get through the 50 minutes. She did so and functioned very well. Thus she turned a potentially defeating situation into a coping experience. She learned not only that she was expected to be at work each day but that she could meet that expectation.

By the use of role-playing and the experiential approach, students have been able to work through many problems that occur in real job situations. The students learn to relate better with one another; they come to understand that, no matter how antagonistic they may feel toward others, their feelings, if displayed or acted upon at work, will cost them their jobs; they hang up the fight in the hallway with their other symptoms and leave it there until after work. In addition, they learn that, as employees, they need to cooperate and help one another. They become less concerned about the boundaries—doing only their assigned tasks—and, as the semester progresses, they assume responsibility for "The Company" as a whole, often helping the slower members of the group finish their work. If the timekeeper is absent, someone assumes the responsibility, often without prompting, so that business can proceed as usual. They are required to teach whoever succeeds them in the jobs of timekeeper, bookkeeper, and banker the duties of that position. They are thorough and patient in this cooperative effort. They learn to recognize one another's weaknesses and will do what they can to compensate in order to be supportive.

Equally, the experiential approach provides the means for learning to relate to the boss, a word that evoked giggles or anger at the beginning of the semester. Authority figures are often a focus of conflict for emotionally disturbed people. Although not sacrificing requisite understanding, the teacher does not practice the tolerance, concern, and patience to which students have become accustomed in their interactions with hospital and school staff. The teacher should share with students the difficulty of maintaining this role and ask them for feedback. With this kind of open, honest relationship the students help the teacher to determine their strengths and, at the same time, they help in the development of the strengths of the teacher. Through growing together in these experiences, the teacher can begin to expect more from the students. For instance, they are expected to follow directions without undue repetition. Occasionally directions are stated in the form of orders; not all bosses say "please" nor give employees their full attention. Teacher attention is withdrawn slowly, with the explanation that bosses have their own work to do. The teacher should also persistently refuse to answer any questions that students could answer for themselves with the proper effort.

A more difficult area is the handling of anger. Often young people quit a job because, "The boss yelled at me." When students are irresponsible, the teacher should try to respond with as much open anger as they are able to accept. Many students seem to believe that anger is their prerogative and adults should always be fair and calm. The teacher should explore ways in which students can express themselves assertively without being destructive to their positions and, at the same time, develop some acceptance of the anger of others. These confrontations are unpleasant and energy-consuming but of inestimable value to the students. The roles and the job structure may be artificial but, if everyone contracts to play the game the best he or she can, the experience can be beneficial in providing the basis for present achievement as well as future success.

Summary

The combination of a cognitive approach (including all the academic material time will allow) and an experiential approach (including role-playing and the job structure) can provide a learning-growth experience for adolescents. The concept is not without difficulties. It is a structure which requires more of a teacher's time than a traditional approach and a higher energy investment. Role-playing takes energy;

dealing with emotionally laden issues directly and openly also demands higher output. Besides the increased demands for time and energy, the unusual structure requires creativity on the part of all involved. Where does one find the additional time, energy, and creativity for such an undertaking? It is to be found by being constantly aware of the successes to be experienced by both the student and the teacher. They are many and gratifying. Students begin to recognize the relevancy of other school subjects, begin to formulate future career plans, and modify their educational plans accordingly. They begin seeking jobs and report successes not only in obtaining them but also in being able to keep them. They are able to relate simulated situations to the real situations they encounter and are able to use these experiences to their advantage. They learn to draw on their strengths and control their symptoms. Their self-images are improved and they begin to see the potential for becoming self-sustaining, independent adults. Who could ask for a greater return on an investment?

Source Material

BOOKS

The amazing adventures of Harvey Crumbaker: Skills for Living Unit 1. Lakeshore Curriculum Materials Centers, 2695 East Dominguez Street, P. O. Box 6261, Carson, California 90749, 1978.

Kimórell, G., & Vineyard, B. S. *Succeeding in the world of work.* Bloomington, Ill.: McKnight, 1975.

Match, S. D. *Fill in the blanks.* Mafex Associates, Inc., 90 Cherry Street, Johnstown, Pennsylvania 15902, 1974.

U. S. Department of Labor. *Occupational outlook handbook.* Washington, D. C.: Bureau of Labor Statistics, 1979.

Washburn, W. Y. *Vocational entry-skills for secondary students.* San Rafael, Calif.: Academic Therapy Publications, 1975.

MAGAZINES

Career World. Curriculum Innovations, Inc., Highwood, Illinois 60040.

Occupational Outlook Quarterly. U. S. Department of Labor, Bureau of Labor Statistics, Washington, D. C. 20212.

Sourcebook—A Magazine for Seniors. 13–30 Corporation, 1005 Maryville Pike, Knoxville, Tennessee 37920.

On Your Own: A Guide to Get Started after High School. 13–30 Corporation, 505 Market Street, Knoxville, Tennessee 37920.

GAMES

Managing Your Money. Cuna Mutual Insurance Society, P. O. Box 391, Madison, Wisconsin 53701.

Steady Job—A Vocational Orientation Game. Mafex Associates, Inc., 90 Cherry Street, Johnstown, Pennsylvania 15902.

PAMPHLETS

Careers for a changing world. New York Life Insurance Company, Box 51, Madison Square Station, New York, New York 10010.

Heads or tails. Center Grafics, Newbury Park, California 91320.

McGravie, A. V. *The job in your future.* Chicago: Science Research Associates.

CASSETTES

The World of Work: "On the Job." EDI Educational Design, Inc., 47 West 13th Street, New York, New York 10011.

KITS

Semi-Skilled Careers Kit. Careers, Largo, Florida 33540.

DIRECTORIES

Wiley, D., & Block, A. L. *Career Information Directory.* Information Systems and Service, Inc., P. O. Box 1237, Milwaukee, Wisconsin 53201.

Adolescent Drug and Alcohol Abuse

17

Robert A. Jardin
Peter W. Ziebell

HISTORICAL PERSPECTIVE

The so-called epidemic of drug and alcohol abuse by adolescents of the middle sixties was countered by intensive programs and massive funding in the early to middle seventies. In the eighties it seems to be an established personal/social phenomenon routinely faced by adolescents as they seek resolution of dependency/autonomy conflicts. Nevertheless, there is no substantial evidence that large numbers of adolescents are failing because of drug and alcohol abuse, only that those adolescents who would have failed without drugs now often present their failure in concert with drug use. Because drug abuse has been so foreign and alarming to the adult society, the label *epidemic*, implying a virulent impact, was applied.

In Montgomery County, Maryland, a separate Office of Drug Control was established for drug program planning, development, and monitoring; within four years over $2,000,000 in program funds were used to combat drugs. However, since the maximum point of development, programs established to combat drugs have largely changed their emphasis from drug abuse to the emotional and behavioral disorders of adolescents and their families. The Office of Drug Control no longer exists; yet, because of the ongoing anxiety about drugs, there is now a vast network of service programs which go far beyond what would have existed without the drug "epidemic."

Educators, parents, police, and helping professionals have reacted during this time with feelings of helplessness, panic, social hysteria, biased misinformation, angry retaliation, blaming, and resignation. Despite political, institutional, community, and parental efforts, drug abuse has largely stabilized while alcohol abuse among adolescents has increased. In general little has changed over these 15 years, although narcotic abuse (heroin, barbituates) has abated and acid and speed abuse has become increasingly rare. Use of hallucinogens (such as LSD) has decreased except for an increase in the use of PCP.

Full identification of the causes of alcohol and drug use and abuse would involve identifying the causes of most human problems. Drug use fulfills adolescent efforts to cope, and those adolescents who have many problems are especially vulnerable to the coping mechanism of alcohol and drug abuse.

There seems to be a close correlation between adolescent alcohol and drug abuse and society's trend to seek chemical solutions for life's distress. Increases in social, institutional, and family disorganization have led adolescents to feel a sense of depersonalization and an increase in the complexity of life; resistance and rebellion against the inculcation of established values and morals has occurred without the correspondent establishment of acceptable new values and morals. Many adolescents try drugs but for those who experience serious difficulty in coping with personal and family disorganization and, equally important, educational conflict and failure, drug use is particularly problematic. The drug abuse by these disturbed adolescents not only expresses their rebellion and reaction against their position but also, for the short term, comforts and protects them against the distress of their feelings. Heavy drug users manifest a depressed existential state devoid of long-range goals and meaning and remain caught by the relief provided by alcohol and drugs and their need to vent frustration against their families, their institutions, and their society.

Today, increasingly, adolescents present the acting-out behaviors of truancy, deliberate school failure, and serious alcohol and drug abuse, complicating the effective application of traditional counseling and psychotherapy. Traditional mental health services and educational counseling reveal a generalized ineffectiveness with these youth. Counselors, therapists, parents, educators, and justice system personnel who accept the need for changes actively seek alternative approaches.

Juvenile civil-rights legislation has tended to remove all but delinquent adolescent offenders from the controls and support formerly available to parents and educators. Although a persuasive argument can be made for requiring parents and educators to play a more responsible role in resolving adolescent problems, many of these individuals have had to face the limits of their own resources in dealing with their self-destructive, rebelling youth. However, even with the risk that the application of more severe parental and educational controls might increase the incidence of adolescent rebellion, the pernicious drift toward societal versus parental responsibility clearly needed to be reversed.

During the past several decades, a shift has occurred in the role and function of children within the family. In the past children were often considered economic assets, however, now they are more likely to be perceived as sources of personal satisfaction for their parents which, in turn, increases the potential for inordinate symbiotic relationships between parent and child, with variable degrees of frustration and rejection as adolescents struggle with predominant relationship/autonomy conflicts. Often parents of alcohol- and drug-abusing youth come to feel unhappy in their parenting role and in frustration vent their displeasure on their youth. Frequently, the juvenile justice system and particularly educational institutions are blamed for failing to provide the necessary support and controls. Parents criticize school and courts, schools criticize parents, and courts criticize parents and schools. This criticism often gets caught in a cycle of blame that is further demoralizing to educators, justice system workers, and certainly the parents and adolescents themselves.

DRUGS: THE INDIVIDUAL AND THE PEER GROUP

The vast majority of heavy drug users is drawn from the 20% of total student population that would predictably (without drug use) be maladjusted, underachieving, and generally nonproductive in the school setting. Therefore any discussion of potential drug abusers must attend to examples of failure-prone youth. Any prescription for approaching existing drug users/abusers must include specific attention to preventive actions which should be taken prior to the incidence of use and abuse. The authors of this chapter advocate active, early intervention by all segments of the failure-prone youth's life system. The following examples of potential drug users are presented in the hope that educators will recognize that because of pre-existing or early school-developed conflicts, these youth are unlikely to adjust to the school learning experience. It is the responsibility of educational institutions to explore ways of modifying its traditions and bureaucracy in an attempt to meet reasonably the educational needs of these failure-prone youth as well as to insist on an interinvolvement of all the significant parts or systems relating to pre-school, primary-school, and secondary-school problem youth.

One can identify many "types" of youth that present patterns of behavior with a reasonably high probability of later alcohol and drug use and abuse. Such adolescents are predisposed to cling close to peers with similar levels of disillusionment and to form groups that subscribe to self-perpetuated values (such as rebelling against parents and schools). The parents of these youth experience alienated, noncommunicative relationships with their adolescents, many times ineffectively contesting those values propagated by the youth and his or her peers. At the same time the peer group increasingly reinforces undisciplined, irresponsible tendencies that enhance the likelihood of drug abuse. In early adolescence such peer groups foster increasingly generalized alienation toward authority causing a deterioration of authority within the school environment and job dissatisfaction among educators. Attempts to "manage" these acting-out adolescents within the educational environment have met with mixed success, but too often result in a frustrating failure for the teacher.

Interestingly, these same youth who overtly reject the necessity of educational accomplishment and its relationship to wealth and position are very much conditioned to be voracious consumers desiring the privileges and advantages that go with responsible and successful adulthood. Youth that abuse drugs and alcohol usually fail educationally and personally and never develop the inner strength and resources necessary for success in adulthood. Many of these youth may "bottom-out" in late adolescence or young adulthood and discontinue alcohol and drug abuse only to find themselves seriously handicapped in participating meaningfully in relationships and work roles. Such a situation often leads to a return to alcohol and/or drugs.

Educators are early observers of all types of abuse-prone youth. For the purposes of example, categories of youth will be identified but the reader should not assume that such categories are sacrosanct; rather they are overlapping and variably interrelated.

Isolated Students

The isolated adolescent often presents symptoms of emotional problems in relation to the immediate family and always presents such symptoms in the ability to find a comfortable relationship with peers. Rejecting, disorganized home environments foster a concept of personal worthlessness and anticipated rejection and failure within the educational setting. Often physiological abnormalities, such as obesity, smallness, largeness, or extreme awkwardness, discriminate against the child's participation within the school social environment and the play environment outside of school. Children who have conflicts with peers but not with family may well become isolated but adequate or superior learners; nevertheless, they remain troubled children who have great anxieties about their self-worth. Their distress is critical in puberty when they often find themselves left out of positive peer relationships. They are self-conscious and basically without the skills necessary to impress their peers and establish their value as members of the peer group. After a miserable early adolescence such youth may find the only peer group accepting them is composed of similarly disillusioned youth among whom the joining behavior often involves rebellion, alcohol, and drug experimentation. Their introduction to marijuana (usually the drug of induction) may produce a welcomed sense of increased self-confidence, elation, and even self-worth; they often feel able to talk and participate much better when "high." These youth experience a sense of increased togetherness, belonging, and importance while in this altered-consciousness state and usually feel uncomfortable and ineffective when they are not drugged. Thus, while drug and alcohol experimentation may be initiated with apprehension and fear as a joining requirement, drug use comes to play an equally important role in providing a sense of emotional support and well being that these youth otherwise do not have.

The Symbiotic Student

The symbiosis-prone child evolves from a highly fused, emotional interaction, usually with his or her mother. Such children usually come from middle-or upper-class families where the typical pattern is of an emotionally distant, vocationally driven father who provides little emotional support for his children and usually less for his wife. Women who marry such men usually do so out of dependency needs that seek resolution in a strong, confident-appearing man; unfortunately, such men often are incapable of providing the close and emotionally warm relationship these women require. Such women are not prone to seek resolution through a career or a vocational outlet; rather they focus their need for emotional acceptance and meaning upon the children.

In many cases, this kind of family system produces a relationship in which the message between the child and mother is "you make me extremely important and I will make you extremely important." The mother's sense of emotional fulfillment and self-worth comes through her role of being a mother and she demands that her child's behavior reflect her as a worthwhile mother. This type of relationship produces many serious neurotic patterns early in life wherein the child receives emotional and material rewards for performing in a manner which reflects the mother's worth. Often, upon entering school, there is a difficult adjustment period in which separation of the child from the mother is traumatic both for the mother and the child. However, once the child learns that very much the same relationship can be established with his or her teacher, security sets in, and the child begins to perform as an ideal child for the teacher. This child always raises his or her hand when the teacher asks a question, always volunteers for any chore that the teacher may need to have done, and generally behaves in a way that mirrors to the teacher all of the wishes he/she may have for a student in that classroom. The message the teacher falls into giving verbally and nonverbally establishes the symbiotic child as the model student, thereby virtually destroying any chance the child has of being a participating member of the peer group. However, this child really does not want to be a member of the peer group; he or she would much rather be close and interinvolved with the teacher. Often this child is seen as a perfect student and gets superior grades throughout elementary school. When the child enters the intermediate grades (or in some cases not until entrance into high school), an extraordinary "Kaboom" phenomenon occurs. "Kaboom!": an explosion occurs and the child rebels. The child recognizes that he or she has no sense of a separate self and is totally dependent on adults, particularly his or her mother. He or she therefore rejects all previous behaviors. The message then given to him or her and others is "the only behavior I can afford to use is that behavior which I'm sure would be unacceptable to all these people I have been behaving for." Typically this type of adolescent jumps into drug use as a flag-raising ceremony. The child's mother may be frantic, frustrated, and panicked because of the loss of her perfect child. The young person who was seen as the model of student perfection in elementary school becomes the menace of his or her classmates. All of the manipulative skills that he or she had in previous behaviors (doing what people want) are retained and used to set forth eloquent anti-establishment, pro-drug kinds of proposals. He or she is often well researched in anti-establishment, drug-taking theories, can argue well and attract quite a following of other youth who see the position as desirable. This student usually (but not always) abandons his or her academic achievement-motivated behavior.

The Learning Disabled Student

The child who in early childhood develops either transitional or permanent, unrecognized learning disabilities often finds his or her sense of self-worth and effectiveness under serious attack in the primary-grade experience. This child can be approached in the learning environment in a way that prevents serious decimation of the child's sense of worth and effectiveness. Too often, however, failure to properly diagnose the disability or to handle remediation with thoughtfulness leaves the child disliking and resisting the educational experience. Even when diagnosed properly, the learning-disabled child is usually unavoidably labeled through special placements. Unfortunately, no matter how sensitive and supportive the teachers, it is difficult to avoid the taunting labels of peers and the disappointment of parents.

Often the child exhibits passive/aggressive behaviors which present a powerful resistance to the learning process. The passive/aggressive behaviors often seep into other learning skills not related to the learning disability. Even in grade school such youth often vent their displeasure against their teachers and the school environment by presenting significant behavior problems. If such youth do not have a secure sense of self to fight back, they may withdraw and present the symptoms of the isolated child.

Youth prone to fight back in elementary school gravitate early to authority-resistant peer groups during late elementary and early intermediate school years and are likely to incorporate alcohol and drug abuse as a symptom of their situation.

The Disadvantaged Student

Parents overwhelmed by the problems created by limited education and low-income and low-status employment sometimes react to their situation with violence, alcohol or drug abuse, and with child neglect or abuse. Because of the intellectual deprivation which evolves from the neglect situation, youth from such families often are identified as slow learners. In contrast, other youth are neglected because of the commitment of both mother and father to all-consuming career goals leaving little energy for involvement with their children. As a result of the lack of involvement, such children often feel unwanted, become depressed, and function as slow learners. Both types of neglected children may present drug and alcohol use in the later elementary school years and truancy, alcohol and drug abuse, and assaultive behavior throughout adolescence. Parents of these children usually are not disposed to seek help for either themselves or their children nor are they supportive of the schools. In adolescence, delinquent acts predictably occur, resulting in juvenile records and possibly culminating in episodes of detention.

A closely parallel group is represented by the culturally deprived child, usually a result of racial, ethnic, or class prejudice. The children of some of these families may have such insufficient preparation for formal education that they are placed in a slow learner category even though technically their intellectual ability would contraindicate such placement. Like the learning disabled child, they often develop appropriate personal strengths prior to school and experience many of the negative feedback conditions upon entering school. Because these children may have experienced less parental supervision and involvement because of the family's economic stress, they often have developed characteristics of choosing and managing their own activities; this produces conflicts with the controls applied in the classroom and, when compounded with the slow learner label, may lead to various types of classroom disruption.

Those youth who fail to integrate and compete successfully with more advantaged youth achieve at a minimal level but are socially promoted and enter the intermediate school system a year or two older than their classmates. In the intermediate school system they may begin truanting with gang-type liaisons (which may eventually lead to suspension or expulsion) from school. Their introduction to drugs often occurs fortuitously rather than as a choice of antibehavior. Often drugs are introduced to these children at a very early age because of the minimally supervised family and community situations. In some cases these children may become alcohol and drug abusers in the elementary years. As individuals in their peer group, they carry on a day-by-day existential survival which usually results in reactive-impulsive behaviors which may attract the attention of the legal authorities of the community. As they go into later adolescence, they may become sellers of drugs largely because they are willing to take the risks involved in order to have spending money or because there is status in selling drugs to other students. These youth generally end up in various correctional institutions before they reach adulthood and some unfortunately never make an adequate adjustment to living in an open society.

Questions and Responses

We come to two questions in further exploring the substance abuse problem. The first is: What can be done to modify, correct, or prevent certain personal/social situations from turning into drug-and alcohol-oriented situations? The other question is: How do we develop approaches and programs which help deal therapeutically with those people who already are so dependent upon alcohol or drug use that they require assistance? A preventive approach cannot continue to be ignored. All aspects of the society should establish priorities which focus on modifying the kinds of family, social, and educational situations that give rise to such problems later in life.

The response of government, communities, and families to adolescent alcohol and drug abuse tends to be emotionally reactive, with tinges of panic and hysteria. This reaction complicates a studied, rational view of effective forms of prevention and treatment for drug-abusing young people. Communities often subscribe to the law as a course of prevention. Persons who advocate law as the main deterrent to alcohol and drug abuse believe that many adolescents choose not to use drugs because of the fear of discovery and of consequent legal actions. A significant part of the community usually also sees that adolescent alcohol and drug abuse is a symptom of personal distress. Adolescents are very reluctant to face the fact that alcohol and drug use can be extremely harmful and they tend toward the unrealistic view that if they really cared to, they could discontinue the use of alcohol and drugs at any time. Traditional forms of treatment tend to be dependent upon the individual's willingness to see himself as in difficulty and upon a willingness to go through the anxiety and problems that may surround change.

The Educational Environment

The young student's introduction to school and the development of a self-concept as a learner is of paramount importance during elementary years. During adolescence the established self-concept of the individual has significant impact on the potential for alcohol and drug use/abuse. Positive approaches to coping with the incipient negative self-concept in the learning situation may, in many cases, significantly modify the incidence of later drug abuse. Students need repeated success experiences in school learning situations. School-negative students are likely to feel increasingly insignificant and incapable of facing the challenge of school, the primary source of achievement and performance in their lives. Too often when a student comes to anticipate and interpret the school as a primary source of failure or negative labeling, he or she will withdraw or rebel.

On entering adolescence those students who have developed a negative reaction toward school (or to any authority structure) will require a psychosocial educational setting that explores self, peers, and family as well as factual educational content and teaching style. Such programming may be through a separate class, a school within a school, or a separate school. In effect, such a strategy requires a therapeutic balance of educational efforts, probably a conjoint health/education programming effort.

Unfortunately schools exist within a linear paradox. They are often considered responsible for ignoring or even enhancing the use and abuse of drugs because they fail to confront and demand responsible behavior from students and their parents. The other institutions of the community, such as police, courts, human service agencies, or private or public mental health agents, often appear to educators and parents as less helpful. Thus, school and parents often come to feel alone in dealing with alcohol and drug abuse, with little or no support from the community and its treatment and intervention services.

Basically the student must come to seek and develop alternatives that contraindicate continued dependence on chemical solutions. In previous years it was assumed the individual student could not be expected to stop using mood-altering substances until he or she discovered a substitute; the psychological dependence upon drugs results from filling a need. Continued failure by some drug- and alcohol-abusing students to fully participate in and profit from alternatives has moved professionals to realize that continued use of alcohol and drugs while participating in alternative programs seriously detracts from the interest and energy the student has to apply to the alternative. Educators and counselors increasingly realize that abstinence from drug use is vital to benefiting from alternative programming.

Drug and alcohol use during school time often results in suspension or expulsion; this too may lead to some brief change in behavior. However, new behavior patterns are not likely to last unless the student's self-concept and success is enhanced through special settings where hope and confidence can be instilled. Successful programs, whether contained classes, separate schools, or residential treatment centers, require a systemic program perspective.

Reactions to alcohol and drug abuse are exercises in futility if the approach is not totally integrated and supported by the entire school system. Teachers and other concerned individuals must know what information is supported by fact and what stems from myth and rumor. At one time much information given to students was emotionally or deliberately distorted to threaten or scare them from using drugs. Such scare tactics tended to threaten and scare the adults far more than the youth. Actually, youth use their peers as authenticators of the benefits and liabilities of specific drug use. They need honest and accurate information about drugs and alcohol because distorted information is often used to deny legitimate information.

A 1979–80 Drug Task Force in Montgomery County, Maryland (a 30-member group of students, teachers, parents, police, health officials, and judges), recognized that drugs and alcohol permeated every facet of the school and community and that drug and alcohol use was a way of life for many youth. The Task Force recommended that school drug rules be strictly and consistently enforced (they had not been); that comprehensive drug education be provided to police and teachers (it had not been); that health, juvenile service, and police personnel work together with consistency (they had not been); that drug and alcohol education be provided from kindergarten through high school (it had not been); and that students begin to deal with the "why" of drug abuse rather than facts only. To accomplish this, schools must have: (a) systemic planning and coordination; (b) protection of the school environment from the use, possession, and distribution of drugs and alcohol; (c) counseling and treatment interrelated and intrasupportive of the educational process; and (d) concerted cooperation and coordination among parents, school, and other private and/or public services and agencies of the community.

WHAT EDUCATORS CAN AND SHOULD DO

The bottom line in the battle against drug abuse is what is going to be done by all concerned with the problem. This is in contrast to the approach of understanding the "why" of drug abuse. This is not to imply that understanding of the causes of drug abuse, as briefly outlined earlier, is not important; such a body of knowledge is essential to all concerned with the problem. Yet, in trying to understand the why, we often lose sight of the need to focus on the reality of the problem itself and on what can be done.

A successful action plan to combat adolescent drug abuse must be holistic and systemic in approach. The whole as well as the parts and the interaction of the parts must be understood and approached in order to have an effective action plan.

The parts or subsystems of the whole that must be addressed are as follows: the family system of the adolescent; the peer system of the adolescent; the adolescent's own idiosyncratic self-system; the situational or environmental system of the adolescent; and the community system of which the adolescent is a part. How much the parts or systems support each other and how much they interrelate becomes that adolescent's whole cognitive and emotional perception of reality. Each part or system must not only have its own action plan to combat drug abuse, but that plan must be positively correlated and synchronized with the action plan of other parts of the whole in order to change the whole. Each part must be understood independent of and in relation to the other parts.

The Educator and the Family System

Ask "how does (as opposed to why) this family system support a drug-abusing family member?" The "why" approach could provide us with a list of causes that relate to drug abuse but would not address the fact that many individuals from similar families come through intact and functioning without resorting to drug abuse. The "how" approach can help the family focus on action, behavior, and responsibility. For educators, this approach toward confronting an adolescent's drug-abuse problem involves collaborating with the family to establish and activate interventions and actions required to stop the drug-abusing behavior. The message given to the family is that the school can do its part only if the family, as the primary change agent, does its part; but correspondingly the family can most effectively do its part only if the school does its part. Systematic efforts are required and blaming is avoided.

The control for remediation of the problem is placed in the parents' hands; yet they are expected to continue working collaboratively with the school system. Schools accept responsibility for drug control and remediation within the school environment.

Educators must expect the parents to be responsible for their child's behavior and they must serve as a consultative, supportive resource to that parent/family. It requires saying to the parents, "Your child has a drug problem. What are you doing or what do you want to do about it? What do you want us to do to support you?" Educators must know and communicate clearly what the school can or cannot do as well as know or have access to staff who know the available referral treatment sources. Families must be told that, if they do not follow through, they and their child, not the schools, pay the long-range consequences. As stated earlier, holding the family responsible is not synonymous with blaming, for although this approach centers on the family's role, it can only be a constructive, worthwhile approach if viewed and operated through an interactional context. More important it can be constructive only if the family (parents) are helped to see that there is hope and a way in which they can get help for themselves and their child.

Those educators activating parental responsibility must become knowledgeable about family dynamics. Actions and intervention must be based upon an assessment of the family system and the role the student plays in his or her family.

Families in which the student has a drug-abuse-related problem typically display four or more of the following traits:

1. Unclear rules governing all facets of family life, chores, expectations.
2. Unclear or inconsistent consequences for broken rules.
3. Parents who are unable to agree on rules and consequences or who contradict each other's rules and consequences.
4. Fixed parental roles such as the mother as protector and comforter and the father as disciplinarian.
5. Father overinvolved in work often with a peripheral role to the family; mother (whether she works outside the home or not) overinvolved with the children.
6. No common time each day, such as dinner time, where the family gets together and communicates.
7. When the family is together, such as dinner time, time is usually filled with conflict and negativity.
8. Parents reluctant to establish a sense of values or afraid of verbalizing them because they might sound "old fashioned."

9. Communication is one-sided in the family; children prohibited from voicing their opinions.

10. Little parental interest shown in children's school work and extracurricular activities.

11. Parents discourage the child from bringing friends home.

12. Parents lack information about things that impinge on their children's lives (including drug usage).

13. Parents who take no stand against drugs or who use and abuse drugs themselves.

14. Parents that use their child as a confidant, placing extra worries on the child.

15. Parents that will not let their children grow up or who fail to prepare them for leaving home.

16. A home where there is little sense of caring and love.

Initially families may need help in venting their feelings about the problem. In helping the family to define or articulate the problem from their own point of view, educators should encourage them to discuss the type of support or help they need from the school. It is equally important for educators to express the problem from the school's point of view and to tell parents how they can support the school. Helping the family to think through an approach for solving the problem is essential. A referral to support services for those parents who need additional services may be necessary. It is beneficial if family, school administrators, teachers, and counselors can agree on an approach to solving the problem.

Before an approach is outlined, schools must clearly differentiate between dealing with drugs as a control issue and dealing with drug abuse as a treatment and treatment-referral concern. In terms of control, schools should have a clear policy that states "drugs and alcohol will not be tolerated in the schools." There should be a policy which refers all students observed (as opposed to suspected) in the use and possession or selling of drugs while on school property to the school administration and then to the police or law enforcement agencies. Most often suspension or expulsion is necessary.

Besides a clear articulation of the legal issue (including required actions by educators), the school must deal with the problem of how to get adolescents suspected of having drug-abuse problems into treatment. The following is an outline of possible steps in a systemic holistic approach to this problem.

Step 1: Identification. Often the classroom teacher is the first one to suspect that a student has a drug problem. Recognition of the problem often is *not* because the student looks "high" or "stoned" but is a result of the students' changing or unacceptable behavior. This may include such behaviors as falling asleep in class, not completing school work, skipping classes, and disruptive classroom behavior. These behaviors should be focused upon because they can be readily and concretely addressed. Of course these behaviors do not always indicate drug or alcohol abuse. (a) Once these behaviors are identified, the teachers make a referral to the guidance office, other school helping service, or administrative staff. (b) It is usually helpful for the school guidance person to clearly rule out the teacher's behavior as a cause for a student's acting out. Usually a teacher can be excluded as the major cause of the student's acting out if the teacher has few problems with most other students. Sometimes a teacher may be contributing to the problem but is not its direct cause. In such cases, intervention at the classroom level will not be sufficient to change the situation. (c) It is essential that the teacher, an administrator, and the student come together to clearly define unacceptable behavior and that the student be told that a parental conference will be called.

Step 2: *Calling a parental conference*. Both parents should be called about the problem and told that the school expects them to come in. The following guidelines will be helpful in getting parents to come. (a) Clearly define the problem behavior and ask for the parents' help and input as a way of precluding the escalation of the problem. (b) If resistance is met, identify the possible outcomes of problem escalation. (c) Spend as little time as possible on the telephone discussing the problem. Insist on an appointment, stressing that the problem could get out of hand beyond your level of action. (d) If there are two parents at home, stress the need for both parents to come in. This is to insure that both parents work together and to rule out one parent's sabotaging a school-parent agreement. (e) Make sure the teacher and other appropriate school staff are present for the conference and that they are clearly in agreement in defining the problem from the school's point of view. However, do not include so many school personnel that parents are likely to be overwhelmed. (f) Allow at least one hour for meeting with parents plus another half-hour for a parent/teacher/counselor follow-up with the student.

Step 3: *Focus of parental conference*. Purposes of parental conferences are: (a) to define the problem and make the problem a concern of the parents; (b) to get parents to state what they are now doing and what they plan to do about the problem; (c) to get parents to state what they want the school to do and how they are going to support the school in its effort; and (d) to get parents to agree on getting and following through with outside help if such help is warranted.

Essential in accomplishing the above is to clearly, without any "you are at fault" messages, make the resolution of the child's problem a conjoint child/parental responsibility, using the school as an ancillary resource in carrying out that responsibility. There are useful communication strategies in working with parents, such as: (a) Ask parents how they handle problems at home. Get specific: when he/she does such, you do such, and then what? (b) Clearly identify whether parents have rules; if they do not, emphasize why rules are important. (c) Determine whether parents agree on the rules and what they do to follow up if rules are broken. (d) If there are no clear-cut rules, relate this to the school's situation. For instance, say "I think it's especially difficult to get John to follow rules in the classroom since there do not seem to be clear-cut rules for him at home. Although this may work for you at home, it doesn't for us here. What do you suggest we could do to see that he obeys the rules here at school?" (e) Keep the discussion focused on the student's unacceptable behavior at school and on what the parents can do about it in concert with the school. (f) Try to come up with a parent-initiated and school-supported plan of action.

Parents who make no rules or who give inappropriate or inconsistent consequences are behaving in many ways like immature and irresponsible children. Such families almost certainly need more long-term help than most schools can give. Nevertheless, the message in the parental conference should be to clearly hold parents responsible to develop and carry through with their part of the plan of action. We cannot expect students to be responsible if we cannot get adults to act responsibly as parents.

Step 4: *Family conference*. After a plan of action has been determined, have the student come into the room. Have the *parents* present to their child an analysis of the problem and the agreed-upon plan of action.

If the parents cannot come up with a plan of action, *do not hold the family conference*. Schedule a second parental conference within a week with the expectation that the parents will come in with a definite plan. In some cases it is helpful to end such a first session with some strategy which heightens family concern for the problem such as: (a) should the child continue to act out before the next session, he/she will be suspended for a day; (b) for severe cases, the child may be suspended, or expelled until the next parental conference.

Step 5: Follow-up: Network and transfer sessions. If part of the parental plan is to get help, the school must follow through to see that it is obtained. One way this can be done is for the educator to ask to be included in the first session with the treatment agent (an effective but seldom-used strategy). This serves several purposes. First, it provides a clear message to treatment professionals and agencies that the school is recognizing its responsibility as one system interfacing with another. Second, parents and professionals receive the message that the school does indeed expect follow-through. Third, it makes clear that the school as well as the family will play a continuing role. Therapists who are unwilling to allow such participation may be questionable as referral sources.

As an important part of follow-up, it is necessary for the schools and the parents to have a clear understanding of their future relationship. For example, future misbehavior in school should result in immediate parental notification and a family/school conference. Schools should also keep parents informed periodically of the positive performance and behavior of the adolescent. Too often educators fail to notify parents about student social and academic successes.

An essential objective in the above approach is the expansion of the network of responsibility. Little will be gained if the student's problem is seen as his or hers alone or if the student continues to see the problem as solely the school's problem. The school certainly has a role and responsibility but only in the context of the larger familial and community system of which the student is a part.

The community system. It is important that the larger community network (the neighborhood, the parents of the adolescent's friends, the school, and the mental health treatment system itself) *not* support drug-abusing behavior.

A school system must take a stand against the possession, use, and sale of drugs on school premises. The parents in turn must support a strong anti-drug/alcohol school system policy in order for the policy to be effective. Denial of this supportive interrelationship means support of drug-abusing behavior.

Parents should also be supportive of each other in their anti-drug and alcohol posture. Neighbors, those with young children as well as those with no children, should be supportive of parents with teenagers. Unfortunately, in many urban-suburban communities, there is no such support network. Neighbors do not know one another and parents do not know the parents of their children's friends. This lack of support aids drug and alcohol-abusing behavior.

The school. The school cannot carry out its anti-drug role without the community. Thus, the school must assume some responsibility for the community.

First, the school must set up a process of developing and enforcing a "no drugs in the school" policy. The school in doing this should have a committee composed of school personnel, parents (representatives from junior/senior high-school PTAs might be used), public and private agency personnel (juvenile court, health, or mental health), and police to help draft such a policy. Once drafted, each PTA group should get all parents to vote on the implementation of the policy. The school policy should include a "Policy Monitoring Committee" to insure uniform and consistent implementation and adherence to the Board of Education–approved program.

The above procedure will result in broad acceptance and involvement and will help to insure that the school system, parents, and related agencies carry out their roles and responsibilities regarding that policy. A principal who is reluctant to carry out the policy because it acknowledges the existence of drug problems in the school is served notice by the parental constituency that he or she is expected to and will be supported in carrying out that policy. Parents who question the right of the school to have such a policy are informed that the larger community backs the school in enforcing the policy.

In short, insuring the enforcement of a community-backed "no drugs in school" policy puts in place another important element in a holistic approach to combating drug abuse. The limits of such a policy are clear. It does not insure that young people will not use drugs, but it does to a reasonable extent insure that the schools will become increasingly drug free. Those students that use and abuse drugs certainly can continue to do so before or after school and off of school grounds, but the policy does reduce or eliminate the pervasive drug culture subsystem that often exists in many schools. Those students that have experienced peer intimidation to use drugs will benefit from the decrease of drug availability in school.

Another important part of a school system's battle against alcohol and drug abuse is a program of formal drug and alcohol education provided to students from kindergarten through the twelve grades. It is important that such a program be age appropriate and include more than pharmacology. Educational ramifications of drug usage, value clarification, decision-making skills, and psychological, sociological, and peer pressure aspects of drug abuse should be included as well. Teachers should be well trained and knowledgeable in the field and the subject should be integrated into a well-planned health-related series.

The juvenile justice system. An effective "no illegal substances" school policy is one that takes the school out of a judgment role. The observed use or sale of drugs and possession of drugs should have a clear set of consequences. For the first offense these consequences may include suspension, notification of parents, and a report of the incident to the police. Involvement of the police is essential, for the law has been broken. Educators must work closely with the police and juvenile justice system to develop a clear set of guidelines and expectations of how both the police and the juvenile justice system will support the position of the school. In many jurisdictions, the police have considerable latitude as to whether the juvenile is formally or informally charged. Optimally this latitude works in the best interests of a student and his or her family. In working with a juvenile, the goal should be to help and treat, as opposed to punish. Thus police can often informally retain a case if the charge is a minor one (that is, it is a first offense, the parents are supportive, or the child appears to have "learned a lesson"). In some cases, the police even handle more severe incidents informally because, from a judicial point of view, the charge will not hold up in juvenile court for a variety of reasons, such as violation of due process, rules of evidence, and so forth. Nevertheless, to an adolescent and his or her family, the inconvenience of going through the police station case processing, even if the charge is not forwarded, is in itself a deterrent. It is important that the processes used by the police are understood and backed by the school system. Communication and understanding between police, juvenile courts, and the school should help to avoid the kinds of misunderstandings that result in a school system's saying "we refer drug offenders to the police and they never do anything" or in the police saying "the school refers kids to us with petty, irrelevant, and unsubstantiated charges." Similarly, with such a relationship the school and police are unlikely to complain that "the juvenile court makes a mockery of our authority by not properly disciplining juvenile offenders." Schools need to understand and accept that there are limits to what the police and the rest of the juvenile justice system can do in terms of clearly defining and consistently applying procedures, guidelines, roles, and expectations.

The mental health treatment system. A school's ability to combat drug abuse effectively must also be tied to and coordinated with the mental health treatment system. Two issues are important to consider regarding the school's role, responsibility, and posture. First, as part of its "no drugs in school" policy, the school should have a clear set of guidelines that encourage treatment of students (and their families) who seek help for a drug- or alcohol-abuse problem and for students suspected of having a drug- or alcohol-abuse problem. Treatment is particularly important for students who present other symptoms, such as school failure, persistent hostility to authority, chronic truancy, and so forth. Treatment should be encouraged and kept separate from the more punitive consequences of drug use. There should be a school-based person, for example, a school counselor or school nurse, that a young person could go to and to whom a teacher can refer a student suspected as a substance abuser. Confidentiality should be maintained in these cases. There should be clear guidelines protecting these students from being treated in a punitive or legal way, as would occur in cases of possession. The message to students should be "if you have a substance-abuse problem and need help, we will help you and your family obtain such assistance."

School systems should become aware of the mental health services available to help drug and substance abusers and should make referrals only to those agencies and professionals that are committed to working *with* the school and the family. Of course, the school has no ultimate control over the treatment choice a family makes; however, it does have control over its recommendations of treatment resources. Those agencies that do not want to work collaboratively with the schools or that never have the time for case coordination conferences or that wish to work only with very motivated students and families should be avoided.

Parents as members of a community. Those neighbors or other parents with which a family co-exists—though often without any meaningful interaction—must be a part of the action plan. Because neighbors and other parents are so rarely involved, parents often feel "isolated." Communities most afflicted by this type of isolation, such as urban areas and their suburbs, often consider the school to be the one identifiable symbol of community wholeness. If a school fails to help this important parent and community system unite, defeat is likely in the battle against drug abuse. The group which develops the school drug policy should be expanded to include members of the religious community, business community, and other neighbors with varied ethnic, class, and racial backgrounds. This group should develop a "Community Bill of Responsibility" that focuses on counteracting community disorganization through actions and responsibilities in support of families. For example, the "Bill" could include statements similar to the following:

(1) As parents we encourage other parents and members of the business and general community to contact us if they see our children engaged in any questionable behavior.

(2) As parents we welcome calls from parents of our children's friends.

(3) At all times, we will expect our children to let us know where they are.

(4) We will check with other parents to assure that parties and other events are properly supervised. We encourage our teenagers (17 and below) to have parties without drugs or alcohol at our own homes and we will not sanction our teenagers' attendance at any party where such substances are permitted.

(5) We support the right of parents to be parents and expect our children to respect the rules of our family.

(6) We expect our children to attend school and try their best. If they no longer want to go to school, they will be expected to go to work and pay their fair share of room and board.

If a high school is interested in mobilizing parents against drug abuse, two basic strategies will be needed. First, a list of potential abusers must be made. Every perceptive school staff member knows which young people are known as "pot heads." Often these students sit together in the school cafeteria (as do the "jocks," the "intellectuals," and others), come to school together, and leave school together. The school administration can call the parents of such students and, while making it clear that they are not accusing the student, ask them to attend a meeting of parents concerned about their children and drugs. Maybe one or two parents would be willing to organize the meeting. At the meeting, school personnel should encourage parents to discuss how they can support one another in creating a drug-free environment. Since these parents have children who know and socialize with one another, this may be the first step toward parents' uniting in constructive action to combat drug abuse in their communities.

The second step in getting the community involved is a school-sponsored community meeting to combat drug abuse. The first part of the community meeting could be spent informing the parents of the nature of the problem and how they are needed. The second part of the meeting could divide parents into groups based on their children's probable interaction. Parents of students from the same feeder junior high schools might be grouped together or parents of students riding the same bus to school or parents living in the same area. In the groups, parents might be encouraged to talk about how isolated they feel or how out-of-control they can become with regard to their children and their children's friends. They can also discuss how they can be supportive of one another and develop their own "Bill of Responsibilities" regarding substance abuse and related destructive behavior. Finally, these parents can be encouraged to discuss a follow-up commitment to continue their dialogue, support, actions, and planning.

Conclusion

The school, as both a respected social institution and a primary influence in the lives of young people, has a unique opportunity to elicit support from all segments of the social systems surrounding substance-abusing youth. To do so will take commitment and determination. Unfortunately, a tremendous sense of hopelessness and helplessness vis-à-vis the drug "epidemic" must be overcome. However, once a holistic approach is embraced and all systems impacting these youth are mobilized, the sense of isolation felt by many will begin to wane. The powerlessness felt by subsystems previously operating alone will be replaced by a sense of unity and control. Against this united, systemic attack, the power of adolescent, peer-supported drug and alcohol abuse will greatly diminish.

References

Guerin, P. J., Jr. *Family therapy, theory and practice.* New York: Gardner Press, 1979.

Haley, J. *Problem solving theory.* San Francisco: Jossey-Bass, 1977.

Kaufman, E., & Kaufman, P. N. (Eds.). *Family therapy of drug and alcohol abuse.* New York: Gardner Press, 1979.

Manatt, M. *Parents, peers, and pot.* Alcohol, Drug Abuse, and Mental Hygiene Administration, Public Health Service, National Institutes on Drug Abuse, 5600 Fishers Lane, Rockville, Maryland, DHEW Publication No. (ADM) 79-812, 1979.

Minuchin, S. *Families and family therapy.* Cambridge: Harvard University Press, 1974.

Satir, V., Stachowiak, J., & Taschman, A. *Helping families to change.* New York: Jason Aronson, 1977.

Supportive Therapies

18

E. Lakin Phillips

There has been an enormous proliferation of counseling and psychotherapy theories and practices during the past decade (Harper, 1975; Parloff, 1977; Phillips, 1977; Phillips, Gershenson & Lyons, 1977). There have also developed a number of supportive, auxiliary, or alternative modes of therapy and counseling (Lester, 1977). Most of the papers and articles about supportive therapies spring from the arts—music, poetry, art, and dance—but some increase in interest is related to more objective areas of study, such as use of the computer. This chapter will review a number of supportive therapies, from a wide variety of settings, which have both classroom and clinical applications.

Before describing the various supportive therapies, some attention should be given to the notion of "support" in this context. Are supportive therapies always adjunctive and auxiliary, or only supportive in the sense of bolstering up, of being consonant with some principal therapeutic modality such as face-to-face, verbal therapy (Lester, 1977)? Are supportive therapies brought in when regular therapy bogs down or in lieu of regular therapy? Do supportive therapies "piggy-back" main avenues of therapy such as behavior therapy, psychoanalysis, or nondirective therapy?

There appears to be no clear definition of supportive therapy. It may function as the main modality of a therapy, as an auxiliary to one, or it may be an equally important parallel course of therapy in relation to any other regular, verbal, face-to-face therapy. Supportive therapies may also be used in combination with one another: dance and music, art and drama, drama and dance, and so on; sometimes these combinations work apart from any kind of regular therapy and sometimes in juxtaposition to it. The patterns are constantly changing since the promulgators of supportive therapies are "doing their own thing" and pay little attention to broad theoretical, research, or clinical considerations of how supportive therapies fit into the larger picture. There is sometimes great excitement among the supportive therapy promoters, enough to carry these therapists along their own paths without regard to how the therapies arose, what their essential functions might be, how they could be improved upon, how they could be explicitly woven into other therapeutic contents, how they might be researched, or how they might be applicable to selective types of fairly well-defined patient or client populations. However, major modalities of regular, face-to-face therapy have never accomplished much in answering these more searching questions, so we cannot expect the supportive therapies to open new theoretical or clinical leads; we can only hope that they contribute somewhat to the versatility of therapists of all persuasions and develop ways of contacting patients or clients that speak to the relatively unique needs of different people and set people on pathways toward self-exploration, self-development, and behavior change.

Regardless of any possible superficiality one might attribute to supportive therapies, they may be viewed positively as contributing to an enlarged data-base for studying and bringing about behavior or personality change. If painting, dance, or music can lead a person to self-expression, self-development, and change without using verbal conceptualizations, then we have learned something about personality and behavior change in the process. Many changes are not mediated by words or verbal conceptualizations and occur as a result of stimulation and reinforcement between the person and his/her social environment. There are no a priori reasons, then, why supportive therapies—many of which lack either verbally controlled face-to-face interactions or verbal conceptualizations and communications—should not "work" in many settings with different types of clients or patients. A look at some of their characteristic strengths and weaknesses follows.

WRITING THERAPY

Writing as a wholly independent therapy was probably first used by Phillips and his students in the early 1960s (Phillips & Wiener, 1966; Test, 1964). This is not to say that writing was not previously used in supplemental ways or in connection with temporary halts in the usual psychotherapy or counseling routine (Alston, 1957; Burton, 1965; Freud, 1959; Kew & Kew, 1963); but writing as a modality during which the therapist and patient never meet nor otherwise interact, in which the usual therapeutic relationship is largely suspended, was probably first utilized by Phillips. That writing could *wholly* substitute for face-to-face interaction is, itself, remarkable, for all of the meaning, the nuances, the easy give-and-take of interview interaction, the subtleties of social exchange are wholly suspended. Both therapist and patient form notions of the other, but they are based on no first-hand contact and may be more mythical and inferential than realistic. For better or worse, relationships are minimal in writing therapy and completely subservient to the written word.

A set of criteria was offered by Phillips and Wiener (1966) for the conduct of writing therapy. These included: allowing the patient (client) to write freely about any topic; limiting the protocol to about one hour's writing (to simulate regular interview times of 50–60 minutes); requiring the patient to come to the clinic and write in a notebook rather than from his/her home or elsewhere; and the keeping of the whole protocol (by both patient and therapist) in this notebook in a locked file, accessible to no other person. Writing is scheduled one or two times per week in most cases. As a rule, also, the therapist replies to the patient in terms of a theoretical structure that includes the following: Ask for more information if a point seems vague or incomplete in the patient's writing; explain to the patient what his/her behavior *might* have meant or implied (providing structure for the reported behavior, such as "You must have been terribly angry with her" or "You write in reference to John as if you felt he imposed on you much of the time—is that correct?" and so forth); relate previous writings to current ones in order to tie up loose ends in the patient's thinking and observations; pull together apparently similar items and label them ("All of these interactions with your mother suggest you are too dependent upon her and hesitate to act without her expressed approval?" or "Now you're ticked off with Bob and Ralph, Jane and Susan—what goes with all these interactions?"). Usually the therapist marks and numbers significant words, phrases, or passages in the margins in order to provide handy references to the client and to get replies which are as specific as possible in the return writing. Often too the writing therapy is conducted for one semester since that period of time generally lends itself well to the schedules of the student (client/patient) and the therapist; but exceptions do occur and some writing therapy efforts can be conducted on a monthly basis for up to two or three years.

In an early study done by Test (Phillips & Wiener, 1966), it was shown that face-to-face, group, and writing therapy produced similar results psychometrically (on the MMPI), and similar grade increases over a semester's time; writing therapy held a barely reliable edge over the other therapies among university students seeking help for personal, social, or academic problems. However, writing therapy was more conservative in the use of therapist time and showed less attrition than did the other therapies. In this study, clients were assigned on a rotational basis to individual therapy, group therapy, or writing.

Phillips et al. (1977) studied writing therapy among 17 college students and reported gains in four areas of measurement: reduced MMPI scores on depression and psychasthenia, more outgoing and less introspective on the Edwards Personal Preference Schedule, gains in self-understanding and self-management according to the clients' own self-ratings, and improved problem-statement and problem-solving as judged by independent judges reading the client's first, fifth, and ninth protocols in a series of 10 time-limited writing sessions.

Informal reports on the use of writing therapy among prison inmates, high-school "drop-outs," and vocational-school students indicate that all clients liked and responded well to writing, attrition was relatively low, all queried said they would resume or continue writing were it possible, and 90% said they would recommend its usefulness to others (Phillips, 1977a).

One of the advantages of writing, as well as with some other forms of supportive therapy, is its economy in time. If clients or patients are writing, using the tape recorder, or engaging in some bibliotherapy, these activities can be scheduled at any time; a review of the protocol or a report by the therapist can be arranged at the therapist's convenience; and replies or reports or suggestions by the therapist can also be scheduled at will. Usually the amount of time a therapist spends in reviewing and replying to writing therapy is about 15 to 20 minutes per client protocol (based on an hour's writing).

A decided advantage for training is also seen in the use of writing therapy. The fledgling therapist has time to consider the protocol, check his/her reply over with a supervisor, and see continuity in the patient's progress (or lack of it) over time. The whole record is right there, hence obscurity and obfuscation are reduced and the therapy may go more directly to the heart of the problem. This advantage also works to support research. One can study the patient's use of adjectives (negative or positive), references to self and others, problem-solving tactics, distress and relief signs, the length of the protocol, the number of different or similar problems, and many other issues. Since the written protocol is a "natural" product of the client's behavior, one is always close to the life of the person seeking help and artificialities of time, place, and convenience in the life of the patient are overcome.

Although writing therapy has been used as a wholly independent and nonsupplementive form of therapy, there is no reason that it cannot be combined with any other supportive or major therapeutic undertaking. Indeed, in the history of the use of writing as a form of therapy, it has been mostly used in supportive or adjunctive roles (Lester, 1977); it is important to realize that it can be used in either way—supportive or as the major undertaking—and that its versatility is just now being realized (Lester, 1977; Phillips, 1977a; 1977b; Phillips et al., 1977).

Teachers can use writing in several ways: By asking students to keep brief written logs on their emotional states; by having the student write about his/her emotional reactions to classroom, social, and academic issues; and by conducting regular exchanges in written form with or without face-to-face exchanges. These efforts could greatly enhance the teacher's role and effectiveness in meeting student emotional needs in lieu of the teacher's personal investment of time with the student. Especially useful with new students, handicapped learners, or those with debilitating personal, social, or emotional problems, writing is a direct avenue of personal expression and one with considerable impact on student and teacher.

BIBLIOTHERAPY

Perhaps the most voluminous literature among all the supportive therapies is to be found under the topic of "bibliotherapy" (Baron, 1978; Berry, 1978; Hynes, 1975). Here the client/patient/reader is referred to relevant printed material, tailored as much as possible to the individual's needs and interests. Most effort in this area of supportive work finds its way into published lists of books, pamphlets, articles and the like, thought to be of value for the client.

The use of bibliotherapy—or, more accurately, the printed word—does not lend itself well to research and not much research has been done on it. However, one might question clients or patients as to the seeming relevance of books or articles read, get ratings on the value of the readings, make checklists of the ideas found (and used) from printed material, and obtain narrative accounts on how the printed materials were of help. These approaches to the use of bibliotherapy materials have not been extensively pursued; approaches to research that establish a more finite set of references covering common problems in realistic, practical, and instructive ways are needed.

The rationale for bibliotherapy is that others have experienced and thought extensively about the kinds of problems the current client is presenting, that these printed materials are fairly thorough and systematic accounts of the problems at hand, and that through vicarious experiences can come emotional relief, problem-solving, and the development of better attitudes on the patient's part. Inherent in the use of bibliotherapy is the observation, also found in writing therapy, that what is written down is somehow more viable than spoken words. We speak far more than we write; writing is a distillation of what one might say or what one has thought. The pointedness of the written word, its "official" status, and its terseness are all advantages if the message is at all on the mark. This seems to be true whether one is referring to his/her own writing or to the writing of others. The written word has an almost biblical significance. It might be noted that "It is written . . ." is a common expression connoting authority, truth, and relevance. Bibliotherapy capitalizes on this bias to a considerable extent.

An additional value is that extant literature in lieu of personal consultation—or along with such consultation—can help the person with emotional problems. The commonality in personal distress is striking, and the relevance of many written accounts of how persons have experienced, overcome, and grown through such distress can often be communicated reasonably well to the naive subject. Themes may range from "pep talks" through emotional grappling with serious problems to actual problem-solving techniques (Phillips, 1977b). Mostly, however, from published bibliographies of bibliotherapy the references are on an experiential basis and the initial approach to bibliotherapy is usually taken on these grounds.

Recent years have shown some growth in studying attitude change as a function of assigned readings. McClaskey (1971) studied bibliotherapy among emotionally disturbed patients. Tobias (1973) referred persons to behavioristic writings as his approach to bibliotherapy among weight-control patients. White (1973) used bibliotherapy among black persons in helping roles. Zucaro (1972) employed the assignment of written materials to change negative attitudes toward blacks. These studies are significant for several reasons: They show that behavior or attitude change can be promoted by and through the printed word, that some attitude change is associated with behavior change, especially in matters relating to self-control. Above all, these studies show that bibliotherapy effects can be researched, a matter of some consequence.

Raising the issue of research on bibliotherapy brings up the question of certain classical works in bibliotherapy and the thought that has been given to this form of therapy. Appel (1944) wrote about bibliotherapy, along with interpretive therapy and the use of poetry therapy, over thirty years ago, thus displaying an early sensitivity to the issues posed by bibliotherapy and a recognition of the need for research on this (then) promising modality. Even earlier Bryan (1939) raised the question as to whether there could be a science of bibliotherapy and concluded that there might well be. An early article on the use of bibliotherapy among hospitalized patients and adolescents appeared many years ago. Schneck (1945) noted that research was needed and that then-current trends might be expected to produce research reports on bibliotherapy.

Berry's recent activities in bibliotherapy (Berry, 1978) recognizes clearly the need for more empirical research. He and his students have begun to do pilot work on the use of bibliotherapy among college-age adolescents seeking help for emotional problems or pursuing self-development ends.

In summary, it might be said that bibliotherapy is emerging as a major thrust among current therapies; it is not simply filling a passive role as a supportive or supplementary therapy. Research studies are beginning to emerge, and the use of assigned readings is spreading to ever-wider populations, with an emphasis on adolescents, although applicability to all age groups and circumstances seems evident. How well bibliotherapy can lead to behavior change—weight control, better problem-solving in interpersonal contexts, decision-making about important events in life, stopping smoking, developing social skills appropriate to common social contexts, and so forth—remains to be seen. It may be that reading about others' experiences in specific areas is different from a more general attitude change (such as becoming less depressed) and that combining bibliotherapy with explicit programs of a behavioral nature will further extend bibliotherapy into new and more penetrating directions. At least bibliotherapy can serve many useful emotional relief purposes; in time it may be extended to a host of more specific problems, especially among adolescents whose social skills and high-level peer pressures need to be dealt with in every-day situations (Phillips, 1978).

Bibliotherapy lends itself well to the teacher's use with students. Students can pursue references on their own, teachers can supply book, article, and pamphlet lists, and the library can set aside special sections for "self-reference" reading. Important, though, is not just the supplying of bibliographic materials, but the feedback from the students on what is helpful and how it can be pursued.

POETRY THERAPY

The use of poetry in therapeutic settings is a natural spinoff from bibliotherapy. In fact, many bibliotherapy reference lists include articles on poetry therapy. Poetry therapy, like bibliotherapy, has enjoyed a resurgence in recent years (Baron, 1978; Berry, 1978; Hynes, 1976). Sometimes the line between the two approaches using the printed word are not drawn; they are used interchangeably.

Aside from reading the poetry of others for therapeutic purposes, there is always the use of poetry written and discussed in therapy by the patient or poetry written by patients and discussed in group settings.

Many uses are cited for poetry from a psychotherapeutic standpoint: It can help reintegrate the alienated patient into society, serve empathic, cathartic, and curative ends (Anant, 1975). Anant suggests using poetry therapy in four stages: listening to poetry read aloud, the actual recitation of the poetry, assimilation of its meaning, and the feeling or emotional responses from one's own life that emanate from these contacts with poetry.

Andrews (1975) has written similarly of the use of poetry. Sharing poetic images promotes a feeling of dignity and helps to objectify feelings and thoughts. In this way poetry is a kind of carrier of emotional messages leading toward the objectification of emotions.

As one might expect from a "depth" psychology standpoint, the use of poetry and other supportive efforts is said to help make the unconscious conscious (Heninger, 1977). Whether such results are obtained or even necessary remains moot; what is common, however, is that once the patient or client has a medium of expression suitable to his/her taste, the utilization of the medium to express the self is certainly common and valid. One might center in on emotional expression, Heninger observed, by taking a word or phrase that is emotionally laden and working it over poetically; the word or phrase might be the patient's own product or from the writings of others.

Lerner (1976a) points up the similarities between poetry therapy and other arts used in therapy—dance, music, painting—and asserts that these convections need to be explored; especially if we are to move to more clarity about what poetry therapy is, or might become, or if the therapists wish to move toward an integration of all the arts in relation to psychotherapy.

In another article, Lerner (1976b) relates poetry therapy to semantics and suggests that the role of semantics be clearly noted. Among the important strictures here are the familiar Korzybsky statements that the word is not the thing, the map is not the territory, and the symbol is not the thing symbolized. Lest one confuse words with things, Lerner cites caution, and this differentiation might well make the use of words (poetry) more therapeutic. Perhaps in poetry therapy words are used to speak more about feelings than about things.

Poetry therapy in groups is a natural approach (Pietropinto, 1975). Poetry may help not only the individual to emotional clarification and expression but in group settings, Pietropinto says, this benefit of poetry is enhanced. The person writes, presents, and discusses his/her poetry in the group setting and receives the same benefits from other group members. People learn that their respective concerns are shared, they are not alone, and the sharing has a cathartic value. Following such a disclosure of one's emotions, it might be expected that changes in overt behavior will occur, but this is a matter that needs to be researched.

Putzel (1975) discussed the use of poetry from different psychotherapeutic vantage points: Freudian, Jungian, and humanistic-gestalt. She puts more emphasis on the process of writing a poem and less on it as a product and relates poetic criticism to the poetry per se rather than to the poet personally. This author branches into discussing the nature of poetry, the nature of man, and other broad philosophical problems, thereby raising to a high level the whole of therapeutic poetry.

In a brief article, Ross (1975) waxes somewhat grand in discussing poetry therapy, explaining how poetry is part of 14 different therapeutic approaches and that it is a safe way of promoting self-discovery and self-expression. He discusses the anthropology of poetry, its linguistic and cognitive aspects, and how poetry relates to one's state of emotional release and freedom.

Silverman (1977) suggests the use of poetry to determine mental illness, personality functioning, and behavioral manifestations. He considers poetry an important ancillary tool in psychological, educational, and rehabilitation programs and stresses its self-disclosure aspects.

Poetry therapy has been used more as a supportive therapy than as a major modality, and it has often been used in active conjunction with verbal, face-to-face therapy. Too often, however, one is left with the feeling that poetry in therapy reaches for ultimate emotional states, for the revelation of inner feelings, and for profound self-disclosure. If one thinks of simple rhymes, jingles, and rhythmic statements, one is reminded that any such poetic efforts may have a communicative effect on the listener and on the producer. Popular songs are full of trite poetry, yet they seem to have an effect on people. More work is needed on how effective it is to put feelings and ideas into rhymed (and unrhymed) verse, to share these with others, and to use the simple self-disclosure aspects to enhance communication. The systematic study of poetry might well include the use of poetry one has written exclusively for oneself as well as poetry written with the intention of sharing it with others. If poetry is truly effective as a revealer of mood and of feeling and a promoter of personality and behavior change, these benefits might well come as readily in individual therapy (or in individual settings without formal psychotherapy) as they would in group therapy or shared settings.

The writing of poetry is a natural vehicle for the teacher. Classroom exercises in English, as well as other subjects, lend themselves well to poetry writing and discussions. A portion of English classes, group therapy writing, and other mental hygiene efforts can readily include poetry written by established poets or by the participants. Emphasis should not be on poetry qua poetry, that is, the technical aspects of poetry and verse but on the communicative value for the participants. Teachers can keep notebooks of these contributions and in a few semesters' time can produce a substantial contribution to the use of poetry in emotional communication in the classroom.

DANCE THERAPY

The generalization that seems to emerge in reading about all kinds of supportive therapies is that any self-expression that is truly spontaneous and genuine can have therapeutic benefits. People suffer in life because of conflicts and frustrations, but often they *continue* to suffer because of lack of communication, disclosure, and self-expression. Any modality that can help overcome these inhibitions and broaden the basis for facing feelings and taking actions would seem to be beneficial.

Dance is a natural form of human expression. Children dance spontaneously in many of their play activities and as they sing and display their emotions. Learning to dance is an important adolescent social skill, and dancing as a form of communicating with others is common throughout life. To dance, to share movement and grace, and to express how one feels should, on a priori grounds, be a productive therapeutic modality.

More often than not, dance therapy is openly considered to be supportive of other therapies, but it is also said to extend regular, face-to-face therapy by putting emphasis on self-expression, on overt movement, and on the social setting (Anderson, 1975).

People who are tense show the tension bodily—they walk stiffly, display a strained countenance, gesture abruptly and inappropriately, and so on (Goldner, 1976). Dance therapy promotes muscular relaxation which is itself often cathartic. Relaxing the body helps one to feel less angry and tense; the use of specific movements in dance "frees up" the extremities and puts them to uses unrelated to vigilance, stress, and aggressiveness. People might also be so tense as to suffer pain, especially in the dorsal spine and in the cervical spine areas; dance therapy can help to relax these areas of the body and to bring to the person's attention how tense and constricted she/he might have been.

Dance therapy fits in group settings as well as in individual ones (Hecox, Levine & Scott, 1976). In such cases physical therapy activities are combined with dance and accompanied by music. Programs attempt to thrust the body into space, to combine thoughts about what one wants to do with his/her body and various movements that actualize or symbolize the covert processes. One lives out and dances out one's covert feelings. According to Hecox et al. (1976), dance works well with rehabilitative patients in the adolescent and early adult years since there are many social motivations and reinforcers for dancing at these age levels.

In researching the value of dance therapy in a day-care center, Marek (1976) compared experimental group members in a six-week dance course with controls of the same background having verbal therapy only. Change measures were the Tennessee Self-Concept Scale and the Movement Dimension Scale, the latter including self-report and ratings by others. Although the results did not differentially support dance therapy as superior to verbal therapy, both groups did show gains in physical expression.

Sandel (1975) wrote about integrating dance therapy into other psychological treatment. Dance was used to provoke discussion of how the patients felt in relation to both their regular therapy and in relation to dance as a supportive therapeutic activity.

Although dance is a prospectively interesting and natural form of self-expression, just how it ties in with changes in behavior, including feelings, is moot. Too little research has been done on the actual benefits from dance therapy in contrast to either regular, face-to-face, verbal therapy or other artistic and supportive forms of therapy. Perhaps one possible answer concerning the efficacy of dance therapy will come from people choosing dance or, indeed, any other form of expressive therapy of a supportive nature. It is possible that supportive therapy modalities, especially among youth, are likely to contribute more to change if the modality is one of some importance to the person. Thus, perhaps one should offer many kinds of supportive therapy and let the patients choose their expressive style.

Dance is carried on already in most school settings. How easy it would be to encourage teachers to exhibit dance as emotional expression (thrust for anger or assertiveness, bending and cowering for retreat, jumping for joy, and so on). Let a class use as many emotions as possible in dance form and elaborate upon them for therapeutic purposes. Not a word need be spoken—the movements will tell all!

ART THERAPY

Art therapy has shown an enormous growth in interest and application in recent years. Many universities now have formal programs in which it can be practiced in rehabilitation centers, hospitals, day-care units, and in conjunction with individual and group psychotherapy. Art therapy has thus far made a larger and more convincing impression of its value than any other form of expressive, artistic, or supportive therapy.

Art is useful in establishing communication between the patient and his/her environment, especially the interpersonal environment. Goldberg (1976) reports on a case of a 14-year-old adolescent girl with predominant symptoms relating to echolalia; the use of paints, magic markers, and clay over a period of several months resulted in better communication between the girl and her therapist.

Art exhibits were combined with music and dance therapy among adolescent inmates of a correctional institution (Ney, 1976). The art programs helped the patients overcome inhibitions in self-expression, concentration, and feelings of self-adequacy. The author states that artistic expression aids in releasing self-expression (overcoming inhibitions), encouraging concentration and focus of attention, improving self-esteem, and facing up to and working through feelings.

Ratcliff (1977) did a study of fifteen 17-year-old high-school students comparing an "Old Masters Art College" (OMAC) art therapy technique with controls who received no such special art instruction. Results indicated a positive change in self-perception among those having the OMAC program as compared to the controls. The OMAC program is not a traditional art therapy procedure and may well recommend itself better to research activities than the less well-structured art therapy in common use.

Art therapy programs were supplemented by the use of videotape among hospitalized patients, day-care center patients, and a storefront adolescent counseling center. The videotape presentation of the art work served to promote discussion of the perceptual development of the patients (all groups) as well as to encourage "psychotherapeutic insight." The video supplement was said to have encouraged discussion, helped with focus on significant problems, and aided in putting emotional matters into perspective.

Wolff (1975) used art therapy in a community mental health center as a truly supplementary form of therapy. Art therapy did not replace regular therapy but served as an encouragement to "get therapy" among out-patients who otherwise might not have come in for counseling or therapy. Wolff reports the program was useful with adolescents as well as with parents, church officers, and school children.

Art therapy, unlike dance, music, and drama therapy, nets a specific, objective product. The works of art therapy stand for themselves: original expressions, examples of problem areas depicted in art, changes in the product over time, and the ability to correlate art therapy works with other, independent assessments of change such as tests, self-reports, and independent observations. There should, then, be more research on art therapy. The emphasis on all forms of artistic, supportive therapies is on disinhibiting the patients or clients and on encouraging the expression of feelings, attitudes, and experiential matters. While all of these are good and resourceful aims, the mere expression of feelings may not lead to personality and/or behavior change. It appears that self-expression when inhibited or when poorly controlled (as with impulsive disorders) does block behavior change, but the occurrence of disinhibited self-expression does not itself lead to change. Most writers on the subject of artistic forms of self-expression used therapeutically equate improved self-expression with general change. This is a topic that needs considerable research, especially among adolescents, who provide remarkable examples of both strong inhibition (schizoid withdrawal) and impulsivity (acting out, interpersonal aggressiveness, and so forth). Would self-expression which comes from the supplementary artistic therapies teach *control* to the impulsive persons and emotional *release* or disinhibition to the suppressed ones in the same way? Are some artistic forms of expression better for one than for the other? Is there a trigger-release factor in both inhibited and impulsive forms of personal and social behavior? These and related questions are important for assessing the value of supplemental forms of artistic therapy.

In a more practical and less research-centered way, art therapy could abound in classroom and general school settings. Students could volunteer for art therapy and then talk about their products in the light of their concerns; teachers could build considerable repertories of skills in encouraging, promoting, and assessing the value of art therapy for the normal as well as for the emotionally disturbed student.

DRAMA THERAPY

Drama, as discussed here, does not include the more well-known and frequently practiced "psychodrama," but rather combinations of verbal scenarios, dance, music, and movement as used with children and adolescents (Morgan, 1975). Improvisation is encouraged but the exact role of drama vis-à-vis each person and his/her problems remains unspecified.

Drama has also been used to cover a mixed bag of "body therapies": bioenergetics, structural integration, structural patterning, the Alexander technique, the Feldenkrais system, polarity therapy, the Lomi school, breath awareness, sensory awareness, massage, yoga, aikido, and so on. The differences and overlaps among such a plethora of offerings is baffling, and how each, as drama or bodily self-expression, comes over psychologically in terms of the patient's problems, especially among adolescents who display many "free-floating" concerns, is equally moot. One might just as well refer to a variety of rock-climbing and mountain-climbing activities as therapeutic (which they might well be!) by referring to precipitous mountains, jagged rocks, rocks over streams, climbing with and without ropes, and so on ad infinitum. Certainly there must be a central concern in dramatic forms of therapy and self-expression; whether one rubs his/her body in one place or another, stretches one or another group of muscles, exercises with and without aids, and so on, might make little or no difference. How to differentiate the therapy, as such, from the improved interpersonal contact that would presumably occur in any social gathering for any viable and common purpose is a difficult matter and one that needs much research (Shinoda, Matsumoto, Tokuyama, & Takeuchi, 1975). Only when the specific contributions of given therapeutic modalities can be associated with described before/after changes in personality can we begin to identify some reliable therapeutic gain. Meanwhile new forms of self-expressive therapy will continue to proliferate—which no one should oppose—claiming a wide variety of benefits, mostly subjective. A skeptical reader is needed for most of this literature (Rappaport, 1975; Shinoda et al., 1975).

To the teacher, however, technicalities of research with some overlap in methods and other nuances of knowledge acquisition should not act as a deterrent in the school or classroom. Drama, as therapy, can draw on original scripts or Shakespeare or the current cinema and stage and contribute much to self-expression. Words and gestures can combine to deliver a strong emotional message—for both the actor and the viewer.

MUSIC THERAPY

In a naive way, music has always been therapeutic. Music catches moods easily and well, is associated with profound past experiences and memories, and is integrated into the general culture to provide support for common forms of experience: jubilation, celebration, sorrow, pensiveness, and so on. We use music to create and sustain psychological states. Can we use music to change unwanted states (depression, for example) and to move the person to more positive levels of spirit, activity, and accomplishment? The answers to that question are far from complete.

Alvin (1975) asserts that music has always been used therapeutically for the physically handicapped and the mentally ill. Music can be used to bring diverse interests and people together to share a common purpose.

Music, as a socializer and strong social reinforcer (Arnold, 1975), has been used with other forms of psychotherapy, such as transactional analysis, to accompany highly structured experiences in group settings. Arnold used music to accompany Berne's six ways of structuring time as a basic focus. Weaving music (or other forms of therapy) into extant therapy with specific objectives in mind might be a way of optimizing the stronger aspects of both regular, formal therapy and self-expression.

Campbell (1976a, 1976b) reports on multiple uses of music with handicapped persons and on the training of music therapists. Since music often utilizes words, the words might replace or supplement verbalizations in psychotherapy, she states.

Popular music was used with teenagers in group therapy (Frances & Schiff, 1976) and was found to initiate interest in the group, promote the expression of opinion and feelings, and facilitate longer-range social contacts.

Using music for its rhythmic and psychomotor features has been reported on by Gollinitz (1975) as a way of supplementing and supporting motor, linguistic, cognitive, and psychological deficiencies among children and adolescents. Music was considered useful since it is economical, fits well with any other form of therapy, is nondoctrinaire, and is a universal experience outside of therapy.

Developmental problems among children and adolescents submit well to music therapy (Purvis & Samet, 1976); music was applied to a curriculum divided into four areas: academics, communication, behavior, and socialization.

McQueen (1975) reported on experimental work with music therapy among mentally handicapped children and adolescents. He used music to help the students increase their awareness of objects in the environment and of the environment itself. Experimental subjects, he reports, demonstrated a higher percentage of identification of the objects and environmental aspects of their lives among populations in two hospital settings. Music, in terms of its rhythm and lyricism, helped to identify the objects, associate them with other experiences, and solidify these memories for later use.

Music therapy might be researched more fully in terms of the types of music used—standard works of music identifying certain moods and attitudes; music used to identify materials to be learned by stressing their rhythmic and lyrical features (rhyming songs about common experiences); music as self-expression; and music as a social reinforcer. Utilizing music in a broad, undifferentiated way might not produce personality or behavior change, especially since music, more than art, drama, or dance, lends itself to moods. Also, since there is much extant music, drawing on it could greatly improve the uses of music for therapeutic purposes. It does appear that music as a medium of human experiences is far broader than its utilization in any therapeutic way; if that is true, music as an art form for personal and group expression may challenge therapists for years.

The classroom teacher could ask, "What mood does this poetry (play or other literary offering) suggest and what music shall we use with it?" Or the music teacher could play various musical compositions, ask students to "name the mood" or spirit of the music, and move toward a consensus. It could be that in a group setting music would set the pace and exemplify or encourage emotional/social contacts among participants.

THE COMPUTER

More objective forms of supportive therapy can also be considered. The computer, properly utilized, may refine some aspects of formal therapy (Lester, 1977). The computer is able to accept, collate, refine, and extend through inference many of the therapeutic processes extant in other forms of therapy. The computer adds a dimension of resourcefulness not found in the artistic forms of self-expression but at the same time it cannot accept just any data that might be offered by more artistic-based therapies. Whatever thinking occurs on the part of the therapist can presumably be simulated by the computer (Cassell & Blum, 1969; Chick, 1970; Fowler, 1968; Friedman, 1973).

The computer has been utilized in a number of ways in psychotherapy: In processing clinical records and in extracting needed data from larger masses of data; in making clinical decisions; in interviewing for specific purposes; in behavior therapy; and in vocational guidance. The computer is less biased, more resourceful, has better recall, can act more quickly to render decisions, can produce predictive data against which the client can measure his chances in one or another course of events, and can collate and store information on an extensive number of cases better than can any person or record-keeping system. Computers are, however, expensive and may not yield personal satisfaction to the clients receiving help (Melbus, Hershenson, & Vermillion, 1973). They also may not cover all the exigencies of importance in the lives of some people. A computer could, however, operate as the workhorse for a high percentage of those seeking help, particularly for limited problems, and then could be supplemented advantageously by the personal attention of therapists in more economical and focused ways.

The use of computers in training novice therapists might be considered (Loehlin, 1968). The computer could simulate a few common characteristics of a narrow range of clients and the tyro therapist could try out his/her reactions. Ways to structure and react to questions, the setting of limited goals, suggesting ways of working on goals, and ways of evaluating the possible attainment of goals could be programmed by the computer and, once learned, transferred by the novice therapist to additional cases. The computer in this instance would be acting like a very wise supervisor of therapy. Problems posed by high-school and college students, especially in the area of the handicapped, could be assimilated readily by the computer. To some extent these youthful populations can be expected to respond well to the structured way in which computers work and offer information.

In actual use the computer has some beneficial as well as unfavorable aspects (Greist, Gustafson, Strauss, Rowse, Laughren, & Chiles, 1973; Holtzman, 1960; Weizenbaum, 1976). On the beneficial side it might be time-shared by a number of therapists or counselors in various agencies, colleges, or universities to economic advantage; it might help to identify over time those cases that would respond most favorably to the computer itself; it could, correspondingly, identify those who are not yet ready to use the computer; and its value for many kinds of follow-up data and assessment would be enormously better than traditional studies of these types.

The classroom teacher has little or no recourse to computers but studying about their uses and abuses might help inform the teacher in various ways. The relative frequency of some kinds of problems in school settings—discipline problems, self-management problems, social withdrawing tendencies, and so forth—might be programmed in ways helpful not only to the students involved but might instruct teachers on more economical ways to intervene in many problem areas. Computers structure events and the structuring can be very helpful to all who are engaged in counseling roles.

THE TELEPHONE

It is surprising that the telephone has not been utilized more often in therapy and counseling, especially with adolescents who have a strong penchant for the phone as a medium of social exchange and reinforcement (Lester, 1973). The main use of the telephone has arisen from the development of "hot line" counseling and referral services conducted by universities and by community mental health centers mostly for emergency services. The present writer has informally used the telephone to advantage in a number of cases of psychotherapy: To make up for a lost appointment, to provide an alternative to a patient wishing to discuss very embarrassing content in other than a face-to-face setting, to provide for a needed interim appointment, and to meet a crisis that required immediate decision-making.

The telephone as a crisis resource has often been used in suicide prevention (Lester & Brockopp, 1973; McDonough, 1975). The interim, stop-gap use may be the optimal one for the telephone, and it may be the principal way in which the phone can contribute to therapy which no other modality can offer. Despite these advantages of the telephone, some ways in which its use might be contraindicated are as follows: If its use allows the therapy to become too impersonal; if it is used only to deal with crises to the neglect of longer-range issues; and if it is used as a way of avoiding relating to the therapist a more immediate concern. The phone may also be used to introduce and promote anonymity and to "shop around" for consultation that agrees with one's own biases, possibly postponing or preventing more salient therapeutic work. However, any modality or device (the computer, for example) can be misused; it is up to the professional to optimize the advantages of the telephone and not succumb to its transient characteristics.

Telephone calls may be sustained over time, however, in lieu of face-to-face meetings and thus serve a useful purpose even in the vein of continuing therapy. Like writing therapy, telephone therapy could sustain a therapeutic undertaking if both or all parties concurred on its relevance. As used, however, the phone is a supportive and adjunctive modality; recognizing its importance in this light and not trying to make it into something it is not allows the phone to be a truly helpful therapeutic modality.

Teachers and counselors have to guard their time jealously and intercession by phone may or may not be propitious. Individual cases and teacher/counselor considerations will have to dictate the appropriate uses of the phone, but it is an ever-ready resource if used judiciously.

COMBINED OR MIXED
SUPPORTIVE THERAPIES

Holding to the notion that even blends of supportive therapies (music, dance, dramas, painting) are still adjunctive, it might be likely that more combinations and meldings of therapies are indicated. Several supportive therapies working together might even be considered a major therapeutic undertaking without the usual support from formal therapy.

If music is used to accompany dance and drama to express feelings and explicate problem statements, this may be all that is needed for some people. Adolescents, often less able to communicate openly than adults or children, may find combinations of expressive movement, rhythm, and song much to their liking.

Edelstein and Kneller (1976) combined art, music, and group discussion techniques. The expressive modalities—art and music—led to topics for discussion, opened up avenues of self-observation and self-appraisal, and possibly suggested actions that individuals or groups can pursue. These authors report that once the expressive modalities stimulate emotions, discussions flow easier and may include confrontations (between self and self, and self and others), interpretations, and perhaps insights into one's behavior. No empirical data were offered; however, hunches along these lines may in time stimulate research or suggest how to focus on the most appropriate ways to integrate various expressive and supportive therapeutic modalities.

Gibson (1975) looked at the combining of modalities as a way of finding out how they might fit best with certain types of patients. She studied ten treatment modalities and the preferences for these among clinicians and therapists. Optimum treatment modalities were agreed upon by the clinicians/therapists for five patient groups. Art therapy was judged to be most effective with youthful drug offenders, among children with educational problems, and with moderately depressed patients. Perhaps, if these findings are significant—and they will need to be checked on other populations of clinicians and patients—one could envision training therapists in several modalities so that such a therapist could function optimally, at least in an adjunctive role, among a wide assortment of patients. There is no reason to think that "talking therapy" has always to carry the therapeutic burden; it, too, may become supplemental at times.

Price and Moos (1975) sought a taxonomy of treatment programs based on a study of 144 such programs; these programs were measured in terms of 10 dimensions of ward atmosphere. They identified six clusters of treatment programs: therapeutic community, relationship oriented, action oriented, insight oriented, control oriented, and disturbed behavior. Perhaps some of the various supportive modalities discussed in this paper might fit into these various clusters and find a match between the type of ward or hospital atmosphere, on the one hand, and therapeutic modality, on the other. The versatility of supportive therapies, irrespective of the one used (behavior modification, insight-oriented dynamic therapy, or others), might then be tested more empirically in a structured, descriptive context that could make good sense of all treatment methods. The juxtaposition of modalities, major and minor, might be a step toward defining more clearly therapeutic objectives, actions, and outcomes.

The use of multiple modes of therapy in biofeedback was examined by Rosenboom (1976). He located 23 articles on biofeedback as it relates to music, graphic arts, theater, film, and video production. Biofeedback data were converted into musical or visual presentations. Rosenboom's work suggests further how a therapeutic approach—biofeedback in this case—might be modified to use directly and cogently various supportive therapeutic modalities and perhaps to select among these supportive modalities those optimal for various patients. Once a conceptual posture has been arrived at through some major psychotherapeutic theory—hypothetically based on any of a number of offerings such as behavior therapy, psychodynamic therapy, Rogerian therapy, and so forth—the supportive therapies could be brought in at opportune times with different kinds of patients (differing in age or complaints, for example) and tested to determine the most efficacious models for combining major and secondary therapeutic modalities. Some would argue that biofeedback is itself a necessary and probably sufficient condition for behavior change: Some kind of feedback has to be available to the person in order to know what one's behavior means, whether this feedback information is in the form of music, drama, graphic presentations, dance, movement, or something else. The value of the supportive modality, then, would hinge on the relevance of the feedback to the person's problem, his/her life situation, and capacity to use the information fed back.

As part of a general supplemental approach to therapy, tape recorders, TV, and video tapes may be utilized (Lester, 1977). These particular devices for supplementing (or perhaps augmenting) regular therapy reside mostly in visual and oral areas; they can be viewed as a logical extension of face-to-face, verbal therapy. TV and video scripts are written for special problem areas, for social skills instruction (Phillips, 1978), and for supervisory help to therapists conducting formal or conventional verbal therapy of whatever persuasion. Sometimes tape recordings might be used in lieu of face-to-face meetings in the context of regular therapy (Denholtz, 1970; Lester, 1977). It is possible, of course, for tape recorders to be used entirely without regular verbal therapy, or for video or TV to be used in the manner of regular therapy (with these modalities the therapist and patient "see" each other over the screen supplemental to, or in lieu of, face-to-face meetings). The playback of the TV script, the video or oral tape recording, can afford both therapist and patient re-runs of the previous sessions and can better prepare both of them for upcoming sessions (Phillips, 1977a). In fact, informal use of the tape recorder between regular verbal sessions helps to clarify moot points, to let the patient know how she/he sounds, and to help construct more salient issues for subsequent sessions (Phillips, 1977a).

Summary and Conclusion

A number of tentative generalizations can be made concerning supportive or adjunctive therapeutic modalities, especially among the young. First, supportive therapeutic modalities have been in evidence for many years, although their more explicit use has shown a groundswell recently; this is particularly true of art, writing, diary, and log techniques, but it is becoming true for music, dance, and drama modalities as well.

Second, supportive therapies may play a role secondary to regular therapies, but the supportive methods may at times take over the major thrust of the therapy or become so necessary that their role is not aptly described as supportive; this is especially true of art therapy, perhaps somewhat for music and drama therapy, and may also be true for therapy via computer.

Third, the impression should not be gained that supportive therapies are always ends in themselves, even if they assume more than a supportive role, since most settings of a therapeutic nature encourage the participants to talk about their poetry, their music, dance, or art efforts. There is no inhibition on talking about or verbally conceptualizing the supplemental therapy efforts.

A fourth point is that the literature emphasizes primarily the emotional-release characteristics of the supplemental therapies; these therapies are expressive in nonverbal ways, especially at the outset of any given therapeutic effort, and are said to give rise to better self-understanding as a result of the release of previously inhibited and nonverbalized emotions. One could speculate that if the various forms of verbal psychotherapy were wholly sufficient in their efforts, no forms of indirect, supportive, nonverbal therapies would be needed. On the other hand, proponents of supportive therapies, especially those based on the arts, might counter by saying that no matter how efficient or effective verbal therapies are, they can never touch the same emotional areas as the artistic or expressive therapies.

Fifth, research on supportive therapies is scattered and not consistent in showing encouraging results. The research is often not conducted very systematically with control groups or adequate descriptions of populations or of methods used. It may be impossible at this juncture to standardize (if that is indeed needed) the conduct of art therapy. To expect or require a formalization of art therapy might be inimical to its objectives. However, some more structuring of its methods and aims might well be pursued. Dance, poetry, drama, and music and combinations of these therapies will be more systematically researched when therapists become more interested in the evaluation of results.

Sixth, the more structured supportive or adjunctive roles played by TV, video, and tape recorders, by writing therapy, and by the computer may lend themselves more readily to research and evaluation. The published studies indicate more research has been done on these methods, and there is encouragement from the available research to pursue them further.

The greatest need among the supportive therapies is for more research. Research may show that emotional release is a necessary but not sufficient condition for therapeutic change; that supportive and expressive therapies may constitute the *introduction* to therapeutic change but some kind of conceptualizing, generalizing, and applicative change to wider situations is sorely needed. (This is also true for regular, formal therapies.)

The most encouraging sign is that supportive therapies may lead to new data collection areas or enlarge the data base, compared to formal therapies. Words may reflect or touch upon only certain areas of human experience; dance, art, and music may enlarge the approach to significant emotional content and provide the potential for emotional release and consequent behavior change not found elsewhere in therapy, especially among less verbal youth and handicapped populations.

The proliferation of various forms of supportive therapy will probably continue; the therapist should, therefore, be aware that proponents of supportive therapies often display enthusiasm for their creations beyond their proven value. Supportive therapies, especially as they appear to the patients as unconventional, novel, and creative may indeed be a better way to start therapy than the usual formal approach, especially for youthful and handicapped populations: the supportive therapies at least appear to take them as they are more often than do the formal therapies. At this time, the supportive therapies are more challenging than they are convincing, more novel than proven, and more varied than formalized or structured; whether all these postures are useful and fruitful remains to be seen.

References

Alston, E. Psychoanalytic psychotherapy conducted by correspondence. *International Journal of Psychoanalysis*, 1957, *38*, 32–50.

Alvin, J. *Music therapy*. New York: Basic Books, 1975

Anant, S. S. The use of poetry in psychotherapy. *Psychological Studies*, 1975, *20*, 31–41.

Anderson, W. Dance therapy as a mode of treatment. *Human Behavior*, 1975, *4*, 56–60.

Andrews, M. Poetry programs in mental hospitals. *Perspectives in Psychiatric Care*, 1975, *13*, 17–18.

Appel, K. E. Psychiatric therapy: Explanatory or poetic therapy, interpretive therapy and bibliotherapy. In J. McV. Hunt (Ed.), *Personality and the behavior disorders*, vol. 2. New York: Ronald Press, 1944.

Arnold, M. Music therapy in a transactional analysis setting. *Journal of Music Therapy*, 1975, *12*, 104–120.

Baron, M. P. *The cumulative and immediate effects of unstructured (journal) and structured (bipolar checklist) self-evaluation writing upon self-evaluation and self-actualization of male and female college students.* Unpublished doctoral dissertation, University of New Mexico, 1978.

Berry, F. M. *A summary of experience in the field of bibliotherapy*. Columbus, Ga.: Columbus College, 1978.

Bryan, A. I. Can there be a science of bibliotherapy? *Library Journal*, 1939, *64*, 773–776.

Burton, A. The use of written productions in psychotherapy. In L. Pearson (Ed.), *The use of written communications in psychotherapy*. Springfield, Ill.: Charles C Thomas, 1965.

Campbell, J. Communication between the different therapeutic fields. *British Journal of Music Therapy*, 1976a, *7*, 1.

Campbell, M. What is music therapy? *British Journal of Music Therapy*, 1976b, *7*, 20–22.

Cassell, R., & Blum, L. Computer-assisted counseling for the prevention of delinquent behavior among teenagers and youth, *Social Science Research*, 1969, *54*, 72–79.

Chick, J. *Innovations in the use of career information*. Boston: Houghton-Mifflin, 1970.

Denholtz, M. The use of tape recordings between therapy sessions, *Journal of Behavior Therapy and Experimental Psychiatry*, 1970, *1*, 139–144.

Edelstein, E. L., & Kneller, D. A combined art therapy group, *Israel Annals of Psychiatry and Related Disciplines*, 1976, *14*, 322–332.

Fowler, R. MMPI computer interpretation for college counseling, *Journal of Psychology*, 1968, *69*, 201–207.

Frances, A., & Schiff, M. Popular music as a catalyst in the induction of therapy groups for teenagers. *International Journal of Group Psychotherapy*, 1976, *26*, 393–398.

Freud, S. Analysis of a phobia in a five-year-old boy. *Collected papers*, vol. 3. New York: Basic Books, 1959, pp. 149–289.

Friedman, R. A computer-based program for simulating the patient-physician encounter. *Journal of Medical Education*, 1973, *48*, 92–97.

Gibson, G. L. A survey of treatment modalities used by mental health clinicians and activity therapists. *Hospital and Community Psychiatry*, 1975, *26*, 441–443.

Goldberg, M. The relationship of art therapy to the symptoms of echolalia. *Art Psychotherapy*, 1976, *3*, 7–10.

Goldner, J. L. Musculoskeletal aspects of emotional problems, *Southern Medical Journal*, 1976, *69*, 6–8.

Gollinitz, G. Fundamentals of rhythmic-psychomotor music therapy. *Acta Paedopsychiatrics*, 1975, *41*, 130–134 (Basel).

Greist, J., Gustafson, D., Strauss, F., Rowse, G., Laughren, T., & Chiles, J. A computer interview for suicide risk prediction. *American Journal of Psychiatry*, 1973, *130*, 1327–1332.

Harper, R. *The new psychotherapies.* Englewood Cliffs, N.J.: Prentice-Hall, 1975.

Hecox, B., Levine, E., & Scott, D. Dance in physical rehabilitation, *Physical Therapy*, 1976, *56*, 919–924.

Heninger, O. E. Poetry therapy: Exploration of a creative righting maneuver. *Art Psychotherapy*, 1977, *4*, 39–40.

Holtzman, W. Can the computer supplant the clinician? *Journal of Clinical Psychology*, 1960, *16*, 119–122.

Hynes, Arleen. *Bibliography of bibliotherapy reference materials, 1970–1975.* Washington, D.C.: St. Elizabeth's Hospital, 1976.

Kew, C., & Kew, C. Writing as an aid in pastoral counseling and psychotherapy. *Pastoral Psychology*, 1963, *14*, 37–43.

Lerner, A. A look at poetry therapy. *Art Psychotherapy*, 1976c, *3*, i–ii.

Lerner, A. Poetry therapy and semantics. *ETC: A Review of General Semantics*, 1976b, *33*, 417–422.

Lester, D. *The use of alternative modes for communication in psychotherapy.* Springfield, Ill.: Charles C Thomas, 1977.

Lester, D., & Brockopp, G. *Crisis intervention and counseling by telephone.* Springfield, Ill.: Charles C Thomas, 1973.

Loehlin, J. *Computer models of personality.* New York: Random House, 1968.

McClaskey, H. C. *Bibliotherapy with emotionally disturbed patients: An experimental study.* (Doctoral dissertation, *Dissertation Abstracts International*, 1971. (University Microfilms No. 71-8523)

McDonough, J. The evaluation of hotlines and crisis phone centers. *Crisis Intervention*, 1975, *6*, 2–19.

McQueen, J. C. Two controlled experiments in music therapy. *British Journal of Music Therapy*, 1975, *6*, 2–8.

Marek, P. A. *Dance therapy with adult day hospital patients.* Doctoral dissertation, *Dissertation Abstracts International*, 1976. (University Microfilms No. 76-11069)

Melbus, G., Hershenson, D., & Vermillion, M. Computer assisted versus traditional vocational counseling with high and low readiness clients. *Journal of Vocational Behavior*, 1973, *3*, 137–144.

Morgan, D. Combining Orff-Schulwerk with creative dramatics for the retarded. *Therapeutic Recreation Journal*, 1975, *9*, 54–56.

Ney, T. Integrated arts program reported in corrections, *American Journal of Correction*, 1976, *38*, 8–9.

Parloff, M. The psychotherapy marketplace. In A. Rosenfeld (Ed.), *Mind and supermind.* New York: Holt, Rinehart & Winston, 1977.

Phillips, E. L. *Counseling and psychotherapy: A behavioral approach.* New York: Wiley, 1977a.

Phillips, E. L. *Day to day anxiety management.* New York: Krieger, 1977b.

Phillips, E. L. *The social skills basis of psychopathology: Alternatives to abnormal psychology and psychiatry.* New York: Grune & Stratton, 1978.

Phillips, E. L., Gershenson, J., & Lyons, G., On time-limited writing therapy, *Psychol. Reports*, 1977, *41*, 707–712.

Phillips, E. L., Gershenson, J., & Lyons, G. D. On time-limited writing therapy. *Psychological Reports*, 1978.

Phillips, E. L., & Wiener, D. N. *Short-term psychotherapy and structured behavior change*. New York: McGraw-Hill, 1966.

Pietropinto, A. Poetry therapy in groups. *Current Psychiatric Therapies*, 1975, *15*, 221–232.

Price, R. H., & Moos, R. H. Toward a taxonomy of inpatient treatment environments. *Journal of Abnormal Psychology*, 1975, *84*, 181–188.

Purvis, J., & Samet, S. *Music in developmental therapy: A curriculum guide*. Baltimore: University Park, 1976.

Putzel, J. *Toward alternative theories of poetry therapy*. Doctoral dissertation. *Dissertation Abstracts International*, 1975. (University Microfilms No. 75-27520)

Rappaport, B. S. Carnal knowledge: What the wisdom of the body has to offer psychotherapy. *Journal of Humanistic Psychology*, 1975, *15*, 49–70.

Ratcliffe, E. R. The Old Masters Art College: An art therapy technique for heuristic self-discovery. *Art Psychotherapy*, 1977, *4*, 29–32.

Rosenboom, D. *Biofeedback and the arts: Results of early experiments* (2nd ed.). Vancouver, Canada: ARC Publications, 1976.

Ross, R. Unlocking the doors of perception: Poetry the healer. *Psychotherapy: Theory, Research and Practice*, 1975, *12*, 255–257.

Sandel, S. L. Integrating dance therapy into treatment. *Hospital and Community Psychiatry*, 1975, *26*, 439–441.

Schneck, J. M. Bibliotherapy and hospital library activities for neuropsychiatric patients: A review of the literature, *Psychiatry*, 1945, *8*, 207–228.

Shinoda, K., Matsumoto, Y., Tokuyama, T., & Takeuchi, T. Features found in the process of psychodramatic therapy, *Bulletin of the Ministry of Justice Research Institute*, 1975, *18*, 117–127 (Tokyo).

Silverman, H. L. Creativeness and creativity in poetry as a therapeutic process. *Art Psychotherapy*, 1977, *4*, 19–28.

Test, L. *A comparative study of four approaches to short-term psychotherapy*. Unpublished doctoral dissertation, George Washington University, Washington, D.C., 1964.

Tobias, L. L. *The relative effectiveness of behavioristic biblio-therapy. Contingency contracting and suggestions of self-control in weight reduction*. Doctoral dissertation, *Dissertation Abstracts International*, 1973. (University Microfilms No. 73-10068)

Weizenbaum, J. *Computer power and human reason*. San Francisco: Freeman, 1976.

White, J. O. *The assessment of a program in bibliotherapy for black helpers*. Doctoral dissertation, *Dissertation Abstracts International*, 1973. (University Microfilms No. 73-17474)

Wolff, R. A. Therapeutic experiences through group art expression, *American Journal of Art Therapy*, 1975, *14*, 91–98.

Zucaro, B. J. *The use of bibliotherapy to affect attitude change toward American Negroes*. Doctoral dissertation, *Dissertation Abstracts International*, 1973. (University Microfilms No. 27216)

Epilogue

James J. Wawrzyniak
Judy Smith
Gwen Blacklock Brown

A major message presented throughout this book is that educators of adolescents with behavior disorders should focus on helping their students become responsible for their own behaviors and futures. Such responsible behavior, it has been argued, is best fostered when students are supported in participating in the development of their own educational objectives and plans. In keeping with the philosophy of full student participation, the editors of this text asked a student to contribute his perspective on current educational practices. Thus, this chapter begins with a statement written by a young man who, while in high school, bore the label "behaviorally disordered." Although his statement provides teachers with only a few concrete suggestions, it makes clear that educators must demonstrate their commitment to students by finding ways to engage them fully in the learning process and by consistently expecting successful and responsible behavior.

JIM'S PERSPECTIVE

When I was in high school, I had a lot of troubles and problems and conflicts. Others classified me as behaviorally disordered, and I guess I would have to agree that they were right. Lots of us were disordered in one way or another. It was a wonder that I ever made it as long as I did. What with getting thrown out repeatedly, or just not bothering to go, or being bored all day, school was not in my top ten of favorite things to do, and it was a lot easier to avoid it than to participate in it.

The first high school I attended was in a very large metropolitan area in the south, located in an upper-middle-class neighborhood. The school building was very nice; it was fairly new and had not been subject to the abuse of time and students, who can run a building down pretty fast. There was a stadium with an outdoor track, two large baseball fields, a gym with a basketball court, volleyball court, a complete weight room, adequate dressing rooms with showers, tennis courts, and enough coaches to show you how to use all of them. The school population was about a thousand in grades 8 through 12; about 65% of us rode buses to school while the rest walked or came by car. The classes never had more than 30 students, but some classes were larger than others because they were required courses, because the teachers were popular, or because they had a reputation for being easy to pass to acquire credit. We had some required courses, such as English, math, and history, and others that were electives, like art, music, and foreign languages.

The second high school I attended was the only public high school serving a large county in the same state. The 800 students came from a wide variety of economic backgrounds, from poverty levels to the upper class, and most of us rode a fair distance to school on a county bus. The school building itself was old and funky, in bad shape. When it was built, all the heat, water, and steam pipes that were run along the ceilings had been left exposed. It was like going to school in a basement.

Transferring to this school was like culture shock. I sat in classes with students who couldn't even read. I knew guys who failed so consistently that, after spending three years trying to get out of junior high school, they would be promoted to high school because the teachers finally got tired of having them around.

So there was this difference between the two schools: the people in the county school seemed to have more learning problems than the people in the city school, but maybe this was because so many of them were disadvantaged in the first place. Still, there were more similarities than differences, and my experiences in these schools, while not at all consistent, had a certain pattern.

Drug use was common among students. I would say that 75% of us used some type of drug sooner or later. One year the city school I mentioned had the distinction of being the one with the highest rate of drug abuse in the county. That was the year that people were falling out in class, in the halls, everywhere—from taking downers. I watched my best friend overdose in history class and be taken off to the hospital to have his stomach pumped.

Most teachers had no idea when we were loaded, and the few who did often said nothing about it. Only on rare occasions would a teacher turn a student in; it's hard to prove that a student is actually high or on an illegal drug, when he could just as well have been up all night and very sleepy.

A large number of students were really wild, and the teachers were pretty lenient about it. On top of that, often when the school did take action, the student's parents were immediately there to threaten whoever had punished their child. (Being a school principal can be dangerous!) Most of the time, the teachers and administration let a lot of things go by. I'd come to class after just having smoked a joint, and, as soon as I would be in the room, this would be obvious. But most of the teachers would say nothing; I guess it was easier to do nothing. This was certainly okay with everybody I knew. Who wanted to hear a bunch of static about smoking a joint? So what? It was no big deal—happened all the time.

Consequences for offensive students were a matter of the individual response of the individual teacher, not any overall policy. The kind of punishment or lack of it usually depended on the teacher who caught you, and some teachers were nicer than others about this. Others wouldn't hesitate to throw you out of class and tell you never to return. The principals reflected this, too. They were fair in their dealings with me, often throwing me out of school (which I deserved) but, at the same time, trying to encourage me by being lenient on other occasions.

I used to get stoned and go to class and get into all kinds of things in the textbooks. Most of the time, though, the things that I read were not the same things that the teacher was talking about. I never had much of a problem going into class high and still completing an assignment. As for my grades, I had a B average when I wasn't being failed for missing too many days.

Of all the contradictions I felt and observed, the one about failing for missing over ten days of class made me the most furious. The high school had a rule that automatically failed any student who skipped more than ten days; I ran into that one from time to time. Even though I had missed ten days, my teachers would tell me that my grades were good enough to pass. But I would fail. It wasn't that I couldn't do the work; it was that the county needed a head count so it could get more money from the state to support the school. No students, no money—so we had to be physically present or fail.

Why, then, did I continue to skip classes? For one thing, I guess I wasn't very mature. For another thing, sometimes I couldn't stand being in the place, and at other times it all seemed so meaningless. Another factor was that I got away with it most of the time. In three years, I never attended one assembly program and rarely went to homeroom and cut a lot of other classes, too. Actually, I got away with most of this because I suppose that no one noticed that I was absent or didn't care whether I was there or not. From time to time, though, all of this would catch up with me, and I would be placed in detention hall or would be expelled for several days. I never understood this kind of contradiction either: I would have thought that the authorities would want to make certain we came to school, not send us home as a measure to improve attendance.

Most of the time, I was bored with the subjects we were to study. They seemed to have no use when applied to day-to-day living, and day-to-day living was what I wanted to find out about. We'd be studying algebra, for instance, while I'd be wanting to know how to fill out an income tax form or balance my checkbook. In history class, after so many "Columbus discovered America" classes (when it really was a Viking), it was easy for me to lose interest, knowing that there was a whole world out there to be looked at. Also, I've always been a voracious reader and will read almost anything. So I would find myself filling in large gaps in textbooks with knowledge I had gained from reading outside of class. It was strange to be sitting in class reading some textbook account of something and saying to myself, "Hey, wait a minute; this isn't right. They forgot this; they didn't mention that; they didn't explain why this happened."

I think most teachers and textbooks are geared to a certain level of knowledge. When students want to go beyond that level, or around it, only a few teachers have the time, patience, and understanding to let them go. In the schools I attended, an occasional teacher might recognize a student who wanted more but would still be unable to give that extra moment that was needed. The teacher was restricted by large classes or, as was often the case, by having to spend time keeping discipline. Both of these things seemed to put a big dent in the teacher's effectiveness.

There were classes where the teacher was so involved in combat with two or three students that the rest of the group were virtually ignored. This, in turn, made it boring—but easy to pass. I've had teachers who would pass you if you just simply came to class and sat there quietly. All you had to do was avoid giving them a hard time, and they would leave you alone also.

Most of my teachers bored me, and this was often due to what seemed to be apathy with their jobs. This had a great effect on me insofar as my attitude toward their classes was concerned. When all a teacher does is give you endless "read and answer the questions" assignments, it's hard to take an interest. Most of the teachers I knew used a combination of oral notes and textbook information, with tests every so often to see how you were doing. With some teachers, it was "read the textbook and show up for exams," and, for me, those were the easiest classes. Most teachers followed the same program, class after class, year after year, and the only change would be a new textbook every so often.

On the other hand, there were some teachers who, upon seeing that some approach would probably put us to sleep or that a text was out of date, would try to supplement the course with information that was more up to date and interesting. This might be in the form of newspapers, television or news magazines like *Time* or *National Geographic*. This usually made for an interesting class and made it easier to relate what was being taught to what was happening in the world. A few teachers really encouraged me by allowing me to study and work on a more individual level. They would help as much as they could but would leave me to work on my own. This was a good arrangement and it enabled me to progress at my own rate and explore things that interested me. However, this arrangement would never last very long and didn't occur in many classes, so I would find myself becoming more and more detached.

Some teachers were receptive to students' questions and understanding of students' problems. Some were tolerant of a more relaxed and informal student-teacher relationship in the classroom, where ideas and comments were encouraged, regardless of their nature. But, on the whole, most of them were there to "teach" and that was that. I usually felt that, if I needed some type of help or advice, I should just go somewhere else and not bother them. This is not to say that all teachers were like this; there was always a teacher or counselor whom I knew I could go to, but there were never enough of these people to reach everyone who needed help. Looking back, I'm pretty sure most of us really did need help, but either didn't know how to go about getting it or couldn't find it. Also, by the time you asked for help, it was often too late.

What to do about all of this? I cannot think of any *one* thing that could be changed to remedy these problems. It would take a lot of changing of attitudes about education, drugs, teaching methods, teachers, students, and so forth—right down to what the purpose of a high-school education should be.

Students should show more self-discipline and be more honest with themselves about the effects of their behavior on themselves and other people. Sometimes I think we go out of our way to make enemies of people in authority.

Schools should be more human, and students should be able to do some learning on the outside, instead of in the confinement that can seem like prison. Schools should be responsible about students' learning problems; if a student is in the tenth grade and still cannot even read, then something should be done about it.

Teachers should be more open to students; they should not let things get out of hand in class, but they shouldn't set up a war with the students, either. Teachers who do nothing about problems become part of the problems. Finally, if people are going to teach, they should take pride in their work; there is nothing worse than a teacher who hates the students. I felt hated more than once; it made me feel sad and mean at the same time, and this came from feeling guilty, but I became more guilty all the time. I don't believe that students generally hate any certain people or things about school in a specific way. For me, the way I was then, I began to see myself as required to be part of a system for not much reason other than to keep the system going, and that was what I hated. I still have that feeling about a lot of things in life. Although it didn't occur to me then, I suppose that many teachers feel the same way. Even if I had thought about that a long time ago, I don't think it would have changed anything, because I doubt that I could have gotten that idea out in the open with any teachers. Saying it now is probably the best reason for writing down what I recall about high school.

THE EDITORS' PERSPECTIVE

The kind of guilt that Jim felt is similar to the kind of guilt that teachers feel when they cannot help students. Like Jim, most teachers experience the frustration of knowing they have done something wrong or not done something they should, but too often they have no certain knowledge of where the real problem lies or how to solve it. In their daily interactions teachers and students have expectations of one another that frequently are not met. However, hopelessness and guilt in both students and teachers must continually be contradicted. As has been argued throughout this text, such hopeless feelings in students can be challenged by providing them with learning experiences at which they can be successful and by gradually stretching the requirements for success. A learning environment which insures daily success and challenge for students also diminishes a teacher's sense of hopelessness and frustration. Similarly, teacher support groups which enable teachers to share information and successes with their peers can be helpful in keeping teachers' attitudes positive and hopeful. With sensitive leadership, such groups also can help teachers to examine their tendency to assume the entire responsibility for student failure. There are, of course, limits to what teachers can accomplish within the current context of secondary education. However, while recognizing the limits of their responsibility is essential, teachers, as well as all other educational personnel, must be encouraged to energetically seek solutions to their educational problems.

It is especially important to examine more closely the overall secondary-school system to determine how it contributes to adolescent problems and how it might be structured to help adolescents maximize their constructive potentials. While many creative structural changes may be developed, it is already apparent that "mainstreaming" troubled adolescents will succeed only if class groups are smaller than the current norm. To achieve the appropriate education promised by Public Law 94–142, teacher attention must be divided among smaller numbers of students so that individualized goals and instruction are possible.

The goals of adolescent education center on career and vocational preparation, skills in socialization, and the knowledge, attitudes, and behaviors essential to success in the world. Education should offer varied opportunities for students to practice these developing capabilities in realistic situations. It is becoming apparent that more of secondary education should take place in the community where learning tasks are likely to seem relevant to students. Under good supervision, community-based education could provide students with excellent opportunities to translate knowledge into competence and to gain a strong sense of belonging to the larger social order. Moreover, since the inappropriate behaviors exhibited by many students are situationally specific and often are more frequently manifested in schools than in other places, changes in the types of learning environments available might help some students to reduce the frequency of these behaviors.

It is hoped that, as alternative learning environments become available, the match between the student, the environment, and the instructional approach will be made with increasing insight and skill. The population described as behaviorally disordered actually consists of several subsets of students, each with distinct behavioral characteristics. However, corresponding differences in the instructional strategies and environments best suited to these subsets of students have yet to be clearly established. Educators at all levels need to give attention to this problem.

In seeking solutions to current educational problems, teachers need to counter their tendency to rely solely on college level researchers and teacher educators. Unfortunately, like classroom teachers, such professionals are just beginning their search for answers to the problems of educating adolescents with behavior disorders. Classroom teachers best know the problems and they are in a perfect position to try different strategies and evaluate their effectiveness. Thus, it is essential that teachers share widely their successes and that they observe and discuss strategies with other successful teachers. Furthermore, educational writers can foster rapid progress in this field by offering teachers more opportunities to publish their successes in journals and texts read by other teachers.

This text represents a beginning effort toward the establishment of a sound and comprehensive body of knowledge related to educating adolescents with behavior disorders. The individuals who contributed their perspectives and suggestions come from widely varying backgrounds, but they all share a commitment to better educational services for adolescents with behavior disorders. The editors hope that the ideas presented here will be helpful to those practitioners who share this commitment and that these ideas will generate new perspectives and suggestions, which in turn receive wide circulation. Educators at every level, parents, and all involved professionals must see themselves as cooperating participants in student change, educational change, and social change.

Contributors

Robert B. Ashlock served as elementary school teacher and principal in Indiana before beginning his work in higher education. With the B.S. and M.S. from Butler University and the Ed.D. from Indiana University, he came to the College Park campus of the University of Maryland in 1965 where he was instrumental in establishing the Arithmetic Center and its graduate program in elementary school mathematics, including a clinic program for children having difficulty learning mathematics. He addresses professional meetings frequently and has a number of professional publications, including *Error Patterns in Computation*. He is currently president of the Research Council for Diagnostic and Prescriptive Mathematics.

Betty Delfs Bowling is a special educator at the Southard School, which provides educational services to the patients at the Children's Hospital, Children's Division of the Menninger Foundation in Topeka, Kansas. She was a child-care worker for five years and has been a teacher for twenty years. She taught in public school systems for three years and the remainder of her teaching career has been devoted to working with emotionally disturbed adolescents at the Southard School. She teaches English, careers, and a life skills course. She holds a B.Ed. degree from Washburn University in Topeka, Kansas, and a M.A. in special education of emotionally disturbed children from Kansas State University. She wishes to thank her son and daughter and the students in her classes for sharing their experiences with her, thereby laying the groundwork for the development of the careers course.

Gwen Brown received her Ed.D. degree from the University of Virginia in 1975. Her studies concentrated on the education of emotionally disturbed children, with Dr. James Kauffman serving as her advisor. After leaving Virginia, she became an assistant professor in the University of Maryland's graduate program for teachers of emotionally disturbed children. She completed postdoctoral work at American University's Rose School under the supervision of Dr. Nicholas Long. Most recently she served as the national advocate for parents and emotionally disturbed students at the Bureau of Education for the Handicapped in Washington, D.C. Currently, she is writing, counseling, and teaching at the University of Delaware on a part-time basis while giving the larger part of her attention to her new daughter, Ellie Brown.

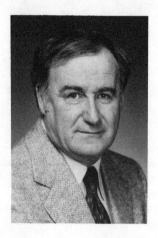

John F. Cawley is professor of education at the University of Connecticut, Storrs, where he has been teaching since 1964. Previously he taught at the University of Kansas, at Syracuse University, and at Norwich Free Academy in Connecticut. He received his Ph.D. from the University of Connecticut in 1962. Dr. Cawley is a member of the NCTM (National Council of Teachers of Mathematics) and numerous professional societies in the fields of special education, psychology, and rehabilitation. He is associate editor of the *Exceptional Children* journal and a member of the Research Council on Exceptional Children. Dr. Cawley has to his credit more than 50 monographs, books, articles, and miscellaneous publications. Each year since 1964 he has been awarded two or more grants from the U.S. Office of Education or other agencies such as USPHS, OEOM, SRSM. The grants, totalling almost four million dollars, have enabled him to carry on extensive research and field-testing with retarded, learning-disabled, and average children.

Gary M. Clark, Ed.D. is professor of special education at the University of Kansas where he specializes in personnel preparation in the area of career/vocational programming for the handicapped. His professional experiences have included work as a secondary public-school teacher, guidance counselor, vocational rehabilitation counselor, teacher educator, author, and consultant. He has directed a 4-year special project funded by the Bureau of Education for the Handicapped known as the Habilitation Personnel Training Project and is currently co-director of the Mid-west ReTool Consortium: Career Education for the Handicapped. His most recent publication in the area of career education is *Career Education for the Handicapped in the Elementary School.*

Douglas Cullinan is an assistant professor in the Department of Learning and Development at Northern Illinois University. He has taught emotionally disturbed and mentally retarded pupils in public schools, and educationally handicapped delinquents in a state detention facility. He has published on various topics related to special education for children and adolescents. Dr. Cullinan is associated with Project ExCEL, a Child Service Demonstration Center in learning disabilities, and serves as associate editor of *Exceptional Children*. Dr. Cullinan received a B.A. in psychology (1966), and an M.A. (1968) and Ed.D. (1974) in special education from the University of Virginia.

Michael H. Epstein is an associate professor at San Diego State University. He is also currently project director of Project ExCEL, a Child Service Demonstrating Center in learning disabilities. Dr. Epstein has taught learning and behaviorally handicapped pupils and has authored numerous journal articles and books dealing with handicapped children and adolescents, particularly in the areas of cognitive tempo, behavior disorders, and applied behavior analysis. Dr. Epstein received a B.S. degree in business (1969) and an M.S. Ed. degree in special education (1971) from American University, and an Ed.D. in special education from the University of Virginia (1975).

Stanley A. Fagen is staff development consultant for Montgomery County Public Schools, Maryland, His previous positions include that of supervisor of professional development, Mark Twain School, Montgomery County; director of psychology training, Childrens Hospital of D.C.; school psychologist at Hillcrest Childrens Center, Washington, D.C.; chief child psychologist at Walter Reed General Hospital; and faculty appointments at the American University, Trinity College, George Washington University, and the Washington School of Psychiatry. Dr. Fagen has written extensively in the areas of teacher training, psychoeducational management, and teaching self-control. He received a B.S. degree from Brooklyn College in 1957, a M.A. from the University of Pennsylvania in 1959, and a Ph.D. degree in clinical child psychology from the University of Pennsylvania in 1963. Dr. Fagen lives with his wife and three daughters in Silver Spring, Maryland.

Barbara Gantley is a learning disabilities resource teacher for Fauquier County, Virginia. Prior to this position, Mrs. Gantley spent four years teaching emotionally disturbed adolescents in both residential and day-care facilities, including Atlantic Academy in Norfolk, Virginia.

Robert A. Jardin, Ph.D., is chief of the Alternatives and Counseling Program, Montgomery County Health Department, Maryland, and maintains a part-time private practice in family therapy. He was formerly assistant chairman of the Department of Education and Director, Counselor Education and Psychology Graduate Program, the American University, Washington, D.C. He has also served as a counselor to delinquent youth in San Francisco, as a consultant to learning disabled youth in the U.S. Army, and a psychologist consultant to the Bureau of Indian Affairs School System.

Roger Kroth received his B.A. and M.A. from the University of Iowa and his Ed.D. from the University of Kansas. He has taught and counseled in the public schools and was director of guidance and testing in the Wichita Public Schools. After graduating from the University of Kansas, he remained on staff in the Department of Special Education for four years at the University of Kansas Medical Center. In 1972, he became a member of the University of New Mexico, Department of Special Education where he is currently a professor and director of the Parent Involvement Center. He has authored and co-authored three books on parent/teacher communications. His latest article is "Unsuccessful Conferencing (Or We've Got to Stop Meeting Like This)."

John Lloyd is assistant professor in the Department of Special Education and academic program coordinator for the Learning Disabilities Research Institute at the University of Virginia. His previous activities include classroom teaching with atypical learners of many different ages and diagnostic labels, involvement in developing social-learning-based parent training procedures, and teaching and conducting research while on the faculty at Northern Illinois University. He received a B.A. in English literature from California State University at Los Angeles (1971) and an M.S. (1974) and Ph.D. (1976) from the University of Oregon.

Nicholas J. Long was born in Detroit, Michigan, in 1929. Currently, he is a professor of special education at the American University and training director of Community Mental Health, Area A, Children's Day Treatment Program, the Rose School. Dr. Long was educated at Wayne State University, where he received a B.S. degree in preschool and elementary education in 1952, and at the University of Michigan, where he received a M.A. degree in child development in 1954 and a Ph.D. degree in educational psychology. Among his special interests in research into the education and management of behavior-disordered children are life-space interviewing, sociometric analysis, management of surface behavior, and analysis of the conflict cycle. Dr. Long is the co-author of *Conflict in the Classroom* and *Teaching Children Self-Control*. In addition, he directed the research and production of a teacher training videotape series.

Richard L. McDowell received his Ed.D. from the University of Kansas in 1969. Dr. McDowell is presently a professor of special education and coordinator for the area of emotional and behavioral disorders for the Department of Special Education at the University of New Mexico in Albuquerque. His professional experiences include being a teacher in both regular and special education; a school psychologist; a director of special education; psychologist and educational consultant for the Adolescent Unit at the Osawatomie State Mental Hospital; a consultant to many programs (public and private) in the areas of emotional and behavioral disorders, secondary education for the emotionally disturbed adolescent, behavior management, and parent involvement; and assistant professor and coordinator for the area of emotional disorders for the Department of Special Education at the University of Cincinnati.

C. Michael Nelson currently is professor of special education at the University of Kentucky. Prior to receiving his Ed.D. from the University of Kansas in 1969, he taught special education at the secondary level and was a psychologist at the Children's Rehabilitiation Unit, University of Kansas Medical Center. Dr. Nelson has published books, chapters, and articles on behavior disorders and special education methods. His major interests are behaviorally disordered adolescents, field-based teacher training, consultation as a support system for children and teachers in the mainstream.

E. Lakin Phillips is a clinical psychologist who received his Ph.D. from the University of Minnesota, Institute of Child Welfare, 1949. He has worked in a number of psychological fields: clinical psychology, child development, psychotherapy and counseling, test development, and more recently in the behavior modification field. Dr. Phillips has written eleven books—the three most recent, and of most interest in the present connection, are *Day To Day Anxiety Management*; *Counseling & Psychotherapy: A Behavioral Approach*; and *The Social Skills Basis of Psychopathology: Alternatives to Abnormal Psychology and Psychiatry*—and some 80-odd articles, reviews, and convention presentations. Dr. Phillips's research, writing, and clinical work have always been strongly behavioral, beginning with his early work on psychotherapy and with the publication in 1962 of *Educating Emotionally Disturbed Children*, with Norris G. Haring. As a professor of psychology and director of the counseling center, George Washington University, founder and executive director of the School for Contemporary Education, Dr. Phillips remains active in special education as well as other clinical areas of practice and research.

Lewis Polsgrove has held positions as a clinical, child, counseling, and school psychologist as well as a teacher of behaviorally disordered and learning disabled children. After completing his doctoral training at the University of Kentucky, he accepted his present position as assistant professor in the Special Education Department at Indiana University. Dr. Polsgrove teaches courses in the areas of behavior disorders and learning disabilities and has published a number of research articles and papers related to teaching academic and behavioral self-management skills to children and youth. He is currently a principal investigator of a U.S.O.E.-funded model program in the Indianapolis public schools for training mildly handicapped secondary students in basic academic and social skills.

Susie R. Rice is currently with Atlantic Academy, a private school serving residential adolescents at Tidewater Psychiatric Institute in Norfolk, Virginia, where she has been an educator-administrator for over 5 years. She formerly taught public school in the Tidewater, Virginia area for 8 years and was actively involved with the Girl Scouts of Greater Tidewater. She holds a B.S. in psychology and a M.S.Ed. in counseling from Old Dominion University. She recently served as president for the Virginia Council for Children with Behavioral Disorders.

Terry L. Rose is an associate professor of special education at the University of Alabama–Birmingham. He has taught learning and behaviorally handicapped pupils in public schools and has authored journal articles and book chapters dealing with applied behavior analysis and handicapped learners. Dr. Rose received a B.A. degree in special education-mental retardation (1973) from the University of South Florida and an M.Ed. (1974) and a Ph.D. (1977) in special education-emotional disturbance and learning disabilities from the University of Florida.

Marian Shelton is a professor in the Department of Special Education at the University of New Mexico. She received her B.A. from Southern Methodist University and her M.A. and Ph.D. from the University of Oklahoma. Dr. Shelton has a varied background. She has taught the mentally handicapped, the learning disabled, and the behaviorally disordered. She has worked with high-school students in poverty programs and evaluated Head Start Programs in midwest and southwest United States. Her special interests in teaching, speaking, and writing include affective education, nonverbal communication, verbal communication, and sex education. Publications include articles in journals, manuals for public school programs, films, and attitude scales.

Richard L. Simpson is an associate professor of special education at the University of Kansas and the University of Kansas Medical Center. In addition, he is the director of the Severe Personal Adjustment Project, a Bureau of Education for the Handicapped demonstration program for severely emotionally disturbed children and adolescents. Prior to university teaching Dr. Simpson worked as a special education teacher and psychologist. Dr. Simpson has conducted research and published in the areas of parent education, management techniques, assessment procedures, and procedures for modifying the attitudes of ordinary children toward the handicapped.

Judy Smith is director of the Dissemin/Action project, a national significance project funded by the U.S.O.E. Division of Personnel Preparation and located in Falls Church, Virginia. She has had seven years' clinical and educational experience in private psychiatric settings where she worked with children, adolescents, and adults. She holds a current postgraduate professional teaching certificate in the State of Virginia, with endorsements in special education for emotionally disturbed students, K-12, and in English in the secondary schools. She was the developer and original director of Atlantic Academy, a private school for seriously disturbed adolescents at two locations in the Tidewater area of Virginia.

James J. Wawrzyniak is a 19-year-old resident of Baton Rouge, Louisiana. Between 1975 and 1978, he attended public high schools in a different state. Later he completed his secondary education by means of the high-school equivalency examination, after which he attended college for a year and a half. He currently works as a truck driver for an office supply firm in Baton Rouge. This chapter contains his first attempt to write for publication.

Dr. Raymond E. Webster, director of Pupil Personnel Services and Special Education at Northeast Area Regional Education Services (NARES), received his M.A. degree in school psychology from Rhode Island College, his M.S. in child clinical psychology from Purdue, and his Ph.D. from the University of Connecticut. He formerly taught learning disabled children and regular education children in the Providence, Rhode Island, Public Schools. He is a former school psychologist and assistant professor at Rhode Island College. Dr. Webster was recently appointed to the adjunct faculty of the Department of Educational Psychology at the University of Connecticut. He is the author of numerous articles in the area of information processing and reading and mathematics disabilities.

Frank H. Wood is presently a professor in the Department of Psychoeducational Studies at the University of Minnesota. His primary activities are the training of teachers to work with seriously behaviorally disordered and emotionally disturbed students and research on procedures appropriate for use by teachers of such students. From 1975–1979, he directed a federally funded Advanced Institute for Trainers of Teachers for Seriously Emotionally Disturbed Children and Youth that issued a series of publications on topics important in this field. Dr. Wood has taught regular elementary and high-school classes as well as special classes of students with severe learning and adjustment problems.

Edward A. Wynne is a sociologist and associate professor, College of Education, Chicago Circle Campus, University of Illinois. Before receiving his degree from the University of California, Berkeley, he was a practicing labor lawyer and spent several years as an administrator in government anti-poverty programs. His academic field of specialization is socialization to adulthood—how children and adolescents learn (or are socialized into) the skills and attitudes that make them effective and emotionally mature adults. Dr. Wynne is incoming editor of *Character*, an interdisciplinary journal being developed to publish materials concerned with socialization to adulthood. His most recent book is *Growing Up Suburban*.

Robert Zabel is an assistant professor of special education at Kansas State University where he is responsible for training teachers for behavior disordered children. He received a Ph.D. in educational psychology from the University of Minnesota in 1977, an M.Ed. from National College of Education in 1973, and a B.A. from Grinnell College in 1969. In between these experiences, he has been an elementary classroom teacher, child-care worker in residential treatment, and a high-school resource teacher for behavior disordered and learning disabled students.

Peter W. Ziebell, M.S., is chief project officer, Montgomery County Health Department, Maryland, and maintains a conjoint family therapy practice in Virginia. He has formerly been deputy director of the Montgomery County, Maryland, Office of Drug Control; director of Montgomery County's Drug Education School; and director of Karma Girls (a residential treatment center in Montgomery County). Prior experience also includes positions as chief psychologist at Lapeer State Hospital, Lapeer, Michigan; assistant dean of students at the University of Michigan at Flint; and psychologist with the U.S. Army.

Author Index

Subject Index